S0-AHO-914
HANDBOOKS

BRITISH COLUMBIA

ANDREW HEMPSTEAD

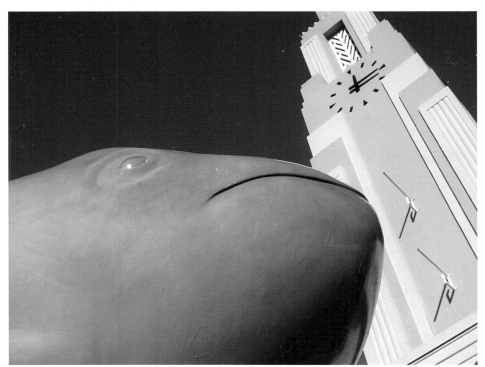

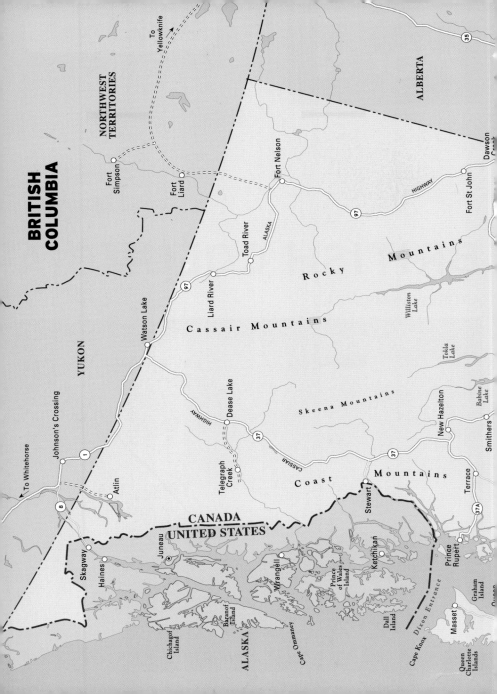

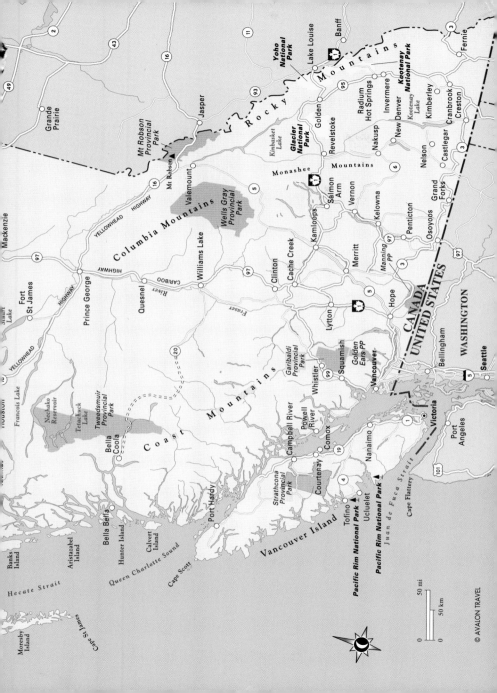

DISCOVER BRITISH COLUMBIA

British Columbia, the westernmost province of Canada, stretches from the Pacific Ocean to the towering heights of the Rocky Mountains – almost twice the size of California, yet with a population half the size of Los Angeles. Sandwiched in between is some of this planet's most magnificent scenery: an enormous variety of terrain including towering mountain ranges, ancient glaciers, endless rivers, crystal clear lakes, rugged coastline, old-growth temperate rainforests, hundreds of islands, and even a desert. Wildlife is abundant and accessible throughout. The forests provide a home for bears, moose, deer, and elk. The ocean is alive with whales, dolphins, and all manner of other sea life.

A major attraction for many is the province's climate, one that is a lot less extreme than the rest of Canada. Yes, it does rain a lot

Mount Robson, Central British Columbia

along the coast, but the upside is that the surrounding mountains and warm ocean currents ensure mild winters and pleasantly warm summers. And while it rarely snows at sea level, winter enthusiasts are spoiled for choice, with alpine resorts scattered through all regions. For those who like to mix up their recreation, the region offers a special treat: Many golf courses are open through winter, and you can try glacier skiing midsummer in Whistler.

Settled by Europeans just 200 years ago, British Columbia has been home to civilization for thousands of years. While world-class facilities such as the Museum of Anthropology and the Royal BC Museum do an admirable job of preserving native culture, there are opportunities to experience these ancient lifestyles by visiting abandoned villages, tasting indigenous dishes, and learning about the meaning-filled art. Totem poles are the most recognized form

Old Town, Victoria

of Pacific Northwest culture, and these can be seen everywhere from local parks to remote islands. Native artwork is held in high regard around the world, with wide-ranging collections available for viewing and purchase in downtown galleries and in locations as far removed from the city as local co-ops within native villages.

The province's largest city is Vancouver, a splendid conglomeration of old and new architectural marvels, parks and gardens, and sheltered beaches on the coast in the southwestern corner of the province. The provincial capital is old-world Victoria, perched at the southeastern tip of Vancouver Island, just across the Strait of Georgia from Vancouver. Victoria boasts an intriguing mixture of old English architecture, customs, and traditions, along with modern attractions, cosmopolitan restaurants, and an infectious joie de vivre.

But most of British Columbia lies away from the cities, in the surrounding vastness. The protected coastal waterways, the rugged west coast of Vancouver Island, the famous Canadian Rockies and many other mountain ranges, the remote northern wilderness,

Columbia River Valley wilderness cabin, Canadian Rockies

and the intriguing Queen Charlotte Islands provide experiences you'll never forget, along with enough ooh-and-aah scenery to keep even the most jaded jet-setter in awe. In these wild areas, you'll find endless opportunities for hiking or climbing, viewing the abundant wildlife, fishing in the hundreds of lakes and rivers, and skiing and boarding any of the dozens of resorts.

And while wilderness beckons to many, you don't need to be that adventurous to enjoy the province. In the last couple of decades, Okanagan wineries have gained a high profile, and there's a wealth of native culture in which to immerse yourself – or you can step back in time at historic towns and parks scattered from north to south. There are magnificent gardens, world-class art galleries, and hundreds of museums.

British Columbia welcomes over 20 million overnight visitors annually, who combine to contribute almost $10 billion to the economy (making tourism the province's second biggest income earner). An excellent tourism infrastructure reflects the importance of the industry. Excellent visitor centers are found in almost every

killer whale in Johnstone Strait, Vancouver Island

town. Accommodations range from good-value backpacker lodges to upscale hotels and lodges that grace the pages of glossy travel magazines. Those who like to sleep under the stars are spoilt for choice with over 1,000 campgrounds to choose from. Serious foodies try to outdo one another with their interpretation of Pacific Northwest dining trends, but the casual visitor need think of only one word when ordering: seafood. Salmon tops the "must try" list, whether it's bought from a fishing boat to be baked on an open fire or ordered with fancy toppings in a downtown restaurant.

The book you hold has evolved greatly since the first edition was published in 1989, and so has British Columbia. It's always been one of the most beautiful, exciting, and inspirational places on this planet. But now it's also one of the world's hottest tourist destinations. Reading through these pages will give you a taste of what to expect, but words can only do so much. You will need to visit to truly experience the wonders of British Columbia.

wildflowers in E. C. Manning Provincial Park

Contents

MAP CONTENTS

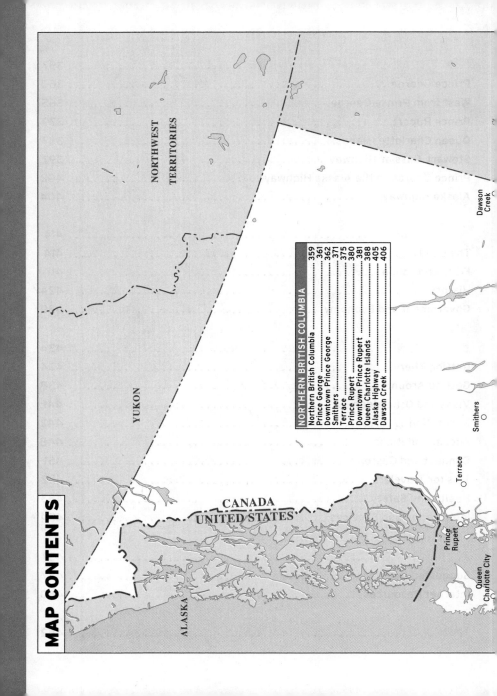

NORTHWEST
TERRITORIES

YUKON

ALASKA

CANADA
UNITED STATES

Dawson
Creek

Smithers

Terrace

Prince
Rupert

Queen
Charlotte City

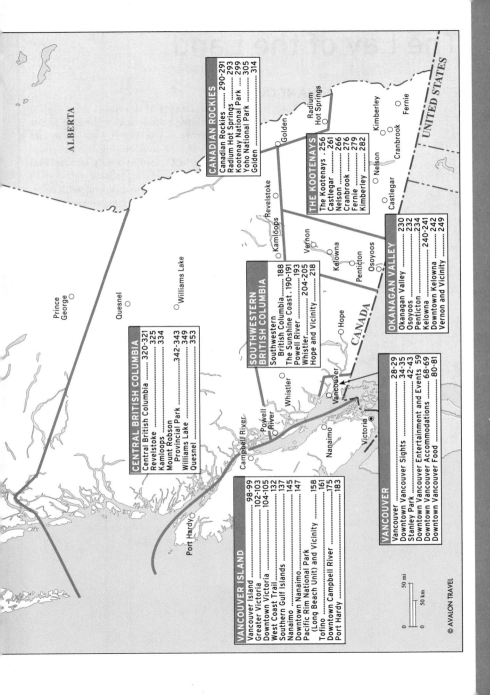

ALBERTA

UNITED STATES

CANADA

Prince George

Quesnel

Williams Lake

Hope

Vernon

Kelowna

Penticton

Osoyoos

Nelson

Castlegar

Kimberley

Cranbrook

Fernie

Radium Hot Springs

Golden

Revelstoke

Kamloops

Whistler

Powell River

Campbell River

Nanaimo

Vancouver

Victoria

Port Hardy

50 mi
50 km
0

© AVALON TRAVEL

The Lay of the Land

VANCOUVER

Let your mind fill with images of dramatic, snowcapped mountains rising high above a modern city clinging to the coastline. A downtown core of century-old buildings and steel-and-glass skyscrapers overlooking the busy waterways. Manicured suburbs fringed by sandy beaches and rocky shorelines. Protected areas of magnificent old-growth forests and brilliant flower gardens overflowing with color. An outdoors-loving population, keen to take advantage of its magnificent surroundings. One of the world's greatest anthropology museums, as well as a world-class museum dedicated to the region's nautical history. Top-notch accommodations to suit all tastes and budgets. Dynamic dining options from legendary diners to purveyors of distinctive West Coast cuisine. These are the magnificent images of Vancouver, British Columbia's largest city, with a population of two million.

VANCOUVER ISLAND

Victoria, the elegant capital of British Columbia on the southern tip of Vancouver Island, couldn't be more different from its neighbor, Vancouver. Victorians will be quick to tell you that the weather is nicer and the pace is slower than over on the mainland. And they are right on both accounts. But the city also projects an intriguing mixture of images, old and new. Well-preserved old buildings line inner-city streets; ancient totem poles sprout from shady parks; restored historic areas house trendy shops, offices, and exotic restaurants; double-decker buses and horse-drawn carriages compete for summer trade; and the residents keep alive the original traditions and atmosphere of Merry Olde England. Beyond city limits, the rest of Vancouver Island beckons, with an array of outdoor experiences that range from hiking the rugged West Coast Trail to surfing the waves of Long Beach.

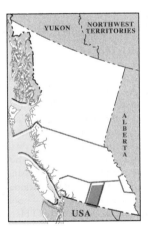

SOUTHWESTERN BRITISH COLUMBIA

Exploring the southwest portion of mainland British Columbia is like taking three very different vacations. From Vancouver, the Sunshine Coast spreads out to the north. Reaching the Sunshine Coast is slightly complicated by ferry-only access, but this also contributes to the charm of its old-fashioned resort towns, which attract families, scuba divers, and sun-loving Canadians. North of Vancouver, the Sea to Sky Highway leads right into the heart of Whistler, a hip, outdoorsy resort town of epic proportions. Summer will keep you busy while winter will captivate you, especially if skiing and snowboarding are your thing. Traveling east from Vancouver, the road forks—head through the scenic Fraser River Canyon to central British Columbia or follow the U.S. border along a winding mountain highway that passes through E. C. Manning Provincial Park before emerging at the Okanagan Valley.

OKANAGAN VALLEY

Tucked into the south-central portion of the province is the gorgeous Okanagan Valley. Around 180 kilometers (112 miles) from end to end, this super-fertile area is dotted with orchards and wineries, the latter a major attraction. But if the only thing you know about wine is that you like it, no worries—wine tasting in the Okanagan is a completely unsnobby affair. The entire valley positively brims with bustling tourist towns, world-class golf courses, marvelous resorts, and enough fun parks to keep the kids busy for an entire vacation. Cruise Highway 97, the valley's main thoroughfare, to hit all the hot spots: the major cities of Penticton, Kelowna, and Vernon; the most celebrated wineries; and the best beaches; as well as lesser-known highlights like Historic O'Keefe Ranch and Silver Star Mountain Resort.

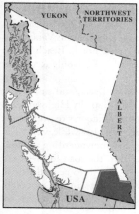

THE KOOTENAYS

Named for the native people who were the original inhabitants of the southeastern corner of British Columbia, the Kootenay region is overwhelmingly beautiful—in a monotonous mountain-and-lakes kind of way. Alpine snowfields feed mighty rivers and massive lakes, creating a **recreational playground** for anglers, canoeists, and kayakers. The largest population center is **Nelson,** a historically important mining center that absorbs a little earthiness from its counterculture vibe. Spend time exploring the ghost town of **Sandon,** step back in time at **Fort Steele Heritage Town,** and wrap up your Kootenay wanderings with a soak at **Ainsworth Hot Springs.** Throughout the mountains many parks merit special attention: White Grizzly Wilderness for the opportunity to view grizzly bears, **Kokanee Creek** to watch fish spawning along a shallow creekbed, and **Akamina-Kishinena** for its solitude.

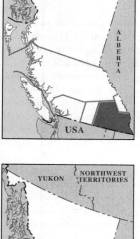

CANADIAN ROCKIES

As you make your way east from the Kootenay region, the mountains become more dramatic—welcome to the Canadian Rockies. I leave the famous national parks you've heard about—Banff and Jasper—for another day, concentrating on the British Columbia side of the mountains, a vast area of wilderness where wildlife is abundant and hiking trails reach all the most scenic locales. The region—and in my opinion, Canada's wilderness—is at its most breathtaking at **Lake O'Hara,** in **Yoho National Park.** Adjacent **Kootenay National Park** offers up more magnificent Canadian wilds, along with hot springs, while **Mount Assiniboine's** remoteness is a blessing for those looking for solitude. Within and beyond the national parks, creature comforts are still just a credit card away—book your accommodations at Emerald Lake Lodge or Lake O'Hara Lodge and you'll want for nothing.

CENTRAL BRITISH COLUMBIA

Cutting a swath across the province, the central region of British Columbia is extremely diverse. In the east is a series of glaciated mountain ranges where the highest peaks are protected by two national parks: **Glacier** (not to be confused with its namesake park in the United States) and **Mount Revelstoke,** where wilderness adventures are extremely accessible and the commercialism of the Canadian Rockies is nonexistent. The heart of central British Columbia is dominated by lakes, including **Shuswap Lake.** For westbound travelers, the scenery changes dramatically west of **Salmon Arm,** as mountains make way for sagebrush-covered hills. In the heart of this desertlike landscape is the city of Kamloops. From **Kamloops,** head northeast to wildlife-rich **Wells Gray Provincial Park** and the high peaks of **Mount Robson Provincial Park,** or west and then north through the ranching country of the **Cariboo.**

NORTHERN BRITISH COLUMBIA

The northern half of British Columbia is for the adventurous. For starters, it's a long way from anywhere else. Secondly, you won't see any famous attractions or scenic wonders. Instead, you'll find **lakes and forest** and lots of both. For anglers, opportunities to catch a trophy-sized trout or steelhead are almost endless. The many small towns provide excellent access to outdoor activities, as well as a little bit of pioneering history. The coastline of northern British Columbia is mostly inaccessible from land. But where highways do push down to the ocean, such as at **Prince Rupert** and **Stewart,** scenic rewards for driving to the end of the road abound. For a real adventure, jump aboard a ferry at Prince Rupert for the **Queen Charlotte Islands,** where totem pole villages abandoned by the fearless Haida are slowly being reclaimed by nature.

Planning Your Trip

Planning a trip can be overwhelming, but don't let it be. The first thing you should do is forget about any preconceived notions you have about travel to Canada—or more precisely British Columbia—and instead focus on the experience. Of course you'll want to visit the museums of Vancouver, take afternoon tea in Victoria, explore the region's six national parks, and maybe even try surfing off Long Beach, but try to think less about specific "sights" and open yourself to discovery.

Start by trying to identify the places you want to see, which parks you just can't miss, the towns that sound most appealing, and how much money you want to spend. Once you have put together an outline of your trip, book lodging—as far in advance as possible—especially if you're traveling in July or August.

It is possible to visit British Columbia without your own vehicle (or a rental), but you'll be confining yourself to the major cities and relying on public transportation and guided tours to get around. Driving is more practical, especially if you plan on visiting the parks and pursuing outdoor endeavors. Even though wilderness dominates the interior, central, and northern regions, British Columbia is dotted with towns and cities linked by well-traveled highways.

WHEN TO GO

Deciding when in the year you'll be visiting British Columbia usually depends on your own schedule, but the following thoughts may help you decide the best time to visit.

While British Columbia can be visited year-round, there are two major influxes of visitors: one in the warmer months and the other in winter. Summer revolves around activities such as hiking, biking, swimming, canoeing, fishing—just about anything you can do outdoors. In winter, the focus is on skiing and snowboarding.

The high season for travel to British Columbia is most definitely summer, or more precisely July and August. This is the time of year when parks come alive with campers, the lakes and streams with anglers, the mountains with hikers, the woods with wildlife, and the roadsides with stalls selling fresh produce. Summer daytime temperatures in Vancouver average a pleasant 23°C (73°F), while the provincial hot spot, the Okanagan Valley, experiences temperatures in the 30s (86–102°F) on many days.

Spring and fall are excellent times to visit British Columbia. While April–June is considered a shoulder season, in many ways the province is at its blooming best in spring. Crowds are at a minimum, the days are long, golfers hit the links in shirts and shorts, and lodging rates throughout the province are reduced. May in the Okanagan Valley is a delight, especially for travelers who enjoy wine festivals.

Fall (mid-Sept.–Nov.) can be tremendous, particularly September, with lingering warm temperatures and a noticeable decrease in crowds immediately after the long weekend at the beginning of the month. While fall colors in general lack the intensity of those in the eastern provinces and New England, larch turn a brilliant yellow throughout high alpine areas in late September.

The two major cities, Vancouver and Victoria, can be visited year-round, with some outdoor activities—golfing, biking, hiking, and more—possible in the dead of winter on Vancouver Island. Alpine resorts throughout the province begin opening in December, and most have seasons extending through to April (or early June in the case of Whistler).

The **best snow conditions** are January–February, although for winter enthusiasts looking for a combination of good snow and warmer weather, March is an excellent time of year to visit.

WHAT TO TAKE

You'll have little use for a suit and tie in British Columbia. Instead, **pack for the outdoors.** At the top of your must-bring list should be walking or hiking boots. If you buy shoes especially for the trip, make sure you wear them once or twice before leaving home, just to make sure they are comfortable. In summer, temperatures rarely drop below freezing anywhere in the province, so you don't need a down jacket or winter boots. But be geared up for a variety of weather conditions, especially at the change of seasons. Do this by preparing to dress in layers, including at least one pair of fleece pants and a heavy long-sleeved top. Bring sunglasses and a wide-brimmed hat to provide protection from the strong sunlight. Gloves and a wool hat are a good idea if you're camping. For dining out, casual dress is accepted at all but the most upscale restaurants in Vancouver and Victoria. Don't forget your swimming costume—for taking a dip in the warm waters off Vancouver Island or soaking in a hot tub up at a ski resort. Finally, bug spray is a summer necessity, but you can pick up the brands that are most effective once you arrive.

Winter temperatures vary greatly throughout the region. Golfers hitting the links on Vancouver Island in January will undoubtedly be warmly dressed, but they *will* be golfing. In the interior and through the northern half of the province, January brings extremely cold temperatures. For this climate, plan to dress in layers, starting with long thermal underwear. The best type of outer layer combines breathable, wind-resistant pants and a jacket. Warm boots with new liners, lined mittens, and a wool hat are a must. If you're traveling from warmer climes, purchasing all the winter necessities in Vancouver is a good idea.

Electrical appliances from the United States work in Canada, but those from other parts of the world will require a current converter (transformer) to bring the voltage down to 120. Many travel-size shavers, hair dryers, and irons have built-in converters.

Choosing a suitcase or backpack is also important. Think about the type of traveling you'll be doing before making a final decision. A midsize suitcase with wheels is best for carting through airports and lugging around hotels. Fold-over bags are good for keeping formal clothing wrinkle-free, but unless you're in town on business or attending a snazzy function, you probably won't require much in the way of dressy clothing. Besides, this type of suitcase is a bother to pack and unpack.

Airlines allow at least one piece of carry-on luggage per person, which must be small enough to fit in the overhead compartments. (Most luggage stores have guidelines to help you choose the right size.) Pack your carry-on with valuables, medications, smaller breakable items, a sweater, reading material, and vital documents (driver's license, credit card, passport, a printout of your reservations, etc.). Even if you're traveling by bus, train, or your own vehicle, it's a good idea to keep all these things in an easy-to-reach carry-on-style bag. The most convenient carry-on bags are small backpacks, which can double as day packs for sightseeing or hiking.

Explore British Columbia

THE BEST OF BRITISH COLUMBIA

Two weeks in British Columbia allows the opportunity to travel throughout the province, including to the northern region. Of course, you could also pad your itinerary with more time in Vancouver and Victoria—and that's what many travelers do—but I encourage you to get adventurous and travel farther afield. In the following itineraries, I assume you have your own vehicle or will be renting one.

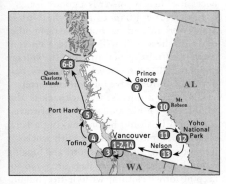

Day 1

Arrive in **Vancouver** for a two-night stay. Spend the rest of your first day exploring **Gastown** and the waterfront area. Rent a bike for an evening ride through **Stanley Park**.

Day 2

Spend the day in **Whistler**, returning to Vancouver in time for dinner atop **Grouse Mountain**.

Day 3

Catch a ferry to **Victoria** and visit capital sights such as the **Royal BC Museum** and **Butchart Gardens**.

Day 4

Make **Tofino** your final destination on Day 4. Even with a visit to **Cathedral Grove** and a short walk along the driftwood-strewn beaches of **Pacific Rim National Park**, you

will have time to enjoy a relaxing evening in Tofino.

Day 5

Make your way north up the island to **Telegraph Cove**. Go whale-watching and continue north to **Port Hardy**.

Day 6

The ferry from Port Hardy gets into Prince Rupert in the late afternoon, linking up with the ferry to the Queen Charlotte Islands.

Day 7

Even after 24 hours and two ferry trips, you'll be invigorated by the uniqueness of the **Queen Charlotte Islands**.

Day 8

You have all day to visit **Naikoon Provincial Park** and cross to Sandspit. Ferries depart the Queen Charlotte Islands for the mainland in the evening (book a cabin to get a good night's rest on board).

Day 9

Arriving in **Prince Rupert** at dawn, take breakfast in Cow Bay while waiting for the **Museum of Northern British Columbia** to open. Head west, stopping at 'Ksan Historical Village. Aim for an overnight stay in Prince George, but don't push it (the more driving you get done today, the quicker you will reach the mountains the following day).

Day 10

After the long haul across northern British Columbia, the first views of the Canadian Rockies are a relief. As **Mount Robson** comes into view, you will be wowed.

Day 11

Drag yourself away from Mount Robson and head south to Kamloops, then east along the TransCanada Highway to **Revelstoke**. Even if you're not a railway buff, **Craigellachie** (site of the last spike on the transcontinental railway) is a pleasant stop.

Day 12

Drive the Meadows in the Sky Parkway and

continue east to **Yoho National Park**. This may be the night for a splurge at the **Emerald Lake Lodge.**

Day 13

Head south through the Columbia Valley. Stop at the **Creston Valley Wildlife Management Area** before continuing to Nelson.

Day 14

It's a seven-hour drive to Vancouver from Nelson. En route, the **wineries, golf courses,** and abundance of **water sports** in the Okanagan Valley will tempt you to linger a day or two longer.

FOCUS ON VANCOUVER AND VICTORIA

Trying to figure out the best way to see the highlights of British Columbia by looking at a map or flipping through this guidebook can be daunting. If all you have is one week, you must face reality: You're not going to see it all. This itinerary balances a little bit of everything—the major cities, mountains, and the ocean—without putting a ridiculous amount of mileage on your vehicle.

Day 1

Head north from Vancouver airport and loop around Point Grey to the **Museum of Anthropology,** a wonderful introduction to the history of the Pacific Northwest. Duck through the old-growth forest behind the museum to get a feel for the city's natural splendor. Check in to your hotel and take an evening stroll through **Gastown.**

Day 2

Even if you hit **Stanley Park** as the sun first rises, you'll find that many locals have beaten you on their morning jog. Cross to the North Shore and take the **Grouse Mountain Skyride.** Drive the Sea to Sky Highway to **Whistler.** Spend the evening at your leisure exploring the resort village.

Day 3

Catch the ferry from Horseshoe Bay to

Nanaimo, on Vancouver Island. Drive across to Tofino, making a stop at Cathedral Grove.

Day 4

Book a whale-watching tour for the morning, and then take a beach walk in Pacific Rim National Park before returning to Nanaimo for the night.

Day 5

Detour from the Island Highway at Crofton Bay to catch a ferry to Salt Spring Island. Enjoy lunch at an outdoor café in Ganges, then make the short ferry hop to Victoria.

Day 6

Today is a walking day, so leave your vehicle at your accommodation and make your way to the Inner Harbour. The Royal BC Museum is a must-see, Market Square and the surrounding streets are interesting to explore, and Barb's Place is perfect for lunch. Still hungry? Head to Oak Bay for afternoon tea.

Day 7

Arrive at Butchart Gardens at opening time—before the bus tour crowd arrives—then return to Vancouver by ferry. You'll arrive in time for an afternoon flight home.

SKI ESCAPES

If you enjoy winter sports, you could spend an entire season exploring British Columbia. But you only have one week—hence this itinerary, which stops at the best-known resorts, detours to some lesser-known places, and finishes up with a round of golf, just because you can.

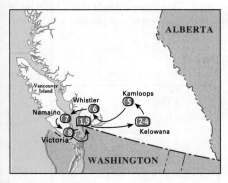

Day 1

You probably don't feel like doing much after arriving in Vancouver, but I urge you to suit up and head for Grouse Mountain, where the ski runs are lighted for night skiing and the views back down across British Columbia's largest city are breathtaking.

Day 2

Head east, through the Fraser River Valley, to Kelowna. Spend the afternoon browsing through town or visiting a local winery. Spend the night at Big White Ski Resort.

Day 3

Hit the slopes of Big White, where the trails suit all abilities and where kids will love the toboggan runs.

Day 4

Families should spend an extra day in the Okanagan Valley, especially those with younger children who will gravitate to the Happy Valley Adventure Centre. Experienced skiers looking to indulge in British Columbia's legendary powder should drive to Rossland on Day 3 and spend Day 4 knee-deep in the deepest snow this side of a helicopter.

Day 5

Regardless of your Day 4 itinerary, spend Day 5 enjoying the slopes of Silver Star before driving through Kamloops to Sun Peaks Resort.

Day 6

Drive to Whistler via Vancouver. You'll have a few spare hours to visit a couple of Vancouver's better-known indoor attractions—like the Maritime Museum.

Day 7

Skiers and boarders should rise early for a full day's skiing. Rather than trying to cover the entire resort, concentrate your efforts on either Whistler or Blackcomb Mountain. Drive to Horseshoe Bay and make the short hop across Georgia Strait to Nanaimo.

Day 8

Spend the day at Mt. Washington Alpine Resort, then choose a heritage home bed-and-breakfast in downtown Victoria for your final night in Canada.

Day 9

Take advantage of Victoria's balmy winter weather by booking a morning tee time at a local links. Return to Vancouver by ferry—or take a floatplane for a treat.

FROM HIGH TEA TO LOW TIDE

So you have just one week and want to concentrate your time on Vancouver Island? Not a problem. This itinerary mixes high tea with low tide to create a trip that has something for everyone. For many people, hiking the West Coast Trail is a major reason for traveling to the island, but because the route takes a minimum of four days to traverse, I leave it as an option that you could include in an extended tour of the island.

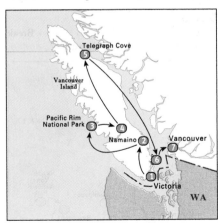

ploring Victoria. Fans of flowers won't want to miss Butchart Gardens, and history buffs should spend an hour or so in the Royal BC Museum. Either way, head to Oak Bay for a traditional afternoon tea.

Day 2

Drive north to Nanaimo. Walk along the harborfront, book an afternoon dive at one of the local wrecks, or go bungee jumping. Leave Nanaimo behind by late afternoon, heading for the west coast. Stop at Cathedral Grove to admire the old-growth forest. Stay in Tofino tonight.

Day 1

After catching a ferry across Georgia Strait from Vancouver, spend your first day ex-

Day 3

Juggle your schedule to include both a whale-watching trip in Clayoquot

Sound and a hike in Pacific Rim National Park. Spend another night in Tofino, or mix it up and move down the coast to Ucluelet.

Day 4
Drive to Port Alberni and take a cruise aboard the MV *Lady Rose*. After returning to port, families may want to book a night at one of Parksville's many beachside resorts, while anglers could continue on to Campbell River.

Day 5
Telegraph Cove will be a highlight of your time on Vancouver Island—even if you don't take a whale-watching trip.

Day 6
Head south to Crofton Bay and catch the ferry to Salt Spring Island. Spend the night on the largest of the Southern Gulf Islands, or continue to pretty Galiano Island.

Day 7
Go kayaking, take a hike, or spend a relaxing morning soaking up island life—just read the timetable carefully to ensure the direct ferry back to Vancouver will arrive well before your scheduled departure home.

ROAD TRIPPING

Truckers make the trip between Calgary and Vancouver in 12 or so hours. Many travelers heading to Vancouver from Alberta also drive the route nonstop, while others overnight along the way. But you're on vacation, so plan on expanding the drive to a weeklong sojourn that will—eventually—get you to Vancouver.

Day 1
Depart Calgary (Alberta) and try not to be tempted by the wonders of Banff National Park (leave them for another time) as you enter the mountains and head to Yoho National Park. Explore the Yoho Valley by road, then head to Emerald Lake for an afternoon walk. If you don't feel like splurging on a park accommodation, continue to Golden.

Day 2
Ride the Kicking Horse Mountain Resort gondola, then hit the highway for Glacier National Park. Even from the highway, this park is spectacular, so unless you're a keen hiker or it's getting late in the day, continue to Revelstoke. Take in an outdoor evening concert in Grizzly Plaza.

Day 3
Drive south from Revelstoke to Nelson. Break up the trip with a short detour to Sandon,

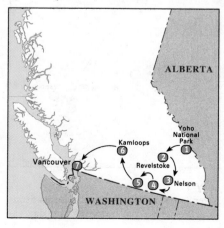

British Columbia's only ghost town, and to watch spawning kokanee at Kokanee Creek Provincial Park. You'll find plenty of choices for dinner in Nelson.

Day 4

Driving through the West Kootenays is a delight, although a roller-coaster highway means the trip takes longer than you might imagine. Stop for a swim in Christina Lake en route.

Day 5

Spend the day at your leisure in the Okanagan Valley. Near Osoyoos, the Nk'Mip Desert Cultural Centre is an interesting stop, unless it's a super-hot day—then stay close to the water or join a winery tour.

Day 6

Head north from Vernon. Silver Star Mountain Resort will leave you with pleasant memories of the Okanagan. Cut across to Kamloops via Highway 97. Stop at Historic O'Keefe Ranch. Spend the night in Kamloops, taking in the Two River Junction dinner theater.

Day 7

Give the direct Coquihalla Highway a miss and travel down the Fraser River Canyon to Hope. Suburban Vancouver is approaching, so if you feel like stalling the inevitable onslaught of city traffic, take a walk through the Othello-Quintette Tunnels.

VANCOUVER

If you view this gleaming mountain- and sea-dominated city for the first time on a beautiful sunny day, you're bound to fall for it in a big way. See it on a dull, dreary day when the clouds are low and Vancouver's backyard mountains are hidden, and you may come away with a slightly less enthusiastic picture—you'll have experienced the "permagray," as residents are quick to call it with a laugh.

But even gray skies can't dampen the city's vibrant, outdoorsy atmosphere. By day, the active visitor can enjoy boating right from downtown, or perhaps venture out to one of the nearby provincial parks for hiking in summer and skiing and snowboarding in winter. More urban-oriented visitors can savor the aromas of just-brewed coffee and freshly baked bread wafting from cosmopolitan sidewalk cafés, join in the bustle at seaside markets, bake on a local beach, or simply relax and do some people-watching in one of the city's tree-shaded squares. By night, Vancouver's myriad of fine restaurants, hip nightclubs, and world-class performing arts venues beckon visitors to continue enjoying themselves on into the wee hours. Vancouver also holds an abundance of world-class attractions, and many smaller gems that are easy to miss. The hardest part will be working out how to best fit all of the activities into your itinerary.

PLANNING YOUR TIME

Deciding how best to spend your time in Vancouver is a personal thing: Outdoorsy budget travelers will spend their days (and money) in different ways from a honeymooning

HIGHLIGHTS

(Canada Place: Its towering white sail-like architecture is a city landmark, taking pride of place along the Vancouver waterfront (page 32).

(Gastown: The cobbled streets of Gastown make up Vancouver's main tourist precinct. The only official attraction is the steam clock, but there are many buildings of historic interest (page 36).

(Granville Island: Interested in the arts? Want to learn about the history of fishing? Do you enjoy browsing through market stalls? You'll find all this and more on this bustling island (page 40).

(Stanley Park: This massive chunk of downtown has been protected in its forested, old-growth state for all time (page 41).

(Vancouver Maritime Museum: The city's nautical past is on display at this museum, with attractions for all ages (page 45).

(VanDusen Botanical Garden: Garden lovers will be in their element at a formal garden in the heart of one of Vancouver's most upscale neighborhoods (page 45).

(Museum of Anthropology: Inspired by the longhouses of First Nations people, this museum houses a stunning collection of totem poles and related arts and crafts (page 46).

(Grouse Mountain Skyride: Catch views

extending across the city to Mount Baker in Washington State. Plentiful on-mountain activities make this a good half-day excursion (page 50).

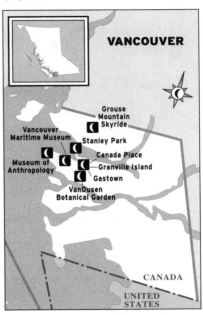

LOOK FOR **(** TO FIND RECOMMENDED SIGHTS, ACTIVITIES, DINING, AND LODGING.

couple looking to kick back and relax for a few days. But this is one of the true joys about visiting Vancouver—there really is something for everyone.

Regardless of whether you have a weekend or a full week scheduled for Vancouver, plan on rising early and heading out to Stanley Park for a walk or ride at least once. Visit the major museums—Vancouver Museum, **Vancouver Maritime Museum,** and the **Museum of Anthropology**—in the mornings. Leave the afternoons for outdoor pursuits that can be

active (kayaking on False Creek), educational (Capilano Salmon Hatchery), or breathtaking (**Grouse Mountain Skyride**). Luckily, many attractions are clustered around downtown, with others such as **Granville Island** and the city's three major museums farther out but easily reached by public transportation. Try to arrange your sightseeing schedule around the weather. If the forecast calls for a rainy day, concentrate on the museums, leaving the North Shore and Stanley Park for a sunny day.

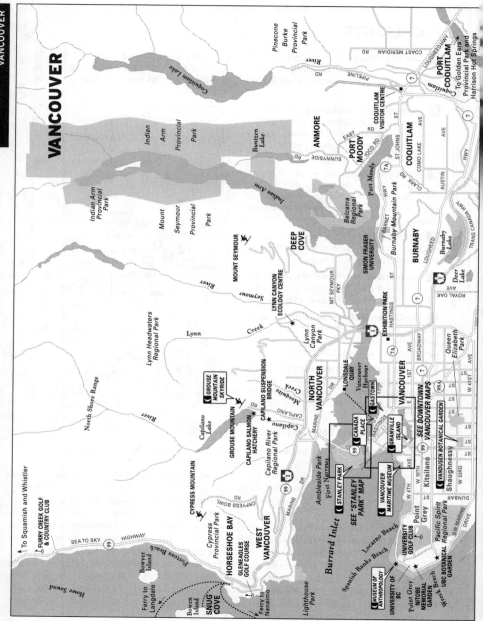

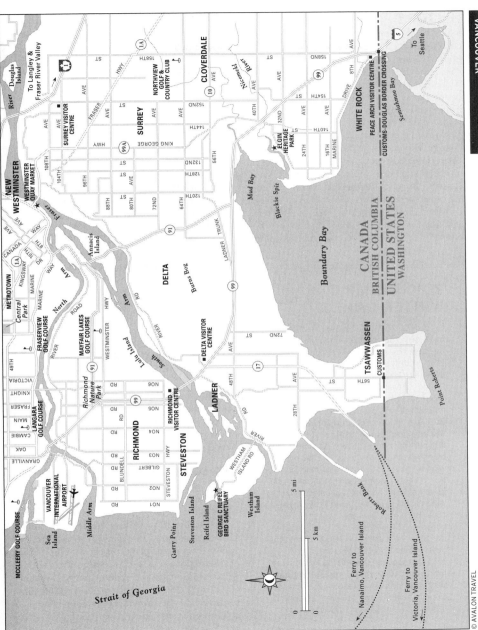

© AVALON TRAVEL

HISTORY

The first Europeans to set eyes on the land encompassing today's city of Vancouver were gold-seeking Spanish traders who sailed through the Strait of Georgia in 1790. Although the forested wilderness they encountered seemed impenetrable, it had been inhabited by humans since becoming ice-free some 10,000 years earlier.

Not to be outdone, the Brits sent Captain George Vancouver to the area in 1792. Vancouver cruised through the Strait of Georgia in search of a northwest passage to the Orient, charting Burrard Inlet and claiming the land for Great Britain in the process. As stories of an abundance of fur-bearing mammals filtered east, the fur companies went into action. The North West Company sent fur trader/explorer Simon Fraser overland to establish a coastal trading post. In 1808 he reached the Pacific Ocean via the river that was later named for him, and he built a fur fort on the riverbank east of today's Vancouver. In 1827, the Hudson's Bay Company established its own fur fort on the Fraser River, 48 kilometers east of present-day Vancouver. Neither of these two outposts spawned a permanent settlement.

Vancouver Is Born

It wasn't until the discovery of gold up the Fraser River in the late 1850s that settlement really took hold in the area. The town of New Westminster, just southeast of present-day Vancouver, was declared British Columbia's first capital in 1866.

The settlement of Vancouver began with the establishment of a brickworks ("Bricks? Why on earth make bricks when we've got all these trees?" said the Woodcutters' Union spokesman) on the south side of Burrard Inlet. Sawmills and related logging and lumber industries followed, and soon several boomtowns were carved out of the wilderness. The first was Granville (now downtown Vancouver), which the original settlers called Gastown after one of its earliest residents, notorious saloon owner "Gassy Jack" Deighton. In 1886 Granville, population 1,000, became the City of Vancouver. Not long thereafter, fire roared through the timber city. Just about everything burned to the ground, but with true pioneering spirit Vancouver was rebuilt at lightning speed.

A Growing City

In 1887, the struggling city got a boost with the arrival of the first transcontinental railroad. Selected as the western terminus for the Canadian Pacific Railway, Vancouver suddenly became Canada's transportation gateway to the Orient and an important player in the development of international commerce around the Pacific Rim. Additionally, the opening of the Panama Canal in 1915 created the perfect outlet for transporting the province's abundant renewable resources to North America's East Coast and Europe, resulting in further development

2010 OLYMPIC WINTER GAMES

On July 2, 2003, Vancouver was named host city for the XXI Olympic Winter Games. The dates are February 12-28, 2010, with the Paralympic Games following March 12-31. Venues are split between Vancouver and Whistler, 120 kilometers (75 miles) to the north. The opening ceremony will take place at the 55,000-seat BC Place Stadium downtown. Vancouver will also host figure skating, speed skating, curling, hockey, freestyle skiing, and freestyle snowboarding. The latter two will take place at Cypress Mountain, on the North Shore. Alpine and Nordic skiing, ski jumping, bobsledding, luge, and skeleton will take place in and around the Whistler area. Both locations will host athletes in purpose-built villages. It is estimated that the games will attract 6,700 athletes and officials and 250,000 visitors.

The **Vancouver Organizing Committee for the 2010 Olympic and Paralympic Winter Games** (www.vancouver2010.com) is the main body overseeing the planning, organizing, and staging of the games.

© ANDREW HEMPSTEAD

looking across to Vancouver's West End from Kitsilano

of the port facilities and a population boom. Granville Island and the far reaches of Burrard Inlet sprawled with industry, the West End developed as a residential area, the University of British Columbia grew in stature, and the opening of the Lions Gate Bridge encouraged settlement on the north side of Burrard Inlet.

Recent Times

From what began just 120 years ago as a cluster of ramshackle buildings centered around a saloon, Vancouver has blossomed into one of the world's greatest cities. While the city holds onto the largest port on North America's West Coast, boasting 20 specialized terminals that handle more tonnage than any other port in Canada, it is now a lot less reliant on its traditional economic heart for its growth. Even after the technology bust, the high-tech industry continues as the fastest-growing sector of Vancouver's economy. Worth $5 billion in 2004, this knowledge-based industry has both revitalized the local economy and created a major shift in government thinking. Tourism contributes over $5 billion annually to the local economy, with finance, real estate, insurance, and manufacturing also forming large slices of the local economic pie. Vancouver is also North America's second-largest movie-making center. Worth $1 billion annually to the city, this exciting industry employs up to 50,000 people on as many as 30 simultaneous productions.

ORIENTATION

Vancouver isn't a particularly easy city to find your way around, although an excellent transit system helps immensely. **Downtown** lies on a spit of land bordered to the north and east by Burrard Inlet, to the west by English Bay, and to the south by False Creek, which almost cuts the city center off from the rest of the city. Due to the foresight of city founders, almost half of the downtown peninsula has been set aside as parkland.

The **City of Vancouver** officially extends south and west from downtown, between Burrard Inlet and the Fraser River, and encompasses the trendy beachside suburb of **Kitsilano** (known as "Kits" to the locals) and **Point Grey,** home of the University of British Columbia. To the east, the residential sprawl continues, through the suburbs of **Burnaby, New Westminster,** and **Coquitlam,** which have a combined population of well over 250,000.

Farther south, the low-lying Fraser River delta extends all the way south to the border. Between the north and south arms of the river is **Richmond,** home of Vancouver International Airport. South of the south arm is the mostly industrial area of **Delta,** as well as **Tsawwassen,** departure point for ferries to Vancouver Island.

Southeast of the Fraser River lies **Surrey,** another of those never-ending suburbs, this one with a population of 349,000. The sprawl continues east from Surrey. With Vancouver growing at an incredible rate, and as development to the south and north are restricted (by the international border and the Coast Mountains), there's nowhere to go but east. From Surrey, the TransCanada Highway passes through the Fraser River Valley and towns such as **Langley** (pop. 85,000), **Abbotsford** (pop. 110,000), and **Chilliwack** (pop. 65,000)—all now part of the city sprawl.

Across Burrard Inlet to the north of downtown, **North Vancouver** is a narrow developed strip backed up to the mountains and connected to the rest of the city by the Lions Gate Bridge. To its west are **Horseshoe Bay,** departure point for Sunshine Coast and Vancouver Island ferries, and **West Vancouver,** an upscale suburb.

Sights

As British Columbia's largest city, Vancouver holds an abundance of world-class attractions, as well as many smaller gems that are easy to miss. Whether you're interested in visiting museums or exploring mountain peaks, you will find plenty to do in Vancouver—the hardest part will be working out how to best fit them into your itinerary. Luckily, many attractions are clustered around downtown, with others such as Granville Island and the city's three major museums farther out but easily reached by public transportation. Try to arrange your sightseeing schedule around the weather. If the forecast calls for a rainy day, concentrate on the museums, leaving the North Shore and Stanley Park for a sunny day.

DOWNTOWN
Granville Street was Vancouver's first commercial corridor, and if today you stand at its junction with West Georgia Street, you're as close to the "center" of the city as it's possible to be. From this busy intersection Granville Street extends north toward Burrard Inlet as a pedestrian mall, leading through the central business district to Canada Place and the main tourist information center. Vancouver Art Gallery, all major banking institutions, shopping centers, and the city's best hotels are within a three-block radius of this intersection. To the south, between Dunsmuir and Robson Streets, is the **theater district** and Library Square. **Yaletown,** the hot spot for tech companies, is farther south, bordered by Homer, Drake, and Nelson Streets. East along the waterfront from Canada Place, and still within easy walking distance of the Granville and Georgia Streets intersection, is the oldest part of the city, **Gastown.** Beyond Gastown, North America's third-largest **Chinatown** is a hive of activity day and night. On the opposite side of the central business district is the **West End** and enormous **Stanley Park,** reached by walking along **Robson Street,** a two-kilometer-long (1.2-mile-long) strip of boutiques and restaurants.

◖ Canada Place
The stunning architectural curiosity with the billowing 27-meter-high (88-foot-high) Teflon-coated fiberglass "sails" on Burrard Inlet—the one that looks as if it might weigh anchor and cruise off into the sunset at any moment—is

© ANDREW HEMPSTEAD

Canada Place

Canada Place, a symbol of Vancouver and a city icon. Built as the Canada Pavilion for Expo86, this integrated waterfront complex is primarily a convention center and cruise-ship dock. The Vancouver Convention and Exhibition Centre, which makes up the bulk of the complex, has been expanded to triple its size at adjacent Burrard Landing, in a half-billion-dollar expansion project that has changed the face of the downtown waterfront. The original complex at the foot of Burrard Street also houses the luxurious 405-room Pan Pacific Hotel (the glass marvel with domed top), restaurants, shops, and an IMAX theater. Start your self-guided tour at the information booth near the main entrance; then allow at least an hour to wander through the complex. Don't miss walking the exterior promenade—3.5 city blocks long—for splendid views of the harbor, the North Shore, the Coast Mountains, and docked Alaska-bound cruise ships.

Vancouver Art Gallery

Francis Rattenbury, architect of Victoria's Empress Hotel and many other masterpieces, designed Vancouver's imposing neoclassical-revival courthouse, which now houses Vancouver Art Gallery (750 Hornby St., 604/662-4700; daily 10 A.M.–5:30 P.M., until 9 P.M. on Tues. and Thurs., closed Mon. Oct.–May; adult $19.50, senior $15, student $14, child $6.50). The gallery houses a large collection of works by Canada's preeminent female artist, **Emily Carr,** who was born on Vancouver Island in 1871 and traveled the world honing her painting and drawing skills before settling in Vancouver in 1906. Her style reflects the time she spent with the native peoples of the Pacific Northwest coast, but she was also influenced by techniques acquired during periods when she lived in London and Paris. Carr combined these influences to create unique works, and the gallery is well worth visiting for these alone. The Carr collection is on the third floor, along with the works of many other local artists. The gallery also holds pieces by contemporary artists from both North America and Europe as well as an impressive collection of historical art.

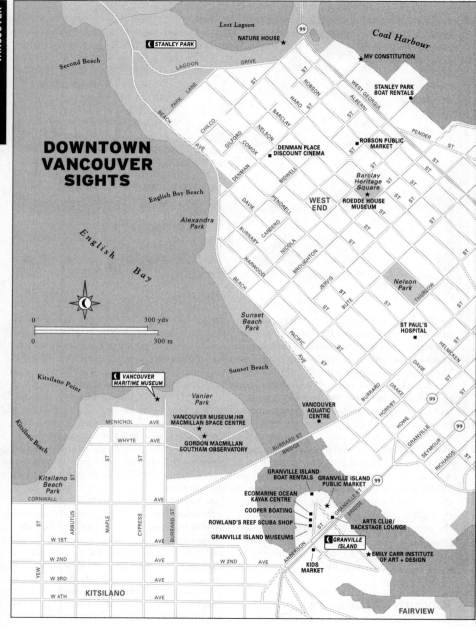

DOWNTOWN VANCOUVER SIGHTS

Lost Lagoon

☾ STANLEY PARK

NATURE HOUSE ★

Coal Harbour

Second Beach

★ MV CONSTITUTION

LAGOON   DRIVE

STANLEY PARK
BOAT RENTALS

PARK   LANE

ROBSON ST

WEST GEORGIA ST

ALBERNI ST

BEACH   AVE

PENDER   ST

CHILCO

GILFORD

NELSON

HARO ST

BARCLAY

COMOX

DENMAN PLACE
DISCOUNT CINEMA ★

★ ROBSON PUBLIC
MARKET

English Bay Beach

DENMAN

BIDWELL

Barclay
Heritage
Square ★
ROEDDE HOUSE
MUSEUM

Alexandra
Park

DAVIE

PENDRELL

WEST
END

BURNABY

CARDERO

NICOLA

E n g l i s h   B a y

HARWOOD

BROUGHTON

Nelson
Park

BEACH

JERVIS ST

BUTE ST

THURLOW ST

0   300 yds

0   300 m

Sunset
Beach
Park

PACIFIC   AVE

ST PAUL'S
HOSPITAL ■

Kitsilano Point

Sunset Beach

DAVIE ST

HELMCKEN ST

☾ VANCOUVER
MARITIME MUSEUM ★

Vanier
Park

VANCOUVER MUSEUM /HR
MACMILLAN SPACE CENTRE ★

BURRARD ST

DRAKE ST

HORNBY ST

HOWE ST

GRANVILLE ST

SEYMOUR ST

RICHARDS ST

99

Kitsilano
Beach

McNICHOL   AVE

WHYTE   AVE

GORDON MACMILLAN
SOUTHAM OBSERVATORY ★

VANCOUVER
AQUATIC
CENTRE ■

99

Kitsilano
Beach
Park

CORNWALL

BURRARD ST
BRIDGE

GRANVILLE ISLAND
BOAT RENTALS

GRANVILLE ISLAND
PUBLIC MARKET

99

ECOMARINE OCEAN
KAYAK CENTRE ■

GRANVILLE ST

GRANVILLE
BRIDGE

ARBUTUS ST

MAPLE ST

CYPRESS ST

BURRARD ST

AVE

COOPER BOATING ■

ROWLAND'S REEF SCUBA SHOP ■

ARTS CLUB/
BACKSTAGE LOUNGE

W 1ST

AVE

GRANVILLE ISLAND MUSEUMS ■

ANDERSON ST

☾ GRANVILLE
ISLAND

YEW ST

W 2ND

AVE   W 2ND   AVE

EMILY CARR INSTITUTE ★
OF ART + DESIGN

W 3RD

AVE

KIDS
MARKET ■

W 4TH   AVE

KITSILANO

FAIRVIEW

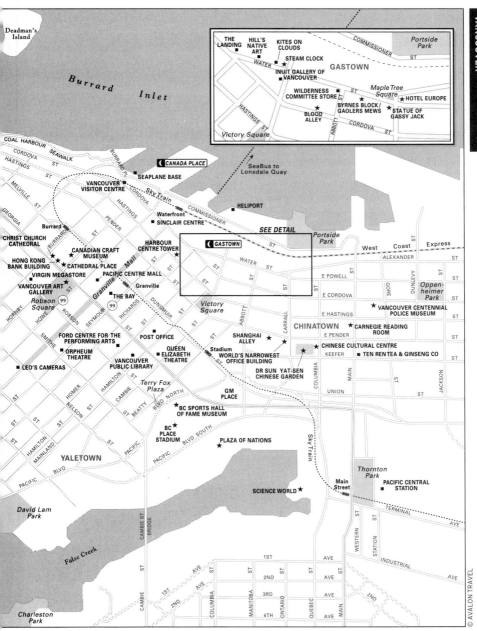

Deadman's Island

Burrard Inlet

DETAIL:
THE LANDING
HILL'S NATIVE ART
KITES ON CLOUDS
COMMISSIONER ST
Portside Park
WATER ST
STEAM CLOCK
GASTOWN
INUIT GALLERY OF VANCOUVER
WILDERNESS COMMITTEE STORE
Maple Tree Square
BYRNES BLOCK / GAOLERS MEWS
HOTEL EUROPE
BLOOD ALLEY
HASTINGS ST
STATUE OF GASSY JACK
ABBOT ST
CORDOVA ST
Victory Square

COAL HARBOUR
SEAWALK
CORDOVA ST
HASTINGS ST
MELVILLE ST
GEORGIA
CANADA PLACE
SEAPLANE BASE
VANCOUVER VISITOR CENTRE
SkyTrain
CORDOVA
HASTINGS
PENDER
COMMISSIONER
SeaBus to Lonsdale Quay
HELIPORT
Waterfront
SINCLAIR CENTRE
SEE DETAIL
GASTOWN
Portside Park
West Coast Express
ALEXANDER ST
Burrard
CHRIST CHURCH CATHEDRAL
BURRARD
HARBOUR CENTRE TOWER
WATER ST
E POWELL ST
GORE
DUNLEVY
Oppenheimer Park
HONG KONG BANK BUILDING
CANADIAN CRAFT MUSEUM
CATHEDRAL PLACE
VIRGIN MEGASTORE
PACIFIC CENTRE MALL
E CORDOVA ST
VANCOUVER ART GALLERY
Granville Mall
Granville
THE BAY
Victory Square
E HASTINGS
VANCOUVER CENTENNIAL POLICE MUSEUM
Robson Square 99
DUNSMUIR
CHINATOWN
CARRALL
CARNEGIE READING ROOM
HORNBY
HOWE
ROBSON
SEYMOUR
RICHARDS
99
ABBOT
E PENDER
ST
FORD CENTRE FOR THE PERFORMING ARTS
POST OFFICE
SHANGHAI ALLEY
CHINESE CULTURAL CENTRE
KEEFER
TEN REN TEA & GINSENG CO
SMITHE
ORPHEUM THEATRE
QUEEN ELIZABETH THEATRE
Stadium
WORLD'S NARROWEST OFFICE BUILDING
MAIN
JACKSON
LEO'S CAMERAS
VANCOUVER PUBLIC LIBRARY
DR SUN YAT-SEN CHINESE GARDEN
COLUMBIA
HAMILTON
Terry Fox Plaza
UNION ST
CAMBIE
NELSON
BEATTY
GM PLACE
BLVD NORTH
BC SPORTS HALL OF FAME MUSEUM
BC PLACE STADIUM
BLVD SOUTH
PLAZA OF NATIONS
SkyTrain
Thornton Park
PACIFIC CENTRAL STATION
HAMILTON
MAINLAND
YALETOWN
PACIFIC
PACIFIC BLVD
SCIENCE WORLD
Main Street
TERMINAL AVE
David Lam Park
CAMBIE ST BRIDGE
COLUMBIA ST
MANITOBA ST
ONTARIO ST
QUEBEC ST
MAIN ST
WESTERN ST
STATION ST
INDUSTRIAL AVE
False Creek
1ST AVE
2ND AVE
3RD AVE
4TH AVE
2ND
Charleston Park

Near the Art Gallery

Diagonal from the art gallery is the **Canadian Craft Museum** (639 Hornby St., 604/687-8266; Mon.–Sat. 10 A.M.–5 P.M., Thurs. until 9 P.M., Sun. noon–5 P.M.; adult $5, senior $3), which catalogs the history of arts and crafts throughout the ages. Mediums displayed include glass, wood, clay, metal, and fabric. The emphasis is on Canadian work, but a couple of other displays and touring exhibitions bring an international feel to the museum. As you'd expect, the gift shop offers an excellent choice of unique craft items at reasonable prices. Entry is free Thursday evenings after 5 P.M.

Cathedral Place is worth visiting for an intriguing sculpture, *Navigational Device,* in the lobby. Next door to Cathedral Place is the **Hongkong Bank** building, which features a massive 27-meter-long (89-foot-long) aluminum pendulum in the lobby. Next door again, on the corner of West Georgia and Burrard Streets, is **Christ Church Cathedral.** When built in 1895, it was in the heart of a residential area. Over the ensuing century, it was engulfed by modern developments and is today Vancouver's oldest church, attracting more sightseers than believers.

◖ Gastown

Three blocks east of Canada Place, Gastown is a marvelous place to spend a few hours. It was the birthplace of Vancouver, officially named Granville in 1870 but always known as Gastown, for saloon owner "Gassy Jack" Deighton.

The Great Fire of 1886 destroyed almost all of Gastown's wooden buildings, but the district was rebuilt in stone and brick. By the 1960s, this historic district held nothing more than decrepit Victorian-era buildings and empty warehouses. A massive rejuvenation program commenced, and today historic Gastown is one of the city's most popular tourist attractions. Tree-lined cobblestone streets and old gas lamps front brightly painted, restored buildings housing galleries, restaurants, and an abundance of gift and souvenir shops.

Most of the action centers along **Water Street,** which branches east off Cordova Street

and slopes gently toward the site of Gassy Jack's original saloon (now the Alhambra Hotel). As you first enter Water Street, you're greeted by **The Landing,** a seven-story heritage building that has had its exterior restored to its former glory and its interior transformed from a warehouse to a shopping arcade. Continuing down the hill, on the corner of Water and Cambie Streets, is a **steam clock,** one of only two in the world (the other is a replica of this, the original one). Built by a local clock maker in the mid-1970s, it is powered by a steam system originally put in place to heat buildings along a 10-kilometer-long (6.2-mile-long) underground pipeline that snakes through downtown. Watch for the burst of steam every 15 minutes, which sets off steam whistles to the tune of Westminster chimes. Continue east along Water Street to the 1899 **Dominion Hotel,** then half a block south down Abbott Street to **Blood Alley,** the hangout of many infamous late-19th-century rogues. Most buildings still standing along Water Street were built immediately after the Great Fire of 1886, but the **Byrnes Block** (2 Water St.) is generally regarded as the oldest; it stands on the site of Deighton House, Gassy Jack's second and more permanent saloon.

Water Street ends at the cobbled **Maple Tree Square,** at the intersection of Water, Carrall, Powell, and Alexander Streets. A bronze **statue of Gassy Jack** watches over the square and the site of his original saloon from the top of a whiskey barrel. The **Alhambra Hotel,** which occupies the actual saloon site, was built in 1886 from bricks used as ballast in ships that sailed into Burrard Inlet.

CHINATOWN

The heart of Chinatown has moved eastward over the years and is now centered on the block bordered by Main, East Pender, Gore, and Keefer Streets. With a population exceeding 30,000, it is the second largest Chinese community in North America and one of the largest outside Asia.

Stroll through the neighborhood to admire the architecture—right down to the pagoda-roofed telephone booths—or to seek out one of the

VANCOUVER VIEWS

Whenever I visit a city for the first time, I like starting off by finding a viewpoint that lets me see the layout of the city. In Vancouver, the obvious option to get your bearings is to take a flightseeing trip in a helicopter or floatplane, but this also means paying out big bucks. Instead, consider one of the following less-expensive options.

DOWNTOWN

For immediate orientation from downtown, catch the high-speed, stomach-sinking glass elevator up the outside of 40-story Harbour Centre Tower (555 W. Hastings St., 604/689-0421; summer daily 8:30 A.M.–10:30 P.M., the rest of the year daily 9:30 A.M.–9 P.M.; adult $13, senior $11, student $9). The ride takes less than a minute and ends at the **Vancouver Lookout,** an enclosed room 167 meters (548 feet) above street level, from where views extend as far away as Mt. Baker, 140 kilometers (87 miles) to the south. Walk around the circular room for 360-degree views and read interpretive panels describing interesting facts about the panorama below and beyond. Keep your receipt and you can return at any time during the same day (the top of the tower is a great place to watch the sun setting over the Strait of Georgia).

DOWN ON THE WATERFRONT

From Vancouver Visitor Centre, continue down Burrard Street to **Canada Place** and wander around the west side promenade for neck-straining views of the city close up, as well as of North Vancouver and the rugged mountains beyond. For a look at the skyline and sparkling Canada Place from sea level, take the SeaBus from the adjacent Waterfront Station across Burrard Inlet to **Lonsdale Quay** ($3).

STANLEY PARK

Drive, walk, or cycle Stanley Park's 10-kilometer (6.2-mile) **Seawall Promenade** to appreciate the skyline to the east, the busy shipping lanes of First Narrows to the north, and the sandy beaches of English Bay to the west. Sunsets from **English Bay Beach,** in the West End, are delightful.

NORTH SHORE

The best views from the north side of Burrard Inlet are gained by taking the **Grouse Mountain Skyride** (Nancy Greene Way, 604/984-0661; adult $33, senior $31, youth $19, child $12) up the slopes of Grouse Mountain. The panorama extends back across the inlet to downtown and beyond to Mt. Baker, in Washington State, and west to Vancouver Island. In summer, the gondola departs from the base station every 10 minutes 10 A.M.–10 P.M.

Head west along Highway 1 from the Grouse Mountain turnoff to Cypress Bowl Road. At the second switchback there's a particularly good city skyline view. Continue west to Horseshoe Bay, then return to the city along Marine Drive, which parallels Burrard Inlet, providing many glimpses of the city skyline. At **Lighthouse Park,** along this route, English Bay, Stanley Park, and Kitsilano Beach are laid out in all their glory from Point Atkinson.

UPTOWN

South of downtown, the **Kitsilano** foreshore provides that well-known view of the city skyline backed by the Coast Mountains. The south side of the city is relatively flat. The high point is 152-meter (500-foot) **Little Mountain,** in Queen Elizabeth Park, where the city skyline and abruptly rising mountains contrast starkly with the residential sprawl of Vancouver.

© ANDREW HEMPSTEAD

The view across the city from Vancouver Lookout is spectacular.

multitude of restaurants. You'll find markets and genuine Cantonese-style cuisine east of Main Street and tamer Chinese-Canadian dishes along Main Street and to the west. Chinatown is an exciting place any time of year, but it's especially lively during a Chinese festival or holiday, when thronging masses follow the ferocious dancing dragon, avoid exploding firecrackers, sample tasty tidbits from outdoor stalls, and pound their feet to the beat of drums.

The district's intriguing stores sell a mind-boggling array of Chinese goods: wind chimes, soy sauce, teapots, dried mushrooms, delicate paper fans, and much, much more. Along Main Street several shops sell ginseng, sold by the Chinese ounce (38 grams). Cultivated ginseng costs from $10 per ounce, while wild ginseng goes for up to $400 per ounce. In addition to selling the herb, the staff at **Ten Ren Tea and Ginseng Co.** (550 Main St., 604/684-1566) explains ginseng preparation methods to buyers and offers tea tasting as well.

To get to Chinatown from downtown, catch bus 19 or 22 east along Pender Street. Try to avoid walking along East Hastings Street at all times; it's Vancouver's skid row, inhabited by unsavory characters day and night.

Chinese Cultural Centre

This cultural center (50 E. Pender St., 604/658-8850) is the epicenter of community programs for the local Chinese population, but holds interest for outsiders. Around the corner from the main entrance, the distinctive museum and archives building (555 Columbia St., 604/658-8880; Tues.–Sun. 11 A.M.–5 P.M.; adult $5, senior $3) catalogs the history of Chinese Canadians in Vancouver. The center also sponsors activities ranging from bonsai displays to cooking classes; admission varies according to what's going on.

Dr. Sun Yat-Sen Classical Chinese Garden

Gardening enthusiasts won't want to miss this peaceful and harmoniously designed garden behind the Cultural Centre (578 Carrall St., 604/662-3207; summer 9:30 A.M.–7 P.M. daily,

the rest of the year 10 A.M.–6 P.M. daily; adult $8.75, senior and student $7). Designed by artisans from Suzhou, China—a city famous for its green-thumbed residents—the garden features limestone rockeries, a waterfall and tranquil pools, and beautiful trees and plants hidden away behind tall walls. The garden is styled around Taoist traditions of balance and harmony, achieved through the use of buildings, rocks, plants, and water. The buildings and other manmade elements, including wood-carvings and sculptures, were shipped from China. This was the first authentic classical Chinese garden built outside China, and it remains to this day the largest.

Adjacent to the gardens is **Dr. Sun Yat-Sen Park,** where admission is free.

Sam Kee Building

Opposite the entrance to Dr. Sun Yat-Sen Classical Chinese Garden is the Sam Kee Building (8 W. Pender St., corner of Carrall St.), best known as the world's narrowest office building. When city developers widened surrounding streets in 1912, the Chinese consortium that owned the lot decided to proceed with its planned building, just making it narrower than at first planned. The result is a building 1.8 meters (approximately six feet) wide, noted in the *Guinness Book of Records* as the "narrowest building in the world."

FALSE CREEK

False Creek, the narrow tidal inlet that almost cuts downtown off from the rest of the city, has undergone enormous changes over the last 25 years and is now a bona fide tourist attraction. Once Vancouver's main industrial area, False Creek was transformed for Expo86 with the construction of the Plaza of Nations (which held the Expo's BC Pavilion) and Expo headquarters, now Science World.

BC Place Stadium

A Vancouver landmark, this 55,000-seat stadium (777 Pacific Blvd., 604/669-2300) will be the center of attention in 2010 for the opening ceremonies of the Olympic Winter Games.

In the meantime, it comes alive for home games of the BC Lions, one of the Canadian Football League teams, and is the venue for major trade shows, concerts, and other big events.

At Gate A you'll find the **BC Sports Hall of Fame and Museum** (604/687-5520; Tues.–Sun. 10 A.M.–5 P.M.; adult $6, senior and child $4). Displays in the Hall of Champions catalog the careers of British Columbia's greatest sports achievers, such as CART racer Greg Moore and skier Nancy Greene. The most moving displays are dedicated to cancer victim Terry Fox and wheelchair-bound Rick Hanson, whose courage in the face of adversity opened the eyes of all Canadians in the late 1970s and early 1980s, respectively.

Science World

This impressive, 17-story-high, geodesic-shaped silver dome (it's best known locally as "the golf ball") stands above the waters of False Creek on the southeast side of city center (1455 Quebec St., 604/443-7440; daily 10 A.M.–5 P.M., until 6 P.M. weekends) is home to Science World, a museum providing exhibitions that "introduce the world of science to the young and the young at heart." The three main galleries explore the basics of physics, natural history, and music through hands-on displays, while a fourth gallery holds an ever-changing array of traveling exhibits. The Science Theatre shows the feature *Over Canada,* a high-definition aerial tour over Canada accompanied by the sounds of Canadian musicians. The Omnimax theater, with one of the world's largest such screens (27 m/89 ft. wide), features science-oriented documentaries. Admission to Science World is adult $16, senior or student $13, child $11; in combination with a ticket to one Omnimax film, admission is $21, $18, and $16 respectively.

The most enjoyable way to get to Science World is aboard a False Creek Ferry from Granville Island or the Vancouver Aquatic Centre. If you don't want to take the ferry, you can drive to the west end of Terminal Avenue—plenty of parking is available—or take the SkyTrain to Main Street Station and then walk across the street.

© ANDREW HEMPSTEAD

Science World is locally known as "the golf ball."

$15, child $11), and the third largest in North America. More than 8,000 aquatic animals and 600 species are on display, representing all corners of the planet, from the oceans of the Arctic to the rain forests of the Amazon. The Wild Coast exhibit features local marine mammals, including sea lions, dolphins, and seals. Pacific Canada is of particular interest because it contains a wide variety of sealife from the Gulf of Georgia, including the giant fish of the deep, halibut, and playful sea otters who frolic in the kelp. In the Amazon Rainforest, experience a computer-generated hourly tropical rainstorm and see numerous fascinating creatures, such as crocodiles and piranhas as well as bizarre misfits like the four-eyed fish. The Tropical Gallery re-creates an Indonesian marine park, complete with colorful sealife, coral, and small reef sharks. Outside, large pools hold beluga whales—distinctive, pure white marine mammals—and sea lions, which can be viewed from above or below ground.

Until the mid-1990s, Stanley Park was home to a zoo; what remains is the **Children's Farmyard,** where you can see all types of domesticated animals. It's linked to the aquarium by a short walking path and is open daily 10 A.M. until dusk.

Getting Around the Park

Even at a casual pace, it's possible to walk the seawall in less than three hours, but it's easy to spend a whole day detouring to the main attractions, taking in the panoramas from the many lookouts, or just relaxing on the benches and beaches along the way. Even if you find the Lycra-clad cyclists racing around the seawall on their thousand-dollar bikes intimidating, exploring the park by bike is easy and fun (allow one hour to ride the seawall). At the corner of Robson and Denman streets, several shops rent decent bikes for under $25 for a full day. They include **Bayshore Bicycles** (745 Denman St., 604/688-2453) and **Spokes Bicycle Rental** (1798 W. Georgia St., 604/688-5141).

Between mid-March and October, **Stanley Park Horse-Drawn Tours** (604/681-5115; adult $25, senior and student $24, child $15)

leave regularly from the information booth, on a one-hour tour in a 20-person carriage.

Between June and mid-September, the city bus system operates a free shuttle around the park and to all major park attractions, with downtown pickups at Canada Place, Gastown, and major hotels.

SOUTH OF DOWNTOWN

Officially divided into 18 municipalities, the City of Vancouver encompasses the entire peninsula, including the area south of downtown, a largely residential area that extends west to Point Grey and the University of British Columbia. Vancouver's three largest museums and a number of public gardens lie south of downtown.

Vancouver Museum

Regional history from Precambrian times to the present comes to life at Vancouver Museum (1100 Chestnut St., 604/736-4431; daily 10 A.M.–5 P.M., Thurs. until 9 P.M., closed Monday in winter; adult $10, senior and student $8, child $6.50) in Vanier Park. The West Coast Archaeology and Culture galleries hold ravishing masks, highly patterned woven blankets, and fine baskets. The Gateway to the Pacific Gallery details European exploration of British Columbia—both by land and by sea. The 50s Gallery depicts the 1950s, where a shiny 1955 Ford Fairlane is displayed and black-and-white TVs screen popular shows of the time. The complex also holds a gift shop and a self-serve restaurant overlooking Vanier Park. To reach the museum, catch bus number 2 or 22 on Burrard Street and get off after Burrard Street Bridge at the Cornwall and Cypress Street stop, or catch a ferry to Vanier Park from Granville Island or the Aquatic Centre at Sunset Beach.

H. R. MacMillan Space Centre

Children especially will love the H. R. MacMillan Space Centre (1100 Chestnut St., 604/738-7827; summer daily 10 A.M.–5 P.M., closed Mon. the rest of the year; adult $15, senior or student $10.75, child $10.75), in the same building as the museum. The main features are displays related to planet Earth, the surrounding universe, and space exploration. Throughout the day, the GroundStation Canada Theatre shows 20-minute audiovisual presentations that explore the universe. The Space Centre also presents a popular laser rock music show in the H. R. MacMillan Planetarium Wednesday–Sunday at 9 P.M., with additional shows on Friday and Saturday nights at 10:30 P.M.; $8.65 per person.

Gordon MacMillan Southam Observatory

Adjacent to the museum complex is the Gordon MacMillan Southam Observatory (604/738-7827; donation), which is open for public stargazing Friday–Saturday, sunset to midnight, when the skies are clear.

◖ Vancouver Maritime Museum

Just a five-minute stroll from Vancouver Museum is Vancouver Maritime Museum (1905 Ogden Ave., 604/257-8300; summer daily 10 A.M.–5 P.M., the rest of the year Tues.–Sat. 10 A.M.–5 P.M. and Sunday noon–5 P.M.; adult $10, child $7.50), at the end of Cypress Avenue. Filled with nautical-themed displays that showcase British Columbia's seafaring legacy, exhibits chronicle everything from the province's first European explorers and their vessels to today's oceangoing adventurers, modern fishing boats, and fancy ships. Beyond the front desk is a historical Royal Canadian Mounted Police (RCMP) vessel, *St. Roch,* which fills the first main room. Now a National Historic Site, the *St. Roch* was the first patrol vessel to successfully negotiate the infamous Northwest Passage. Children tend to gravitate toward the back of the museum to the Maritime Discovery Centre, where they can dress up as a fisherman, try their hand at navigation, and crawl through a pirate's cave.

◖ VanDusen Botanical Garden

This 22-hectare (54-acre) garden (5251 Oak St. at 37th Ave., 604/878-9274) is home to more than 7,500 species from every continent except Antarctica. It's the place to feast your eyes on more than 1,000 varieties of rhododendrons,

KITSILANO

Named for a Squamish chief and known simply as "Kits" to locals, Kitsilano is a trendy beachside suburb southwest of downtown boasting a young, active population. Extending south to West 16th Avenue and west to Alma Street from Burrard Street, its main attractions are two not-to-be-missed museums in **Vanier Park.** This park extends from Burrard Street Bridge to Maple Street and is a popular spot for walkers, joggers, and cyclists. It's home to the famous Bard on the Beach summertime theater. Green space continues beyond Vanier Park to **Kitsilano Beach,** facing English Bay. Vancouver's most popular beach, this spot attracts hordes of bronzed (and not-so-bronzed) bodies to its long sandy beach, warm shallow waters, spectacular mountain views, the city's largest outdoor pool, beach volleyball, and surrounding cafés and restaurants.

Away from the Kitsilano waterfront are two main shopping and dining precincts: West 4th Avenue between Burrard and Balsam Streets, and Broadway between Larch and Collingwood Streets.

as well as roses, all kinds of botanical rarities, winter blossoms, and an Elizabethan hedge maze. Look for the display board near the front entrance to see what's best for the time of year in which you're visiting. The complex also includes a shop selling cards, perfumes, soaps, potpourri, and all kinds of gifts with a floral theme. The garden is open daily in summer 10 A.M.–8 P.M., in April and October 10 A.M.–6 P.M. daily, and the rest of the year 10 A.M.–4 P.M. daily. Admission April–September is adult $8.25, senior $6, youth $6.25, child $4.25; the rest of the year it's adult $6, senior and student $4.25, child $2.40. To get there by bus, take number 17 south along Burrard Street. Oak Street runs parallel to Granville Street; access to the garden is on the corner of East 33rd Avenue.

Queen Elizabeth Park

Less than two kilometers (1.2 miles) from VanDusen Botanical Garden, this 53-hectare (130-acre) park sits atop 152-meter (500-foot) **Little Mountain,** the city's highest point, with magnificent views of Vancouver and the Coast Mountains. The park is a paradise of sweeping lawns, trees, flowering shrubs, masses of rhododendrons—a vivid spectacle in May and June—formal flower gardens (including a rose garden in the park's southwest corner), sunken gardens in the old quarry pits, and mature plantings of native trees from across Canada. Public facilities include tennis courts and a pitch-and-putt golf course.

The highlight of the park is the magnificent **Bloedel Floral Conservatory** (604/257-8584; summer Mon.–Fri. 9 A.M.–8 P.M. and Sat.–Sun. 10 A.M.–9 P.M., the rest of the year daily 10 A.M.–5:30 P.M.; adult $4.60, senior $3.20, child $2.20), a glass-domed structure rising 40 meters (130 feet) and enclosing a temperature-controlled, humid tropical jungle. The park's main entrance is by the junction of 33rd Avenue West and Cambie Street; to get there from downtown take bus number 15 south on Burrard Street.

UNIVERSITY OF BRITISH COLUMBIA

The UBC campus sprawls across **Point Grey,** the westernmost point of Vancouver and the southern extremity of Burrard Inlet. It enjoys a spectacular coastal location, surrounded by parkland laced with hiking trails. Many of the trails provide access to the beach. The campus encompasses more than 400 hectares (990 acres) and serves up to 35,000 students at one time.

◖ Museum of Anthropology

Containing the world's largest collection of arts and crafts of the Pacific Northwest native peoples, this excellent on-campus museum should not be missed (6393 Northwest Marine Dr., 604/822-5087; summer daily 10 A.M.–5 P.M., the rest of the year Tues.–Sun. 11 A.M.–5 P.M.; adult $9, senior and student $7). Designed by innovative Canadian architect Arthur Erickson,

the ultramodern concrete-and-glass building perches on a high cliff overlooking the Pacific Ocean and mimics the post-and-beam structures favored by the Coast Salish.

The entrance is flanked by panels in the shape of a Bent-box, which the Salish believed contained the meaning of life. Inside, a ramp lined with impressive sculptures by renowned modern-day carvers leads to the Great Hall, a cavernous 18-meter (59-foot) room dominated by towering totem poles collected from along the coast and interspersed with other ancient works. A museum highlight is the collection of works by Haida artist Bill Reid, which includes *The Raven and the First Men.* Carved from a four-ton chunk of yellow cedar, drenched in natural light, and raised above sand from the Queen Charlotte Islands, this piece is simply breathtaking. Other displays include intricate carvings, baskets, ceremonial masks, fabulous jewelry, and European ceramics. The museum holds more than 200,000 artifacts, most of which are stored in uniquely accessible research collections. Instead of being stored in musty boxes out back and available only to anthropologists, the collections are stored in the main museum—in row upon row of glass-enclosed cabinets and in drawers that visitors are encouraged to open. Details of each piece are noted in binders.

Outside, a deliciously scented woodland path on the left side of the museum leads to a reconstructed Haida village and some contemporary totem poles with descriptive plaques.

If you have your own vehicle, make sure you have a fistful of change to park in the lot beside the museum ($1 for every 20 minutes). The museum is open until 9 P.M. on Tuesday, with admission by donation after 5 P.M.

University Gardens

Just south of the Museum of Anthropology is the serene **Nitobe Memorial Garden** (604/822-9666; mid-March to October daily 10 A.M.–6 P.M.; adult $5, senior $4, child $2.50), named for and dedicated to a prominent Japanese educator. Spread over one hectare (2.5 acres), this traditional Japanese garden of shrubs and miniatures has two distinct sections: the Stroll Garden, laid out in a form that symbolizes the journey through life, and the Tea Garden, the place to contemplate life from a ceremonial teahouse. The garden is surrounded by high walls (which almost block out the noise of traffic from busy Marine Drive), making it a peaceful retreat. Outside of summer, the garden is open limited hours (Mon.–Fri. 10 A.M.–2:30 P.M.), but admission is by donation.

Also on campus is the delightful **UBC Botanical Garden** (6804 Marine Dr., 604/822-4208; adult $7, senior $5, child $3). Set among coastal forest, the 44-hectare (110-acre) garden dates to the turn of the 20th century and features eight separate sections, which hold around 10,000 species of trees, shrubs, and flowers. The various gardens have themes of specific regions or environments, including Canada's largest collection of rhododendrons in the Asian Garden; a BC Native Garden alive with the plants, flowers, and shrubs found along the Pacific Northwest coast; and a display of mountain plants from the world's continents in the Alpine Garden. Thriving in Vancouver's mild climate, the garden offers something of interest year-round, with the main season running mid-March to mid-October, when it's open 10 A.M.–6 P.M. (the rest of the year 10 A.M.–5 P.M.). From the Museum of Anthropology, follow Marine Drive south for 2.4 kilometers (1.5 miles) to 16th Avenue.

RICHMOND

The city of Richmond (population 170,000) sprawls across **Lulu Island** at the mouth of the Fraser River. Most visitors to Vancouver cross the island on their way north from the United States on Highway 99, or to and from the airport or Tsawwassen Ferry Terminal. Steveston is the main reason to visit Richmond, but on the way, consider escaping the suburban sprawl at **Richmond Nature Park** at the junction of Highways 91 and 99. This 85-hectare (210-acre) park has been left in its natural state; the only development consists of trails leading to ponds and fens. The park is open daily during daylight hours.

Steveston

On Lulu Island's southwestern extremity, the historic fishing village of Steveston is a lively spot worth a visit. In the 1880s it had more than 50 canneries and was the world's largest fishing port. One block south of Moncton Street and a short walk from the old cannery is a redeveloped stretch of harborfront that bustles with activity in summer. Casual visitors and local anglers mingle at fishing-supply outlets, shops selling packaged seafood products, boutiques, and restaurants. Below the main wharf, fishing boats sell the day's catch—halibut, salmon, ling cod, rock cod, crab, and shrimp—to the general public at excellent prices. The fishermen are friendly enough, chatting happily about their catch and how best to cook it up.

On the harborfront you'll find the **Gulf of Georgia Cannery National Historic Site** (12138 4th Ave., 604/664-9009; June–Sept. daily 10 A.M.–5 P.M., spring and fall Thurs.–Mon. same hours; adult $7.15, senior $5.90, child $3.45), a cannery that operated between 1894 and 1979. Another historic site, the **Britannia Heritage Shipyard** (5180 Westwater Dr., 604/718-8050; May–Sept. Tues.–Sun. 10 A.M.–6 P.M., the rest of the year weekends noon–4 P.M.) is reached by following the signs east along Moncton Street. Dating to 1885, the actual Britannia Shipyard building is currently being restored, but it is surrounded by four already restored buildings from the same era, five others in various states of disrepair, and a variety of interesting wooden vessels.

Naturally, seafood is the specialty at harborfront restaurants, all with outdoor tables. The most casual option is a take-out meal from **Sockeye City Diner** (Fisherman's Wharf, Bayview Rd., 604/275-6790); order at the window and spread out your feast on the wharf or dock. On a floating dock down toward the cannery is **Pa Jo's** (604/204-0767; summer daily 11 A.M.–8 P.M.), cooking up classic battered fish and chips with a wedge of lemon for around $9. Tables are set on the dock as well as on the wharf high above.

To get to Steveston, take Highway 99 to the

Steveston Highway exit, then head west, passing by a magnificent Buddhist temple. Town center is south from the Steveston Highway along the No. 1 Road.

DELTA

Pass under the south arm of the Fraser River via Highway 99 and the George Massey Tunnel, and you'll emerge in the sprawling industrial and residential district of Delta (pop. 100,000). Take Highway 17 (Exit 28) south from Highway 99 and turn right on Ladner Trunk Road to access **Ladner Village** and **Delta Museum and Archives** (4858 Delta St., 604/946-9322; Tues.–Sat. 10 A.M.–4:30 P.M.; donation). This museum tells the story of the area's first inhabitants, the Salish, and the farming and fishing history of more recent times.

George C. Reifel Migratory Bird Sanctuary

Two kilometers (1.2 miles) from Ladner Village along River Road West, cross Canoe Passage

© ANDREW HEMPSTEAD

Blue herons are one of many species at the George C. Reifel Migratory Bird Sanctuary.

on the old wooden bridge to access this coastal wildlife sanctuary (604/946-6980; daily 9 A.M.–4 P.M.; adult $4, senior and child $2). The 350-hectare (800-acre) reserve protects the northern corner of low-lying Westham Island, a stopover for thousands of migratory birds in spring and fall. In the middle of a wide delta at the mouth of the Fraser River, the island is a world away from surrounding urban life. The best time for a visit is during the spectacular snow goose migration, which runs from early November to mid-December. Otherwise, you'll see abundant migratory birdlife anytime between October and April. The island also serves as a permanent home for many bird species, including bald eagles, peregrine falcons, herons, swans, owls, and ducks.

SURREY

The City of Surrey is well within Metro Vancouver but is officially its own incorporated city—with a population of 350,000, it's British Columbia's second largest. Its first settlers were the Stewarts, who built a homestead beside the Nicomekl River in 1894. The original homestead is now the centerpiece of **Elgin Heritage Park** (13723 Crescent Rd., 250/543-3456; Mon.–Fri. 10 A.M.–4 P.M., Sat.–Sun. noon–4 P.M.; free). The farm's original workers' accommodations have been transformed into a weaving center, where textiles are created on antique looms and spinning wheels. Also on the property is a barn full of antique farm machinery and a covered display telling the story of the local crabbing industry. To get there, take the King George Highway exit off Highway 99, then turn onto Elgin Road, which becomes Crescent Road.

White Rock

Named for a 400-ton glacial erratic that sits by the shoreline, this incorporated city of 17,000 is at the main border crossing for Vancouver-bound travelers heading north on Highway 5 from Seattle (Highway 99 north of the border). At the 24-hour checkpoint are duty-free shops and **Peace Arch Provincial Park,** where a stone archway symbolizes the friendly relationship

© ANDREW HEMPSTEAD

Crowds flock to White Rock beaches throughout the summer.

enjoyed between Canada and the United States. Take 8th Avenue west from the first interchange north of the border to reach downtown White Rock, where Marine Drive hugs the coastline for five kilometers (3.1 miles), lined almost the entire way with outdoor cafés, restaurants, old beach houses, and ocean-inspired condominiums. At around 149th Street is the main concentration of restaurants, an information center, and a long pier. The city's namesake lies above the high-tide mark just south of the pier. It is now painted bright white and impossible to miss. The beach is no Caribbean gem, but at low tide, locals flock to the wide expanse of sand to bake in the sun, wade in shallow water, play Frisbee, or skimboard across pools of water.

NORTH SHORE

North of downtown lie the incorporated cities of **North Vancouver** (pop. 48,000) and **West Vancouver** (pop. 43,000), both of which are dramatically sandwiched between the North Shore Range of the Coast Mountains and Burrard Inlet. The North Shore is accessible from downtown via the **Lions Gate Bridge,** but the SeaBus, which runs from Waterfront Station to **Lonsdale Quay,** offers a more enjoyable alternative to getting caught in bridge traffic. At the lively quay, a small information center (to the right as you come out of the SeaBus terminal) dispenses valuable information, and transit buses depart regularly.

Capilano Suspension Bridge

Admission at this North Shore attraction (604/985-7474; summer daily 8 A.M.–dusk, the rest of the year daily 9 A.M.–5 P.M.; adult $24, senior $22, youth $14, child $8.50) is a bit steep, but it's one of Vancouver's most popular sights. The centerpiece is a wood-and-wire suspension bridge spanning a canyon some 70 meters (230 feet) above the Capilano River. Allow at least two hours to walk the bridge, step out onto the numerous cantilevered decks, take the Treetops Adventure suspended walkway, and wander along the forested nature trails. Back near the main entrance, native carvers display their skills in the Big House, and you'll find the requisite gift shop and eateries. To get there by car, cross Lions Gate Bridge, turn east onto Marine Drive and then immediately north onto Capilano Road, continuing to 3735 Capilano, on your left. By bus, take number 246 north on Georgia Street or hop aboard the SeaBus and take bus number 236 from Lonsdale Quay.

Capilano Salmon Hatchery

This is my favorite North Shore attraction—and not only because it's free. If you've always wanted to know more about the miraculous life cycle of salmon, or want some facts to back up your fish stories, visit this hatchery on the Capilano River, just upstream from the suspension bridge (604/666-1790; summer daily 8 A.M.–8 P.M., until dusk the rest of the year). Beside the rushing Capilano River and ensconced in cool rainforest, salmon are diverted through a channel and into manmade spawning grounds. The channel is topped by a metal grate in one section and lined with glass windows in another. This allows up-close viewing of the salmon as they fight the current through their July-to-October run. In addition to the life-cycle displays, an exhibit on fly-fishing holds some interesting old tackle.

◖ Grouse Mountain Skyride

Continuing north, Capilano Road becomes Nancy Greene Way and ends at the base of the Grouse Mountain Skyride (604/980-9311; adult $33, senior $31, youth $19, child $12), North America's largest aerial tramway. For an excellent view of downtown Vancouver, Stanley Park, the Pacific Ocean, and as far south as Mount Baker (Washington), take the almost-vertical eight-minute ride on the gondola to the upper slopes of 1,250-meter (4,100-foot) Grouse Mountain. The gondola runs year-round, departing every 15 minutes, 10 A.M.–10 P.M. in summer (less frequently the rest of the year).

The trip to the top is a lot more than a gondola ride—and it's easy to spend the best part of a day exploring the surrounding area and taking advantage of the attractions included in the price of the ride up. Of the many possible hikes, the one-kilometer (0.6-mile) **Blue Grouse Interpretive Trail** is the easiest and most enjoyable, winding around a lake and through a rainforest. Another trail leads to a fenced area where wolves and bears are rehabilitated after being orphaned. The best-known hike is the **Grouse Grind,** from the base of the gondola to the top. It's so named for a reason: The trail gains more than one kilometer (3,300 feet) of elevation in just 2.9 kilometers (1.8 miles). Other summit activities include a fun but touristy logging show, chairlift rides, a First Nations longhouse with dancing and storytelling, and wide-screen movie presentations of the outdoor wonders of British Columbia and local wildlife.

Lynn Canyon Park

On its way to Burrard Inlet, Lynn Creek flows through a deep canyon straddled by this 240-hectare (930-acre) park. Spanning the canyon is the "other" suspension bridge. The one here is half as wide as its more famous counterpart over the Capilano River, but it's a few meters higher and, best of all, it's free. An ancient forest of Douglas fir surrounds the impressive canyon and harbors several hiking trails. Also visit **Lynn Canyon Ecology Centre** (604/981-3103, daily 10 A.M.–5 P.M.; free), where displays, models, and free slide shows and films explore plant and animal ecology.

Lynn Canyon Park is seven kilometers (4.3 miles) east of the Capilano River. To get there by car, take the Lynn Valley Road exit off Highway 1, east of the Lions Gate Bridge. By public transport, take the SeaBus to Lonsdale Quay, then bus 228 or 229.

Mount Seymour Provincial Park and Vicinity

Hikers and skiers flock to this 3,508-hectare (8,670-acre) park 20 kilometers (12.4 miles) northeast of downtown. The park lies off Mt. Seymour Parkway, which splits east off the TransCanada Highway just north of Burrard Inlet. The long and winding access road to the park climbs steadily through an ancient forest of western hemlock, cedar, and Douglas fir to a small facility area at an elevation of 1,000 meters (3,300 feet). From the parking lot, trails lead to the summit of 1,453-meter (4,770-foot) Mount Seymour; allow one hour for the two-kilometer (1.2-mile) trek to the summit.

Cypress Provincial Park

This 3,012-hectare (7,440-acre) park northwest of downtown encompasses a high alpine area in the North Shore Mountains. To get to the park, take the TransCanada Highway 12 kilometers (7.5 miles) west of Lions Gate Bridge and turn north onto Cypress Bowl Road (Exit 8). Even the park access road up from the Trans-Canada Highway is worthwhile for the views. At the second switchback, **Highview Lookout** provides a stunning panorama of the city, with interpretive panels describing the surrounding natural history. Just beyond the third switch-back is another lookout, along with picnic tables. At the 12-kilometer (7.5-mile) mark, the road splits. Go straight ahead to reach Cypress Bowl ski area, where summer season over the next years will be a hive of activity as the area is redeveloped in preparation for hosting free-style skiing and snowboarding events of the 2010 Olympic Winter Games. From the main day lodge, well-marked hiking trails radiate out like spokes. One easy trail leads under the Black Chair (to the left as you stand in front of the day lodge) and passes a small alpine lake before ending after 1.3 kilometers (0.8 mile) at a lookout; allow one hour maximum for the round-trip. The 2.3-kilometer (1.4-mile) circuit to Yew Lake gains less elevation and is barrier free.

Lighthouse Park

On a headland jutting into Howe Sound, Lighthouse Park lies eight kilometers (five miles) west of the Lions Gate Bridge. Trails lead through the park to coastal cliffs and a lighthouse that guides shipping into narrow Burrard Inlet. Views from the lighthouse grounds are spectacular, extending west over the Strait of Georgia and east to Stanley Park and the Vancouver skyline.

Horseshoe Bay

The pretty little residential area of Horseshoe Bay offers plenty to see and do while you wait for the Vancouver Island or Sunshine Coast ferry. If you and your trusty vehicle are catching one of the ferries, buy your ticket at the car booth, move your automobile into the lineup, and then explore the town. Several restaurants, a bakery, a supermarket, a pub, and a couple of good delis cater to the hungry and thirsty. A stroll along the beautiful waterfront marina is a good way to cool your heels and dawdle away some waiting time.

EAST FROM DOWNTOWN

When you leave Vancouver and head due east, you travel through the most built-up and heavily populated area of British Columbia, skirting modern commercial centers, residential suburbs, and zones of heavy industry. Greater Vancouver extends almost 100 kilometers (62 miles) along the Fraser Valley, through mostly residential areas. The main route east is the TransCanada Highway, which parallels the Fraser River to the south, passing through Burnaby, Langley, and Abbotsford. The original path taken by this highway crosses the Fraser River at New Westminster, the capital of British Columbia for a short period in the 1860s.

Burnaby

Immediately east of downtown, Burnaby was incorporated as a city in 1992 (its population of 200,000 makes it British Columbia's third largest city), but in reality it's part of Vancouver's suburban sprawl. The TransCanada Highway bisects Burnaby, but access is easiest via the SkyTrain, which makes four stops within the city. Among these stops is **Metrotown,** which is Vancouver's largest shopping mall.

Burnaby Village Museum is a four-hectare (10-acre) open-air museum (604/293-6500; May–early September 11 A.M.–4:30 P.M.; adult $10, senior and youth $7.50, child $5) that lies in Deer Lake Park, on the south side of the TransCanada Highway; to get there take Exit 33 south, then turn left onto Canada Way and right onto Deer Lake Avenue. The village is a reconstruction of how a BC town would have looked in the first 20 years of the 1900s, complete with more than 30 shops and houses, heritage-style gardens, a miniature railway, and costumed staff. The highlight is a historic carousel with 30 restored wooden horses.

Burnaby Mountain Park

On the north side of the TransCanada Highway is Burnaby Mountain Park, which surrounds the campus of **Simon Fraser University,** the province's second-largest campus. Centennial Way (off Burnaby Mountain Parkway) leads to the park's high point, where views extend down Burrard Inlet to North Vancouver and its stunning mountain backdrop. Also at the summit is a collection of totem poles, some Japanese sculptures, a rose garden, and a restaurant. The university itself is worthy of inspection. Its unique design of "quadrants" linked by a massive fountain-filled courtyard is typical of architect Arthur Erickson, who was partly responsible for its design. The **Museum of Archaeology and Ethnology** (8888 University Dr., 604/291-3325; Mon.–Fri. 10 A.M.–4 P.M.; donation) holds a collection of native artifacts gathered from along the Pacific Northwest coast.

Golden Ears Provincial Park

Encompassing 62,540 hectares (154,540 acres) of the Coast Mountains, this park extends from the Alouette River, near the suburb of Maple Ridge, north to Garibaldi Provincial Park. To get to the main facility areas, follow Highway 7 east out of the city for 40 kilometers (25 miles) to Maple Ridge, then follow signs north. Much of the park was logged for railway ties in the 1920s, but today the second-growth montane forest—dominated by western hemlock—has almost erased the early human devastation.

The park access road follows the Alouette River into the park, ending at Alouette Lake. The river and lake provide fair fishing, but the park's most popular activity is hiking. **Lower Falls Trail** begins at the end of the road and leads 2.7 kilometers (1.7 miles) along Gold Creek to a 10-meter (33-foot) waterfall; allow one hour each way. Across Gold Creek, **West Canyon Trail** climbs 200 vertical meters (660 feet) over 1.5 kilometers (0.9 miles) to a viewpoint of Alouette Lake.

New Westminster

"New West," as it's best known, is a densely populated residential area 15 kilometers (9.3 miles) southeast of downtown. Because of its strategic location, where the Fraser River divides, it was declared the capital of the mainland colony in 1859 and then the provincial capital in the years 1866–1868. Only a few historic buildings remain, and the old port area has been totally overtaken by modern developments. Although still a busy inland port, the north side of the river, along Columbia Street, was redeveloped in the late 1980s, with a riverside promenade linking attractive stretches of green space to **Westminster Quay Market.** Although it's open for very unmarket-like hours (it doesn't open until 9:30 A.M.), it holds an interesting selection of fresh produce, take-out food stalls, and specialty shops. Out front is the **Samson V,** built in 1937 and the last remaining paddle wheeler left on the river when it was retired in 1980. It's now open for public inspection (June–Aug. daily noon–5 P.M.). Beside the market is the **Fraser River Discovery Centre** (788 Quayside Dr., 604/521-8401; Tues.–Sat. 10 A.M.–4 P.M.; free), which describes the river and its importance to the development of New Westminster.

Sports and Recreation

WALKING AND HIKING
Stanley Park

Vancouver is not a particularly good city to explore on foot, but it does have one redeeming factor for foot travelers: Stanley Park, an urban oasis crisscrossed with hiking trails and encircled by a 10-kilometer (6.2-mile) promenade that hugs the shoreline. Along the way are many points of interest, benches, and interpretive plaques pointing out historical events. Allow three hours for the entire circuit. The promenade can be walked in either direction, but those on bikes and skates must travel counterclockwise. It is *always* packed, especially in late afternoon and on weekends.

Away from the Seawall Promenade, you'll find most trails a lot less busy. A good alternative to exploring one long section of the promenade is to ascend the steps immediately north of Lions Gate Bridge to Prospect Point (and maybe stop for a snack at the café), then continue west along the Merilees Trail, which follows the top of the cliff band to Third Beach. Along the way, an old lookout point affords excellent views of Siwash Rock and the Strait of Georgia.

The isthmus of land linking the park to the rest of the downtown peninsula is less than one kilometer (0.6 miles) wide, but it's mostly taken up by Lost Lagoon. A 1.5-kilometer (0.9-mile) trail (30 minutes round-trip) encircles this bird-filled body of water. In the heart of the park is Beaver Lake, a small body of water that is alive with birds throughout summer. Trails lead into this lake from all directions, and it can easily be walked around in 20 minutes.

False Creek

From English Bay Beach, a promenade continues along English Bay to Sunset Beach and Vancouver Aquatic Centre. The small ferries that operate on False Creek, extending service as far west as the Aquatic Centre, open up several

© ANDREW HEMPSTEAD

False Creek has a number of walking combinations with a view of the marina.

walking combinations around False Creek. Granville Island is a good starting point. No official trails go around the island, but if you walk east from the market, you pass a community of floating houses and go through a grassed area to Lookout Hill. Continue around the island and you'll come across a small footbridge leading to the mainland. From this point, it's seven kilometers (4.3 miles) around the head of False Creek, passing Science World and the Plaza of Nations, then closely following the water to the foot of Hornby Street for the short ferry trip back across to Granville Island; allow two hours without stopping.

Pacific Spirit Regional Park and Vicinity

This 762-hectare (1,880-acre) park on the Vancouver peninsula offers 35 kilometers (22 miles) of hiking trails through a forested environment similar to that which greeted the first European settlers more than 200 years ago. A good starting point is the Park Centre (16th Ave. W., west of Blanca St., 604/224-5739; Mon.–Fri. 8 A.M.–4 P.M.), which has a supply of trail maps. The entire park is crisscrossed with trails, so although getting seriously lost is impossible, taking the wrong trail and ending up away from your intended destination is easy. One good trailhead is opposite a residential area in the east of the park, at the junction of Imperial Road and King Edward Avenue. From this point, the Imperial Trail heads west through a forest of red cedar and fir, crosses Salish Creek, then emerges on Southwest Marine Drive, across the road from a plaque that notes the many explorers who contributed to opening up Vancouver to European settlement. From this lofty viewpoint, the view extends across the Strait of Georgia. This trail is 2.8 kilometers (1.7 miles) one-way; allow two hours for the round-trip. In the same vicinity as the trailhead detailed above, at the west end of 19th Avenue, a short boardwalk trail leads to Camosun Bog, home to a great variety of plants and birds.

BICYCLING

Stanley Park is *very* popular with cyclists; among its network of bike paths is the popular Seawall Promenade, which hugs the coast for

biking in Stanley Park

© ANDREW HEMPSTEAD

10 kilometers (6.2 miles). Bike travel is in a counterclockwise direction. On the south side of English Bay, a cycle path runs from Vanier Park to Point Grey and the university, passing some of the city's best beaches on the way.

Near the entrance to Stanley Park, where Robson and Denman Streets meet, you'll find a profusion of bike-rental shops. These include **Bayshore Bicycles** (745 Denman St., 604/688-2453) and **Spokes Bicycle Rental** (1798 W. Georgia St., 604/688-5141), while back toward Canada Place is **Seawall Adventure Centre** (1095 West Waterfront Rd., 604/233-3500).

GOLF

Vancouver is blessed with more than 50 courses, most of which are open to the public. It is often quoted that in Vancouver it is possible to ski in the morning and golf in the afternoon, and because most courses are open year-round, this really is true.

There's a pitch-and-putt golf course in **Stanley Park** (604/681-8847; daily 8 A.M.–6:30 P.M.). With 18 holes under 100 yards each, the course makes a fun diversion. Greens fees are $9.75 per round, plus $1 per club for rentals.

One of the best courses open to the public is the **University Golf Club** (5185 University Blvd., Point Grey, 604/224-1818), featuring fairways lined with mature trees. Greens fees are $60 midweek and $70 on weekends (those over 60 pay a discounted rate of $45 Mon.–Fri. before noon).

Vancouver Parks and Recreation operates three 18-hole courses on the south side of the city: **McCleery Golf Course** (7188 McDonald St., Southlands, 604/257-8191) has a flat, relatively easy layout with wide fairways; **Fraserview Golf Course** (7800 Vivian Dr., Fraserview, 604/257-6923), rebuilt in the late 1990s, winds its way through a well-established forest; and **Langara Golf Course** (6706 Alberta St. off Cambie St., South Cambie, 604/713-1816) is the most challenging of the three. Each course offers club rentals, carts, and lessons, and all but Langara have driving ranges. Greens fees at all three courses are $52–55 during the week and $55–58 on weekends. Make bookings up to five days in advance by calling 604/280-1818, or call the courses directly on the day you want to play.

Water comes into play on 13 holes of the **Mayfair Lakes & Country Club** (5460 No. 7 Rd., Richmond, 604/276-0505), but its most unique feature is the salmon, which spawn in Mayfair's waterways. Greens fees are $79 Mon.–Thurs., $89 Friday and weekends, with twilight and off-season rates discounted as low as $39.

Beyond Porteau Cove is **Furry Creek Golf and Country Club** (604/922-9461 or 888/922-9462), generally regarded as the most scenic course in the Vancouver region. Immaculately manicured, the course is bordered on one side by the driftwood-strewn beaches of Howe Sound and on the other by towering mountains. It is relatively short, at just over 5,486 meters (6,000 yards), but water comes into play on many holes, including one where the green juts into the sound and is almost an island. On summer weekends, greens fees are $110, with the price of a round decreasing to $95 midweek and as low as $60 the rest of the year.

WATER SPORTS
Swimming and Sunbathing

All of Vancouver's best beaches are along the shoreline of English Bay; 10 have lifeguards on duty through the summer 11:30 A.M.–8:45 P.M. Closest to downtown is **English Bay Beach,** at the end of Denman Street. Flanked by a narrow strip of parkland and a wide array of cafés and restaurants, this is *the* beach for people-watching. From English Bay Beach, the Seawall Promenade leads north to **Second** and **Third Beaches,** both short, secluded stretches of sand. To the south is **Sunset Beach,** which is most popular with families.

Swimmers take note: Even at the peak of summer, the water here only warms up to about 17°C (63°F), tops. If that doesn't sound enticing, continue to the south end of Sunset Beach to **Vancouver Aquatic Centre** (1050 Beach Ave., 604/665-3424; adult $5, senior $3.50, child $2.50). Inside is a 50-meter heated pool, saunas, whirlpools, and a small weight room.

On the south side of English Bay, **Kitsilano Beach** offers spectacular views back across the bay to downtown and the mountains beyond. Take a dip in the adjacent public pool, which is 137 meters (450 feet) long and was built in 1931. The beach and pool are an easy walk from both Vanier Park and a False Creek Ferries dock.

Canoeing and Kayaking

Granville Island is the center of action for paddlers, and the calm waters of adjacent False Creek are the perfect place to practice your skills. For the widest choice of equipment, head to **Ecomarine Ocean Kayak Centre** (1668 Duranleau St., 604/689-7575), which rents single sea kayaks from $34 for 2 hours or $59 for 24 hours, and double sea kayaks and canoes from $46 for 2 hours, $89 for 24 hours. Both companies also teach kayaking.

The **Indian Arm** of Burrard Inlet allows for a real wilderness experience, right on the city's back doorstep. This 22-kilometer (13.7-mile) fjord cuts deeply into the North Shore Range; the only development is at its southern end, where the suburb of Deep Cove provides a takeoff point for the waterway. **Deep Cove Canoe and Kayak Centre** (2156 Banbury Rd., Deep Cove, 604/929-2268; Apr.–Oct.) rents canoes and kayaks for $32 for two hours for a single kayak. If you'd prefer to take a tour, contact **Lotus Land Tours** (604/684-4922 or 800/528-3531), which charges $165 per person for a full-day tour, including downtown hotel pickups, a salmon barbecue on an uninhabited island, and instruction.

SKIING AND SNOWBOARDING

While Vancouver is the gateway to world-renowned Whistler/Blackcomb (see *Whistler* in the *Southwestern British Columbia* chapter), the city boasts three other alpine resorts on its back doorstep. They don't offer the terrain or facilities of Whistler, and their low elevations can create unreliable conditions, but a day's skiing or boarding at any one of the three sure beats being stuck in the hustle and bustle of the city on a cold winter's day.

Grouse Mountain

Towering above North Vancouver, the cut slopes of this resort (604/980-9311, www .grousemountain.com) can be seen from many parts of the city, but as you'd expect, on a clear day views from *up there* are much more spectacular. To get there, take Capilano Road north from the TransCanada, following it onto Nancy Greene Way, from which a gondola lifts you up 1,000 vertical meters (3,280 feet) to the slopes. Four chairlifts and a couple of T-bars serve 24 runs and a vertical rise of 365 meters (1,200 feet). Advanced skiers and boarders shouldn't get too excited about a day on the slopes here—even the runs with names like Purgatory and Devil's Advocate are pretty tame—but schussing down the slopes of Grouse Mountain after dark is an experience you won't soon forget. Lift tickets are adult $47, youth and senior $37, child $21. Night skiing (after 4 P.M.) costs adult $37, youth and senior $31, and child $19 until closing at 10 P.M.

Cypress Mountain

The eyes of the world will be on this small resort (604/926-5612, www.cypressmountain .com) on Vancouver's North Shore when it hosts the freestyle skiing and snowboarding events of the 2010 Olympic Winter Games. It currently offers about 34 runs across a vertical rise of 534 meters (1,750 feet). Lift tickets are adult $48, senior and child $23.

Cypress also caters to cross-country skiers and snowshoers, with 16 kilometers (10 miles) of groomed and track-set trails, some of which are lit for night skiing. A package of cross-country ski rentals, a lesson, and trail pass costs $70. Snowshoe rentals are $18 per day. If none of the above appeals, consider spending a few hours whizzing down the slopes of the Snow Tube Park; $13 per person includes all-day use of the Tube Tow and a tube.

To get to the resort, take the TransCanada Highway 12 kilometers (7.5 miles) west from Lions Gate Bridge and turn north on Cypress Bowl Road. If you don't feel like driving up the mountain, catch the shuttle bus that departs hourly from Lonsdale Quay and Cypress Mountain Sports in Park Royal Mall, West Vancouver; $15 round-trip. For a snow report, call 604/419-7669.

Mount Seymour

With the highest base elevation of Vancouver's three alpine resorts, Seymour's (604/986-2261, snow report 604/718-7771, www.mount seymour.com) snow is somewhat reliable, but the area's relatively gentle terrain will be of interest only to beginning and intermediate skiers and boarders. Four chairlifts serve 20 runs and a vertical rise of 365 meters (1,200 feet). Daily lift passes are adult $39, senior $27, child $19. You can also rent snowshoes ($16) and tramp along the resort's trail system ($6 for a day pass), but the Friday night guided snowshoe walk ($32) is a real treat—and not only because of the chocolate fondue at the end. The resort is in Mount Seymour Provincial Park. To get there, head north off the TransCanada Highway 15 kilometers (9.3 miles) east of the Lions Gate Bridge, following the Mt. Seymour Parkway to Mt. Seymour Road. Call the resort for a shuttle schedule from the North Shore; $9 per person round-trip.

SPECTATOR SPORTS

Vancouverites love their sports—not just being involved themselves, but supporting local teams. With a long season and outside activities curtailed by the winter weather, ice hockey—known in Canada simply as "hockey"—draws the biggest crowds (although the official national sport is lacrosse), but the city also boasts professional football, baseball, and soccer teams.

Hockey

In 1911 the world's second (and largest) artificial ice rink opened at the north end of Denman Street, complete with seating for 10,000 hockey fans. The local team, then known as the Vancouver Millionaires, played in a small professional league, and in 1915 Vancouver won its first and only **Stanley Cup,** the holy grail of professional ice hockey. The **Vancouver**

Canucks (604/899-7400, www.canucks.com) today play at General Motors Place (across from BC Place Stadium on Griffith Way) through a season running from October to April; ticket prices range $38–120.

Football

The **BC Lions** (604/589-7627, www.bclions .com) are Vancouver's Canadian Football League (CFL) franchise. American football fans might be surprised by some of the plays because the rules are slightly different from those of the National Football League (NFL). And no, you're not imagining things: The playing field is larger than those used in the game's American version. Last winning the Grey Cup in 2006, the Lions play out of BC Place Stadium, on the south side of downtown at the corner of Robson and Beatty Streets. The season runs June–November, with most games played in the evening; tickets range $25–75.

Soccer

Vancouver is a soccer stronghold, and with two professional teams and dozens of intracity leagues, it is always well represented on the national team. Vancouver's professional men's soccer team, the **Whitecaps** (604/899-9283, www.whitecapsfc.com) play in the USL-1 of the United Soccer League, competing against teams across North America through the summer. Local women players are represented in the W League and are also known as the Whitecaps. Both teams play at Burnaby's Swangard Stadium with a season that runs May–August. Game day tickets are in the $9–24 range.

Horse Racing

Thoroughbred racing takes place in the Pacific National Exhibition grounds six kilometers (3.7 miles) east of downtown at **Hastings Park Racecourse** (corner of Renfrew and McGill Streets, 604/254-1631, www.hastingspark .com), as it has done for more than 100 years. Full betting and a variety of dining facilities are offered. The season runs late April–November, with the first race starting at 1:03 P.M. The biggest races fall near the end of the season, including the BC Derby on the last Saturday in September. General admission is free, or pay $8 for entry to the clubhouse.

TOURS

If you don't have a lot of time to explore Vancouver on your own, or just want an introduction to the city, consider taking one of the many tours available—they'll maximize your time and get you to the highlights with minimum stress.

Bus Tours

Gray Line (604/879-3363 or 800/667-0882, www.grayline.ca) offers a large variety of tours. The four-hour Deluxe Grand City Tour, which includes Stanley Park, Chinatown, Gastown, Robson Street, and English Bay, costs adult $62, child $42. Another option with Gray Line is a downtown loop tour aboard an old English double-decker bus (mid-Apr.–Oct.). You can get on and off as you please at any of the 21 stops made on the two-hour loop. Tickets cost adult $35, senior $32, child $18. Gray Line also has tours to Grouse Mountain (late Mar.–Oct.; adult $93, child $62). Ticket prices include pickups at major downtown hotels.

Vancouver Trolley Company

From the main pickup point, a trolley-shaped booth at the top end of Gastown, this company (157 Water St., 604/801-5515 or 888/451-5581) operates an old-fashioned trolley through the streets of downtown Vancouver. The two-hour City Attractions Loop Tour stops at 23 tourist attractions, from Stanley Park in the north

to Science World in the south. Trolleys run April–October daily 9 A.M.–4 P.M., coming by each stop every half hour. Tickets are adult $35, senior $32, child $18.50. Reservations aren't necessary.

Harbor Cruises

From June to September, **Harbour Cruises** (604/688-7246 or 800/663-1500) offers a 75-minute tour of bustling Burrard Inlet on the paddle wheeler MV *Constitution.* Tours depart from the north foot of Denman Street, up to three times daily between April and October; adult $25, senior and student $21, child $10. In the evening (June–Sept. at 7 P.M.), the paddle wheeler heads out onto the harbor for a three-hour Sunset Dinner Cruise. The cruise (adult $70, child $60) includes dinner and, if booked through Gray Line (604/879-3363), hotel transfers.

While puttering around False Creek on a small ferry is an inexpensive way to see this part of the city from water level, **False Creek Ferries** (604/684-7781) also offers a 40-minute guided tour of the historic waterway for just $9 per person. Departures are daily 10 A.M.–5 P.M. from Granville Island.

Flightseeing

Flightseeing tours of the city are offered by **Harbour Air** (604/274-1277, www.harbour-air .com) from its seaplane base on the west side of Canada Place. Options range from a 20-minute flight over downtown ($100 pp) to a full day trip to Victoria, including time at Butchart Gardens ($269 pp).

Entertainment and Events

There's never a dull moment in Vancouver when it comes to nightlife. The city's unofficial entertainment district extends southwest along Granville Street from Granville Street Mall and south from this strip to False Creek. Cinemas line Granville Street Mall, and beyond the mall is a smattering of nightclubs, with the main concentration of these in Yaletown. Performing

arts and concert venues are scattered throughout the city, but the three largest—Ford Centre for the Performing Arts, Queen Elizabeth Theatre, and BC Place Stadium—are south of Granville Street along Georgia Street.

For complete listings of all that's happening around the city, pick up the free *Georgia Straight* (www.straight.com), the offspring

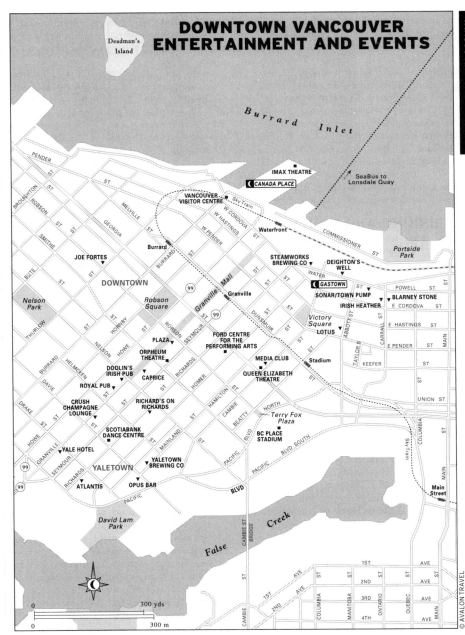

DOWNTOWN VANCOUVER ENTERTAINMENT AND EVENTS

VANCOUVER

Deadman's Island

Burrard   Inlet

IMAX THEATRE
SeaBus to Lonsdale Quay
CANADA PLACE

VANCOUVER VISITOR CENTRE
SkyTrain
W CORDOVA
W HASTINGS
W PENDER
Waterfront
Portside Park
COMMISSIONER ST

PENDER
ST
BROUGHTON
ROBSON
MELVILLE
GEORGIA
SMITHE
ST
Burrard

JOE FORTES
STEAMWORKS BREWING CO
DEIGHTON'S WELL
WATER
GASTOWN
POWELL   ST
BLARNEY STONE
E CORDOVA   ST

BUTE
DOWNTOWN
Robson Square
Granville
SONAR/TOWN PUMP
IRISH HEATHER
E HASTINGS   ST

Nelson Park
99
Granville Mall
Victory Square
LOTUS
E PENDER   ST

NELSON
THURLOW
HORNBY
HOWE
SEYMOUR
99
DUNSMUIR
ABBOTT ST
CARRALL ST
TAYLOR S
KEEFER   ST
MAIN

PLAZA
FORD CENTRE FOR THE PERFORMING ARTS
Stadium

ORPHEUM THEATRE
RICHARDS
MEDIA CLUB
UNION ST

DOOLIN'S IRISH PUB
CAPRICE
HOMER
QUEEN ELIZABETH THEATRE

ROYAL PUB
HAMILTON
CAMBIE
BEATTY
NORTH
Terry Fox Plaza
COLUMBIA

CRUSH CHAMPAGNE LOUNGE
RICHARD'S ON RICHARDS
BC PLACE STADIUM

SCOTIABANK DANCE CENTRE
MAINLAND
BLVD
BLVD SOUTH

YALE HOTEL
YALETOWN
YALETOWN BREWING CO
PACIFIC
PACIFIC
MAIN
Main Street

ATLANTIS
OPUS BAR
PACIFIC
BLVD

DRAKE
DAVIE
HELMCKEN
BURRARD
HOWE
GRANVILLE
SEYMOUR
RICHARDS

David Lam Park
CAMBIE ST
False   Creek
BRIDGE

300 yds
300 m

1ST   AVE
2ND   AVE
1ST
2ND
3RD   AVE
4TH   AVE
COLUMBIA
MANITOBA
ONTARIO
QUEBEC
MAIN
CAMBIE

© AVALON TRAVEL

of an entertainment rag started by the flower children of the late 1960s. Friday and weekend editions of Vancouver's two daily newspapers, the *Province* and the *Vancouver Sun,* offer comprehensive entertainment listings.

As in all other major cities across Canada (and the United States), **Ticketmaster** (604/280-3311, www.ticketmaster.ca) has a monopoly on advance ticket sales to major entertainment events; have your credit card ready. **Tickets Tonight** (200 Burrard St., 604/684-2787, www.ticketstonight.ca; daily 10 A.M.–6 P.M.) sells half-price tickets the day of major performances. You must purchase them in person from the booth inside the downtown information center.

DRINKING AND DANCING
Ever since "Gassy Jack" Deighton set up the city's first liquor outlet (a barrel of whiskey set atop a crude plank bar) in the area that became known as Gastown, Vancouver has had its favorite watering holes.

Gastown
In the historic building, The Landing, **Steamworks Brewing Co.** (375 Water St., 604/689-2739; daily 11:30 A.M.–10 P.M.) is the perfect place to relax with a beer from the in-house brewery. The atmosphere is casual yet stylish, and you'll have great views across Burrard Inlet. Down the hill is **Deighton's Well** (127 Water St., 604/669-7219), with a few tables streetside and a larger room out back that hosts occasional live music. At the far end of Gastown, the lively **Blarney Stone** (216 Carrall St., 604/687-4322) frequently resounds with rowdy Irish party bands. The evening crowd here is older and often single. In the same vein, across the road is the **Irish Heather** (217 Carrall St., 604/688-9779), renowned for its Guinness.

Yaletown and Granville
Yaletown Brewing Co. (1111 Mainland St., 604/681-2739) is the premier drinking hole for the hip population of inner-city Yaletown. The in-house brewery produces a variety of excellent beers, there's a great patio, and the food is of a high standard for a pub. Also in Yaletown,

the **Opus Bar** (350 Davie St., 604/642-0557) serves up strong cocktails and imported beer in a sizzlingly hip setting off the lobby of the Opus Hotel.

In the same vicinity but with a very different atmosphere is the old **Yale Hotel** (1300 Granville St., 604/681-9253), primarily a blues venue but a pleasant place for a quiet drink even without the music. Walk back toward downtown from the Yale to the **Royal Pub** (1025 Granville St., 604/685-5335) to join the throngs of young backpackers drinking up nightly specials before retiring to the upstairs hostel. **Doolin's Irish Pub** (654 Nelson St., 604/605-4343) dispenses mugs of Guinness and hearty food (such as ploughman's lunch for $8) daily from 11:30 A.M.

The small but always lively **Stamp's Landing Neighbourhood Pub** (610 Stamp's Landing, 604/879-0821) overlooks False Creek just east of Granville Island and a short ferry trip from Yaletown. Aside from beer and liquor, Stamp's offers delicious snacks to keep you going, live music on weekends, and great sunset views of the harbor.

West End
Toward the West End, **Joe Fortes Seafood and Chophouse** (777 Thurlow St., 604/669-1940) boasts a great bar, complete with a wide range of beers and a condensed menu from the adjacent restaurant. In the same part of town, at street level of the Best Western, **Checkers** (1755 Davie St., 604/682-1831) is a popular sports bar, this one with a distinctive checkered decor and live rock on weekends.

Nightclubs
Nightclubs change names and reputations regularly, so check with the free entertainment newspapers or the website www.clubvibes.com for the latest hot spots. Naturally, weekends are busiest, with the most popular clubs having cover charges up to $20 and long lines after 9 P.M. Downtown nightclubs are concentrated at the southern end of downtown along and immediately south of Granville Street. Best known is Dick's on Dicks, **Richard's on**

Richards (1036 Richards St., 604/687-6794) has been a staple of the Vancouver nightclub scene for more than 20 years. It's most popular with the late-20s and over-30 crowds. The music is live through the week, with DJs spinning discs on weekends. The dance floor is always high energy. The best place to escape the crowd is the second-floor shooter bar, which has a good view back down to the dance floor. One of the hottest nightclubs in recent years has been **Atlantis** (1320 Richards St., 604/662-7077). The centerpiece is a massive dance floor, featuring a hanging light system that produces incredible effects. Music varies from hip-hop to progressive. Since the early 1990s, **Bar None** (1222 Hamilton St., 604/689-7000) has been attracting a young, single crowd. Live music is featured during the week (Thursday is especially busy) and DJ-spun tunes on the weekends. Drink prices at Bar None are higher than at most other local venues.

Up the hill from the above clubs, at **Crush Champagne Lounge** (1180 Granville St., 604/684-0355), the retro feel attracts an over-30 crowd. A house band plays through the week, whereas weekends are the domain of name acts. At **Stone Temple** (1082 Granville St., 604/488-1333), a DJ spins hip-hop, retro, and Top 40 discs nightly until 4 A.M. Weekends are busy, but crowds thin during the week, when you can expect drink specials and various promotions. In a converted movie theater toward the central business district, **Plaza** (881 Granville St., 604/646-0064) tried to appeal to the upmarket dance club crowd, but now has more of a rave atmosphere with a DJ spinning house, trance, or whatever's hot in the music scene, on Fridays and Saturdays, and playing anything British on Thursdays. Nearby, and also in a converted movie theater, **Caprice** (967 Granville St., 604/681-2114) combines a lounge and food service with a multilevel nightclub with a friendly vibe.

Rock

The world's biggest rock, pop, and country acts usually include Vancouver on their world tours, and the city's thriving local music industry

© ANDREW HEMPSTEAD

The Yale Hotel is a classic blues venue.

supports live bands at a variety of venues. Most big-name acts play BC Place Stadium, the Orpheum, or Queen Elizabeth Theatres. Attracting a huge crowd every night of the week, at the classic **Roxy** (932 Granville St., 604/331-7999), two house bands play rock-and-roll music from all eras to a packed house during the week, with imported bands on weekends. The young, hip crowd, good music, and performance bartenders make this the city's most popular live music venue, so expect a line, especially after 9 P.M. on weekends; cover charges range $5–10.

Jazz and Blues

The **Coastal Jazz and Blues Society** (604/872-5200, www.coastaljazz.ca) maintains a listing of all the city's jazz and blues events.

Serious blues lovers should head to the historic **Yale Hotel** (1300 Granville St., 604/681-9253), which has hosted some of the greatest names in the business, including Junior Wells and Stevie Ray Vaughan. The hotel offers plenty of room for everyone, whether you want to get up and dance or shoot pool in the back. Sunday is the only night without live performances, although a jam session starts up around 3 P.M. on Saturday and Sunday afternoons. Drinks are expensive, and a $5–15 cover charge is collected Thursday–Saturday nights.

Comedy

Yuk Yuk's (Century Plaza Hotel, 1015 Burrard St., 604/696-9857) offers comedy nights Wednesday–Saturday. Admission costs $5 on Tuesday (amateur night), $8–22 the rest of the week. **Lafflines** (26 4th St., New Westminster, 604/525-2262) offers a similar program and attracts acts from throughout Canada. Wednesday through Sunday, the Arts Club (604/738-7013) hosts the **Vancouver Theatresports League** of improvised comedy on its New Revue Stage, Granville Island.

PERFORMING ARTS
Theater

Vancouver has theaters all over the city—for professional plays, amateur plays, comedy, and "instant" theater. In total, the city boasts 30 professional theater companies and more than 20 regular venues.

The **Centre in Vancouver for Performing Arts** (777 Homer St., 604/602-0616, www .centreinvancouver.com) hosts the biggest of musical hits. Designed by renowned architect Moshe Safdie, the modern wonder features a five-story glass lobby flanked by granite walls. The trilevel theater seats more than 1,800 and boasts North America's largest stage. Matinees cost from $50 while evening shows range $55–90. A smaller facility is the **Chan Centre for the Performing Arts** (6265 Crescent Rd., Point Grey, 604/822-2697), comprising three stages including the 1,400-seat Chan Shun Concert Hall.

One of the great joys of summer in the city is sitting around Malkin Bowl in Stanley Park watching **Theatre under the Stars** (604/687-0174, www.tuts.bc.ca). Since 1934 these shows have drawn around 1,000 theater-goers nightly, with performances usually musically oriented. The setting itself, an open amphitheater, surrounded by towering Douglas fir trees, is as much of an attraction as the performance. The show runs June–August Monday–Saturday at 7 P.M. Tickets (adult $28, child $24) go on sale at noon daily from a booth beside the bowl. Another summer production is **Bard on the Beach** (604/739-0559, www.bardonthebeach.org), a celebration of the works of Shakespeare that takes place in huge, open-ended tents in Vanier Park. Tickets are well priced at just $17–31.

The **Arts Club Theatre** (1585 Johnston St., 604/687-1644, www.artsclub.com) always offers excellent theater productions at the **Granville Island Stage.** Productions range from drama to comedy to improv. Tickets run $21–35; book in advance and pick up your tickets at the door 30 minutes before showtime. Another venue for the Arts Club is the restored **Stanley Industrial Alliance Theatre** (2750 Granville St.), south of the island at 12th Avenue.

Since its inception in 1964, the **Playhouse Theatre Company** has grown to become the city's largest theater company. Seven productions are performed each year, ranging from classical to contemporary, with 8 P.M. start times and tickets ranging $50–75. Matinees (2 P.M.) cost from $45. The company is based at the **Playhouse Theatre** (corner of Hamilton and Dunsmuir Streets, 604/873-3311).

Music and Dance

The **Queen Elizabeth Theatre** (630 Hamilton St., 604/665-3050) is the home of **Vancouver Opera** (604/683-0222); tickets begin at $35 and rise to $90 for the best seats. The theater also hosts a variety of music recitals and stage performances.

The historic **Orpheum Theatre,** on the corner of Smithe and Seymour Streets, dates to 1927 and houses its original Wurlitzer organ. Now fully restored, the theater provides excellent acoustics for the resident **Vancouver Symphony** (604/684-9100), as well as for concerts by the professional **Vancouver Chamber Choir** (604/738-6822) and the amateur **Vancouver Bach Choir** (604/921-8012).

CINEMAS

Cineplex Odeon (604/434-2463) operates 20 cinemas in Vancouver. Call or check the two daily papers for locations and screenings. Admission to first-run screenings is about $10.

If you're staying at a Robson Street or West End accommodation, head over to **Denman Place Discount Cinema** (corner of Denman St. and Comox St., 604/683-2201) for first- and second-run hits for $2.50–5. For foreign and Canadian indie films, check out **Pacific Cinematheque** (1131 Howe St., 604/688-8202).

At the far end of Canada Place, the **IMAX Theatre** (604/682-4629) provides spectacular movie entertainment and special effects on a five-story-high screen with wraparound surround sound. Films are generally on the world's natural wonders and last around 45 minutes, with two or three features showing each day, beginning around noon. Ticket prices range $10–14.50 per screening, or catch a double feature for a few bucks extra.

SHOPPING

Vancouver has shopping centers, malls, and specialty stores everywhere. Head to Gastown for native arts and crafts, Robson Street for boutique clothing, Granville Street Mall for department stores, Granville Island for everything from ships' chandlery to kids' clothing, Yaletown for the trendy clothes of local designers, the east side for army-surplus stores and pawnbrokers, Chinatown for Eastern foods, and the junction of Main Street and East 49th Avenue for Indian goods.

Gastown

Sandwiched between the many cafés, restaurants, and tacky souvenir stores along Water Street are other stores selling Vancouver's best selection of native arts and crafts. One of the largest outlets, **Hill's Native Art** (165 Water St., 604/685-4249) sells $10 T-shirts, towering $12,000 totem poles, and everything in between, including genuine Cowichan sweaters and carved ceremonial masks. The **Inuit Gallery of Vancouver** (206 Cambie St., 604/688-7323) exhibits the work of Inuit and Northwest Coast native artists and sculptors. Among the highlights are many soapstone pieces by carvers from Cape Dorset, a remote Inuit village in Canada's new territory of Nunavut. The **Wilderness Committee Store** (227 Abbott St., 604/683-2567) features environmentally friendly souvenirs, including shirts, posters, and calendars.

Granville Island

Arts-and-crafts galleries on Granville Island include **Wickaninnish Gallery** (1666 Johnston St., 604/681-1057), which sells stunning native art, jewelry, carvings, weavings, and original paintings, and **Gallery of BC Ceramics** (1359 Cartwright St., 604/669-3606), showcasing the work of the province's leading potters and sculptors. Head to the **Umbrella Shop** (1550 Anderson St., 604/697-0919) if it looks like there's rain in the forecast.

Duranleau Street is home to many maritime-based businesses, adventure-tour operators, and charter operators. The **Quarterdeck** (1660 Duranleau St., 604/683-8232) stocks everything from marine charts to brass shipping bells. To buy a sea kayak or canoe (from

$1,100 secondhand), head to **Ecomarine Ocean Kayak Centre** (1668 Duranleau St., 604/689-7575). This shop also carries related equipment, books, and nautical charts. The city's leading dive shop is **Rowand's Reef Scuba Shop** (1512 Duranleau St., 604/669-3483), with sales, repairs, rentals, and plenty of information on local dive spots.

A small stretch of West Broadway, between Main and Cambie Streets, holds Vancouver's largest concentration of outdoor equipment stores. The largest of these, and the largest in British Columbia, is **Mountain Equipment Co-op** (130 W. Broadway, 604/872-7858). Like the American R.E.I. stores, it is a cooperative owned by its members; to make a purchase, you must be a member (a one-time charge of $5).

Per capita, residents of Vancouver buy more books than the residents of any other North American city, and they buy them from a huge number of bookstores scattered throughout the city.

Duthie Books (2339 W. 4th Ave., Kitsilano, 604/732-5344) and **Blackberry Books** (1663 Duranleau St., 604/685-6188) are two popular independents.

Vancouver has three excellent bookstores specializing in travel-related literature; all are close to each other in the area between Granville Island and Point Grey. They are **Wanderlust** (west of Cypress St. at 1929 W. 4th Ave., Kitsilano, 604/739-2182), **The Travel Bug** (3065 W. Broadway, 604/737-1122, www.travelbugbooks .ca), and **International Travel Maps and Books** (530 W. Broadway, 604/879-3621). The latter is part bookstore, part distributor, part publisher, with a particularly good selection of maps.

Vancouver has some fantastic secondhand bookstores, including a few specializing entirely in nonfiction. The largest concentration lies along West Pender Street between Richards and Hamilton Streets. **Macleod's Books** (455 W. Pender St., 604/681-7654) stocks a wide range of antique titles, including many of the earliest works on Western Canada. On the corner of W. Hastings and Hamilton Streets is **Stephen C. Lunsford Books** (604/681-6830), with plenty of old Canadian nonfiction titles.

FESTIVALS AND EVENTS

Whether it's a celebration of local or international culture, the arts, sporting events, or just a wacky long-time tradition, there's always a reason to party in Vancouver. Many of the most popular festivals are held during summer, the peak visitor season, but the rest of the year is the main season for performances by the city's dance, theater, and music companies, and not-to-be-missed events such as the Christmas Carol Ships Parade.

Tickets for most major events can be booked through **Ticketmaster** (www.ticketmaster.ca); for the arts, call 604/280-3311; for sporting events, call 604/280-4400.

Spring

The spring event schedule kicks off in a big way the third week of March with the **Vancouver Playhouse International Wine Festival** (604/872-6622, www.playhousewinefest.com). Hosted by various downtown venues, it is one of North America's largest, bringing together representatives from more than 150 wineries and 14 countries.

The **Vancouver Sun Run** (604/689-9441, www.sunrun.com) is a 10-kilometer (6.2-mile) run (or walk) through the streets of downtown on the third Sunday in April. Attracting over 45,000 participants, it is Canada's largest (and the world's third largest) such run. For more serious runners, the **Vancouver Marathon** (604/872-2928, www.bmovanmarathon.ca) takes place two Sundays later.

The streets of New Westminster come alive in late May for **Hyack Festival** (604/522-6894, www.hyack.bc.ca), in celebration of spring and the history of British Columbia's one-time capital. Farther east, the country comes to the city for one of British Columbia's biggest rodeos, the **Cloverdale Rodeo and Exhibition** (604/576-9461, www .cloverdalerodeo.com) on the third weekend of May.

The third week of May is the **Vancouver International Children's Festival** (604/708-5655, www.childrensfestival.com), at Vanier Park; it's a kid's paradise, with face painting, costumes, plays, puppetry, mime, sing-alongs, storytelling, and fancy-hat competitions.

Summer

Two of summer's most popular cultural events take place from mid-June to late in the season, meaning you can enjoy them at any time through the warmer months. **Bard on the Beach** (604/739-0559, www.bardonthebeach .org) comprises three favorite Shakespeare plays performed in open-ended tents in Vanier Park, allowing a spectacular backdrop of English Bay, the city skyline, and the mountains beyond. Tickets are well priced at just $17–26.50 for 1 P.M. and 4 P.M. matinees and from $31 for 7:30 P.M. evening performances. The other event, the **Kitsilano Showboat** (604/734-7332), takes place at nearby Kitsilano Beach. Amateur variety acts have been taking to this stage since 1935. Performances are Monday, Wednesday, and Friday nights over a 10-week summer season.

The **Alcan Dragon Boat Festival** (604/688-2382, www.adbf.com) comes to False Creek on the third weekend in June. In addition to the races, a blessing ceremony and other cultural activities take place in and around the Plaza of Nations.

The last week of June, Vancouver taps its feet to the beat of the annual **Vancouver International Jazz Festival** (604/872-5200, www.coastaljazz.ca), when more than 1,500 musicians from countries around the world gather to perform traditional and contemporary jazz at 40 venues around the city.

Canada Day is July 1. The main celebrations—music, dancing, and fireworks—are held at Canada Place, but if you head out to the **Steveston Salmon Festival** (604/718-8094, www.stevestonsalmonfest.ca), you'll come across a massive salmon barbecue, food fair, children's festival, drag racing, and more.

The middle weekend of July, Jericho Beach Park draws lots of folks to the **Vancouver Folk Music Festival** (604/602-9798, www.thefestival .bc.ca). In addition to the wonderful music, the festival features storytelling, dance performances, live theater, and a food fair.

On the first Sunday in August, the **Vancouver Pride Parade** (604/687-0955, www.vancouverpride.ca) culminates a week of gay pride celebration. It runs along Denman Street, ending at Sunset Beach, where there's entertainment and partying.

Year after year, Vancouverites await with much anticipation the early August **Celebration of Light** (604/641-1193, www .celebration-of-light.com), the world's largest musical fireworks competition. Each year, three countries compete: Each has a night to itself (the last Saturday in July, then the following Wednesday and Saturday), putting on a display that lasts up to an hour from 10:15 P.M.; then on the final night (second Wednesday in August), the three competing countries come together for a grand finale. The fireworks are let off from a barge moored in English Bay, allowing viewing from Stanley Park, Kitsilano, Jericho Beach, and as far away as West Vancouver. Music that accompanies the displays can be heard around the shoreline; if you're away from the action tune your radio to 101.1 FM for a simulcast.

Summer's busy event schedule winds up at the Pacific National Exhibition Grounds with **The Fair (Pacific National Exhibition)** (604/253-2311, www.pne.bc.ca) in late August. A highlight of this agricultural exposition is the twice-daily RCMP musical ride, a precision drill performed by Canada's famous Mounties.

Fall

Beginning the second week of September, the **Vancouver International Fringe Festival** (604/257-0350, www.vancouverfringe.com) schedules around 550 performances by 80 artists from around the world at indoor and outdoor stages throughout Granville Island.

The **Vancouver International Film Festival** (604/685-0260, www.viff.org) is held late in September and features more than 300 of the very best movies from around 60 countries at theaters across downtown. One month later, literary types congregate on Granville Island for the **Vancouver International Writers Festival** (604/681-6330, www.writersfest.bc.ca).

Winter

Through the month of December, VanDusen Botanical Garden is transformed each evening by over 80,000 lights and seasonal displays such as a nativity scene during the **Festival of Lights** (604/878-9274, www.vandusengarden .org). Another popular pre-Christmas event is the **Carol Ships Parade of Lights** (604/878-8999, www.carolships.org). For three weeks leading up to Christmas Eve, the waterways of Vancouver come alive with the sounds of the festive season as each night a flotilla of up to 80 boats, each decorated with colorful lights, sails around Burrard Inlet, Port Moody, Deep Cove, and around English Bay to False Creek, while onboard carolers sing the songs of Christmas through sound systems that can clearly be heard from along the shoreline.

While most normal folk spend New Year's Day recovering from the previous night's celebrations, up to 2,000 brave souls head down to English Bay Beach and go *swimming*. The information hotline for the **Polar Bear Swim** is 604/665-3418, but all you really need to know is that the water will be *very* cold. The stupidity starts at 2:30 P.M.

Accommodations

Whether you're looking for a luxurious room in a highrise hotel, a downtown dorm, or a historic bed-and-breakfast, Vancouver has accommodations to suit all tastes and budgets. Downtown hotel room rates fluctuate greatly depending on supply and demand, much more so than bed-and-breakfast and motel rates in suburban locations. Demand throughout the city, but especially downtown, is highest in summer and on weekdays, so if you're looking to save a few bucks, plan on being in town in the cooler months (May and September are my favorite times to be in Vancouver), or stay at a business hotel as part of a weekend package. One word of warning: If you plan to have a vehicle, prepare yourself for parking fees of up to $25 per day in the downtown area; ask if weekend rates include free parking—they often do.

The following recommendations reflect my favorites in various price categories throughout the city. You won't find every downtown hotel mentioned here, and outside of downtown only convenient and good-value choices are included.

DOWNTOWN
Under $50

As you may imagine, the only downtown accommodations in this price range are backpacker lodges. For those on a budget, they are a great way to stay in the heart of the action and to mingle with like-minded travelers from around the world.

HI-Vancouver Downtown (1114 Burnaby St., 604/684-4565 or 888/203-4302, www .hihostels.ca; members $27.50, nonmembers $31.15, private rooms $66.50–74 s or d) is typical of the new-look facilities operated by Hostelling International, the world's largest and longest-running network of backpacker accommodations. The complex offers a large kitchen, a library, a game room, public Internet access, a travel agency, bike rentals, bag storage, and laundry facilities. The dormitories hold a maximum of four beds but are small.

Once the entertainment center of the city, Granville Street is still lined with old theaters and hotels. Many of these facilities have been renovated, including the Royal Hotel, which is now **HI-Vancouver Central** (1025 Granville St., 604/685-5335 or 888/203-8333, www .hihostels.ca), complete with its own downstairs bar with nightly drink and food specials (giving it more of a party atmosphere than the HI hostel on Burnaby Street) and similar rates to HI–Vancouver Downtown.

Privately owned backpacker lodges in Vancouver come and go with predictable regularity. One exception is **Samesun Vancouver** (1018 Granville St., 604/682-8226 or 877/972-6378, www.samesun.com), which is excellent in all respects. Typical of inner-city hostels the world over, rooms in this old four-story building are small, but each has been tastefully decorated, and the communal lounge and kitchen areas serve guests well. Other facilities include a separate TV room, wireless and modem Internet access, and a rooftop patio. Rates are $24 per person in a dormitory (maximum four beds) or $45–70 for a private room.

$50-100

The **YWCA** (733 Beatty St., 604/895-5830 or 800/663-1424, www.ywcahotel.com; $64–137 s or d) is popular with female travelers, couples, and families who don't want to spend a fortune on accommodations but don't like the "backpacker scene" at regular hostels. It's a few blocks from Vancouver's business core, but the modern facilities and choice of nearby restaurants more than compensate for the walk. More than 150 rooms are spread over 11 stories. Each room has a telephone, and the private rooms have televisions. Communal facilities include two kitchens, three lounges, and two laundries. Guests also have use of the nearby YWCA Health and Wellness Centre, which houses a pool and gym.

In this price range, you also move into the domain of older hotels—some good, some bad. Of these, the **⊂ Victorian Hotel** (514 Homer St., 604/681-6369 or 877/681-6369, www .victorianhotel.ca) is one of the best choices. Guest rooms have only basic amenities, but they are comfortably furnished and light on the wallet. The central location and complimentary breakfast make them an even better value. Rooms that share bathrooms are $99–109 s or d, those with en suites and lovely bay windows are $139–159.

Like the Victorian Hotel, the three-story **Kingston Hotel** (757 Richards St., 604/684-9024 or 888/713-3304, www.kingstonhotel vancouver.com) is around 100 years old and has been extensively renovated. Most of the 55 rooms share bathrooms ($68 s, $78 d) but have a sink with running water, while en suite rooms are $115–145 s or d.

$100-150

Spending $100–150 per night will get you a room in one of the older downtown motels, most of which are southwest toward Granville Island, a 10-minute walk from the central business district. If you're looking for weekend or off-season lodgings, check the websites of the $200-plus recommendations below for rates that fall easily into this price range.

The best value of downtown accommodations advertising rack rates in this price range is **Bosman's Hotel** (1060 Howe St., 604/682-3171 or 888/267-6267, www.bosmanshotel .com; $145 s or d), offering 100 fairly standard, midsized rooms and older facilities, including an outdoor pool and restaurant. Parking and wireless Internet are free.

A colorful paint job and bright fabrics can do a lot to reinvent an old hotel, and you won't find a better example than the centrally located **Howard Johnson Hotel Downtown** (1176 Granville St., 604/688-8701 or 888/654-6336, www.hojovancouver.com; from $149 s or d).

$150-200

Least expensive of the central business district hotels is **Days Inn Vancouver** (921 W. Pender St., 604/681-4335 or 877/681-4335, www .daysinnvancouver.com; from $189 s or d). The 85 rooms are small, and surrounding highrises block any views. But each room is decorated in bright and breezy pastel colors, and coffeemakers are provided. There's also an in-house restaurant.

Although guest facilities at **Ramada Downtown Vancouver** (435 W. Pender St., 604/488-1088 or 888/389-5888, www.ramada downtownvancouver.com; from $199 s or d) are limited compared to other properties in this price category, like the Days Inn, the location is central. An old hotel, its 80 rooms are small, but they are well appointed and come with everything from hair dryers to Nintendo. Look for the retro neon sign out front.

$200-250

The best reason to stay at the **Century Plaza Hotel** (1015 Burrard St., 604/687-0575 or

VANCOUVER

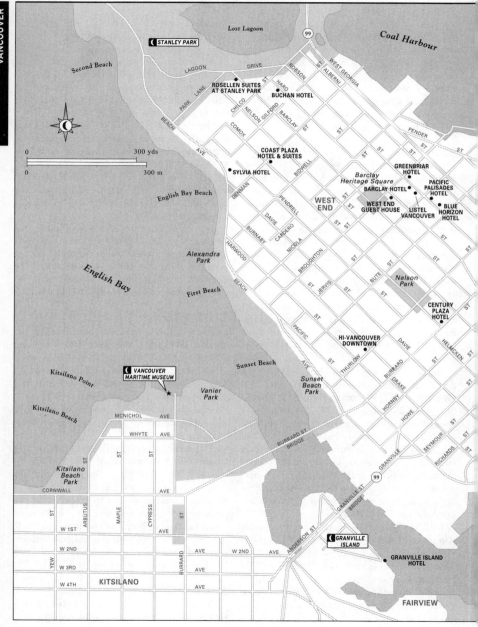

Lost Lagoon

Coal Harbour

☾ STANLEY PARK

99

Second Beach

LAGOON DRIVE

WEST GEORGIA

ROBSON ST ALBERNI

PARK LANE

BEACH

ROSELLEN SUITES
AT STANLEY PARK

HARO

BUCHAN HOTEL

CHILCO NELSON GILFORD BARCLAY ST

PENDER

ST

ST

ST

ST

ST

ST

ST

COMOX

0   300 yds

0   300 m

COAST PLAZA
HOTEL & SUITES

BIDWELL

GREENBRIAR
HOTEL

English Bay Beach

SYLVIA HOTEL

DENMAN

Barclay
Heritage Square

BARCLAY HOTEL

PACIFIC
PALISADES
HOTEL

WEST
END

WEST END
GUEST HOUSE

LISTEL
VANCOUVER

BLUE
HORIZON
HOTEL

ST

ST

PENDRELL

DAVIE

Alexandra
Park

BURNABY

CARDERO

NICOLA

ST

English Bay

HARWOOD

BROUGHTON

ST

BUTE

Nelson
Park

First Beach

BEACH

JERVIS

ST

ST

ST

ST

CENTURY
PLAZA
HOTEL

ST

Sunset Beach

PACIFIC

HI-VANCOUVER
DOWNTOWN

DAVIE

HELMCKEN

Kitsilano Point

☾ VANCOUVER
MARITIME MUSEUM

Sunset
Beach
Park

THURLOW

BURRARD

ST

ST

Kitsilano Beach

Vanier
Park

AVE

DRAKE

ST

★

MCNICHOL AVE

HORNBY

WHYTE AVE

BURRARD ST
BRIDGE

HOWE

ST

ST

Kitsilano
Beach
Park

ST

SEYMOUR

RICHARDS

ST

AVE

GRANVILLE

CORNWALL

99

YEW

ARBUTUS

MAPLE

CYPRESS

ST

W 1ST

W 2ND

ST

GRANVILLE ST
BRIDGE

BURRARD

W 2ND

AVE

AVE

ANDERSON ST

☾ GRANVILLE
ISLAND

W 3RD

AVE

W 4TH

KITSILANO

AVE

GRANVILLE ISLAND
HOTEL

FAIRVIEW

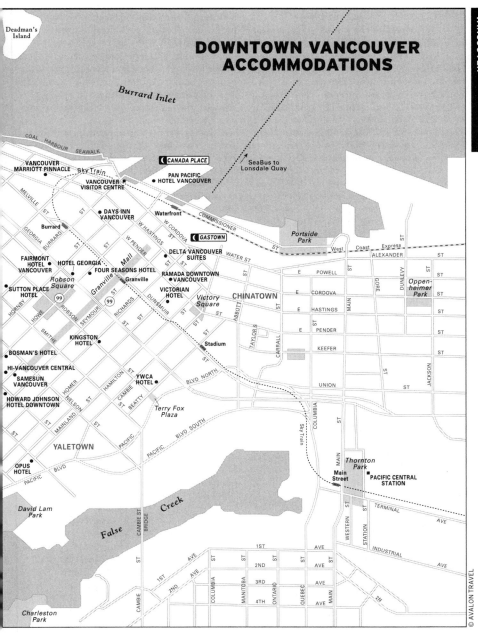

DOWNTOWN VANCOUVER ACCOMMODATIONS

Deadman's Island

Burrard Inlet

COAL HARBOUR SEAWALK

Canada Place

SeaBus to Lonsdale Quay

VANCOUVER MARRIOTT PINNACLE

Sky Train

VANCOUVER VISITOR CENTRE

PAN PACIFIC HOTEL VANCOUVER

MELVILLE ST

DAYS INN VANCOUVER

Waterfront

GEORGIA

Burrard

BURRARD ST

W HASTINGS ST

W CORDOVA ST

GASTOWN

Portside Park

West Coast Express

FAIRMONT HOTEL VANCOUVER

HOTEL GEORGIA

W PENDER ST

DELTA VANCOUVER SUITES

WATER ST

ALEXANDER ST

POWELL ST

FOUR SEASONS HOTEL

Granville

RAMADA DOWNTOWN VANCOUVER

E CORDOVA ST

GORE

DUNLEVY

Oppen-heimer Park

Robson Square

Mall

Granville St

SUTTON PLACE HOTEL

99

VICTORIAN HOTEL

CHINATOWN

E HASTINGS ST

MAIN

99

Victory Square

E PENDER ST

HOWE

SMITHE

RICHARDS

DUNSMUIR ST

ABBOTT

CARRALL

TAYLORS

KEEFER ST

JACKSON ST

KINGSTON HOTEL

SEYMOUR ST

Stadium

BOSMAN'S HOTEL

HI-VANCOUVER CENTRAL

SAMESUN VANCOUVER

HAMILTON ST

BLVD NORTH

UNION ST

YWCA HOTEL

HOWARD JOHNSON HOTEL DOWNTOWN

HOMER

NELSON ST

CAMBIE

BEATTY

Terry Fox Plaza

MAINLAND ST

BLVD SOUTH

YALETOWN

PACIFIC

PACIFIC

COLUMBIA ST

OPUS HOTEL

PACIFIC BLVD

Main Street

Thornton Park

PACIFIC CENTRAL STATION

David Lam Park

CAMBIE ST

BRIDGE ST

Creek

False

TERMINAL AVE

WESTERN ST

STATION ST

INDUSTRIAL AVE

1ST

2ND AVE

1ST ST

AVE

Charleston Park

CAMBIE

1ST

2ND

AVE

COLUMBIA

MANITOBA

3RD AVE

ONTARIO

4TH AVE

QUEBEC

AVE

MAIN

2N

800/663-1818, www.century-plaza.com; $245–600 s or d) is the Absolute Spa, a favorite haunt of movie stars in Vancouver on location. Each of the 236 kitchen-equipped rooms is comfortable, but not as opulent as the spa facility. Other amenities include a café, steakhouse restaurant, and lounge.

Granville Island Hotel (1253 Johnston St., 604/683-7373 or 800/663-1840, www.granville islandhotel.com; $230 s, $240 d) enjoys a fabulous location on the island of the same name immediately south of downtown. Contemporary and elegant, the rooms are spacious and furnished with Persian rugs, marble-floored bathrooms, and modern necessities, such as high-speed Internet access. Most also have water views. Other facilities include a fitness center, rooftop hot tub, sauna, and kayak rentals from the on-site marina. There's also an in-house brewery and excellent restaurant specializing in West Coast cuisine.

$250-300

None of the 225 "suites" at **Delta Vancouver Suites** (550 W. Hastings St., 604/689-8188 or 888/890-3222, www.deltahotels.com), in the heart of downtown, are equipped with a kitchen, but each is spacious and has a separate bedroom and comfortable lounge area. In-room business facilities include a work desk stocked with supplies, two phone lines, high-speed Internet access, and personalized voice mail. Other guest facilities include a health club, an indoor pool, saunas and a whirlpool, and a restaurant. Rack rates are $299 s or d, but because this hotel is aimed primarily at business travelers, greatly reduced weekend and package rates are offered.

$300-400

Generally regarded as one of the world's hippest hotels, the (**Opus Hotel** (322 Davie St., Yaletown, 604/642-6787 or 866/642-6787, www.opushotel.com; $389–529 s or d) fills a distinct niche in the Vancouver scene as a megacool place to stay. This means vibrant colors, striking decor, clean-lined furnishings, 250-count linens, 27-inch TVs, CD players,

luxurious bathrooms filled with top-notch bath products, valet-only parking, and upscale dining and drinking off the brightly minimalist lobby. Rooms are decorated in themes linked to five Lifestyle Concierges (choose your favorite when booking online) and come in a variety of configurations, including one daring layout with the bathroom on the floor-to-ceiling windowed outer wall.

Drawing a mix of upscale business travelers and international vacationers, the **Vancouver Marriott Pinnacle** (1128 W. Hastings St., 604/684-1128 or 800/207-4150, www.marriott .com; from $309 s, $329 d) is an excellent choice in the downtown core. Dating to 2000, this full-service property features 434 spacious rooms, each with stylish furniture, elegant bathrooms, a writing desk full of office supplies, two telephones (including a cordless) with voice mail and Internet access, a coffeemaker, ironing facilities, and also an umbrella for Vancouver's occasional rainy days. Guests also enjoy complimentary use of the hotel's health club, which features a 17-meter (60-foot) indoor pool, a hot tub, a sauna, and a large outdoor patio area.

Fairmont Hotels and Resorts, best known for landmark accommodations such as the Fairmont Empress in Victoria and the Fairmont Banff Springs in Banff, operates two properties in the downtown area. The copper-roofed **Fairmont Hotel Vancouver** (900 W. Georgia St., 604/684-3131 or 866/540-4452, www .fairmont.com) is the company's Vancouver flagship and a downtown landmark—you can't help but notice the distinctive green copper roof, the gargoyles, and the classic, Gothic château-style architecture of this grand old dame. Facilities include restaurants, a comfortable lounge, an indoor pool, saunas, a weight room, health facilities, 24-hour room service, ample parking, and a large staff to attend to your every whim. The smallish standard rooms start at $370 s or d, but upgrading to a larger Fairmont Room is only a few dollars extra, and several good-value packages are offered year-round.

Memories of another era pervade at the (**Hotel Georgia** (801 Georgia St., 604/682-

5566 or 800/663-1111, www.hotelgeorgia
.bc.ca), across the road from the art gallery and
kitty-corner to the Hotel Vancouver. Built in
1927 in a Georgian revival style, this 313-room
grand old dame underwent massive renovations
in 2007. Original oak furnishings, the oak-
paneled lobby, and the brass elevator have been
restored, and all facilities have been upgraded,
including a fitness center and various eating
establishments. In summer, rooms cost $369–
399 s or d during the week, while on weekends
breakfast and a late checkout are included in the
rate of $319. Outside of summer, rooms start at
$200, including breakfast on weekends.

Over $400

One block from the city end of Robson Street is
the super-luxurious, European-style **C** **Sutton
Place Hotel** (845 Burrard St., 604/682-5511
or 866/378-8866, www.suttonplace.com;
from $455 s or d), one of only a handful of
properties in North America to get a precious
five-diamond rating from the American Automobile Association. This, Vancouver's most
elegant accommodation, features original European artworks in public areas and reproduc-
tions in the 396 rooms and suites. Rooms are
furnished with king-size beds, plush bathrobes,
ice dispensers, and two phone lines, and guests
enjoy a twice-daily maid service, complete
with fresh flowers. Other facilities include spa
services, an indoor pool, a business center, an
English gentlemen's club–style lounge bar, and
Fleuri, an upmarket restaurant.

Since the world's first Four Seasons Hotel
opened in Toronto in 1961, the company has
expanded into 20 other countries, gaining a
reputation for the best in comfort and service.
The Vancouver **Four Seasons Hotel** (791 W.
Georgia St., 604/689-9333 or 800/819-5053,
www.fourseasons.com; $425 s, $455 d) is no
exception, getting a five-diamond rating from
the American Automobile Association. The 372
spacious rooms are luxuriously appointed, with
guests enjoying fresh flowers, a wide range of in-
room amenities, and twice-daily housekeeping.

For all of the modern conveniences along
with unbeatable city and harbor views, head for
the sparkling **Pan Pacific Hotel Vancouver**
(Canada Place, 604/662-8111 or 800/937-1515,

© ANDREW HEMPSTEAD

The Pan Pacific Hotel Vancouver provides breathtaking harbor views.

www.panpacific.com). It's part of the landmark Canada Place (the top 8 floors of the 13-story complex are guest rooms), whose Teflon sails fly over busy, bustling sidewalks and a constant flow of cruise ships. Each of the 504 spacious rooms boasts stunning views, contemporary furnishings, a luxurious marble bathroom, and in-room video checkout. Facilities include a pool, an extra-charge health club, Sails Restaurant, and Cascades Lounge. Both the restaurant and lounge offer great views. The rack rate for the least expensive City View rooms is $490, but the hotel website regularly sells rooms with water views for around $400.

ROBSON STREET

Robson Street—with its sidewalk cafés, restaurants open until the wee hours, and fashionable boutiques—provides a great alternative to staying right downtown. Although you'll generally get a better value for your money and pay less for parking in this part of the city, the rates quoted below aren't discounted as much (if at all) on weekends, unlike the downtown business traveler–oriented hotels.

$100-150

Built in the 1920s, the European-style **Barclay Hotel** (1348 Robson St., 604/688-8850, www .barclayhotel.com; $125–135 s or d) has 80 medium-size rooms, a small lounge, and an intimate restaurant. The rooms are stylish in a slightly old-fashioned way; each holds a comfortable bed, a writing desk, a couch, and an older television.

The **Greenbrier Hotel** (1393 Robson St., 604/683-4558 or 888/355-5888, www.green brierhotel.com; $139–179 s or d) looks a bit rough on the outside, but each of the 32 units has a large living area, full kitchen, and separate bedroom. One block farther toward Stanley Park, the **Riviera Hotel** (1431 Robson St., 604/685-1301 or 888/699-5222, www.rivieraonrobson .com; $128 s, $148 d) offers similar facilities.

Built at the turn of the 20th century, the **West End Guest House** (1362 Haro St., 604/681-2889, www.westendguesthouse.com; $145–265 s or d) has been lovingly refurbished in Victorian-era

colors and furnished with stylish antiques to retain its original charm. Each of the eight guest rooms has a brass bed complete with cotton linens and a goose-down duvet, an en suite bathroom, a television, and a telephone. Guests can relax either in the comfortable lounge or on the outdoor terrace and have the use of bikes. After dishing up a full cooked breakfast (included in the rates), the friendly owners will set you up with a wealth of ideas for a day of sightseeing. Parking and use of bikes are free.

$150-200

At the 214-room **Blue Horizon Hotel** (1225 Robson St., 604/688-1411 or 800/663-1333, www.bluehorizonhotel.com; from $169 s or d), facilities include an indoor lap pool, a fitness room, a sauna, a restaurant, and a café. All 214 rooms are large, brightly lit, and have a work desk, coffeemaking facilities, and an in-room safe. One quirk of the layout is that every room is a corner room, complete with private balcony. To take advantage of this, you should request a room on floors 15–30 ($179–199 s or d).

$200-250

❰ **Pacific Palisades Hotel** (1277 Robson St., 604/688-0461 or 800/663-1815, www.pacific palisadeshotel.com) is touted as being a cross between "South Beach (Miami) and Stanley Park," a fairly apt description of this chic Robson Street accommodation. Originally a luxury apartment building, the entire hotel now has a beachy, ultra-contemporary feel: Each of the 233 spacious rooms is decorated with sleek furnishings and a dynamic color scheme. Many have views and all have a large work desk, super-comfortable beds, a coffeemaker, and high-speed Internet access. Amenities include a lounge and stylish restaurant, a fitness center, an 18-meter (59-foot) indoor lap pool, a variety of business services, and newspapers and coffee in the lobby each morning. Rack rates are a reasonable $225–250 s or d (from $280 for a suite) in summer, discounted year-round on the website and up to 50 percent in winter. Parking is $26 per day.

Diagonally opposite Pacific Palisades, **Listel**

Vancouver (1300 Robson St., 604/684-8461 or 800/663-5491, www.listel-vancouver.com) is an elegant full-service lodging best known for its innovative use of original and limited-edition Northwest Coast artwork in many of the 130 rooms. Rooms are well appointed and highlighted by contemporary furnishings, goose-down duvets, and luxurious bathrooms. Summer rates for a regular room are $240 s or d, while rooms on the two Museum Floors, which in addition to artworks feature separate bedrooms and bay windows, are $300.

WEST END

The few accommodations at the west end of downtown are near some fine restaurants, close to Stanley Park and English Bay, and a 25-minute walk along bustling Robson Street from downtown proper.

$50-100

A hostel for grown-ups, the three-story **Buchan Hotel** (1906 Haro St., 604/685-5354 or 800/668-6654, www.buchanhotel.com) is in a quiet residential area one block from Stanley Park. Built in 1926, the hotel boasts an atmosphere today that is friendly, especially in the evening, when guests gather in the main lounge. On the downside, the rooms are small and sparsely decorated. Rates for rooms with shared bathroom facilities are $75 s, $80 d and those with private bathrooms start at $90 s, $98 d.

$100-150

Overlooking English Bay and the closest beach to downtown, the old-style funky 1912 **⟨ Sylvia Hotel** (1154 Gilford St., 604/681-9321, www.sylviahotel.com) is a local landmark sporting a brick and terra-cotta exterior covered with Virginia creeper vine. It's popular with budget travelers looking for something a little nicer than a hostel, with rates ranging $110–325 s or d (the less expensive rooms are fairly small), with more expensive rooms featuring fantastic views, separate bedrooms, and full kitchens.

Over $200

Families especially will like **Rosellen Suites**

at Stanley Park (2030 Barclay St., 604/689-4807 or 888/317-6648, www.rosellensuites.com), located in a residential area right by Stanley Park. Each of the 30 extra-spacious units features modern furnishings, a separate living and dining area, a full kitchen, and modern conveniences such as stereos and voice mail. Rates are $209 for a one-bedroom unit, $239 for a two-bedroom unit, and $269–399 for larger units with fireplaces and private patios.

A couple of blocks from English Bay and surrounded by good dining choices, **Coast Plaza Hotel & Suites** (1763 Comox St., 604/688-7711 or 800/716-6199, www.coasthotels.com; $255 s or d) is a full-service hotel with 267 rooms on 35 levels. As a former apartment tower, its rooms are spacious; all have balconies, in-room coffee, free local calls, and free Internet access, and most feature kitchens. Amenities include a health club, an indoor pool, room service, a bistro, and a lounge.

NORTH SHORE

The best reason to stay on the North Shore is to enjoy the local hospitality at one of the many bed-and-breakfasts, but plenty of hotels and motels are also scattered through this part of the city.

$100-150

Perfect as a jumping-off point for a ferry trip to the Sunshine Coast or Vancouver Island is the **Horseshoe Bay Motel** (6588 Royal Ave., 604/921-7454; $105 s or d), 12 kilometers (7.5 miles) west of the Lions Gate Bridge, tucked below the highway in Horseshoe Bay and right by the BC Ferries terminal.

$150-200

Gracious **Thistledown House** (3910 Capilano Rd., North Vancouver, 604/986-7173 or 888/633-7173, www.thistle-down.com; $150–275 s or d) has been restored to resemble a country-style inn. Each of the five guest rooms has been tastefully decorated and has its own character, an en suite bathroom, and a balcony, and many delightful touches, such as homemade soap. If you're going to splurge, request the Under the Apple Tree room, which features a king-size bed, a split-level sitting room, and a large bathroom complete with a whirlpool tub. Rates include a gourmet breakfast served in the dining room and afternoon tea served in the cozy lounge or landscaped gardens, depending on the weather.

Yes, it's a chain motel, but at the **Holiday Inn Express Vancouver North Shore** (1800 Capilano Rd., 604/987-4461 or 800/663-4055, www.holiday-inn.com), you know exactly what you're paying for: a smartly decorated room with a light breakfast included in the rates of $189 s or d. An outdoor pool is a bonus.

Over $200

If you don't have transportation but don't want to stay downtown, the **Lonsdale Quay Hotel** (123 Carrie Cates Court, North Vancouver, 604/986-6111, www.lonsdalequayhotel.com; $205–300 s or d) is a good choice. It enjoys an absolute waterfront location above lively Lonsdale Quay Market and the SeaBus terminal, making it just 12 minutes to downtown by water. Each of the 70 rooms is equipped with modern furnishings and amenities that normally only come with a more expensive downtown room.

KITSILANO AND VICINITY

Hip Kitsilano and surrounding suburbs are Vancouver's most upscale residential neighborhoods south of Burrard Inlet. Accommodations in this part of the city are nearly all bed-and-breakfasts, and these are my favorites.

Under $50

If you're on a budget and don't need to stay right downtown, **HI-Vancouver Jericho Beach** (1515 Discovery St., Point Grey, 604/224-3208 or 888/203-4303, www.hi hostels.ca; May–Sept.) is a good alternative. The location is fantastic—in scenic parkland behind Jericho Beach, across English Bay from downtown, and linked to extensive biking and walking trails. Inside the huge white building are separate dorms for men and women, rooms for couples and families, a living area with tele-

vision, a café, and a kitchen. Members pay $23 per night, nonmembers $27 for a dorm bed, or $63 and $71 respectively for a double room. To get there, take Northwest Marine Drive off 4th Avenue West and turn right down Discovery Street at the arts center.

$100-150

Tucked away near the east end of Pacific Spirit Regional Park (closest park access is two blocks north at 33rd Ave.) is **Pacific Spirit Guest House** (4080 West 35th Ave., off Dunbar St., 604/261-6837 or 866/768-6837, www.vanbb .com; $95 s, $105 d), a budget-priced bed-and-breakfast. Choose between the guest room with a king-size bed or one with garden views. All guests are welcome to relax in the lounge and help themselves to tea and coffee, or take advantage of the large collection of books and music in the library. In the morning, a huge, multicourse breakfast will set you up for a day of sightseeing.

On the southern edge of Shaughnessy, **Beautiful B&B** (428 West 40th Ave., just off Cambie St., 604/327-1102, www.beautiful bandb.bc.ca) is a colonial-style two-story home set on a high point of land where views extend across the city to the North Shore Range. Both Queen Elizabeth Park and VanDusen Botanical Garden are within walking distance. The house is decorated with antiques and fresh flowers from the surrounding garden. Two rooms share a bathroom ($135–175 s or d), while the Honeymoon Suite features a fireplace, panoramic views, and a huge en suite bathroom complete with soaker tub ($245 s or d).

KINGSWAY

Kingsway, a main thoroughfare linking downtown to Burnaby, is lined with a smattering of inexpensive motels—perfect if you want to save a few dollars and like the convenience of being a short bus ride from downtown.

$50-100

At the bottom of the price spectrum is the **2400 Motel** (2400 Kingsway 604/434-2464 or 888/833-2400), an old roadside-style place with basic rooms, cable TV, and coffee and newspapers offered in the office each morning. Rates start at $80 s or d, with kitchenettes for $105 and two-bedroom units from $115 for four adults.

$100-150

C Pillow Suites (2859 Manitoba St., Mt. Pleasant, 604/879-8977, www.pillow.net) is a unique lodging three blocks west of the Kingsway and a few hundred meters east of city hall. The six suites are spread through three adjacent, colorfully painted heritage houses. Each unit is fully self-contained with a kitchen, an en suite bathroom, a telephone, cable TV, a fireplace, and a private entrance. Rates range from $125 for the Country Store, formerly a corner store and now filled with brightly painted appliances, to $265 for a complete three-bedroom house that sleeps six comfortably.

Closest of the Kingsway accommodations to the city center is the **Howard Johnson Plaza** (395 Kingsway, 604/872-5252 or 800/663-5713, www.biltmorehotelvancouver.com; $89 s, $109 d). It's been a few years now since this seven-story hotel was renovated, but each of the 96 rooms holds modern conveniences such as Internet access and electronic card-lock doors, and there's an outdoor pool.

Within walking distance of a SkyTrain station is **Days Inn-Vancouver Metro** (2075 Kingsway, 604/876-5531 or 800/546-4792, www.daysinn.com; $129–149 s or d), comprising 66 rooms opening to a private and quiet courtyard. The renovated rooms are typical of the Days Inn properties, with a simple, contemporary feel, and each has amenities such as hairdryers and coffeemakers.

RICHMOND (VANCOUVER INTERNATIONAL AIRPORT)

The following Richmond accommodations are good choices for those visitors who arrive late at or have an early departure from the international airport. All accommodations detailed in this section offer complimentary airport shuttles.

$100-150

The **Coast Vancouver Airport Hotel** (1041 Southwest Marine Dr., 604/263-1555 or 800/716-6199, www.coasthotels.com; $129–189 s or d) lies farther from the airport (toward the city) than the rest of the lodgings detailed in this section, but with free airport transfers, free long-term parking, and in-house dining, it is still aimed directly at airport travelers.

Three kilometers (1.9 miles) from the airport, the **Holiday Inn Express Vancouver Airport** (9351 Bridgeport Rd., 604/273-8080 or 888/831-3388, www.holiday-inn.com) is a typical modern, multistory airport hotel, with large and comfortably furnished rooms. The rates of $149 s or d include a light breakfast.

$150-200

Radisson President Hotel and Suites (8181 Cambie Rd., 604/276-8181 or 888/201-1718, www.radissonvancouver.com) is a sprawling complex of 184 guest rooms, a fitness center, an indoor pool, and several restaurants. The rooms are spacious and well appointed, making the rates of $189 s or d, including breakfast, reasonable. Travelers 55 and older get a much better deal—they pay from $139 s or d.

Hilton Vancouver Airport (5911 Minoru Blvd., 604/273-6336 or 800/445-8667, www.hilton.com; $199–329 s or d), Vancouver's only Hilton Hotel, lies five kilometers (3.1 miles) south of the airport near the Richmond shopping district. The moderately sized rooms are each outfitted with a work desk, two phone lines, and a coffeemaker, and each has a private balcony. Other facilities include a fitness center, a heated outdoor pool, a whirlpool tub, and two tennis courts.

Over $200

Right at the international airport, the modern **Fairmont Vancouver Airport** (3111 Grant McConachie Way, 604/207-5200 or 888/540-4441, www.fairmont.com; $249–449 s or d) offers 398 rooms equipped with remote-controlled everything, right down to the drapes; fog-free bathroom mirrors; and floor-to-ceiling soundproofed windows. Other more traditional hotel conveniences include a huge work center, a health club (where swimmers take to the self-adjusted current of a lap pool), and the Spa at the Fairmont massage and treatment facility.

The **Delta Vancouver Airport** lies on Sea Island (3500 Cessna Dr., 604/278-1241 or 888/890-3222, www.deltahotels.com). This 415-room hotel, part of the upscale Delta Hotel chain (but without a Signature Club floor), offers the high standard of rooms and service expected of an international-style hostelry. Fitness facilities are adequate but limited, and there's a small outdoor pool. A lobby restaurant opens daily for breakfast, while the Elephant & Castle enjoys a riverside location and is open daily for lunch and dinner. Rack rates could be a bit cheaper (from $250 s or d), and they are if you book online.

DELTA

Separated from Richmond by the south arm of the Fraser River, Delta is a continuation of Vancouver's sprawl. It's an ideal place to stay if you're planning to get an early-morning jump on the crowds for the ferry trip over to Vancouver Island, or if you're arriving from the United States and don't feel like tackling city traffic after a long day's drive.

$50-100

The **Delta Town & Country Inn** (6005 Hwy. 17, 604/946-4404 or 888/777-1266, www.delta inn.com; $99 including breakfast) is ideally situated and an excellent value. It's at the junction of Highway 99 and Highway 17, halfway between the airport and the ferry terminal, but the setting is parklike and quiet, with most of the 50 rooms enjoying views over extensive gardens and a landscaped pool area. In addition to the large pool, facilities include tennis courts, a restaurant, and a sports bar.

BURNABY AND THE FRASER VALLEY
$50-100

The least expensive motel in the sprawling suburban area of Burnaby, immediately east of downtown, is the **401 Motor Inn** (2950 Boundary Rd., 604/438-3451 or 877/438-

3451, www.401inn.com; $80 s, $90 d). From the TransCanada Highway eastbound, take Exit 28A south onto Boundary Road or westbound Exit 28B onto the Grandview Highway and take Boundary Road to the south; either way it's less than 200 meters (220 yards) from the highway and on the left.

Falling in the same price range, the **Happy Day Inn** (7330 6th St., 604/524-8501 or 800/665-9733, www.happydayinn.com; $80–104 s, $84–104 d) is farther east (almost in New Westminster). Rooms are brightly decorated, and each of the 32 rooms is air-conditioned. Amenities include a small fitness facility and a sauna. To get there take Edmonds Street east from the Kingsway to 6th Street.

Over $100

Within walking distance of the huge Metrotown shopping complex, **Ramada Hotel & Suites Metrotown** (3484 Kingsway, 604/433-8255 or 888/228-2111, www.ramadahotel vancouver.com) has free wireless Internet, a business center, a heated outdoor pool (summer only), a café, a restaurant, and a lounge. Each of the 123 spacious rooms has two TVs and coffee-making facilities. Rates start at $119 s, $139 d, while larger rooms that sleep four are $179.

Holiday Inn Express Vancouver Metrotown (4405 Central Blvd., 604/438-1881 or 888/465-4329, www.holiday-inn.com; $189 s or d) is part of Vancouver's biggest shopping complex and is connected to downtown by the SkyTrain. The 100 spacious rooms are spread over six stories in this contemporary hotel. Facilities include a wide range of recreational amenities, including an outdoor swimming pool, a tennis court, and a fitness center.

CAMPGROUNDS

You won't find any campgrounds in the city center area, but a limited number dot the suburbs along the major approach routes. Unless otherwise noted, the campgrounds below are open year-round.

North

The closest campground to downtown is

Capilano RV Park (295 Tomahawk Ave., North Vancouver, 604/987-4722, www .capilanorvpark.com). To get there from downtown, cross Lions Gate Bridge, turn right on Marine Drive, right on Capilano Road, and right again on Welch Street. From Highway 1/99 in West Vancouver, exit south on Taylor Way toward the shopping center and turn left over the Capilano River. It's about an hour walk to downtown from the campground, over Lions Gate Bridge and through Stanley Park. Amenities include a 13-meter (43-foot) pool, a big hot tub, a TV and games room, and a laundry facility. Sites are equipped with 15- and 30-amp power as well as sewer, water, cable, and telephone hookups. These sites range $37–52 per night. It gets crowded in summer, so even though there are more than 200 sites, you'll need to book well ahead to be assured of a site.

Of the provincial parks immediately north of the city, the only one with a campground is **Golden Ears,** 40 kilometers (25 miles) northeast from downtown, near the suburb of Maple Ridge. To get there, take Highway 7 from downtown through Coquitlam and Pitt Meadows to Maple Ridge, and follow the signs north on 232nd Street. The park holds almost 400 sites in two campgrounds near Alouette Lake. Facilities include hot showers, flush toilets, and a picnic table and fire ring at each site; $22 per night. Traveling north on Highway 99 toward Whistler, **Porteau Cove Provincial Park,** 20 kilometers (12 miles) north of Horseshoe Bay, offers 60 sites in a pleasant wooded setting with mountain views. Through summer, sites are $22, discounted to $17 the rest of the year.

South

Parkcanada (4799 Nulelum Way, Delta, 604/943-5811, www.parkcanada.com) is very convenient to the BC Ferries terminal at Tsawwassen, a 30-minute drive south of the city center. The campground has a small outdoor pool, but next-door is a much larger waterpark—perfect for the kids. Other amenities include a store with groceries and some RV supplies, laundry facilities, a lounge, and free showers.

Unserviced sites, suitable for tents, are $24; serviced sites range $25.50–32. To get there, follow the ferry signs from Highway 99 and turn right off Highway 17 at 52nd Street. Take the first left, and you're there.

Farther south along Highway 99 is **Peace Arch RV Park** (14601 40th Ave., 604/594-7009, www.peacearchrvpark.com; tents $20, hookups $29.50), which sprawls over four hectares (10 acres) between White Rock and Delta, 10 kilometers (6.2 miles) from the Douglas Border Crossing (take Exit 10—King George Highway—north from Highway 99, then the first right, 40th Avenue). The well-tended facilities include a heated pool, a playground and minigolf, a game room, coin-operated showers, and a laundry.

East

Adjacent to Burnaby Lake Regional Park, **Burnaby Cariboo RV Park** (8765 Cariboo Place, Burnaby, 604/420-1722, www.bcrvpark .com; tents $33, hookups $44–50) offers top-notch facilities, including a large indoor heated pool, fitness room, whirlpool tub, sundeck, playground, lounge, barbeque area, grocery store, and laundry facility. The park is 17 kilometers (10.6 miles) east of downtown. To get there, take Exit 37 (Gaglardi) from the TransCanada Highway, turn right at the first traffic light, take the first left, and then first right into Cariboo Place. The Production Way SkyTrain station is an eight-minute walk from this campground.

Farther east, **Dogwood Campground & RV Park** (15151 112th Ave., Surrey, 604/583-5585, www.dogwoodcampgrounds.com; $25–33) is 35 kilometers (22 miles) from downtown. It's right beside the TransCanada Highway; to get there from downtown, take Exit 48 and cross back over the highway, turning left onto 154th Street. Eastbound travelers (heading toward the city) should take Exit 50, turn north over the highway, and follow 160th Street north to 112th Avenue. Turn left and follow this street to the end. Facilities are adequate and modern, but basic, and include a pool, playground, and laundry.

Food

With an estimated 2,000 restaurants and hundreds of cafés and coffeehouses, Vancouver is a gastronomical delight. The city is home to more than 60 different cultures, so don't be surprised to find a smorgasbord of ethnic restaurants. The local specialty is West Coast or "fusion" cuisine, which combines fresh Canadian produce, such as local seafood and seasonal game, with Asian flavors and ingredients, usually in a healthy, low-fat way. Vancouver has no tourist-oriented, San Francisco–style Fisherman's Wharf, but however and wherever it's prepared, seafood will always dominate local menus. Pacific salmon, halibut, snapper, shrimp, oysters, clams, crab, and squid are all harvested locally.

DOWNTOWN

Downtown Vancouver has so many good dining options that it is a shame to eat in a food court, but like in cities around the Western world, they are a good place for a fast, reliable, and inexpensive meal. The southwest corner of the Pacific Centre (at Howe and Georgia Streets, diagonally opposite the art gallery) holds a glass-domed food court with many inexpensive food bars and seating indoors and out.

Family Dining

Of course, if you have a family, you're welcome at most restaurants. These are simply recommendations that specialize in keeping all ages happy—without breaking the bank.

Although this book purposely ignores the fast-food chains, **White Spot** is worthy of inclusion. The first White Spot restaurant—a drive-in—opened in Vancouver at the corner of Granville Street and 67th Avenue, South Granville, in 1928, dishing up hamburgers and milk shakes. Today, 50 White Spots across Canada still offer burgers—including the famous Triple O—as well as everything from pastas to stir-fried vegetables. For a sample, visit White Spot's downtown location (1616 W. Georgia St., 604/681-8034, daily for breakfast, lunch, and dinner).

At the bottom end of Gastown, the uniquely decorated **Brothers Restaurant** (1 Water St., 604/683-9124; daily for lunch and dinner) features monastery-like surroundings of wood, brick, stained glass, chandeliers, and monkish murals. Enjoy delicious soups (try the Boston clam chowder), salads, sandwiches, and a variety of entrées (from $15)—all served by waiters appropriately dressed in monk attire—accompanied by congregational sing-alongs and laser-light shows. The daily lunch specials are a good value, as are the early dinner deals available Monday–Thursday before 6 P.M.

The **Old Spaghetti Factory** (53 Water St., 604/684-1288; daily for lunch and dinner) is a family-friendly favorite offering lunch entrées from $7 and dinner entrées from $12, including salad, bread, dessert, and coffee.

Pacific Northwest

With its prime waterfront location between Canada Place and Gastown, **Aqua Riva** (200 Granville St., 604/683-5599) features stunning views across Burrard Inlet to the North Shore Range through floor-to-ceiling windows. It's less touristy than you may imagine, and well priced for the high standard of food offered. The least expensive way to enjoy the dramatic view is with a pizza baked in a wood-fired oven ($14–18). Other mains, mostly seafood and including a delicious alderwood-grilled wild salmon, are generally under $30 (pastas average $22). Lunch mains, including a wide variety of gourmet sandwiches, range $11–24.

At Gastown's busiest intersection, opposite the crowd-drawing steam clock, is **Water Street Cafe** (300 Water St., 604/689-2832; daily 11:30 A.M.–9:30 P.M.), in the 1906 Edward Hotel. Unlike dining at most other Gastown eateries, you won't feel like you're in the touristy quarter of Vancouver. White linens, dark blue carpets, and lots of polished woodwork ooze style, while service is professional. Most important, the food is well priced and delicious. The wild salmon topped with hazelnuts and a maple butter sauce ($24) is a good choice, or go for something lighter, such as the prawn and papaya salad ($17.50). A good selection of pastas ($14–17) provides a break from seafood.

To enjoy creative Pacific Northwest cooking dominated by local seafood in an absolute waterfront location, make reservations at fashionable **Nu** (1661 Granville St., 604/646-4668; daily lunch and dinner). Tables are inside or out, and the whole building is over the water, allowing great views of the bustling False Creek waterway below. Prices are more reasonable than you might imagine: starter fried oysters accompanied by a lager shooter are $3.90 each, wine poached pear salad is $10.90. Mains are as varied as a chilled seafood salad ($30) and melt-in-your-mouth braised pork belly with a yam dumpling ($23). Save room for the passionfruit pudding ($6.50).

Seafood

Slick and chic, **Coast** (1257 Hamilton St., Yaletown, 604/685-5010; daily from 5:30 P.M.) is a cavernous dining room that bristles with energy. It was formerly a warehouse, but the

---

DOWNTOWN DINING CLASSICS

While the best known of Vancouver's restaurants are judged by their food, the service, the decor, and the crowd they attract, none of that matters to the following places. At the places listed here, though, you can expect hearty portions, inexpensive prices, and, at all except the infamous Elbow Room, friendly service.

The **Elbow Room,** one block south of Granville Street (560 Davie St., 604/685-3628, Mon.-Fri. 7:30 A.M.-3:30 P.M., Sat.-Sun. 8:30 A.M.-4 P.M.), is a Vancouver institution where portions are huge and the prices reasonable ($8 for the Lumberjack breakfast), but it's the service that you'll remember long after the meal. Feel like coffee? Get it yourself. A glass of water, maybe? "Get off your ass and get it yourself," a sign declares. The waiters take no nonsense, and the constant banter from the open kitchen, if not memorable, is at least unique. But it's all in good fun, and if you get abused you'll join a long list of celebrities whose photos adorn the walls. If you don't finish your meal, you must make a donation to a local charity; if it's a pancake you can't finish, you're advised to "just rub it on your thighs, because that's where it's going anyway!" Sunday morning is when the kitchen and wait staff are at their wittiest.

"Quality Food, Snappy Service" is the catch-cry at **The Templeton** (1087 Granville St., 604/685-4612; daily 9 A.M.-11 P.M.), which has been serving downtown locals since 1934. Eat at the low counter or in the vinyl booths, each with a small jukebox, and enjoy traditional diner fare as well as more exotic creations, such as grilled ahi tuna with a dab of pineapple salsa on top and a side of organic greens ($14). Wash it down with a banana split ($8). Breakfasts go for under $8, lunches range $6-11, and dinners are all under $18. On Friday, movies are screened off the back wall.

In the same vicinity, Davie Street north of Granville holds a couple of classic diners, including **Hamburger Mary's** (1202 Davie St., 604/687-1293), complete with chrome chairs, mirrored walls, and an old jukebox. Delicious hamburgers attract the crowds to Mary's; starting at $5.50, they aren't particularly cheap, but they come with fries, and extras such as salad are just $1. Breakfast ($5 for eggs, bacon, hash browns, and toast) begins daily at 7 A.M., and the last burgers are flipped in the early hours of the morning. Wash down your meal with one of Mary's famous milkshakes.

Vancouver's oldest restaurant, the **Only Café,** between downtown and Chinatown (20 E. Hastings St., 604/681-6546; daily 11 A.M.-8 P.M.), has been serving bargain-basement seafood for over 80 years. The decor is very 1950s, with two U-shaped counters, two duct-taped booths, and no bathrooms, but the food is always fresh and cooked to perfection. Up the hill from the Only Cafe, beyond Main Street, is the **Ovaltine Café** (251 E. Hastings St., 604/685-7021; daily 6 A.M.-midnight), easily spotted by the classic neon sign hanging out front. This classic diner has been serving up cheap chow for over 50 years.

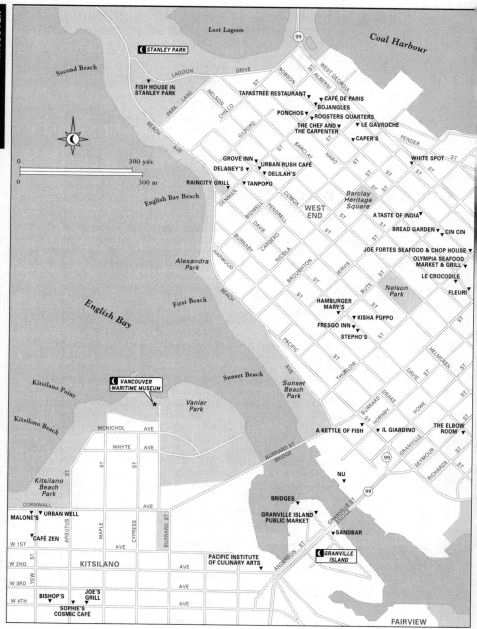

Lost Lagoon

Coal Harbour

Second Beach

STANLEY PARK

LAGOON   DRIVE

FISH HOUSE IN
STANLEY PARK

WEST GEORGIA

ROBSON
ALBERNI

TAPASTREE RESTAURANT

CAFÉ DE PARIS
BOJANGLES
PONCHOS   ROOSTERS QUARTERS
THE CHEF AND   LE GAVROCHE
THE CARPENTER
CAPER'S

PENDER

BEACH

AVE

NELSON

CHILCO

GILFORD

BARCLAY

HARO

WHITE SPOT

GROVE INN
DELANEY'S

URBAN RUSH CAFÉ
DELILAH'S

RAINCITY GRILL   TANPOPO

DENMAN

BIDWELL

PENDRELL

COMOX

Barclay
Heritage
Square

WEST
END

A TASTE OF INDIA

English Bay Beach

300 yds

300 m

DAVIE

CARDERO

NICOLA

BREAD GARDEN   CIN CIN

JOE FORTES SEAFOOD & CHOP HOUSE
OLYMPIA SEAFOOD
MARKET & GRILL
LE CROCODILE

Alexandra
Park

HARWOOD

BURNABY

BROUGHTON

JERVIS

BUTE

Nelson
Park

FLEURI

First Beach

BEACH

HAMBURGER
MARY'S
KISHA POPPO

FRESGO INN
STEPHO'S

English Bay

PACIFIC

AVE

THURLOW

DAVIE

HELMCKEN

Sunset Beach

Sunset
Beach
Park

VANCOUVER
MARITIME MUSEUM

Vanier
Park

Kitsilano Point

BURRARD

DRAKE

HORNBY

HOWE

Kitsilano Beach

MCNICHOL   AVE

WHYTE   AVE

A KETTLE OF FISH   IL GIARDINO

THE ELBOW
ROOM

GRANVILLE

SEYMOUR

RICHARDS

Kitsilano
Beach
Park

ST

MAPLE

CYPRESS

AVE

BURRARD ST
BRIDGE

99

NU

CORNWALL

MALONE'S   URBAN WELL

CAFÉ ZEN

W 1ST

ARBUTUS

AVE

BRIDGES

GRANVILLE ISLAND
PUBLIC MARKET

99

GRANVILLE ST
BRIDGE

SANDBAR

W 2ND

KITSILANO   AVE

PACIFIC INSTITUTE
OF CULINARY ARTS

ANDERSON

GRANVILLE
ISLAND

W 3RD

YEW

AVE

W 4TH

BISHOP'S

JOE'S
GRILL

AVE

SOPHIE'S
COSMIC CAFÉ

FAIRVIEW

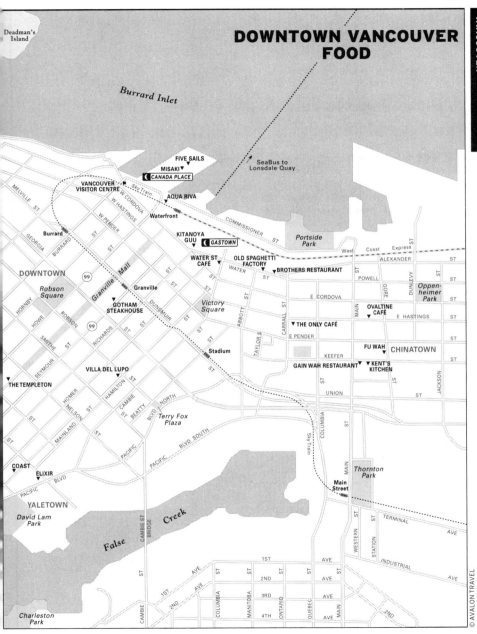

DOWNTOWN VANCOUVER FOOD

Deadman's Island

Burrard Inlet

FIVE SAILS ▼
MISAKI ▼
CANADA PLACE

SeaBus to
Lonsdale Quay

VANCOUVER
VISITOR CENTRE
AQUA RIVA

Waterfront

MELVILLE ST
W CORDOVA
W HASTINGS
W PENDER

Burrard

GEORGIA

SkyTrain

KITANOYA
GUU
GASTOWN

COMMISSIONER ST

Portside
Park

West   Coast   Express   ST

WATER ST
CAFÉ ▼
OLD SPAGHETTI
FACTORY
WATER   ST
▼BROTHERS RESTAURANT

ALEXANDER   ST

DOWNTOWN   99

Robson
Square

Granville

Granville Mall

GOTHAM
STEAKHOUSE

DUNSMUIR

Victory
Square

ABBOTT

CARRALL

POWELL

E CORDOVA

GORE

DUNLEVY

Oppen-
heimer
Park

ST

ST

99

RICHARDS   ST

HORNBY
HOWE
ROBSON
SMITHE

TAYLOR

Stadium

MAIN

OVALTINE
CAFÉ

E HASTINGS

ST

ST

▼ THE ONLY CAFÉ

E PENDER

KEEFER

FU WAH ▼

CHINATOWN

ST

SEYMOUR   ST

VILLA DEL LUPO

HAMILTON   ST

GAIN WAH RESTAURANT ▼   ▼ KENT'S
KITCHEN

JACKSON

▼
THE TEMPLETON

HOMER
NELSON   ST

CAMBIE
BEATTY   ST

BLVD NORTH

UNION

ST

ST

Terry Fox
Plaza

MAINLAND   ST

PACIFIC   ST

PACIFIC   BLVD SOUTH

COLUMBIA   ST

MAIN   ST

Thornton
Park

▼
COAST

▼ ELIXIR

PACIFIC   BLVD

SkyTrain

Main
Street

YALETOWN

David Lam
Park

CAMBIE ST BRIDGE

False   Creek

WESTERN   ST
STATION   ST

TERMINAL

AVE

INDUSTRIAL   AVE

1ST   AVE

ST

ST

ST

2ND   AVE

1ST

2ND

AVE

CAMBIE

COLUMBIA ST

MANITOBA ST

ONTARIO ST

QUEBEC ST

MAIN ST

3RD   AVE

4TH   AVE

2ND

Charleston
Park

© AVALON TRAVEL

industrial feel has been softened with a light color scheme and modern furnishings. The menu of fresh seafood is a knockout from beginning to end. Start with a seafood nectar, such as clam chowder with smoked bacon ($8), which comes with chunks of sourdough bread for dipping. Then move onto entrées such as tempura-battered halibut with aromatic spiced fries ($23) or one of the seasonal grill choices ($28–34) that may include ahi tuna or wild salmon.

One of Vancouver's finest seafood restaurants is ◖ **A Kettle of Fish** (900 Pacific St., 604/682-6853; lunch Mon.–Fri., dinner daily), near the Burrard Street Bridge. The casual decor features café-style seating and abundant greenery, while the menu swims with schools of piscatory pleasures. New England clam chowder ($10) is one of more than 20 appetizers, while traditionally prepared entrées, such as grilled Arctic char with a grainy mustard glaze ($24) and Dungeness crab ($36), make up the main menu. The extensive wine list is especially strong on white wines—the perfect accompaniment for a feast of seafood.

At Canada Place is **Five Sails,** in the Pan Pacific Vancouver Hotel (604/891-2892; daily 6–10 P.M.). The fabulous setting and harbor views are reflected in the prices. The menu features dishes originating in the chef's French homeland, but steers away from using fusion techniques that are prevalent in many of Vancouver's better restaurants.

Steak

Steak lovers who feel like a splurge should consider **Gotham Steakhouse** (615 Seymour St., 604/605-8282; daily from 5 P.M.). The cavernous room holding this restaurant is divided into a restaurant and a bar, meeting in the middle under a 13-meter-high (43-foot-high) arched ceiling. With furnishings of thick leather seats, dark-colored hardwood tables, and plush velvet carpet, both sections exude the atmosphere of a private gentlemen's club. If the steak here isn't the best in Vancouver, servings are certainly the most generous, especially the signature dish, a $49.95 porterhouse. Other mains range $26–50, earning Gotham awards

from city magazines as the "Best Restaurant when Someone Else Is Paying."

European

For Vancouver's finest French cuisine, go to the small, intimate **Le Crocodile** (909 Burrard St., 604/669-4298; lunch Mon.–Fri., dinner Mon.–Sat.), which has won innumerable awards over its two decades as one of Vancouver's premier restaurants. Named after a restaurant in the owner's hometown, Le Crocodile is elegant, but not as intimidating as its reputation. The smallish menu relies heavily on traditional French techniques, which shine through on appetizers (or entrées as they are properly called at Le Crocodile), such as wild mushroom soup with truffle oil ($7.50) or frogs legs sautéed in a chive butter sauce ($12), and on mains like grilled beef tenderloin with peppercorn sauce ($34).

◖ **Fleuri,** in the Sutton Place Hotel (845 Burrard St., 604/642-2900), is one of Vancouver's best hotel restaurants, and you needn't spend a fortune to enjoy dining in what is generally regarded as one of the world's best hotels. Every afternoon, high tea—complete with scones and cream, finger foods, and nonalcoholic beverages—costs $22. The dinner menu is French influenced (mains $25–34), with a magnificent seafood buffet offered on Friday and Saturday nights. Fleuri is also regarded as having one of the city's best Sunday brunch spreads (adult $39, child $19.50), complete with live jazz. Adjacent to the restaurant is the elegant Gerald Lounge, the perfect spot for a predinner drink.

Of Vancouver's many Italian restaurants, one of the most popular is **Il Giardino** (1382 Hornby St., 604/669-2422; Mon.–Fri. noon–2:30 P.M. and daily 6–11 P.M.), in a distinctive yellow Italian-style villa. The light, bright furnishings and enclosed terrace provide the perfect ambience for indulging in the featured Tuscan cuisine. Expect to pay $12–16 for lunch entrées, $16–33 for dinner.

Elixir, in the Opus Hotel (322 Davie St., 604/642-6787; Mon.–Sat. 6:30 A.M.–2 A.M., Sunday 6:30 A.M.–midnight) is a stylish, energetic bistro at the street level of Vancouver's hippest hotel. The contemporary French menu blends easily with the young, money-to-burn crowd—and prices are not as outrageous as you may imagine. The three-course "Express Dinner" ($30) changes nightly, while al a carte choices include delicious sablefish poached in a port reduction ($28).

Japanese

Kitanoya Guu (375 Water St., 604/685-8682; daily 11:30 A.M.–10:30 P.M.) is a groovy Japanese restaurant with an energetic chef who oversees the needs of mostly young, always loud, patrons. Known in Japan as *izakaya*-style dining, the atmosphere is informal, with a menu that encourages sharing. It's similar to a North American neighborhood pub, but instead of wings and nachos, choices include *harumaki* (spring rolls), *shiso-age* (chicken and plum sauce wrapped in thin bread), and *maguro* (tuna with avocado and mango sauce).

At the opposite end of the Japanese dining experience spectrum, **Misaki** (in Canada Place, 604/891-2893; Tues.–Fri. noon–1:30 P.M., Tues.–Sat. 6–9 P.M.) offers the peace and tranquility of a classy Tokyo restaurant. The cuisine combines traditional Japanese and contemporary fusion cooking, with most dishes using local seasonal produce.

DAVIE STREET

The downtown end of Davie Street, between Burrard and Bute Streets, holds many coffeehouses and inexpensive dining options. It is a popular after-hours haunt, with many places open 24 hours to cater to the nightclub crowd. Typical is **Fresgo Inn** (1138 Davie St., 604/689-1332), a cavernous self-serve cafeteria where breakfast is bargain priced and hamburgers cost from $3.50. A longtime favorite, once open 24 hours, it now closes at 3 A.M. Monday–Saturday and at midnight on Sunday. On the corner of the next intersection, at Bute Street, is **Hamburger Mary's** (1202 Davie St., 604/687-1293; daily at 7 A.M.), a classic 1950s-style diner (it actually opened in 1979), complete with chrome chairs, mirrored walls,

and an old jukebox. Wash down your meal with one of Mary's famous milkshakes.

Expect to wait for a table at **Stepho's** (1124 Davie St., 604/683-2555, daily noon–11:30 P.M.), one of Vancouver's best-value restaurants. Locals line up here to enjoy the atmosphere of a typical Greek taverna, complete with terra-cotta floors, white stucco walls, arched doorways, blue-and-white tablecloths, travel posters, and lots of colorful flowering plants. All of the favorite Greek dishes are offered, such as souvlakis or a steak and Greek salad combination for around $10, and portions are generous.

Kisha Poppo (1143 Davie St., 604/681-0488; daily 11:30 A.M.–midnight) serves up Westernized Japanese food in a sterile diner-style atmosphere, but the price is right. All-you-can-eat soup, starters, sushi, hot mains such as teriyaki, and dessert are offered through lunch ($11 pp) and dinner ($19).

CHINATOWN

Dining in Chinatown offers two distinct options: traditional eateries, where you'll find the locals, and the larger, Westernized restaurants that attract Westerners and a younger Chinese crowd. A perfect combination of the two is **Kent's Kitchen** (232 Keefer St., 604/669-2237), a modern café-style restaurant where the service is fast and efficient, the food freshly prepared, and the prices incredibly low. The most expensive combination is a large portion of shrimp and sweet-and-sour pork, which along with rice and pop is $8.50 (and could easily feed two people). Tiny **Gain Wah Restaurant** (218 Keefer St., 604/684-1740) is typical of the many hundreds of noodle houses found in Hong Kong. In Asia, noodle houses cater to the thriftier segment of the population, and although this is a Westernized version of those across the Pacific, dining here is still extremely inexpensive. The restaurant is best noted for *congee,* a simple soup of water extracted from boiling rice. A bowl of congee costs $1.50, with flavorings an additional $0.25–2.

Around the corner from Keefer Street, Gore Street is less Westernized; beyond the large fish market you'll find **Fu Wah** (525 Gore St.,

604/688-8722), which has a ridiculously inexpensive lunchtime dim sum menu.

ROBSON STREET

Linking downtown to the West End, Robson Street holds the city's largest concentration of eateries. In addition to several fine-dining restaurants, cafés sprinkle the sidewalks with outdoor tables—perfect for people-watching.

Cafés and Coffeehouses

It's been said that Vancouver is addicted to coffee, and walking along Robson Street, it would be hard to disagree. The street harbors multiple outlets of the main coffeehouse chains, including 6 **Starbucks** (of 100 citywide) and 4 of the city's 20 **Blenz** outlets.

One of the best spots in all of Vancouver for coffee and a light snack is at one of the 10 **Bread Garden** cafés scattered throughout Metro Vancouver. In this part of the city, the Bread Garden is half a block off busy Robson Street (812 Bute St., 604/688-3213). It's open 24 hours a day and is always busy—so much so that patrons often need to take a number and wait for service. The coffee is great, as are the freshly baked muffins and pastries. Salads and healthy sandwiches are also available.

At the west end of Robson Street, **Caper's** (1675 Robson St., 604/687-5288) is a cavernous store selling groceries and premade meals for the health-conscious. Caper's also has an in-house bakery, deli, and juice bar.

Seafood

Half a block off Robson, 🔳 **Joe Fortes Seafood and Chophouse** (777 Thurlow St., 604/669-1940; daily 11:30 A.M.–10:30 P.M.) is a city institution and is always busy with the young and beautiful set. The comfortable interior offers elegant furnishings, bleached-linen tablecloths, a rooftop patio, and an oyster bar where you can relax while waiting for your table. At lunch, the specialty grilled fish goes for $15–20. The dinner menu is slightly more expensive, although midweek "blue plate" specials such as jambalaya (Tuesday) are well

priced. In warmer weather, request a table on the rooftop patio.

Although the oysters at Joe's are hard to beat, those at the **Olympia Seafood Market and Grill** (820 Thurlow, 604/685-0716; daily 11 A.M.–7 P.M.), one block away, come pretty close. What was originally a fish market—and still looks like one—now sells cooked fish and chips (boxed, with a slice of lemon, for $7–10), either to take out or to enjoy at the short counter. You can still get fresh and packaged seafood to go: everything from marlin to caviar is on the menu.

European

The Chef and the Carpenter (1745 Robson St., 604/687-2700) serves great country-French cuisine in an intimate yet relaxed atmosphere. Portions are large, but save room for the delicious desserts. Main meals range $18–22. Open weekdays for lunch and daily for dinner (reservations required).

Generally regarded as one of Canada's finest French restaurants 🔳 **Le Gavroche** (1616 Alberni St., 604/685-3924; daily from 5:30 P.M.) is romantic, yet not as pretentious as you may assume. Ensconced in a century-old home, tables are spread through the second floor, with some spilling onto a terrace. Caesar salad ($9) is created tableside, after which you can order mains such as mustard-crusted rack of lamb ($32) or grilled sablefish topped with a fennel puree ($32). Tasting menus (three courses $45, four courses $55, five courses $60) are a popular option. The wine list is one of the most thoughtful in Vancouver.

Named for a traditional Italian toast, **CinCin** (1154 Robson St., 604/688-7338; lunch Mon.–Fri., daily from 5 P.M.) is a Mediterranean-style restaurant with a loyal local following. The centerpiece of the dining room is a large open kitchen, with a wood-fired oven and a rotisserie in view of diners. The heated terrace fills up quickly but is the place to watch the Robson Street action from above. The specialty is fancy pizza (from $15), but the oven is also used to cook dishes like rack of lamb broiled in a rosemary marinade ($34), and ahi tuna

DINING IN STANLEY PARK

The simplest way to enjoy a meal in Stanley Park is by having a picnic – smoked salmon, a selection of cheeses, a loaf of sourdough bread – you know the drill. But for something a little more formal, three restaurants are all excellent alternatives, for lunch or dinner.

The least expensive place to eat in Stanley Park is **Prospect Point Café,** near the south end of Lions Gate Bridge (604/669-2737; summer daily 11 A.M.-8 P.M., shorter hours the rest of the year), with a large deck that allows sweeping views across to the North Shore. Grilled salmon (around $20) is the specialty, but you can also order dishes such as a Bavarian smokie ($8) and a smoked salmon Caesar salad ($13). Get there by driving along the Stanley Park loop road or by walking up the steps from the sea-level promenade.

Between Second and Third Beaches, **Sequoia Grill** (Ferguson Point, 604/669-3281, daily 11:30 A.M.-2:30 P.M., 5-9:30 P.M.) is an intimate restaurant of connected rooms with bright, elegant surroundings set among towering trees. Healthy, contemporary cooking is the order of the day. Look for starters

such as carrot and ginger soup ($7) and mains that range from maple-marinated cedar plank salmon ($25) to pan-seared venison smothered in apricot chutney ($29). Vegetable sides are extra (be careful with the oven-roasted cherry tomatoes – they can be very hot). Reservations aren't generally necessary during the day, but reserve a table on the heated patio to enjoy the evening sunset.

The **Fish House in Stanley Park** (8901 Stanley Park Dr., 604/681-7275; daily 11 A.M.-9 P.M.) lies in a parklike setting in the southwest corner of the park, away from the crowded promenade and surrounded by a bowling green and tennis courts. The atmosphere is as refined as at the Sequoia Grill, but a more traditional menu attracts a slightly older crowd. All of the usual seafood dishes are offered, as well as a few unique choices. A meal could go something like this: crispy prawn spring rolls to start, maple-glazed salmon as a main, and Pavlova (meringue topped with whipped cream and fruit) for dessert. Expect to pay around $45 for this or a similar combination.

($36). Grilled dishes are similarly priced, while pastas range $14–24.

East Indian
A Taste of India (1282 Robson St., 604/682-3894; daily 11 A.M.–midnight) stands out along this strip of fashionable boutiques and trendy cafés. The decor—complete with plastic flowers—is nothing to write home about, but this restaurant is worth visiting for its wide selection of traditional East Indian dishes at reasonable prices.

WEST END
Denman Street is the center of the dining action in this trendy part of downtown. Toward the English Bay end of Denman Street, there is a definite seaside atmosphere, with many cafés and restaurants offering water views and attracting droves of beach-lovers in their summer wear.

Cafés and Cheap Eats
Raised a few steps from street level, **Urban Rush Café** (1040 Denman St., 604/685-2996; daily 7 A.M.–10 P.M.) is a large, busy café with a long row of outdoor tables. Across the road is **Delany's** (1105 Denman St., 604/662-3344), part of a small local coffeehouse chain.

Opposite Denman Place Mall, near the crest of Denman Street, a couple of older-style places have survived, offering old-fashioned service and good value. The least expensive of these for breakfast is the **Grove Inn** (1047 Denman St., 604/687-0557; daily 7 A.M.–11 P.M.), where the breakfast special is $5 before 10 A.M.

For chicken cooked to perfection, head over the hill to **Rooster's Quarters** (836 Denman St., 604/689-8023; Mon.–Thurs. from noon, Fri.–Sun. from 4:30 P.M.), a casual eatery chock-full of chicken memorabilia. A full chicken with accompanying vegetables and fries (for two) is a reasonable $17.

At the street's north end is **Bojangles** (785 Denman St., 604/687-3622), a small café on a busy intersection. More than the usual coffee house, Bojangles offers simple cooked breakfasts ($5–7) and gourmet sandwiches ($6).

West Coast

You'll find contemporary West Coast cuisine at **Delilah's** (1789 Comox St., 604/687-3424; daily from 5:30 P.M.). One of Vancouver's longtime favorite restaurants, Delilah's features well-prepared dishes that take advantage of seasonal produce and locally harvested seafood served in an elegant European-style setting. The fixed-price two-course dinner costs from $29, depending on the season; a four-course feast ($41) is also offered. Start your evening meal with one of Delilah's delicious martinis.

The innovative menu and extensive by-the-glass wine list at nearby **Raincity Grill** (1193 Denman St., 604/685-7337; daily 11:30 A.M.–2:30 P.M. and 5–10:30 P.M.) have gained this restaurant numerous awards. The interior is stylish and table settings more than adequate, but the views across English Bay through large windows are most impressive (on the downside, inside can get crowded and noisy). The menu changes with the season but always includes seafood and carefully selected local ingredients, such as free-range chicken from Fraser River Valley farms. Lunch entrées (the salad of smoked steelhead is a particular treat) are $10–17, dinner (such as roasted loin of lamb with potato puree, green beans, and mint jus) ranges $21–33. Sweet treats include a tasty rhubarb crumble ($8.50).

Mexican

Ponchos (827 Denman St., 604/683-7236; daily 5–11 P.M.) is a friendly, family-run Mexican restaurant where the walls are decorated with colorful ponchos, you eat from tiled tables, and a guitar-playing singer serenades diners between courses. The menu is extremely well priced, with authentic Mexican

food costing from $7 and combination meals for around $16.

European

The atmosphere at **Tapastree Restaurant** (1829 Robson St., 604/606-4680; daily for dinner) is inviting and cozy, and the service is faultless, but the food really shines: the tapas-only menu features choices such as vegetarian antipasto, prawns with grilled pesto, and salmon baked in a Dijon crust, most of which are under $12.

Around the corner, **Café de Paris** (751 Denman St., 604/687-1418; Mon.–Fri. 11:30 A.M.–2 P.M., daily 5:30–10 P.M.) is an intimate yet casual city-style French bistro. Classic French main courses (don't dare call them entrées at this very French restaurant), which change daily, range $25–35, but the daily three-course table d'hôte is the best value at around $45. Wines offered are almost exclusively French.

GRANVILLE ISLAND AND VICINITY

The distinctive yellow building on Granville Island's northern tip is **Bridges** (1696 Duranleau St., 604/687-4400). Here diners have a choice of four dining areas, each with its own menu. The outside dockside menu features typical wide-ranging bistro-style fare of hamburgers, salads, and pastas, as well as basic seafood dishes such as a platter to share for $38. Inside, the bistro offers a similar menu, or eat in the pub and save a few bucks on the same dishes while listening to yachties talking too loud on their cell phones. The upstairs dining room is more formal and is open nightly for a seafood-oriented menu.

Under the Granville Street Bridge, **Sandbar** (1535 Johnston St., 604/669-9030; daily 11:30 A.M.–10 P.M.) is hidden from the main road that loops around the island but well worth searching out. Downstairs features an open kitchen and water views, a world away from the hustle and bustle of the nearby marketplace. The upstairs room features a private deck complete with its own elevated waterfront bar. The menu comprises

If the sun is shining, head to Bridges on Granville Island for food served with a view.

mostly seafood, cooked with a distinct Asian feel. Highly recommended is the Fish Hot Pot ($20), crammed with "whatever's available at the market."

Pacific Institute of Culinary Arts

Students from around the world are attracted to the ◖ Pacific Institute of Culinary Arts (1505 W. 2nd Ave., 604/734-4488), right by the entrance to Granville Island, for its state-of-the-art facilities and world-class teachers led by chef Walter Messiah. Cuisine prepared by these budding chefs is served to the public in the institute's 50-seat dining room. The quality of the food is impossible to fault, and its presentation is also impeccable. Lunch is offered weekdays 11:30 A.M.–2 P.M. and dinner Monday–Saturday 6–9 P.M. The three-course set menus are a bargain at $24 and $36, respectively. It's à la carte daily except on Friday, when an extravagant seafood buffet is offered. Desserts and pastries produced by the institute's bakery classes are also tempting and are offered

Monday–Saturday 8 A.M.–7 P.M. at the café-style bakery.

Granville Island Market

This market, on Johnston Street, bustles with locals and tourists alike throughout the day. In the tradition of similar European markets, shopping here is an unpretentious and practical affair, with lots of talking, poking, and inquiring at stalls selling fresh meats, seafood, fruit and vegetables, and cheeses and at specialty stalls stocked with prepackaged goodies to go. At the Burrard Inlet end of the market, you'll find a variety of takeout stalls, and while there's a large expanse of indoor tables, most people head outside to enjoy their meal among the sights and sounds of False Creek. It is difficult not to mention the **Stock Market** (604/687-2433) when recommending a stall to grab lunch. Specializing in soups and broths to take home, this place serves one soup steaming hot each day (if Red Snapper Chowder is the choice of the day, you're in for a real treat). The market is officially open daily 9 A.M.–6 P.M., but some food stalls open earlier and others later.

KITSILANO

The main concentration of restaurants on the south side of False Creek is in Kitsilano, along West 4th Avenue between Burrard and Vine Streets. This part of the city was the heart of hippiedom in the 1970s, and while most restaurants from that era are long gone, a few remain, and other, newer additions to the local dining scene reflect that period of the city's history.

Healthy Eating

Capers Community Market (2285 W. 4th Ave., 604/739-6676; daily 8 A.M.–10 P.M.) is a large grocery-style store crammed with natural and organic foods. Off to one side is the Gourmet Deli & Bakery, with its own courtyard patio, where you can fill up at the salad bar, or order everything from muffins to smoked salmon wraps.

Cool and Casual

Retro-hip **Sophie's Cosmic Café** (2095 W. 4th Ave., at Arbutus St., 604/732-6810; daily 8 A.M.–9:30 P.M.) typifies the scene with a definite cosmic look, but also provides a good value and fast, efficient service. Standard bacon and eggs is $7 and omelets are around $10. The rest of the day, check the blackboard above the food-service window for dishes such as a nut and herb burger ($8.50). Expect to wait for a table on Sunday morning.

Joe's Grill (2061 W. 4th Ave., 604/736-6588; daily 7 A.M.–10 P.M.), one block east of Sophie's, has survived from the 1960s, serving up typical greasy spoon fare at good prices. A breakfast of eggs, bacon, and hash browns is $6; the daily soup-and-sandwich special is just $7; the milkshakes are to die for; and coffee refills are free. In diner tradition, seating is at tables or booths.

West Coast

At the **Livingroom Bistro** (2958 W. 4th Ave., 604/737-7529; daily from 5:30 P.M.), the menu may reflect modern tastes, but as a throwback to days gone by in Kitsilano, the atmosphere is typically bohemian. The owners have cleverly created a classy restaurant using retro-style furnishings, right down to mismatched plates. The starters are perfect for sharing, including delicious cheddar and potato pierogi ($7). For mains, the vegetarian dishes—think portobello mushrooms stuffed with corn and couscous ($12)—shine, and things only get better with hearty choices like a palate-pleasing brie- and apricot-stuffed chicken breast for a very reasonable $17.

Vegetarian

A throwback to the hippie era of the 1960s is **Naam** (2724 W. 4th Ave., 604/738-7151), at Stephens Street, a particularly good natural-food restaurant in a renovated two-story private residence. Boasting large servings, excellent service, and an easygoing atmosphere that has become legendary, it's open 24 hours a day, every day of the week. Veggie burgers start at $5, full meals range $8–14.

Mexican

At Maple Street, **Las Margaritas** (1999 W. 4th Ave., 604/734-7117) is open for lunch (around $8) and dinner ($10–14) and boasts "mild or wild, we can add all the octane you wish." The decor is California-style south-of-the-border: white stucco walls, Mexican hats, tile floor, tile-topped tables, and an outdoor deck. Start with a bowl of chips and salsa, move on to the grilled salmon burrito ($13.25), and throw back a couple of margaritas along the way.

Farther west, near McDonald Street, **Topanga Café** (2904 W. 4th Ave., 604/733-3713; Mon.–Sat. 11:30 A.M.–10 P.M.) offers less expensive California-style Mexican dishes in a home-style atmosphere. Most main meals are under $17, including massive chicken burritos, complete with rice, beans, and corn chips for $6.

European

The much-lauded **Bishop's** (2183 W. 4th Ave.,

604/738-2025; daily 5:30–10 P.M.) is very French in all aspects. Owner and longtime Vancouver restaurateur John Bishop makes all diners feel special, personally greeting them at the door, escorting them to their table, and then describing the menu and wine list as required. Elegant surroundings, parched-white linen, and soft jazz background music complete the picture. The menu features French classics but changes as seasonal produce becomes available, such as salmon and halibut, Fraser River Valley vegetables, and fruits from the Okanagan Valley. Expect to pay around $120 for three courses for two, sans drinks. Reservations are required.

Continuing west, **Quattro on Fourth** (2611 W. 4th Ave., 604/734-4444, daily from 5 P.M.) exudes an elegant yet casual atmosphere, and the walls are lined with cabinets filled with wines from around the world. An outdoor deck features table settings set amid flowers and shrubbery. The menu emphasizes traditional country-style Italian cooking, including simple pastas ($18–22) and specialty dishes ($25–37), such as a delicious prawn-and-scallop ravioli ($26.50).

WEST BROADWAY

Broadway runs parallel to 4th Avenue, which is five blocks farther south. The restaurants listed below are farther east than those along West 4th Avenue and are generally less trendy, appealing to those looking for value.

Pacific Northwest

One of only three Canadian restaurants with the Relais Gourmand designation, **Lumière** (2551 W. Broadway, 604/739-8185; daily for dinner) is one of Vancouver's finest eateries. In the minimalist room, you'll enjoy superb French cooking with a young, smartly dressed crowd. Most diners gravitate to classic dishes such as duck breast poached in olive oil with pan-seared foie gras on the side. Expect to pay $23–35 per main.

Feenie's (2563 W. Broadway, 604/739-7115; daily for lunch and dinner) is owned by one of Canada's top young chefs, Robert Feenie, who also oversees the kitchen at adjacent Lumière.

The casual lounge bar buzzes with liveliness, with hip locals sipping martinis at the big red bar or tucking into dishes such as a Feenie's Weenie ($9) or a slab of shepherd's pie filled with duck confit ($17) at comfortable booths. Things get serious in the main dining room, where single dishes start at $15 and the multicourse Chef's Tasting Menu is $120.

Asian

Nakornthai (401 W. Broadway, at Yukon St., 604/874-8923; daily for lunch and dinner) specializes in the cuisine of Thailand, where many dishes are based on thick, coconut milk–based sauces. Pork is a staple in Thai cooking, prepared here in many different ways. The restaurant is small but clean, well decorated, and bright and airy. It's also inexpensive, with hearty lunch specials from just $6.

One block north of West Broadway at Granville Street is **C Vij's** (1480 11th Ave., 604/736-6664; daily from 5:30 P.M.), one of Vancouver's most acclaimed Asian restaurants. Vikram Vij, the East Indian owner, combines the spicy flavors of his homeland with local tastes, creating a menu that appeals to everyone. Presentation and service are of the highest standard, but the food really makes this restaurant stand out. Appetizers are all under $15, and mains, such as halibut poached in buttermilk and saffron broth, range $21–28. No reservations are taken, and getting a table often involves a wait, which says something about a place in a nondescript building within one block of a kilometer-long strip of other restaurants.

NORTH SHORE

If you've crossed Burrard Inlet on the Sea-Bus, visit **Lonsdale Market** for local produce, including a couple of market stalls selling seafood fresh from the trawlers.

The pick of spots for breakfast or lunch in suburban West Vancouver, west of Lonsdale Quay and the Lions Gate Bridge, is **Savary Island Pie Company** (1533 Marine Dr., 604/926-4021; daily 6 A.M.–7 P.M.). Join the line at this super-popular café and order a slice of focaccia pizza ($4) or a generous slab

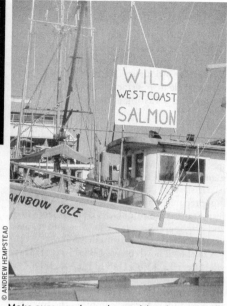

© ANDREW HEMPSTEAD

Make sure you try salmon at least once while in Vancouver.

of chicken potpie ($8.50), saving room for an oatmeal cookie or brownie.

Seafood

On the north side of Burrard Inlet, **◖ Salmon House on the Hill** (2229 Folkstone Way, West Vancouver, 604/926-3212; daily 11:30 A.M.– 2:30 P.M. and 5–10 P.M.) offers a relaxed atmosphere and provides panoramic views across Burrard Inlet to Stanley Park and the city center from its elevated mountainside location. The cavernous interior is full of Northwest Coast native arts and crafts, including a dugout canoe suspended over the main dining area. For an appetizer, the seafood chowder ($8) is my recommendation. It's not a huge serving, but it is thick and delicious. Another good starter is the sample platter of salmon prepared in various ways ($18). The house specialty of salmon barbecued over an open-flame, alderwood-fired grill is also hard to pass by. And the price for this signature dish is right at just $25. To get there, take the 21st Street exit off Upper Levels Highway to Folkstone Way, and turn left on Ski Lift Road.

Information and Services

TOURIST OFFICES
Downtown

The city's main information center is **Vancouver Visitor Centre,** right downtown in the heart of the waterfront district one block from Canada Place (Plaza Level, 200 Burrard St., 604/683-2000; May–Sept. daily 8:30 A.M.– 6 P.M., the rest of the year Mon.–Sat. 8:30 A.M.– 5:30 P.M.). Brochures line the lower level, while on the upper level specially trained staff provide free maps, brochures, and public transportation schedules; book sightseeing tours; and make accommodations reservations. Look for public transportation information and timetables to the right as you enter the center.

South

If you approach Vancouver from the south on Highway 5 (Highway 99 in Canada), the first official information center you'll come to is the **Peace Arch Provincial Visitor Centre** (summer 8 A.M.–8 P.M., the rest of the year 9 A.M.–5 P.M.), immediately north of the border and right beside the highway. A currency exchange is on-site.

Farther north along Highway 99, **Richmond Visitor Centre** (604/271-8280 or 877/247-0777, www.tourismrichmond.com; Mar.–June daily 9:30 A.M.–5 P.M., July–Aug. daily 9 A.M.–7 P.M., Sept. daily 9:30 A.M.–5 P.M.) is right by the highway, to the right as you emerge on the north side of the George Massey Tunnel under the Fraser River. It's operated by Tourism Richmond.

North

A handy source of information north of the harbor is the small information center in the

VANCOUVER

historic building beside Lonsdale Quay, which is open in summer daily 9 A.M.–6 P.M.

East

If you're approaching the city from the east along Highway 1, **Chilliwack Visitor Centre** (44150 Luckakuck Way, 604/858-8121 or 800/567-9535, www.tourismchilliwack.com) is a good place to stop, stretch your legs, and gather some brochures.

Across the Fraser River from Surrey, Tourism New Westminster (604/526-1905, www .tourismnewwestminster.org) operates **New Westminster Visitor Centre** (604/526-1905) in the riverfront market at 810 Quayside Drive. This location is out of the way for highway travelers, but if you do make the detour, take Brunette Avenue south from Exit 40 off the TransCanada Highway.

Operated by the local chamber of commerce, **Coquitlam Visitor Centre** (1209 Pinetree Way, 604/464-2716, www.tricitieschamber .com) is also by Highway 7, at the north side of its intersection of Highway 7A. As well as Coquitlam and Port Coquitlam, the center represents Port Moody and the wilderness areas to the north.

EMERGENCY SERVICES

For emergencies, call 911. For medical emergencies, contact the downtown **St. Paul's Hospital** (1081 Burrard St., 604/682-2344), which has an emergency ward open 24 hours a day, seven days a week. Other major hospitals are **Vancouver General Hospital** (899 W. 12th Ave., 604/875-4111) and **Lions Gate Hospital** (231 E. 15th St., 604/988-3131). **Seymour Medical Clinic** (1530 W. 7th Ave., 604/738-2151) is open 24 hours. For emergency dental help, call the **AARM Dental Group** (1128 Hornby St., 604/681-8530). For the **Royal Canadian Mounted Police (RCMP)**, call 911 or 604/264-3111.

COMMUNICATIONS
Postal Service

Vancouver's **main post office** is at 349 W. Georgia St. (604/662-5722), open Mon.–Sat.).

Postal Station A (757 W. Hastings St.) and the branch at **Bentall Centre** (595 Burrard St.) are also open on Saturdays.

Visitors can have their mail sent to them c/o General Delivery, Postal Station A, Vancouver, BC V3S 4P2, Canada. The West Hastings Street post office will hold the mail for two weeks and then return it to the sender.

Internet Access

All of Vancouver's major hotels have in-room modem or wireless Internet access, but for those not traveling with a laptop, head to any Blenz café. If you have a vehicle, kill two birds with one stone at **Cold Coin Laundry** (3496 W. Broadway, 604/737-9642; daily 7 A.M.–10 P.M.), which has laundry facilities, public Internet access ($5 per hour), and better coffee than you may imagine.

Libraries

Vancouver Public Library (350 W. Georgia St., 604/331-3600; year-round Mon.–Thurs. 10 A.M.–9 P.M., Fri.–Sat. 10 A.M.–6 P.M., Sun. 1–5 P.M.) is a magnificent facility dominated by an elliptical facade containing a glass-walled promenade rising six stories above a row of stylish indoor shops and cafés. Once inside, you'll soon discover that the city also found enough money to stock the shelves; the library holds more than one million books. More than 20 other affiliated libraries are spread across the city. Call 604/331-3600 or go to www.vpl.vancouver .bc.ca for addresses and opening hours.

Newspapers

Vancouver's two newspapers are the *Province* (www.vancouverprovince.com), published daily except Saturday, and the *Vancouver Sun* (www.vancouversun.com), published daily except Sunday.

Many free publications are distributed throughout the city. The weekly *Georgia Straight* (www.straight.com) features articles on local issues, as well as a full entertainment rundown for the city. The *Westender,* also a weekly, spotlights downtown issues and has good restaurant reviews. The weekly *Terminal*

VANCOUVER

City (www.terminalcity.ca) and, for the hip set, *Loop* both have offbeat articles and music and entertainment diaries.

PHOTOGRAPHY

One-hour film processing is offered by dozens of outlets throughout Vancouver. Two of the most reliable are **London Drugs,** with branches throughout Metro Vancouver (call 604/872-8114 for the location nearest to you), and **Lens and Shutter,** which has an outlet at 2912 West Broadway, 604/736-3461. **Leo's Cameras** (1055 Granville St., 604/685-5331; Mon.–Fri. 9 A.M.–5 P.M., Sat. 10 A.M.–4 P.M.) has an excellent selection of new and used camera equipment, with knowledgeable staff on hand to answer any questions.

Getting There

AIR

Vancouver International Airport (www.yvr .ca) is on Sea Island, 15 kilometers (9.3 miles) south of the Vancouver city center. Over 16 million passengers pass through the terminal annually. The three-story international terminal and adjacent domestic terminal hold coffee shops and restaurants, car-rental agencies, a post office, currency exchanges, newsstands, gift shops, and duty-free shops. Numerous information boards provide a quick airport orientation, and an information booth on Level 3 of the international terminal offers tourist brochures, bus schedules, and taxi information.

The **Vancouver Airporter** (604/946-8866 or 800/668-3141, www.yvrairporter .com) leaves the arrivals level of both terminals every 15–30 minutes 6:30 A.M.–11:30 P.M. daily, shuttling passengers along three routes between the airport and more than 40

Pacific Central Station is the Vancouver terminus of all long-distance rail and bus services.

© ANDREW HEMPSTEAD

downtown accommodations and Pacific Central Station. The one-way fare is adult $13.50, senior $10.50, child $6.25, with a slight discount offered for a round-trip purchase. Buy tickets from the driver or from the ticket offices on the arrivals levels of both terminals. A cab from the airport to downtown takes from 25 minutes and runs around $35.

RAIL

Vancouver is served by **VIA Rail** (416/366-8411 or 888/842-7245, www.viarail.ca) passenger trains from across the country and is the terminus for the **Rocky Mountaineer** (604/606-7245 or 800/665-7245, www.rocky mountaineer.com). For details on both these services, including schedules and pricing, go to the *Essentials* chapter of this book.

The Vancouver terminus of all VIA Rail services is **Pacific Central Station** (1150 Station St.), two kilometers (1.2 miles) southeast of downtown, an $8 cab ride or just a few minutes on the SkyTrain from any of the four downtown stations. Inside the station you'll find a currency exchange, cash machines, lockers, a newsstand, information boards, and a McDonald's restaurant. The Rocky Mountaineer terminates behind Pacific Central Station off Terminal Avenue (1755 Cottrell St.).

BUS

All long-distance Greyhound bus services terminate in Vancouver at **Pacific Central Station,** two kilometers (1.2 miles) southeast of downtown at 1150 Station Street.

Quick Shuttle (604/940-4428 or 800/665-2122, www.quickcoach.com) operates a regular bus service to Pacific Central Station and major downtown Vancouver hotels from downtown Seattle (US$36 one-way) and SeaTac Airport (US$49 one-way).

Getting Around

TRANSLINK

TransLink (604/953-3333, www.translink .bc.ca) operates an extensive network of buses, trains, and ferries that can get you just about anywhere you want to go within Vancouver. The free brochure *Discover Vancouver on Transit* is available from all city information centers and is an invaluable source of information.

Buses run to all corners of the city 5 A.M.–2 A.M. daily. Transfers are valid for 90 minutes of travel in one direction.

SkyTrain is a computer-operated (no drivers) light-rail transit system that runs along 28 kilometers (17.3 miles) of elevated track from downtown Vancouver through New Westminster and over the Fraser River to King George Highway in Surrey. It stops at 20 stations along its 39-minute route. The four city-center stations are underground but are clearly marked at each street entrance.

The double-ended, 400-passenger **SeaBus** scoots across Burrard Inlet every 15–30 minutes, linking downtown Vancouver to North Vancouver in just 12 minutes. The downtown terminus is Waterfront Station, beside Canada Place and a five-minute walk from the Vancouver Visitor Centre. The terminal in North Vancouver is at Lonsdale Quay, where you can catch TransLink buses to most North Shore sights.

On weekdays 5:30 A.M.–6:30 P.M. the city is divided into three zones, and fares vary adult $2.25–4.50, senior $1.50–3 for each sector (Zone 1 encompasses all of downtown and Metro Vancouver; Zone 2 covers all of the North Shore, Burnaby, New Westminster, and Richmond; and Zone 3 extends to the limits of the TransLink system). At other times (including all weekend), travel anywhere in the city costs $2.25 one-way. Pay the driver (exact change only) for bus travel or purchase tickets from machines at any SkyTrain station or SeaBus terminal. Request a free transfer from the driver if required. A **DayPass** costs adult $8, senior $6, and allows unlimited travel for one day anywhere on the TransLink system. They are available at all SeaBus and SkyTrain stations and FareDealers (convenience stores such as 7-Eleven and Mac's) throughout the city.

Disabled Access

TransLink's small **HandyDART** buses (604/430-2692) provide door-to-door wheelchair-accessible service for about the same price you'd pay on regular buses. Many other city buses are equipped with wheelchair lifts, and all SkyTrain stations as well as the SeaBus and West Coast Express are fully wheelchair accessible. The best source of further information is the *Rider's Guide to Accessible Transit,* available by calling Translink (604/953-3333).

FERRY

Apart from the SeaBus (see previous section *TransLink*), the only other scheduled ferry services within the city are on False Creek. Two private companies, **Granville Island Ferries** (604-684-7781) and **Aquabus** (604/689-5858), operate on this narrow waterway. From the main hub of Granville Island, 12- to 20-passenger ferries run every 15 minutes daily 7 A.M.–10 P.M. to the foot of Hornby Street, and under the Burrard Street Bridge to the Aquatic Centre (at the south end of Thurlow St.) and Vanier Park (Vancouver Museum). Every 30–60 minutes both companies also run down the head of False Creek to Stamps Landing, the Plaza of Nations, and Science World. Fares range $2.50–5 each way, with discounts for seniors and kids; schedules are posted at all docking points.

TAXI

Taxi cabs are easiest to catch outside major hotels or transportation hubs. Fares in Vancouver are a uniform $2.50 flag charge plus $1.45 per kilometer (plus $0.30 per minute when stopped). Trips within downtown usually run under $10. The trip between the airport and downtown is $35. A 10–15 percent tip to the driver is expected. Major companies include **Black Top** (604/683-4567 or 800/494-1111); **Vancouver Taxi** (877/871-1111); and **Yellow Cab** (604/681-1111 or 800/898-8294).

Several wheelchair-accommodating taxi cabs are available from Vancouver Taxi. The fares are the same as those for regular taxis.

CAR

An excellent public transit system makes up for the fact that Vancouver isn't the world's most driver-friendly city, especially downtown, where congestion is a major problem, particularly during rush hour. West Georgia Street is a particular trouble spot, with traffic from all directions funneling onto Lions Gate Bridge to cross to the North Shore. Many downtown streets are one-way and lack left-turn lanes, adding to the congestion. On a larger scale, Vancouver lacks any real expressways, meaning a torturous trip through downtown to get anywhere on the North Shore.

Parking

Downtown metered parking costs $1 per 30 minutes but is often difficult to find during business hours. Most shopping centers have underground parking, and a few multistory parking lots are scattered throughout the city core (including between Water and Cordova Streets, Gastown; access from either side). These cost from $5 per hour and from $20 per day, with discounts for full-day parking for early arrivals. One place you'll be assured of finding parking is under the downtown hotels, which generally charge $5–8 per hour for nonguests. Guests at these same hotels pay up to $30 per 24-hour period for parking; often, weekend hotel rates include free parking. Throughout the residential areas of downtown, parking in many streets is designated for permit-holding residents only—look for the signs or expect to be towed.

VANCOUVER ISLAND

Vancouver Island, the largest isle in North America's Pacific, stretches for more than 450 superb kilometers (280 miles) off the west coast of mainland British Columbia. Victoria, the provincial capital, lies at the southern tip of the island. Its deeply entrenched British traditions make Victoria unique among North American cities.

The rest of the island draws scenery buffs, outdoor adventurers, wildlife watchers, and students of northwest native culture. A magnificent chain of rugged snowcapped mountains, sprinkled with lakes and rivers and pierced by deep inlets, effectively divides the island into two distinct sides: dense, rain-drenched forest and remote surf- and wind-battered shores on the west, and well-populated, sheltered, beach-fringed lowlands on the east.

Much of the lush, green island is covered with dense forests of Douglas fir, western red cedar, and hemlock. The climate, stabilized by the Pacific Ocean and warmed by the Japanese current, never really gets too hot or too cold, but be prepared for cloudbursts, especially in winter.

PLANNING YOUR TIME

Many visitors to Victoria spend a few nights in the city as part of a longer vacation that includes the rest of Vancouver Island. At an absolute minimum, plan on spending two full days in the capital, preferably overnighting at a character-filled bed-and-breakfast. Regardless of how long you'll be in the city, much of your time will be spent in and around the Inner Harbour, a busy waterway surrounded

HIGHLIGHTS

◖ **Fairmont Empress:** You don't need to be a guest at this historic hotel to admire its grandeur. Plan on eating a meal here for the full effect (page 101).

◖ **Royal BC Museum:** If you visit only one museum in Victoria, make it this one, where you can come face-to-face with an Ice Age woolly mammoth (page 101).

◖ **Goldstream Provincial Park:** Laced with hiking trails, Goldstream Provincial Park is a great escape from the city. If you're visiting in late fall, a trip to the park is worthwhile to view the spectacle of spawning salmon (page 111).

◖ **Butchart Gardens:** Even if you have only one day in Victoria, make time to visit one of the world's most delightful gardens (page 112).

◖ **West Coast Trail:** Winding through 77 kilometers (48 miles) of old-growth forest,

and with the Pacific Ocean close at hand, this ambitious walk is one of the world's great long-distance hikes (page 131).

◖ **Galiano Island:** Each of the Southern Gulf Islands has its own charms, but a personal favorite for kayaking is Galiano Island (page 141).

◖ **Pacific Rim National Park:** Canada isn't renowned for its beaches, but this park protects some magnificent stretches of sand (page 158).

◖ **Telegraph Cove:** It's worth the drive to Telegraph Cove on northern Vancouver Island just to wander around the postcard-perfect boardwalk village, but you'll also want to take a tour boat in search of orca whales (page 180).

◖ **Alert Bay:** On Cormorant Island, Alert Bay is a hotbed of native history. A cultural center and some of the world's tallest totem poles are highlights (page 182).

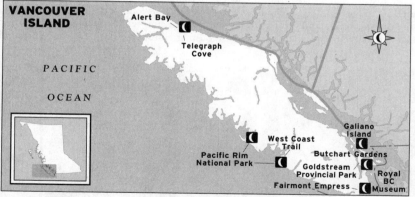

LOOK FOR ◖ TO FIND RECOMMENDED SIGHTS, ACTIVITIES, DINING, AND LODGING.

© ANDREW HEMPSTEAD

Victoria's Inner Harbour

by the city's top sights and best restaurants. At the top of the must-see list is the **Royal BC Museum,** which will impress even the biggest museophobes. Victoria's most visited attraction is **Butchart Gardens,** an absolutely stunning collection of plants that deserves at least half a day of your time. **Goldstream Provincial Park** and the scenic waterfront drive between downtown and Oak Bay are two outdoor destinations you should figure into your schedule.

Exploring Vancouver Island beyond Victoria requires some advance planning and an idea of where you want to end up. If you have just a day to spare, you can take the oceanside drive west from Victoria to Port Renfrew or travel north as far as Nanaimo, but to explore the island farther you should schedule at least two days and preferably more. The Southern Gulf Islands, linked to Victoria by ferry and float-plane, make a good overnight trip from the capital (my favorite is **Galiano Island**). Plan on at least two nights out from Victoria to do the west coast town of Tofino and the adjacent **Pacific Rim National Park** justice. Incorporating other parts of the province into an itinerary that includes Vancouver Island is easy. The most obvious and useful option is to do your thing on Vancouver Island and then catch a ferry from Comox to Powell River (covered in the *Southwestern British Columbia* chapter), and then drive down the Sunshine Coast to Vancouver. A more ambitious loop is to drive to Port Hardy, taking time to go whale-watching from **Telegraph Cove** and immerse yourself in native culture at **Alert Bay,** and catch the ferry from the northern tip of Vancouver Island to Prince Rupert (see *Northern British Columbia*), then return to Vancouver through the central portion of the province.

VANCOUVER ISLAND

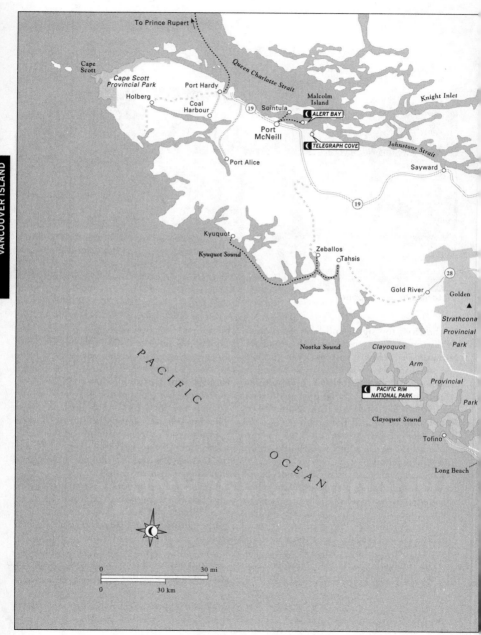

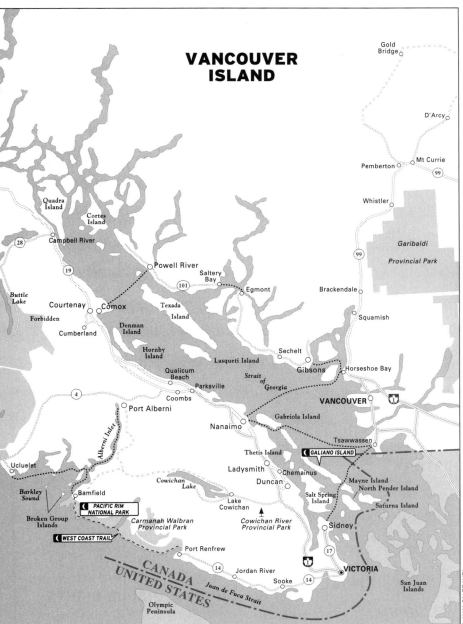

VANCOUVER ISLAND

Gold Bridge

D'Arcy

Pemberton   Mt Currie   99

Whistler

Garibaldi

Provincial Park

Quadra Island

Cortes Island

28

Campbell River   Powell River   Saltery Bay   Egmont   Brackendale   99   Squamish

19

101

Buttle Lake

Courtenay   Comox   Texada Island   Sechelt

Forbidden   Denman Island   Lasqueti Island   Gibsons   Horseshoe Bay

Cumberland   Hornby Island   Qualicum Beach   Strait of Georgia

Parksville   Coombs

4   Port Alberni   Nanaimo   Gabriola Island   VANCOUVER

Alberni Inlet   Thetis Island   Tsawwassen   GALIANO ISLAND

Ucluelet   Ladysmith   Chemainus   Mayne Island   North Pender Island

Barkley Sound   Bamfield   Cowichan Lake   Duncan   Salt Spring Island   Saturna Island

PACIFIC RIM NATIONAL PARK   Lake Cowichan   Cowichan River Provincial Park

Broken Group Islands   Carmanah Walbran Provincial Park

WEST COAST TRAIL   Sidney

17

Port Renfrew

CANADA   14   Jordan River   VICTORIA

UNITED STATES   Juan de Fuca Strait   Sooke   14   San Juan Islands

Olympic Peninsula

Victoria

Many people view the city for the first time from the Inner Harbour, coming in by boat the way people have for almost 150 years; as the boat rounds Laurel Point, Victoria sparkles into view. Ferries, fishing boats, and seaplanes bob in the harbor, with a backdrop of manicured lawns and flower gardens, quiet residential suburbs, and striking inner-city architecture. Despite the pressures that go with city life, easygoing Victorians still find time for a stroll along the waterfront, a round of golf, or a night out at a fine restaurant.

Victoria doesn't have as many official sights as Vancouver, but this isn't a bad thing. Once you've visited must-sees like the Royal BC Museum and Butchart Gardens you can devote your time to outdoor pursuits such as whale-watching, a bike ride through Oak Bay, or something as simple as enjoying a stroll along the beach. You will be confronted with oodles of ways to trim bulging wallets in Victoria. Some commercial attractions are worth every cent, others are routine at best, although the latter may be crowd-pleasers with children, which makes them worth considering. Discovering Victoria's roots has been a longtime favorite with visitors, but some locals find the "more English than England" reputation tiring. Yes, there's a tacky side to some traditions, but high tea, double-decker bus tours, and exploring formal gardens remain true joys in Victoria.

HISTORY

In 1792, Captain George Vancouver sailed through the Strait of Georgia, noting and naming Vancouver Island. But this had little effect on the many indigenous communities living along the shoreline. Europeans didn't see and exploit the island's potential for another 50 years, when the Hudson's Bay Company established control over the entire island and the mainland territory of "Columbia."

Fort Victoria

Needing to firmly establish British presence on the continent's northwest coast, the Hudson's Bay Company built Fort Victoria—named after Queen Victoria—on the southern tip of Vancouver Island in 1843. Three years later, the Oregon Treaty fixed the U.S.–Canada boundary at the 49th parallel, with the proviso that the section of Vancouver Island lying south of that line would be retained by Canada. To forestall any claims that the United States may have had on the area, the British government went about settling the island. In 1849, the island was gazetted as a Crown colony and leased back to the Hudson's Bay Company. Gradually land around Fort Victoria was opened up by groups of British settlers brought to the island by the company's subsidiary, Puget Sound Agricultural Company. Several large company farms were developed, and Esquimalt Harbour became a major port for British ships.

The Growth of Victoria

In the late 1850s gold strikes on the mainland's Thompson and Fraser Rivers brought thousands of gold miners into Victoria, the region's only port and source of supplies. Overnight, Victoria became a classic boomtown, but with a distinctly British flavor: Most of the company men, early settlers, and military personnel firmly maintained their homeland traditions and celebrations. Even after the gold rush ended, Victoria remained an energetic bastion of military, economic, and political activity, and was officially incorporated as a city in 1862. In 1868, two years after the colonies of Vancouver Island and British Columbia were united, Victoria was made capital. Through the two world wars, Victoria continued to grow. The commencement of ferry service between Tsawwassen and Sidney in 1903 created a small population boom, but Victoria has always lagged well behind Vancouver in the population stakes.

INNER HARBOUR SIGHTS

The epicenter of downtown Victoria is the foreshore of the Inner Harbour, which is flanked by the parliament buildings, the city's main museum, and the landmark Fairmont Empress Hotel. Government Street leads uphill from the waterfront through a concentration of touristy shops and restaurants, while parallel to the west, Douglas Street is the core of a smallish central business district.

Above the northeast corner of the harbor is the **Victoria Visitor Centre** (812 Wharf St., 250/953-2033, www.tourismvictoria.com), the perfect place to start your city exploration. Be sure to return to the Inner Harbour after dark, when the parliament buildings are outlined in lights and the Empress Hotel is floodlit.

Fairmont Empress

Overlooking the Inner Harbour, the pompous, ivy-covered 1908 Fairmont Empress (721 Government St., 250/384-8111 or 800/257-7544, www.fairmont.com) is Victoria's most recognizable landmark. Its architect was the well-known Francis Rattenbury, who also designed the parliament buildings, the Canadian Pacific Railway (CPR) steamship terminal (now housing the wax

Fairmont Empress

© ANDREW HEMPSTEAD

museum), and Crystal Garden. It's worthwhile walking through the hotel lobby to gaze—head back, mouth agape—at the interior razzle-dazzle, and to watch people-watching people partake in traditional afternoon tea. Browse through the conservatory and gift shops, drool over the menus of the various restaurants, see what tours are available, and exchange currency if you're desperate (banks give a better exchange rate).

Royal BC Museum

Canada's most visited museum and easily one of North America's best, the Royal British Columbia Museum (675 Belleville St., 250/356-7226, summer daily 9 A.M.–6 P.M., the rest of the year daily 9 A.M.–5 P.M.) is a must-see attraction for even the most jaded museum-goer. Its fine Natural History Gallery displays are extraordinarily true to life, complete with appropriate sounds and smells. Come face-to-face with an Ice Age woolly mammoth, stroll through a coastal forest full of deer and tweeting birds, meander along a seashore or tidal marsh, and then descend into the Open Ocean Exhibit via submarine—a very real trip that's not recommended for claustrophobics. The First Peoples Gallery holds a fine collection of artifacts from the island's first human inhabitants, the Nuu-chah-nulth (Nootka). Many of the pieces were collected by Charles Newcombe, who paid the Nuu-chah-nulth for them on collection sorties in the early 1900s. Modern human history is also explored here in creative ways. Take a tour through time via the time capsules; walk along an early-1900s street; and experience hands-on exhibits on industrialization, the gold rush, and the exploration of British Columbia by land and sea in the Modern History and 20th Century Galleries. Museum admission outside of summer is a very worthwhile adult $15, senior and youth $10. In summer, admission jumps to around adult $25.50, senior $19.50, child $17.50, which includes access to a world-class traveling exhibit.

Part of the complex is the **National Geographic Theatre,** showing nature-oriented IMAX films daily 9 A.M.–8 P.M. (additional charge).

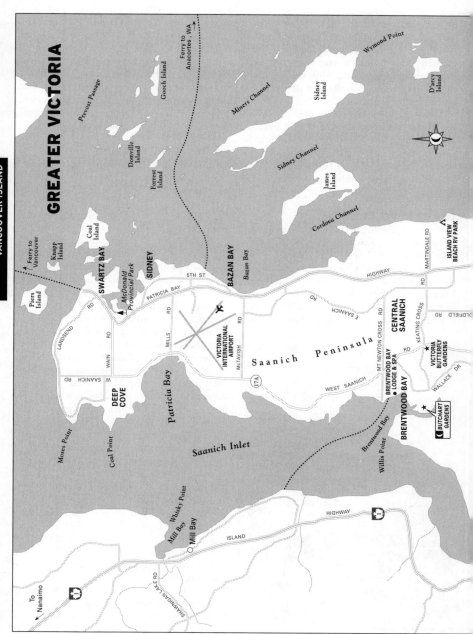

GREATER VICTORIA

Ferry to Anacortes, WA

Wymond Point

Prevost Passage

Gooch Island

Miners Channel

Sidney Island

D'arcy Island

Domville Island

Sidney Channel

Forrest Island

James Island

Cordova Channel

ISLAND VIEW BEACH RV PARK

Ferry to Vancouver

Coal Island

Knapp Island

SWARTZ BAY

SIDNEY

BAZAN BAY

Bazan Bay

MARTINDALE RD

McDonald Provincial Park

5TH ST

HIGHWAY

Piers Island

PATRICIA BAY

RD

OLDFIELD RD

LANDSEND RD

RD

MILLS RD

E SAANICH RD

KEATING CROSS RD

CENTRAL SAANICH

VICTORIA INTERNATIONAL AIRPORT

McTAVISH RD

Saanich   Peninsula

MT NEWTON CROSS RD

VICTORIA BUTTERFLY GARDENS

WAIN RD

SAANICH RD

17A

WEST SAANICH RD

BRENTWOOD BAY LODGE & SPA

WALLACE DR

DEEP COVE

Patricia Bay

BRENTWOOD BAY

BUTCHART GARDENS

Moses Point

Coal Point

Saanich Inlet

Brentwood Bay

Willis Point

Whisky Point

Mill Bay

Mill Bay

ISLAND

HIGHWAY

To Nanaimo

SHAWNIGAN LAKE RD

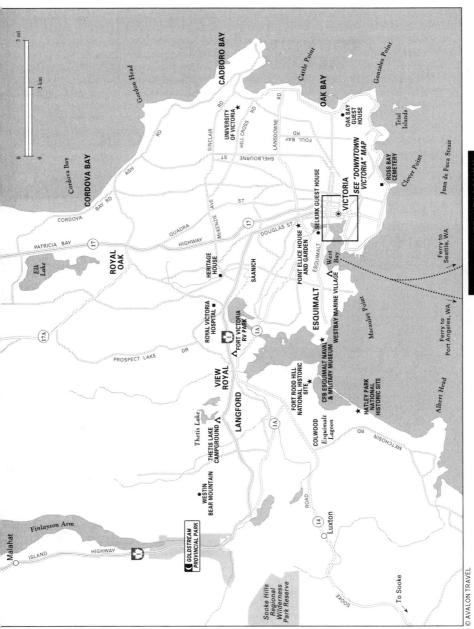

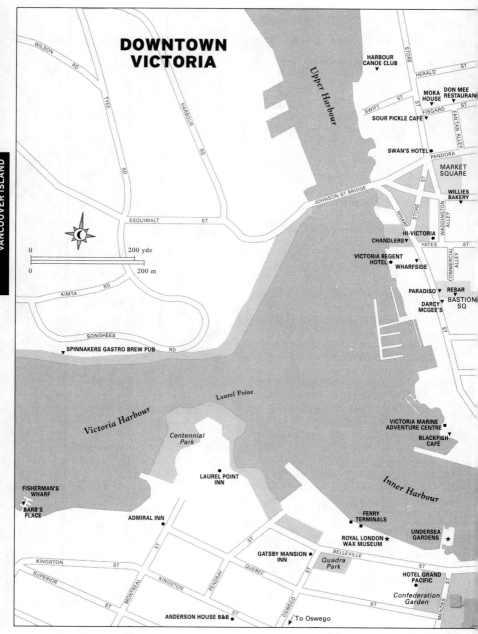

DOWNTOWN VICTORIA

Upper Harbour

WILSON RD
TYEE RD
HARBOUR RD

HARBOUR CANOE CLUB ▼
HERALD ST
STORE ST
MOKA HOUSE ▼
DON MEE RESTAURAN
SWIFT ST
FISGARD ST
SOUR PICKLE CAFÉ ▼
FANTAN ALLEY

SWAN'S HOTEL ●
PANDORA

MARKET SQUARE

WILLIES BAKERY ▼
WADDINGTON ALLEY

JOHNSON ST BRIDGE

ESQUIMALT ST

WHARF ST
STORE ST
YATES ST

HI-VICTORIA ●
CHANDLERS ▼

COMMERCIAL ALLEY

VICTORIA REGENT HOTEL ● ■ WHARFSIDE

PARADISO ▼ REBAR ▼
BASTION SQ
DARCY MCGEE'S ●

0 ____ 200 yds
0 ____ 200 m

KIMTA RD

SONGHEES RD
▲ SPINNAKERS GASTRO BREW PUB

Victoria Harbour

Laurel Point

Centennial Park

VICTORIA MARINE ADVENTURE CENTRE ▼
BLACKFISH CAFÉ ▼

LAUREL POINT INN ●

Inner Harbour

FISHERMAN'S WHARF
BARB'S PLACE ◆

ADMIRAL INN ●

FERRY TERMINALS ■

UNDERSEA GARDENS ★

ROYAL LONDON WAX MUSEUM ★

GATSBY MANSION INN ●
BELLEVILLE ST
Quadra Park

HOTEL GRAND PACIFIC ●

KINGSTON ST
SUPERIOR ST
MONTREAL ST
KINGSTON ST
PENDRAY ST
QUEBEC ST
OSWEGO ST

Confederation Garden
MENZIES ST

ANDERSON HOUSE B&B ●
↓ To Oswego

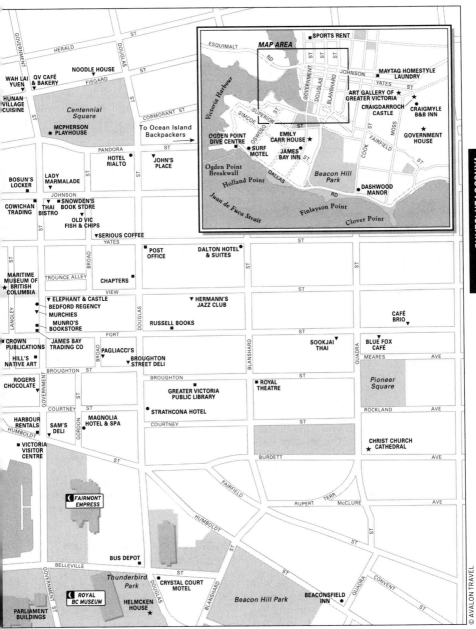

Thunderbird Park

Around the Museum

In front of the museum, the 27-meter (89-foot) **Netherlands Centennial Carillon** was a gift to the city from British Columbia's Dutch community. The tower's 62 bells range in weight from 8 to 1,500 kilograms (18 to 3,300 pounds) and toll at 15-minute intervals daily 7 A.M.–10 P.M.

On the museum's eastern corner, at Belleville and Douglas Streets, lies **Thunderbird Park,** a small green spot chockablock with authentic totem poles intricately carved by northwest coast native peoples. Best of all, it's absolutely free. Beside Thunderbird Park is **Helmcken House** (10 Elliot St., 250/361-0021; summer daily noon–4 P.M.; adult $5, senior $4, child $3), the oldest house in the province still standing on its original site. It was built by Dr. J. S. Helmcken, pioneer surgeon and legislator, who arrived in Victoria in 1850 and aided in negotiating the union of British Columbia with Canada in 1870. Inside this 1852 residence you'll find restored rooms decorated with Victorian period furniture, as well as a collection

of the good doctor's gruesome surgical equipment, which will help you appreciate modern medical technology.

Parliament Buildings

Satisfy your lust for governmental, historical, and architectural knowledge all in one by taking a free tour of the harborside Provincial Legislative Buildings, a.k.a. the parliament buildings. These prominent buildings were designed by Francis Rattenbury and completed in 1897. The exterior is British Columbia Haddington Island stone, and if you walk around the buildings you'll no doubt spot many a stern or gruesome face staring down from the stonework. Walk through the main entrance and into the memorial rotunda, look skyward for a dramatic view of the central dome, and then continue upstairs to peer into the legislative chamber, the home of the democratic government of British Columbia. Free guided tours are offered every 20 minutes, 9 A.M.–noon and 1–5 P.M. in summer, less frequently (and Mon.–Fri. only) in winter. Tour times differ according to the goings-on inside; for current times, call the tour office at 250/387-3046.

Laurel Point

For an enjoyable short walk from downtown, continue along Belleville Street from the parliament buildings, passing a conglomeration of modern hotels, ferry terminals, and some intriguing architecture dating back to the late 19th century. A path leads down through a shady park to Laurel Point, hugging the waterfront and providing good views of the Inner Harbour en route. If you're feeling really energetic, continue to **Fisherman's Wharf,** where an eclectic array of floating homes are tied up to floating wharves.

Royal London Wax Museum

Along the waterfront on Belleville Street, across the road from the parliament buildings, is the former CPR steamship terminal, now the Royal London Wax Museum (470 Belleville St., 250/388-4461; daily 9 A.M.–5 P.M., until 7:30 P.M. in summer). As you enter the grandly ornate building, pay the admission (adult $10, senior $9, child $5) to the cashier on the right. Inside the attraction proper is a series of galleries filled with around 300 wax figures: British royalty, famous folks such as Mother Teresa and Albert Einstein, Canadian heroes like courageous cancer victim Terry Fox, and Arctic explorers. About halfway through, choose between Storybook Land or the Chamber of Horrors. If you have children (or even if you don't), you may want to bypass the latter. The hideous story of Madame Tussaud and her work that led to the famous London wax museum is interesting, but other displays are gruesome at best.

Pacific Undersea Gardens

On the water beside the wax museum, Pacific Undersea Gardens (490 Belleville St., 250/382-5717; summer daily 9 A.M.–8 P.M., the rest of the year daily 10 A.M.–5 P.M.; adult $9.50, senior $8.50, child $5.50) is of dubious value. Local species on display include tasty snapper, enormous sturgeon, schools of salmon, and scary wolf eels. Scuba divers miked for sound make regular appearances at the far end.

OLD TOWN

The oldest section of Victoria lies immediately north of the Inner Harbour between Wharf and Government Streets. Start by walking north from the Inner Harbour along historic Wharf Street, where Hudson's Bay Company furs were loaded onto ships bound for England, gold seekers arrived in search of fortune, and shopkeepers first established businesses. Cross the road to cobblestoned **Bastion Square**, lined with old gas lamps and decorative architecture dating from the 1860s to the 1890s. This was the original site chosen by James Douglas in 1843 for Fort Victoria.

Maritime Museum of British Columbia

At the top (east) end of Bastion Square, the Maritime Museum (250/385-4222; daily 9:30 A.M.–4:30 P.M., until 5 P.M. in summer; adult $8, senior $5, child $3) traces the his-

tory of seafaring exploration, adventure, commercial ventures, and passenger travel through displays of dugout canoes, model ships, Royal Navy charts, figureheads, photographs, naval uniforms, and bells. One room is devoted to exhibits chronicling the circumnavigation of the world, and another holds a theater.

Other Old Town Sights

Centennial Square, bounded by Government Street, Douglas Street, Pandora Avenue, and Fisgard Street, is lined with many buildings dating from the 1880s and '90s, refurbished in recent times for all to appreciate. Don't miss the 1878 **city hall** (fronting Douglas Street) and the imposing Greek-style building of the Hudson's Bay Company. Continue down Fisgard Street into colorful **Chinatown.** It's a delicious place to breathe in the aroma of authentic Asian food wafting from the many restaurants. Poke through the dark little shops along Fisgard Street, where you can find everything from fragile paper lanterns and embroidered silks to gingerroot and exotic canned fruits and veggies, then cruise Fan Tan Alley, the center of the opium trade in the 1800s.

SOUTH OF THE INNER HARBOUR

Emily Carr House

In 1871 artist Emily Carr was born in this typical upper-class 1864 Victorian-era home (207 Government St., 250/383-5843; mid-May–Sept. daily 11 A.M.–4 P.M.; adult $5.50, senior and student $4.50, child $3.25). Carr moved to the mainland at an early age, escaping the confines of the capital to draw and write about the British Columbian native peoples and the wilderness in which she lived. She is best remembered today for her painting, a medium she took up in later years.

Beacon Hill Park

This large, hilly city park—a lush, sea-edged oasis of grass and flowers—extends from the back of the museum along Douglas Street out to cliffs that offer spectacular views of Juan de Fuca Strait and, on a clear day, the distant

VANCOUVER ISLAND

© ANDREW HEMPSTEAD

Beacon Hill Park

Olympic Mountains. Add a handful of rocky points to scramble on and many protected pebble-and-sand beaches, and you've found yourself a perfect spot to indulge your senses. Catch a sea breeze and gaze at all the strolling, cycling, dog-walking, and pram-pushing Victorians passing by.

ROCKLAND

This historic part of downtown lies behind the Inner Harbour, east of Douglas Street, and is easily accessible on foot.

Christ Church Cathedral

On the corner of Quadra and Courtney Streets, Christ Church Cathedral (250/383-2714) is the seat of the Bishop of the Diocese of British Columbia. Built in 1896, in 13th-century Gothic style, it's one of Canada's largest churches. Self-guided tours are possible Monday–Friday 8:30 A.M.–5 P.M. and Sunday 7:30 A.M.–8:30 P.M. In summer, the cathedral sponsors free choral recitals each Saturday at 4 P.M. The park next to the cathedral is a shady haven to rest weary feet, and the gravestones make fascinating reading.

Art Gallery of Greater Victoria

From Christ Church Cathedral, walk up Rockland Avenue through the historic Rockland district, passing stately mansions and colorful gardens on tree-lined streets. Turn left on Moss Street and you'll come to the 1889 Spencer Mansion and its modern wing, which together make up the Art Gallery of Greater Victoria (1040 Moss St., 250/384-4101; daily 10 A.M.–5 P.M., Thurs. 10 A.M.–9 P.M.; adult $12, senior $10, child $2). The gallery contains Canada's finest collection of Japanese art, a range of contemporary art, an Emily Carr gallery, and traveling exhibits, as well as a Japanese garden with a Shinto shrine. The Gallery Shop sells art books, reproductions, and handcrafted jewelry, pottery, and glass.

Government House

Continue up Rockland Avenue from the art gallery to reach Government House, the official residence of the lieutenant governor, the queen's representative in British Columbia. The surrounding gardens, including an English-style garden, rose garden, and rhododendron garden, along with green velvet lawns and picture-perfect flower beds, are open to the public throughout the year. On the front side of the property, vegetation has been left in a more natural state, with gravel paths leading to benches that invite pausing to take in the city panorama.

Craigdarroch Castle

A short walk up (east) from the art gallery along Rockland Avenue and left on Joan Crescent brings you to the baronial four-story mansion known as Craigdarroch Castle (1050 Joan Crescent, 250/592-5323; summer daily 9 A.M.–7 P.M., the rest of the year daily 10 A.M.–4:30 P.M.; adult $11.75, senior $10.75, child $3.75). The architectural masterpiece was built in 1890 for Robert Dunsmuir, a wealthy industrialist and politician who died just before the building was completed.

© ANDREW HEMPSTEAD

Craigdarroch Castle, one of Victoria's grandest residences, is open to the public for tours.

SCENIC ROUTE TO OAK BAY

This route starts south of the Inner Harbour and follows the coastline all the way to the University of Victoria. If you have your own transportation, this is a must-do in Victoria; if you don't, most city tours take in the sights detailed here. You can take Douglas Street south alongside Beacon Hill Park (described earlier) to access the coast, but it's possible to continue east along the Inner Harbour to the mouth of Victoria Harbour proper, passing the Canadian Coast Guard Base and the **Ogden Point Breakwall,** the official start of the Scenic Drive (marked by blue signs). The breakwall is only three meters (10 feet) wide, but it extends for 800 meters (0.5 mile) into the bay. It's a super-popular stroll, especially in the early morning.

For the first few kilometers beyond the breakwall, the Olympic Mountains in Washington State are clearly visible across the Strait of Georgia, and many lookouts allow you to stop and take in the panorama, including **Clover Point.** A few hundred meters beyond Clover Point, **Ross Bay Cemetery** is the final resting place of many of early Victoria's most prominent residents. Continuing east, Dallas Road takes you through quiet residential areas, past small pebble beaches covered in driftwood, and into the ritzy mansion district east of downtown, where the residents have grand houses, manicured gardens, and stunning water views.

Continue through the well-manicured fairways of Victoria Golf Club on Gonzales Point to Cadboro Bay, home to the **Royal Victoria Yacht Club.** The **University of Victoria** lies on a ridge above Cadboro Bay; from here head southwest along Cadboro Bay Road and then Yates Street to get back downtown, or north and take Sinclair Road and then Mackenzie Avenue to reach Highway 17, the main route north up the Saanich Peninsula toward famous Butchart Gardens.

THE GORGE WATERWAY

This natural canal leads north from the Inner Harbour to Portage Inlet, a small saltwater lake beside Highway 1. The best way to see the Gorge is from sea level, aboard a

© ANDREW HEMPSTEAD

Victoria Harbour Ferry

Victoria Harbour Ferry (250/708-0201). This company runs funky little 12-passenger vessels (round-trip tour adult $20, senior $18, child $10) to a turnaround point at Gorge Park by the Tillicum Road Bridge.

Point Ellice House

Built in 1861, this restored mansion (2616 Pleasant St., 250/380-6506, May–mid-Sept. daily 10 A.M.–4 P.M.; adult $6, child $3) sits amid beautiful gardens along the Gorge on Point Ellice, less than two kilometers (1.2 miles) from the Inner Harbour. The house's second owner, Peter O'Reilly, a successful entrepreneur and politician, bought it in 1868 and entertained many distinguished guests there. Original Victorian-era artifacts clutter every nook and cranny of the interior, but the best reason to visit is to enjoy a traditional English afternoon tea served 11 A.M.–3 P.M. (adult $22, child $11, includes a tour). To get there from the Inner Harbour, jump aboard a Victoria Harbour Ferry (10 minutes and $3.50 each way), or by road take Government or Douglas Street north from downtown, turn left on Bay Street, and turn left again on Pleasant Street.

Craigflower Manor

Completed in 1856 using local lumber, this stately home on the Gorge Waterway was the home of one of the island's first farmers. Surrounded by commercial and residential sprawl, the scene today is a far cry from what it was in the 1800s, when the grand home was a social hub for Victorian socialites and naval officers from nearby Esquimalt. You can wander through the grounds and ask questions of volunteers, who tend to gardens filled with the same vegetables and herbs that the original owners planted, and ask to peek inside the main residence. Directly across the Gorge Waterway is Craigflower Schoolhouse, dating from a similar era as the manor and built from lumber cut from a steam-powered sawmill operated by the Mackenzie family. To reach Craigflower, take Gorge Road (Hwy. 1A) north from downtown to the Craigflower Bridge (around four kilometers/2.5 miles). The schoolhouse is on the left, and the manor is across the bridge on the right.

WEST OF DOWNTOWN
CFB Esquimalt Naval & Military Museum

This small museum (250/363-4312; summer daily 10 A.M.–3:30 P.M., the rest of the year Mon.–Fri. 10 A.M.–3:30 P.M.; adult $2, senior and child $1) lies within the confines of **CFB Esquimalt,** on Esquimalt Harbour west of downtown. A couple of buildings have been opened to the public, displaying naval, military, and general maritime memorabilia. To get there from downtown, take the Johnson Street Bridge and follow Esquimalt Road to Admirals Road; turn north, and then take Naden Way and you're on the base. Follow the museum signs.

Hatley Park National Historic Site

Hatley Park (2005 Sooke Rd., 250/391-2666; daily 10 A.M.–8 P.M.; adult $9, senior $8, child free) is a sprawling estate established over 100 years ago by James Dunsmuir, the then premier of British Columbia. The site has also been used as a military college and is currently part of Royal Roads University. Visitors are invited to tour the classic Edwardian-style garden, as well as a rose garden and a Japanese garden, and stroll through an old-growth forest that extends to Esquimalt Lagoon. Dunsmuir's imposing 40-room mansion is also open for guided tours (daily 10 A.M.–3:45 P.M.; adult $15, senior $14, child $7, includes garden access).

Fort Rodd Hill National Historic Site

Clinging to a headland across the harbor entrance from CFB Esquimalt, this picturesque site (603 Fort Rodd Hill Rd., Colwood, 250/478-5849; Mar.–Oct. daily 10 A.M.–5:30 P.M., Nov.–Feb. daily 9 A.M.–4:30 P.M.; adult $4, senior $3.50, child $2) comprises **Fort Rodd,** built in 1898 to protect the fleets of ships in the harbor, and **Fisgard Lighthouse,** which dates to 1873. It's an interesting place

to explore; audio stations bring the sounds of the past alive, workrooms are furnished as they were at the turn of the 20th century, and the lighthouse has been fully restored and is open to visitors. To get there from downtown, take the Old Island Highway (Gorge Road) and turn left on Belmont Road and then left onto Ocean Boulevard. By bus, take number 50 from downtown, then transfer to bus 52.

◀ Goldstream Provincial Park

Lying 20 kilometers (12 miles) from the heart of Victoria, this 390-hectare (960-acre) park straddles Highway 1 northwest of downtown. The park's main natural feature is the Goldstream River, which flows north into the Finlayson Arm of Saanich Inlet. Forests of ancient Douglas fir and western red cedar flank the river; orchids flourish in forested glades; and at higher elevations forests of lodgepole pine, western hemlock, and maple thrive.

The park's highlight event occurs late October through December, when chum, coho, and chinook salmon fight their way upriver to spawn themselves out on the same shallow gravel bars where they were born four years previously. Bald eagles begin arriving in December, feeding off the spawned-out salmon until February. From the picnic area parking lot, two kilometers (1.2 miles) north of the campground turnoff, a trail leads 400 meters (440 yards) along the Goldstream River to **Freeman King Visitor Centre** (250/478-9414; daily 9 A.M.–5 P.M.), where the life cycle of salmon is described.

Even if the salmon aren't spawning, Goldstream is a great place to visit. The most popular destination is **Goldstream Falls.** The trail leaves from the back of the park campground and descends to the picturesque falls in around 300 meters (200 yards). Noncampers should park at the campground entrance; from there it's 1.2 kilometers (0.7 mile) to the falls. One of the park's longer hikes is the **Goldmine Trail,** which begins from a parking lot on the west side of Highway 1 halfway between the campground and the picnic area. This trail winds two kilometers (1.2 miles) each way through

© ANDREW HEMPSTEAD

Goldstream Provincial Park

a mixed forest of lodgepole pine, maple, and western hemlock, passing the site of a short-lived gold rush and coming to **Niagara Falls,** a poor relation of its eastern namesake but still a picturesque flow of water.

Park admission is $1 per vehicle per hour to a maximum of $3 for a day pass.

SAANICH PENINSULA

The Saanich Peninsula is the finger of land that extends north from downtown. It holds Victoria's most famous attraction, Butchart Gardens, as well as Victoria International Airport and the main arrival point for ferries from Tsawwassen. If you've caught the ferry over to Vancouver Island from Tsawwassen, you'll have arrived at **Swartz Bay** on the northern tip of the Saanich Peninsula; from here it's a clear run down Highway 17 to downtown Victoria. If you've been in Goldstream Provincial Park (described earlier this chapter) or are traveling down the island from Nanaimo on Highway 1, head north or south, respectively, to **Mill Bay,** where a ferry departs regularly for **Brentwood**

Bay on the Saanich Peninsula. Ferries run in both directions nine times daily 7:30 A.M.–6 P.M. Peak one-way fares for the 25-minute crossing are adult $5.50, child $2.75, vehicle $13.65. For exact times, contact **BC Ferries** (250/386-3431, www.bcferries.com).

🄲 Butchart Gardens

Carved from an abandoned quarry, these delightful gardens are Victoria's best-known attraction. They're approximately 20 kilometers north of downtown (800 Benvenuto Dr., Brentwood Bay, 250/652-4422, www.butchartgardens.com). The gardens are open every day of the year from 9 A.M., closing in summer at 10 P.M. and in winter at 4 P.M., with varying closing hours in other seasons. Admission in summer is adult $25, youth 13–17 $12.50, children 5–12 $3; admission in winter is around 60 percent of those rates.

A Canadian cement pioneer, R. P. Butchart built a mansion near his quarries. He and his wife, Jennie, traveled extensively, collecting rare and exotic shrubs, trees, and plants from around the world. By 1904 the quarries had been abandoned, and the couple began to beautify them by transplanting their collection into formal gardens interspersed with concrete footpaths, small bridges, waterfalls, ponds, and fountains. The gardens now contain more than 5,000 varieties of flowers, and the extensive nurseries test-grow some 35,000 new bulbs and more than 100 new roses every year. Go there in spring, summer, or early autumn to treat your eyes and nose to a marvelous sensual experience (many a gardener would give both hands to be able to work in these gardens). Highlights include the Sunken Garden (the original quarry site) with its water features and annuals; the formal Rose Garden, set around a central lawn; and the Japanese Garden, from where views extend to Saanich Inlet. In winter, when little is blooming and the entire landscape is green, the basic design of the gardens can best be appreciated. Summer visitors are in for a special treat on Saturday nights (July and August only), when a spectacular fireworks display lights up the garden.

Butchart Gardens is one Victoria attraction you won't want to miss.

© ANDREW HEMPSTEAD

Victoria Butterfly Gardens

In the vicinity of Butchart Gardens, Victoria Butterfly Gardens (corner of Benvenuto Dr. and W. Saanich Rd., 250/652-3822; summer daily 9 A.M.–5 P.M., March–mid-May and October daily 9:30 A.M.–4:30 P.M.; adult $11, senior $10, child $5.75) offers the opportunity to view and photograph some of the world's most spectacular butterflies at close range. Thousands of these beautiful creatures—species from around the world—live here, flying freely around the enclosed gardens and feeding on the nectar provided by colorful tropical plants. You'll also be able to get up close and personal with exotic birds such as parrots and cockatoos.

Sidney

The bustling seaside town of Sidney lies on the east side of the Saanich Peninsula, overlooking the Strait of Georgia. As well as being the departure point for ferries to the San Juan Islands (Washington), Sidney has a charming waterfront precinct anchored by the impressive Sidney Pier Hotel & Spa. It's a pleasant spot to explore on foot—enjoying the many outdoor cafés, walking out onto the pier, and soaking up the nautical ambience. From the marina, **Sidney Harbour Cruise** (250/655-5211) runs four tours daily around the harbor and to a couple of the inner Gulf Islands ($18 pp).

TOURS

The classic way to see Victoria is from the comfort of a horse-drawn carriage. Throughout the day and into the evening, **Victoria Carriage Tours** (250/383-2207 or 877/663-2207) has horse carriages lined up along Menzies Street at Belleville Street awaiting passengers. A 30-minute tour costs $90 per carriage (seating up to six people), a 45-minute tour costs $130, or take a 60-minute Royal Tour for $170. Tours run 9 A.M.–midnight and bookings aren't necessary, although there's often a line.

Big red double-decker buses are as much a part of the Victoria tour scene as horse-drawn carriages. These are operated by **Gray Line** (250/388-6539 or 800/663-8390) from beside the Inner Harbour. There are many tours to

The Inner Harbour is a hub of recreational activity.

choose from, but to get yourself oriented while also learning some city history, take the 90-minute Grand City Drive Tour. It departs from the harborfront every half hour 9:30 A.M.–4 P.M.; adult $25, child $15. The most popular of Gray Line's other tours is the one to Butchart Gardens ($49, including admission price).

On the Water
Victoria Harbour Ferry (250/708-0201) offers boat tours of the harbor and Gorge Waterway. The company's funny-looking boats each seat around 20 passengers and depart regularly 9 A.M.–8:15 P.M. from below the Empress Hotel. The 45-minute loop tour allows passengers the chance to get on and off at will. Costs are adult $20, senior $18, child $10, or travel just pieces of the entire loop for adult $4, child $2 per sector.

SPORTS AND RECREATION
All of Vancouver Island is a recreational paradise, but Victorians find plenty to do around their own city. Walking and biking are

especially popular, and from the Inner Harbour, it's possible to travel on foot or by pedal power all the way along the waterfront to Oak Bay.

Hiking and Biking
If you're feeling energetic—or even if you're not—plan on walking or biking at least a small section of the Scenic Marine Drive, which follows the shoreline of Juan de Fuca Strait from Ogden Point all the way to Oak Bay. The section immediately south of downtown, between Holland Point Park and Ross Bay Cemetery, is extremely popular with early-rising locals, who start streaming onto the pedestrian pathway before the sun rises. Out of town, **Goldstream Provincial Park,** beside Highway 1, and **East Sooke Regional Park,** off Highway 14 west of downtown, offer the best hiking opportunities. You can rent bikes at **Sports Rent,** just north of downtown (1950 Government St., 250/385-7368; from $6–8 per hour, $25–35 per day).

Whale-Watching
Heading out from Victoria in search of whales is something that can be enjoyed by everyone. Both resident and transient whales are sighted during the local whale-watching season (mid-April to October), along with sea lions, porpoises, and seals. Trips last 2–3 hours, are generally made in sturdy inflatable boats with an onboard naturalist, and cost $75–100 per person. Recommended operators departing from the Inner Harbour include **Cuda Marine** (250/383-8411 or 888/672-6722), **Great Pacific Adventures** (250/386-2277 or 877/733-6722), **Orca Spirit Adventures** (250/383-8411 or 888/672-6722), and **Prince of Whales** (250/383-4884 or 888/383-4884). **Sea Quest Adventures** (250/655-4256 or 888/656-7599) is based in Sidney, on the Saanich Peninsula, and offers whale-watching cruises on the Strait of Georgia. The waters here are calmer than those experienced on trips departing the Inner Harbour. This company has kayak tours and rentals.

Kayaking
Daily through summer, **Ocean River Sports**

(1824 Store St., 250/381-4233 or 800/909-4233, www.oceanriver.com) organizes guided three-hour paddles in the Inner Harbour ($60 pp). They also offer kayaking courses, sell and rent kayaks and other equipment, and offer overnight tours as far away as the Queen Charlotte Islands. **Sports Rent** (1950 Government St., 250/385-7368) rents canoes, kayaks, and a wide range of other outdoor equipment. Expect to pay about $35 per day and from $145 per week for a canoe or single kayak.

Scuba Diving

Close to downtown Victoria lie several good dive sites, notably the Ogden Point breakwall. At the breakwall, **Ogden Point Dive Centre** (199 Dallas Rd., 250/380-9119, www.dive victoria.com) offers rentals, instruction, and a daily (10 A.M.) guided dive. Other amenities include lockers and showers.

To access the great diving in the Straits of Georgia and Juan de Fuca, you'll need to charter a boat. One particularly interesting site lies in the shallow waters off Sidney, just north of Victoria, where a 110-meter (360-foot) destroyer escort was scuttled especially for divers.

Swimming and Sunbathing

The best beaches are east of downtown. At **Willows Beach,** Oak Bay, most of the summer crowds spend the day sunbathing, although a few hardy individuals brave a swim; water temperature here tops out at around 17°C (63°F). Closer to downtown, at the foot of Douglas Street, the foreshore is mostly rocky, but you can find a couple of short, sandy stretches here and there. **Elk Lake,** toward the Saanich Peninsula, and **Thetis Lake,** west of downtown along Highway 1, are also popular swimming and sunbathing spots. Within walking distance of downtown, **Crystal Pool** (2275 Quadra St., 250/361-0732) has an Olympic-size pool as well as diving facilities, a kids' pool, sauna, and whirlpool.

ENTERTAINMENT AND EVENTS

Victoria has a vibrant performing arts community, with unique events designed especially for the summer crowds. The city lacks the wild nightlife scene of neighboring Vancouver, but a large influx of summer workers keeps the bars crowded and a few nightclubs jumping during the busy season. The city does have more than its fair share of British-style pubs, and you can usually get a good meal along with a pint of lager. The magazine **Monday** (www .mondaymag.com) offers a comprehensive arts and entertainment section.

Performing Arts

Dating to 1914, the grand old **McPherson Playhouse** (known lovingly as "the Mac" by local theatergoers) hosts a variety of performances. It's in Centennial Square, at the corner of Pandora Avenue and Government Street. The Mac's sister theater, the **Royal Theatre,** across downtown at 805 Broughton Street, began life as a roadhouse and was used as a movie theater for many years. Today it hosts stage productions and a variety of musical recitals. For schedule information and tickets at both theaters, call the Royal & McPherson Theatres Society (250/386-6121 or 888/717-6121, www.rmts.bc.ca).

Performing arts on a smaller scale can be appreciated at the **Belfry Theatre,** in a historic church (1291 Gladstone St., 250/385-6815, www.belfry.bc.ca) that offers live theater October–April; tickets $26–33 per person.

Pacific Opera Victoria (250/385-0222, www.pov.bc.ca) performs three productions each year (usually Oct.–Apr.) in the McPherson Playhouse. Tickets run $20–65. The **Victoria Operatic Society** (250/381-1021) presents opera year-round at the McPherson Playhouse; call for a current schedule.

Drinking and Dancing

The **Strathcona Hotel** (919 Douglas St., 250/383-7137) is Victoria's largest entertainment venue, featuring four bars, including one with a magnificent rooftop patio (with a volleyball court) and the Sticky Wicket, an English bar complete with mahogany paneling. Closer to the Inner Harbour is **Swans Hotel** (506 Pandora St., 250/361-3310; daily from 11 A.M.), which brews its own beer. Unlike many other smaller brewing operations, this one uses traditional ingredients and methods, such as allowing the brew to settle naturally rather than be filtered. The main bar is a popular hangout for local businesspeople and gets busy weeknights 5–8 P.M. A few blocks farther north and right on the water is the **Harbour Canoe Club** (450 Swift St., 250/361-1940), popular with the younger downtown business crowd and with a great deck. Also offering magnificent water views is **Spinnakers Gastro Brewpub,** across the Inner Harbour from downtown (308 Catherine St., 250/384-6613; daily 11 A.M.–2 A.M.). Opening in 1984 as Canada's first brewpub, Spinnakers continues to produce its own European-style ales, including the popular Spinnakers Ale. The original downstairs brewpub is now a restaurant, while upstairs is now the bar. Most important, both levels have outdoor tables with water views.

Victoria's many English-style pubs usually feature a wide variety of beers, a congenial atmosphere, and inexpensive meals. The closest of these to downtown is the **James Bay Inn** (270 Government St., 250/384-7151). Farther out, **Six Mile House** (494 Island Hwy., 250/478-3121) is a classic Tudor-style English pub that was extensively restored in 1980. To get there, head west out of the city along Highway 1 and take the Colwood exit.

Most of Victoria's nightclubs double as live music venues attracting a great variety of acts. **Legends,** in the Strathcona Hotel (919 Douglas St., 250/383-7137), has been a city hotspot for more than 30 years. It comes alive with live rock-and-roll some nights and a DJ spinning the latest dance tunes on other nights. In the same hotel, **Big Bad John's** is the city's main country music venue. At the bottom of Bastion Square, **D'Arcy McGee's** (1127 Wharf St., 250/380-1322) is a great place for lunch or an afternoon drink, while after dark it dishes up live rock to a working class crowd. Across the road, below street level at the Wharfside complex, the **Boom Boom Room** (1208 Wharf St., 250/381-2331; closed Sunday), with bright lights and a large dance floor, is a longtime

favorite with the dance crowd. Other popular nightclubs are **Hugo's** (625 Courtney St., 250/920-4846), which offers live music before 10 P.M. before transforming to a dance club, and **Plan B** (1318 Broad St., 250/384-3557), a small venue with attitude.

Victoria boasts several good jazz venues. The best of these is **Hermann's Jazz Club** (753 View St., 250/388-9166; Wed.–Sat.). **Steamers** (570 Yates St., 250/381-4340) draws diverse acts, but generally features jazz and blues on Tuesday and Wednesday nights. Check the Victoria Jazz Info Line (250/388-4423, www.vicjazz.bc.ca) for a schedule of local jazz performances.

Spring Festivals and Events

Officially, of course, February is still winter, but Victorians love the fact that spring arrives early on Canada's West Coast, which is the premise behind the **Flower Count,** the last week in February. While for other Canadians summer is a long way off, locals count the number of blossoms in their own yards, in parks, and along the streets. Totals in the millions are tabulated and gleefully reported across Canada.

The birthday of Queen Victoria has been celebrated in Canada since 1834 and is especially relevant for those who call her namesake city home. The Inner Harbour is alive with weekend festivities that culminate in a downtown **Victoria Day Parade** that takes two hours to pass a single spot. (Although Queen Victoria's actual birthday was May 24, the event is celebrated with a public holiday on the Monday preceding May 25.)

More than 300 musicians from around the world descend on the capital for **Jazzfest International** (250/388-4423, www.vicjazz .bc.ca), held the last week of June. Venues are scattered throughout the city.

Although most visitors associate Victoria with afternoon tea at the Empress, cowboys know Victoria as an important early-season stop on the rodeo circuit. Sanctioned by the Canadian Professional Rodeo Association, the **Luxton Pro Rodeo** (250/478-4250, www

.rodeocanada.com), the third weekend in May, features all traditional events as well as trick riding and a midway. Access to Luxton Rodeo Grounds, west of the city toward Sooke, is free, with admission to the rodeo costing $12.

Hosted by the Royal Victoria Yacht Club on the last weekend of May and with more than 60 years of history behind it, the **Swiftsure International Yacht Race** (250/592-9098, www.swiftsure.org) attracts thousands of spectators to the shoreline of the Inner Harbour to watch a wide variety of vessels cross the finish line in six different classes, including the popular pre-1970 Classics division.

Summer Festivals and Events

One of summer's most popular events, especially with arts-loving locals, is the **Symphony Splash** (250/385-9771, www.symphony splash.com), on the first weekend of August. The local symphony orchestra performs from a barge moored in the Inner Harbour to masses crowded around the shore. This unique musical event attracts upwards of 40,000 spectators, who line the shore or watch from kayaks.

On the middle weekend of August, the water comes alive with colorful dragon boats for the **Victoria Dragon Boat Festival** (250/704-2500, www.victoriadragonboat.com), with 90 teams competing along a short course stretching across the Inner Harbour. Onshore entertainment includes the Forbidden City Food Court, classic music performances, First Nations dancing, and lots of children's events.

Running 12 days in late August, the **Victoria Fringe Theatre Festival** (250/383-2663, www.victoriafringe.com) is a celebration of alternative theater, with more than 350 acts performing at six venues throughout the city, including outside along the harbor foreshore and inside at the Conservatory of Music on Pandora Street. All tickets are around $10.

SHOPPING

Victoria is a shopper's delight. Most shops and all major department stores are generally open Monday–Saturday 9:30 A.M.–5:30 P.M. and stay open for late-night shopping Thursday and

Friday nights until 9 P.M. The touristy shops around the Inner Harbour and along Government Street are all open Sunday. Government Street is the main strip of tourist and gift shops. The bottom end, behind the Empress Hotel, is where you'll pick up all those tacky T-shirts and such. Farther up the street are more stylish shops, such as **James Bay Trading Co.** (1102 Government St., 250/388-5477), which specializes in native arts from coastal communities; **Hill's Native Art** (1008 Government St., 250/385-3911), selling a wide range of authentic native souvenirs; and **Cowichan Trading** (1328 Government St., 250/383-0321), featuring Cowichan sweaters. Traditions continue at **Rogers Chocolates** (913 Government St., 250/384-7021), which is set up like a candy store of the early 1900s, when Charles Rogers first began selling his homemade chocolates to the local kids.

Old Town

In Old Town, the colorful, two-story **Market Square** courtyard complex was once the haunt of sailors, sealers, and whalers, who came ashore looking for booze and brothels. It's been jazzed up, and today shops here specialize in everything from kayaks to condoms. Walk out of Market Square on Johnson Street to find camping supply stores and the interesting **Bosun's Locker** (580 Johnson St., 250/386-1308), filled to the brim with nautical knickknacks. Follow Store Street north from Market Square to find a concentration of arts-and-crafts shops along Herald Street. In the vicinity, **Capital Iron** (1900 Store St., 250/385-9703) is the real thing. Housed in a building that dates to 1863, this business began in the 1930s by offering the public goods salvaged from ships. In the 80-odd years since, it's evolved into a department store stocking an eclectic variety of hardware and homeware products.

Bookstores

Don't be put off by the touristy location of **Munro's Bookstore** (1108 Government St., 250/382-2464 or 888/243-2464), in a magnificent neoclassical building that originally opened as the Royal Bank in 1909. It holds a comprehensive collection of fiction and non-fiction titles related to Victoria, the island, and Canada in general. Munro's may be the grandest bookstore in town, but it's not the largest. That distinction goes to **Chapters** (1212 Douglas St., 250/380-9009, open Mon.–Sat. 8 A.M.–11 P.M., Sun. 9 A.M.–11 P.M.). **Crown Publications** (106 Ontario St., 250/386-4636, www.crownpub.bc.ca) is a specialty bookstore with a great selection of western Canadiana and maps. In seaside Oak Bay, **Ivy's Bookshop** (2188 Oak Bay Ave., 250/598-2713) is a friendly little spot with a selection ranging from local literature to current best sellers.

For secondhand and rare West Coast and nautical titles, search out **Russell Books** (734 Fort St., 250/361-4447). Also, **Snowden's Bookstore** (619 Johnson St., 250/383-8131) holds a good selection of secondhand titles.

ACCOMMODATIONS

Victoria accommodations come in all shapes and sizes. A couple of downtown hostels cater to travelers on a budget, while a surprising number of convenient roadside motels have rooms for under $100. Bed-and-breakfasts are where Victoria really shines, with more than 300 at last count. You'll be able to find bed-and-breakfast rooms for under $100, but to fully immerse yourself in the historic charm of the city, expect to pay more. In the same price range are boutique hotels such as the Bedford Regency—older hotels that have been restored and come with top-notch amenities and full service. Most of the upscale hotel chains are not represented downtown; the city has no Four Seasons, Hilton, Hotel Inter-Continental, Hyatt, Marriott, Radisson, or Regent.

In the off-season (Oct.–May), nightly rates quoted here are discounted up to 50 percent, but occupancy rates are high as Canadians flock to the country's winter hot spot. No matter what time of year you plan to visit, arriving in Victoria without a reservation is unwise, but especially in the summer months, when gaggles of tourists compete for a relative paucity of rooms.

Under $50

In the heart of downtown Victoria's oldest section, and just a stone's throw from the harbor, is the 108-bed **HI-Victoria** (516 Yates St., 250/385-4511 or 888/883-0099, www.hihostels .ca). Separate dorms and bathroom facilities for men and women are complemented by two fully equipped kitchens, a large meeting room, a lounge, a library, a game room, travel services, public Internet terminals, and an informative bulletin board. Members of Hostelling International pay $21 per night, nonmembers $25; a limited number of private rooms range $52–60 s or d.

Housed in the upper stories of an old commercial building, **Ocean Island Backpackers Inn** lies a couple of blocks from downtown (791 Pandora Ave., 250/385-1788 or 888/888-4180, www.oceanisland.com; dorms $25, private rooms from $30 s, $70 d). This is a real party place—exactly what some young travelers are looking for, but annoying enough for some to generate letters to harried travel writers. On the plus side, the lodging is clean, modern, and welcoming throughout. Guests have use of kitchen facilities, a laundry room, and a computer for Internet access. There's also plenty of space to relax, such as a reading room, music room (guitars supplied), television room, and street-level bar open until midnight.

$50-100

The centrally located **Hotel Rialto** (1450 Douglas St., 250/383-4157 or 800/332-9981, www.hotelrialto.ca) is one of Victoria's many old hotels, this one dating to 1911 and five stories high. Guests have use of a coin laundry, and downstairs is a café and restaurant. The 50 guest rooms are basic and small, but comfortable. One drawback is that half the rooms share bathrooms ($65 s or d). Larger en suite rooms are $109 s or d.

If you have your own transportation, ◖ **Selkirk Guest House** (934 Selkirk Ave., 250/389-1213 or 800/974-6638, www .selkirkguesthouse.com; $95–130 s or d) is a good choice. This family-run accommodation is in an attractive historic home on the south side of the Gorge Waterway just under three kilometers (1.9 miles) from downtown (cross the Johnson Street Bridge from downtown and take Craigflower Road). While the house has been extensively renovated and offers comfortable accommodations, it's the waterfront location that sets this place apart from similarly priced choices. Younger travelers will love the trampoline and tree house.

In a quiet residential area immediately east of downtown, **Craigmyle B&B Inn** (1037 Craigdarroch Rd., Rockland, 250/595-5411 or 888/595-5411, bandbvictoria.com; from $65 s, $95–200 d) has been converted from part of the original Craigdarroch Estate (it stands directly in front of the famous castle). This rambling 1913 home is full of character, comfortable furnishings, and lots of original stained-glass windows. An inviting living room with a TV, a bright sunny dining area, and friendly longtime owners make this a real home away from home. Check-in is 2–6 P.M.

In the heart of the city center, the six-story 1913 **Strathcona Hotel** (919 Douglas St., 250/383-7137 or 800/663-7476, www.strathcona hotel.com) holds a variety of bars, including a couple of the city's most popular, as well as 86 guest rooms. They are sparsely furnished but clean and comfortable. In summer, rates start at $95 s or d, but it's worth upgrading to the much larger Premier Rooms ($120 s or d). Rates include a light breakfast.

The alternative to taking Highway 1 out of the city is to travel along Gorge Road (Hwy. 1A), where you'll find the vaguely castle-like **Oxford Castle Inn** (133 Gorge Rd., 250/388-6431 or 800/661-0322, www.oxfordcastleinn .com), which charges $90–160 for standard motel rooms with balconies; some have kitchens. Amenities include an indoor pool, a hot tub, and a sauna.

$100-150

◖ Heritage House (3808 Heritage Lane, 250/479-0892 or 877/326-9242, www.heritage housevictoria.com; from $135 s or d), a beautiful 1910 mansion surrounded by trees and gardens, sits in a quiet residential area near Por-

tage Inlet, five kilometers (3.7 miles) northwest of the city center. Guests choose from several outstanding rooms, one with a view of Portage Inlet from a private veranda. Enjoy the large communal living room and a cooked breakfast in the elegant dining room. Heritage Lane is not shown on any Victoria maps; from the city center, take Douglas Street north to Burnside Road East (bear left off Douglas). Just across the TransCanada Highway, Burnside makes a hard left (if you continue straight instead you'll be on Interurban Road). Make the left turn and continue down Burnside to just past Grange Road. The next road on the right is Heritage Lane.

East of downtown in the suburb of Oak Bay, the Tudor-style **Oak Bay Guest House** (1052 Newport Ave., 250/598-3812 or 800/575-3812, www.oakbayguesthouse.com; $139–189 s or d) has been taking in guests since 1922. It offers 11 smallish antique-filled rooms, each with a private balcony and a bathroom. The Sun Lounge holds a small library while the Foyer Lounge features plush chairs set around an open fireplace. Rates include a delicious four-course breakfast.

Every time I visit Victoria I expect to see that the old **Surf Motel** (290 Dallas Rd., 250/386-3305, www.surfmotel.net) has been demolished, but it's still there, offering priceless ocean and mountain views for a reasonable $135 s or d (discounted to $95 Nov.–Mar.). It's south of the Inner Harbour; take Oswego Road from Belleville Street.

One block from Douglas Street is the 1867 **Dalton Hotel & Suites** (759 Yates St., 250/384-4136 or 800/663-6101, www.dalton hotel.ca), Victoria's oldest hotel. Millions of dollars have been spent restoring the property, with stylish wooden beams, brass trim and lamps, ceiling fans, and marble floors reviving the Victorian era. The restored Boutique Rooms ($155–205 s or d) are absolutely charming with large beds and lovely bathrooms. Some rooms at the Dalton haven't been renovated in years. Sold as Standard Rooms (you won't find pictures on the website), they are a little overpriced at $115–125 d. The Dalton offers some attractive off-season, meal-inclusive deals—just make sure you know which class of room you'll be in.

Also right downtown, and kitty-corner to the bus depot, is the old **Crystal Court Motel** (701 Belleville St., 250/384-0551), with 56 park-at-the-door-style motel rooms, half with kitchenettes. As you'd expect with any accommodation falling into this price category in such a prime position, the rooms are fairly basic; costs are $109 s or d, $135 for a kitchenette. Ask for a nonsmoking room when making your reservation.

Traveller's Inn (www.travellersinn.com) is a local chain of 11 inexpensive properties strung out along the main highways into downtown. The two best choices are **Traveller's Inn Downtown** (1850 Douglas St., 250/381-1000 or 888/254-6476) and **Traveller's Inn City Center** (1961 Douglas St., 250/953-1000 or 888/877-9444). Rates at both are $109.95 s, $119.95 d in July and August, discounted at other times of the year and throughout the week outside of summer. These rates include a light breakfast.

On the Saanich Peninsula, just off the main highway between the ferry terminal and downtown, and on the road into downtown Sidney, is **Cedarwood Inn & Suites** (9522 Lochside Dr., 250/656-5551 or 877/656-5551, www.cedarwoodinnandsuites.com), highlighted by a colorful garden with outdoor seating overlooking the Strait of Georgia. Regular motel rooms go for $119 s or d, but providing a better deal are the individually furnished log cottages, some with full kitchens ($159 s or d).

$150-200

If you're looking for a modern feel, centrally located **Swans Suite Hotel** (506 Pandora Ave., 250/361-3310 or 800/668-7926, www.swanshotel.com) is an excellent choice. Located above a restaurant/pub complex that was built in the 1880s as a grain storehouse, each of the 30 split-level suites holds a loft, full kitchen, dining area, and bedroom. The furnishings are casual yet elegantly rustic, with West Coast artwork adorning the walls and fresh flowers in every room. The rates of $199 for a studio, $289 for a one-bedroom suite, and $359 for a two-bedroom suite are a great value. In the off-season, all rooms are discounted up to 40 percent.

Separated from downtown by Beacon Hill Park, **Dashwood Manor** (1 Cook St., 250/385-5517 or 800/667-5517, www.dashwoodmanor.com), a 1912 Tudor-style heritage house on a bluff overlooking Juan de Fuca Strait, enjoys a panoramic view of the entire Olympic mountain range. The 11 guest rooms are elegantly furnished, and hosts Dave and Sharon Layzell will happily recount the historic details of each room. Rates range from $195 s or d up to $285 for the Oxford Grand, which holds a chandelier, stone fireplace, and antiques.

Four blocks from the Inner Harbour, the 1905 **Beaconsfield Inn** (988 Humboldt St., 250/384-4044 or 888/884-4044, www.beaconsfieldinn.com; $189–329 s or d) is exactly what you may imagine a Victorian bed-and-breakfast should be. Original mahogany floors, high ceilings, classical moldings, imported antiques, and fresh flowers from the garden create an upscale historic charm throughout. Each of the nine guest rooms is individually decorated in a style evoking the Edwardian era. After checking in, you'll be invited to join other guests for afternoon tea in the library and then be encouraged to return for a glass of sherry before heading out for dinner. As you may expect, breakfast—served in a formal dining room or more casual conservatory—is a grand affair.

In the oldest section of downtown, surrounded by the city's best dining and shopping opportunities, is the **Bedford Regency** (1140 Government St., 250/384-6835 or 800/665-6500, www.bedfordregency.com), featuring 40 guest rooms of varying configurations. Stylish, uncluttered art deco furnishings and high ceilings make the standard rooms ($165 s or d) seem larger than they really are. A better deal are the deluxe rooms and suites, which provide more space and better amenities for only slightly more money (from $180 s or d). The downstairs Belingo Lounge is the perfect place to relax with a glass of Pacific Northwest wine.

$200-250

Very different from Victoria's traditional accommodations is the contemporary **Oswego** (500 Oswego St., 250/294-7500 or 877/767-9346, www.oswegovictoria.com; from $220 s or d). Within walking distance of the Inner Harbour, the guest rooms have a slick West Coast feel, and each has a full kitchen with stainless steel appliances. Rooms on the upper floors have water views, including the two three-bedroom Penthouse Suites. Other highlights include a fitness room, underground parking, and a bistro.

Dating to 1897, **Gatsby Mansion Inn** (309 Belleville St., 250/388-9191 or 800/563-9656, www.gatsbymansioninn.com; $215–309 s, $245–319 d), across the road from the Inner Harbour, has been elegantly restored, with stained-glass windows, a magnificent fireplace, lots of exposed wood, crystal chandeliers under a gabled roof, and antiques decorating every corner.

Around the southern end of the Inner Harbour, the **Admiral Inn** (257 Belleville St., 250/388-6267 or 888/823-6472, www

Gatsby Mansion Inn

.admiral.bc.ca; $209–229 s or d) has motel-style rooms within walking distance of the main attractions and best restaurants. Spacious rooms come with a balcony or patio, while extras include free parking, a light breakfast, and kitchens in many rooms.

Sitting on a point of land jutting into the Inner Harbour, the **Laurel Point Inn** (680 Montreal St., 250/386-8721 or 800/663-7667, www.laurelpoint.com; from $249 s or d) offers a distinct resort atmosphere within walking distance of downtown. Two wings hold around 200 rooms (those in the south wing are newer); each room has a water view and private balcony, and even the standard rooms have a king-size bed. Amenities include an indoor pool, beautifully landscaped Japanese-style gardens, a sauna, a small fitness facility, two restaurants, and a lounge.

Enjoying an absolute waterfront location right downtown is the **Victoria Regent Hotel** (1234 Wharf St., 250/386-2211 or 800/663-7472, www.victoriaregent.com). The exterior of this renovated building is nothing special, but inside, the rooms are spacious and comfortable. The best-value rooms at the Regent are the suites, which include a full kitchen, a balcony, and a daily newspaper; $269 s or d, or $299 with a separate bedroom and water view. Regular rooms are $200 s or d.

$250-300

The ◖ **Magnolia Hotel & Spa** (623 Courtney St., 250/381-0999 or 877/624-6654, www.magnoliahotel.com) is a European-style boutique hotel just up the hill from the harbor. It features an elegant interior with mahogany-paneled walls, Persian rugs, chandeliers, a gold-leafed ceiling, and fresh flowers throughout public areas. The rooms are each elegantly furnished and feature floor-to-ceiling windows, heritage-style furniture in a contemporary room layout, richly colored fabrics, down duvets, a work desk with cordless phone, and coffeemaking facilities. The Magnolia is also home to an Aveda Lifestyle Spa, two restaurants, and a small in-house brewery. Rates of a reasonable $269 s or d include a light breakfast, a daily newspaper, passes to a nearby fitness facility, and (unlike most other downtown hotels) free parking.

A few blocks back from the Inner Harbour is **Andersen House Bed and Breakfast** (301 Kingston St., 250/388-4565 or 877/264-9988, www.andersenhouse.com; $275–295 s or d). Built in the late 19th century for a retired sea captain, the house features large high-ceilinged rooms all overlooking gardens that supply the kitchen with a variety of berries and herbs. Each room has an en suite bathroom, a private entrance, and a CD player (complete with CDs). In the traditions of its original owner, the house is decorated with furnishings from around the world, including contemporary paintings.

Holding a prime waterfront position next to the parliament buildings is the 300-room **Hotel Grand Pacific** (463 Belleville St., 250/386-0450 or 800/663-7550, www.hotelgrandpacific.com; from $259, $309 with water views). Amenities include spa services, a health club, a variety of restaurants and lounges, and a currency exchange.

The Westin Bear Mountain (1999 Country Club Way, 250/391-7160 or 888/533-2327, www.bearmountain.ca; from $269 s or d) is a small part of an ambitious real estate and recreational development that sprawls over the namesake mountain summit about a 30-minute drive from downtown. Access is from Exit 14 of Highway 1 off Millstream Road. Over 150 rooms are spread through two buildings, and all have luxurious touches such as slate floors, deep soaker tubs, and super-comfortable beds. The main lodge holds a spa facility and multiple dining options, while a separate building is home to a health club and an outdoor heated pool. Rooms also have balconies and many have full kitchens. Check online for golf packages from $200 per person.

Over $300

The grand old **Fairmont Empress** (721 Government St., 250/384-8111 or 800/257-7544, www.fairmont.com) is Victoria's best-loved accommodation. Covered in ivy and with only magnificent gardens separating it from the Inner Harbour, it's also in the city's best location. Designed by Francis Rattenbury in 1908, the Empress is one of the original Canadian Pacific Railway hotels. Rooms are offered in 90 different configurations, and like other hotels of the era, most are small, but each is filled with Victorian period furnishings and antiques. The least expensive Fairmont rooms start at $329, but if you really want to stay in this Canadian landmark, consider upgrading to an Entrée Gold room. Although not necessarily larger, these rooms have views, a private check-in, nightly turndown service, and a private lounge where hors d'oeuvres are served in the evening; $429–499 includes a light breakfast. If you can't afford to stay at the Empress, plan on at least visiting one of the restaurants or the regal Bengal Lounge.

You'll feel like you're a million miles from the city at **Brentwood Bay Lodge & Spa** (849 Verdier Ave., Brentwood Bay, 250/544-2079 or 888/544-2079, www.brentwoodbaylodge.com; $369–699 s or d), an upscale retreat overlooking Saanich Inlet. At Brentwood, one of only three Canadian properties with a Small Luxury Hotels of the World designation, you will want for nothing. You can learn to scuba dive, take a water taxi to Butchart Gardens, enjoy the latest spa treatments, or join a kayak tour. The 33 rooms take understated elegance to new heights. Filled with natural light, they feature contemporary West Coast styling (lots of polished wood and natural colors), the finest Italian sheets on king-size beds, and private balconies. Modern conveniences like DVD entertainment systems, high-speed Internet access, and free calls within North America are a given. Dining options include a wood-fired grill, an upscale restaurant, a coffee bar, and a deli serving picnic lunches.

Campgrounds
WEST

The closest camping to downtown is at **Westbay Marine Village** (453 Head St., Esquimalt, 250/385-1831 or 866/937-8229, www.westbay.bc.ca), across Victoria Harbour from downtown. Facilities at this RV-only campground include full hookups and a laundry room. It is part of a marina complex comprising floating residences and commercial businesses, such as fishing charter operators and restaurants. Water taxis connect the "village" to downtown. Rates range $30–45 per night, depending on the view (the $45 sites have unobstructed views across to the Inner Harbour).

Fort Victoria RV Park (340 Island Hwy., 250/479-8112, www.fortvictoria.ca; $30–32) is six kilometers (3.7 miles) northwest of the city center on Highway 1A. This campground provides full hookups (including cable TV), free showers, laundry facilities, and opportunities to join charter salmon-fishing trips.

NORTH ALONG HIGHWAY 1

Continuing west from the campgrounds just detailed, Highway 1 curves north through **Goldstream Provincial Park** (19 kilometers/11 miles from downtown) and begins its up-island journey north. The southern end of the park holds 161 well-spaced campsites scattered through an old-growth forest—it's one of the most beautiful settings you could imagine close to a capital city. The campground offers free hot showers but no hookups. Sites are $22 per night.

In Malahat, seven kilometers (4.3 miles) farther north along Highway 1, is **Victoria West KOA** (250/478-3332 or 800/562-1732, www.victoriakoa.com; mid-May to mid-Sept.; tenting $34, hookups $36–42, cabins from $74). Facilities include free showers, an outdoor pool, a laundry room, a store, and a game room.

SAANICH PENINSULA

If you're coming from or heading for the ferry terminal, consider staying at **McDonald Provincial Park,** near the tip of the Saanich Peninsula 31 kilometers (19 miles) north of the city center. Facilities are limited (no showers or hookups); campsites are $17 per night.

Also on the peninsula, halfway between downtown Victoria and Sidney, is **Island View Beach RV Park** (Homathko Dr., 250/652-0548), right on the beach three kilometers (1.9

miles) east of Highway 17. Sites are $25–33, and you'll need lots of quarters for the showers.

FOOD

Victoria doesn't have a reputation as a culinary hot spot, but for the past decade things have improved greatly, with the opening of numerous restaurants serving top-notch cuisine with influences from around the world. Local chefs are big on produce organically grown and sourced from island farms. Seafood—halibut, shrimp, mussels, crab, and salmon—also features prominently on many menus. You will still find great interest in traditional English fare, including afternoon tea, which is served everywhere from motherly corner cafés to the Fairmont Empress. English cooking in general is much maligned but worth trying. For the full experience, choose kippers and poached eggs for breakfast, a ploughman's lunch (crusty bread, a chunk of cheese, pickled onions), and then roast beef with Yorkshire pudding (a crispy pastry made with drippings and doused with gravy) in the evening.

Cafés and Cheap Eats

While Victoria is generally associated with high tea, there are some serious coffee lovers in the capital. A good percentage of these consider **Moka House** (540 Fisgard St., 250/381-4933; Mon.–Sat. 6:30 A.M.–9 P.M., Sun. 7 A.M.–7 P.M.) as pouring the best coffee. As a bonus, bagels are excellent and wireless Internet is free. Also recommended by the caffeine crowd is **Serious Coffee** (632 Yates St., 250/380-8272; Mon.–Fri. 6:30 A.M.–10 P.M., Sat.–Sun. 8 A.M.–10 P.M.), also with free wireless Internet and lots of comfortable seating.

In the heart of downtown, **Broughton Street Deli** (648 Broughton St., 250/380-9988; Mon.–Fri. 7:30 A.M.–4 P.M.) occupies a tiny space at street level of a historic red brick building. Soups made from scratch daily are $4 and sandwiches just $5.

At the foot of Bastion Square, a cobbled pedestrian mall, quiet **Paradiso** (10 Bastion Square, 250/920-7266; Mon.–Fri. 7 A.M.–6 P.M., Sat. 8 A.M.–6 P.M., Sun. 9 A.M.–6 P.M.)

serves a range of coffees, pastries, and muffins. The Paradiso's outdoor tables are reason enough to stop by.

Lady Marmalade (608 Johnson St., 250/381-2872; Tues.–Sat. 8:30 A.M.–10 P.M., Sun.–Mon. 8:30 A.M.–4 P.M.) is a small, funky café with a delightful array of breakfast choices (think brie and avocado eggs Benedict) and healthy lunches, including a tangy Thai salad.

Well worth searching out is the **Blue Fox** (919 Fort St., 250/380-1683; daily from 7 A.M.), where there's nearly always a lineup for tables. Breakfast includes Eggs Benedict Pacifico (with smoked salmon and avocado) and Apple Charlotte (French toast with apples and maple syrup). At lunch, try an oversized Waldorf salad or a curried chicken burger with sweet date chutney. Almost everything is under $12.

Bakeries

In Old Town, **Willies Bakery** (537 Johnson St., 250/381-8414) is an old-style café offering cakes, pastries, and sodas, with a quiet cobbled courtyard in which to enjoy them. Ignore the dated furnishings at the **Dutch Bakery** (718 Fort St., 250/383-9725; closed Sunday) and tuck into freshly baked goodies and handmade chocolates.

Diner-Style Dining

While tourists flock to the cafés and restau-

TREATING YOURSELF TO AFTERNOON TEA

Afternoon tea, that terribly English tradition that started in the 1840s as a midmeal snack, is one ritual you should definitely partake in while visiting Victoria. Many North Americans don't realize that there is a difference between afternoon tea and high tea, and even in Victoria the names are sometimes used in place of one another. Afternoon tea is the lighter version, featuring fine teas (no tea bags) accompanied by delicate crustless sandwiches, scones with clotted cream and preserves, and a selection of other small treats. High tea (traditionally taken later in the day, around 6 P.M.) is more substantial – more like dinner in North America.

The best place to immerse yourself in the ritual is at one of the smaller tearooms scattered around the outskirts of downtown. You can order tea and scones at the **James Bay Tea Room** (332 Menzies St., 250/382-8282), but apart from the faux-Tudor exterior, it's not particularly English inside. Instead, continue on to Oak Bay to the **Blethering Place Tearoom** (2250 Oak Bay Ave., 250/598-1413; daily 11 A.M.–6 P.M.), which looks exactly like a tearoom should, right down to the regulars blethering (chatting) away with the friendly staff in white aprons. Tea and scones is $6, a full afternoon tea is $15, or pay $17 and end the procession of food with a slab of trifle.

White Heather Tea Room (1885 Oak Bay Ave., 250/595-8020; Tues.-Sat. 9:30 A.M.-5 P.M.) is a smaller, more homely setting, with a great deal of attention given to all aspects of afternoon tea – right down to the handmade tea cozies.

If the sun is shining, a pleasant place to enjoy afternoon tea is **Point Ellice House,** a historic waterfront property along the Gorge Waterway (250/380-6506, May-mid-Sept. daily 11 A.M.-3 P.M.). The price of adult $22, child $11 includes a tour of the property. As you'd expect, it's a touristy affair at **Butchart Gardens** (see *Sights*; 800 Benvenuto Dr., Brentwood Bay, 250/652-4422; daily from noon), where afternoon tea is $25 (with Cornish pastries, quiche, and more).

The **Fairmont Empress** (721 Government St., 250/389-2727) offers the grandest of grand afternoon teas, but you pay for it: $55 per person. Still, it's so popular that you must book at least a week in advance through summer and reserve a table at one of seven sitting times between noon and 5 P.M.

Finally, **Murchies** (1110 Government St., 250/381-5451), in the heart of the tourist precinct, sells teas from around the world as well as tea paraphernalia such as teapots, gift sets, and collector tins. The adjacent café pours teas from around the world in a North American-style coffeehouse.

rants of the Inner Harbour and Government Street, Douglas Street remains the haunt of lunching locals. Reminiscent of days gone by, **John's Place** (723 Pandora Ave., 250/389-0711; Mon.–Fri. 7 A.M.–9 P.M., Sat.–Sun. 8 A.M.–10 P.M.), just off Douglas Street, serves excellent value for those in the know. The walls are decorated with movie posters, old advertisements, and photos of sports stars, but this place is a lot more than just another greasy spoon restaurant. The food is good, the atmosphere casual, and the wait staff actually seems to enjoy working here. It's breakfast, burgers, salads, and sandwiches throughout the week, but weekend brunch is busiest, when there's nearly always a line spilling onto the street.

Opposite Beacon Hill Park, the **Beacon Drive-In** (126 Douglas St., 250/385-7521; daily all meals) dishes up the usual collection of cooked breakfasts and loaded burgers, with so-so milkshakes to wash it all down.

The **James Bay Inn** (270 Government St., 250/384-7151l; daily 7 A.M.–9 P.M.) has a downstairs restaurant with disco decor, friendly staff, and a predictable wide-ranging menu that suits the tastes of in-house guests (who receive a 15 percent discount on their food) and hungry locals avoiding the waterfront area.

Casual Dining

Right across from the information center, and drawing tourists like a magnet, is **Sam's Deli** (805 Government St., 250/382-8424; daily 7:30 A.M.–10 P.M.). Many places nearby have better food, but Sam's boasts a superb location and a casual, cheerful atmosphere that makes it perfect for families. The ploughman's lunch, a staple of English pub dining, costs $9.50, while sandwiches (shrimp and avocado is an in-house feature) are in the $6.50–11 range and salads are all around $10.

Touristy **Wharfside Eatery** (1208 Wharf St., 250/360-1808) is a bustling waterfront complex with a maritime theme and family atmosphere. Behind a small café section and a bar is the main dining room and a two-story deck, where almost every table has a stunning water view. The lunch menu covers all bases,

with dishes in the $12–24 range. Seafood starters to share include a tasting plate of salmon and mussels steamed in a creamy tomato broth. The lunchtime appetizers run through to the evening menu (same prices), which also includes wood-fired pizza ($21–25 for two people), standard seafood dishes under $30, and a delicious smoked chicken and wild mushroom penne ($22.50). The cheesecake is heavenly.

In Old Town, the small **Sour Pickle Café** (1623 Store St., 250/384-9390; Mon.–Fri. 7:30 A.M.–4:30 P.M.) comes alive with funky music and an enthusiastic staff. The menu offers bagels from $2.50, full cooked breakfasts from $7, soup of the day $5, healthy sandwiches $7–8.50, and delicious single-serve pizzas for around $10.

Seafood

Victoria's many seafood restaurants come in all forms. Fish and chips is a British tradition and is sold as such at **Old Vic Fish & Chips** (1316 Broad St., 250/383-4536; Mon.–Thurs. 11 A.M.–8 P.M., Fri.–Sat. noon–8 P.M.), which has been in business since 1930.

Occupying a prime location on a floating dock amid whale-watching boats, seaplanes, and shiny white leisure craft, the **◖ Blackfish Café** (Wharf St., 250/385-9996) is just steps from the main tourist trail, but it's far enough removed to make it a popular haunt with locals wanting a quiet, casual, waterfront meal. The setting alone makes the Blackfish a winner, but the menu is a knockout. Choose pan-fried oysters ($11.50) or grilled chili-lime marinated prawns to share, and then move on to mains like seafood risotto ($25). The Blackfish opens Monday–Saturday at 6:30 A.M. and on weekends at 7:30 A.M., closing between 7 and 9 P.M. depending on the season. To get there, walk north along the harbor from the information center.

Away from the tourist-clogged streets of the Inner Harbour is **◖ Barb's Place** (Fisherman's Wharf, at the foot of St. Lawrence St., 250/384-6515; daily from 8 A.M.), a sea-level eatery on a floating dock. It's not a restaurant as such, but a shack surrounded by outdoor tables, some protected from the elements by a canvas tent.

The food is as fresh as it gets. Choose cod and chips ($7), halibut and chips ($9.50), or clam chowder ($6), or splash out on a steamed crab ($16). Adding to the charm are surrounding floating houses and seals that hang out waiting for handouts. An enjoyable way to reach Barb's is by ferry from the Inner Harbour.

Pub Meals

Right in the heart of downtown is the **Elephant and Castle** (corner of Government St. and View St., 250/383-5858). This English-style pub features exposed beams, oak paneling, and traditional pub decor. A few umbrella-shaded tables line the sidewalk out front. All the favorites, such as steak and kidney pie and fish and chips, range $9.50–17.50. Open daily for lunch and dinner.

Swan's Hotel is home to an English-style pub (506 Pandora St., 250/361-3310; daily 7 A.M.–1 A.M.) with matching food, such as bangers and mash (sausages and mashed potatoes) and shepherd's pie, all around $10–12. Along with the typical pub pews, the hotel has a glass-enclosed atrium that covers a section of the sidewalk.

While all of the above pubs exude the English traditions for which Victoria is famous, **Spinnakers Brew Pub** (308 Catherine St., Esquimalt, 250/386-2739; daily from 11 A.M.) is in a class by itself. It was Canada's first in-house brewpub, and it's as popular today as when it opened in 1985. The crowds come for the beer but also for great food served up in a casual, modern atmosphere. British-style pub fare, such as a ploughman's lunch, is served in the bar, while West Coast and seafood dishes, such as sea bass basted in an ale sauce, are offered in the downstairs restaurant.

European

The energetic atmosphere at **Café Brio** (944 Fort St., 250/383-0009; daily from 5:30 P.M.) is contagious, and the food is as good as anywhere in Victoria. The Mediterranean-inspired dining room is adorned with lively artwork and built around a U-shaped bar, while out front are a handful of tables on an alfresco terrace. A creative menu combines local, seasonal produce with Italian expertise and flair. The charcuterie, prepared in house, is always a good choice to begin with, followed by wild salmon prepared however your server suggests. Order the chocolate cake smothered in chocolate espresso sauce, even if you're full. Mains range $17–30.

Pagliacci's (1011 Broad St., 250/386-1662; daily 11:30 A.M.–11 P.M.) is known for hearty Italian food, homemade bread, great desserts, and loads of atmosphere. Small and always busy, the restaurant attracts a lively local crowd, many with children; you'll inevitably have to wait for a table during the busiest times (no reservations taken). Pastas ranging $11–25 include a prawn fettuccine topped with tomato-mint sauce. A jazz combo plays Wednesday through Sunday nights.

A good place to go for a well-rounded menu of Greek favorites is **Periklis** (531 Yates St., 250/386-3313). Main courses range $14–25, and almost anything might be happening on the floor—from exotic belly dancers to crazy Greek dancing.

Vegetarian

Rebar (50 Bastion Square, 250/361-9223; Mon.–Sat. 8:30 A.M.–9 P.M., Sun. 8:30 A.M.–3:30 P.M.) is a cheerful, always busy 1970s-style vegetarian restaurant with a loyal local following. Dishes such as the almond burger ($7.50) at lunch and Thai tiger prawn curry ($16) at dinner are full of flavor and made with only the freshest ingredients. Still hungry? Try the nutty carrot cake ($5.50). Children are catered to with fun choices such as banana and peanut butter on sunflower seed bread ($4). It's worth stopping by just for juice: vegetable and fruit juices, power tonics, and wheatgrass infusions are made to order for $5.

Asian

Victoria's small **Chinatown** surrounds a short, colorful strip of Fisgard Street between Store and Government Streets. The restaurants welcome everyone, and generally the menus are filled with all of the familiar Westernized Chinese choices. Near the top (east) end of Fisgard is **QV Cafe and Bakery** (1701 Government St.,

Victoria's Chinatown is small, but it holds a variety of inexpensive restaurants.

250/384-8831), offering inexpensive Western-style breakfasts in the morning and Chinese delicacies the rest of the day. One of the least expensive places in the area is **Wah Lai Yuen** (560 Fisgard St., 250/381-5355; daily 10 A.M.–9 P.M.), a large, simply decorated, well-lit restaurant with fast and efficient service. Named for the Chinese province renowned for hot and spicy food, **Hunan Village Cuisine** (546 Fisgard St., 250/382-0661; Mon.–Sat. for lunch and daily for dinner) offers entrées ranging $8–15. Down the hill a little is **Don Mee Restaurant** (538 Fisgard St., 250/383-1032; Mon.–Fri. for lunch, daily for dinner), specializing in the cuisine of Canton. Entrées run about $7 each, while four-course dinners for two or more diners are a good deal at under $15 per person.

Noodle Box (626 Fisgard St., 250/360-1312; daily 11 A.M.–9 P.M.) started out as a street stall and now has multiple Victoria locations, including along Fisgard Street near the entrance to Chinatown. The concept is simple: an inexpensive noodle bar serving up similar fare to what you'd find on the streets of Southeast Asia. It's a tiny place, with most mains just $10.

If you've never tried Thai cuisine, you're in for a treat at **Sookjai Thai** (893 Fort St., 250/383-9945; Mon.–Fri. 11:30 A.M.–2:30 P.M., Mon.–Sat. 5–9 P.M.). The tranquil setting is the perfect place to sample traditional delights such as *Tom Yum Goong,* a prawn and mushroom soup with a hint of tangy citrus ($9), and baked red snapper sprinkled with spices sourced from Thailand ($16). The snapper is the most expensive main, with several inspiring vegetarian choices all under $10.

Seating just 20 diners, **Thai Bistro** (615 Johnson St., 250/380-7878; Mon.–Sat. 11:30 A.M.–2:30 P.M., daily from 5 P.M.) offers up inexpensive fare, including sweet corn cakes ($5.50) to start and prawns roasted in sweet chili sauce ($13) as a main.

INFORMATION AND SERVICES
Tourist Information
Tourism Victoria (250/953-2033 or 800/663-3883,

www.tourismvictoria.com; year-round daily 9 A.M.–5 P.M.) runs the bright, modern **Victoria Visitor Centre,** which overlooks the Inner Harbour from 812 Wharf Street. The friendly staff can answer most of your questions. They also book accommodations, tours and charters, restaurants, entertainment, and transportation.

Coming off the ferry from Vancouver, stop in at **Sidney Visitor Centre** (10382 Pat Bay Hwy., 250/656-0525; daily 9 A.M.–5 P.M.).

Libraries
Greater Victoria Public Library (735 Broughton St., at the corner of Courtney St., 250/382-7241, www.gvpl.ca) is open Monday–Friday 9 A.M.–6 P.M., Saturday 9 A.M.–1 P.M.

Services
In a medical emergency, call 911 or contact **Victoria General Hospital** (1 Hospital Way, 250/727-4212). For nonurgent cases, a handy facility is **James Bay Medical Treatment Centre** (230 Menzies St., 250/388-9934). The **Cresta Dental Centre** is at 3170 Tillicum Road (at Burnside St.), 250/384-7711. **Shopper's Drug Mart** (1222 Douglas St., 250/381-4321) is open daily 7 A.M.–7 P.M.

The main **post office** is on the corner of Yates and Douglas Streets.

All of Victoria's downtown accommodations have in-room Internet access. Those that don't, like the hostel, have inexpensive Internet booths near the lobby. A good option for travelers on the run is the small café on the lower level of the Hotel Grand Pacific (463 Belleville St.; daily 7 A.M.–7 P.M.), where public Internet access is free with a purchase.

GETTING THERE
Air
Air Canada (604/688-5515 or 888/247-2262, www.aircanada.ca), **Pacific Coastal** (604/273-8666 or 800/663-2872, www.pacific-coastal.com), and **WestJet** (604/606-5525 or 800/538-5696, www.westjet.com) have scheduled flights between Vancouver and Victoria, but the flight is so short that the attendants don't even have time to throw a bag

of peanuts in your lap. These flights are really only practical if you have an onward destination—flying out of Victoria, for example, with Los Angeles as a final destination.

Victoria International Airport is on the Saanich Peninsula, 20 kilometers (12.4 miles) north of Victoria's city center. Once you've collected your baggage from the carousels, it's impossible to miss the rental car outlets (Avis, Budget, Hertz, and National) across the room, where you'll also find a currency exchange and information booth. Outside is a taxi stand and ticket booth for the **AKAL Airport Shuttle Bus** (250/386-2525 or 877/386-2525, www.victoriaairporter.com), running passengers between the airport and major downtown hotels every 30 minutes; $15 per person each way. The first departure from downtown to the airport is 4:30 A.M. A taxi costs approximately $55 to downtown.

Several companies operate seaplanes between downtown Vancouver and downtown Victoria. From Coal Harbour, on Burrard Inlet, **Harbour Air** (604/274-1277 or 800/665-0212, www.harbour-air.com) and **West Coast Air** (604/606-6888 or 800/347-2222, www.westcoastair.com) have scheduled floatplane flights to Victoria's Inner Harbour. Expect to pay around $120 per person each way for any of these flights.

Ferry
BC Ferries (250/386-3431 or 888/223-3779, www.bcferries.com) link the two cities with a fleet of ferries that operate year-round. Ferries depart Vancouver from **Tsawwassen,** south of Vancouver International Airport (allow one hour by road from downtown Vancouver), and from **Horseshoe Bay,** on Vancouver's North Shore. They terminate on Vancouver Island at **Swartz Bay,** 32 kilometers (20 miles) north of Victoria. On weekends and holidays, the one-way fare on either route is adult $11.15, child 5–11 $5.60, vehicle $39; rates for motor vehicles are slightly lower on weekdays, and all fares are reduced mid-September to late June. Seniors travel free Monday–Thursday but must pay for their vehicles. In high season

(late June to mid-September), the ferries run about once an hour 7 A.M.–10 P.M. The rest of the year they run a little less frequently. Both crossings take around 90 minutes. Expect a wait in summer, particularly if you have an oversized vehicle (each ferry can accommodate far fewer large vehicles than standard-size cars and trucks). Limited vehicle reservations ($15 per booking) are accepted at 604/444-2890 or 888/724-5223, or online at www .bcferries.com.

Bus

The main bus depot is behind the Fairmont Empress at 710 Douglas Street. **Pacific Coach Lines** (604/662-7575 or 800/661-1725, www .pacificcoach.com) operates bus service between Vancouver's Pacific Central Station and downtown Victoria, via the Tsawwassen–Swartz Bay ferry. In summer the coaches run hourly 6 A.M.–9 P.M.; $37.50 one-way, $73 round-trip, which includes the ferry fare. The trip takes three and a half hours. This same company also runs buses to the Victoria depot from downtown Vancouver hotels ($41.40 one-way, $81 round-trip) and from Vancouver International Airport ($43 one-way, $84 round-trip).

GETTING AROUND
Bus

Most of the inner-city attractions can be reached on foot. However, the local bus network is excellent, and it's easy to jump on and off and get everywhere you want to go. Pick up an *Explore*

Victoria brochure at the information center for details of all the major sights, parks, beaches, and shopping areas and the buses needed to reach them. Bus fare for travel within Zone 1, which covers most of the city, is adult $2.25, senior or child $1.40. Zone 2 covers outlying areas such as the airport and Swartz Bay ferry terminal; adult $3, senior or child $2.25. Transfers are good for travel in one direction within 90 minutes of purchase. A DayPass, valid for one day's unlimited bus travel, costs adult $7, senior or child $5. For general bus information, call **Victoria Regional Transit System** (250/385-2551) or surf the Internet to www .transitbc.com.

Bike

Victoria doesn't have the great network of bicycle paths that Vancouver boasts, but bike-rental shops are nevertheless plentiful. Try **Sports Rent** (1950 Government St., 250/385-7368) or **Oak Bay Bicycle** (1990 Oak Bay Ave., 250/598-4111). Expect to pay from around $8 per hour, $25 per day. As well as renting bikes, **Harbour Rentals** (directly opposite the information center at 811 Wharf St., 250/995-1661) rents strollers, scooters, and a variety of watercraft.

Taxi

Taxis operate on a meter system, charging $2.75 at the initial flag drop plus around $2 per kilometer. Call **Blue Bird Cabs** (250/382-8294 or 800/665-7055), **Empress Taxi** (250/381-2222), or **Victoria Taxi** (250/383-7111).

Vicinity of Victoria

Two highways lead out of Victoria: Highway 14 heads west and Highway 1 heads north. Highway 14 begins at Sooke, on the outskirts of Victoria, and runs a spectacular coastal route ending in Port Renfrew, 104 kilometers (65 miles) from the capital. Along this ocean-hugging stretch of road are provincial parks, delightful oceanfront lodgings, and a panorama that extends across Juan de Fuca Strait to the snowcapped peaks of

the Olympic Mountains in Washington State. Meanwhile, Highway 1 leads north from Victoria to the towns of Duncan, Chemainus, and Ladysmith, each with its own particular charm. West of Duncan is massive Cowichan Lake, an inland paradise for anglers and boaters, and Carmanah Walbran Provincial Park, protecting a remote watershed full of ancient Sitka spruce that miraculously escaped logging.

SOOKE

About 34 kilometers (21 miles) from Victoria, Sooke (with a silent "e") is best known for a lodge that combines luxurious accommodations with one of Canada's most renowned restaurants, but a couple other diversions are worth investigating as well.

The town spreads along a harbor created by **Whiffen Spit,** a naturally occurring sandbar that extends for over one kilometer (0.6 miles). Take Whiffen Spit Road (through town to the west) to reach the spit. It's a 20-minute walk to the end, and along the way you may spot seals from the shoreline. **Sooke Region Museum** (corner of Sooke and Phillips roads, 250/642-6351; daily 9 A.M.–5 P.M.; donation) lies just beyond Sooke River Bridge. When you've finished admiring the historic artifacts, relax on the grassy area in front or wander around the back to count all 478 growth rings on the cross-section of a giant spruce tree. The museum is also home to **Sooke Visitor Centre.**

Accommodations and Food

Sooke Harbour House (1528 Whiffen Spit Rd., 250/642-3421 or 800/889-9688, www.sookeharbourhouse.com) combines the elegance of an upscale country-style inn with the atmosphere of an exclusive oceanfront resort. The sprawling waterfront property sits on a bluff, with 28 guest rooms spread throughout immaculately manicured gardens. Each of the rooms reflects a different aspect of life on the West Coast, and all have stunning views, a wood-burning fireplace, and a deck or patio. Rates range $399–599 s or d, which includes breakfast and a picnic lunch; off-season, these rates are reduced up to 40 percent. In addition to luxury accommodations, one of Canada's finest dining experiences can be had at Sooke Harbour House. The decor is country-style simple, not that anything could possibly take away from the food and ocean views. The menu changes daily, but most dishes feature local seafood prepared to perfection with vegetables and herbs picked straight from the surrounding garden. Many diners disregard the cost and choose the seven-course Gastronomic Adventure ($100

pp), which represents a wide variety of seafood, including wild sea asparagus harvested from tidal pools below the restaurant. Otherwise, dinner entrées range $28–40, with vegetarians offered at least one choice. The cellar is almost as renowned as the food—it holds more than 10,000 bottles. Reservations essential at this restaurant that opens daily at 5 P.M.

The **17 Mile Pub** (5126 Sooke Rd., 250/642-5942; daily 11 A.M.–10 P.M.) is a charming relic from the past. It dates from an era when travelers heading to Sooke would stop for a meal 17 miles from Victoria's city hall. The walls are decorated with a century's worth of memorabilia, and there's still a hitching post out back. The rotating nightly specials haven't changed for years, but no one seems to mind, especially on Saturday when a prime rib dinner is served for $18. One thing that definitely wasn't on the menu 100 years ago is a delicious sesame-teriyaki-grilled salmon dish ($16).

CONTINUING ALONG HIGHWAY 14 TO PORT RENFREW

The road west from Sooke takes you past pebbly beaches scattered with shells and driftwood, past **Gordon's Beach** to **French Beach Provincial Park** (about 20 kilometers/12 miles from Sooke). Here you can wander down through a lush forest of Douglas fir and Sitka spruce to watch ocean breakers crashing up on the beach. It's a great place for a windswept walk, a picnic, or camping ($14 per night, pit toilets provided). Day use access is $3 per vehicle.

Continuing west, the highway winds up and down forested hills for another 12 kilometers (7.5 miles) or so, passing evidence of regular logging as well as signposted forest trails to sandy beaches. Along this stretch of coast are two great accommodations. The first, three kilometers (1.9 miles) beyond French Beach, is **Point No Point Resort** (10829 West Coast Rd., 250/646-2020, www.pointnopoint resort.com), where 25 cabins each have ocean views, a full kitchen, and a fireplace. Explore the shore out front, relax on the nearby beach, or scan the horizon for migrating whales, with the Olympic Mountains as a backdrop. Rates range $160–260 s or d, with the least expensive cabins older and smaller (you're really paying for the location). Afternoon tea ($18) and full meals (mains $25–30) are available in the lodge restaurant. Two kilometers (1.2 miles) farther west, high upon oceanfront cliffs, **Fossil Bay Resort** (250/646-2073, www.fossilbay.com; $230 s or d) offers six modern cottages, each with a hot tub, private balcony, fireplace, king-size bed, and full kitchen.

Jordan River and Vicinity

When you emerge at the small logging town of Jordan River, take time to take in the smells of the ocean and the surrounding windswept landscape. The town comprises only a few houses, a small logging operation, and an oceanfront park. The park lies on a point at the mouth of the Jordan River. It's not the best camping spot you'll ever come across, but no signs prohibit overnight stays; surfers often spend the night here, waiting for the swells to rise and the long right-handed waves known as Jordans to crank up. Note: **Sports Rent** (1950 Government St., Victoria, 250/385-7368) rents surfboards and wetsuits.

Three kilometers (1.9 miles) west of Jordan River, a 700-meter (0.4-mile) one-way trail leads through Sitka spruce to pebbly **China Beach,** which is strewn with driftwood and backed by a couple of protected picnic sites. Camping (back up by the highway) is $14 per night. The beach and campground have recently been incorporated within 1,277-hectare (3,156-acre) **Juan de Fuca Provincial Park,** which protects a narrow coastal strip between Jordan River and Botanical Beach near Port Renfrew. China Beach is also the beginning of the 47-kilometer (29-mile) **Juan de Fuca Trail,** a coastal hiking route that ends at Port Renfrew.

Port Renfrew

This small seaside community clings to the rugged shoreline of Port San Juan, 104 kilometers (65 miles) from Victoria. An eclectic array of houses leads down the hill to the wa-terfront. Follow the signs to **Botanical Beach,** a fascinating intertidal pool area where low tide exposes hundreds of species of marine creatures at the foot of scoured-out sandstone cliffs. The three-kilometer (1.9-mile) road to the beach is rough and can be impassable in winter.

Accommodations are available at the **Trailhead Resort** in the heart of town (250/647-5468, www.trailhead-resort.com). Its motel rooms are relatively new, basic but practical, with a balcony out front ($105 s or d), or choose to stay in a fully self-contained two-bedroom cabin ($225). On site a store sells camping and fishing gear. Beyond town, at the mouth of the San Juan River, **Port Renfrew Marina and RV Park** (250/647-0002, www .portrenfrewmarina.com; Apr.–Oct.) has un-serviced campsites ($20) but no showers. This place is primarily a marina complex, with boat charters and fishing gear for sale.

WEST COAST TRAIL

The magnificent West Coast Trail meanders 77 kilometers (48 miles) along Vancouver Island's untamed western shoreline, through the West Coast Trail unit of **Pacific Rim National Park.** It's one of the world's great hikes, ex-hilaratingly challenging, incredibly beautiful, and very satisfying—many hikers come back to do it again. The quickest hikers can complete the trail in four days, but by allowing six, seven, or eight days you'll have time to fully enjoy the adventure. The trail extends from the mouth of the Gordon River near Port Renfrew to Pachena Bay, near the remote fishing village of Bamfield on Barkley Sound. Along the way you'll wander along beaches, steep cliff tops, and slippery banks; ford rivers by rope, suspension bridge, or ferry; climb down sandstone cliffs by ladder; cross slippery board-walks, muddy slopes, bogs, and deep gullies; and balance on fallen logs. But for all your efforts you're rewarded with panoramic views of sand and sea, dense lush rainforest, waterfalls cascading into deep pools, all kinds of wild-life—gray whales, eagles, sea lions, seals, and seabirds—and the constant roar and hiss of the Pacific surf pummeling the sand.

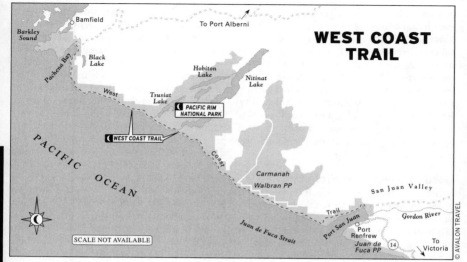

WEST COAST TRAIL

To Port Alberni

Bamfield

Barkley Sound

Pachena Bay

Black Lake

Hobiton Lake

Nitinat Lake

West

Tsusiat Lake

PACIFIC RIM NATIONAL PARK

WEST COAST TRAIL

PACIFIC OCEAN

Coast

Carmanah Walbran PP

San Juan Valley

Gordon River

Trail

Port San Juan

Juan de Fuca Strait

Port Renfrew

Juan de Fuca PP

14

To Victoria

SCALE NOT AVAILABLE

© AVALON TRAVEL

Hiking Conditions

The trail can be hiked in either direction, so take your choice. The first two days out from Gordon River traverse difficult terrain, meaning more enjoyable hiking for the remaining days. The first two days out from Pachena Bay are relatively easy, meaning a lighter pack for the more difficult section.

Hikers must be totally self-sufficient, because no facilities exist along the route. Go with at least two other people, and travel as light as possible. Wear comfortable hiking boots, and take a stove, at least 15 meters (50 feet) of strong light rope, head-to-toe waterproof gear (keep your spare clothes and sleeping bag in a plastic bag), a small amount of fire starter for an emergency, suntan lotion, insect repellent, a first-aid kit (for cuts, burns, sprains, and blisters), and waterproof matches. Rainfall is least likely in the summer; July is generally the driest month, but be prepared for rain, strong winds, thick fog, and muddy trail conditions even then.

Along the trail are two river crossings that are made via ferry. One is at Gordon River outside of Port Renfrew. The other, midway along the trail, crosses Nitinat Narrows, the treach-erous mouth of tidal Nitinat Lake. Ferries run April 15–September 30 daily 9 A.M.–5 P.M. The ferry fees ($15 each) are collected on behalf of private operators in conjunction with the trail permit (see next section). When there is no ferry service (Oct. 1–April 14), the West Coast Trail is closed.

Permits

A quota system is in effect on the trail to reduce the environmental impact caused by overuse. In peak season (mid-June to mid-Sept.) only 52 hikers per day are issued permits to start down the trail (26 from each end). Reservations for 42 of the 52 slots are accepted starting March 1 for the following season; call Tourism BC (250/387-1642 or 800/435-5622; 7 A.M.–6 P.M.). The nonrefundable reservation fee is $25 per person, which includes a waterproof trail map. The remaining 10 spots per day are allocated on a first-come, first-served basis (five from each end; no reservation fee), but expect a wait of up to three days in summer. For one month before and after peak season, there is no quota. Once at Port Renfrew or Bamfield, all hikers must head for the registration office to obtain a trail-use permit ($128.75 per person), pay for the ferry crossings ($30), and attend a 90-minute orientation session.

Getting There

Unless you plan on turning around and returning to the beginning of the trail on foot, you'll want to make some transportation arrangements. Getting to and from either end of the trail is made easier by **West Coast Trail Express** (250/477-8700 or 888/999-2288, www.trailbus.com), departing Victoria daily in the morning to both ends of the trail. The fare between Victoria and Port Renfrew is $45 one-way, while between Victoria and Pachena Bay it's $60. Pickups are made along the way, including from Nanaimo and Port Alberni. Travel between the trailheads costs $60. (If you leave your vehicle at the Port Renfrew end of the trail and return to this point by bus after walking the trail, you won't have to shuttle a vehicle out to remote Bamfield.) Pachena Bay lies 11 kilometers (6.8 miles) from Bamfield, and taxis operate between the two points. West Coast Trail Express also rents camping and hiking gear.

Information

The first step in planning to hike the West Coast Trail is to do some research at the Parks Canada website (www.pc.gc.ca). The invaluable information covers everything you need to know, including an overview of what to expect, instructions on trail-use fees, a list of equipment you should take, a list of relevant literature, tide tables, and advertisements for companies offering trailhead transportation.

Seasonal park information/registration centers are in Port Renfrew (250/647-5434) and Pachena Bay (250/728-3234). The recommended topographic map *West Coast Trail, Pacific Rim National Park—Port Renfrew to Bamfield* is available at most specialty map stores, as well as at the information centers (registration offices) at each end of the trail. The cost of a trail-use permit includes this map.

DUNCAN

Duncan, self-proclaimed "City of Totems," lies at the junction of Highways 1 and 18, about 60 kilometers (37 miles) north of Victoria. The small city of 6,100 serves the surrounding farming and forestry communities of the Cowichan Valley. Native carvers, many from the local Cowichan band, have created some 80 intricate and colorful totem poles here. Look for the poles along the main highway near the information center, beside the railway station in the old section of town, by city hall, and inside local businesses.

Sights

Follow the signs off the main highway to the city center for a quick wander around the renovated **Old Town.** (Free two-hour parking is available by the old railway station on Canada Ave.) Start your totem-pole hunt here or just wander down the streets opposite the railway station to appreciate some of the pleasing older architecture, such as city hall on the corner of Kenneth and Craig Streets. Two distinctly different native carvings stand side by side behind city hall: a Native American carving, and a New Zealand Maori carving donated by Duncan's sister city, Kaikohe.

Apart from the famous totem poles, Duncan's main attraction is the excellent **Quw'utsun' Cultural Centre,** on the south side of downtown (200 Cowichan Way, 250/746-8119; May–Sept. daily 9 A.M.–6 P.M., Oct.–Apr. daily 10 A.M.–5 P.M.; adult $13, senior $11, child $2). Representing the arts, crafts, legends, and traditions of a 3,500-strong Quw'utsun' population spread throughout the Cowichan Valley, this facility features a longhouse, a carving shed, dance performances, a café with native cuisine (and summertime salmon barbecues), and a gift shop selling Cowichan sweaters.

Another local attraction is the 40-hectare (98-acre) **BC Forest Discovery Centre** (one kilometer/0.6 mile north of town, 250/715-1113; Apr.–May and Sept. Thurs.–Mon. 10 A.M.–4:30 P.M., June–Aug. daily 10 A.M.–4:30 P.M.; adult $11, senior $9, child $5). You can catch a ride on an old steam train and puff back in time, through the forest and past a farmstead, a logging camp, and Somenos Lake. Then check out the working sawmill, the restored planer mill, a blacksmith's shop, and forestry and lumber displays. The main museum building holds modern displays pertaining to the industry, including hands-on and interactive computer displays and an interesting audiovisual exhibit. The grounds are a pleasant place to wander through shady glades of trees (most identified) or over to the pond, where you'll find a gaggle of friendly geese awaiting a tasty morsel.

Practicalities

● Sahtlam Lodge and Cabins (5720 Riverbottom Rd. W., 250/748-7738 or 877/748-7738, www.sahtlamlodge.com) is beside the Cowichan River west of town. Three cabins are spread across the property, and each is equipped with an old-style fireplace, a woodstove, and a full kitchen. Rates are $175–190 s or d, with multiple-night stays discounted 30 percent. A breakfast basket delivered daily to your cabin is included. On the south side of the river is the turnoff to **Duncan RV Park and Campground** (2950 Boys Rd., 250/748-8511), which is one block west of the highway, right beside the river. Sites are $19–23; full hookups available.

Always crowded with locals, **Arbutus Cafe** (195 Kenneth St., 250/746-5443) concocts a great shrimp salad for $7, sandwiches and hamburgers for $5–9, and specialty pies from $4.50.

Stop at **Duncan Visitor Centre** (250/746-4636 or 888/303-3337, www.duncancc.bc.ca; Mon.–Sat. 9 A.M.–5 P.M.), on the west side of the highway in Overwaitea Plaza, for the complete rundown on the area.

COWICHAN LAKE AND VICINITY

Flowing into the Strait of Georgia from Cowichan Lake, the Cowichan River is renowned for its salmon and steelhead fishing. Much of its length is protected by **Cowichan River Provincial Park.** The park has three access points, including Skutz Falls, where salmon spawn each fall. Trails are well signposted and link into the TransCanada Trail, which follows the river west to Cowichan Lake.

Cowichan Lake

Don a good pair of walking shoes, grab your swimsuit, sleeping bag, fishing pole, and frying pan, and head west from Duncan to Cowichan Lake, Vancouver Island's second largest lake. The massive, 32-kilometer (20-mile) inland waterway is a popular spot for canoeing, water-skiing, swimming, and especially fishing—the lake and river are well stocked with kokanee and trout (steelhead, rainbow, brown, and cutthroat). Logging roads encircle the lake (75 kilometers/47 miles round-trip) and provide hikers access into the adjacent wilderness, which includes the legendary **Carmanah Valley** (see the sidebar *Carmanah Walbran Provincial Park*).

The sleepy lakeside village of **Lake Cowichan** (pop. 3,200) lies on the eastern arm of Cowichan Lake, 30 kilometers (18.6 miles) from Duncan. Campers have the choice of staying at the local municipal campground, **Lakeview Park** (three kilometers/1.9 miles west of Lake Cowichan, 250/749-6244; $22 per night) or **Gordon Bay Provincial Park,** on the south side of the lake 23 kilometers (14.3 miles) farther west ($22). Both campgrounds have hot showers. **Rail's End Pub** (70 South Shore Rd., 250/749-6755; daily from 11 A.M.) has a good family-style restaurant overlooking the outlet of Cowichan Lake.

On the waterfront is **Cowichan Lake Visitor Centre** (125 South Shore Rd., 250/749-3244, www.cowichanlakecc.ca; daily in summer Mon.–Sat. 9 A.M.–4 P.M., Sun. 1–4 P.M.). The center is a good source of information on fishing conditions and on the logging roads leading to the Carmanah Valley and Port Renfrew.

NORTH TOWARD NANAIMO

Nanaimo is just 45 kilometers (28 miles) north of Duncan—less than 30 minutes along the divided highway—but several small towns invite short detours along the way.

Chemainus

The town of Chemainus (pop. 700) bills itself as "The Little Town that Did." Did what, you ask? Well, Chemainus has always been a

CARMANAH WALBRAN PROVINCIAL PARK

If you're looking for a day trip to escape the tourist-clogged streets of Victoria, you can't get any more remote than the **Carmanah Valley.** Eyed by logging companies for many years, the Carmanah and adjacent Walbran Valley were designated a provincial park in 1995, providing complete protection for the 16,450-hectare (40,650-acre) watershed. For environmentalists, creation of the park was a major victory because this mist-shrouded valley extending all the way to the rugged west coast holds an old-growth forest of absolute wonder. Many 800-year-old Sitka spruce and 1,000-year-old cedar trees – some of the world's oldest – rise up to 95 meters (300 feet) off the damp valley floor here. Others lie where they've fallen, their slowly decaying moss- and fern-cloaked hulks providing homes for thousands of small mammals and insects.

The only way to reach the park is via Lake Cowichan, following the south shore of Cowichan Lake to Nitinat Main, a logging road that leads south to Nitinat Junction (no services). There the road is joined by a logging road from Port Alberni. From this point, Nitinat Main continues south to a bridge across the Caycuse River. Take the first right after crossing the river. This is Rosander Main, a rough road that dead-ends at the park boundary. The park is signposted from Nitinat Junction, but the signs are small and easy to miss.

From the road's-end parking lot, a rough 1.3-kilometer (0.8-mile) hiking trail (30 minutes each way) descends to the valley floor and Carmanah Creek. From the creek, trails lead upstream to the Three Sisters (2.5 km/1.5 miles; 40 minutes), through Grunt's Grove to August Creek (7.5 km/4.6 miles; two hours), and downstream through a grove of Sitka spruce named for Randy Stoltmann, a legendary environmentalist who first brought the valley's giants to the world's attention (2.4 km/1.5 miles; 40 minutes).

sleepy little mill town; its first sawmill dates back to 1862. In 1982, MacMillan Bloedel shut down the town's antiquated mill, which employed 400 people, replacing it a year later with a modern mill employing only 155 people. Chemainiacs did not want their town to die. Needing tourists, they hired local artists to cover many of the town's plain walls with larger-than-life murals depicting the town's history and culture. The result was outstanding. In 1983, the town received a First Place award at a downtown revitalization competition held in New York.

Follow the signs to Chemainus from Highway 1 and park at **Waterwheel Park,** central to local activities and eateries, and a pleasant downhill walk to the waterfront. Also at the park is **Chemainus Visitor Centre** (9758 Chemainus Rd., 250/246-3944; May–Sept. daily 9 A.M.–5 P.M.), where you'll see the first enormous mural—a street scene. From there you can explore the rest of Chemainus on foot, following the yellow footprints into town. Walk down to shady, waterfront **Heritage Park,** passing a mural information booth (where there's a small replica of the waterwheel that powered the original 1862 sawmill) and a detailed map of the town.

The **Chemainus Theatre Festival** (9737 Chemainus Rd., 250/246-9820 or 800/565-7738) is a year-round production of international musical hits. It runs Wednesday–Saturday with tickets ranging $29–36 ($48–58 with dinner). **Chemainus Tours** (250/246-5055) operates horse-drawn carriage rides around town, passing all of the murals along the route. The rides depart from Waterwheel Park every half hour; adult $10, child $5.

One of many inviting downtown cafés is **Dancing Bean Café** (9752 Willow St., 250/246-5050), which opens daily at 8 A.M. and stays open late when presenting live musical performances. The coffee is the best in town, while the wraps, salads, soups, and grilled panini are all healthy and delicious.

Ladysmith

The trim little waterfront village of Ladysmith has a couple of claims to fame. The first is its location straddling the 49th parallel, the invisible line separating Canada from the United States. After much bargaining for the 1846 Oregon Treaty, Canada got to keep all of Vancouver Island despite the 49th parallel chopping the island in two. The second claim is a little less historically important: Ladysmith was the birthplace of TV starlet Pamela Anderson.

Southern Gulf Islands

Spread throughout the Strait of Georgia between mainland British Columbia and Vancouver Island, this group of islands is within Canadian territory but linked geologically to the San Juan Islands, immediately to the south. Five of the islands—Salt Spring, the Penders, Galiano, Mayne, and Saturna—are populated, and each is linked to the outside world by scheduled ferry service. **Gulf Islands National Park** protects pockets of land on Mayne and Saturna islands, the Penders, and 14 uninhabited islands.

The mild, almost Mediterranean climate, beautiful scenery, driftwood-strewn beaches, quaint towns, and wide-ranging choice of accommodations combine to make the islands popular in summer, when laidback locals share their home with flocks of visitors. Still, there's plenty of room to get away from the hustle, with mile after mile of remote coastline and easily reached peaks beckoning to be explored. After kayaking, biking, or hiking, the best way to end the day is at one of the many island restaurants, feasting on salmon and crab brought ashore that morning.

Getting There and Around

The main transportation provider is **BC Ferries** (250/386-3431 or 888/223-3779, www.bcferries .com), which operates scheduled year-round services between the Southern Gulf Islands and out to the islands from both Vancouver Island and Vancouver. The main departure points are Swartz Bay, 32 kilometers (20 miles) north of Victoria, and Tsawwassen, on the south side of Vancouver. All ferries take vehicles (including RVs), motorcycles, bicycles, canoes, and kayaks. It's important to check the timetables (online or posted at each terminal), because some ferries are nonstop and others make up to three stops before reaching the more remote islands. Also try to avoid peak periods, such as Friday and Sunday afternoons. Aside from that, simply roll up and pay your fare.

Regardless of the final destination, the round-trip fare from Swartz Bay (Victoria) to any of the Southern Gulf Islands is a reasonable adult $7.70, child $3.85, vehicle $26.50. Interisland travel is charged on a one-way basis: adult $4.15, child $2.10, vehicle $8.50. The fare system is designed to be flexible; for example, if you plan to travel to Galiano Island from Swartz Bay, with a stop on Salt Spring Island on the way out, you would pay the interisland fare departing Salt Spring and then use the return portion of the main ticket from Galiano, for a total of $11.85 per person.

From the mainland Tsawwassen terminal (south of downtown Vancouver), the fare is the same regardless of which island you travel to: one-way adult $11.75, child $5.90, vehicle $43.35.

SALT SPRING ISLAND

Largest of the Southern Gulf Islands, 180-square-kilometer (70-square-mile) Salt Spring (pop. 10,000) lies close to Vancouver Island, immediately north of Saanich Inlet. Ferries link the south and north ends of the island to Vancouver Island, and myriad roads converge on the service town of **Ganges.** The island is home to many artisans, along with hobby farmers, retirees, and wealthy Vancouverites who spend their summers at private getaways.

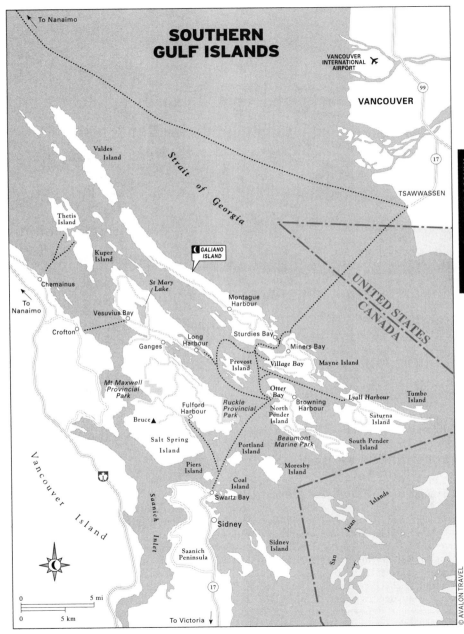

SOUTHERN GULF ISLANDS

To Nanaimo

VANCOUVER INTERNATIONAL AIRPORT ✈

VANCOUVER

99

Valdes Island

Strait of Georgia

17

TSAWWASSEN

Thetis Island

Kuper Island

GALIANO ISLAND

UNITED STATES
CANADA

Chemainus

St Mary Lake

To Nanaimo

Vesuvius Bay

Montague Harbour

Sturdies Bay

Crofton

Ganges

Long Harbour

Miners Bay

Prevost Island

Village Bay

Mayne Island

Mt Maxwell Provincial Park

Otter Bay

Lyall Harbour

Tumbo Island

Fulford Harbour

Ruckle Provincial Park

North Pender Island

Browning Harbour

Bruce ▲

Saturna Island

Salt Spring Island

Beaumont Marine Park

South Pender Island

Piers Island

Portland Island

Moresby Island

Vancouver Island

Saanich Inlet

Coal Island

Swartz Bay

Sidney

San Juan Islands

Sidney Island

Saanich Peninsula

17

0   5 mi
0   5 km

To Victoria ↓

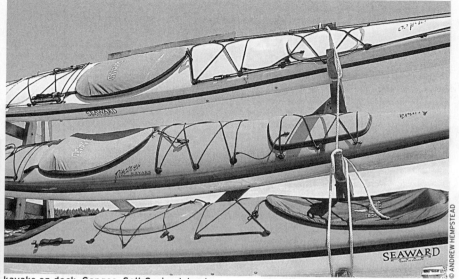

© ANDREW HEMPSTEAD

kayaks on dock, Ganges, Salt Spring Island

Ganges

Ask any longtime local and they'll tell you the island's main town, Ganges, is overcommercialized. But it's still quaint, and well worth visiting—at the very least to stock up with supplies. Set around a protected bay, the original waterfront buildings have undergone a colorful transformation, and where once you would have found boat-builders you now can browse through art galleries, shop for antiques, or dine on innovative cuisine. One of the most eye-catching shops is the boardwalk gallery featuring the whimsical painting of Jill Louise Campbell. On a smaller scale, **Mahon Hall** (114 Rainbow Rd., 250/537-0899; mid-May to mid-Sept. daily 10 A.M.–5 P.M.) is filled with arty booths, while the Saturday market in Centennial Park showcases the work of local artists. Head to **Salt Spring Books** (104 McPhillips Ave., 250/537-2812) to pick up some holiday reading or check your email on the public-access computers. Within walking distance of the waterfront, at the end of Seaspring Drive, is **Mouat Park,** a quiet reprieve from the bustle.

Exploring the Rest of the Island

Even if you've never kayaked, plan on joining a tour with **Island Escapes** (163 Fulford-Ganges Rd., 250/537-2553). Get a feel for paddling on the two-hour tour ($45), enjoy the calm evening water on the Sunset Paddle ($60), or spend a full-day ($150) exploring the coastline, with a break for a picnic lunch on a remote beach.

Landlubbers have plenty to see on Salt Spring. From the Fulford Harbour ferry terminal, take Beaver Point Road east to 486-hectare (1,200-acre) **Ruckle Provincial Park.** The access road ends at the rocky headland of Beaver Point, from where trails lead north along the coastline, providing great views across to North Pender Island. The land that's now protected as a park was donated to the province by the Ruckle family, whose 1876 farmhouse still stands.

Along the road north to Ganges, small **Mount Maxwell Provincial Park** protects the slopes of its namesake mountain. A rough unsealed road off Musgrave Road leads to the 588-meter (1,930-foot) summit, from where views extend south across the island to Vancouver Island and east to the other Gulf Islands. South of Mount Maxwell is 704-meter (2,300-foot) **Mount Bruce,** the island's highest peak.

Accommodations and Camping

Maple Ridge Cottages (301 Tripp Rd., 250/537-5977, www.mapleridgecottages.com; $145–185 s or d) is on the banks of St. Mary Lake, a largish body of fresh water that holds a hungry population of bass and trout that can be caught right from the shoreline. For me, the allure of the wooden cottages is the location, but their rustic charm brings back families year after year. Relax on the deck while your catch of the day cooks on the barbecue for the full effect. Free use of canoes and kayaks is a popular bonus.

Salt Springs Spa Resort (1460 North Beach Rd., 250/537-4111 or 800/665-0039, www.saltysprings.com) commands lots of attention for its spa services, but the accommodations are also noteworthy. Each spacious unit features lots of polished wood topping out in a vaulted ceiling, plus a modern kitchen, a fireplace, and a two-person spa tub filled with mineral water. Guests have use of rowboats, mountain bikes, a game room, and a barbecue area. Summer rates are $200–260, discounted as low as $110 in winter.

The campground in **Ruckle Provincial Park** conceals 78 sites in a forest of Douglas fir overlooking Swanson Channel. The camping area is a short walk from the parking lot, making this place unsuitable for RVs; $14 per night. On the north side of the island on St. Mary Lake, **Lakeside Gardens Resort** (1450 North End Rd., 250/537-5773, www.lakesidegardensresort.com; Apr.–Nov.) offers campsites with full hookups for $25, rustic waterfront cabanas that share bathrooms for $65, and self-contained cottages for $135.

Food

Head to Ganges and wander around the waterfront for the island's widest choice of dining options. In the heart of the action is the **C Tree House Café** (106 Purvis Lane, 250/537-5379; daily 8 A.M.–10 P.M.). The "tree" is a plum tree

© ANDREW HEMPSTEAD

VANCOUVER ISLAND

The Ganges waterfront is lined with cafés and restaurants.

and the "house" is the kitchen. Most people dine outside in the shade of the tree, choosing freshly made dishes such as salmon frittata ($11) for breakfast, tuna melt on sourdough ($8.50) at lunch, or Thai chicken curry ($14) in the evening.

Around the corner from the Tree House is **La Cucina e Terrazza** (Mouat's Landing, 250/537-5747; 11 A.M.–9 P.M.), where the atmosphere is refined casual. The winsome menu ranges from Italian favorites such as gorgonzola linguine ($16) to locally inspired dishes such as a duo of grilled salmon and halibut ($24). Sit inside for the wonderful smells wafting from the kitchen or outside to soak up the harbor views.

Information

Salt Spring Island Visitor Centre (121 Lower Ganges Rd., 250/537-4223 or 866/216-2936, www.saltspringtoday.com) is in downtown Ganges, on the main road above the marina. It's open in summer daily 8 A.M.–6 P.M., the rest of the year Mon.–Fri. 8:30 A.M.–4:30 P.M.

Getting There

Salt Spring has two ferry terminals with year-round service to two points on Vancouver Island. If you're traveling up from Victoria, the Swartz Bay terminal is the most convenient departure point, with 10–12 departures daily for **Fulford Harbour,** a 20-minute drive south of Ganges. Sailings are even more frequent on the 20-minute run between Crofton, near the Vancouver Island town of Duncan, and **Vesuvius Bay,** at the island's north end. Interisland ferries depart from a third terminal, at **Long Harbour,** east of Ganges.

From the mainland, sailings depart the Tsawwassen terminal (south of downtown Vancouver) bound for Long Harbour. Direct sailings take 80 minutes, while those that make stops at other Gulf Islands take up to three hours—so check a timetable before boarding.

THE PENDERS

It's just a short hop by ferry from Salt Spring Island to **Otter Bay** on North Pender Island. Originally, North and South Pender Islands were joined, but around 100 years ago a canal was dredged between the two as a shipping channel. Today, a rickety wooden bridge forms the link. Between them, the two islands are home to 2,000 people, most of whom live on North Pender. The island has dozens of little beaches to explore, with public roads providing ocean access at more than 20 points. One of the nicest spots is **Hamilton Beach** on Browning Harbour.

Accommodations and Camping

The least expensive way to enjoy an overnight stay on North Pender Island is to camp at **Prior Centennial Campground** (mid-May to mid-Oct.; $14), a unit of Gulf Islands National Park. Sites are primitive, with no showers or hookups, but the treed location is excellent. The facility is located six kilometers (3.7 miles) south of the ferry terminal.

The island's premier accommodation is the **Oceanside Inn** (4230 Armadale Rd. five kilometers/3.1 miles from the ferry terminal, 250/629-6691 or 800/601-3284, www

.penderisland.com). Each room is elegantly furnished, and a wide balcony takes advantage of the waterfront location. Off-season rates start at $159 s or d, rising to $169–239 in summer. Rates include breakfast, use of a fitness room, and small luxuries such as fluffy bathrobes.

Other Practicalities

The commercial hub of the Penders is the **Driftwood Centre,** a citylike shopping mall overlooking cleared pastureland south of the ferry terminal. In addition to gas, groceries, booze, and a bank are several eateries, including a super-busy bakery. For something a little more substantial, move along the mall to the contemporary **Pistou Grill** (250/629-3131; Tues.–Sat. 11:30 A.M.–2:30 P.M. and 5:30–8 P.M.) for surprisingly innovative cooking that includes slow-braised lamb shank with rosemary jus ($22).

Pender Island Visitor Centre (250/629-6541; summer daily 9 A.M.–6 P.M.) is a small booth up the hill from the ferry terminal.

MAYNE ISLAND

Separated from Galiano Island by a narrow channel, Mayne Island is just 21 square kilometers (eight square miles) in area. Its year-round population of fewer than 1,000 triples in summer, but the island never really seems crowded. Ferries dock at village-less **Village Bay;** all commercial facilities are at nearby **Miners Bay,** which got its name during the Cariboo gold rush when miners used the island as a stopping point. From the ferry terminal, narrow roads meander to all corners of the island, including to **Georgina Point Lighthouse,** which was manned between 1885 and 1997. Island beaches are limited to those at **Oyster Bay,** but visitors can enjoy interesting shoreline walks or take the road to the low summit of Mount Park for panoramic views. For something a little different, wander through **Dinner Bay Park,** where a small Japanese garden takes pride of place.

The best island kayaking originates from the sandy beach in Bennett Bay, which is within Gulf Islands National Park. From its base at

Blue Vista Resort (see *Accommodations and Camping*), **Mayne Island Kayaking** (563 Arbutus Dr., 250/539-2463) provides rentals and kayak drop-offs.

Accommodations and Camping

The least expensive island accommodation is **Springwater Lodge** (Village Bay Rd., 250/539-5521, www.springwaterlodge.com), an old hotel overlooking Active Pass from the west side of Village Bay. Rooms are basic at best and bathrooms are shared, but at $40 s or d you know what you're getting. Beside the hotel are four well-equipped cabins that go for $95 per night. The inn also has a restaurant that's open daily for all three meals.

Across the road from protected Bennett Bay, the emphasis at **Blue Vista Resort** (563 Arbutus Dr., 250/539-2463 or 877/535-2424, www.bluevistaresort.com; $95–140 s or d) is on outdoor recreation, with hosts Doug and Leslie Peers operating a kayak rental and tour company. Rooms are practically furnished, with separate bedrooms, cooking facilities, and decks surrounded by native forest.

Set on four hectares (10 acres) overlooking a protected waterway and less than two kilometers (1.2 miles) south of the ferry terminal is **Oceanwood Country Inn** (630 Dinner Bay Rd., 250/539-5074, www.oceanwood.com). Paths lead through the very private property, past herb and rose gardens, and down to the water's edge. Within the lodge are four communal areas, including a well-stocked library, a comfortable lounge, and a restaurant (see *Other Practicalities*). Each of the 12 rooms has its own character; some have a private balcony, others a deck or hot tub, and the largest features a split-level living area, luxurious bathroom, and private deck with hot tub. Rates start at $179 s or d; rooms with ocean views range $249–349. A cooked breakfast and tea and coffee throughout the day are included.

Camping at **Mayne Island Eco Camping** (359 Maple Dr., Miners Bay, 250/539-2667, www.mayneisle.com; $12 per person) is pleasant but primitive. Spread around the back of a short beach, some sites are right on the water,

whereas others are spread throughout the forest. Facilities include outhouses, a (hot) waterfed "tree" shower, and kayak rentals. Part of the same property is the two-bedroom **Seal Beach Cottage** (same contact information), which rents for $150 per night.

Other Practicalities

No-frills, short-order grills are the order of the day at the old **Springwater Lodge** (Village Bay Rd., 250/539-5521). Head to the **Sunny Mayne Bakery Café** (Miners Bay, 250/539-2323; daily 7 A.M.–6 P.M., until 7 P.M. on weekends) for freshly baked breads, picnic hampers, sumptuous cakes and pastries, healthy sandwiches, and the island's best coffee concoctions.

The bright and breezy dining room at the **Oceanwood Country Inn** (630 Dinner Bay Rd., 250/539-5074) is primarily the domain of registered guests, but each evening at 6 P.M. the doors open to all for a four-course table d'hôte dinner ($55 per person) that includes a choice from two entrées that focus on creative presentations of local produce and seafood.

The website www.mayneislandchamber.ca is loaded with useful information, including links to current weather conditions, accommodations, services, and, for those who fall in love with island living, real estate agents.

Stock up on reading material at **Miners Bay Books** (478 Village Bay Rd., 250/539-3112).

◖ GALIANO ISLAND

Named for a Spanish explorer who sailed through the Strait of Georgia more than 200 years ago, this long, narrow island—27 kilometers (17 miles) from north to south but only a few kilometers wide—has some delightful beaches and good kayaking. Most of the population (1,000) lives in the south, within a five-minute drive of the ferry terminal at **Sturdies Bay.**

Montague Harbour Provincial Park

Climbing out of Sturdies Bay, roads tempt exploration in all directions. Take Porlier Pass Road to reach Montague Harbour Provincial Park,

VANCOUVER ISLAND

© ANDREW HEMPSTEAD

The shoreline of Galiano Island is dotted with remote coves.

which protects an 89-hectare (210-acre) chunk of coastal forest and a beach of bleached-white broken seashells. You can walk out along the beach and return via a forested trail in around 20 minutes. At the end of the beach are middens, manmade piles of empty shells that accumulated over centuries of native feasting. The island is dotted with many less-obvious access points, many of which aren't even signposted. The beach below Active Pass Road is typical: Look for the power pole numbered 1038 and make your way down the steep trail to a protected cove. Ask at the information center or your accommodation for a full listing of similar spots.

Kayaking

The best way to explore local waterways is with **Gulf Island Kayaking** (250/539-2442), based at the marina in Montague Harbour. Three-hour guided tours, either early in the morning or at sunset, are $50. Another tour takes in the local marinelife on a six-hour paddle for $75. Those with previous experience can rent a kayak; $48–60 per day for a single or $70–95 for a double.

Golf

Galiano Golf Club (St. Andrews Dr., 250/539-5533) is typical of the many courses on the Southern Gulf Islands, with nine holes, inexpensive greens fees ($20), a relaxed atmosphere, and a clubhouse offering rentals and meals.

Accommodations and Camping

Many of the travelers you'll meet on the ferry trip to Galiano will be staying for a week or more in an island cottage. If this style of vacation sounds ideal to you, check www.galiano island.com for a choice of rentals, but do so well before planning your visit because the best ones fill fast. **Paradise Rock Ocean Front Cottage** (310 Ganner Dr., 250/539-3404; $150 per night) is typical in all respects—water views from a private setting, self-contained, and a deck with a propane barbecue—except that it can be rented for as few as two nights.

Set on Sturdies Bay waterfront is the **Bellhouse Inn** (29 Farmhouse Rd., 250/539-5667 or 800/970-7464, www.bellhouseinn .com; $135–195), an 1890s farmhouse that has been taking in travelers since the 1920s. Each of the three guest rooms has water views, and the most expensive room features a hot tub, private balcony, and fireplace. Rates include a full breakfast and personal touches such as tea or coffee delivered to the room before breakfast.

You'll see the magnificent gardens of the **◖ Galiano Inn** (134 Madrona Dr., 250/539-3388 or 877/530-3939, www.galianoinn.com), at the head of Sturdies Bay, before the ferry docks. The elegant guest rooms infused with European charm come in two sizes (Queen, $249; King, $299) and all have views extending down the bay to Mayne Island. Other highlights include private balconies, super-comfortable beds, plush robes, luxury bathrooms with soaker tubs, and extras such as CD players and coffeemakers. The inn is also home to the **Madrona del Mar Spa,** the place to get pampered with a soothing hot stone massage or kick back in the seaside hot tub. Guests can also book a variety of tours aboard the inn's own motor cruiser, including wine-tasting on nearby Saturna Island.

The campground in **Montague Harbour Provincial Park,** 10 kilometers (6.2 miles) from the ferry, is one of the best in the Southern Gulf Islands. Sites are set below a towering forest of old-growth cedar and fir trees and open to a white shingle beach that is aligned perfectly to watch the setting sun. As with all provincial park campgrounds, facilities are limited to picnic tables, pit toilets, and drinking water; $17 per night and no reservations taken. The gates are open mid-April to mid-October.

Food

To immerse yourself in island life, plan on dining at the **Grand Central Emporium** (2470 Sturdies Bay Rd., 250/539-9885; daily 7 A.M.–3:30 P.M. and for dinner Tues.–Sun.), which is decorated in lumberjack artifacts and has seating ripped from old buses. Free-range eggs are the prime ingredient in the omelets, which are huge (ham and Swiss cheese for $10). Sandwiches and burgers dominate the lunch menu. In the evening, the blackboard dinner menu

(mains around $20) reflects whatever is in season, often with live music playing in the background. While you're waiting for a ferry—or even if you're not—line up at the **Max & Moritz** food wagon, in front of the parking lot at the ferry terminal, for a combination of German and Indonesian dishes, such as *nasi goreng* (fried rice), $5.

The stellar food is reason enough to dine at **Atrevida** (Galiano Inn, 134 Madrona Dr., 250/539-3388), but the unobstructed water views cost no extra. Although the upscale dining room has a touch of Old World elegance, the cooking is healthy and modern, with a seasonal menu that uses fresh island produce and local seafood. Professional service and an impressive wine list round out what many regard as the finest restaurant on the Southern Gulf Islands. In summer, a sunken patio buzzes with activity as locals and visitors from outlying islands enjoy lunchtime barbecues in a cultured garden setting.

Information

Right at the ferry terminal is **Galiano Island Visitor Centre** (250/539-2233, www.galiano-island.com; July–Aug. daily 9 A.M.–5 P.M.). The Southern Gulf Islands have a surprising number of bookstores, and none are better than **Galiano Island Books** (Madrona Dr., 250/539-3340; daily 10 A.M.–5 P.M.), down the first left after exiting the terminal area. Stop by for works by island writers as well as Canadiana, children's titles, and some great cooking books that use local ingredients.

SATURNA ISLAND

Most remote of the populated Southern Gulf Islands, Saturna protrudes into the heart of Georgia Strait and features a long, rugged northern coastline and over half its land area within Gulf Islands National Park. It offers a range of accommodations, but other services are limited (no banks or bank machines) and ferries only stop by a couple of times a day.

From the ferry dock at **Lyall Harbour,** the island's main road loops east and then south along the coastline for 14 kilometers (8.7 miles), ending at **East Point Regional Park.** Here you can go swimming or simply admire the sweeping views across the border to the San Juans. Before the park, **Winter Cove** is another picturesque diversion. On Canada Day (July 1), everyone gathers on this beach for a lamb barbecue.

Accommodations and Food

Most accommodations on Saturna Island are in private home bed-and-breakfasts. A short walk from where the ferry docks is **Lyall Harbour B&B** (121 E. Point Rd., 250/539-5577 or 877/473-9343, www.lyallharbour.com; $100 s, $130 d). Each of the three guest rooms is spacious and features modern furnishings, a fireplace, and a deck with ocean views; breakfast is served in a sun-drenched solarium.

Overlooking Boot Cove and also within walking distance of the dock is **Saturna Lodge** (130 Payne Rd., 250/539-2254 or 866/539-

2254, www.saturna.ca; May–Oct.). Right on the water, this modern accommodation offers seven guest rooms, a hot tub, a lounge with fireplace, and extensive gardens. Rates range $135–195 including breakfast. Within the lodge a small restaurant has a big reputation for seafood and local game and produce. The owners are involved in various projects around the island, including **Saturna Island Vineyards** (Harris Rd., 250/539-5139; May–Oct. daily 11:30 A.M.–4 P.M.), which sources pinot noir, merlot, and chardonnay grapes from four island vineyards. Stop by the barn-shaped cellar door for tastings and a tour.

Off East Point Road, **Saturna's Café** (Narvaez Bay Rd., 250/539-2936) is open daily except Tuesday 9:30 A.M.–2 P.M. and Wednesday–Monday for dinner from 6 P.M. Expect simple home-style cooking, a casual ambience, and friendly service.

Nanaimo and Vicinity

Nanaimo (pronounced na-NYE-mo) sprawls lazily up and down the hilly coastal terrain between sparkling Nanaimo Harbour and Mount Benson, on the east coast of Vancouver Island 110 kilometers (69 miles) north of Victoria. With a population of 78,000, it's the island's second largest city and one of the 10 largest cities in British Columbia. It's also a vibrant city enjoying a rich history, mild climate, wide range of visitor services, and direct ferry link to both of Vancouver's ferry terminals.

The **Nanaimo Parkway** bypasses the city to the west along a 21-kilometer (13-mile) route that branches off the original highway 5 kilometers (3.1 miles) south of downtown, rejoining it 18 kilometers (11 miles) north of downtown.

SIGHTS

Downtown Nanaimo lies in a wide bowl sloping down to the waterfront, where forward thinking by early town planners has left wide expanses of parkland. Down near the water, the Civic Arena building makes a good place to

park your car and go exploring on foot. Right in front of the Civic Arena is **Swy-A-Lana Lagoon,** a unique manmade tidal lagoon full of interesting marinelife. A promenade leads south from the lagoon to a bustling downtown marina filled with commercial fishing boats and leisure craft. Beside the marina is a distinctive mastlike sculpture that provides foot access to a tiered development with various viewpoints. Up in downtown proper, many historic buildings still stand, most around the corner of Front and Church Streets and along Commercial Street. Look for hotels dating to last century, the Francis Rattenbury–designed courthouse, and various old commercial buildings. Up Fitzwilliam Street are the 1893 St. Andrew's Church and the 1883 railway station.

The Bastion

Overlooking the harbor at the junction of Bastion and Front Streets stands the Bastion, a well-protected fort built in 1853 by the Hudson's Bay Company to protect employees and

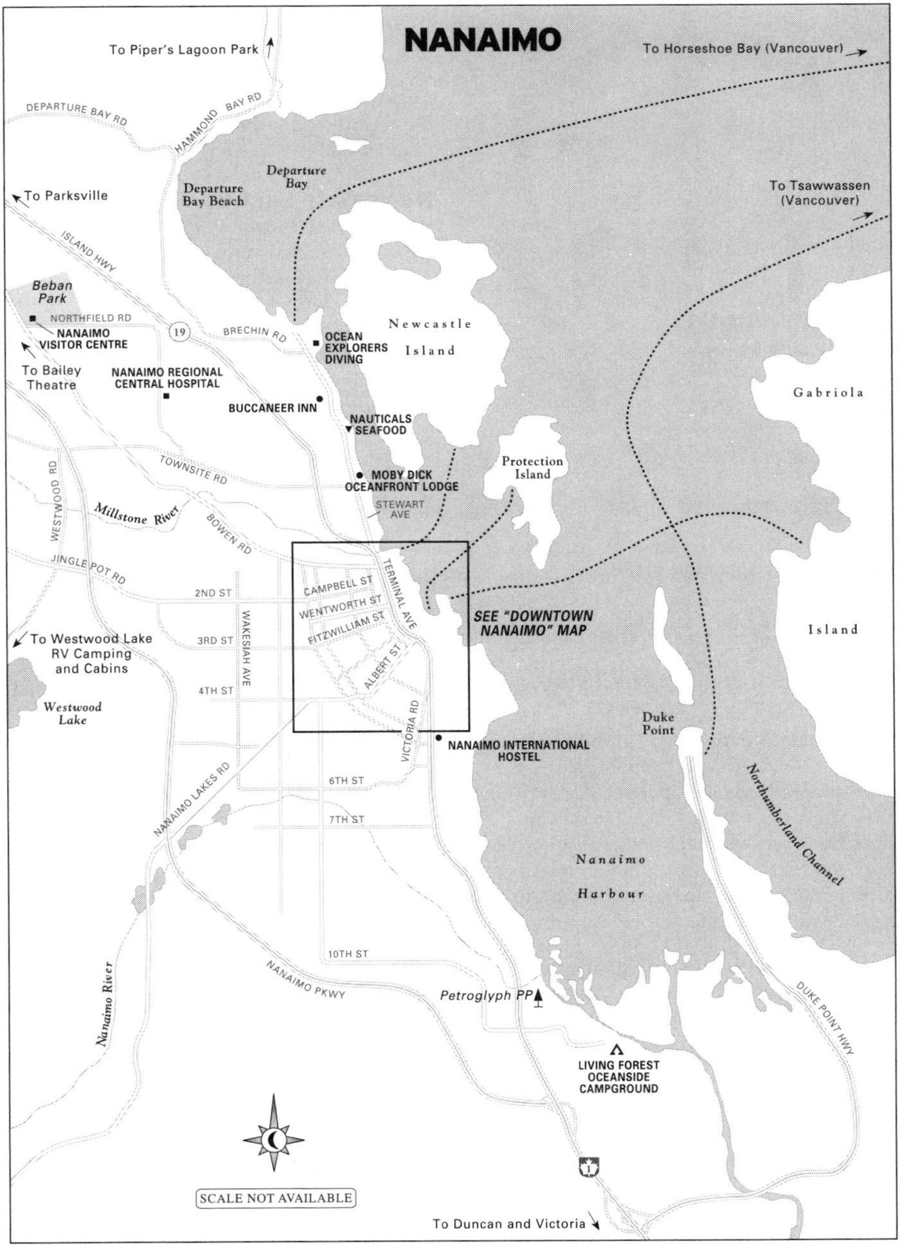

NANAIMO

To Piper's Lagoon Park ↑

To Horseshoe Bay (Vancouver) →

DEPARTURE BAY RD

HAMMOND BAY RD

To Parksville ↖

ISLAND HWY

Departure
Bay Beach

Departure
Bay

To Tsawwassen
(Vancouver) →

*Beban
Park* ■

NORTHFIELD RD

**NANAIMO
VISITOR CENTRE** ↖

To Bailey
Theatre

(19)

BRECHIN RD

**NANAIMO REGIONAL
CENTRAL HOSPITAL** ■

● **OCEAN
EXPLORERS
DIVING**

Newcastle

Island

Gabriola

BUCCANEER INN ■

**NAUTICALS
▼ SEAFOOD**

TOWNSITE RD

WESTWOOD RD

Millstone River

BOWEN RD

● **MOBY DICK
OCEANFRONT LODGE**

STEWART
AVE

Protection
Island

JINGLE POT RD

To Westwood Lake
RV Camping
and Cabins ↙

2ND ST

CAMPBELL ST

WENTWORTH ST

FITZWILLIAM ST

TERMINAL AVE

*SEE "DOWNTOWN
NANAIMO" MAP*

Island

*Westwood
Lake*

3RD ST

4TH ST

WAKESIAH AVE

ALBERT ST

*Duke
Point*

NANAIMO LAKES RD

VICTORIA RD

● **NANAIMO INTERNATIONAL
HOSTEL**

6TH ST

7TH ST

Northumberland Channel

Nanaimo River

10TH ST

NANAIMO PKWY

Nanaimo

Harbour

Petroglyph PP ▲

DUKE POINT HWY

∧ **LIVING FOREST
OCEANSIDE
CAMPGROUND**

✦

SCALE NOT AVAILABLE

(1)

To Duncan and Victoria ↓

VANCOUVER ISLAND

© AVALON TRAVEL

the Bastion, a fort built in 1853

their families against an attack by natives. Originally used as a company office, arsenal, and supply house, the fort today houses the **Bastion Museum** (June–Aug. daily 10 A.M.–4 P.M.; $1). For the benefit of tourists, a group of local university students dressed in appropriate gunnery uniforms and led by a piper parades down Bastion Street daily at 11:45 A.M. in summer. The parade ends at the Bastion, where the three cannons are fired out over the water. It's the only ceremonial cannon firing west of Ontario. For a good vantage point, be there early.

Nanaimo District Museum

Across Front Street from the harbor is the Nanaimo Museum (100 Museum Way, 250/753-1821; summer daily 10 A.M.–5 P.M., the rest of the year Tues.–Sat. 10 A.M.–5 P.M.; adult $2, senior $1.75, child $0.75). Walk around the outside to appreciate harbor, city, and mountain views, as well as replica petroglyphs of animals, humans, and spiritual creatures. Then allow at least an hour for wandering through the displays inside, which focus on life in early

Nanaimo and include topics such as geology, native peoples, pioneers, and local sporting heroes. An exhibit on the coal-mining days features a realistic coalmine from the 1850s. Don't miss the impressive native carvings by James Dick.

Newcastle Island Provincial Marine Park

Newcastle Island is a magnificent chunk of wilderness separated from downtown Nanaimo by a narrow channel. It's mostly forested, ringed by sandstone cliffs and a few short stretches of pebbly beach. Wildlife inhabitants include deer, raccoons, beavers, and more than 50 species of birds.

When Europeans arrived and began mining coal, they displaced natives who had lived on the island for centuries. Coal was mined until 1883, and sandstone—featured on many of Nanaimo's historic buildings—was quarried here until 1932. The pavilion and facilities near the ferry dock date to the 1940s. Back then, the island was a popular holiday spot, at one point even boasting a floating hotel.

A 7.5-kilometer (4.7-mile) walking trail (allow 2–3 hours) encircles the island, leading to picturesque Kanaka Bay, Mallard Lake, and a lookout offering views east to the snowcapped Coast Mountains.

Nanaimo Harbour Ferry (877/297-8526; no reservations) departs for the island from Maffeo-Sutton Park in summer every 20 minutes 9 A.M.–9 P.M. on the hour, with fewer sailings in May and September. The round-trip fare is adult $8, senior or child $4, bicycle $3.

Other Parks

Along the Millstone River and linked by a trail to the waterfront promenade, 36-hectare (89-acre) **Bowen Park** remains mostly in its natural state, with stands of Douglas fir, hemlock, cedar, and maple. It's home to beavers and birds, and even deer are occasionally sighted within its boundaries. Street access is from Bowen Road.

On the road into downtown Nanaimo from the south, two kilometers (1.2 miles)

north of the Nanaimo Parkway intersection, **Petroglyph Provincial Park** features a short trail leading to ancient petroglyphs (rock carvings). Petroglyphs, found throughout the province and common along the coastal waterways, were made with stone tools, and they recorded important ceremonies and events. The petroglyphs protected by this park were carved thousands of years ago and are believed to represent human beings, animals (real and supernatural), bottom fish, and the rarely depicted sea wolf, a mythical creature that's part wolf and part killer whale.

Along Hammond Bay Road, north of downtown and beyond Departure Bay, is **Piper's Lagoon Park,** encompassing an isthmus and a rocky headland that shelter a shallow lagoon. A trail from the parking lot leads to the headland, with views of the mainland across the Strait of Georgia. Continuing north, more trails lead through **Neck Point Park** to rocky beaches and oceanside picnic areas.

RECREATION
On and Under the Water

The obvious way to appreciate the harbor aspect of Nanaimo is by boat. To arrange a cruise, wander down to the marina below the Bastion and inquire among the fishing and sightseeing charter boats, or stop by the Nanaimo Visitor Centre and ask for a list of local guides and charters, plus current prices. **Nanaimo**

NANAIMO'S WORLD CHAMPIONSHIP BATHTUB RACE

On the third Sunday of every July the waters off Nanaimo come alive for the World Championship Bathtub Race (250/753-7223, www.bathtubbing.com), the grand finale of the annual Nanaimo Marine Festival. The idea for the race was conceived back in 1967, when the chairman of the city's Canada Centennial Committee, Frank Ney, was asked to come up with a special event for the occasion. Bathtub racing was born over a cup of coffee, and Ney went on to be elected mayor of Nanaimo.

Originally, competitors raced across the Strait of Georgia between Nanaimo and Kitsilano Beach, Vancouver. Today, they leave from downtown, racing around Entrance and Winchelsea Islands to the finish line at Departure Bay in a modified bathtub fitted with a 7.5-horsepower outboard motor. The racers are escorted by hundreds of boats of the more regular variety, loaded with people just waiting for the competitors to sink! Every bathtubber wins a prize: a golden plug for entering, a small trophy for making it to the other side of the strait, and a silver plunger for the first tub to sink! These days, the sport and the festivities around it have grown enormously, attracting tens of thousands of visitors to Nanaimo. And "tubbing," as the locals call it, has spread to other provincial communities, where preliminary races qualify entrants for the big one.

Harbour Ferry (877/297-8526; April to mid-Oct.) takes passengers on a 45-minute narrated cruise of the harbor. During the cruise, you might spot seals, bald eagles, blue herons, and cormorants. Cruises cost adult $17, senior $15, child $9. The departure point is the Fisherman's Market.

A great variety of dives can be accessed from Nanaimo, including several vessels that have been sunk especially for diving enthusiasts, such as the HMAS *Cape Breton* and HMAS *Saskatchewan,* both 120-meter (400-foot) Navy destroyer escorts. The much smaller *Rivtow Lion,* a rescue tug, was scuttled in the shallow waters of Departure Bay, making it a popular spot for novice divers. Marinelife is also varied, with divers mixing with harbor seals, anemones, sponges, salmon, and "tame" wolf eels. Near the Departure Bay ferry terminal, **Ocean Explorers Diving** (1690 Stewart Ave., 250/753-2055, www.oceanexplorersdiving .com) is a well-respected island operation, offering equipment rentals, charters, guided tours (from $60 per dive including air), lessons, and accommodation packages.

ENTERTAINMENT

Lovers of the arts will find Nanaimo to be quite the cultural center, especially since the opening of the **Port Theatre** (125 Front St., 250/754-8550, www.porttheatre.com) in 1998. This magnificent 800-seat theater in an architecturally pleasing circular concrete-and-glass building opposite the harbor showcases theater productions, musicals, and music performances by a wide range of artists. The **Nanaimo Theatre Group** (250/758-7246) presents live performances at the Port Theatre as well as in the Bailey Theatre (2373 Rosstown Rd.).

The best place in Nanaimo for a quiet drink in a relaxing atmosphere is upstairs in the **Lighthouse Pub** (50 Anchor Way, 250/754-3212), built out over the water in front of downtown. This casual pub gets busy in summer, with nightly drink specials, a pool table, and a good selection of pub food. For nautical atmosphere, head over to the **Dinghy**

Dock Marine Pub, moored at Protection Island (250/753-2373); ferries depart regularly from Nanaimo Boat Basin.

The **Nanaimo Art Gallery** (150 Commercial St., 250/754-1750; Tues.–Sat. 11 A.M.– 5 P.M.) displays and sells works by a diverse range of island artists.

ACCOMMODATIONS
Under $50
A few of Nanaimo's older motels offer rooms under $50 outside of summer, but only **Nanaimo International Hostel** (65 Nicol St., 250/753-1188, www.nanaimohostel.com) falls into this price range year-round. In a converted house, this accommodation enjoys a convenient location three blocks from the train station and seven blocks from the bus depot. The hostel operates year-round, providing dormitory-style accommodations, as well as campsites, a kitchen, laundry facilities, a TV room, and bicycle rentals. Guests can get discounts at many local restaurants and attractions. All beds are $19; register after 4 P.M.

$50-100
On an island of overpriced accommodations, two places, both on the same street in Nanaimo, stand out as being an excellent value. The first of these, across from the waterfront and within easy walking distance of downtown and the Departure Bay ferry terminal, is the two-story **Buccaneer Inn** (1577 Stewart Ave., 250/753-1246 or 877/282-6337, www.buccaneerinn.com). Bedecked by a nautical-themed mural and colorful baskets of flowers, the motel is surrounded by well-maintained grounds, a sundeck, picnic tables, and a barbecue facility. The rooms are spacious and brightly decorated, and each has a desk, coffeemaking facilities, a small fridge, and Internet connections. The smallest rooms are $70 s or d, while kitchen suites, some with gas fireplaces, start at $110 s or d. The Fireplace Suite, complete with a wood-burning fireplace, soaker tub, and separate bedroom, is $190. Off-season rates range $60–140. Friendly owner/operators provide a wealth

of information on the local area (as does the motel website).

A few blocks toward downtown from the Buccaneer is the **Moby Dick Oceanfront Lodge** (1000 Stewart St., 250/753-7111 or 800/663-2116, www.mobydicklodge.com). This four-story waterfront motel faces Newcastle Island, offering water views from every room. The rooms are extra large, and each has a kitchen and private balcony, making the rates of $85 s, $95 d an extremely good value.

$100-150
As you'd expect, accommodations right downtown are more expensive than those farther out. A bit nicer than you'd expect from the bland exterior, the **Best Western Dorchester Nanaimo Hotel** (70 Church St., 250/754-6835 or 800/661-2449, www.dorchesternanaimo .com) offers water views and a rooftop terrace from a central location. Rooms in this historic building won't win any design awards, but they are relatively modern, many have water views, and wireless Internet access is free. Rack rates are $120–160, but online specials usually have rooms at $100, even in summer.

Also right downtown, the **Coast Bastion Inn** (11 Bastion St., 250/753-6601 or 800/716-6199, www.coasthotels.com) is a full-service, 179-room hotel with an exercise room, a café, the contemporary Minnoz Restaurant, and water views from every room. Advertised rates are from $149 s or d, but like other properties in this chain, search their website for packages that offer decent discounts, even in summer.

Camping
Two commercial campgrounds lie within 10 kilometers (6.2 miles) of the city center, but the nicest surroundings are in the provincial park out on **Newcastle Island** (www.newcastleisland.ca; see *Sights*), connected to downtown by regular passenger ferry service. The island isn't suitable for RVers, but it's ideal for those with a lightweight tent. Facilities include picnic tables and a barbecue shelter. Sites are $14.

The closest of the commercial campgrounds to downtown is **Westwood Lake RV Camping** and Cabins (380 Westwood Rd., 250/753-3922, www.westwoodlakecampgrounds.com). Set on the edge of beautiful Westwood Lake, it features canoe rentals, a barbecue area, a game room, a laundry facility, and hot showers. Unserviced sites are $22, hookups $27, and basic rooms for $70 s or d ($85 with linen).

Living Forest Oceanside RV & Campground (6 Maki Rd., 250/755-1755, www.campingbc.com) is set on 20 hectares (49 acres) of coastal forest at the braided mouth of the Nanaimo River south of downtown. The location is delightful and facilities modern, including a laundry room, a general store, a game room, and coin showers. Tent sites are $23, serviced sites $24–33, with the best of these large pull-through sites enjoying water views.

FOOD

First things first. This is the place to try a delicious chocolate-topped **Nanaimo Bar,** a layered delicacy that originated in this city. Try the **Nanaimo Bakery** (2025 Bowen Rd., 250/758-4260, Mon.–Fri. 7:30 A.M.–4:40 P.M.).

Cafés and Cheap Eats

If you're wandering along the harbor and looking for a spot to relax with a hot drink, you won't do better than **Javawocky** (90 Front St., 250/753-1688, Mon.–Fri. from 6:15 A.M., Sat.–Sun. from 7 A.M.), overlooking the harbor. It offers all of the usual coffee drinks, great milkshakes, inexpensive cakes and pastries, and light lunchtime snacks. Another downtown haunt with good coffee (and muffins) is **Perkins** (234 Commercial St., 250/753-2582; Mon.–Fri. 6:30 A.M.–5 P.M., Sat. 7 A.M.–5 P.M.).

Pirate Chips (1 Commercial St., 250/753-2447; daily 11:30 A.M.–9 P.M., weekends until 3 A.M.) is a funky little takeout place where you can load up on hearty servings of fries with various toppings, and even try a deep-fried chocolate bar.

In the heart of downtown, tiny **Tina's Diner** (187 Commercial St., 250/753-5333; Mon.–Tues. 9 A.M.–3 P.M., Wed.–Fri. 8 A.M.–2 P.M., Sat.–Sun. 9 A.M.–2 P.M.) offers a cooked breakfast for under $5 before 10 A.M. Also

downtown is the **Modern Café** (221 Commercial St., 250/754-5022; daily 11 A.M.–11 P.M.), which isn't, and has hearty, no-frills cooking.

Seafood

Head down to the marina at the foot of Wharf Street for seafood straight from the fishing boats. You can buy salmon, halibut, cod, snapper, shrimp, crabs, mussels, or whatever the day's catch might be at reasonable prices—perfect if you're camping or have a motel room with a kitchen (many local accommodations also have outdoor barbecue facilities). Also at the marina is **Troller's** (250/741-7994; daily from 11 A.M.), with tables and chairs set up around a small takeout counter on one of the arms of the floating dock. Expect to pay $7–10 for fish and chips.

A little more stylish is **Nauticals Seafood** (1340 Stewart Ave., 250/754-8881; daily from 11:30 A.M.), along the road to the Departure Bay ferry terminal and with outdoor tables on the back deck enjoying sweeping water views. The seafood-dominated menu includes a British Columbia platter and well-priced mains, such as poached halibut smothered in hollandaise sauce for under $20.

Other Restaurants

The menu at **Tania's** (75 Front St., 250/753-5181; Sun.–Mon. 11 A.M.–3 P.M., Tues.–Sat. 11 A.M.–midnight) takes inspiration from around the world, with island-sourced produce used whenever possible; try the chili- and lime-crusted rack of lamb ($24). The ambiance is casual and laidback, with live music some evenings adding to the charm.

Dinghy Dock Marine Pub (250/753-2373; daily 11 A.M.–11 P.M., later on weekends) offers a unique dining experience: The floating restaurant is moored at nearby Protection Island. Well known for great food and plenty of seagoing atmosphere, the pub also hosts live entertainment on Friday and Saturday nights from May to September. To get to the restaurant, take a ferry from Nanaimo Boat Basin. Ferries depart hourly 9:10 A.M.–11:10 P.M.; for information, call 250/753-8244.

© ANDREW HEMPSTEAD

Troller's, on the marina, provides the perfect setting for enjoying a meal of fish and chips.

For some of the best Mexican food on the island, head for **Gina's Mexican Café,** behind the courthouse (47 Skinner St., 250/753-5411; daily for lunch and dinner). Although it's on a back street, the building itself, a converted residence, is hard to miss: The exterior is painted shades of purple and decorated with a fusion of Mexican and maritime memorabilia.

Old Quarter

Up Fitzwilliam Street from the center of town, in the Old Quarter, is a concentration of quality eateries, including **Bocca Café** (427 Fitzwilliam St., 250/753-1797; Mon.–Fri. 7 A.M.–6 P.M., Sat. 8 A.M.–6 P.M., Sun. 8 A.M.–5 P.M.), an inviting little space that is a favorite with locals looking for a little style. From the delicious coffee and muffins in the morning to freshly made sandwiches at lunch, everything is delightful. Tables lining a covered walkway are especially popular. Across the road is **McLeans Specialty Foods** (426 Fitzwilliam St., 250/754-

0100; Mon.–Fri. 9:30 A.M.–5:30 P.M., Sat. 10 A.M.–5 P.M., Sun. 11 A.M.–4 P.M.), which is chock-full of local produce, including an incredible selection of cheeses. Also on offer are gourmet foods from around the world.

INFORMATION AND SERVICES

Nanaimo is promoted to the world by **Tourism Nanaimo** (250/756-0106 or 800/663-7337, www.tourismnanaimo.com). The main **Nanaimo Visitor Centre** (2290 Bowen Rd., Mon.–Fri. 9 A.M.–5 P.M., Sat.–Sun. 10 A.M.–4 P.M.) is in an imposing, historic log building north of downtown and off the main highway in the grounds of Beban Park.

For maps, nautical charts, and books about Vancouver Island, visit **Nanaimo Maps and Charts** (8 Church St., 250/754-2513). Numerous used bookstores can be found along Commercial Street.

The main **post office** is on Front Street in

the Harbour Park Mall. For emergencies, head to **Nanaimo Regional Central Hospital** (1200 Dufferin Cres., 250/754-2141). If you need a pharmacy, go to the **Pharmasave** (2000 North Island Hwy., Brooks Landing Mall, 250/760-0771).

GETTING THERE

BC Ferries (250/386-3431 or 888/223-3779, www.bcferries.com) operates regular services between Vancouver and Nanaimo along two different routes. Ferries leave Vancouver's Tsawwassen terminal up to eight times a day for the two-hour trip to Nanaimo's **Duke Point** terminal, 20 minutes south of downtown and with direct access to the highway that bypasses the city. Through downtown, at the north end of Stewart Avenue, is the **Departure Bay** terminal. This facility contains a large lounge area with a café and large-screen TVs. Ferries from Vancouver's Horseshoe Bay terminal leave up to 11 times a day for Departure Bay. Fares on both routes are the same: peak one-way travel costs adult $11.15, child $5.60, vehicle $39. Limited reservations are taken via the website ($15 plus ferry fare).

West Coast Air (604/606-6888 or 800/347-2222) and **Harbour Air** (250/714-0900) fly daily between Vancouver and the seaplane base in downtown Nanaimo; $75 one-way.

The **Greyhound** bus depot is at the rear of the Howard Johnson hotel (corner of Terminal Ave. and Comox Rd., 800/753-4371). Buses depart regularly for points north and south of Nanaimo and west to Port Alberni and Tofino.

GETTING AROUND

Nanaimo Regional Transit System (250/390-4531) buses run daily. The main routes radiate from the Harbour Park Mall (at the south end of downtown) north to Departure Bay, west to Westwood Lake, and south as far as Cedar. An all-day pass is $5.75.

Rental car agencies in Nanaimo include **Avis** (250/716-8898), **Budget** (250/754-7368), **Discount** (250/758-5171), **Hertz** (250/245-

8818), **National** (250/758-3509), and **Rent-a-wreck** (250/753-6461).

GABRIOLA ISLAND

Like the Southern Gulf Islands, Gabriola (pop. 3,500) is partly residential, but also holds large expanses of forest, abundant wildlife, and long stretches of unspoiled coastline. The ferry from Nanaimo docks at Descanso Bay, on the west side of the island.

Take Taylor Bay Road north from the ferry terminal to access the island's best beaches, including those within tiny **Gabriola Sands Provincial Park.** Walk out to the park's southern headland to view sandstone cliffs eroded into interesting shapes by eons of wave action. North and South Roads encircle the island, combining for a 30-kilometer (18.6-mile) loop that's perfect for a leisurely bike ride. Many scenic spots invite you to pull off—at petroglyphs, secluded bays, and lookouts. **Drumbeg Provincial Park** protects the island's southeast corner, where a short trail through dense forest leads to a secluded bay.

Practicalities

For romantic-themed bed-and-breakfast accommodation, **Marina's Hideaway** (943 Canso Dr., 250/247-8854 or 888/208-9850, www .marinashideaway.com; $145 s or d), overlooking Northumberland Channel, is an excellent choice. Each of the two spacious guest rooms in this magnificent waterfront home has a king-size bed, gas fireplace, private entrance, and balcony.

Basic services are available a little over one kilometer (0.6 miles) from the ferry terminal on North Road. There you'll find a café, a grocery store, and the **Gabriola Island Visitor Centre** (250/247-9332, www.gabriolaisland.org; mid-May–mid-Sept. daily 9 A.M.–6 P.M.).

BC Ferries (250/386-3431) schedules 15 sailings daily between the terminal off Front Street in Nanaimo (downtown, across from Harbour Park Mall) and Gabriola Island. The trip takes 20 minutes each way. The peak round-trip fare is adult $6.60, child $3.30, vehicle $16.70. For a taxi, call **Gabriola Island Cabs** (250/247-0049).

Highway 4 to the West Coast

From Nanaimo, it's 35 kilometers (21.7 miles) northwest up Highway 19 to one of Vancouver Island's main highway junctions, where Highway 4 spurs west to Port Alberni and the island's west coast. Follow Highway 4 to its end to reach **Pacific Rim National Park,** a long, narrow park protecting the wild coastal strip and some magnificent sandy beaches, and **Tofino,** a picturesque little town that makes the perfect base for sea kayaking, whale-watching, or fishing excursions.

Englishman River Provincial Park

After turning off Highway 19, make your first stop here, where Englishman River—full of steelhead, cutthroat, and rainbow trout—cascades down from high Beaufort Range snowfields in a series of beautiful waterfalls. Within the park you'll find a picnic area, easy hiking trails to both the upper and lower falls, crystal-clear swimming holes, and plenty of campsites among tall cedars and lush ferns ($17 per night; no showers).

To get there, turn off Highway 4 on Errington Road, three kilometers (1.9 miles) west of the highway junction, and continue another nine kilometers (5.6 miles), following signs.

Coombs

What started just over 30 years ago as a simple produce stand has grown into the **Old Country Market** (250/248-6272; daily 8 A.M.–9 P.M.), the lifeblood of Coombs, along Highway 4A west of Nanaimo. Before moving inside the market building, you'll want to stand out front and look upward, where several goats can be seen contentedly grazing along the roof line, seemingly oblivious to the amused, camera-clicking visitors. Inside is a selection of goodies of epic proportions: a bakery, a deli, an ice cream stand, and a wealth of healthy island-made produce. Behind the main building and in an adjacent property are rows of arty shops selling everything from pottery to jewelry to kites.

On the west side of Coombs, at the junction of Highways 4 and 4A, is **Creekmore's Coffee** (2701 Alberni Hwy., 250/752-0158; Mon.–Fri. 6:30 A.M.–6 P.M., Sat. 8 A.M.–6 P.M., Sun. 9 A.M.–4 P.M.). This unassuming place pours freshly roasted coffee as good as any on the island.

Little Qualicum Falls Provincial Park

This 440-hectare (1,090-acre) park lies along the north side of the highway, 10 kilometers (six miles) west of Coombs. The park's main hiking trail leads alongside the Little Qualicum River to a series of plummeting waterfalls. Take your fishing pole along the riverside trail and catch a trout, stop for an exhilarating dip in one of the icy emerald pools, and stay the night in a sheltered riverside campsite ($17 per night; no showers). The source of the Little Qualicum River is **Cameron Lake,** a large, deep-green, trout-filled body of water just outside the western park boundary.

Cathedral Grove

At the west end of Cameron Lake, Highway 4 dives into one of the last remaining easily accessible stands of old-growth forest in British Columbia. The tallest trees are protected by **MacMillan Provincial Park.** The road through the park is narrow, so take extra care pulling into the main parking lot. From this point, a 500-meter (0.3-mile) trail leads through a majestic stand of 200- to 800-year-old Douglas firs that rise a neck-straining 70 meters (230 feet) from the forest floor.

PORT ALBERNI AND VICINITY

If you hit Port Alberni on a cloudy day, you won't know what you're missing—until the sky lifts! Then beautiful tree-mantled mountains suddenly appear, and Alberni Inlet and the Somass River turn a stunning deep blue. Situated at the head of the island's longest inlet, Port Alberni is an industrial town of 19,500 centered around the forestry industry. The

Alberni Harbour Quay is the colorful epicenter of the Port Alberni waterfront.

town's three mills—lumber, specialty lumber, and pulp and paper—are its main sources of income. The town is also a port for pulp and lumber freighters, deep-sea vessels, and commercial fishing boats.

Despite all the industry, Port Alberni has much to offer, including interesting museums, nearby provincial parks, and a modern marina filled with both charter fishing boats and tour boats, including the famous MV *Lady Rose.*

Sights

Follow the signs from Highway 4 to brightly decorated **Alberni Harbour Quay** at the end of Argyle Street. For a great view of the quay, harbor, marina, inlet, and surrounding mountains, climb the clock tower. Also on the quay is the **Forestry Visitor Centre,** operated by the logging giant Weyerhaeuser (250/720-2108; summer daily 9:30 A.M.–5:30 P.M., the rest of the year Fri.–Sun. 11 A.M.–4 P.M.), where you can view interpretive displays on logging, milling, and replanting, and arrange tours through

local industry. Off Argyle Street is Industrial Road, which leads to the **Maritime Discovery Centre,** ensconced in a red-and-white lighthouse (250/723-6164; mid-June to early Sept. daily 10 A.M.–5 P.M.; donation). Children will love the hands-on displays that explore the importance of the ocean to the town's history.

Alberni Harbour Quay is also the starting point for the **Alberni Pacific Railway,** which runs twice a day Thursday–Monday to **McLean Mill National Historic Site** (250/723-1376; July–Aug. daily 10 A.M.–5 P.M.). The site has Canada's only steam-powered sawmill, and it still works, so you can watch workers milling lumber through the clunky contraption. Admission to the site is adult $7.50, child $5.50— or pay adult $29, child $10 for a ticket that includes the train ride. To get to the mill under your own steam, take Highway 4 west through town and turn north on Beaver Creek Road.

Find out more about the origins of the famous West Coast Trail, see a collection of Nuu-chah-nulth artwork, or tinker with a variety of operating motorized machines from the forestry industry at the **Alberni Valley Museum** (corner of 10th Ave. and Wallace St., 250/723-2181; Tues.–Sat. 10 A.M.–5 P.M.; donation).

MV *Lady Rose*

The *Lady Rose* (250/723-8313 or 800/663-7192, www.ladyrosemarine.com), a vintage Scottish coaster, has been serving the remote communities of Alberni Inlet and Barkley Sound since 1949 as a supply and passenger service. But because of the spectacular scenery along the route, the cruise is also one of the island's biggest tourist attractions. Depending on the time of year, orcas and gray whales, seals, sea lions, porpoises, river otters, bald eagles, and all sorts of seabirds join you on your trip through magnificent Barkley Sound. The vessel is also a great way to reach the remote fishing village of Bamfield and the only way to reach the Broken Group Islands (see the sidebar *Broken Group Islands*).

Year-round, the MV *Lady Rose* departs Alberni Harbour Quay Tuesdays, Thursdays, and Saturdays at 8 A.M., reaching Kildonan at 10 A.M. and Bamfield at 12:30 P.M., then departing Bamfield at 1:30 P.M. and docking back in Port Alberni at 5:30 P.M. In summer, sailings are also made to Bamfield on Sunday, with a special stop for kayakers in the Broken Group Islands. If you want to stay longer in Bamfield, accommodations are available (see *Bamfield* section following). June–September an extra route is added to the schedule, with the vessel departing Mondays, Wednesdays, and Fridays at 8 A.M. for the Broken Group Islands, arriving at Ucluelet at 1 P.M. for a 90-minute layover before returning to Port Alberni around 7 P.M. One-way fares from Port Alberni are Kildonan $20, Bamfield $29, Broken Group Islands (Sechart) $29, Ucluelet $32. Children under 16 travel for half-price. In summer the *Lady Rose* does a roaring business—book as far ahead as possible.

Fishing

Along with at least one other Vancouver Island town, Port Alberni claims to be the "Salmon Capital of the World." The fishing in Alberni Inlet is certainly world-class, but probably no better than a handful of other places on the island. The main salmon runs occur in fall, when hundreds of thousands of salmon migrate up Alberni Inlet to their spawning grounds.

To get the rundown on fishing charters, head down to the full-service **Port Alberni Marina** (5104 River Rd., 250/723-8022; daily in summer dawn to dusk, winter 9 A.M.–5 P.M.). The owners, local fishing guides, have put together all kinds of printed information on local fishing. They know all of the best spots and how to catch the lunkers. Expect to pay $350 for two people, $380 for three for a six-hour guided morning charter; $220 for two, $250 for three for a four-hour guided afternoon charter.

Accommodations and Camping

Within walking distance of the quay is **Bluebird Motel** (3755 3rd Ave., 250/723-1153 or 888/591-3888), which charges $69 s, $79 d for reliable but unsurprising rooms. Right downtown, each of the large guest rooms at the **Hospitality Inn** (3835 Redford St., 250/723-8111 or 877/723-8111, www.hospitality innportalberni.com; $130 s, $135 d) is air-conditioned and features a comfortable bed and a writing desk. Amenities include a heated outdoor pool, a fitness room, and a restaurant.

The best camping is out of town, at **Underwood Cove Marina** (250/723-9812) right on Alberni Inlet. Choose between open and wooded full-facility sites ($16–28 per site) in a relatively remote setting with sweeping views of the inlet from a sandy log-strewn beach. To get there take 3rd Avenue south to Ship Creek Road, and follow that for 14 kilometers (8.7 miles). **Stamp River Provincial Park,** northwest of Port Alberni, enjoys a beautiful location on the river of the same name; $17 per site. To get there follow Highway 4 west, and immediately after crossing Kitsuksus Creek, take Beaver Creek Road north for 14 kilometers (8.7 miles).

Food

At any time of day, the best place to find something to eat is down at Alberni Harbour Quay, where you'll find several small cafés with outdoor seating. While researching this edition I headed for **McMuggin's** (5440 Argyle St., 250/723-1166), where huge sandwiches (around $6) are made to order on bread baked daily on the premises—and when my wife tried my accompanying milkshake ($3.50), she wished she had ordered one too. At the entrance to the quay is **Blue Door Cafe** (5415 Argyle St., 250/723-8811; daily from 6 A.M.), a small old-style place that's a real locals' hangout. Breakfasts are huge; an omelet with all the trimmings goes for $6–7.50, and bottomless self-serve coffee is an extra buck. The clam chowder ($5.50) is also good. Through downtown to the west, the **Westwind Pub** (4940 Cherry Creek Rd., 250/724-1324) is a nautical-themed bar with a good selection of reasonably priced meals.

Information

On the rise above town to the east is **Port Alberni Visitor Centre** (2533 Redford St., 250/724-6535 or 866/576-3662; summer daily

VANCOUVER ISLAND

8 A.M.–6 P.M., the rest of the year Mon.–Fri. 9 A.M.–5 P.M.). This excellent facility is a great source of information on Pacific Rim National Park, transportation options to Bamfield, and all west coast attractions. The best source of pretrip planning is the Alberni Valley Chamber of Commerce website (www.avcoc.com).

BAMFIELD

One of the island's most remote communities, this tiny fishing village lies along both sides of a narrow inlet on Barkley Sound. Most people arrive here aboard the **MV Lady Rose** from Port Alberni (see previous section), but the town is also linked to Port Alberni by a rough 100-kilometer (62-mile) logging road. It's well worth the trip out to go fishing, explore the seashore, or just soak up the atmosphere of this picturesque boardwalk village. Bamfield is also the northern terminus of the **West Coast Trail** (see the *West Coast Trail* section earlier this chapter).

Practicalities

On the boardwalk, but across the channel from the road side of the village, **Bamfield Lodge** (250/728-3419, www.bamfieldlodge.com) comprises self-contained cabins set among trees and overlooking the water. The cabins are $110 per night, which includes boat transfers from across the channel. The lodge owners also operate a restaurant and a charter boat for fishing and wilderness trips.

WEST FROM PORT ALBERNI

Highway 4 west from Port Alberni meanders through unspoiled mountain wilderness, and you won't find a gas station or store for at least a couple of hours. The highway skirts the north shore of large Sproat Lake, whose clear waters draw keen trout and salmon anglers. Along the highway, camping at **Sproat Lake Provincial Park** is $17 per night. Provided they're not out squelching a fire, you can also see the world's largest water bombers—Martin Mars Flying Tankers—tied up here. Originally designed as troop carriers for World War II, only five were ever built and only two remain, both here at Sproat Lake. Used to fight wildfires, these massive flying beasts—36 meters (118 feet) long and with a wingspan of more than 60 meters (200 feet)—skim across the lake, each filling its tank with 27 tons of water.

Highway 4 splits at a point 91 kilometers (56.5 miles) from Port Alberni, leading 8 kilometers (5 miles) south to Ucluelet or 34 kilometers (21 miles) north through Pacific Rim National Park to Tofino.

UCLUELET

A small town of 1,800 on the northern edge of Barkley Sound, Ucluelet (pronounced yoo-CLOO-let) has a wonderfully scenic location between the ocean and a protected bay. Like nearby Tofino, the remote town grew as a logging and fishing center, but unlike with its neighbor, tourism has been slower to catch on. You can enjoy all of the same pursuits as in Tofino—beachcombing, whale-watching, kayaking, and fishing—but in a more low-key manner.

The Nuu-chah-nulth people lived around the bay where Ucluelet now sits for centuries before the arrival of Europeans (in their language, the town's name means "people with a safe landing place"). During the last century or so, Ucluelet has also been a fur sealers' trading post and a logging and sawmill center, but fishing remains the steady mainstay, as evidenced by the town's resident fishing fleet and several fish-processing plants.

Sights and Recreation

Drive through town to reach **He-tin-kis Park,** where a short trail leads through a littoral (coastal) rainforest to a small stretch of rocky beach. The park and beach are part of the **Wild Pacific Trail,** an ambitious project that will eventually wander along the coastline all the way to Pacific Rim National Park. You can take the trail or continue southward by vehicle to reach the end of the road. The lighthouse here is not the world's most photogenic, but it gets the job done—keeping ships from running ashore along this stretch of particularly treacherous coastline.

Many visitors who choose to stay in Ucluelet

do so for the fishing, particularly for chinook salmon (Feb.–Sept.) and halibut (May–July). The fall runs of chinook can yield fish up to 20 kilograms (44 pounds), and the town's busy charter fleet offers deep-sea fishing excursions as well as whale-watching trips.

Accommodations and Camping

If you're looking at sharing inexpensive accommodations with an outdoorsy crowd, reserve a bed at **Surfs Inn** (1874 Peninsula Rd., 250/726-4426, www.surfsinn.ca), contained within a restored home along the main road into town. Communal facilities include a lounge with wood-burning fireplace, a modern kitchen, and plenty of space to store bikes and surfboards. Guest room options are dorm beds

($27 pp), one double bed ($65), an en suite with water views ($125), or a self-contained cabin ($250).

Terrace Beach Resort (1002 Peninsula Rd., 250/726-2901 or 866/726-2901, www .terracebeachresort.ca) is the first in what will surely be a wave of Tofino-style accommodations in Ucluelet. The weathered "eco-industrial" exterior is a little deceiving, as the guest rooms feature West Coast contemporary styling throughout livable units that range from one-bedroom motel rooms to multistory oceanfront cabins, linked by elevated boardwalks and all enclosed in an old-growth forest. Rates for the smallest start at $99 s or d, but if it's off-season, consider upgrading to one of the cabins for $199 s or d ($349 in summer). Don't be

VANCOUVER ISLAND

THE BROKEN GROUP ISLANDS

These 100 or so forested islands in the mouth of Barkley Sound, south of Ucluelet, once held native villages and some of the first trading posts on the coast. Now they're inhabited only by wildlife and visited primarily by campers paddling through the archipelago in canoes and kayaks. The islands offer few beaches, so paddlers come ashore in the many sheltered bays.

Marinelife abounds in the cool and clear waters: Seals, porpoises, and gray whales are present year-round. Birdlife is also prolific: Bald eagles, blue herons, and cormorants are permanent residents, and large numbers of loons and Canada geese stop by on their spring and fall migration routes.

The archipelago extends almost 15 kilometers (9.3 miles) out to sea from Sechart, the starting point for kayakers. The protected islands of **Hand, Gibraltar, Dodo,** and **Willis** all hold campsites and are good destinations for novice paddlers. Farther out, the varying sea conditions make a higher level of skill necessary. Predictably, a westerly wind blows up early each afternoon through summer, making paddling more difficult.

The best way to reach the Broken Group Islands is aboard the **MV Lady Rose** (250/723-8313 or 800/663-7192, www.ladyrosemarine

.com) from Port Alberni or Ucluelet. Based in Port Alberni, this historic vessel departs Alberni Harbour Quay June–September, Monday, Wednesday, and Friday at 8 A.M., dropping kayakers at **Sechart,** the site of a whaling station and now home to **Sechart Lodge** (book in conjunction with the tour boat; $125 s, $190 d including meals). Originally an office building for a local forestry company, the lodge was barged to the site and converted to basic but comfortable guest rooms and a restaurant. The *Lady Rose* then continues to Ucluelet, departing that village at 2 P.M. and making another stop at Sechart before returning to Port Alberni. In July and August, an additional Sunday sailing departs Port Alberni at 8 A.M., stopping at Sechart and returning directly to Port Alberni. The one-way fare between Port Alberni and Sechart is $29; between Ucluelet and Sechart it's $20.

The company that operates the boat also rents kayaks ($35–50 per day), which are left at Sechart so you don't have to pay a transportation charge. If you bring your own kayak, the transportation charge is $15-20 each way. The trip out on this boat is worthwhile just for the scenery, with the Ucluelet sailing passing right through the heart of the archipelago.

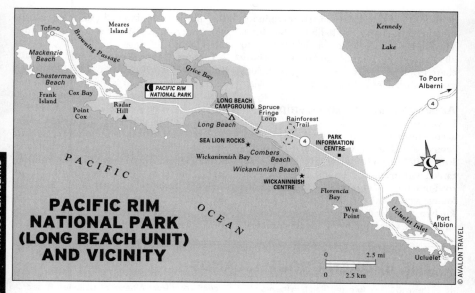

PACIFIC RIM NATIONAL PARK (LONG BEACH UNIT) AND VICINITY

surprised to see actor Jason Priestly wandering through the forest—he and his family own the lodge.

At unique **Canadian Princess Resort** (1943 Peninsula Rd., 250/598-3366 or 800/663-7090, www.obmg.com, from $105 s or d), you can spend the night aboard the 75-meter (240-foot) steamship *Canadian Princess,* which is permanently anchored in Ucluelet Harbour. The least expensive rooms aboard this historic gem are small and share bathroom facilities, but they're still a decent value. The resort also offers modern, more expensive onshore rooms and has a large fleet of boats for fishing charters. Most people staying here do so on a multinight fishing package, costing from $359 per person for two nights.

Island West Resort (160 Hemlock St., 250/726-7515, www.islandwestresort.com) has its own marina right on the inlet and serves as the base of operations for a wide range of charter boats. The resort also has a good restaurant and pub. In the height of summer, rooms—each with full kitchen—run from a reasonable $108 s or d. Campers should backtrack to **Ucluelet Campground,** along the way into

town (260 Seaplane Base Rd., 250/726-4355, www.ucluecampground.com; March–Oct.; $29–38 per site).

Food

Get your morning caffeine fix along with a chocolate-cluster muffin at **Cynamoka Coffee House** (1536 Peninsula Rd., 250/726-3407; daily 7 A.M.–6 P.M.). It's through town, up a steep driveway to the right. Anglers head to the pub or restaurant at **Island West Resort** (250/726-7515). Locals congregate at **Smiley's** (1922 Peninsula Rd., 250/726-4213) for breakfast, lunch, and dinner and for its bowling lanes. If you're camping or have access to a barbecue, stop at **Oyster Jim's** (2480 Pacific Rim Hwy., 250/726-7350) to pick up fresh oysters that open naturally over hot coals.

◖ PACIFIC RIM NATIONAL PARK

Named for its location on the edge of the Pacific Ocean, this park encompasses a long, narrow strip of coast that has been battered by the sea for eons. The park comprises three units, each different in nature and accessed in different ways. The section at the end of Highway 4 is the **Long Beach Unit,** named for an 11-kilometer (6.8-mile) stretch of beach that dominates the landscape. Accessible by vehicle, this is the most popular part of the park and is particularly busy in July and August. To the south, in Barkley Sound, the **Broken Group Islands Unit** (see the sidebar) encompasses an archipelago of 100 islands, accessible by the MV *Lady Rose* from Port Alberni. Farther south still is the **West Coast Trail Unit,** named for the famous 77-kilometer (48-mile) hiking trail between Port Renfrew and Bamfield (see the *West Coast Trail* section earlier in this chapter).

Flora and Fauna

Like the entire west coast of Vancouver Island, Pacific Rim National Park is dominated by littoral rainforest. Closest to the ocean, clinging to the rocky shore, a narrow windswept strip of Sitka spruce is covered by salty water year-round. These forests of spruce are compact and low-growing, forming a natural windbreak for the old-growth forests of western hemlock and western red cedar farther inland. The old-growth forests are strewn with fallen trees and lushly carpeted with mosses, shrubs, and ferns.

The park's largest land mammal is the black bear, some of which occasionally wander down to the beach in search of food. Also present are blacktail deer, raccoons, otters, and mink. Bald eagles are year-round residents, but the migratory birds arrive in the largest numbers—in spring and fall, thousands of Canada geese, pintails, mallards, and black brants converge on the vast tidal mudflats of **Grice Bay,** in the north of the park beyond the golf course.

Long Beach

Ensconced between rocky headlands is more than 11 kilometers (6.8 miles) of hard-packed white sand, covered in twisted driftwood, shells, and the occasional Japanese glass fishing float. Dense rainforest and the high snowcapped peaks of the Mackenzie Range form a beautiful backdrop, while offshore lie craggy surf-battered isles home to myriad marinelife. You

can access the beach at many places, but first stop at the renovated **Wickaninnish Interpretive Centre** (250/726-4212; mid-March–mid-June daily 10:30 A.M.–6 P.M., mid-June–Aug. 8 A.M.–8 P.M., Sept.–mid-Oct. 10 A.M.–6 P.M.), which overlooks the entire beach from a protected southern cove. This is the place to learn about the natural and human history of both the park and the ocean through exhibits and spectacular hand-painted murals.

Camping

The park's campground fills up *very* fast every day through summer, because it's in a marvelous location behind **Green Point,** a beautiful bluff above the beach. Facilities include drive-in sites, washrooms, picnic tables, an evening interpretive program, and plenty of firewood, but no showers or hookups. Mid-March to mid-October, walk-in sites are $16.80 per night and all other sites are $22.75. Some sites can be reserved through the Parks Canada Campground Reservation Service (877/737-3783, www .pccamping.ca) for a small additional fee. The closest commercial campgrounds are in Ucluelet and Tofino.

one of the many wild west coast beaches

VANCOUVER ISLAND

Information and Services

The **Park Information Centre** is in the ocean-front **Wickaninnish Centre** (250/726-4212; mid-Mar.–mid-June daily 10:30 A.M.–6 P.M., mid-June–Aug. 8 A.M.–8 P.M., Sept.–mid-Oct. 10 A.M.–6 P.M.).

There are no stores or gas stations in the park, but supplies and gas are available in Ucluelet and Tofino. The **Wickaninnish Restaurant** (250/726-7706; mid-March–mid-Oct. daily 10:30 A.M.–6 P.M.), in the Wickaninnish Interpretive Centre, overlooks the wide sweeping bay for which it's named. It's not particularly cheap (lunch entrées $12–21), but the views are magnificent, and even if you don't indulge in a full meal, it's a great place to sip coffee while watching the ocean. Sunday brunch is particularly popular.

Park Fee

You're not charged a fee just to travel straight through the park to Tofino, but if you stop anywhere en route, a strictly enforced charge applies. A one-day permit is adult $6.90, senior $5.90, child $3.45.

Tofino

The bustling fishing village of Tofino sits at the end of a long narrow peninsula, with the only road access to the outside world being winding Highway 4. The closest town of any size is Port Alberni, 130 kilometers (81 miles) to the east (allow at least 2.5 hours); Victoria is 340 kilometers (211 miles) distant.

Fishing has always been the mainstay of the local economy, but Tofino is one of the fastest growing tourism hotspots in the province. In winter it's a quiet, friendly community with a population of fewer than 1,900. In summer the population swells to several times that size and the village springs to life: fishing boats pick up supplies and deposit salmon, cod, prawns, crabs, halibut, and other delicacies of the sea, and cruising, whale-watching, and fishing boats, along with seaplanes, do a roaring business introducing visitors to the natural wonders of the west coast.

The town lies on the southern edge of sheltered **Clayoquot Sound,** known worldwide for an ongoing fight by environmentalists to save the world's largest remaining coastal temperate forest. Around 200,000 hectares (494,000 acres) of this old-growth forest remain; several parks, including **Clayoquot Arm Provincial Park, Clayoquot Plateau Provincial Park, Hesquiat Peninsula Provincial Park, Flores Island Provincial Park,** and **Maquinna Marine Provincial Park** have resulted from the Clayoquot Sound Land Use Decision. An influx of environmentally conscious residents over the last two decades has added flavor to one of the West Coast's most picturesque and relaxing towns, and because many aware residents like Tofino exactly the way it is, it's unlikely that highrise hotels or fast-food chains will ever spoil this peaceful coastal paradise.

SIGHTS AND RECREATION

Tofino is best known for whale-watching, kayaking, and the long sandy beaches south of town, but a couple of interesting diversions are well worth a stop.

Sights

Eagle Aerie Gallery (350 Campbell St., 250/725-3235; summer daily 9 A.M.–9 P.M., the rest of the year daily 9:30 A.M.–5:30 P.M.) features the eye-catching paintings, prints, and sculptures of Roy Henry Vickers, a well-known and highly respected Tsimshian artist. You can watch a video about the artist and then browse among the artworks, primarily native Canadian designs and outdoor scenes with clean lines and brilliant colors. If you fall for one of the most popular paintings but can't afford it, you can buy it in card or poster form. The gallery is built on the theme of a West Coast

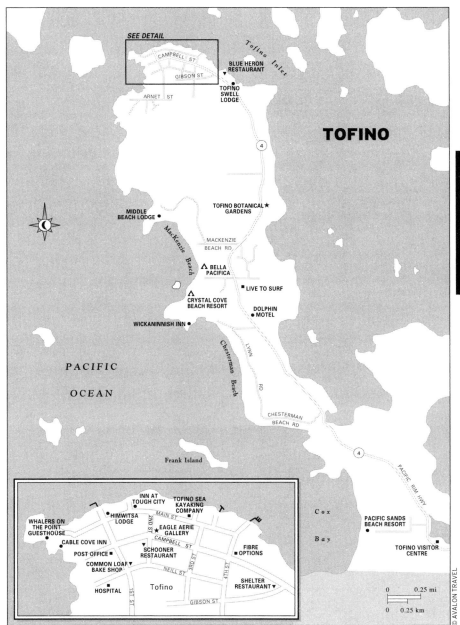

VANCOUVER ISLAND

TOFINO

SEE DETAIL

Tofino Inlet

CAMPBELL ST

GIBSON ST

BLUE HERON
RESTAURANT

TOFINO SWELL
LODGE

ARNET ST

4

TOFINO BOTANICAL ★
GARDENS

MIDDLE
BEACH LODGE ●

MacKenzie Beach

MACKENZIE
BEACH RD

⋀ BELLA
PACIFICA

■ LIVE TO SURF

⋀ CRYSTAL COVE
BEACH RESORT

DOLPHIN
● MOTEL

WICKANINNISH INN ●

Chesterman Beach

LYNN
RD

PACIFIC

OCEAN

CHESTERMAN
BEACH RD

4

PACIFIC RIM HWY

Frank Island

INN AT
TOUGH CITY

TOFINO SEA
KAYAKING
COMPANY

MAIN ST

HIMWITSA
LODGE

2ND ST

WHALERS ON
THE POINT
GUESTHOUSE

EAGLE AERIE ★
GALLERY

CABLE COVE INN

CAMPBELL ST

3RD ST

FIBRE
■ OPTIONS

POST OFFICE ■

SCHOONER
RESTAURANT ▼

COMMON LOAF ▼
BAKE SHOP

NEILL ST

4TH ST

■ HOSPITAL

Tofino

SHELTER
RESTAURANT ▼

1ST ST

GIBSON ST

C o x

B a y

PACIFIC SANDS
BEACH RESORT

TOFINO VISITOR
CENTRE

0   0.25 mi

0   0.25 km

© AVALON TRAVEL

© ANDREW HEMPSTEAD

Chesterman Beach

native longhouse, with a carved and painted exterior and interior totem poles.

Developed by knowledgeable locals, **Tofino Botanical Gardens** (1084 Pacific Rim Hwy., 250/725-1220; daily 9 A.M.–dusk; adult $10, child under 13 free), just before town, showcases local flora with the emphasis on a fun, educational experience. One garden is devoted to native species you would find in the adjacent national park and another to plants you can eat (but aren't allowed to). This is the only botanical garden I've visited where a colorfully painted camper van from the 1970s is incorporated into a display. Another botanical point of interest is the massive cedar tree on the right-hand side of the road as you enter town. Estimated to be more than 800 years old, the tree is kept from toppling over by wire stays.

Sun, Sand, and Surf

If you fancy a long walk along a fabulous shell-strewn stretch of white sand, like to sit on craggy rocks watching the waves disintegrate into white spray, or just want a piece of sun all your own to lie in and work on your tan, head for **Chesterman Beach,** just south of Tofino. From that beach, at low tide you can walk all the way out to **Frank Island** to watch the surf pound the exposed side while the tide creeps in and cuts you off from civilization for a few hours. The turnoff (not marked) to Chesterman Beach is Lynn Road, on the right just past the Dolphin Motel as you leave Tofino. Follow the road and park at one of three small parking lots; the parking lot at the corner of Lynn and Chesterman Beach Roads is closest to Frank Island.

Surfers wanting to hit the water should head south of town to **Live to Surf** (1180 Pacific Rim Hwy., 250/725-4464, www.livetosurf .com). The shop rents surfboards for $25 per day and wetsuits for $20, and offers lessons for $55 per person. The staff will also tell you where the best surf can be found, and if there's no surf, they'll tell you how good it was last week. Check their website for west coast surf reports. **Surf Sister** (625 Campbell St., 250/725-4456 or 877/724-7873) is Canada's only all-women surf school.

Whale-Watching

Each spring around 20,000 Pacific gray whales migrate between Baja and Alaska, passing through the waters off Tofino between March and May. Most of them continue north, but some stay in local waters through summer. Their feeding grounds are north of Tofino within **Maquinna Marine Park.** During the spring migration and some feeding periods, gray whales are also frequently sighted in the calm inland waters around **Meares Island,** just off Tofino.

Whale-watching is one of the most popular activities in town, and companies search out whales to watch them cruise up the coast, diving, surfacing, and spouting. On the whale-watching trips, you'll likely spy other marinelife as well; look for sea lions and puffins sunning themselves on offshore rocks, dolphins and harbor seals frolicking in the bays and inlets, and majestic bald eagles gracefully swooping around in the sky or perching in the treetops. Trips depart mid-February to October and generally last 2–3 hours. Expect to pay about $100 per person. (See the following *Local Charter Operators* section for contact numbers.)

Hot Springs

Pamper yourself and take a boat or floatplane to **Hotsprings Cove,** Vancouver Island's only hot spring. Water bubbles out of the ground at a temperature of 87°C (189°F), tumbles over a cliff, and then drops down through a series of pools—each large enough for two or three people—and into the sea. Lobsterize yourself silly in the first pool, or go for the ultimate in hot/cold torture by immersing yourself in the last pool, where at high tide you'll be slapped by breathtakingly refreshing ocean waves.

Several companies offer excursions out to the hot springs (see next section for contact numbers), and although prices vary slightly, expect to pay around $80–90 for a six- to seven-hour trip departing around 10 A.M., with about three hours ashore at the hot springs and the chance to see whales en route. **Tofino Air,** based at the 1st Street dock (250/725-4454), offers a scenic 15-minute flight to the hot springs by floatplane; $140 per person round-trip, minimum three persons.

Local Charter Operators

The streets of downtown Tofino hold a profusion of charter operators offering a wide variety of trips. All those listed here go whale-watching and head out to Hotsprings Cove. Other options include a tour of Meares Island and fishing charters. For details, head to any of the following: **Adventures Pacific** (120 4th St., 250/725-2811 or 888/486-3466), **Jamie's** (606 Campbell St., 250/725-3919 or 800/667-9913), **Remote Passages** (71 Wharf St., 250/725-3330 or 800/666-9833), **Sea Trek** (445 Campbell St., 250/725-4412 or 800/811-9155), **Seaside Adventures** (300 Main St., 250/725-2292 or 888/332-4252), or the **Whale Centre** (411 Campbell St., 250/725-2132 or 888/474-2288), where a gray whale skeleton is on display. Even with all of these operators, business is brisk, so book ahead if possible.

Sea Kayaking

Exploring the waters around Tofino by sea kayak has become increasingly popular in recent years. **Tofino Sea Kayaking Company** (320 Main St., 250/725-4222, www.tofino -kayaking.com) has designed tours to meet the demand and suit all levels of experience. Excursions range from a 2.5-hour harbor paddle ($54 per person) to a four-day trip to a remote lodge on Vargas Island ($780 per person). The company's experienced staff will also help adventurous, independent paddlers plan an itinerary—many camping areas lie within a one-day paddle of Tofino. Single kayak rentals are $48 for one day or $40 per day for two or more days; double kayaks are $84 and $74, respectively. Rental prices include all accessories. At the company base, right on the harbor, is a shop selling provisions, accessories (such as marine charts), and a wide range of local literature. Also here are a coffee shop, a bookstore, and a few rooms renting for $75 s, $85 d per room per night.

Pacific Rim Whale Festival

Tofino and Ucluelet join together each spring to put on the annual Pacific Rim Whale Festival (www.pacificrimwhalefestival.org), which features educational shows and special events in the adjacent national park, a native song and dance festival, a parade, crab races, plays at the local theater, dances, concerts, a golf tournament, and a multitude of events and activities in celebration of the gray whale spring migration. The festival takes place the last two weeks of March.

ACCOMMODATIONS AND CAMPING

Tofino boasts plenty of accommodations, both in town and south along the beach-fringed coastline, but getting a room or campsite in summer can be difficult if you just turn up, so book as far ahead as possible. Like elsewhere in the province, high season rates apply late June to early September. A month either side of this time and you'll enjoy big discounts when the weather is still warm enough to take advantage of Tofino's outdoor attractions. Winter in Tofino is known as the "storm-watching season," when rates are reduced up to 50 percent, although no one can guarantee the big storms.

Under $50

Tofino's least expensive accommodation is **Whalers on the Point Guesthouse** (81 West St., 250/725-3443, www.tofinohostel.com). Affiliated with Hostelling International, it is a world away from hostels of old, appealing to all travelers. The building is a stylish log structure, with a stunning waterfront location, of which the communal lounge area takes full advantage. Other facilities include a modern kitchen, a laundry room, a large deck with a barbecue, a game room, and bike rentals. Dorm beds are $27 for members ($29 for nonmembers). Private rooms with shared bathrooms cost $85 s or d ($90 for nonmembers).

$50-100

Of Tofino's regular motels, least expensive is the **Dolphin Motel**, on the road into town

(1190 Pacific Rim Hwy., 250/725-3377, www.dolphinmotel.ca; $95–139 s or d).

$100-150

Continuing into town beyond the Dolphin Motel, **Tofino Swell Lodge** (341 Olsen Rd., 250/725-3274, www.tofinoswell.com; $95 s, $110 d) is above a busy marina. This seven-room motel offers well-decorated rooms, shared use of a fully equipped kitchen and living room (complete with stereo, TV, and telescope), and pleasant gardens with incredible views of Tofino Inlet, tree-covered Meares Island, and distant snowcapped mountains.

Out of town to the south are several ocean-front resorts. Of these, ◖ **Middle Beach Lodge** (250/725-2900 or 866/725-2900, www.middlebeach.com) does the best job of combining a unique West Coast experience with reasonable prices. It comprises two distinct complexes: At the Beach, more intimate, with its own private beach, and the other, At the Headlands, with luxurious self-contained chalets built along the top of a rugged headland. A short trail links the two, and guests are welcome to wander between them. Outdoor settings are scattered throughout the property. Rates for At the Beach start at $140, ocean views and a balcony from $180, and all rates include a gourmet continental breakfast served in a magnificent common room. Rates for At the Headlands start at $165 rising to over $400 for a freestanding cabin. This part of the complex has a restaurant with a table d'hôte menu offered nightly.

$150-200

Overlooking the water right downtown is **The Inn at Tough City** (350 Main St., 250/725-2021, www.toughcity.com), a newer lodging constructed with materials sourced from throughout the region. The bricks, all 30,000 of them, were salvaged from a 100-year-old building in Vancouver's historic Gastown, while stained-glass windows, hardwood used in the flooring, and many of the furnishings are of historical value. The rooms are decorated in a stylish heritage color scheme, and

The Inn at Tough City

beds are covered in plush down duvets. Summer rates are $170–230 s or d, discounted as low as $100 in winter.

In the best location in town, right beside the main dock, is **Himwitsa Lodge** (300 Main St., 250/725-3319 or 800/899-1947, www.himwitsa .com). No expense has been spared in the four contemporary upstairs suites, each with hot tub, comfortable lounge and writing area, TV and videocassette player, fully equipped kitchen, and private balcony with spectacular ocean views. Summer rates are $180–250 s or d.

Over $200

Cable Cove Inn (201 Main St., 250/725-4236 or 800/663-6449, www.cablecoveinn .com; $210–305 s or d) has a Main Street address, but you'd never know it sitting on the private deck of your ocean-facing room. It's tucked away in a quiet location overlooking a small cove, yet it's only a two-minute walk from the center of town. Well furnished in a casual yet elegant style, each of the six rooms features a private deck and a fireplace. A continental breakfast is included in the rates, while spa services are extra.

You'll find cheaper places to stay in Tofino, but you won't find a lodge like **◖ Pacific Sands Beach Resort** (Cox Bay, 250/725-3322 or 800/565-2322, www.pacificsands .com), which is perfect for families and outdoorsy types who want to kick back for a few days. Set right on a popular surfing beach eight kilometers (five miles) south of town, guest units come in a variety of configurations, starting with one-bedroom, kitchen-equipped suites that rent from $235 per night in summer ($160 in winter). Some of these hold a prime beachfront location—ask when booking. The best units are the newest: two-level timber-frame villas equipped with everything from surfboard racks to stainless steel kitchen appliances ($475–505). The heated floors and gas fireplaces are a plus during the winter storm-watching season. Pacific Sands is a family-run operation, which translates to friendly service and repeat guests who have been visiting since childhood (and still bring their surfboards).

If you subscribe to one of those glossy travel mags, you've probably read about the ◖ **Wickaninnish Inn** (Osprey Lane, Chesterman Beach, 250/725-3100, www.wickinn.com; from $465 s or d), which is regarded as one of the world's great resorts—and regularly features at the top of Top Ten lists. Just for good measure, the in-house Pointe Restaurant is similarly lauded. Everything you've read is true: If you want to surrender to the lap of luxury in a wilderness setting, this is the place to do it. Designed to complement the rainforest setting, the exterior post-and-beam construction is big and bold, while the interior oozes West Coast elegance. Public areas such as the restaurant, an upscale lounge, a relaxing library, and a downstairs TV room (plasma, of course) make the resort feel like a world unto itself, but the guest rooms will really wow you. Spread throughout two wings, each of the 76 rooms overflows with amenities, including fireplaces, oversized soaker tubs, super-comfortable beds, and furniture made from recycled old-growth woods, but the ocean views through floor-to-ceiling windows will captivate you most. The menu of spa treatments is phenomenal—think hot stone massage for two in a hut overlooking the ocean, a full-body exfoliation, or a sacred sea hydrotherapy treatment. The Wickaninnish is a five-minute drive south of Tofino, but who cares? You won't want to leave.

Camping

All of Tofino's campgrounds are on the beaches south of town, but enjoying the great outdoors comes at a price in this part of the world, with some campsites costing more than $50 per night. Best of the bunch is **Bella Pacifica Campground** (250/725-3400, www.bella pacifica.com; mid-Feb.–mid-Nov.; $35–46), which is right on MacKenzie Beach and offers protected tent sites, full hookups, coin-operated showers, and a laundry room.

Along the same stretch of sand, **Crystal Cove Beach Resort** (250/725-4213, www .crystalcovebeachresort.com) is one of the province's finest campgrounds. Facilities are modern, with personal touches such as com-

plimentary coffee each morning and a book exchange. Many of the sites are in a private, heavily wooded area (unserviced $42, hook-ups $52).

FOOD

Tofino has grocery stores, fish and seafood stores, bakeries, and a variety of cafés and restaurants, many of them serving locally caught seafood. The **Common Loaf Bake Shop** (180 1st St., 250/725-3915; daily 8 A.M.–6 P.M.) is a longtime favorite with locals (delicious cinnamon rolls for $2.40); sit outside or upstairs, where you'll have a magnificent view down Tofino's main street and across the sound.

The **Schooner Restaurant** (331 Campbell St., 250/725-3444; daily 9 A.M.–3 P.M. and 5–10 P.M.) has been dishing up well-priced seafood for 50 years. Over time the menu has gotten more creative (soya-marinated salmon baked on a cedar plank), but old favorites (grilled halibut) still appear. Expect to pay $9–16 for starters and $22–34 for a main. Also of note is the service, which is remarkably good for a tourist town.

In Weigh West Marine Resort's **Blue Heron Restaurant** (634 Campbell St., 250/725-3277), you can savor delicious smoked salmon and clam chowder for $8, and seafood or steak dinners for $23–28. In the same complex is a pub with inexpensive meals and water views.

In an unassuming building near the entrance to town, the **Shelter Restaurant** (601 Campbell St., 250/725-3353; daily from 5:30 P.M.) brings some big-city pizzazz to tiny Tofino. Inside you'll find an open dining room with imaginative treats such as crab fritters ($14) and prosciutto-wrapped halibut ($32).

South of Tofino, the ◖ **Pointe Restaurant** (Wickaninnish Inn, Osprey Lane, Chesterman Beach, 250/725-3100; daily from 7:30 A.M.) is simply superb in every respect. It's built on a rocky headland, and you'll find the sweeping ocean views from anywhere within the circular dining room as good as those of any restaurant in Canada (ask for a window table when reserving). At breakfast, sparkling wine and orange juice encourages holiday spirit, or get serious by ordering eggs Benedict with smoked salmon ($16). The lunch and dinner menus highlight seafood and island produce. Lunch includes seafood chowder ($13) and a wild salmon BLT ($17). A good way to start dinner is with seared scallops ($13) or roasted oysters ($3.50 each), before moving on to the steamed halibut ($32) or smoked black cod ($36). Rounding out a world-class dining experience is the impeccable service and a wine list that's dominated by Pacific Northwest bottles.

INFORMATION AND SERVICES

Tofino Visitor Centre (250/725-3414, www .tofinobc.org; summer Sun.–Thurs. 10 A.M.– 4 P.M., Fri.–Sat. 10 A.M.–6 P.M.) is along the Pacific Rim Highway, eight kilometers (five miles) before town.

Within the waterfront Tofino Sea Kayaking Company base, **Wildside Booksellers** (320 Main St., 250/725-4222) stocks an excellent selection of natural history and recreation books.

The **post office,** a **laundry facility,** and

Tofino General Hospital (250/725-3212) are all on Campbell Street.

GETTING THERE AND AROUND

Tofino Bus (461 Main St., 250/725-2871 or 866/986-3466, www.tofinobus.com) runs one bus daily between Victoria and Tofino, making pickups at both Nanaimo ferry terminals. The fare from Victoria is $65. Three times daily, this company runs a bus between Tofino and Ucluelet ($10 each way), with stops made at lodges and hiking trails along the way.

Orca Airways (604/270-6722 or 888/359-6722, www.flyorcaair.com) flies from its base at Vancouver's South Terminal to Tofino year-round. Although it doesn't offer any scheduled flights, **Tofino Air,** based at the foot of 1st Street (250/725-4454), provides scenic floatplane flightseeing and charters.

Getting around town is easiest on foot. You can rent bikes from **Fiber Options** (corner of 4th and Campbell Streets, 250/725-2192) for $30 per day; blend in with the locals by adding a surfboard rack for $8.

Oceanside

Back on the east side of the island, the Inland Island Highway north of the Highway 4 junction bypasses Oceanside, a stretch of coast that has developed as a popular holiday area, with many beaches, resorts, and waterfront campgrounds.

PARKSVILLE

Unspoiled sand fringes the coastline between Parksville (pop. 11,000) and Qualicum Beach. Parksville Beach claims "the warmest water in the whole of Canada." When the tide goes out along this stretch of the coast, it leaves a strip of sand up to one kilometer (0.6 miles) wide exposed to the sun. When the water returns, voilà: sand-heated water.

Rathtrevor Beach Provincial Park, a 347-hectare (860-acre) chunk of coastline just south of the town center, features a fine two-

kilometer (1.2-mile) sandy beach, a wooded upland area, nature trails, and bird-watching action that's particularly good in early spring, when seabirds swoop in for an annual herring feast. The children will probably want to stop at **Riptide Lagoon** (1000 Resort Dr., 250/248-8290; daily 10 A.M.–9 P.M.), near the park entrance. This over-the-top mini-golf complex costs $7.50 per game for adult, $5 children.

Accommodations and Camping

Parksville's many accommodations have been developed for vacationing families—with weekly rentals of self-contained units within walking distance of the water. Overlooking Craig Bay on the southeast side of town, **Ocean Sands Resort** (1165 Resort Dr., 250/954-0662 or 877/733-5969, www.oceansandsresort.ca;

$199–299 s or d) is typical. Guests swim in the warm ocean water out front or in the heated pool, while children make the most of the playground. Most of the units enjoy sweeping ocean views and separate bedrooms. All have full kitchens and comfortable living areas. Rates start at $100 outside summer. Guest rooms at **Tigh-Na-Mara Seaside Spa Resort** (1155 Resort Dr., 250/248-2072 or 800/663-7373, www.tigh-na-mara.com; $180–339) are smaller but the resort itself has more facilities, including two adventure playgrounds, mountain bike rentals, a large swimming pool, two restaurants, and a large spa facility.

Right off Parksville's waterfront downtown strip is **Surfside RV Resort** (200 North Corfield St., 250/248-9713 or 866/642-2001, www.surfside.bc.ca), packed with families throughout summer. It has all of the usual facilities in a prime oceanfront locale (although no surf as the name may suggest). Sites range $45–58, with the more expensive ones lining the beachfront. At **Rathtrevor Beach Provincial Park,** south of downtown off Highway 19A (take Exit 46 from the south), campers choose the natural setting over modern facilities (no hookups). Walk-in tent sites are $14, pull-throughs $22.

Food

Step away from the beach scene at **Pacific Brimm** (123 Craig St., 250/248-3336; Mon.–Sat. 6 A.M.–10 P.M., Sun. 8 A.M.–9 P.M.), an inviting café that's halfway between relaxed and refined. In addition to all the usual coffee choices, you'll find a good selection of loose-leaf teas and delicious oversized cinnamon buns.

After soaking up the elegance of the Grotto Spa at Tigh-Na-Mara Seaside Spa Resort, plan on moving upstairs to the resort's **Treetop Tapas & Grill** (1155 Resort Dr., 250/248-2072), where you are encouraged to relax in your robe over a lunch of bite-size tapas. Visit the resort's other restaurant, the **Cedar Room** (daily 7 A.M.–9:30 P.M.), for classic Pacific Northwest cooking at reasonable prices (dinner mains all under $30).

Information

Traveling north from Nanaimo, take Exit 46 from Highway 19 and follow Highway 19A for just under one kilometer (0.06 mile) to reach **Parksville Visitor Centre** (Hwy. 19A, 250/248-3613, www.visitparksvillequalicum beach.com; July–Aug. daily 8 A.M.–8 P.M., the rest of the year Mon.–Sat. 9 A.M.–5 P.M.). Adjacent to the information center is the outdoor **Craig Heritage Park** (250/248-6966; mid-May to early Sept. daily 10 A.M.–4 P.M.; free), comprising historic buildings such as a post office and church.

QUALICUM BEACH AND VICINITY

This beach community (pop. 7,000) is generally quieter than Parksville, but it shares the same endless sands of Georgia Strait and attracts the same droves of beachgoers, sun worshippers, anglers, and golfers on summer vacation. You can stay on Highway 19 (bypassing Parksville) and take the Memorial Avenue exit to reach the heart of the town, but a more scenic option is to continue along the old coastal highway through Parksville. This route is lined with motels, resorts, and RV parks. The attractive downtown area, locally known as "the Village," is away from the beach area up Memorial Avenue.

Sights and Recreation

The beach is the main attraction. Park anywhere along its length and join the crowd walking, running, or biking along the promenade. At low tide, the beach comes alive with people in search of sand dollars.

Between Parksville and Qualicum Beach, **Milner Gardens and Woodland** (2179 Island Hwy. W., 250/752-6153; May–Aug. daily 10 A.M.–5 P.M., April and Sept. Thurs.–Sun. 10 A.M.–5 P.M.; adult $10, child $6) protects a historic oceanfront estate that includes a 24-hectare (60-acre) old-growth forest and over 500 species of rhododendrons. Afternoon tea is served in the main house daily, 1–4 P.M.

If you appreciate high-quality arts and crafts, detour off the main drag at this point and head

Crowds gather on the streets of Qualicum Beach for the Show & Shine each Father's Day.

for the **Old School House Arts Centre** (122 Fern Rd. W., 250/752-6133; Mon. noon– 4 P.M., Tues.–Sat. 10 A.M.–4:30 P.M., Sun. (summer only) noon–4 P.M.). The gallery occupies a beautifully restored 1912 building, while working artist studios below allow you a chance to see wood carving, printmaking, pottery, weaving, painting, and fabric art in progress. Don't miss a stop at the gallery shop, where all kinds of original handcrafted treasures are likely to lure a couple of dollars out of your wallet.

Through town to the west, take Bayswater Road inland a short way to reach the government-operated **Big Qualicum Hatchery** (215 Fisheries Rd., 250/757-8412), where a wooded trail leads to holding tanks and an artificial spawning channel.

The year's biggest event is the Father's Day (mid-June) **Show & Shine** (250/248-1015), which sees Qualicum's streets filled with antique and hot rod cars from throughout North America.

Horne Lake Caves

If you can drag yourself away from the beach, consider a half-day detour inland to one of Vancouver Island's most intriguing natural attractions, Horne Lake Caves, which are protected as a provincial park. To get there, continue along the old coastal highway for 11 kilometers (6.8 miles) beyond Qualicum Beach and turn off at the Horne Lake Store, following the road for 16 kilometers (10 miles) west to Horne Lake. Two caves are open for exploration without a guide. There's no charge for entering these caves, but you'll need a helmet and light source, which can be rented for $8. Several different guided tours of the more interesting caves are offered. The 90-minute Family Cavern Tour of Riverbend Cave includes a short walk as well as underground exploration and explanation (adult $20, child $17). All caves are open mid-June to September daily 10 A.M.– 4 P.M. A private contractor (250/757-8687, www .hornelake.com) runs the tours using qualified guides. The company also operates the campground ($17–22 per night), has canoes for rent, and organizes a variety of educational programs such as rock-climbing and guided nature walks.

Accommodations and Camping

Old Dutch Inn (2690 Island Hwy. W., 250/752-6914 or 800/661-0199, www.olddutch inn.com; $110–140 s or d) is across the road from the ocean and within walking distance of Qualicum Beach Golf Club. Amenities include an indoor pool, sauna and whirlpool, and a restaurant with lots of outdoor seating. The rooms could be nicer, but the location can't be beat.

Looking for a place to stay like no other you've ever experienced? Then make reservations at **Free Spirit Spheres** (420 Horne Lake Rd., 250/757-9445, www.freespirit spheres.com; $150 s or d). Accommodation consists of perfectly round, three-meter-wide (10-foot-wide) wooden spheres hanging from towering old-growth trees. Each comprises a small flat area, a shortish bed, windows, and a door that opens to a walkway connected to

VANCOUVER ISLAND

the ground. Bathrooms are shared and also at ground level.

Give the central campgrounds a miss and continue 16 kilometers (10 miles) northwest from Qualicum Beach to **Qualicum Bay Resort** (5970 Island Hwy. W., 250/757-2003 or 800/663-6899, www.resortbc.com). Separated from the water by a road, facilities at this family-oriented resort include a manmade swimming lake, a playground, a game room, an ice cream stand, and a restaurant. Tent sites are $15, hookups $26–30, camping cabins (no linen, shared bathrooms) $35, and basic motel rooms $85–140 s or d.

Food

Lefty's (710 Memorial Ave., 250/752-7530; Sun.–Thurs. 8 A.M.–8 P.M., Fri.–Sat. 8 A.M.–9 P.M.) is a contemporary, bistro-style restaurant where the menu is filled with dishes made from fresh, locally sourced ingredients. At lunch, enjoy a mandarin and chicken wrap for $8, while at dinner, mains such as mango-ginger-glazed salmon are mostly under $20. Adding to the appeal is friendly service and a row of outdoor tables.

One of the few remaining houses set right on the waterfront has been converted to the ◖ **Beach House Café** (2775 Island Hwy. W., 250/752-9626; daily 11 A.M.–2 P.M. and 5–9:30 P.M.). Plan to eat outside on the glassed-in patio and order grilled salmon cakes ($12), spicy goulash ($18.50), or curried shrimp ($18).

Information

For the complete rundown on this stretch of the coast, stop in at **Qualicum Beach Visitor Centre** (corner Hwys. 19A and 4, 250/752-9532 or 866/887-7106, www.qualicum .bc.ca), on the promenade as you enter town from the southeast.

OFFSHORE ISLANDS
Denman Island
Buckley Bay, 35 kilometers (22 miles) northwest of Qualicum Beach, is the departure point for ferries across Bayne Sound to

Denman Island. Like all ferries through the Strait of Georgia, they are operated by **BC Ferries** (250/335-0323) and require no reservations. The service runs hourly 7 A.M.–11 P.M. and costs adult $6.05, child $3.05, vehicle $14.50. Ten minutes after leaving Buckley Bay you'll be driving off the ferry and onto this rural oasis, similar to the Southern Gulf Islands in appearance, sans the crowds. Fishing, hiking, biking, bird-watching, and scuba diving are prime draws here, and you'll also find good beaches, parks, and an artisan community along narrow winding roads.

Within walking distance of the ferry is Denman Village, boasting several early-20th-century heritage buildings. Across the island, 23-hectare (57-acre) **Fillongley Provincial Park** features forested trails, long stretches of beach, and 10 campsites for $17. At **Boyle Point Provincial Park** in the south, an 800-meter (0.5-mile) loop trail (15 minutes round-trip) leads to a lookout with views across to Chrome Island, where a lighthouse stands.

Hornby Island

This small, seldom-visited island has great beaches, especially along crescent-shaped Tribune Bay, where the longest stretch of sand is protected by 95-hectare (235-acre) **Tribune Bay Provincial Park.** Continue beyond that park and take St. John's Point Road to 287-hectare (710-acre) **Helliwell Provincial Park,** on a rugged, forested headland where trails lead through an old-growth forest of Douglas fir and western red cedar to high bluffs. Allow 90 minutes for the full five-kilometer (3.1-mile) loop.

Neither of the island's provincial parks have campgrounds. Instead, stay at the beautifully located **Tribune Bay Campsite** (250/335-2359, www.tribunebay.com; June–mid-Sept.), where tent camping is $32 and powered sites are $38. Amenities include coin-operated showers and a playground, and the facility is within walking distance of a general store and bike rental shop. Right by the ferry dock, **Hornby Island Resort** (4305 Shingle Spit Rd., 250/335-0136) offers boat rentals, tennis courts, a restaurant and pub, and a laundry room. The motel rooms

($110) have water views but need renovating, the cabins (July–Aug. $950 per week, the rest of the year $125 per night) are perfect for families who need to spread out, and a limited number of RV sites ($32 per night) are off to one side.

Every hour, 8 A.M.–6 P.M., a small ferry departs the southern end of Denman Island for Hornby Island, a short, 10-minute run across Lambert Channel. The fares are the same as the Buckley Bay–Denman Island run.

Comox Valley

The three communities of **Courtenay, Cumberland,** and **Comox** lie in the beautiful Comox Valley, nestled between Georgia Strait and high snowcapped mountains to the west. The valley lies almost halfway up the island, 220 kilometers (137 miles) from Victoria, but direct flights to the mainland have created a mini-boom in recent years, especially since Westjet started offering inexpensive flights between Calgary (Alberta) and Comox. The three towns merge into one, but each has its own personality: Courtenay, the staid town with a compact downtown core and all the visitor services you need; Cumberland, away from the water but historically charming nonetheless; and Comox, a sprawl of retiree housing developments and golf courses that extends across a wide peninsula to the ocean.

COURTENAY

The valley's largest town and a commercial center for local farming, logging, fishing, and retirement communities, Courtenay (pop. 22,000) extends around the head of Comox Harbour. It's not particularly scenic but has a few interesting sights and plenty of highway accommodations. It was named for Captain George Courtenay, who led the original surveying expedition of the area in 1848.

Sights

As you enter Courtenay from the south, you pass all sorts of restaurants, the information center, and motel after motel. Continue into the heart of town and you come to the pleasing downtown area with its cobbled streets, old-fashioned lamps, brick planters full of flowers, and numerous shops. The main attraction

downtown is **Courtenay and District Museum** (207 4th St., 250/334-0686; May–Aug. Mon.–Sat. 10 A.M.–5 P.M., Sun. noon–4 P.M., the rest of the year Tues.–Sat. 10 A.M.–4:30 P.M.; donation). The highlight is a full-size replica of an *elasmosaur.* The original—12 meters (39 feet) long and 80 million years old—was found at the nearby Puntledge River. Daily in July and August and Saturday only April–June and September, the museum leads tours out to the site, on which you have the chance to dig for your very own fossil (adult $25, senior $20, child $15). Other museum exhibits include a series of realistic dioramas and a replica of a bighouse containing many native artifacts and items, some formerly belonging to prominent

FORBIDDEN PLATEAU

This high plateau west of the Comox Valley was "forbidden" according to ancient legend. The village of Comox was threatened by Cowichan warriors many moons ago, so the Comox men sent the women and children up the mountain to be out of harm's way. When the danger was over, the men went up to collect their families, but they had disappeared without a trace – and were never seen again. Not knowing how or why the party disappeared off the face of the planet, the plateau became for the Comox a fearful and forbidden place. But judging by the number of hikers who explore Forbidden Plateau and return to tell the tale, the legend has been put to rest.

chiefs. Finish up in the gift shop, which is well stocked with local arts and crafts.

From downtown, cross the bridge to the totem pole–flanked entrance to **Lewis Park,** at the confluence of the Puntledge and Tsolum Rivers. The two rivers join here to form the very short Courtenay River.

Mt. Washington Alpine Resort

To outsiders, Vancouver Island is not usually associated with snow sports, but locals know they don't need to leave their island home to enjoy world-class skiing and boarding at Mt. Washington Alpine Resort (250/338-1386 or 888/231-1499, mountwashington.ca), 35 kilometers (22 miles) northwest of Courtenay. The scope and popularity of the resort is remarkable—it ranks fourth in British Columbia for the number of skier days and has a modern base village with more than 3,500 beds—but not surprising, considering it receives an annual snowfall of nine meters (30 feet) and temperatures that remain relatively warm compared to the interior of British Columbia. Seven chairlifts serve 370 hectares (915 acres), with the vertical rise a respectable 500 meters (1,640 feet) and the longest run just under two kilometers (1.2 miles). Other facilities include a terrain park and a half-pipe. Lift tickets are adult $58, senior $43, and child $32.

Between July and mid-October, the resort welcomes outdoor enthusiasts who come to hike through alpine meadows, ride the chairlift (adult $15, senior $12, child $10), mountain bike down the slopes, or go trail riding through the forest. A wealth of other activities are on offer—from mini-golf to a bungee trampoline—making it a good place to escape the beachy crowd for a day or two. Inexpensive summer packages (see the website) encourage overnight stays.

Kayaking

Comox Valley Kayaks (2020 Cliffe Ave., 250/334-2628 or 888/545-5595) offers a sunset paddle for $48, three-hour sea-kayaking lessons for $55 per person, and full-day guided trips from $95. Or rent a kayak for some exploration by yourself, around the local waterways or out on nearby Denman and Hornby Islands; $35–65 for 24 hours. The company also rents canoes—great for nearby Comox Lake—for $38 per day.

Accommodations and Camping

The valley's least expensive motels are strung out along the highway (Cliffe Ave.) as you enter Courtenay from the south. The 67-room **Anco Motel** (1885 Cliffe Ave., 250/334-2451, www.ancomotelbc.com; $65 s, $75 d) is typical, with an outdoor pool and high-speed Internet access as a bonus.

Overlooking Gartley Bay south of Courtenay is **Kingfisher Oceanside Resort** (4330 Island Hwy. S., 250/338-1323 or 800/663-7929, www.kingfisherspa.com), set around well-manicured gardens and a large heated pool right on the water. The resort also holds a spa facility, yoga lounge, bar with outdoor seating, and restaurant renowned for its West Coast cuisine (and a great Sunday brunch buffet). Accommodation choices are in regular rooms, each with a private balcony ($170 s or d), or newer beachfront suites, each with a fireplace, hot tub, and kitchen ($240–455 s or d).

An excellent choice for campers looking for a vacation vibe is **Seaview Tent and Trailer Park** (685 Lazo Rd., Comox, 250/339-3976), within walking distance of the beach. Unserviced sites are $22–26, hookups $32–38. To get there from the highway, take Comox Road through downtown Comox and turn right onto Balmoral Avenue (which leads into Lazo Rd.).

Food

In the heart of downtown, the **Union Street Grill** (477 5th St., 250/897-0081; Mon.–Fri. 11 A.M.–9 P.M., Sat.–Sun. 11:30 A.M.–9 P.M.) dishes up well-priced global choices that include a delicious jambalaya ($15.50) and expertly prepared fish from local waters ($14–19). Save room for a slice of chocolate mocha fudge cake ($6). In the vicinity, the **Rose Tea Room** (180 5th St., 250/897-1007;

Mon.–Sat. 10 A.M.–5 P.M.) is a friendly little place where older locals catch up over simple sandwiches, scones and tea, and decadent rocky road brownies.

Occupying one of Courtenay's original residences, the **Tomäto Tomäto** (1760 Riverside Lane, 250/338-5406; daily for lunch and dinner) sits among landscaped gardens of a much more modern Old House Village Suites & Hotel. The menu is filled with tempting yet well-priced Pacific Northwest choices. You could start with local clams steamed open in a creamy white-wine sauce ($12), then move on to halibut wrapped in prosciutto ($23) as a main.

Information

Comox Valley Visitor Centre (2040 Cliffe Ave., 250/334-3234, www.comox-valley -tourism.com; summer daily 8:30 A.M.–6 P.M., the rest of the year Mon.–Fri. 9 A.M.–6 P.M.) is on the main highway leading into Courtenay—look for the totem pole out front.

CUMBERLAND

Coal was first discovered in the Comox Valley in 1869, and by the mid-1880s extraction of the most productive seam was going ahead, near present-day Cumberland. The mine was operated by the Union Colliery Co., which brought in thousands of Chinese workers. Cumberland's Chinatown was once home to 3,000 people, second in size only to San Francisco's Chinatown. **Cumberland Museum** (2680 Dunsmuir St., 250/336-2445; daily 9 A.M.–5 P.M., closed Sun. outside summer; $3) is a small but excellent facility, with interesting historic photos. Below the museum is a re-created mine shaft open to the public. Before leaving, pick up a heritage walking-tour brochure and ask for directions to the overgrown remains of the Chinese settlement, which lies around 1.6 kilometers (one mile) west of the museum.

COMOX

The population of Comox is quoted at 13,000, and there's certainly enough room for everyone, but you'd never know it, driving along forested roads that lead to golf courses, retirement communities, and a magnificent stretch of coastline. To reach Comox's small downtown area, take Comox Road eastward after crossing the Courtenay River along Highway 19A.

Filberg Heritage Lodge and Park

Through downtown is a highlight of the valley, Filberg Heritage Lodge (Comox Ave. at Filberg Rd., 250/339-2715). A high hedge hides the property from the outside world, but the grounds are open daily dawn to dusk, and no admission is charged to wander through the beautifully landscaped grounds that stretch down to Comox Harbour. At the bottom of the garden is the main house, built by a logging magnate in 1929. Filled with period antiques and quirky architecture, it's open for inspection in summer daily 11 A.M.–5 P.M. (admission $4).

In early August, the **Filberg Festival** features gourmet food, free entertainment, and unique arts and crafts from the best of BC's artisans.

Within the grounds, facing the water, is a small café (Mon.–Fri. 11 A.M.–3 P.M., Sat.–Sun. 11 A.M.–5 P.M.), with picnic tables spread out under mature trees. A delightful setting more than makes up for the uninspiring café fare.

Other Sights

Take Pritchard Road north from Filberg Lodge and you'll eventually reach the Canadian Forces Base, which doubles as the local airport for commercial flights. Cross Knight Road to reach **Comox Air Force Museum,** at the entrance to Comox Air Force Base (Ryan Rd., 250/339-8162; daily 10 A.M.–4 P.M.; donation). The museum isn't huge, but it is chock-full of Air Force memorabilia. Once you've gone through the indoor displays, you'll want to wander down to the Airpark (May–Sept. daily 10 A.M.–4 P.M.), a five-minute walk south, where around a dozen planes from various eras are parked.

© ANDREW HEMPSTEAD

The white cliffs at Kye Bay are off the main tourist path, but worth visiting for their distinctive geological origins.

On the other side of the runway is **Kye Bay,** a wide strip of sand that is perfect for families. To the east, beyond the headland, are intriguing **white cliffs.** At the end of an ancient ice age, as the sheet of ice that covered this region retreated, it stalled, leaving behind a massive mound of finely ground glacial silt. Wind and water action in the ensuing years have uncovered the silt, forming white cliffs that stand in stark contrast to the surrounding bedrock. To reach Kye Bay from the airport, head east on Knight Road (past the entrance to the main terminal) and take Kye Bay Road around the south end of the runway.

Another interesting spot is **Seal Bay Nature Park,** north of downtown along Anderton and then Waveland Roads. The park protects one of the region's few undeveloped stretches of coastline. Trails lead through a lush forest of Douglas fir and ferns to a pleasant, rocky beach where bald eagles and seals are often sighted.

Getting There
BC Ferries (250/386-3431, www.bcferries .com) sails four times daily between Comox and Powell River, allowing mainlanders easy access to mid-island beaches and snow slopes and saving visitors to northern Vancouver Island from having to backtrack down to Nanaimo or Victoria. To get to the terminal, stay on Highway 19 through Courtenay, then take Ryan Road east to Anderton Road. Turn left and follow the signs down Ellenor Road. The regular one-way fare for this 75-minute sailing is adult $9.05, child $4.55, vehicle $30.85.

NORTH TOWARD CAMPBELL RIVER
An enjoyable place to pitch a tent, **Miracle Beach Provincial Park** is about three kilometers (1.9 miles) off the main highway, 23 kilometers (14.3 miles) north of Courtenay. Highlights include a wooded campground, a sandy beach, good swimming and fishing, and nature trails. Look for porpoises and seals at the mouth of Black Creek, orcas in the Strait of Georgia, black-tailed deer, black bear, and raccoons in the park, and seabirds and crabs along the shoreline. In summer you can take a nature walk with a park naturalist, participate in a clambake or barbecue, or watch demonstrations and films at the Miracle Beach Nature House. Campsites cost $22 per night.

A few kilometers north of Miracle Beach and 18 kilometers (11.2 miles) south of Campbell River is **Salmon Point Resort** (2176 Salmon Point Rd., 250/923-6605 or 866/246-6605, www.salmonpoint.com), also offering great views of the Strait of Georgia and the snow-capped peaks of the Coast Mountains. Facilities are excellent, including a restaurant overlooking the water, a couple of recreation rooms (one for adults only), fishing guide service and tackle, boat rentals ($120 per day), a heated pool, heated bathrooms, and a laundry room. All campsites sit among small stands of pines; tents $27.50, hookups $28–33. Cottages range $90–175 per night.

Northern Vancouver Island

The northern section of Vancouver Island is mountainous, heavily treed, dotted with lakes, riddled with rivers and waterfalls, and almost completely unsettled. Just one main highway serves the region, although hundreds of kilometers of logging roads penetrate the dense forests. The gateway to the north is **Campbell River,** another small city that proudly calls itself the "Salmon Capital of the World." From this point north, the Island Highway follows a winding route over mountains and through valleys, first hitting the coast near **Telegraph Cove,** one of Canada's most photogenic communities and the departure point for orca-watching trips to the nutrient-rich waters of Johnstone Strait and Robson Bight. The island's northernmost town is **Port Hardy,** terminus for ferries heading north to Prince Rupert and the gateway to the wild west coast and **Cape Scott Provincial Park.**

CAMPBELL RIVER

A gateway to the wilderness of northern Vancouver Island, this city of 30,000 stretches along Discovery Passage 260 kilometers (162 miles) north of Victoria and 235 kilometers (146 miles) southeast of Port Hardy. Views from town—of tree-covered Quadra Island and the magnificent white-topped mountains of mainland British Columbia—are superb, but most visitors come for the salmon fishing. The underwater topography creates prime angling conditions; Georgia Strait ends just south of Campbell River, and Discovery Passage begins. The waterway suddenly narrows to a width of only two kilometers (1.2 miles)

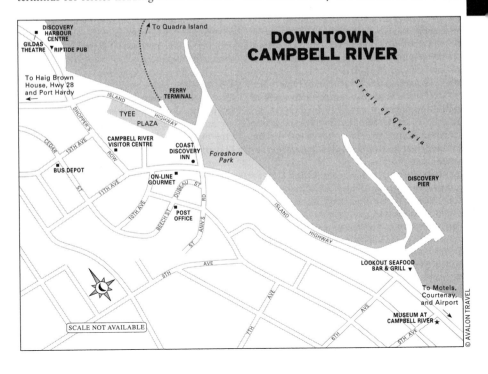

DOWNTOWN CAMPBELL RIVER

DISCOVERY HARBOUR CENTRE
GILDAS THEATRE ▾RIPTIDE PUB

To Quadra Island

To Haig Brown House, Hwy 28 and Port Hardy ←

FERRY TERMINAL

ISLAND

TYEE PLAZA

HIGHWAY

SHOPPER'S ROW

CEDAR ST

13TH AVE

CAMPBELL RIVER VISITOR CENTRE

COAST DISCOVERY INN

Foreshore Park

Strait of Georgia

BUS DEPOT

ST

11TH AVE

ON-LINE GOURMET

DUBEAU ST

ISLAND

DISCOVERY PIER

10TH AVE

BEECH ST

POST OFFICE

ST ANN'S RD

HIGHWAY

AVE

9TH

LOOKOUT SEAFOOD BAR & GRILL ▾

7TH AVE

AVE

To Motels, Courtenay, and Airport

6TH AVE

MUSEUM AT CAMPBELL RIVER ★

5TH AVE

SCALE NOT AVAILABLE

© AVALON TRAVEL

between Vancouver and Quadra Islands, causing some of the strongest tides on the coast, attracting bait fish, and forcing thousands of migrating salmon to concentrate off Campbell River, much to every angler's delight.

Sights

The best place to absorb some of the local atmosphere is **Discovery Pier.** The 180-meter (590-foot) pier is fun to walk on whether you're into fishing or not. Its benches and protected shelters allow proper appreciation of the marina, strait, mainland mountains, and fishing action, even on wet and windy days.

The **Museum at Campbell River** (470 Oceanside Island Hwy., 250/287-3103; May–Sept. daily 10 A.M.–5 P.M., the rest of the year Tues.–Sun. noon–5 P.M.; $5) sits on four hectares (10 acres) overlooking Discovery Passage. First check out the photos and interesting written snippets that provide a look at Campbell River's early beginnings. Then feast your eyes on mystical artifacts, a huge collection of masks, exciting artwork, baskets, woven articles, carved-wood boxes, colorful button blankets, petroglyphs, and totem poles. Other displays center on sportfishing and local pioneers. Worth watching in the museum's theater is *Devil Beneath the Sea,* a documentary cataloging the destruction of nearby Ripple Rock by the world's largest non-nuclear explosion. Finish up in the gift shop, where you can buy stunning native prints, masks, postcards, and other paraphernalia.

Soak up native culture at the **Gildas Theatre** (Discovery Harbour Centre, 1370 Island Hwy., 250/287-7310). Through song, dance, and storytelling, performers tell the story of a young Laichwiltach man who learns about the world of spirits by traveling beyond the confines of his village. Performances run mid-June–mid-September Tuesday–Saturday at 4 P.M., with an extra show at 1 P.M. on Saturday. Admission is adult $18, child $9.

Accommodations

Along the highway south of town, only the road separates several motels from Discovery Passage. If you want to save your money for a fishing charter, no worries—book a room at the 22-room **Big Rock Motel** (1020 South Island Hwy., 250/923-4211 or 877/923-4211; $58 s, $68 d, $86 with a kitchen), your average two-story, cinder-block motel. Continuing north, you'll come to the **Best Western Austrian Chalet** (462 South Island Hwy., 250/923-4231 or 800/667-7207, www.bwcampbellriver.com), with a wide range of facilities including an indoor pool, a sauna, a restaurant and pub, and even a putting green. Rates start at $130 s or d ($30 extra for an ocean view). Right downtown, **Coast Discovery Inn** (975 Shopper's Row, 250/287-7155 or 800/663-1144, www.coasthotels.com; $145 s, $155 d) is a full-service hotel with a fitness room, restaurant, and pub.

Bed-and-breakfast accommodations are provided at **Haig-Brown House** (2250 Campbell River Rd., 250/286-6646; May–Oct.; $80 s, $95 d), the modest 1923 riverside home of famed angler and author Roderick Haig-Brown. The old antique-filled house has changed little over time and the grounds are a delightful place to relax. The three guest rooms share a bathroom.

Camping

Many campgrounds line the highway south of town, and although they're close to the water, the surroundings are generally nothing special. One of the better choices is **Campbell River Fishing Village and RV Park** (260 South Island Hwy., 250/287-3630, www.fishingvillage.bc.ca), two kilometers (1.2 miles) south of downtown. As the name suggests, it's set up for anglers, with boat rentals, guided charters, rentals (everything from rods to depth sounders), a tackle shop, and fish-freezing facilities. Other amenities include a playground, laundry, and communal fire pit. Sites are $20–25 per night. Less commercial options with limited facilities include **Elk Falls Provincial Park,** six kilometers (3.7 miles) west of town on Highway 28, and **Loveland Bay Provincial Park,** on the shore of Campbell Lake 20 kilometers (12 miles) west of town; $17 and $14, respectively.

Other Practicalities

One of the best places to go for a meal is the two-story **Lookout Seafood Bar & Grill** (921 South Island Hwy., 250/286-6812; daily 11 A.M.–10 P.M.), overlooking Discovery Pier and the marina from an absolute waterfront location. The house specialty is, of course, seafood, including clam chowder for $6.50, a Cajun scallop and bacon burger for $9, and fish and chips for around $14. Continuing north along the harborfront is **Riptide Pub** (1340 South Island Hwy., 250/830-0044; daily for lunch and dinner), which is a good place for a full meal, although it doesn't take full advantage of its waterfront location (unless you score a table on the glassed-in patio). The sleek interior is a little nicer than you may imagine, while the food is exactly what you'd expect: fresh scallops, oysters, mussels, halibut, and salmon (mains $14–24). Save room for a slice of cheesecake.

Park in the large parking lot of **Tyee Plaza** and you're within easy walking distance of the information center and all services. At the front of the parking lot is **Campbell River Visitor Centre** (1235 Shopper's Row, 250/287-4636; summer daily 8 A.M.–8 P.M., the rest of the year Mon.–Fri. 9 A.M.–5 P.M.). Besides providing tons of brochures, free tourist papers, and information on both the local area and Vancouver Island in general, the knowledgeable staff can answer just about any question on the area you could think up. For other information, contact **Campbell River Tourism** (250/286-1616, www.campbellrivertourism.com). Other plaza tenants include banks, a big-box grocery store, a laundry, and various family-style eateries. Across from the plaza is the **post office** (Beech St.) and **On-Line Gourmet** (970 Shoppers Row, 250/286-6521; closed Sunday), where you can check your email for a small charge. The **hospital** is at 375 2nd Avenue (250/287-7111).

Campbell River Airport, off Erickson Road 20 kilometers (12 miles) south of downtown, is served by **Pacific Coastal** (800/663-2872) from Vancouver. For transportation between the airport and accommodations, call the **Campbell River Airporter** (250/286-3000). From Victoria, **Greyhound** (509 13th Ave., 250/287-7151) operates 3–5 buses daily to Campbell River, with at least one continuing north to Port Hardy timed to link with the ferry departing for Prince Rupert. Local rental car agencies include **Budget** (250/923-4283), **National** (250/923-1234), and **Rent-a-wreck** (250/287-8353).

QUADRA ISLAND

A 10-minute ferry ride across Discovery Passage from downtown Campbell River takes you to Quadra Island (pop. 2,700), which blends beautiful scenery, native culture, and upscale fishing lodges to create a unique and worthwhile detour from your up-island travels. The ferry docks in the south of the island, where most of the population resides. This narrow peninsula widens in the north to an unpopulated area where provincial and marine parks protect a wealth of wildlife. Marinelife around the entire shoreline is widespread; orcas cruise Discovery Passage, and seals and sea lions are commonly spied in surrounding waters.

Sights and Recreation

Captain Vancouver may have been the first European to step onto the island when he made landfall at **Cape Mudge** in 1792, but the island had been inhabited by native people for many centuries before. Learn about the island's long and rich native history at the **Nuyumabales Cultural Centre** (Cape Mudge Village, 250/285-3733; summer Mon.–Sat. 10 A.M.–4:30 P.M., Sun. noon–4:30 P.M., the rest of the year Tues.–Sat. 10 A.M.–4:30 P.M.; adult $6, senior and child $4). This excellent facility displays a wide variety of ceremonial dresses used in potlatches, as well as masks and other native artifacts. Native petroglyphs found at the island's southern end have been moved to the museum grounds and can be viewed at any time.

At the island's southern tip, **Cape Mudge Lighthouse** was built in 1898 to prevent shipwrecks in the wild, surging waters around the point. On the east coast is **Heriot Bay,** the name of both a cove and the island's largest community. Narrow Rebecca Spit, site of **Rebecca Spit Marine Park,** protects a beach-lined bay from the elements. Roads lead north from Heriot Bay to the island's wild northern reaches, where you can go hiking to the low summit of **Chinese Mountain** (three kilometers/1.9 miles; allow one hour each way), around **Morte Lake** (five kilometers/3.1 miles; allow 90 minutes for the loop), and in the far north to **Newton Lake** from Granite Bay (four kilometers/2.4 miles; 75 minutes each way).

Practicalities

Near Cape Mudge Lighthouse is 🄲 **Tsa-Kwa-Luten** (250/285-2042 or 800/665-7745, www.capemudgeresort.bc.ca). This magnificent waterfront lodge was built by the local Kwagiulth people, and its centerpiece is the foyer, built in the style of a bighouse (a traditional meeting place) using locally milled woods. Each of the 35 spacious rooms is decorated in a Northwest native theme, and each has a private balcony with water views. Rates start at a reasonable $130 s or d, with meal packages available. The lodge coordinates fishing charters and cultural activities, and its restaurant specializes in native foods.

For campers, the best option is the charming **We Wai Kai Campsite** (250/285-3111, www.wwkampsite.ca; mid-May–mid-Sept.), set along a pleasant sandy beach at the head of Heriot Bay. Regular sites are $25, or pay $5 extra for water views.

BC Ferries (250/286-1412) offers services from Campbell River to the island, every hour on the hour 6 A.M.–11 P.M.; round-trip fare is adult $6.05, child $3.05, vehicle $14.75. For a cab, call **Quadra Taxi** (250/285-3598).

CORTES ISLAND

Accessible by ferry from Quadra Island, Cortes Island (pronounced cor-TEZ—it was named by an early Spanish explorer) is a relatively remote place, closer to the mainland than to Vancouver Island. Few visitors venture out here, but those who do are rarely disappointed. Aside from three small villages, the island remains in its natural state. **Manson's Landing Provincial**

Park is a beautiful little spot sandwiched between a large tidal lagoon and the forested shoreline of **Hague Lake.** In the south of the island is **Smelt Bay Provincial Park,** another great spot for swimming, beachcombing, and taking in the unique island environment.

Practicalities

Accommodations on the island are limited, so unless you plan to camp, make reservations before coming over. **Smelt Bay Provincial Park,** 25 kilometers (15.5 miles) from the ferry terminal, offers campsites for $14 per site. Closer to the terminal, **Gorge Harbour Marina Resort** (Hunt Rd., Gorge Harbour, 250/935-6433, www.gorgeharbour.com) offers tent sites ($20) and full hookups ($28) beside the island's main marina, as well as four rooms ($75 s or d includes use of a kitchen), kayak and boat rentals, fishing charters, and a restaurant.

The island has no official visitor center. You can get an idea of island life by checking out the online version of the local newspaper (www.cortesisland.com), which has everything you'll need to know for a visit, as well as things you probably don't want to know, such as where to purchase the annual calendar of naked residents.

The ferry trip between Heriot Bay on Quadra Island and Cortes Island takes 40 minutes. **BC Ferries** (250/286-1412) operates scheduled service between the two islands six times daily, with the first departing Quadra Island at 9 A.M. and the last departing Cortes Island at 5:50 P.M. Peak round-trip fare is adult $7.10, child $3.55, vehicle $18.05.

HIGHWAY 28

Running across the island through the northern section of magnificent Strathcona Provincial Park, Highway 28 is another road worth traveling for the scenery alone. The first place to stop is 1,087-hectare (2,690-acre) **Elk Falls Provincial Park,** six kilometers (3.7 miles) west of Campbell River. Here you can follow a forested trail to waterfalls, go swimming and fishing, and stay the night in a wooded campsite (Apr.–Oct.; $14).

Strathcona Provincial Park

British Columbia's oldest and Vancouver Island's largest park, Strathcona preserves a vast 250,000-hectare (617,800-acre) wilderness in the northern center of Vancouver Island. Vancouver Island's highest peak, 2,220-meter (7,280-foot) **Golden Hinde**, is within the park. The peak was named for Sir Francis Drake's ship, in which he circumnavigated the world in the 1570s (some believe he would have sighted the peak from his ship).

You'll get a taste of Strathcona's beauty along Highway 28, but to get into the park proper, turn south off Highway 28 halfway between Campbell River and Gold River. This access road hugs the eastern shore of **Buttle Lake,** passing many well-marked nature walks and hiking trails. One of the first is the short walk (10 minutes each way) to **Lupin Falls,** which are more impressive than the small creek across from the parking lot would suggest. Continuing south along the lakeshore past driftwood-strewn beaches, you'll come to the **Karst Creek Trail** (two-kilometer/1.2-mile loop; allow 30 minutes), which passes through a karst landscape of sinkholes and disappearing streams. At the lake's southern end, where the road crosses Thelwood Creek, a six-kilometer (3.7-mile) trail (2.5 hours each way) climbs a steep valley to **Bedwell Lake** and surrounding alpine meadows.

As the road continues around the lakeshore, look for **Myra Falls** across the water. After passing through the Westmin Resources mining operation, the road ends on the edge of an old-growth forest. From this point, explore on foot by taking the **Upper Myra Falls Trail** (three kilometers/1.9 miles; one hour each way) to a lookout point above the falls.

Apart from numerous picnic areas along the shore of Buttle Lake, the only facilities within the park are two campgrounds. **Buttle Lake Campground** is beside Buttle Lake, just west of the junction of Highway 28 and the park access road. **Ralph River Campground** is farther south, on the shore of Buttle Lake. Both have pit toilets, picnic tables, and fire rings, and both charge $14 per night.

Gold River

Those looking for a glimpse of Vancouver Island away from the touristy east coast will find the 90-kilometer (56-mile) drive west from Campbell River to Gold River (pop. 1,700) both enjoyable and interesting. Boat tours into Nootka Sound make the trip even more worthwhile.

Beyond the west boundary of Strathcona Provincial Park, Highway 28 descends along the Heber River to its confluence with the Gold River, where the town of Gold River lies. Built in 1965 to house employees of a pulp mill, it was the first all-electric town in Canada. The natural highlight of Gold River is **Upana Caves,** but unless you're a spelunker, chances are you've never heard of them. The caves, accessed 16 kilometers (10 miles) west of town from Head Bay Forest Road, are the largest cave system north of Mexico and include a river that flows underground for 150 meters (500 feet) through eroded limestone bedrock. Meanwhile, anglers and kayakers head out to Muchalat Inlet, while golfers walk the fairways of the town's nine-hole course simply because it's there.

Rooms at the **Ridgeview Motor Inn** (395 Donner Ct., 250/283-2277 or 800/989-3393, www.ridgeview-inn.com; $95–130 s or d) were a lot nicer than expected, and each comes with a fridge, TV, and phone. A light breakfast is included in the rates. The adjacent pub/restaurant serves decent food and has an outdoor eating area with fantastic valley views. The **Lions Campground,** on the edge of town, has unserviced sites for $12.

At the entrance to town, stop at the **Gold River Visitor Centre** (Muchalat Dr., www.goldriver.ca; mid-May–Aug. daily 9 A.M.–4:30 P.M.).

Cruising Nootka Sound

The best reason to travel west from Campbell River is to take a cruise along Muchalat Inlet to Nootka Sound. The **MV Uchuck III** (250/283-2325, www.mvuchuck.com), a converted World War II minesweeper, departs year-round from the dock at the end of Highway 28 (14 kilometers/8.7 miles west from Gold River). Its primary purpose is dropping supplies at remote west coast communities and logging camps, but interested visitors are more than welcome and are made to feel comfortable by the hardworking crew. The main sailing departs June–Sept. every Monday at 9 A.M. for **Tahsis** and **Zeballos,** with an overnight stop in the latter included in the rate of $225 s, $355 d ($75 for children). The one-way fare to Zeballos is $40 (but you'll need to make lodging arrangements because the return trip departs the following morning). A second sailing departs year-round Thursday at 7 A.M., heading out to the open ocean and up the coast to **Kyuquot.** This is also an overnight trip, with meals and accommodations included in the price of $280 s, $430 d ($105 for children). A third sailing departs mid-June to mid-September every Wednesday at 10 A.M., visiting two points of historical interest: the spot where in 1778 Captain James Cook and his crew became the first Europeans to land on the West Coast, and **Friendly Cove,** where in 1792 Captain George Vancouver and Don Juan Francisco de la Bodega y Quadra negotiated possession of Nootka Sound territory. Fare for this six-hour tour is adult $60, senior $55, child $30.

NORTH TO PORT MCNEILL

Highway 19, covering the 235 kilometers (146 miles) between Campbell River and Port Hardy, is a good road with plenty of straight stretches and not much traffic. Passing through relatively untouched wilderness, with only logged hillsides to remind you of the ugliness humanity can produce with such ease, it's almost as though you've entered another world, or at least another island. Stop at all of the frequent rest areas for the best views of forested mountains, white peaks, sparkling rivers and lakes, and cascading waterfalls.

After taking a convoluted inland route for 130 kilometers (81 miles), Highway 19 returns to the coastline at Port McNeill, the regional headquarters for three logging companies and home of "the world's largest burl," on the main highway two kilometers (1.2 miles) north of town at the entrance to a logging company office—you can't miss it. The center of town comprises a shopping plaza and an industrial

waterfront development. Port McNeill is also the jumping-off point for ferry trips to Alert Bay and Malcolm Island (see following sections).

◖ TELEGRAPH COVE

Most visitors come to Telegraph Cove to go whale-watching on Johnston Strait (see the sidebar), but the village is well worth the eight-kilometer (five-mile) detour from the highway just east of Port McNeill. Built around a deep sheltered harbor, it's one of the last existing "boardwalk" communities on the island. Many of the buildings stand on stilts and pilings over the water, linked by a boardwalk.

Fewer than 20 people live here year-round, but the population swells enormously during late spring and summer when whale-watching, diving, and fishing charters do a roaring trade, canoeists and kayakers arrive to paddle along Johnstone Strait, and the campground opens for the season. Walk along the boardwalk, passing cabins, kayak rentals, an art gallery, a small interpretive center, the **Killer Whale Café,** the Old Saltery Pub, and a store selling groceries and fishing tackle.

Across Johnstone Strait from Telegraph Cove is **Knight Inlet,** home to a large population of brown bears. **Tide Rip Grizzly Tours** (250/928-3090 or 888/643-9319, www.tiderip .com) has bear-watching tours departing Telegraph Cove daily mid-May to mid-October. For the first two months, when the bears come down to the waterline to feed, the boat doesn't dock, but from mid-August onward, when bears are feeding on salmon, the tour includes two hours spent in a specially built bear-viewing platform. The tour cost is $360 per person ($250 early in the season).

Accommodations and Camping

Many of the buildings on the boardwalk and around the bay have been converted to guest accommodations and can be rented by the night (reserve well in advance) May through mid-October. The quarters range from extremely basic cabins ($100 s or d) to three-bedroom self-contained homes ($280). About the only thing they have in common is the incredible setting.

WHALE-WATCHING IN JOHNSTONE STRAIT

More than 50 whale-watching operations have sprung up around Vancouver Island in recent years, but the opportunity to view orcas (killer whales) close up in Johnstone Strait is unparalleled. These magnificent, intelligent mammals spend the summer in the waters around Telegraph Cove and are most concentrated in **Robson Bight,** where they rub on the gravel beaches near the mouth of the Tsitka River, an area that has been established as a sanctuary for the whales.

Stubbs Island Whale Watching (250/928-3185 or 800/665-3066, www.stubbs-island .com) was the province's first whale-watching company, and continues to lead the way in responsible whale-watching. The company's two boats, *Lukwa* and *Gikumi,* depart daily from Telegraph Cove on 3-4-hour cruises from mid-May to early October. The experienced crew takes you out to view the whales in their natural habitat and to hear their mysterious and beautiful sounds through a hydrophone (underwater microphone). Both boats are comfortable, with covered areas and bathrooms.

The cost of the most popular 1 P.M. cruise is $84 per person. The 9 A.M. and 5:30 P.M. departures are $74. Reservations are required,

and you should call ahead as far as possible to ensure a spot. Dress warmly and don't forget your camera for this experience of a lifetime.

© JIM BORROWMAN

Overlooking the cove, **Wastell Manor** has been restored, with the four well-furnished guest rooms ranging $155–185. Finally, a short walk from the village is a campground with wooded sites as well as showers, a laundry room, a boat launch, and a store. Sites are $21–26. For reservations at any of the above options, contact **Telegraph Cove Resorts** (250/928-3131 or 800/200-4665, www.telegraphcoveresort.com).

MALCOLM ISLAND

This largish island immediately offshore from Port McNeill is home to around 800 people, most of whom live in the village of **Sointula.** The first European settlers were of Finnish descent. They arrived around 1900, after migrating across Canada in search of a remote,

peaceful place to call their own. Meaning "harmony" in Finnish, Sointula evolved as a socialist community in which everyone shared everything. To some extent, these utopian ideals continue to this day, with descendents of the original settlers operating a fleet of fishing boats and the general store as cooperatives. In town, wander along the residential streets and admire the trim homes and well-tended gardens, then walk the three-kilometer (1.9-mile) Mateoja Trail from the end of 3rd Street to a popular bird-watching spot, Big Lake.

Practicalities

One of the many upscale fishing lodges scattered throughout this part of the world is ◀ **Sund's Lodge** (250/973-6381, www.sunds

lodge.com; mid-June to early Sept.), located on a beautiful waterfront property east of Sointula. It is everything a luxurious fishing lodge should be, but it is a completely unpretentious family-run operation. Inside the spacious guest cabins you'll find super-comfortable beds, log furniture, top-notch bathrooms, and original art. Guests stay as part of all-inclusive packages, which include memorable meals and as much guided fishing as you can handle. Drive across the island to **Bere Point** to reach the island's only official campground.

The easiest way to reach Malcolm Island is with **BC Ferries** (250/956-4533), which makes the short run across Broughton Strait from Port McNeil around eight times daily. The round-trip fare is adult $7.10, child $3.55, vehicle $18.05.

◖ ALERT BAY

This fascinating village is the only settlement on crescent-shaped **Cormorant Island,** which lies in Broughton Strait 45 minutes by ferry from Port McNeill. The island's population of 600 is evenly split between natives and non-natives.

Alert Bay holds plenty of history. Captain Vancouver landed there in the late 1700s, and it's been a supply stop for fur traders and gold miners on their way to Alaska, a place for ships to stock up on water, and home base to an entire fishing fleet. Today the village is one of the region's major fishing and marine service centers, and it holds two fish-processing and -packing plants. Half the island is owned by the Kwakiutl, whose powerful art draws visitors to Alert Bay.

Sights

All of the island's numerous attractions can be reached on foot or by bicycle. Start by wandering through the village to appreciate the early-1900s waterfront buildings and the colorful totems decorating **Nimpkish Burial Ground.**

For an outstanding introduction to the fascinating culture and heritage of the Kwakiutl, don't miss the **U'Mista Cultural Centre** (Front St., 250/974-5403; Mon.–Fri. 9 A.M.–5 P.M., Sat. noon–5 P.M.; adult $7, se-

nior $6, child $3). Built to house a ceremonial potlatch collection confiscated by the federal government after a 1921 ban on potlatches, the center contains masks and other Kwakiutl art and artifacts. Take a guided tour through the center, and then wander at your leisure past the photos and colorful displays to watch two award-winning films produced by the center—one explains the origin and meaning of the potlatch. The center also teaches local children the native language, culture, song, and dance.

Also on the north end of the island you'll find the **Indian Bighouse,** the world's second tallest totem pole (it's 53 meters/174 feet high—the tallest is in Victoria), and the historic century-old **Anglican Church.** Take a boardwalk stroll through the intriguing ecological area called **Gator Gardens** to see moss-draped forests, ghostly black-water swamps, and lots of ravens, bald eagles, and other birds.

Practicalities

The island's least expensive accommodation is **Alert Bay Camping** (250/974-5213; $12–18 per night), overlooking Broughton Strait, with a cookhouse and barbecues. The **Nimpkish Hotel** (318 Fir St., 250/974-2324 or 888/646-7547, www.nimpkishhotel.com) has four small, simple rooms ($60 s or d), as well as a restaurant downstairs with tables that sprawl outside to a wide waterfront deck.

BC Ferries (250/956-4533) runs to the island from Port McNeill many times daily, with most sailings stopping en route at Malcolm Island. The peak round-trip fare is adult $7.10, child $3.55. You can take a vehicle over for $18.05 round-trip, but there's no real point because everything on the island is reachable on foot.

Across from the waterfront is **Alert Bay Visitor Centre** (116 Fir St., 250/974-5024; summer daily 9 A.M.–6 P.M., the rest of the year Mon.–Fri. 9 A.M.–5 P.M.).

PORT HARDY

Port Hardy (pop. 4,600) lies along sheltered Hardy Bay, 235 kilometers (146 miles) north of Campbell River and 495 kilometers (308 miles) north of Victoria. It's the largest community north of Campbell River and the terminus for ferries sailing the Inside Passage to and from Prince Rupert.

Sights and Recreation

As you enter the Port Hardy area, take the scenic route to town via Hardy Bay Road. You'll pass several original chainsaw woodcarvings and skirt the edge of peaceful Hardy Bay before entering downtown via Market Street. Stroll along the promenade to reach **Tsulquate Park,** where you can appreciate native carvings and do some beachcombing if the tide is out. Many bald eagles reside around the bay. Another interesting place to spend a little time is the small **Port Hardy Museum** (7110 Market St., 250/949-8143; Tues.–Sat. noon–4:30 P.M.), which holds a predictable collection of pioneer artifacts.

At **Quatse River Hatchery** (Byng Rd., 250/949-9022; Mon.–Fri. 8 A.M.–4:30 P.M.), on the scenic Quatse River, you can observe incubation and rearing facilities for pink, chum, and coho salmon, as well as steelhead. Good

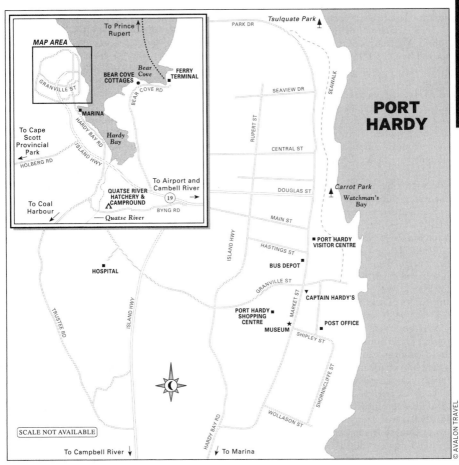

fishing on the river attracts droves of anglers year-round, but the Quatse is by no means the only fishing game in town. With so much water—both salt and fresh—surrounding Port Hardy, visiting anglers probably won't know where to start. Ask at the local sporting-goods store on Market Street for the best fishing spots, or take a fishing charter (inquire at the information center for guides and skippers).

Accommodations and Camping

Accommodations in Port Hardy are limited and often fill up, especially on the night prior to ferry departures. Book ahead.

In a town of boring, overpriced motel rooms, **Bear Cove Cottages** (6715 Bear Cove Hwy., 250/949-7939 or 877/949-7939, www.bearcovecottages.ca) stands out, but because there are only eight of them, you'll need to reserve well in advance. Located right near the ferry terminal 10 kilometers (6.2 miles) out of town, they sit in a neat row high above the ocean with stunning water views. Each modern unit comes with a compact but well-designed kitchen, a fireplace, a bathroom with jetted tub, and a private deck. Between June and September the rates are $160 s or d, while the rest of the year the price drops to $130.

South of downtown, two hotels overlook Port Hardy's busy harbor from the marina. **Glen Lyon Inn** (6435 Hardy Bay Rd., 250/949-7115 or 877/949-7115, www.glenlyoninn.com) has rooms in an original wing for $90 s, $95 d and larger, newer, and much nicer rooms in a 2000 addition for $115 s, $125 d. The adjacent **Quarterdeck Inn** (6555 Hardy Bay Rd., 250/902-0455 or 877/902-0459, www.quarterdeckresort.net) offers harbor views from each of its 40 smallish rooms. Facilities include a fitness room, a sauna, and a laundry room. At $125 s, $145 d (including a light breakfast), and relative to the other town motels, this place is a good value.

Both of Port Hardy's commercial campgrounds are south of town, halfway around Hardy Bay to the ferry terminal. The pick of the two is **Quatse River Campground** (Byng Rd., 250/949-2395 or 866/949-2395, www.quatse campground.com; $18–22), which is operated

in conjunction with the adjacent salmon hatchery. Sites are shaded by a lush old-growth forest, and you can fish in the river right off the camping area—then move over to the communal fire pit and recall stories of the one that got away. In the vicinity is **Sunny Sanctuary Campground** (8080 Goodspeed Rd., 250/949-8111 or 866/251-4556), also on the Quatse River. Facilities include a barbecue shelter, modern bathrooms, firewood and fire rings, and a small store. The open and treed sites are $16–21.

Food

Port Hardy doesn't offer a large variety of dining options. Wander around town and you'll soon see what there is. At **Captain Hardy's** (7145 Market St., 250/949-7133) the advertised breakfast specials are small and come on plastic plates, but cost only about $4. The rest of the day, this place offers good fish and chips from $6.

Dine at the **Oceanside Restaurant,** south of downtown in the Glen Lyon Inn (Hardy Bay Rd., 250/949-3050) for the opportunity to see bald eagles feeding right outside the window. The menu is fairly standard, but well priced, with many seafood choices. It's open daily for breakfast, lunch, and dinner.

Information

The energetic staff at the downtown **Port Hardy Visitor Centre** (7250 Market St., 250/949-7622, www.ph-chamber.bc.ca; summer Mon.–Fri. 8:30 A.M.–6 P.M. and Sat.–Sun. 9 A.M.–5 P.M., the rest of the year Mon.–Fri. 8:30 A.M.–5 P.M.) will happily fill you in on everything there is to see and do in Port Hardy and beyond.

Getting There

Port Hardy Airport, 12 kilometers (7.5 miles) south of town, is served by **Pacific Coastal** (604/273-8666 or 800/663-2872) from Vancouver. It's a spectacular flight, with stunning views of the Coast Mountains for passengers seated on the plane's right side.

Airport facilities include parking ($3 per day), Budget and National rental car outlets, and a small café. **North Island Transport**

(250/949-6300) offers twice-daily bus service between the airport and downtown.

The North Island Transport depot at 7210 Market Street is also the local **Greyhound** (250/949-7532) stop, with once-daily bus service up the length of the island, scheduled to correspond with ferry departures. The departure of the southbound bus links with ferry arrivals. The journey between Victoria and Port Hardy takes a painful nine hours and costs around $130 one-way.

Continuing North by Ferry

Most people arriving in Port Hardy do so with the intention of continuing north with **BC Ferries** (250/386-3431 or 888/223-3779, www.bcferries.com) to Prince Rupert and beyond. The ferry terminal is at Bear Cove, 10 kilometers (6.2 miles) from downtown Port Hardy. Northbound ferries depart at least once every two days, with the run to Prince Rupert taking 13 hours. The service runs year-round, but departures are less frequent outside of summer. Peak one-way fare is adult $116, child

5–11 $58, vehicle $275. (These peak-season fares are discounted up to 40 percent outside of summer.) Cabins are available.

CAPE SCOTT PROVINCIAL PARK

Cape Scott Provincial Park encompasses 22,566 hectares (55,760 acres) of rugged coastal wilderness at the northernmost tip of Vancouver Island. It's the place to go if you really want to get away from everything and everyone. Rugged trails, suitable for experienced hikers and outdoors enthusiasts, lead through dense forests of cedar, pine, hemlock, and fir to 23 kilometers (14.3 miles) of beautiful sandy beaches and rocky promontories and headlands.

To get to the park boundary, you have to follow 67 kilometers (42 miles) of logging roads (remember that logging trucks always have the right-of-way), and then hike in. Near the end of the road is a small Forest Service campground ($8 per night). The hiking trail to **Cape Scott Lighthouse** (23 kilometers/14.3 miles; about eight hours each way) is relatively level, but you'll need stout footwear. A cove east of the cape was once the site of an ill-fated Danish settlement. Around 100 Danes moved to the area in 1896, cutting themselves off from the rest of the world and forcing themselves to be totally self-sufficient. By 1930, the settlement was deserted, with many of the residents relocating to nearby Holberg.

A shorter alternative to the long trek out to the cape is the trail to beautiful **San Josef Bay** at the southern boundary of the park (2.5 kilometers/1.6 miles; 45 minutes each way).

Before setting off for the park, go by the Port Hardy Visitor Centre and pick up the park brochure and detailed logging-road maps for the area. Be well equipped for unpredictable weather, even in midsummer.

South of the park is rugged and remote **Raft Cove.** To get there, turn off seven kilometers (4.3 miles) before the park, following a rough 12-kilometer (7.5-mile) logging road to a slight rise where the road ends. From this point, a narrow and rough trail leads 1.5 kilometers (0.9 mile) to the cove.

heading north with BC Ferries

SOUTHWESTERN BRITISH COLUMBIA

Once you've reluctantly decided to drag yourself away from Vancouver, you'll be confronted by a variety of things to see and do within a day's drive of the city.

Although British Columbia is best known for its mountains, a stretch of coastline northwest of Vancouver is a watery playground perfect for swimming, sunbathing on sandy beaches, canoeing and kayaking, beachcombing, scuba diving, boating, and fishing. Known as the Sunshine Coast, the region is reached by taking a ferry from Horseshoe Bay (west of North Vancouver) then continuing up Highway 101. The highway winds along the Strait of Georgia, passing seaside villages, provincial parks, and marine parks, and ending near Powell River, a large tourist town and service center. Powell River is the gateway to the paddler's paradise at Desolation Sound and on the Powell Forest Canoe Route.

Spectacular Highway 99, the aptly named Sea to Sky Highway, leads you northeast out of Vancouver along the edge of island-dotted Howe Sound. You pass numerous provincial parks before coming to the resort town of Whistler. This year-round outdoor-sports mecca offers outstanding opportunities for hiking, biking, golfing, fishing, and other warm-weather pursuits. But it's best known for its alpine resort: Whistler/Blackcomb, boasting North America's highest lift-served vertical rise.

From Vancouver two routes head east: You can zip along the TransCanada Highway on the south side of the wide Fraser

HIGHLIGHTS

◖ **Gibsons:** The Sunshine Coast is dotted with picturesque villages, none more scenic than Gibsons, where cafés and interesting shops line the rocky foreshore (page 190).

◖ **Savary Island:** The only sandy island in the Strait of Georgia, Savary Island stands out among the hundreds of Gulf Islands for its great beaches (page 197).

◖ **Whistler Gondola:** It's worth riding this gondola regardless of the season, but it is winter skiing and snowboarding that is most spectacular (page 204).

◖ **Othello-Quintette Tunnels:** At a glance, Hope doesn't have much to offer the visitor, but tucked in the mountains behind

town are the Othello-Quintette Tunnels, which wind through a rugged canyon (page 219).

◖ **Hell's Gate:** Even if you don't ride the tramway, Hell's Gate is an interesting and scenic stop along the Fraser Canyon (page 221).

◖ **E. C. Manning Provincial Park:** This ruggedly spectacular park in the Cascade Mountains stretches down to the Canada-U.S. border and has abundant wildlife, including black bear, moose, elk, coyote, and beaver (page 222).

◖ **Grist Mill:** At Keremeos the water-powered mill is a delightful spot to step back in time and learn about the lifestyle of early pioneers (page 226).

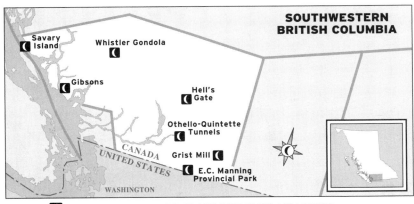

LOOK FOR ◖ TO FIND RECOMMENDED SIGHTS, ACTIVITIES, DINING, AND LODGING.

River, or meander along slower Highway 7 on the north side of the river. Both highways take you through the lush, fertile, and obviously agricultural Fraser Valley, converging at Hope. After exploring Hope's spectacular canyon formations, you have another choice of routes: north along the Fraser River Canyon, northeast to Kamloops along the Coquihalla Highway, or east along Highway 3 to the picturesque lakes and alpine meadows of Manning Provincial Park.

PLANNING YOUR TIME

After exploring Vancouver, you're faced with a decision: Where to next? This chapter covers three of the options, while a fourth, Vancouver Island, is covered in the previous chapter. Your choice of direction is dependent on two main elements: the time of year and your interests. The first option is to jump aboard a ferry for the Sunshine Coast. Rather than backtracking, plan on catching a ferry from Powell River across to Vancouver Island (make the detour to

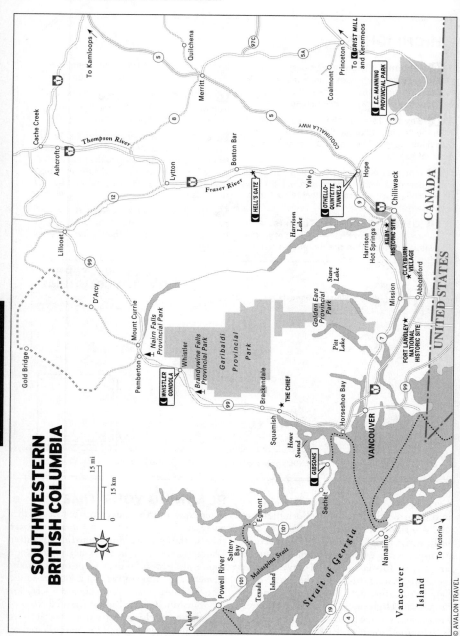

SOUTHWESTERN B.C.

SOUTHWESTERN BRITISH COLUMBIA

0 15 mi
0 15 km

To Kamloops

Cache Creek

Ashcroft

Thompson River

Lillooet

Gold Bridge

D'Arcy

Mount Currie

Pemberton

Gibsons

Lund

Powell River

Saltery Bay

Egmont

Sechelt

Nanaimo

Vancouver Island

To Victoria

Quilchena

Merritt

Lytton

Boston Bar

Fraser River

HELL'S GATE

Yale

Hope

Harrison Hot Springs

Mission

Abbotsford

Chilliwack

Princeton

Coalmont

To GRIST MILL and Keremeos

E.C. MANNING PROVINCIAL PARK

COQUIHALLA HWY

OTHELLO-QUINTETTE TUNNELS

KILBY HISTORIC SITE

CLAYBURN VILLAGE

FORT LANGLEY NATIONAL HISTORIC SITE

Harrison Lake

Stave Lake

Golden Ears Provincial Park

Pitt Lake

Garibaldi Provincial Park

Nairn Falls Provincial Park

Brandywine Falls Provincial Park

WHISTLER GONDOLA

Whistler

Brackendale

THE CHIEF

Squamish

Howe Sound

Horseshoe Bay

VANCOUVER

Malaspina Strait

Texada Island

Strait of Georgia

Vancouver Island

CANADA

UNITED STATES

© AVALON TRAVEL

delightful Lund before you do). Of course, you can make this loop by traveling in the opposite direction—from Vancouver Island to Powell River and down to Vancouver. One important thing to remember is that travel along this strip of coastline takes a lot longer than you may imagine from looking at a map, mostly due to two unavoidable ferry rides.

Regardless of the season, include Whistler in your British Columbia travels. The resort is close enough to Vancouver for a day trip, but it's easy to spend at least a full day exploring the main mountain by gondola, which means if you want to bike, hike, or golf, you'll need at least two days. Winter is high season in Whistler; in return for skiing or boarding some of the world's best-known slopes, you'll be paying big bucks for accommodations. The vast majority of Whistler visitors return to Vancouver,

but the Gold Nugget Route continues north through Lillooet to central British Columbia, eliminating the need to backtrack.

Most travelers heading east from Vancouver do so on their way to the Okanagan Valley, Kamloops, or beyond. But there are many reasons to stop, including Harrison Hot Springs, so plan your time accordingly. Once at Hope, the highway divides, and you're faced with three more options. Heading north is the zippy Coquihalla Highway or the more scenic Highway 1 through the Fraser River Canyon, which passes natural highlights such as Hell's Gate. Also from Hope, Highway 3 veers east along the U.S. border to mountainous E.C. Manning Provincial Park and a string of delightful towns such as Keremeos, where a historic grist mill continues to grind wheat for delicious breads.

The Sunshine Coast

The 150-kilometer-long (93-mile-long) Sunshine Coast lies along the northeast shore of the Strait of Georgia between Howe Sound in the south and Desolation Sound in the north. This rare bit of sun-drenched Canadian coastline is bordered by countless bays and inlets, broad sandy beaches, quiet lagoons, rugged headlands, provincial parks, and lush fir forests backed by the snowcapped Coast Mountains.

The route from Vancouver is punctuated by two ferry rides and offers delightful glimpses of wilderness islands in the Strait of Georgia. Settlement began here in the late 19th century, and as you work your way up this stretch of the coastline, note the odd assortment of place-names left by Coast Salish natives and Spanish and British navigators.

Today the area is a recreation paradise. Boasting Canada's mildest climate, the Sunshine Coast enjoys moderately warm summers and mild winters, with only 940 millimeters (37 inches) of rain annually and 2,400 hours of sunlight—a few more hours than Victoria, the so-called provincial hot spot. Boaters

and kayakers can cruise into beautiful marine parks providing sheltered anchorage and campsites amid some of the most magnificent scenery along the west coast, or anchor at sheltered fishing villages with marinas and all the modern conveniences.

Traveling Along the Coast

Although the Sunshine Coast is part of the mainland, a trip north entails two trips with **BC Ferries** (604/669-1211 or 888/223-3779, www.bcferries.com). From **Horseshoe Bay,** at the west end of Vancouver's North Shore, ferries regularly cross Howe Sound to **Langdale,** the gateway to the Sunshine Coast. From there, Highway 101 runs up the coast 81 kilometers (50.3 miles) to **Earls Cove,** where another ferry crosses Jervis Inlet to **Saltery Bay.** These trips take 40 and 50 minutes respectively and run approximately every two hours between 6:30 A.M. and 11:30 P.M. The ferry charge is adult $9.60, child $4, vehicle $36, which includes one-way travel on both ferries or round-trip travel on just one ferry.

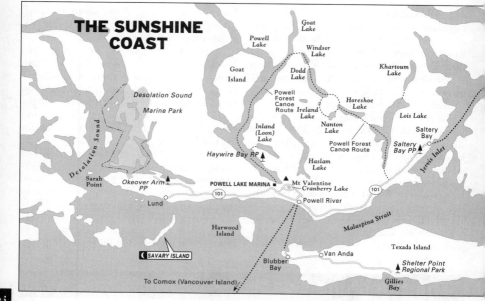

THE SUNSHINE COAST

Goat Lake
Powell Lake
Windsor Lake
Goat Island
Dodd Lake
Khartoum Lake
Desolation Sound Marine Park
Powell Forest Canoe Route
Horeshoe Lake
Ireland Lake
Lois Lake
Saltery Bay
Inland (Loon) Lake
Nanton Lake
Powell Forest Canoe Route
Saltery Bay PP
Haywire Bay RP
Haslam Lake
Desolation Sound
Jervis Inlet
Sarah Point
Okeover Arm PP
POWELL LAKE MARINA
Mt Valentine
Cranberry Lake
101
101
Lund
Powell River
Harwood Island
Malaspina Strait
SAVARY ISLAND
Texada Island
Blubber Bay
Van Anda
Shelter Point Regional Park
Gillies Bay
To Comox (Vancouver Island)

From the terminal at Saltery Bay, Highway 101 continues 35 kilometers (22 miles) to Powell River. From here you can return along the same route or loop back on Vancouver Island via the **Powell River-Comox ferry** (adult $9, child $4.60, vehicle $32).

(Gibsons

A delightful hillside community of 4,000 at the mouth of Howe Sound, Gibsons offers recreation galore. The town has two sections: the original 100-year-old fishing village around the harbor, and a commercial corridor along the highway. Around the harbor, Gower Point Road is a charming strip of seafaring businesses, antique dealers, arty shops, and cafés (this was the setting for the popular 1970s TV series *The Beachcombers*). Down on the harbor itself is a marina and the pleasant Gibsons Seawalk, a 10-minute, scenic meander (lighted at night).

Sunshine Coast Museum (716 Winn Rd., 604/886-8232; Tues.–Sat. 10:30 A.M.–4:30 P.M.) features intriguing pioneer and Coast Salish native displays and holds what must be one of the largest seashell collections on the planet (some 25,000). In summer locals participate in a couple of salmon derbies and revel at the annual **Sea Cavalcade,** which features a swimming race from nearby Keats Island to Gibsons, a parade, and fireworks.

On the main road, **Cedars Inn** (895 Gibsons Way, 604/886-3008 or 888/774-7044, www.thecedarsinn.com; $88 s, $94 d) features a heated outdoor pool, a sauna, a small exercise room, and a restaurant.

Gibsons has a surprisingly good selection of eateries, most in the original part of town on a hill above the marina. For home-style cooking at reasonable prices, try **(Molly's Reach** (647 School Rd., 604/886-9710; breakfast, lunch, and dinner). Food is also offered at the **Waterfront Restaurant** (442 Marine Dr., 604/886-2831; daily 8 A.M.–8 P.M.) overlooking the marina.

At the east entrance to town, **Gibsons Visitor Centre** (900 Gibsons Way, 604/886-2325 or 866/222-3806, www.gibsonsbc.ca; daily 9 A.M.–5 P.M.) is a good first stop for Sunshine Coast information.

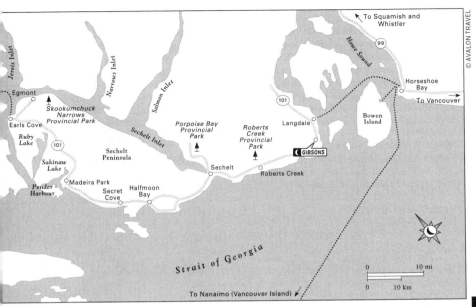

Roberts Creek

About nine kilometers (5.6 miles) north-west of Gibsons is the small artistic community of Roberts Creek (take the lower road off Highway 101), where arts-and-crafts appreciators can often snatch up a bargain. In an old-growth forest, **Roberts Creek Provincial Park,** 14 kilometers (8.7 miles) northwest of Gibsons, holds hiking trails, waterfalls, a picnic ground, and a pebbly beach. Campsites are $14 per night.

The relaxed atmosphere at (**Up the Creek Backpacker's B&B** (1261 Roberts Creek Rd., 604/885-0384 or 877/885-8100, www .upthecreek.ca) is reason enough to rest your head here overnight. Throw in well-priced beds, modern amenities such as a full kitchen and Internet access, and friendly owners, and you'll want to stay longer. Accommodations are in bright dorms ($23 pp) or private rooms ($69 s or d), with a self-serve breakfast an extra $5 per person.

Sechelt and Vicinity

The native cultural center and regional service center of Sechelt (pop. 7,800) perches on the isthmus of the Sechelt Peninsula between the head of Sechelt Inlet and the Strait of Georgia. Logging, fishing, and summer tourism support the town.

One of the area's nicest spots is **Porpoise Bay Provincial Park,** four kilometers (2.5 miles) north of Sechelt via East Porpoise Bay Road. The park offers open grassy areas among forests of fir and cedar, along with a broad, sheltered sandy beach along the eastern shore of Sechelt Inlet. Hiking trails connect the beach with a day-use area and campground, and a woodland trail meanders along the bank of Angus Creek, where chum and coho salmon spawn in fall. The park is a handy base for kayakers and canoeists exploring Sechelt Inlets Provincial Marine Recreation Area. Porpoise Bay and the nearby rivers are also noted for good sportfishing, and oysters and clams are found along the inlet northwest of the park. The 84-site campground ($22) has hot showers. Also on Sechelt Inlet is **Porpoise Bay Charters** (604/885-5950, www.porpoise baycharters.com), a well-established company with kayak rentals and tours, diving charters, and a few waterfront cabins ($105 s or d).

Out of town to the west, **Rockwater Secret Cove Resort** (604/885-7038 or 877/296-4593, www.rockwatersecretcoveresort.com) is an upscale waterfront complex overlooking Halfmoon Bay. It has a wonderful restaurant (for the food and view), lodge rooms from $169 s or d, cabins for $179–229 s or d, and luxurious Tenthouse Suites, nestled in a forest, for $379.

Sechelt Visitor Centre (5790 Teredo St., 604/885-1036; summer daily 9 A.M.–5 P.M., the rest of the year Mon.–Sat. 10 A.M.–4 P.M.) is well signposted along Highway 101.

Pender Harbour

Along the shores of Pender Harbour lie the villages of Madeira Park, Garden Bay, and Irvines Landing. Boating and ocean fishing are popular activities on this stretch of coast, and Ruby and Sakinaw Lakes—between Madeira Park and Earls Cove—are a trout fisher's delight in season. Canoeists head for the chain of eight lakes between Garden Bay and Egmont, where those casting a line will find good fishing for cutthroat trout May–October.

Skookumchuck Narrows Provincial Park

Just before Earls Cove, take the road north to Egmont, then the four-kilometer (2.5-mile) hiking trail (one hour each way) along Sechelt Inlet to a tidal oddity protected as a park. Its name meaning "turbulent water" in Chinook, Skookumchuck protects Narrows and Roland Points and the 400-meter-wide (1,300-footwide) rock-strewn waterway between them. The tides of three inlets roar through this narrow passage four times a day. The resulting rapids and eddies boisterously boil and bubble to create fierce-looking whirlpools—fascinating to see when your feet are firmly planted on terra firma, but very dangerous for inexperienced boaters unfamiliar with the tides. It's a particularly amazing spectacle one hour after the ebb of extra-low spring tides, when the rapids may reach as high as five meters (16 feet) and the water whooshes past at 20 kph (12

mph). At any low tide, you'll also see abundant marine creatures in tidal pools—it's a fascinating spot. Take a picnic lunch, pull up a rock, and enjoy the view.

Earls Cove

Earls Cove marks the end of this section of Highway 101. From here, BC Ferries offers regular service across Jervis Inlet to Saltery Bay. The 16-kilometer (10-mile) crossing takes 50 minutes.

Saltery Bay and Vicinity

Less than two kilometers (1.2 miles) from the Saltery Bay ferry terminal is 140-hectare (346-acre) **Saltery Bay Provincial Park,** one of the Sunshine Coast's diving hot spots. All the best dive spots are accessible as shore dives, including a bronze mermaid. The park is broken into two sections. The southernmost is where the diving takes place, and it also holds a campground ($14 per night). Less than one kilometer (0.6 mile) farther up the road is the park's dayuse area, with picnic tables and a grassed area fronting the rocky foreshore.

Bookended by the park's two sections is **Kent's Beach Resort** (604/487-9386, www.kentsbeach.com; Mar.–Oct.), one of the coast's many old-fashioned, family-friendly oceanfront resorts. In July and August, the eight self-contained cabins are rented by the week ($655–965). The rest of the operating season, you can snag your waterfront getaway for just $90–105 per night. Either way, furnishings are sparse (bring your own bedding), but the setting is unbeatable. Camping is $18–27 per night, with the more expensive sites right on the waterfront.

From Saltery Bay, it's 30 kilometers (19 miles) of winding road to Powell River. Along the way you'll cross Lois River, the outlet for large Lois Lake, and pass a string of coastal communities clinging to the rocky shoreline of Malaspina Strait.

POWELL RIVER

Situated between Jervis Inlet and Desolation Sound along the edge of Malaspina Strait, Powell River (pop. 16,500) is almost surrounded by water. The town is actually a municipality made up of four communities. **Townsite,** the original "Powell River," is occupied by an ugly waterfront pulp mill and a number of boarded-up buildings. A few kilometers south is **Westview,** Powell River's main service center, home to the ferry terminal and information center as well as accommodations and restaurants. The other two official communities are **Wildwood,** north of Townsite, and **Cranberry,** east of Townsite.

Powell River holds one of the world's largest pulp and paper mill complexes and is a thriving center for the region's abundant outdoor-recreation opportunities, including salmon fishing (good year-round), trout fishing, scuba diving, sailing, canoeing, kayaking, and hiking.

Sights

Start your exploration by visiting the excellent **Powell River Historical Museum** across the road from Willingdon Beach (Marine Ave., 604/485-2222; summer daily 10 A.M.–5 P.M., the rest of the year Mon.–Fri. only), which is like wandering back in time. Peruse the vast collection of photographs (the province's third-largest archives) and other displays to find out about this seashore community and to see what the area was like before the town was established.

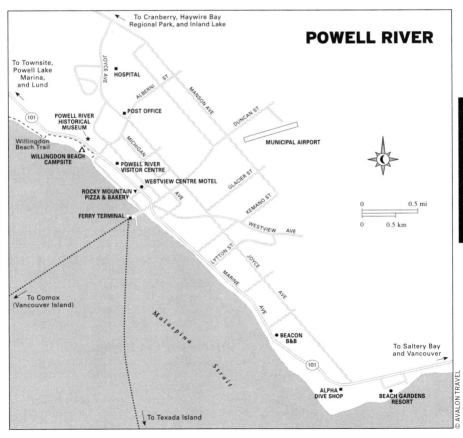

POWELL RIVER

SOUTHWESTERN B.C.

© AVALON TRAVEL

© ANDREW HEMPSTEAD

Powell River Marina

Also see well-preserved artifacts, native carvings and baskets, the shanty home of a hermit who once lived along Powell Lake, and even sand from around the world.

North through the main built-up area is the original town site, built around a bay that still holds a working pulp and paper mill complex. The *Heritage Walk* brochure (available at the information center) will guide you around the interesting array of buildings that date from 1910 to the 1930s. Many—such as the grand Hotel Rodmay and the imposing Federal Building—have been boarded up for decades. Drive along Sycamore Street and you'll see many Craftsman-style homes in varying states of disrepair. **Norske Canada** operates the mill, and tours are available June–September Monday–Friday four times a day. Book through the information center (604/485-4701).

Hiking

While most visitors to Powell River spend their time enjoying water-oriented sports, the hiking around town is also good—and chances are you'll have the trails to yourself.

From Powell River's municipal campground, the 1.2-kilometer (0.7-mile) **Willingdon Beach Trail** spurs north past interpretive boards describing natural features and the uses of old logging machinery scattered along the trail. The trail ends at a viewpoint overlooking historic Townsite and the pulp operations. One of the most popular short local trails is the one-kilometer (0.6-mile) hike up **Mount Valentine,** north of Cranberry. The trail leads to a stunning panoramic view of Malaspina Strait and the Strait of Georgia. Access is from the end of Crown Avenue: Take Manson Avenue east to Cranberry Street, turn left, then turn right on Crown.

Canoeing and Kayaking

The sheltered Sunshine Coast provides plenty of opportunities for good lake and ocean canoeing or kayaking. The most popular canoe trip is the **Powell Forest Canoe Route** (see sidebar), while kayakers find solitude in **Desolation Sound** (see *Lund and Vicinity*).

Mitchell Canoe & Kayak (Myrtle Point Rd., 604/487-1609, www.canoeingbc.com) rents canoes for the Powell Forest Canoe Route. Prices range $50–70 for one day, or $130–210 for five days. The company also rents all the necessary accessories and fishing gear, provides free parking, and runs a shuttle service to and from the put-in ($75).

Although **Powell River Sea Kayak** (Malaspina Rd., 604/483-2160 or 866/617-4444, www.bcseakayak.com) outfits for the Powell Forest Canoe Route, kayaks are its specialty. Single and double kayaks for use around local waterways rent for $44–70 for one day and $84–135 for two days. Guided three-hour tours are $65, a snorkeling tour (wetsuit included) is $49, and overnight sea-kayaking trips start at $395.

Scuba Diving

Known as the "Diving Capital of Canada," the Strait of Georgia provides divers with exceptionally clear, relatively warm water and more than 100 exciting dives mapped by local experts. Conditions are particularly excellent in winter, when visibility reaches 30 meters (98 feet). Expect to see underwater cliffs and abundant marinelife, including sponges, giant octopuses, wolf eels, perch, lingcod, tubeworms, sea anemones, nudibranchs (including intriguing hooded nudibranchs), sea stars, crabs, and tunicates. Seals can be seen year-round, sea lions November–April.

The highlight for wreck divers on the Sunshine Coast is the HMCS *Chaudiere,* sunk in 1993 to form an artificial reef. The hull provides a home for colorful marinelife, and giant holes have been cut through it to enable adventurous divers to do some inside exploration.

Diving gear and a list of charter operators are available at **Alpha Dive Services** (7013 Thunder Bay St., 604/485-6939, www.dive powellriver.com), on the south side of town.

Accommodations and Camping

Powell River doesn't have a great number of motel rooms, so try to reserve a room in advance or plan to camp or head north to Lund

POWELL FOREST CANOE ROUTE

This four- to eight-day backcountry canoe route is a great way to get away from it all, surrounding yourself with tree-covered lowlands and rugged mountain peaks while slipping through fjordlike lakes. Take side trips and you can extend the water distance from 67 kilometers (41.6 miles) to more than 150 kilometers (93 miles), or just do one or two sections of the trail – all the major lakes can be reached by road.

To reach the put-in at **Lois Lake,** take Highway 101 east of Powell River 20 kilometers (12.4 miles) to a logging road that branches north off the highway. Follow that road for one kilometer (0.6 mile), then turn right on the Branch 41 logging road and follow it seven kilometers (4.3 miles) to a primitive lakeside campground. The route includes paddling along part of Lois Lake, then the lengths of **Horseshoe, Dodd, Windsor,** and **Goat Lakes** to **Powell Lake.** Powell Lake Marina is the most popular pull-out point. In total, the route requires 57 kilometers (35.4 miles) of paddling and 10 kilometers (6.2 miles) of portaging. The longest single paddle is 28.5 kilometers (17.7 miles), and the longest portage is 2.5 kilometers (1.6 miles). Carry a tent, stove, and supplies, and stay at one of the 20 Forest Service recreation sites and camping areas along the route. Don't forget your fishing rod and tackle: All the lakes are stocked with cutthroat trout, and some hold rainbow trout and kokanee.

The route's major outfitter is **Mitchell Canoe & Kayak** (Myrtle Point Rd., 604/487-1699, www.canoeingbc.com). Canoe rentals range $50-70 for one day, $130-210 for five days. The company provides all accessories and free car parking, and shuttles paddlers to and from the route. A three-day guided paddle is $355 per person.

For a map and brochure describing the route in detail and to find out present water levels and campfire regulations, contact the **Powell River Visitor Centre** (4690 Marine Ave., Westview, 604/485-4701).

(where you'll also need reservations). A solid cheapie is **Westview Centre Motel** (4534 Marine Ave., 604/485-4023 or 877/485-4023, www.westviewcentremotel.com), where basic rooms sell for $68 s, $78 d per night.

One of the most attractive and relaxing lodgings in Powell River is **Beacon Bed and Breakfast** (3750 Marine Dr., 604/485-5563 or 800/485-5563, www.beaconbb.com), which overlooks Malaspina Strait and the peaks of Vancouver Island two kilometers (1.2 miles) south of the ferry terminal. Within the two-story home are three guest rooms, each with ocean views. Facilities include a lounge area overlooking the water, an outdoor hot tub, Internet access, spa services, and in-room luxuries like fluffy robes. Rates are $89–129 s, $99–139 d, which includes a big breakfast that will set you up for a day of outdoor activities.

The ordinary rooms at **Beach Gardens Resort** (five kilometers/3.1 miles south of the ferry terminal, 7074 Westminster Ave., 604/485-6267 or 800/663-7070, www.beach gardens.com; $105–165 s or d) are more than made up for by amenities like an indoor swimming pool, a sauna, tennis courts, a fitness room, and a marina with boat rentals and divers' air (it's a great place to meet fellow scuba enthusiasts). The resort's waterfront restaurant offers lunchtime buffets and a pub.

Willingdon Beach Campsite (4845 Marine Ave., 604/485-2242) enjoys a great waterfront location one kilometer (0.6 mile) north of the ferry terminal. You'll find sheltered and very popular campsites along the beach, as well as a laundry and washrooms with free hot showers. Basic tent sites are $20, hookups $24–26.

Food

Head to **Rocky Mountain Pizza and Bakery Co.** (4471 Marine Ave., 604/485-9111, Mon.–Sat. from 6:30 A.M., Sun. from 8 A.M.) for great bakery items, coffee as strong (or as weak) as you like it, and daily newspapers. The rest of the day it's pizza, pizza, and more pizza until 6 or 7 P.M., depending on the season. At the entrance to Willingdon Beach, the **Beach Hut** is busy throughout summer serving battered

fish and chips, hamburgers, and the Sunshine Coast's best ice cream.

Manzanita (6243 Walnut St., Townsite, 604/483-2228; Fri.–Mon. for lunch, daily from 5 P.M. for dinner) is within the restored Old Courthouse Inn, a government building dating to 1939. Given its history, the dining room is surprisingly warm, with a cheery ambience and an ever-changing menu of seasonal seafood. Expect to pay from $18 for a dinner main.

At the marina overlooking Powell Lake, north of town, the **Shinglemill** (604/483-2001) is part pub, part restaurant, with the former spilling out onto a wide deck. The pub menu is wide-ranging; a good choice is the seafood chowder served in a sourdough bread bowl ($6.75). In the restaurant, mains like salmon baked in a soy-ginger glaze range $15–24.50. The restaurant is open daily for dinner while the pub is open daily 11 A.M.–11 P.M. Whichever room you choose, you'll be pleasantly surprised by the well-priced wine list.

Information and Services

Powell River Visitor Centre is along the main strip of shops (4690 Marine Ave., 604/485-4701, www.discoverpowellriver.com; summer Mon.–Sat. 9 A.M.–9 P.M. and Sun. 9 A.M.–5 P.M., the rest of the year weekdays only). Coming off the ferry from Vancouver Island, drive up the hill to Marine Avenue and turn left; it's three blocks down on the right. **Powell River Public Library** (4411 Michigan Ave., 604/485-4796; Mon.–Sat. 10 A.M.–5 P.M.) is a good place to hang out on a rainy day.

Head to **River City Coffee** (4801 Joyce Ave., 604/485-0011; daily from 8 A.M.) to check your email.

Getting There and Around

Powell River Municipal Airport is east of town, off Duncan Street. **Pacific Coastal** (604/483-2107 or 800/663-2872) flies at least three times daily between Powell River and its hub at the South Terminal of Vancouver International Airport.

The ferry terminal in Powell River is at the

foot of Duncan Street, right downtown. **BC Ferries** (604/485-2943) has regular sailings between Powell River and Comox on Vancouver Island. One-way fares for the 75-minute sailing are $9, child $4.60, vehicle $32. You can't make reservations—just roll up and join the queue.

Sunshine Coast Transit System (604/885-3234) operates local bus service between Sunshine Coast communities; $2.25 per sector (no Sun. service).

TEXADA ISLAND

A 35-minute ferry trip from the Powell River ferry terminal, Texada is one of the largest of the Gulf Islands (50 kilometers/31 miles from north to south and up to 10 kilometers/6.2 miles wide), but the permanent population is only 1,400 and services are limited. Originally home to a whaling station, the island has also housed a couple of mining operations and a distillery that supplied illegal liquor to the United States during Prohibition.

From the ferry terminal at Blubber Bay, the island's main road winds south for eight kilometers (five miles) to **Van Anda,** a historic village that once boasted saloons, an opera house, and a hospital. Take a walk along Van Anda's Erickson Beach to appreciate the island's natural beauty. Continuing south, the road leads to Gillies Bay and beyond to **Shelter Point Regional Park,** which has some short but enjoyable hiking trails and a sandy spit that leads to a private high-tide island. At low tide, look for colorful starfish along the shoreline, or maybe try your hand digging for clams. Campsites overlooking the water are $17.

Getting to Texada

The short hop over to the island from Powell River with **BC Ferries** (604/485-2943) costs adult $6.25, child $3.75, vehicle $16.50 round-trip. Ferries depart about every two hours 8 A.M.–11 P.M.; no reservations taken.

LUND AND VICINITY

Twenty-eight kilometers (17 miles) north of Powell River, Highway 101 dead-ends at the old wooden wharf of Lund, a tiny fishing village founded in 1889 and named after the Swedish hometown of the first settlers. Lund lies on a secluded harbor backed by the magnificent peaks of the Coast Mountains. Although best known as the gateway to Desolation Sound, it's worth the trip out just for the relaxed atmosphere and surrounding beauty. Wander around the bustling marina, cruise over to the white-sand beaches of Savary Island, or relax with a cold drink on the deck of the Lund Hotel. At the back of the Lund Hotel, **Rockfish Kayak** (604/414-9355) rents kayaks for $45–75 per day; transport the kayaks to Okeover Arm and you're on your way.

Savary Island

A geological quirk created Savary Island, the only sandy island in the Strait of Georgia. While the hundreds of other Gulf Islands are rocky in origin, Savary is composed of glacial till that was left behind after the last ice age. Over time, the island has become forested, but it is still ringed by telltale sandy beaches. A few hundred lucky souls have summer homes on Savary, but most visitors arrive just for the day, traveling by water taxi (604/483-9749), which departs 4–5 times daily for $8.50 per person each way. By the island dock is a café and bike rental outlet. For information on island services, including accommodations, visit www.savary.ca.

Desolation Sound

Desolation Sound was named by Captain Vancouver after his visit in 1792—he was obviously unimpressed, as the name implies. Today, 8,256 hectares (20,400 acres) of the sound are protected as **Desolation Sound Marine Park,** the largest of British Columbia's 50 marine parks. The park also preserves over 60 kilometers (37 miles) of shoreline, a number of offshore islands, the Gifford Peninsula, and a section of mainland that includes Unwin Lake. A wilderness-seeker's paradise, the park is totally undeveloped and without road access. The sound is a popular yachtie hangout and a haven for sea kayakers, who need to be totally self-sufficient here.

The shallow, sheltered waters of **Okeover Arm**—a southern arm of Desolation Sound but outside the park—provide the perfect environment for all kinds of prolific marinelife; try to time your visit with the receding tide. Access is via Malaspina Road, off Highway 101 south of Lund. Forested four-hectare (10-acre) **Okeover Arm Provincial Park** lies on the water; it's a small, rustic park with just a few undeveloped campsites ($14), a pit toilet, and a kayak- and boat-launching ramp, but it's a great spot to camp if you're into canoeing or kayaking.

Accommodations

The only accommodation right in town is the **Historic Lund Hotel** (604/414-0474 or 877/569-3999, www.lundhotel.com; $120–220 s or d), which sits right on the harbor. The historic charm of the original guest rooms has been replaced by contemporary styling and hand-painted murals. The hotel complex holds a pub, restaurant, kayak rental shop, laundry, post office, art gallery, and grocery store.

Historic Lund Hotel

If you're looking for something a little different, choose to stay at **(The Dome** (off Baggi Rd., 604/483-9160, www.magicaldome.com; $140), a five-minute drive from Lund. As far as I know, it's the only place in Canada where you can stay in a geodesic dome—a quirky architectural style that employs dozens of triangular panels to form a rigid spherical structure that creates the most space with the least amount of materials. Inside is a bedroom, loft with second bed, well-equipped kitchen, lounge area, and wood-burning fireplace. Adjacent is a modern bathhouse, complete with sauna.

Set on three hectares (7.4 acres) overlooking Okeover Arm, **(Desolation Resort** (2694 Dawson Rd., 604/483-3592 or 800/399-3592, www.desolationresort.com) offers a wonderful escape at reasonable prices. Accommodation is in freestanding wood chalets set high above the lake edge on stilts. All feature rich-colored wood furnishings, and even the smallest (the bottom half of one unit) has a king-size bed, a large deck, a kitchen, separate living and dining areas, and a barbecue. Rates range from just $149 for the unit detailed above to $360 for four guests sharing a two-bedroom, two-bathroom chalet. Fishing, canoeing, and kayaking are practically right out your door at the private marina.

Food

In addition to a fine choice of accommodations, Lund is home to a couple of the Sunshine Coast's premier restaurants. The food at **Historic Lund Hotel** (604/414-0474) is overshadowed by the views, especially if you talk your way to an outside table. Crab cakes topped with crab salad are a good starter, followed by seafood fettuccine as a main and a slab of mud cake for dessert. Choose this combo and you'll pay around $35—about the same as a main meal in Vancouver.

The upscale **(Laughing Oyster** (Vandermaeden Rd., 604/483-9775; Wed.–Sun. noon–8:30 P.M.) is a hidden gem. In this restaurant overlooking the water from an elevated setting, diners are seated outside on a deck or inside on tiers that allow everyone to enjoy the view.

Starters include oysters prepared in a variety of ways (you can see the restaurant's oyster farm from the deck) and a healthy blue cheese salad. Mains range $18–25 and include a perfectly presented baked halibut dish. Even if you're full, try a slice of melt-in-your-mouth bourbon pecan pie for desert. The Laughing Oyster is a well-signposted, five-minute drive from Lund.

Sea to Sky Highway

The spectacular, aptly named Sea to Sky Highway (Highway 99) runs 105 kilometers (65 miles) between Horseshoe Bay and Whistler. With the almost-vertical tree-covered **Coast Mountains** to the east and island-dotted **Howe Sound** to the west, this newly upgraded, cliff-hugging highway winds precariously through a dramatic glacier-carved landscape.

HORSESHOE BAY TOWARD SQUAMISH
Porteau Cove Provincial Park
On the east shore of Howe Sound, Porteau Cove is best known among the diving fraternity for its artificial reef of four sunken wrecks, but it also offers good swimming and fishing. In addition, the area's strong winds and lack of waves make for perfect windsurfing conditions. The park holds boat-launching and scuba-diving facilities, an ecology information center, picnic tables, and a waterfront campground for tents and RVs. A day pass is $5 per vehicle and camping is $22 per night March–October (free the rest of the year).

Britannia Beach
Small Britannia Beach is worth a stop to visit the **BC Museum of Mining** (604/896-2233; mid-May–early Oct. daily 9 A.M.–4:30 P.M., weekdays only the rest of the year; adult $15, senior and student $12), overlooking Howe Sound. In the early 1930s the Britannia Beach Mine was the British Empire's largest producer of copper, producing more than 600,000 tons. Today it's not a working mine but a working museum. Ever wondered what it's like to slave away underground? Here's your chance to don a hard hat and raincoat, hop on an electric train, and travel under a mountain, without even getting your hands dirty. See fully functional mining equipment, along with demonstrations and displays on the techniques of mining. Then take a step into the past in the museum, where hundreds of photos and artifacts tell the story of the mine.

Continuing North
Straddling the highway, tiny **Murrin Provincial Park** provides good boating, fishing, swimming, and walking trails, as well as steep cliffs that attract novice and intermediate rock climbers. The park has picnic tables but no campsites ($3 per day admission). Farther up the highway, stop at **Shannon Falls Provincial Park** to view the spectacular 335-meter-high (1,100-foot-high) namesake falls from a platform at the base. You can picnic here or hike a few trails. No campsites are available, but just across the road is **Klahanie Campground and RV Park** (604/892-3435, www.klahaniecampground.com; $22–28 per site).

SQUAMISH
Squamish (pop. 15,000), 67 kilometers (42 miles) north of Vancouver and 53 kilometers (33 miles) south of Whistler, enjoys a stunning location at the head of Howe Sound, surrounded by snowcapped mountains. The name Squamish is a native Coast Salish word meaning "mother of the wind"—the town gets stiff breezes year-round, delighting today's sailors and windsurfers. Lumber is still the lifeblood of the area: The town holds four sawmills, and along **Mamquam Blind Channel** on the east side of town you can see logs being boomed in preparation for towing to other mills.

Town Sights
See around 65 vintage rail cars and engines in a

mock working rail yard, complete with a station garden, a replica workers' home, and a restored station at the **West Coast Railway Heritage Park** (Industrial Way, one km from Hwy. 99, 604/524-1011; May–Oct. daily 10 A.M.–5 P.M.; adult $12, child $9.50). In a converted heritage house, **Squamish Valley Museum** (2nd Ave., 604/898-3273; Wed.–Sun.; donation) has the usual collection of local memorabilia. Farther along 2nd Avenue, at Victoria Street, a colorful mural covers the exterior of the Ocean Pub, depicting the natural and human elements of life along the west coast.

Recreation

Although Squamish has a reputation as an industrial town, it is also the center of a growing recreation-based economy. Leading the way is rock climbing on the 762-meter-high (2,500-foot-high) **Stawamus Chief,** clearly visible across the highway from downtown. The "Chief," as it's best known, is one of the world's largest granite monoliths. It formed around 100 million years ago as massive forces

deep inside the earth forced molten magma through the crust—as it cooled, it hardened and fractured, creating a perfect environment for today's climbers. The face offers a great variety of free and aided climbing on almost 1,000 routes, which take in dikes, cracks, slabs, chasms, and ridges. Climbers camp at the base for $11 per night but head into town to the aquatic center to shower and soak in a hot tub ($4 per visit). If you've never climbed or are inexperienced, consider using the services of **Squamish Rock Guides** (604/815-1750, www.squamishrockguides.com) for a variety of courses with equipment supplied; expect to pay around $100 per person for a beginner's climbing course. **Vertical Reality Sports Store** (38154 2nd Ave., 604/892-8248) offers a full range of climbing equipment and sells local climbing guidebooks.

At first it may be difficult to see past the industrial scars along Squamish's waterways, but on the west side of downtown, a large section of the delta where the Squamish River flows into Howe Sound has escaped development. It

Stawamus Chief

comprises tidal flats, forested areas, marshes, and open meadows—and over 200 species of birds call the area home. Hiking trails lace the area, and there are three main access points: Industrial Road, the end of Winnipeg Street, and the end of Vancouver Street, all of which branch off Cleveland Avenue.

Squamish celebrates two very different lifestyles at its major annual events. The last week of June is the **Squamish Mountain Festival** (www.squamishmountainfestival.com), a semi-social gathering of adventure-loving folk who come for the mountain biking, windsurfing, white-water kayaking, rock climbing, and even kite-flying. Then, early in August, Squamish is mobbed by loggers from around the world who congregate for the annual **Squamish Days Logger Sports** (www.squamishdays.org). Don't be too surprised to see people competing at racing up trees, rolling logs, and throwing axes. The show also includes an RV rally, Truck Loggers Rodeo, dances, pageants, and parades.

Accommodations and Camping

The best place to stay around Squamish is ◖ **Dryden Creek Resorts,** six kilometers (3.7 miles) north of town at Depot Road (604/898-9726 or 877/237-9336, www.dryden creek.com). It's on six hectares (14 acres) of landscaped parkland with Garibaldi Provincial Park as a backdrop. Each of the six suite-style studios has a cedar ceiling, large skylights, wireless Internet, and fully equipped kitchen with handcrafted cabinets. Rates of $85 s or d include complimentary coffee and chocolates. The resort's campground offers a choice of forested or creekside sites; unserviced sites $22, hookups $28.

Rooms at the **Garibaldi Budget Inn** (38012 3rd Ave., 604/892-5204 or 888/313-9299) go for just $59 s, $79 d, but if you're planning a big night out across the road at Squamish's infamous Ocean's Pub, you probably don't care that they are ordinary at best. Also right downtown, **Howe Sound Inn** (37801 Cleveland Ave., 604/892-2603 or 800/919-2537, www.howesound.com) is a stylish place with

THE EAGLES OF BRACKENDALE

Squamish itself doesn't have a ton of sights, but if you're in the area during winter, Brackendale, just to the north along Highway 99, is definitely worth a stop. Through the colder months of the year, the river flats behind this sleepy little town are home to a larger concentration of bald eagles than anywhere else on the face of the earth. Over 3,000 of these magnificent creatures descend on a stretch of the Squamish River between the Cheakamus and Mam-quam tributaries to feed on spawned-out salmon that litter the banks. The dead fish are the result of a late-fall run of an estimated 100,000 chum salmon. The birds begin arriving in late October, but numbers reach their peak around late December, and by early February the birds are gone. The best viewing spot is from the dike that runs along the back of Brackendale.

The best place to learn more about these creatures is the **Brackendale Art Gallery** (604/898-3333; Jan. daily noon–5 P.M., weekends only the rest of the year), which has an adjacent bird-watching tower that rises some 11 meters (36 feet) above the surrounding trees. Through January, the gallery is Eagle Count Headquarters, with slide presentations, talks, and other eagle-related activities. Guided walks to the site cost $35 per person. To get to the gallery, follow the main Brackendale access road over the railway tracks, take the first right, and look for the gallery nestled in the trees on the right.

20 modern rooms from $109 s or d. In keeping with the local scene, the inn has a climbing wall, along with underground parking, wireless Internet access, a restaurant, and an in-house brewery.

Information

For detailed information on Squamish, local provincial parks, and Whistler, follow the signs from the highway downtown to **Squamish Visitor Centre** (38551 Loggers Lane, 604/815-4994 or 866/333-2010, www.squamish chamber.com; daily 9 A.M.–6 P.M.). It's part of the Squamish Adventure Centre, home to a theater, an activity booking desk, and a café.

NORTH TOWARD WHISTLER
Garibaldi Provincial Park

This beautiful park encompasses 195,000 hectares (481,850 acres) of pristine alpine wilderness east of Highway 99. Dominated by the snowcapped and glaciated Coast Mountains, the park reaches a high point at 2,678-meter (8,790-foot) **Mount Garibaldi,** named in 1860 after Italian soldier and statesman Giuseppe Garibaldi. Other park features include 2,315-meter (7,600-foot) **Black Tusk,** the **Gargoyles** (eroded rock formations reached by a trail from the park's southern entrance), and a 1.6-kilometer-long (one-mile-long) lava flow above the west side of **Garibaldi Lake.**

Garibaldi is a true wilderness park, with road access only up to the park boundary. From late July through early September, the hiking is fabulous—through forests of fir, red cedar, hemlock, and balsam, across high meadows crowded with spectacular wildflowers, and past bright blue lakes, huge glaciers, and jagged volcanic peaks and lava flows.

Between Squamish and Pemberton, five clearly marked entrance roads lead off Highway 99 to trailheads providing access into the five most popular areas of the park: **Diamond Head, Black Tusk/Garibaldi Lake, Cheakamus Lake, Singing Pass,** and **Wedgemount Lake.** Aside from these five areas, the rest of the park is untouched wilderness, explored only by mountaineers and

experienced cross-country skiers. All major trails have backcountry tent sites.

Alice Lake Provincial Park

Alice Lake, surrounded by a 400-hectare (1,000-acre) park of open grassy areas, dense forests, and impressive snowcapped peaks, is particularly good for canoeing, swimming, and fishing for small rainbow and cutthroat trout. A 1.4-kilometer (0.9-mile) trail encircles the lake, while others lead to three smaller bodies of water; allow 20 minutes for the loop. A campground with showers and picnic tables is open year-round; unserviced sites are $22, powered sites $27. It costs $5 per vehicle for a day pass. The park entrance is 13 kilometers (eight miles) north of Squamish, and the lake just under two kilometers (1.2 miles) from the highway.

Brandywine Falls Provincial Park

If you like waterfalls, stop at this small park 45 kilometers (28 miles) north of Squamish and follow the 300-meter (0.2-mile), five-minute trail from the parking lot. It's the kind of trail that excites all your senses: magnificent frosty peaks high above, dense lush forest on either side, a fast, deep river roaring along on one side, the pungent aroma and cushiness of crushed pine needles beneath your feet. The trail takes you to a viewing platform to see 66-meter-high (220-foot-high) **Brandywine Falls,** where the waters plummet down a vertical lava cliff into a massive swirling plunge pool, then roar down a forest-edged river into a lake. It's most magnificent early in summer. The falls were named in the early part of the 20th century by two railroad surveyors who made a wager on guessing the falls' height, the winner to receive bottles of, you guessed it, brandywine.

Whistler

Magnificent snowcapped peaks, dense green forests, transparent lakes, sparkling rivers, and an upmarket, cosmopolitan village right in the middle of it all: Welcome to Whistler (pop. 10,000), one of the world's great resort towns, just 120 kilometers (75 miles) north of Vancouver along Highway 99. The Whistler Valley has seen incredible development in recent years and is now British Columbia's third most popular tourist destination (behind Vancouver and Victoria), attracting around two million visitors annually. Things will be even busier in February 2010, when Whistler hosts the downhill, Nordic, and sliding events of the Olympic Winter Games. The crowds and the costs might not be for everyone, but there *is* a great variety of things to do in Whistler, and the village takes full advantage of magnificent natural surroundings, making a trip north from Vancouver well worthwhile at any time of year.

Best-known among skiers and boarders, the town is built around the base of one of North America's finest resorts, **Whistler/Blackcomb**, which comprises almost 3,000 hectares (7,400 acres) on two mountains accessed by an ultra-modern lift system. A season stretching from November to early June doesn't leave much time for summer recreation, but in recent years, the "off-season" has become almost equally busy. Among the abundant summertime recreation opportunities: lift-served hiking and glacier skiing and boarding; biking through the valley and mountains; water activities on five lakes; horseback riding; golfing on some of the world's best resort courses; and fishing, rafting, and jet-boating on the rivers. The more sedentary summer visitor can simply stay in bustling **Whistler Village** and enjoy a plethora of outdoor cafés and restaurants.

HISTORY

The history of Whistler as a resort town doesn't *really* begin until the 1960s and is associated almost entirely with the development of the ski area. At this time the only development was a bunch of ramshackle summer holiday houses around Alta Lake (which was also the name of the "town"), population 300. In 1964 the rough and treacherous road linking the valley to Vancouver was finally paved, and in 1965 the Garibaldi Lift Co. began constructing the first lifts on the west side of what was then called London Mountain. The idea of a European-style ski-in, ski-out village was promoted throughout the 1970s, but it wasn't until 1980 that Whistler Village officially opened. The lift system on what became known as Whistler Mountain (after the shrill call of marmots that lived around its summit) had by this time expanded greatly, but the capacity of the resort doubled for the 1980–81 season with the opening of a resort on adjacent Blackcomb Mountain. Throughout the last two decades of the 20th century, on-mountain construction was overshadowed by developments in the valley below: Intrawest spent $25 million on base facilities at Blackcomb, some of the best-known names in the golf world were brought in to

SUMMER SKIING

Just because the calendar, thermometer, and sun's angle say it's summer doesn't mean skiing is months away. Whistler/Blackcomb is one of just two North American resorts offering lift-served summer skiing. Between late June and early August (but very weather-dependent), a T-bar on Blackcomb Mountain's **Horstman Glacier** opens up a small 45-hectare (110-acre) area with a vertical rise of 209 meters (520 feet). The lift opens daily noon-3 P.M.; adult $49, child $25 includes lift transportation from the valley floor. The slopes can get crowded, with local and national ski teams in training and with visitors enjoying the novelty of summer skiing. But if it gets too bad, just go back to the valley floor for golf or water sports.

design championship-standard golf courses, Whistler Village Centre opened in 1995, and the population increased 10-fold in 20 years.

Looking Forward

Overdevelopment is an ongoing concern throughout the valley. The most recent community plan has recommended capping the number of "beds" at 52,500, up from the current number of 42,000. The main reason for a cap on development is a lack of available land. But the demand for both motel rooms and residential lots is seemingly never-ending, pushing up the costs of living and of staying in the village (empty lots sell for up to $4,000,000, and existing homes range $700,000 to $22 million). In addition, Whistler will share hosting duties with Vancouver for the 2010 Olympic Winter Games. Planned venues include the main ski resort and the Callaghan Valley, 16 kilometers (10 miles) south of the village. Check out the latest at www.vancouver2010.com.

Whistler Museum

The best place to learn the full story of development in the valley is the Whistler Museum (4329 Main St., 604/932-2019; summer daily 10 A.M.–4 P.M., the rest of the year Fri.–Sun. 10 A.M.–4 P.M.; adult $2, child $1).

SPORTS AND RECREATION
◖ Whistler Gondola

During the few months that they aren't covered in snow, the slopes of **Whistler/ Blackcomb** come alive with locals and tourists alike enjoying hiking, guided naturalist walks, mountain biking, and horseback riding, or just marveling at the mountainscape from the comfort of the lifts. Die-hard skiers will even find glacier skiing here early in the summer. More than 50 kilometers (31 miles) of hiking trails wind around the mountains, including trails through the high alpine to destinations such as beautiful Harmony Lake (2.5 kilometers/1.6 miles from the top of the gondola; Whistler Mountain) or to the toe of a small glacier (2.5 kilometers/1.6 miles from the top of the gondola; Whistler Mountain).

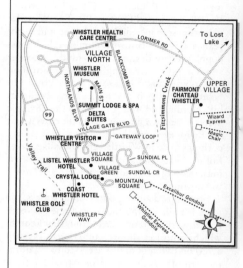

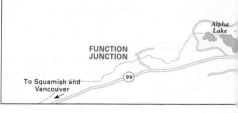

WHISTLER

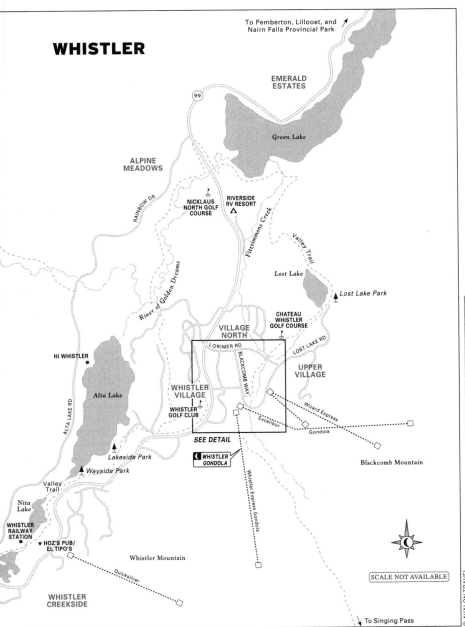

To Pemberton, Lillooet, and
Nairn Falls Provincial Park

EMERALD
ESTATES

99

Green Lake

ALPINE
MEADOWS

RAINBOW DR

NICKLAUS
NORTH GOLF
COURSE

RIVERSIDE
RV RESORT

Fitzsimmons Creek

Valley Trail

Lost Lake

Lost Lake Park

River of Golden Dreams

CHATEAU
WHISTLER
GOLF COURSE

VILLAGE
NORTH

LORIMER RD

LOST LAKE RD

HI WHISTLER

BLACKCOMB WAY

UPPER
VILLAGE

Alta Lake

WHISTLER
VILLAGE

WHISTLER
GOLF CLUB

Wizard Express

ALTA LAKE RD

Excalibur

Gondola

SEE DETAIL

Blackcomb Mountain

WHISTLER
GONDOLA

Lakeside Park

Wayside Park

Whistler Express Gondola

Valley
Trail

Nita
Lake

WHISTLER
RAILWAY
STATION

HOZ'S PUB/
EL TIPO'S

Whistler Mountain

SCALE NOT AVAILABLE

Quicksilver

WHISTLER
CREEKSIDE

To Singing Pass

SOUTHWESTERN B.C.

© BONNY MAKAREWICZ

Take a summer gondola ride to access alpine hiking areas in Whistler.

It's also possible to rent snowshoes for $6 per hour to walk across areas of year-round snowpack. Or for an adrenaline rush, take the gondola up and then bicycle down the mountain with **Backroads Whistler** (604/932-3111, www.backroadswhistler.com).

Rates for the sightseeing lifts are adult $30, senior $24, child $12. A two-day pass is adult $40, senior $34, child $22. Summer lift hours are mid-June to September daily 10 A.M.–5 P.M., during the first couple of weekends of June and October 11 A.M.–4 P.M. These dates vary between the mountains and are totally dependent on snow cover, or the lack of it. Dining facilities are available on both mountains, or grab a picnic basket lunch from any of the delis down in the village. The best source of information is the **Whistler Activity Centre** (4010 Whistler Way, 604/938-2769 or 877/991-9988; daily 8:30 A.M.–5 P.M.).

Hiking

The easiest way to access the area's most spec-

tacular hiking country is to take a sightseeing lift up Whistler or Blackcomb Mountain, but many other options exist. Walking around Whistler Valley you'll notice signposted trails all over the place. **Valley Trail** is a paved walkway/bikeway in summer and a cross-country ski trail in winter. It makes an almost complete tour of the valley, from Whistler Village to **Lost Lake** and **Green Lake,** along the **River of Golden Dreams** to **Alta Lake, Nita Lake,** and **Alpha Lake,** and finally to Highway 99 in the Whistler Creekside area. If you'd rather do a short walk, head for Lost Lake via the two-kilometer (1.2-mile) trail from Parking Lot East at the back of Whistler Village.

Between Whistler and Blackcomb Mountains, a gravel road leads five kilometers (3.1 miles) to the trailhead for the **Singing Pass Trail.** From the parking lot, this trail follows the Fitzsimmons Creek watershed for 7.5 kilometers (4.7 miles) to Singing Pass, gaining 600 meters (2,000 feet) in elevation; allow 2.5 hours each way. From the pass, it's another two kilometers (1.2 miles) to beautiful **Russet Lake,** where you'll find a backcountry campground.

Mountain Biking

Whistler Valley is a perfect place to take a mountain bike—you'd need months to ride all of the trails here. Many of the locals have abandoned their cars for bikes, which in some cases are worth much more than their vehicles! You can see them scooting along **Valley Trail,** a paved walk/bikeway that links the entire valley and is the resident cyclists' freeway. Another popular destination for mountain bikers is beautiful **Lost Lake,** two kilometers (1.2 miles) northeast of Whistler Village.

On the mountain slopes, **Whistler Mountain Bike Park** (mid-May–early Oct.; $47 per day) is perfect for adventurous riders to strut their stuff. Using the lifts to access a vertical drop of 1,200 meters (3,900 feet), it features three "Skill Centres," filled with obstacles for varying levels of skill; a Bikercross Course; and a variety of trails to the valley floor. Run the courses by yourself, or join a group in a guided descent for $70 including bike rental.

If you didn't bring a bike, not to worry—they're available for rent. Rental rates start at around $15 per hour, $40–125 per day. Or perhaps a guided bicycle tour of the local area sounds appealing—it's not a bad idea to have a guide at first. **Backroads Whistler** (604/932-3111, www.backroadswhistler.com) runs a variety of tours, ranging from an easy ride along the valley floor to hard-core downhill riding. This company, along with the following, rent bikes: **Garbanzo Bike & Bean** (base of the Whistler Mountain Bike Park, 604/905-2076), **Spicy** (Rainbow Bldg., Gateway Loop, 604/905-2777), **Sportstop** (4112 Golfers Approach, 604/932-5495), **Bike Whistler Co.** (4205 Village Sq., 604/938-9511), and **Wild Willies** (4240 Gateway Loop, 604/938-8036).

Water Sports

Sunbathers head for the public beaches along the shores of **Alta Lake**—watching all the windsurfers whipping across the water, or beginners repeatedly taking a plunge, is a good source of summer entertainment. Wayside Park at the south end of the lake has a beach, a canoe launch, an offshore pontoon, a grassy area with picnic tables, and hiking/biking trails. At Lakeside Park, also on Alta Lake, **Whistler Outdoor Experience** (604/932-3389, www.whistleroutdoor.com) rents canoes for $24 per hour or $72 per half day, and kayaks for $20 per hour. You can also travel by canoe along the smooth, flowing River of Golden Dreams for $49 ($79 guided) or experience the way in which early explorers traveled by taking a voyager canoe tour ($39 per person).

For a little white-water excitement, try river rafting with **Whistler River Adventures** (604/932-3532 or 888/932-3532, www.whistlerriver.com), which provides guided scenic and white-water tours between the end of May and early September. Outings range from an easy float down the Green River for $69 per person to the white-water thrills of a full-day trip on the Elaho River for $154.

Golf

Whistler boasts four world-class championship

SOUTHWESTERN B.C.

© GREG GRIFFITH / MOUNTAIN MOMENTS PHOTOGRAPHY

Whitewater rafting is a popular summertime pursuit in the Whistler Valley.

golf courses, each with its own character and charm. The entire valley has gained a reputation as a golfing destination, with many accommodations offering package deals that include greens fees. Still, golfing at Whistler is as expensive as anywhere in the country. All of the following courses offer a golf shop with club rentals ($40–50), cart rentals, and a clubhouse with dining facilities. The golfing season runs mid-May to October, so in late spring you can ski in the morning and golf in the afternoon. Designed by Arnold Palmer, **Whistler Golf Club** (between Whistler Village and Alta Lake, 604/932-3280 or 800/376-1777) offers large greens and narrow wooded fairways over a challenging 6,676-yard par-72 layout. Greens fees are $159 (the twilight rate of $99 is offered after 4 P.M.). On the other side of the village, **Fairmont Chateau Whistler Golf Club** (Blackcomb Way, 604/938-2092 or 888/938-2092; greens fees $169) takes advantage of the rugged terrain of Blackcomb Mountain's lower slopes through holes that rise and fall with the lay of the land. The Jack Nicklaus–designed **Nicklaus North** course (just north of Whistler Village, 604/938-9898; $185) is an open layout holding numerous water hazards. It boasts 360-degree mountain vistas and plays to a challenging 6,900 yards from the back markers. Farther up the valley is **Big Sky Golf and Country Club** (604/894-6106 or 800/668-7900; $159), a lengthy par-72 course of over 7,000 yards.

Flightseeing

Nothing beats the spectacular sight of the Coast Mountains' majestic peaks, glaciers, icy-blue lakes, and lush mountain meadows from an unforgettable vantage point high in the sky. **Whistler Air** (604/932-6615 or 888/806-2299) will take you aloft in a floatplane from Green Lake, three kilometers (1.9 miles) north of Whistler Village. A 30-minute flight over the glaciers of Garibaldi Provincial Park costs $129, a 40-minute flight over the Pemberton Ice Cap goes for $159, and an 80-minute flight landing on a high alpine lake runs $209. You can also charter the whole plane (minimum four people) for a remote backcountry adventure.

Skiing and Snowboarding

No matter what your ability, the skiing at **Whistler/Blackcomb,** consistently rated as North America's number-one ski destination, makes for a winter holiday you won't forget in a hurry. The two lift-served mountains, Whistler and Blackcomb, are separated by a steep-sided valley through which Fitzsimmons Creek flows, with lifts converging at Whistler Village. Skiing is over almost 3,000 hectares (7,400 acres), comprising more than 200 groomed runs, hundreds of unmarked trails through forested areas, three glaciers, and 12 bowls. The lift-served vertical rise of Blackcomb is 1,609 meters (5,280 feet), the highest in North America, but Whistler is only slightly lower at 1,530 meters (5,020 feet). In total, the resort has 34 lifts, including three gondolas, 12 high-speed quad chairlifts, five triples, one double, and 12 surface lifts. The terrain is rated Intermediate over 55 percent of the resort, with the remaining 45 percent split evenly between Beginner and Expert. Snowboarders are well catered to with four terrain parks and numerous half-pipes. The length of season is also impressive, running from November to early May, with the Horstman Glacier open for skiing for a few weeks of summer.

For many visitors, the resort can be overwhelming. Trail maps detail all of the marked runs, but they can't convey the vast size of the area. A great way to get to know the mountain is on an orientation tour; these leave throughout the day from various meeting points (ask when and where when you buy your ticket) and are free. **Whistler Blackcomb Ski and Board School** (604/932-3434 or 800/766-0449) is the country's largest ski school and offers various lesson packages and programs, such as the Esprit, a three-day, women's-only "camp" that provides instruction in a variety of disciplines.

Lift tickets are adult $85, senior and youth $71, child $44, and those under seven ski for free. The resort's website (www.whistler blackcomb.com) contains everything you'll need to know about the resort and booking winter accommodation packages, or call the

downhill skiers enjoying a powder day on Blackcomb Mountain

general information desk (604/932-3434 or 800/766-0449). For accommodation information, call Whistler Central Reservations (604/904-7060 or 888/403-4727).

Cross-Country Skiing

Many kilometers of trails wind through snow-covered terrain in the valley. Starting at Whistler Village and running in a long loop past Lost Lake and Green Lake is the **Valley Trail,** a paved walk/bikeway in summer that becomes a popular cross-country ski trail in winter. The biggest concentration of trails lies near Lost Lake and on the adjacent Chateau Whistler Golf Course. Most trails are groomed, while some are track set, and a five-kilometer (3.1-mile) stretch is illuminated for night skiing. The trail system is operated by **Whistler Nordics** (604/932-6436, www.whistler nordics.com), which collects a fee of $15 for a day pass from a ticket booth near Lost Lake, where you'll also find a cozy warming hut.

Heli-Skiing

Heli-skiing is offered by **Whistler Heli-skiing** (Crystal Lodge, 604/932-4105, www.whistler heliskiing.com), which takes strong intermediates and expert adventurers high into the Coast Mountains to ski fields of untracked powder. Rates of $730 include a day's skiing, transportation to and from the heliport north of Whistler Village, a gourmet lunch, and the guide.

Indoor Climbing

The Core (4010 Whistler Conference Centre, 604/905-7625; daily 10 A.M.–10 P.M.) is an indoor climbing wall with varying degrees of slope and an overhang. It costs $17.50 for a day pass, with instruction and equipment rental ($8) extra.

Spas

Whistler Body Wrap (4433 Sundial Pl., Whistler Village, 604/932-4710) offers a wide variety of spa treatments, including massages, facials, body wraps, and salon services. A standard 25-minute massage costs $95, or a full day of treatments—including an herbal body wrap—and lunch costs from $500. **Avello Spa & Health Club** (The Westin Resort & Spa, 4090 Whistler

Way, 604/935-3444) is a more luxurious facility offering all of the same services but at a higher cost.

ENTERTAINMENT AND EVENTS
Drinking and Dancing
Throughout the year you can usually find live evening entertainment in Whistler Village. The **Garibaldi Lift Co. Bar & Grill** (2320 London Lane, 604/905-2220) features live entertainment most nights—often blues and jazz—and good food at reasonable prices. At **Buffalo Bill's** (4122 Village Green, 604/932-6613), expect anything from reggae to rock. For two decades, **Tommy Africa's** (4216 Gateway Dr., 604/932-6090) has been one of the village's hottest nightspots. It's popular with the younger crowd, pumping out high-volume reggae across the valley's most crowded dance floor. Head to **Savage Beagle** (Whistler Village Sq., 604/938-3337) or **Maxx Fish** (Whistler Village Sq., 604/932-1904) nightly between 8 P.M. and 2 A.M. for dance, house, and alternative music.

Black's Pub (Sundial Boutique Hotel, Whistler Village Sq., 604/932-6945) offers more than 90 international beers and a quiet atmosphere in a small upstairs English-style bar. Another more refined watering hole is the **Crystal Lounge** (Crystal Lodge, 4154 Village Sq., 604/932-2221).

Events
The winter season is packed with ski and snowboard races, but the biggest is the **World Ski & Snowboard Festival,** through mid-April (604/938-3399, www.wssf.com). This innovative event brings together the very best winter athletes for the World Skiing Invitational and the World Snowboarding Championship. These are only the flagships of this 10-day extravaganza, which also includes demo days, exhibitions, and a film festival.

Each weekend in May and June and daily through summer, the streets of Whistler come alive with street entertainment such as musicians, jugglers, and comedians. The last weekend of May is the official end of the ski

season up on Blackcomb Mountain, with a **Slush Cup** and live music.

Canada Day, July 1, is celebrated with a parade through Whistler Village. **Whistler Music & Arts Festival,** the second weekend of August, includes lots of free entertainment, including outdoor film screenings and street music.

During **Oktoberfest,** many restaurants and businesses dress themselves up in a Bavarian theme. The festival also features dancing in the streets, and, of course, a beer hall.

ACCOMMODATIONS AND CAMPING
Whistler's accommodations range from inexpensive dorm beds to luxury resort hotels. It's just a matter of selecting one to suit your budget and location preference. Skiers may want to be right in Whistler Village or by the gondola base in Whistler Creekside so that they can stroll out their door, strap on skis, and jump on a lift. (The term "slopeside" describes accommodations within a five-minute walk of the lifts.)

Winter is most definitely high season, with the week after Christmas and all of February and March a high season within a high season, especially for slopeside lodgings or those that are self-contained and capable of sleeping more than two people. These are also the accommodations that discount most heavily outside of winter. For example, at the Delta Whistler Village Suites website (www.deltahotels.com), type in a February date and then a July date under Reservations—rates are a bargain in July and over the top in winter.

Although winter is peak season, most rates quoted here are for summertime.

Reservation Package Deals
If you plan on skiing or golfing, a package deal is the way to go. These can be booked directly through many accommodations, but the following agencies offer a wider scope of choices. **Tourism Whistler** (604/932-0606 or 800/944-7853, www.whistler.com) is one option, as are the following: **Allura Direct** (604/707-6700 or 866/425-5872, www.alluradirect.com/whistler) and **ResortQuest** (604/932-6699 or 877/588-5800, www.resortquest.com).

Under $50

On the western shore of Alta Lake, **HI-Whistler** (5678 Alta Lake Rd., 604/932-5492, www.hihostels.ca) boasts magnificent views across the water to the resort. It's relatively small (just 32 beds), with facilities including a communal kitchen, dining area, and big, cozy living area. Bike and canoe rentals are available. It's understandably popular year-round; members $26 per night, nonmembers $30. Check-in is 4–10 P.M. To get there from the south, take Alta Lake Road to the left off Highway 99 and watch for the small sign on the lake side of the road. **WAVE** (Whistler and Valley Express) transit buses depart Whistler Village and run right past the hostel door.

$50-100

There's nothing on offer in Whistler in this price bracket—it's either a dorm bed or a more expensive hotel room.

$100-150

⟨ **Crystal Lodge** (4154 Village Green, 604/932-2221 or 800/667-3363, www.crystal-lodge.com) stands out as an excellent value in the heart of the action of Whistler Village. Rooms in the original wing are spacious and have a homey feel. Summer rates ($130) are a good value. The north wing holds larger suites that have balconies and modern amenities such as Internet access. Summer rates for these are a still-reasonable $198 s or d. All guests have the use of an outdoor hot tub and heated pool.

$150-200

The modern log cabins at the ⟨ **Riverside RV Resort** (8018 Mons Rd., 604/905-5533 or 877/905-5533, www.whistlercamping.com) aren't spacious, but you're in Whistler, so you'll be spending most of your time hiking, biking, and generally being outdoors anyway. They ooze mountain charm and come complete with a small kitchen and TV/VCR combo for $165 ($175–215 in winter). An on-site grocery store and café save heading into town for food.

© ANDREW HEMPSTEAD

Delta Whistler Village Suites

On the edge of the village and adjacent to one of the valley's best golf courses is **Coast Whistler Hotel** (4005 Whistler Way, 604/932-2522 or 800/663-5644, www.coastwhistlerhotel.com). Each of the 194 rooms is simply but stylishly decorated in pastel colors. Facilities include a heated outdoor pool, an exercise room, a hot tub, a restaurant, and a bar. Summer rates start at a reasonable $179 (from $109 in spring and fall), but the winter rate of $295 s or d is a little steep considering you're away from the ski lifts.

Centrally located **Delta Whistler Village Suites** (4308 Main St., 604/905-3987 or 888/299-3987, www.deltahotels.com) combines the conveniences of a full-service hotel with more than 200 kitchen-equipped units—the only such property in Whistler. Advertised rack rates are $180 s or d (summer), but check the website for promotional deals.

$200-250

In the heart of the action, ⟨ **Listel Whistler Hotel** (4121 Village Green, 604/932-1133 or

800/663-5472, www.listelhotel.com) is a self-contained resort complete with a year-round outdoor pool, outdoor hot tub, restaurant, and laundry. The contemporary-style rooms are $249 s or d through much of the year, rising to $349 in February and March. Check the Listel website for specials.

Over $250

Summit Lodge & Spa (4359 Main St., 604/932-2778 or 888/913-8811, www.summit lodge.com) is a luxurious European Alps–style boutique hotel. Each of the 81 units features comfortable furnishings, a slate floor, a fireplace, a balcony, and a small kitchen. There's also an outdoor heated pool. Off-season rates start at $300 s or d, rising to $450 in winter.

Fairmont Chateau Whistler, at the base of Blackcomb Mountain in Upper Village (604/938-8000 or 866/540-4424, www .fairmont.com), is Whistler's most luxurious lodging, with its own championship golf course, the Vida Wellness Spa, a health club with the best equipment money can buy, tennis courts, and all of the facilities expected at one of the world's best accommodations. The massive lobby is decorated in the style of a rustic lodge, but the rooms couldn't be more different. Each is elegantly furnished and offers great mountain views. In the low season (late spring and fall), rooms start at $300 s or d; peak summer rates start at $380 s or d, winter rates at $460 s or d.

Camping

Enjoying a pleasant location just over two kilometers (1.2 miles) north of the village, **Riverside RV Resort** (8018 Mons Rd., 604/905-5533 or 877/905-5533, www.whistler camping.com) is the only campground within town boundaries. It offers a modern bathroom complex (with in-floor heating), a putting course, a playground, a hot tub, a laundry, a small general store, and a café (daily from 7 A.M.). Sites range $35–50, with a small wooded area set aside for walk-in tent campers. Cabins are $165 ($175–215 in winter).

Out of town, the closest campground is in

Nairn Falls Provincial Park, 28 kilometers (17.4 miles) north. It's open April–November and charges $17 per night. For more facilities, **Dryden Creek Resorts** (50 kilometers/31 miles south, 604/898-9726 or 800/903-4690; $22–28) is a good option.

FOOD

Like the town itself, the dining scene in Whistler is hip, ever-changing, and not particularly cheap. Many small cafés dot the cobbled walkways of Whistler Village, while most bars have reasonably priced pub-fare menus.

For a caffeine fix, **Moguls Cafe** (4208 Village Sq., 604/932-4845; daily from 6:30 A.M.) is as good as any place—it's popular with both locals and visitors, and the outdoor seating catches the morning sun.

Cool and Casual

The rustic decor and great Canadian food at **Garibaldi Lift Co. Bar & Grill,** at the base of the Whistler Village gondola (604/905-2220), has been a big hit since the place opened in 1995. The bar and sundeck are popular après-ski hangouts, and by around 8 P.M. everyone's back for dinner. For Western-style atmosphere with mountain views, head to the **Longhorn Saloon and Grill** (4290 Mountain Sq., 604/932-5999; daily from 11 A.M.) and share a platter of finger food or order your own cut of prime Alberta beef, complete with trimmings, for $18–27.

◖ Citta's Bistro (4217 Village Stroll, Whistler Village, 604/932-4177; daily for lunch and dinner) has been around since Whistler first became a hip destination—and it's as popular today as it ever was. If it's a warm evening, try for a table on the patio and order a gourmet pizza for one ($14–17) to go with a locally brewed beer.

On the south side of Whistler Village, **Hoz's Pub** (2129 Lake Placid Rd., 604/932-5940; daily from 11 A.M.) is popular among locals for its well-priced food and untouristy atmosphere. Look for typical pub fare as well as a few West Coast–inspired choices (beer-battered salmon and chips, $11). If you feel like heading south of the border for dinner, have a beer at Hoz's, then move next door to **El Tipo's** (604/932-4424, daily for dinner) to feast on the valley's best Mexican food. The chicken enchilada ($14) was a real treat. Children will enjoy the funky atmosphere and their own menu.

Steak

For steaks, seafood, a salad bar, fresh hot bread, and plenty of food at a reasonable price, the **Whistler Keg** (Whistler Village Inn & Suites, 4429 Sundial Pl., 604/932-5151; daily from 5:30 P.M.) is a sure thing. The atmosphere is casual, yet the service is slick and refreshingly attentive. Expect to pay from $18 for an entrée. Reservations are not taken.

At **Ⓒ Hy's** (Delta Whistler Village Suites, 4308 Main St., 604/905-5555), you don't need to ask if the steak is good—everything on offer is top-notch AAA Alberta beef, including a signature, not-for-the-faint-hearted 22-ounce porterhouse ($49). The scene is upmarket, with elegant tables set within rich-colored wood walls. Starters range $8–12, with steaks starting at $33.

Pacific Northwest

For an upscale yet casual setting and a wide-ranging menu infused with lots of local seafood and produce, make reservations at **Mountain Club** (4314 Main St., Town Plaza, Village North, 604/932-6009; daily from 5 P.M.). The menu is clearly divided into earth and ocean choices, with most mains under $30.

Ⓒ Araxi (4222 Village Sq., Whistler Village, 604/932-4540; daily from 5 P.M.) consistently wins awards for its creative menu, which takes advantage of produce from around the Lower Mainland yet also manages to offer traditional European dishes. It also boasts a seafood bar and an extensive wine list.

Italian

Restaurant entrepreneur Umberto Menghi operates numerous eateries in Vancouver and two restaurants in Whistler Village. Both are reasonably priced with menus influenced by the cuisine of Tuscany. Check out **Il Caminetto** (4242 Village Stroll, 604/932-4442; daily

from 5 P.M.) and **Trattoria di Umberto** (4417 Sundial Pl., 604/932-5858; summer only for lunch, daily for dinner). The former, named for a fireplace that has been replaced by more tables, has a warm, welcoming atmosphere and an extensive menu of pastas from $22. Fresh flowers and original art add to the appeal. The latter is less expensive and attracts a more casual crowd.

Asian

Reasonably priced Mongolian fare is on the menu at **Mongolie Grill** (4295 Whistler Way, Whistler Village, 604/938-9416; daily from 11:30 A.M.). This is one of the better places to take children. They'll love choosing their own ingredients—meats, vegetables, and so on—with matching sauces, and then watch the speedy chefs fry up the personalized dish in front of them.

Thai One On (4557 Blackcomb Way, 604/932-4822; daily for dinner) serves a mix of modern and traditional Thai cooking in a casual setting. Pad thais and curries are all around $20, or splurge on the *krua muu* (roast pork tenderloin smothered in pineapple and ginger sauce) for $28.

INFORMATION AND SERVICES
Information

The **Whistler Visitor Centre** is centrally located at 4230 Gateway Drive (604/932-5922; daily 9 A.M.–6 P.M.). Also in the village is the **Whistler 2010 Info Centre** (604/932-2010; www.vancouver2010.com; daily 11 A.M.–5 P.M.), where you can learn all about the Olympic Winter Games and the planning and development that goes along with hosting the world's premier sporting event.

Good sources of pretrip planning information are **Tourism Whistler** (www.tourismwhistler.com) and the **Whistler Chamber of Commerce** website (www.whistlerchamber.com).

The two weekly newspapers are good sources of local information: the *Question* (www.whistlerquestion.com) and *Pique* (www.piquenewsmagazine.com).

Services

In Whistler Village you'll find a post office, banks, a currency exchange, a laundry, a supermarket, and a liquor store. **Whistler Health Care Centre** is at 4380 Lorimer (604/932-4911).

Whistler Public Library (4329 Main St., 604/932-5564; Mon.–Sat. 11 A.M.–7 P.M., Sun. 11 A.M.–4 P.M.) has an international selection of newspapers and magazines, as well as free public Internet access.

GETTING THERE

The **Whistler Mountaineer** (604/606-7245 or 877/460-3200, www.whistlermountaineer .com) is a luxury rail service between North Vancouver and Whistler. While the train itself is deluxe in every respect, it's what's outside the large windows that is most memorable: a moving postcard of mountains, ocean, and waterfalls. The trip runs May through mid-October, with departures from North Vancouver daily at 8:30 P.M. Rates are adult $189 round-trip, child $99, or upgrade to the Glacier Dome Car for adult $299, child $209. Rates include snacks and hotel transfers. You can also return to Vancouver by bus, which saves a few bucks and allows you to spend an extra two hours in Whistler.

Whistler has no airport, but you can fly in with **Whistler Air** (604/932-6615 or 888/806-2299, www.whistlerair.ca), which operates scheduled floatplane flights between downtown Vancouver and Green Lake (just north of Whistler Village) for $149 one-way, $249 round-trip. The flight takes around 30 minutes and the baggage limit is 25 pounds plus $1 for every extra pound.

Vancouver International Airport, 130 kilometers (81 miles) to the south, is the main gateway to Whistler. **Perimeter** (604/266-5386 or 877/317-7788, www.perimeterbus .com) provides bus service between the two up to 11 times daily; adult $55, child $35. Buses make stops at some Vancouver hotels and a short rest stop at pretty Shannon Falls. **Greyhound** (800/667-0882, www.whistlerbus .com) runs six buses daily between Vancouver's Pacific Central Station (1150 Station St.) and Whistler Village; $20 one-way, $38 round-trip, with connections from the airport.

GETTING AROUND

Once you're in Whistler, getting around is pretty easy—if you're staying in Whistler Village, everything you need is within easy walking distance. **WAVE** (604/932-4020) operates extensive bus routes throughout the valley daily 6 A.M.–midnight. Routes radiate from Village Exchange in Whistler Village south to Whistler Creekside and as far north as Emerald Estates on the shore of Green Lake. Fare is $1.50, senior and child $1.25 (exact change only). A 10-ride WAVE Card is adult $13, senior and child $11.

For a cab, call **Sea to Sky Taxi** (604/932-3333) or **Whistler Taxi** (604/938-3333).

Rental car agencies in Whistler include **Budget** (604/932-1236) and **Thrifty** (604/938-0302).

The Gold Nugget Route

The route north between Whistler and Lillooet is best traveled in good weather—the scenery is so spectacular, you don't want to miss *anything.* See white-topped peaks all around you and big glacier-colored rivers. If you have the time, stop at provincial parks along the way for always-good scenery and outdoor activities.

Make your first stop north of Whistler at **Nairn Falls Provincial Park,** on the banks of Green River, where a wooded trail leads to a waterfall. Stay overnight at the campground (Apr.–Nov., $14).

Pemberton

This small logging community is growing rapidly as a cheaper housing alternative for Whistler workers, who commute the 32 kilometers (20 miles) south. Surrounded by mountains, trees, lakes, and rivers, Pemberton sits in a fertile valley known for its potatoes. It's only a short distance south of the Lillooet River, a main transportation route to the Cariboo during the 1860s' gold-rush days. Today's visitors mostly leave their gold pans at home, coming mainly to fish or to hike in the beautiful valleys around Pemberton.

The summer-only **Pemberton Visitor Centre** (604/894-6175, www.pemberton chamber.com; mid-May–Sept. daily 9 A.M.– 5 P.M.) is back out of town on Highway 99.

North to Lillooet

From Pemberton you can take one of three routes to Lillooet. Whichever route you decide on, it's important to note that the weather can change rapidly, and even in summer you might find yourself traveling through a sudden snowstorm at higher elevations. However, the scenery makes the effort worthwhile. You'll see beautiful lakes, fast rivers, summer wildflowers, deep-blue mountains, steep ravines, never-ending forests, and vistas in every shade of green imaginable. Campgrounds and picnic areas mark all the best locations.

The most direct way—the route once taken by fortune seekers heading toward the Cariboo goldfields—is paved Highway 99. A few minutes' drive out of Mount Currie, the highway begins switchbacking, as it climbs abruptly into the Coast Mountains and crests at a 1,300-meter-high (4,260-foot-high) pass. Just before the pass is 1,460-hectare (3,600-

acre) **Joffre Lakes Provincial Park,** where a short trail (allow 20 minutes round-trip) leads to Lower Joffre Lake. The trail continues beyond the first lake, making an elevation gain of 400 meters (1,300 feet) before reaching the main body of water, 10 kilometers (6.2 miles) from the highway.

From the pass, Highway 99 loses over 1,000 meters (3,300 feet) of elevation in its descent to Lillooet. Along the way is narrow **Duffey Lake** (the highway itself is referred to locally as the "Duffey Lake Road"), backed by the steep-sided Cayoosh Range. At the north end of the lake is a provincial park with camping ($14 per night).

The second route (summer only) spurs north through Mount Currie following the Birkenhead River, passing the turnoff to 9,755-hectare (24,100-acre) **Birkenhead Lake Provincial Park,** then descending to **D'Arcy.** Beyond this point, the road can get extremely rough, so check conditions in town before setting out. The third, northernmost, and longest route, over 200 kilometers (124 miles) of mostly unpaved road (also summer only), climbs north along the Lillooet River through Pemberton Meadows, over Hurley Pass, and to the historic mining communities of **Gold Bridge** and **Bralorne** before closely following the shore of Carpenter Lake in an easterly direction back to Lillooet.

For information on **Lillooet,** the confluence of the three above routes, see the *Cariboo Country* section of the *Central British Columbia* chapter.

East from Vancouver

FRASER VALLEY

When you leave Vancouver and head due east, you travel through the most built-up and heavily populated area of British Columbia, skirting modern cities, residential suburbs, and zones of heavy industry. However, it's not an unattractive area—the main roads follow the mighty Fraser River through a fertile valley of rolling farmland dotted with historic

villages, and beautiful mountains line the horizon in just about any direction.

You have a choice of two major routes. The TransCanada Highway, on the south side of the Fraser River, speeds you out of southeast Vancouver through Abbotsford and scenic Chilliwack to Hope. Slower, more picturesque Highway 7 meanders along the north side of the Fraser River through **Mission,** named

There are plenty of pleasant stops on the journey through the Fraser Valley.

after a Roman Catholic mission school built in 1861. The town is now known for its Benedictine monastery, which offers a retreat center open to the public. The highway then passes the access road to **Harrison Hot Springs** and crosses over the Fraser River to Hope. In summer you can pick and choose from an endless number of roadside stands selling fresh fruit at bargain prices—the raspberries in July are delectable.

Fort Langley National Historic Site

In 1827, the Hudson's Bay Company established a settlement 48 kilometers (30 miles) upstream from the mouth of the Fraser River as part of a network of trading posts, provision depots, and administrative centers that stretched across western Canada. The original site was abandoned in 1838 in favor of another, farther upstream, where today the settlement has been re-created. When British Columbia became a crown colony on November 19, 1858,

Fort Langley was declared capital, but one year later, the entire colonial government moved to the more central New Westminster. Today the restored riverside **trading post** (604/513-4777; Mar.–Oct. 10 A.M.–5 P.M.; adult $7.15, senior $5.90, child $3.45) springs to life as park interpreters in period costumes animate the fort's history. The park is within walking distance of Fort Langley village, where many businesses are built in a heritage style, and you'll find dozens of antique shops, boutiques, restaurants, and cafés along its main tree-lined street.

To get there, follow Highway 1 for 50 kilometers (31 miles) east from downtown and head north toward the Fraser River from Exit 66 on 232nd Street and then Glover Road. From the highway, it's five kilometers (3.1 miles) to downtown Fort Langley; the fort lies a few blocks east of the main street. It's well posted from Highway 1, but the official address is 23433 Mavis Street, Fort Langley.

East Toward Hope

If you've visited Fort Langley, backtrack south to continue east along the valley. Instead of continuing along Highway 1, cross the transcontinental highway on Glover Road to Langley city center, then head east on Old Yale Road and into an area laced with lazy country roads. If you decide to cross from Highway 1 to Highway 7 at Abbotsford, make the detour to delightful **Clayburn Village,** originally a company town for a local brickworks. As you'd expect, most of the neat houses are built of brick, providing a local atmosphere a world away from the surrounding modern subdivisions. Along the main street, **Clayburn Village Store** (Wright St., Tues.–Sat. 9 A.M.–5 P.M., Sun. noon–5 P.M.) is a general store that has changed little in appearance since opening almost 100 years ago. The highlight is the delicious Devonshire tea, although children will say it's the candy sold from big glass jars. Reach the store by taking Exit 92 north from Highway 1, follow Highway 11 north for six kilometers (3.7 miles), and then head east along Clayburn Road.

It is possible to continue east through Clayburn to **Sumas Mountain Provincial Park** (ask directions at the local general store), or take Exit 95 from Highway 1 to Sumas Mountain Road, then take Batts Road, which climbs steadily up the mountain's southern slopes. From the end of this service road, it's a short climb to the 900-meter (2,950-foot) summit of Sumas Mountain, from which views extend north across the Fraser River and south across a patchwork of farmland to Washington's snow-capped Mount Baker. From the pullout one kilometer (0.6 mile) from the end of the road, a hiking trail descends for 1.6 kilometers (one mile) to forest-encircled Chadsey Lake and a lakeside picnic area.

Kilby Historic Site

Off the beaten track and often missed by those unfamiliar with the area, this historic site (604/796-9576; Apr.–mid-May Thurs.–Sun. 11 A.M.–5 P.M., mid-May–early Sept. daily 11 A.M.–5 P.M.; adult $9, senior $8, youth $7) lies on the north side of the Fraser River, near the turnoff to Harrison Hot Springs, 40 kilometers (25 miles) east of Mission and six kilometers (3.7 miles) west of Agassiz (look for the inconspicuous sign close to Harrison Mills). The fascinating museum/country store, which operated until the early 1970s, is fully stocked with all of the old brands and types of goods that were commonplace in the 1920s and '30s. On the two-hectare (five-acre) riverside grounds are farm equipment, farm animals, a gift shop, and a café serving delicious home-style cooking.

Harrison Hot Springs

Of British Columbia's 60 natural hot springs, the closest to Vancouver is Harrison Hot Springs, on the north side of the Fraser Valley, 125 kilometers (78 miles) east of downtown. Known as the "Spa of Canada," the springs lie on the sandy southern shores of the Lower Mainland's largest body of water, **Harrison Lake.** Since the opening of the province's first resort in 1886, the springs have spurred much surrounding development. Coast Salish were the first to take advantage of the soothing water. Then in the late 1850s, gold miners

stumbled upon the springs. Because of a historical agreement, only the Harrison Hot Springs Resort has water rights, but the hotel operates **Harrison Public Pool** (corner of Harrison Hot Springs Rd. and Esplanade Ave., 604/796-2244; summer daily 8 A.M.–9 P.M., the rest of the year daily 9 A.M.–9 P.M.; adult $9, senior and child $6.50). Scalding 74°C (165°F) mineral water is pumped from its source, cooled to a soothing 38°C (100°F), then pumped into the pool. The lake itself provides many recreation opportunities, with good swimming, sailing, canoeing, and fishing for rainbow trout. Through town to the north is 1,220-hectare (3,010-acre) **Sasquatch Provincial Park,** named for a tall, hairy, unshaven beast that supposedly inhabits the area. The park extends from a day-use area on the bank of Harrison Lake to picturesque tree-encircled lakes, each with road access, short hiking trails, and picnic areas.

Lakeside **Harrison Hot Springs Resort** (100 Esplanade, 604/796-2244 or 800/663-2266, www.harrisonresort.com; $180–260 s or d) is the town's most elegant accommodation, and it offers guests use of a large indoor and outdoor complex of mineral pools, complete with grassed areas, lots of outdoor furniture, and a café. Other facilities include boat and canoe rentals, sailing lessons, and a restaurant and lounge bar. Most of the 323 rooms have private balconies, many with spectacular views across the lake. Within walking distance of the public hot pool and the lake is **Glencoe Motel** (259 Hot Springs Rd., 604/796-2574, www.glencoemotel.com; $70 s, $80 d). The least expensive overnight option is to camp at one of three campgrounds along the road into town or through town in lakeside **Sasquatch Provincial Park.**

Harrison Hot Springs Visitor Centre is beside the main road into town (604/796-3425; summer daily 8 A.M.–6 P.M.).

HOPE AND VICINITY

Locals say "all roads lead to Hope"—and they're right. On a finger of land at the confluence of the Fraser and Coquihalla Rivers,

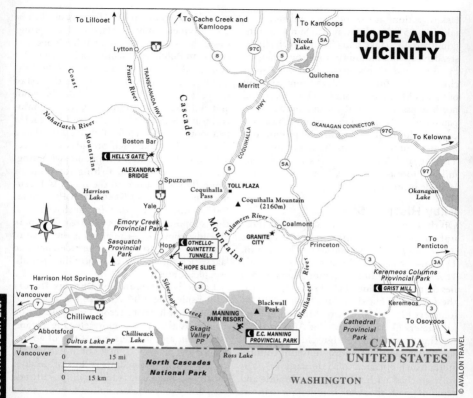

HOPE AND VICINITY

To Lillooet
To Cache Creek and Kamloops
To Kamloops

Lytton
Nicola Lake
97C
8
5
Quilchena
Merritt
Coast Mountains
Cascade
Fraser River
TRANSCANADA HWY
Nahatlatch River
Boston Bar
HELL'S GATE
ALEXANDRA BRIDGE
Spuzzum
Harrison Lake
Yale
Coquihalla Pass
TOLL PLAZA
Coquihalla Mountain (2160m)
OKANAGAN CONNECTOR
97C
To Kelowna
97
Okanagan Lake
Emory Creek Provincial Park
COQUIHALLA HWY
5
5A
Tulameen River
Coalmont
Sasquatch Provincial Park
Hope
OTHELLO QUINTETTE TUNNELS
GRANITE CITY
Princeton
To Penticton
3A
HOPE SLIDE
Harrison Hot Springs
To Vancouver
7
Chilliwack
Silverhope Creek
3
Smitameen River
Keremeos Columns Provincial Park
GRIST MILL
Keremeos
3
To Osoyoos
Abbotsford
Chilliwack Lake
Skagit Valley PP
MANNING PARK RESORT
Blackwall Peak
E.C. MANNING PROVINCIAL PARK
Cathedral Provincial Park
CANADA
To Vancouver
Cultus Lake PP
Ross Lake
UNITED STATES
0   15 mi
0   15 km
North Cascades National Park
WASHINGTON

© AVALON TRAVEL

SOUTHWESTERN B.C.

158 kilometers (98 miles) east of Vancouver, Hope (pop. 6,700) really is a hub. The TransCanada Highway and Highway 7 from Vancouver, the Coquihalla Highway to Kamloops, and Highway 3 from the Okanagan all meet at Hope. Don't be put off by first impressions of the town itself. Surrounded by magnificent mountains and rivers, with a couple of great wilderness areas only a short drive away and an abundance of recreational opportunities, Hope is a great place to spend some time.

Town Sights

To find out more about the history of Hope, visit **Hope Museum** (919 Water Ave., 604/869-7322; May–June daily 9 A.M.–5 P.M., July–Aug. daily 8 A.M.–8 P.M.; donation), in

the same building as the information center. The museum's comprehensive collection of pioneer artifacts is displayed in several re-created settings, including a kitchen, bedroom, parlor, schoolroom, and blacksmith shop. Other exhibits focus on local native crafts and on artifacts from the original Fort Hope and gold-rush days. Outside, climb on the Hope Gold Mill, a restored gold-ore concentrator from the Coquihalla area.

While you're discovering the downtown area, check out the tree-stump art, created by Pete Ryan. The eagle holding a salmon in its claws (in front of the district office) was carved from a tree with root rot, and it was one of the original tree-stump works of art scattered through town.

[Othello-Quintette Tunnels

These five huge tunnels through a steep gorge of **Coquihalla Canyon** were carved out of solid granite by the Kettle Valley Railway, completing a route for the company's steam locomotives between Vancouver and Nelson. The tunnels opened in 1916, but the line was plagued by snow, rock slides, and washouts, and closed for repairs more often than it was open. It was eventually abandoned in 1959. By 1962 the tracks and four steel bridges over the awesome Coquihalla River gorge had been removed. Today a short, tree-shaded walk takes you from the **Coquihalla Canyon Provincial Park** parking lot to the massive, dark tunnels, now a popular tourist attraction. Stroll through them and over the sturdy wooden bridges to admire the gorge and the power and the roar of the Coquihalla River below. If you'd visited the tunnels back in 1981, you would have seen Sylvester Stallone swinging through the canyons during the filming of the first Rambo movie, *First Blood*. To get to the tunnels from downtown, take Wallace Street to 6th Avenue and turn right. Turn left on Kawkawa Lake Road, crossing the Coquihalla River Bridge and railway tracks. At the first intersection take the right branch, Othello Road, and continue until you see a sign to the right (over a rise and easy to miss) pointing to the recreation area. The tunnels are closed November–April.

On the way up to the tunnels, **Kawkawa Lake** is a pleasant body of water with a high concentration of kokanee and a lakeside picnic area.

Skagit Valley Provincial Park

This remote wilderness of 32,577 hectares (80,500 acres) southeast of Hope is bordered to the east by Manning Provincial Park and to the south by the U.S.–Canada border. Access is along the Silver-Skagit Road, which branches south off Flood Hope Road four kilometers (2.5 miles) southwest of Hope. This rough gravel road climbs steadily for 39 kilometers (24 miles) to the park entrance, then continues 22 kilometers (14 miles) farther to the international border and road's end at **Ross Lake Reservoir.**

Through the park, the road follows the Skagit River, which flows northward from Ross Lake Reservoir through a magnificent valley cloaked in spruce, pine, aspen, and maple. Black bears, cougars, wolves, coyotes, deer, beavers, and over 200 species of birds are all present within the park.

Outdoor enthusiasts can hike trails suited mainly to overnight excursions. Skagit River Trail begins just east of where the park access road crosses the river, following the river downstream for 15 kilometers (9.3 miles) to a day-use area beside Highway 3. Fishing in the Skagit River is good for Dolly Varden and rainbow trout. The access road is dotted with day-use areas, including Shawatum, six kilometers (3.7 miles) from the park entrance, which was the site of a bustling town with saloons, restaurants, a sawmill, and a daily newspaper—until it was discovered that the only gold found in the area had been planted.

Hope Slide

On Highway 3, about 18 kilometers (11

© ANDREW HEMPSTEAD

Othello-Quintette Tunnels

miles) southeast of Hope, the effects of one of nature's amazing forces can be seen. On January 9, 1965, a minor earthquake caused a huge section of mountain to come crashing down, filling the bottom of the Nicolum Creek Valley, destroying about three kilometers (1.9 miles) of the Hope–Princeton Highway, and killing four motorists. The highway, viewpoint, and parking area are built over the Hope Slide, but you can still see the slide's treeless boundaries along the south side of the valley.

Accommodations and Camping

Hope doesn't offer much hope if you're looking for upscale lodging. Instead you'll find a motley collection of roadside motels in town and across the TransCanada Highway on Old Hope–Princeton Way. On the latter, **Royal Lodge Motel** (604/869-5358 or 877/500-6620, www.royallodgemotel.ca) has rooms for $70 s, $75 d, with kitchens an extra $8. The much newer **Alpine Motel** (Old Hope–Princeton Way, 604/869-9931 or 877/869-9931; from $80 s, $86 d.) offers large, comfortably furnished rooms, a pool, and a pleasant setting. In a scenic setting four kilometers (2.5 miles) north of Hope, **Beautiful Lake of the Woods Resort** (TransCanada Hwy., 604/869-9211 or 888/508-2211, www.lakewoods-resortmotel .com) sits on a lake with views of the surrounding mountainscape. The property is a resort in name only, but facilities include a restaurant and canoe rentals ($10 per hour). Uninspiring motel rooms are $65 s, $75 d; cabins are $75–115 d.

Along the road up to the tunnels, **Coquihalla Campground** (Kawkawa Lake Rd., 604/869-7119 or 888/869-7118; Apr.–Oct.; unserviced sites $21, hookups $24–32) sits right beside the river. Trees surround most sites, and facilities include hot showers, a barbecue area, a laundry, and a game room.

Other Practicalities

The best place for a coffee is **Blue Moose** (322 Wallace St., 604/869-0729; Mon.–Sat. 8 A.M.–10 P.M., Sun. 9 A.M.–10 P.M.), with a slick polished-wood and sparkling blue interior and free wireless Internet. Panini, wraps, sandwiches, and soups are all well under $10. For something a little more substantial, wander down Wallace Street to the corner of 3rd Avenue, where **The Cutting Board** (604/869-5222; daily for lunch and dinner) serves up creative cooking at reasonable prices. "Irish apples" (baked potatoes stuffed with all manner of ingredients) are under $8, fire-baked lasagna is $12, and baked teriyaki chicken is $14. Out on the highway, **Home Restaurant** (665 Old Hope–Princeton Way, 604/869-5558; daily 7 A.M.–10 P.M.) is the best choice for inexpensive family-style dining.

Right downtown, the friendly staff at **Hope Visitor Centre** (919 Water Ave., 604/869-2021; daily 9 A.M.–5 P.M., with extended summer hours of 8 A.M.–8 P.M.) can help you decide which of the routes to take out of Hope but might also convince you to stay in town a little longer.

FRASER RIVER CANYON

From Hope, the old TransCanada Highway runs north along the west bank of the fast-flowing Fraser River. Although the Coquihalla Highway is a much shorter option for those heading for Kamloops and beyond, the old highway offers many interesting stops and is by far the preferred route for those not in a hurry. Head north through downtown Hope, cross the Fraser River, take the first right, and you're on your way.

The first worthwhile stop is tiny **Emory Creek Provincial Park,** 15 kilometers (9.3 miles) from Hope. Stopping at this quiet riverside park, it's hard to believe that 130 years ago it was the site of Emory City, complete with saloons, a brewery, a large sawmill, and all the other businesses of a bustling frontier gold town. The city had virtually disappeared by the 1890s, and today no hint of its short-lived presence remains. Wander along riverside trails, try some fishing, or stay at one of the wooded campsites ($17).

Yale

This small town of 200 has quite a history. It

started off as one of the many Hudson's Bay Company posts, then became a transportation center at the head of the navigable lower section of the Fraser River. Enormous Lady Franklin Rock blocked the upriver section to steamer traffic, so all goods heading for the interior had to be carried from this point by wagon train along the **Cariboo Wagon Road.** By 1858 Yale was a flourishing gold-rush town of 20,000, filled with tents, shacks, bars, gambling joints, and shops. But when the gold ran out, in the 1890s, so did most of the population, and Yale dwindled to the small forestry and service center it has been ever since. To find out more about Yale's past, visit the **Yale Museum** (Douglas St., 604/863-2324; summer daily 10 A.M.–5 P.M.; adult $5, senior $4, child $3) and the adjacent historic 1863 **St. John's Church.**

If you're looking for a place to spend the night, choose between the downtown, 12-room **Fort Yale Motel** (604/863-2216; $60 s or d) or head back down the highway 12 kilometers (7.5 miles) to the campground at **Emory Creek Provincial Park.** Along the Trans-Canada Highway through town is a small **information booth** (604/863-2324; summer daily 9 A.M.–6 P.M.).

Alexandra Bridge

The treacherous Fraser Canyon posed a major transportation obstacle during the 1850s gold rush. In 1863, Alexandra Bridge, 22 kilometers (14 miles) north of Yale, was completed. However, with the successful completion of the Canadian Pacific Railway line through the canyon, the bridge and the Cariboo Wagon Road fell into disrepair. The popularity of the automobile forced engineers to construct a new suspension bridge in 1926. The new bridge used the original abutments and lasted right up to 1962, when it was replaced by today's bridge on Highway 1. **Alexandra Bridge Provincial Park** now protects a section of the old Cariboo Wagon Road, including the old bridge. The trail down to the bridge makes a good place to get out and stretch your legs.

◖ Hell's Gate

At well-known Hell's Gate, the Fraser River powers its way through a narrow, glacially carved, 34-meter-high (112-foot-high) gorge. When Simon Fraser saw this section of the gorge in 1808, he wrote, "we had to travel where no human being should venture—for surely we have encountered the gates of hell," and the name stuck. In 1914 a massive rockslide rocketed down into the gorge, blocking it even further and resulting in the almost total obliteration of the sockeye salmon population that spawned farther upstream. In 1944 giant concrete fishways were built to slow the waters and allow the spawning salmon to jump upstream—the river soon swarmed with salmon once again. Today you can cross the canyon aboard the 25-passenger **Hell's Gate Airtram** (604/867-9277; early Apr.–mid-Oct. daily 10 A.M.–4 P.M., with extended hours of 10 A.M.–5:30 P.M. July and Aug.; adult $15, senior $12, child $9). Once across the river you can browse through landscaped gardens, learn more about the fishway and salmon, or even try your hand at gold panning. Part of the complex (accessible by tram only) is the **Salmon House Restaurant** (same hours as the tram). I'm always wary of dining rooms associated with commercial attractions, but this place will pleasantly surprise you with a richly delicious salmon chowder ($10) and a variety of salmon mains under $24.

North Toward Cache Creek

Another small town with a gold-rush history, **Boston Bar** is today a popular white-water rafting mecca for those brave enough to float the Fraser River's roaring rapids. A bridge crossing at Boston Bar accesses the **Nahatlatch River,** renowned for white-water kayaking. Along quieter stretches of this river are some great fishing spots, three lakes, and numerous primitive campgrounds. **REO Rafting Adventure Resort** (16 kilometers/10 miles west from Boston Bar, 604/461-7238 or 800/736-7238, www.reorafting.com) offers a few campsites for $20 and tent cabins from $75, or stay in a log cabin and take a raft trip, with all meals included, for $209 per person for one night. As the name suggests, the resort is the base for REO Rafting, but horseback riding, rock climbing, and guided hiking are also offered.

Continuing up the canyon, the narrow highway winds northward for 34 kilometers (21 miles) to **Lytton**, a historic village at the confluence of the Fraser and Thompson Rivers, before spurring eastward and following the Thompson River. This route eventually reaches Cache Creek, the gateway to Cariboo Country (see the *Central British Columbia* chapter), and continues on to the major interior city of Kamloops.

COQUIHALLA HIGHWAY

Opened in 1986, the Coquihalla Highway is the most direct link between Hope and the interior of British Columbia. It saves at least 90 minutes by cutting 72 kilometers (45 miles) from the trip between Hope and Kamloops and bypassing the TransCanada Highway's narrow, winding stretch along the Fraser River Canyon. Along the 190-kilometer (118-mile) route are many worthwhile stops, but only one that's compulsory—a toll plaza at Coquihalla Pass, 115 kilometers (71 miles) from Hope, where $10 is collected from each vehicle.

The highway ascends and descends through magnificent mountain and river scenery to dry semiarid grasslands. You'll cruise through the valleys of the Lower Coquihalla River and Boston Bar Creek, climb to the 1,240-meter (4,070-foot) summit of Coquihalla Pass near Coquihalla Lake, descend along the Coldwater River, then climb the Coldwater's eastern valley slope to Merritt. From Merritt the highway climbs the valleys of the Nicola River and Clapperton Creek to join the TransCanada Highway eight kilometers (five miles) west of Kamloops.

Merritt

This town of 8,000 in the Nicola Valley, 115 kilometers (71 miles) north of Hope, provides the only services along the Coquihalla Highway. It's also the exit point for those heading east to the Okanagan on the Okanagan Connector.

Make your first stop off the highway at

Merritt Visitor Centre, on a high point east of the highway (250/378-0749, www.tourism merritt.com; daily 9 A.M.–5 P.M.). Upstairs in this large log building is an intriguing forestry exhibition, and behind the building is the **Godey Creek Hiking Trail,** which takes you 1.4 kilometers (0.9 mile) each way to a lookout cabin; allow one hour for the round-trip.

Each July, **Merritt Mountain Music Festival** (604/525-3330, www.mountainfest .com) attracts tens of thousands of country-music lovers for a weekend of concerts featuring the biggest names in country music.

Since the Coquihalla Highway opened, many motels have been built around Merritt, but by far the best choice is one of the originals, the ◖ **Quilchena Hotel** (250/378-2611, www.quilchena.com), on Nicola Lake, 20 kilometers (12 miles) east of town on Highway 5A (take Exit 290). Built in 1908 and still part of a working ranch, the property is a destination in itself, with golfing ($19 for 9 holes, $26 for 18), horseback riding ($30 for a one-hour trail ride), swimming, biking (rentals available), canoeing, and fishing. The hotel is a stately old building surrounded by well-tended gardens and oozing Victorian charm. A grand staircase leads up to guest rooms decorated with period antiques, lace curtains, and solid wooden beds. Rates for rooms with shared bathrooms are $69–99 s or d, while en suite rooms are $129–149. Downstairs are a saloon (complete with bullet holes in the bar) and a restaurant serving up beef raised on the hotel ranch.

◖ E. C. MANNING PROVINCIAL PARK

This rugged 70,844-hectare (175,100-acre) park in the Cascade Mountains, 64 kilometers (40 miles) east of Hope along Highway 3, stretches down to the Canada–U.S. border. Highway 3 makes a U through the park—from the northwest to south to northeast sections. But to really appreciate the park, you need to get off the highway—take in the beautiful bodies of water, drive up to a wonderful stretch of high alpine meadows, or hike on the numerous trails.

Summer Recreation

A highlight of the park is the paved road immediately across Highway 3 from Manning Park Resort; it climbs steadily to **Cascade Lookout,** a viewpoint offering a magnificent 180-degree panoramic view. Beyond the lookout, the road turns to gravel and continues climbing for nine kilometers, ending at a parking lot beneath 2,063-meter (6,700-foot) Blackwall Peak. From this area of flower-filled alpine meadows, views extend over the park's remote northern boundary. Take time to soak up the color by taking one of the short trails originating from the parking lot. Or hike **Heather Trail** (10 kilometers/6.2 miles each way; allow three hours) to Three Brothers Mountain. If you're there between late July and mid-August, you won't believe what you're seeing: a rich yellow, orange, and white carpet of wildflowers as far as you can see.

Along Highway 3 are some short, self-guided nature trails, including a 700-meter (0.4-mile) walk (20 minutes) through a stand of ancient western red cedars. The trailhead is Sumallo Grove day-use area, 10 kilometers (6.2 miles) east of where Highway 3 enters the park from the west. Just east of the Visitor Information Centre, on the south side of the road, is the 500-meter (0.3-mile) **Beaver Pond Trail.** If you notice people arriving on foot in this parking lot with worn soles, bent backs, and great big smiles on their faces, give them a pat on the back—they may have just completed one of the world's greatest long-distance hikes. The **Pacific Crest Trail** runs 3,860 kilometers (2,400 miles) from the U.S.–Mexico border to this small and undistinguished trailhead.

Wintertime

The park gets plenty of dry snow for skiing and boarding. At **Manning Park Resort** (250/840-8822 or 800/330-3321, www.manningpark.com), 11 kilometers (6.8 miles) west of Highway 3 along Gibson Pass Road, downhill enthusiasts can take advantage of a 437-meter (1,430-foot) vertical rise served by two chairlifts, a T-bar, and a rope tow. Most runs are for intermediate skiers, but novices and experts will also find suitable terrain. Lift tickets are adult $50, senior and child $25. The resort is geared toward families, with other activities including a skating rink, terrain park, and tubing park, keeping all ages happy. On-hill facilities include a cafeteria, ski school, and ski rentals (from $35 for a full day). A free shuttle bus transfers guests to the ski area from Manning Park Resort, which offers winter packages from $150 for two nights' midweek high-season accommodations and two days' skiing.

Along with 190 kilometers (118 miles) of wilderness trails, cross-country skiers can enjoy 30 kilometers (19 miles) of groomed trails for $17 per day. Cross-country skis rent for $18 per day.

Practicalities

In the heart of the park on Highway 3, **Manning Park Resort** (250/840-8822 or 800/330-3321, www.manningpark.com) is a full-service lodging providing comfortable hotel rooms, cabins, and triplexes, as well as a dining room, a self-serve cafeteria, a small grocery store, and an open fireside lounge. Other facilities include saunas, an indoor pool, a TV room, a fitness center, tennis courts, a coin-operated laundry, and a gift shop. Through summer, rooms in the main lodge are $140–160 s or d, and chalets with kitchens range $165–309. The rest of the year rates are reduced, with rooms from $89 and chalets from $119.

The park's four campgrounds hold 355 sites; in summer, get in early to be assured of snagging one. Each campground provides drinking water and toilets. Firewood is available for a fee. The most popular campground is **Lightning Lakes,** two kilometers (1.2 miles) west of Manning Park Resort on Gibson Pass Road, which has showers; $22 per night. Others include **Coldspring Campground,** on Highway 3 two kilometers (1.2 miles) west of the resort; **Hampton Campground,** on Highway 3 four kilometers (2.5 miles) east of the resort; and **Mule Deer Campground,** four kilometers (2.5 miles) farther east. These three charge $14 per night.

The park's **Visitor Information Centre** (250/840-8836; summer daily

SOUTHWESTERN B.C.

8:30 A.M.–4:30 P.M., weekdays only the rest of the year) is one kilometer (0.6 mile) east of Manning Park Resort. Inside, you'll find displays on recreation opportunities and on the area's natural and cultural history, as well as maps and detailed information about park facilities.

CONTINUING TOWARD THE OKANAGAN VALLEY

From the eastern boundary of E.C. Manning Provincial Park, Highway 3 follows the Similkameen River north to Princeton, then turns sharply southeast to Osoyoos, at the southern end of the Okanagan Valley, a total distance of 158 kilometers (98 miles).

Princeton

At the confluence of the Similkameen and Tulameen Rivers, surrounded by low tree-covered hills, lies the small, friendly ranching town of Princeton (pop. 3,000). **Princeton and District Pioneer Museum** (167 Vermilion Ave., 250/295-7588; Mon.–Fri. 1–5 P.M.) features pioneer artifacts from Granite City, Chinese and Interior Salish artifacts, and a good fossil display.

On the northeast side of Princeton, the stone and concrete ruins of a 1910 cement plant have been incorporated in a unique resort complex, **(Princeton Castle Resort** (Hwy. 5A, 250/295-7988 or 888/228-8881, www.castleresort.com). The cement works was built at a cost of $1 million, yet operated for only one year. In the ensuing decades, the buildings have been reclaimed by nature. Around, through, and over the crumbling ruins grow trees, wild roses, lilacs, and lupines. (Take a look at the concrete paths and steps leading down from the back of the administrative building to the ruins—the concrete is loaded with fossilized shells.) Surrounding the ruins are cabins and chalets of varying configurations, with the larger chalets taking pride of place along a ridge overlooking a sparkling creek. One-bed cabins with no linen and shared bathrooms are $75 s or d, while chalets complete with bathrooms, kitchens, and TV cost from $165. Beyond the ruins, a

© ANDREW HEMPSTEAD

The crumbling remains of "Princeton Castle" are the centerpiece of a unique resort on the outskirts of Princeton.

road leads up to the resort campground, where sites are $25 and tepees (no linen) are rented for $45 per night. Aside from admiring the ruins, children will love the large playground, while all ages can enjoy horseback riding, or canoeing on the small lake. To get there from Princeton, cross the bridge at the north end of Bridge Street, turn right on Old Hedley Road, cross Highway 5, turn left on Five Mile Road, then continue until the sign to the park leads you right.

Just a short stroll from downtown, **Riverside Motel** (307 Thomas Ave. at the north end of Bridge St., 250/295-6232) was built in 1934 as a hunting and fishing lodge. The aptly named motel is right beside the river, and in the height of summer the water level drops to expose a small beach and shallow swimming hole. (Ask the owner to show you a photo of the place taken in 1937—the cabins still look exactly the same.) Each basic cabin has a toilet, a shower, and a kitchen with a fridge, stove, cooking utensils, crockery, and cutlery. Rates are a very reasonable $38–70 s or d.

For a meal, head downtown to the **Princeton Hotel** (258 Bridge St., 250/295-3355); order bistro-style at the small window across from the bar.

At the east entrance to town, **Princeton Visitor Centre** (Hwy. 3, 250/295-3103) is open year-round 9 A.M.–5 P.M., daily in summer but Monday–Friday only the rest of the year.

Coalmont and Beyond

If you want to see some impressive canyon scenery off the main tourist drag, cross the river at the north end of Princeton's Bridge Street and turn left, heading west toward Coalmont for 18 kilometers (11 miles). Coalmont came to the forefront when gold-rush activity moved from Granite City (see sidebar) to this village in 1911. Today, you can't help but notice that the town's residents have a sense of humor. The welcoming sign states that Coalmont has no industry but plenty of activity, in the form of sleeping and daydreaming. It also claims Coalmont has a hot, cold, wet, and dry climate, warns traveling salespeople to stay away, and advises single women that their safety is not guaranteed due to the predominance of bachelors. The attractive 1911 **Coalmont Hotel** (250/295-6066) still serves up beer to thirsty travelers, while quite a number of homes— some with backyards crammed with eclectic collections of rusting mine machinery—line the streets.

The main road through Coalmont winds its way north to Merritt, providing a handy shortcut, if that's the direction you're heading. The only town en route is the hamlet of **Tulameen** (pop. 250). Along the main street, the museum in a one-room log schoolhouse may or may not be open, while at the north end of town, you'll probably have the beach at **Otter Bay Provincial Park** to yourself.

Hedley and Vicinity

From Princeton, Highway 3 takes you on a scenic route through the beautiful **Similkameen River Valley,** which holds lots of places to

camp, in either provincial parks or private campgrounds. Between Princeton and Keremeos the road follows the Dewdney Trail, a 468-kilometer (290-mile) track used in the 1860s to connect Hope with the Wildhorse Creek goldfields. This stretch itself has also been a major mining area, supplying a fortune in gold, silver, nickel, and copper over the years.

One of the richest mines was the Mascot Mine, unique in that the mine entrance was perched 850 vertical meters (2,800 feet) above the mining town of Hedley. To immerse yourself in the history of the mining era wander around the tree-lined streets of Hedley or consider staying at **Colonial Inn B&B** (Colonial Rd., 250/292-8131, www.colonialinnbb.ca; Apr.–Oct.), a historic guesthouse surrounded by mature gardens. Three of the five guest rooms have private bathrooms, and a cooked breakfast is included in the rates of $87 s, $98–109 d. Camping out back is $20.

GRANITE CITY

After the discovery of a gold nugget in Granite Creek back in 1885, a 13-saloon gold-rush city sprang to life on this spot. Soon it was the third-largest city in the province, supporting a population of over 2,000. But the boom was short-lived, and the town was quickly abandoned. What remains of Granite City lies two kilometers (1.2 miles) from Coalmont. To get there, head straight through Coalmont to Granite Creek, turn left on Hope Street, right over the creek, and then follow the road to a fork. Straight ahead is the site of the boomtown, marked by a riverside cairn and the broken-down remains of a few log buildings among wild lilac bushes – it's really up to your imagination to re-create the good ol' days. On the bluff to the north of Granite City (take the right fork and then the first right) is a small graveyard with headstones showing dates from the boom years.

The landscape east of Princeton is different from that to the west, but the change is most pronounced east of Hedley—going from ragged, tree-covered mountains through rolling hills covered in sagebrush and lush, irrigated orchards around Keremeos to desert (complete with lizards, cactus, and rattlesnakes) around Osoyoos on the Canada–U.S. border.

Cathedral Provincial Park

Wilderness hikers and mountaineers should not miss the turnoff to this spectacular 33,272-hectare (82,200-acre) park just west of Keremeos. Access along the 21-kilometer (13-mile) road leading into the park is restricted to guests of **(Cathedral Lakes Lodge** (250/226-7560 or 888/255-4453, www.cathedral-lakes-lodge .com) or those willing to walk. For this reason, most park visitors stay at the resort, which provides accommodations, meals, use of canoes, a recreation room and hot tub, and transportation to and from the base camp. The minimum stay is a two-day package: original cabins and bungalow rooms start at $420 per person, while rooms in the main lodge sell for $450. Rates include all meals and the shuttle ride. The lodge also offers the option of a day trip for $95 per person, which includes the shuttle and lunch.

About 60 kilometers (37 miles) of wilderness trails lead from the resort to a variety of striking and enticingly named rock formations, including Stone City, Giant Cleft, Devil's Woodpile, Macabre Tower, Grimface Mountain, Denture Ridge, and Smokey the Bear. Wander through meadows waving with dainty alpine flowers, climb peaks for tremendous views, fish for trout in sparkling turquoise lakes, and capture on film immense glacier-topped mountains.

KEREMEOS

As you approach mountain-surrounded Keremeos from the west, the road is lined with lush, irrigated orchards and fruit stands, one after another, which is probably what inspired the town's claim to fame as the "Fruit Stand Capital of Canada." Keremeos has one of the longest growing seasons in the province. Try a taste-bud-tingling fruit-juice shake in summer; recommended is the second-to-last stand as you head east out of town. Harvest dates are mid-June to mid-July for cherries, mid-July to early August for apricots, mid-July to early September for peaches, mid-August to mid-September for pears, early August to mid-October for apples, early to mid-September for plums, and early September to early October for grapes.

(Grist Mill

The town's main historic attraction is the Grist Mill (250/499-2888; adult $6, child $3), a restored water-powered mill built in 1877. This is where pioneer Similkameen Valley settlers used to grind locally produced wheat into flour. Costumed interpreters lead tours of the property daily late May–early October, then invite you to try your hand at the many informative and entertaining hands-on displays in the museum

Grist Mill, Keremeos

and visitor center. A pleasant tearoom over-looks garden plots carefully planted to reflect various eras (the pancake breakfast on summer weekends is a treat). Outside of summer, the grounds are open for inspection. To get there, go through town on the main highway, turn north on Highway 3A toward Penticton, then right at the Historic Site sign on Upper Bench Road.

Flour ground at the Grist Mill is used in breads available on-site, as well as at the brightly painted **《 Hanna's Bakery** (614 7th Ave., 250/499-2522; Mon.–Sat. 2 A.M.–5 P.M.), which is difficult to miss driving down Keremeos's main street. Sit inside and check your email or sit out front and watch the world of Keremeos go by as you tuck into a meat pie or sweet treat.

Keremeos Columns

Another local highlight, although it takes some effort to reach, is **Keremeos Columns Provincial Park.** The park is named for a 90-meter (300-foot) cliff of remarkable hexagonal basalt columns rising from a lava base just outside the park boundary (the columns were supposed to be in the park but because of a surveying accident actually stand on private land). Access the viewpoint by taking a steep eight-kilometer (five-mile) logging road off Highway 3 about four kilometers (2.5 miles) north of town (turn right at the Keremeos cemetery), then take another steep six-kilometer (3.7-mile) hike (allow at least three hours one-way) across private property; ask for permission and trail details at the house at the end of the paved road.

OKANAGAN VALLEY

This warm, sunny valley 400 kilometers (250 miles) east of Vancouver extends 180 kilometers (112 miles) between the U.S.–Canada border in the south and the TransCanada Highway in the north. Lush orchards and vineyards, fertile irrigated croplands, low rolling hills, and a string of beautiful lakes line the valley floor, where you'll also find 40 golf courses, dozens of commercial attractions, and lots and lots of people—especially in summer.

The Okanagan Valley's three main cities—Penticton, Kelowna, and Vernon—are spread around long, narrow Okanagan Lake and collectively hold the bulk of interior British Columbia's population. Numerous smaller communities also ring the lakeshore, doubling or tripling in size in July and August when hordes of vacationers turn the valley into one big resort. Most of these summer pilgrims are Canadians from cooler climes, who come in search of guaranteed sunshine, lazy days on a beach, and a take-away tan. In winter, the valley draws pilgrims of another sort: skiers and snowboarders on their way to the world-class slopes flanking the valley.

All the credit for developing the Okanagan into Canada's fruit basket goes to the original planter, Father Charles Pandosy, a French oblate priest who established a mission in the Kelowna area in 1859. Within a couple of years he had successfully introduced apple trees to the district. The trees positively blossomed under his care, thanks to the valley's long five-and-a-half-month growing season, over 2,000 hours of sunshine a year, relatively mild winters, and the ready availability of water. Soon

© ANDREW HEMPSTEAD

HIGHLIGHTS

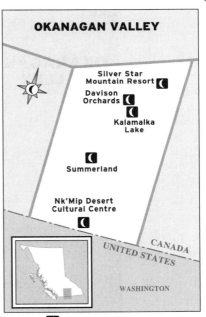

OKANAGAN VALLEY

◖ Nk'Mip Desert Cultural Centre: Native history combined with walking trails through a very un-Canadian desert define this unique attraction (page 231).

◖ Summerland: On a map of the Okanagan, Summerland is just a small dot with an enticing name. But this lakeside hamlet is home to one of the valley's finest wineries (Sumac Ridge) and the departure point for train rides along the Kettle Valley Steam Railway (page 237).

◖ Davison Orchards: Children will love these orchards near Vernon, where they can explore a working farm on a wagon tour (page 250).

◖ Kalamalka Lake: Choosing a favorite Okanagan lake is difficult, but my nod goes to Kalamalka Lake, between Kelowna and Vernon, for its beautiful hue, sandy beaches, and warm clear water (page 250).

◖ Silver Star Mountain Resort: This resort has more than just great skiing and boarding; its gold-rush-style buildings and a packed summer activity program make it a worthwhile destination at any time of year (page 252).

LOOK FOR ◖ TO FIND RECOMMENDED SIGHTS, ACTIVITIES, DINING, AND LODGING.

fruit orchards of all types were springing up everywhere, and today the Okanagan Valley region produces 30 percent of Canada's apples, 60 percent of its cherries, 20 percent of its peaches, half of its pears and plums, and all the apricots in the country.

PLANNING YOUR TIME

Regardless of your approach to the Okanagan Valley, you'll spend time driving Highway 97, which is the main north–south thoroughfare. This highway passes through the four largest towns—from south to north Osoyoos, Penticton, Kelowna, and Vernon—closely parallels Okanagan Lake, and is rarely out of sight of an orchard or vineyard. It's a truly spectacular drive, but don't plan on doing it in one day. You could spend at least one day in and around each population center, mixing traditional sights such as the **Nk'Mip Desert Cultural Centre** at Osoyoos with winery tours, golf, and time out on the beaches. Younger children will revel in the many outdoor activities: Take a wagon ride around **Davison Orchards,** schedule a half-day at a fun park, or get back to nature in one of the many provincial parks.

If you have a beach-loving family in tow on your British Columbia vacation, the Okanagan Valley is the place to plan a break from the rigors of sightseeing. Use my accommodation recommendations scattered through this chapter to choose a lodging that suits your needs and budget, and make reservations as far in

OKANAGAN VALLEY

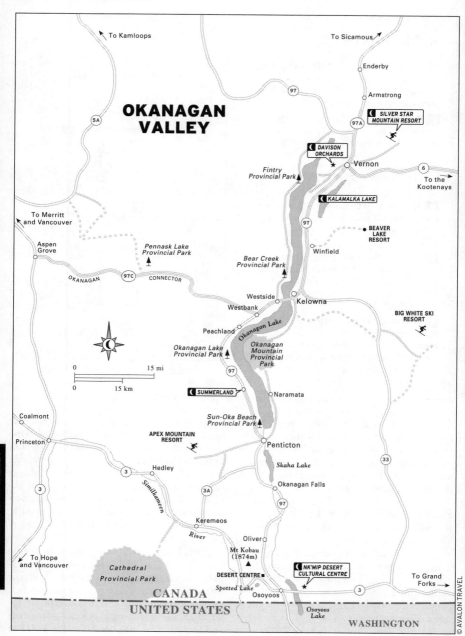

OKANAGAN VALLEY

To Kamloops

To Sicamous

Enderby

Armstrong

97

5A

☾ **SILVER STAR MOUNTAIN RESORT** 🎿

97A

⬛ **DAVISON ORCHARDS**

★

Vernon

Fintry Provincial Park ▲

6

To the Kootenays

☾ **KALAMALKA LAKE**

To Merritt and Vancouver

97

● **BEAVER LAKE RESORT**

Aspen Grove

Pennask Lake Provincial Park ▲

Winfield

Bear Creek Provincial Park ▲

OKANAGAN

97C CONNECTOR

Westside

Westbank

Kelowna

BIG WHITE SKI RESORT 🎿

Peachland

Okanagan Lake

Okanagan Lake Provincial Park ▲

Okanagan Mountain Provincial Park

0   15 mi

0   15 km

97

☾ **SUMMERLAND**

Naramata

Sun-Oka Beach Provincial Park ▲

Coalmont

APEX MOUNTAIN RESORT 🎿

Penticton

Princeton

Skaha Lake

33

3

Hedley

Similkameen

3A

Okanagan Falls

97

3

To Hope and Vancouver

Keremeos

River

Oliver

Mt Kobau (1874m)

DESERT CENTRE ■

☾ **NK'MIP DESERT CULTURAL CENTRE**

★

To Grand Forks →

3

Cathedral Provincial Park

CANADA

Spotted Lake

Osoyoos

UNITED STATES

Osoyoos Lake

WASHINGTON

advance as possible. Even if you haven't set your itinerary for the rest of your travels, having a few days' downtime to look forward to will make your vacation more enjoyable.

As in the rest of British Columbia, July through August is by far the busiest time of year in the Okanagan. This is when temperatures are at their highest and the waterways at their busiest. If you're planning on camping, reserve a spot as far in advance as possible, especially at commercial lakeside campgrounds. As a general rule, the summer weather will be hot and windy along the valley floor, with temperatures cooling off as you climb into the surrounding mountains. Take this into consideration if you don't like the heat, and plan on staying somewhere like Beaver Lake Resort, in the mountains in Kelowna, or **Silver Star Mountain Resort,** near Vernon.

Osoyoos

This town of 4,600 is nestled on the west shore of **Osoyoos Lake,** Canada's warmest freshwater lake (up to 24°C, 75°F in summer). The town also boasts Canada's highest year-round average temperature. The older main street leads down to the lakefront and **Gyro Community Park,** where a floating swimming pool provides the perfect spot for families to cool off.

◖ NK'MIP DESERT CULTURAL CENTRE

The Okanagan Indian Band, whose land spreads along the east side of the lake, are one of the most progressive in North America. They own and operate a number of very successful enterprises; among those most visible to visitors will be the winery, golf course, resort, and campground. Their culture is showcased at this museum (1000 Rancher Creek Rd., 250/495-7901; daily 9:30 A.M.–4:30 P.M., closed Sun. outside summer; adult $12, senior $11, child $8), pronounced "in-ka-meep." Integrated with the surrounding desert, the main building is filled with displays telling the story of the First Nations people and their close relationship with the land. The documentary *Coyote Spirit,* shown regularly in a larger theater, is particularly endearing. There's also a display of desert critters. Outside, interpreters present various programs, including a rattlesnake show-and-talk. Walking trails lead through the desert to viewpoints and past various native structures, all with interpretive panels.

DESERT CENTRE

Across the lake from Nk'Mip, a 100-hectare (250-acre) "pocket desert" has the distinction of being Canada's driest spot, receiving less than 300 millimeters (11 inches) of precipitation annually. It is a desert in the truest sense, complete with sand, cacti, prickly pear, sagebrush, lizards, scorpions, rattlesnakes, and other desert dwellers, including 23 invertebrates found nowhere else in the world. Learn more about this unique landscape at the Desert Centre (250/495-2470 or 877/899-0897; May–early Oct. Wed.–Mon. 10 A.M.–5 P.M.; adult $6, senior $5, child $3), a research and interpretive facility where a boardwalk leads through this very un-Canadian environment. To get there follow Highway 97 north from Osoyoos and take 146th Avenue west.

SCENIC DRIVE

For a bird's-eye view of the lake, take Highway 3 west from town 12 kilometers (7.5 miles), then follow a 20-kilometer (12-mile) gravel road to the 1,874-meter (6,150-foot) summit of **Mount Kobau.** Short trails there lead to viewpoints of the Similkameen and Okanagan Valleys. Along the section of Highway 3 before the turnoff, watch for **Spotted Lake,** a bizarre natural phenomenon on the south side of the road. As summer progresses and the lake's water evaporates, high concentrations of magnesium, calcium, and sodium crystallize, forming colorful circles.

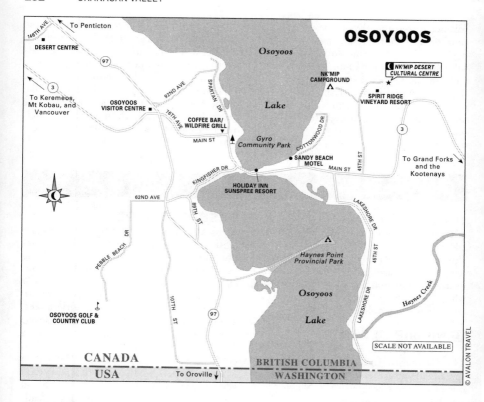

OSOYOOS

SCALE NOT AVAILABLE

© AVALON TRAVEL

ACCOMMODATIONS

In summer, Osoyoos Lake attracts hordes of water lovers and sun worshippers, so getting accommodations can be difficult—especially along the prime stretch of lakefront east of downtown along Highway 3. You'll need to book well in advance to get a room during summer at the **Sandy Beach Motel** (6706 Ponderosa Dr., 250/495-6931 or 866/495-6931, www.sandybeachmotel.com), but you'll be glad you did. Set on a private stretch of sandy beach, the 25 kitchen-equipped units face a grassy courtyard, landscaped with crushed gravel pathways and cacti. Summer rates range $127–254 s or d, dropping as low as $70 in winter. Along the same stretch, but larger and less personal, is **Holiday Inn Sunspree Resort** (Hwy. 3, 250/495-7223 or 877/786-7773, www.holiday

innosoyoos; $189 s or d), with many of the 85 rooms overlooking the resort's private beach. The resort also has a rooftop garden, a fitness center, boat rentals, and a restaurant.

Spirit Ridge Vineyard Resort (1200 Rancher Creek Rd., 250/495-5445 or 877/313-9463, www.spiritridge.ca; from $255 s or d) is part of the Nk'Mip development, overlooking Osoyoos Lake across the water from town. This self-contained resort includes the Nk'Mip cultural center, a golf course, a winery, and an outdoor heated pool and hot tub, and a small section of private beach is easily reached on foot through the vineyard. The spacious guest rooms have modern kitchens, high-speed Internet access, and TV/DVD combos, and most have separate bedrooms. It's worth paying extra for a lake view.

Spirit Ridge Vineyard Resort is one of the valley's premier accommodations.

Camping

Haynes Point Provincial Park protects an extremely narrow low-lying spit that juts into Osoyoos Lake south of downtown. At the far end of the spit is a beautiful campground, with many sites enjoying lakefront settings ($22 per night). Like most other provincial parks, Haynes Point has no showers or hookups, so if you need more amenities, consider **Nk'Mip Campground** (8000 45th St., 250/495-7279,

www.campingosoyoos.com; $29–38). This campground (almost directly opposite downtown Osoyoos) has some sites set along the lake and offers its own private beach.

FOOD

Walk down Main Street and take your pick from various cafés and the usual smattering of Italian and Chinese restaurants. **The Coffee Bar** (8523 Main St.; daily from 7:30 A.M.) features a good range of coffee concoctions in a modern setting. At the same corner is the **Wildfire Grill** (8523 Main St., 250/495-2215; daily for lunch and dinner), which has a quiet patio out back. Expect contemporary takes on traditional dishes, with most dinner mains in the $16–24 range.

Across the lake, **Passa Tempo** is the signature restaurant at Spirit Ridge Vineyard Resort (1200 Rancher Creek Rd., 250/495-8007; daily 7 A.M.–11 P.M.). Talk your way to an outdoor table overlooking the vineyard and lake to enjoy dishes such as grilled bison topped with blue cheese cream. Next door, a winery café (May–Oct.) opens for lunch, with Pacific Northwest-inspired dishes and the same memorable views.

INFORMATION

In a parking lot at the corner of Highways 3 and 97 is **Osoyoos Visitor Centre** (250/495-7142 or 888/676-9667, www.destinationosoyoos.com; summer daily 8:30 A.M.–4:30 P.M., the rest of the year Mon.–Fri.).

Penticton

One of the Okanagan's three major population centers, Penticton (pop. 43,000) lies between the north end of Skaha Lake and the south end of Okanagan Lake. Approaching from the south, you'll see a roadside plaque honoring pioneer Thomas Ellis, who arrived in the valley in 1886, built a great cattle empire, and planted the area's first orchard. Today

fruit orchards are everywhere, and Penticton's nickname is Peach City.

SIGHTS AND RECREATION

The emphasis in Penticton is on sun and sand, but there's also a little history to explore at **Penticton Museum** (785 Main St., 250/490-2451; Mon.–Sat. 10 A.M.–5 P.M.; adult $2, child $1).

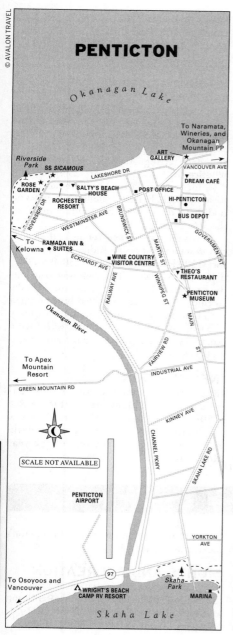

© AVALON TRAVEL

PENTICTON

Okanagan Lake

To Naramata,
Wineries, and
Okanagan
Mountain PP

ART
GALLERY

Riverside
Park   SS SICAMOUS
LAKESHORE DR

VANCOUVER AVE

DREAM CAFÉ

ROSE
GARDEN   SALTY'S BEACH
HOUSE   POST OFFICE

ROCHESTER
RESORT

RIVERSIDE DR

WESTMINSTER AVE

HI-PENTICTON

BUS DEPOT

BRUNSWICK ST

GOVERNMENT ST

To
Kelowna   RAMADA INN &
SUITES

ECKHARDT AVE

WINE COUNTRY
VISITOR CENTRE

MARTIN ST

THEO'S
RESTAURANT

RAILWAY AVE

WINNIPEG ST

PENTICTON
MUSEUM

Okanagan River

FAIRVIEW RD

MAIN
ST

To Apex
Mountain
Resort

GREEN MOUNTAIN RD

INDUSTRIAL AVE

KINNEY AVE

CHANNEL PKWY

SKAHA LAKE RD

SCALE NOT AVAILABLE

PENTICTON
AIRPORT

YORKTON
AVE

97

To Osoyoos and
Vancouver

WRIGHT'S BEACH
CAMP RV RESORT

Skaha
Park

MARINA

Skaha Lake

OKANAGAN VALLEY

Along Okanagan Lake

Wander along the tree-shaded shores of Lake Okanagan to see the **SS *Sicamous*** (1099 Lakeshore Dr. W., 250/492-0403; daily 10 A.M.–4 P.M. extended to 7 A.M.–7 P.M. in summer; adult $5, child $1). This Canadian Pacific Railway sternwheeler operated on Okanagan Lake 1914–1936. Now it rests on the lakeshore, and it's easy to spend an hour wandering through the ship, peeking into the purser's office, admiring the furnishings in the grand dining room, and clambering up to the observation deck.

At the opposite end of Lakeshore Drive (to the east) is the **Art Gallery of the South Okanagan** (199 Marina Way, 250/493-2928; Tues.–Fri. 10 A.M.–5 P.M., Sat.–Sun. noon–5 P.M.; adult $2). The craft shop is a good place to pick up creative treasures and handmade souvenirs. Continue east from the gallery to the local **marina**—another enjoyable spot for a lakeside stroll.

To Naramata

A 14-kilometer (8.7-mile) secondary road runs northeast out of Penticton, skirting the east side of Okanagan Lake and passing through the small community of Naramata. The first of many well-respected wineries along the way is the **Red Rooster Winery** (891 Naramata Rd., 250/492-2424; Apr.–Oct. daily 10 A.M.–6 P.M., Nov.–March daily 11 A.M.–5 P.M.), easily recognized by the mission-style tasting room beside the highway. No tours—instead enjoy a tasting session of the winery's acclaimed pinot gris and chardonnay wines, then soak up the lake views over a cheese platter or slice of quiche on the veranda. Next up is the aptly named **Hillside Estate** (1350 Naramata Rd., 250/493-6274), with an impressive three-story wooden building holding the main winery. Hillside is known for its pinot noir, but it also produces an unusually dry but fruity riesling. It's open for tours daily 10 A.M.–6 P.M. and for lunch daily from 11:30 A.M.

Naramata itself is a charming lakeside village, far removed from the commercialism of Penticton. Access to the lake is somewhat

OKANAGAN WINES

Okanagan wines receive acclaim worldwide, although this success is only recent. In fact, it was doubted that quality grapes could be grown north of the 49th parallel until the late 1980s, when the Canada-United States Free Trade Agreement (now NAFTA) forced local vintners to revisit their quality control. As a result, most of the original hybrid vines were ripped out and replaced with classic European varietals.

The valley's climate – long summer days and cool nights – produces small grapes with a higher-than-usual sugar content, creating intensely flavored and aromatic wines. A wide variety of red and white wine grapes are planted, with the reds thriving in the warmer south end of the valley, where merlot, cabernet franc, and pinot noir grapes produce the best local wines. The entire wine-making process in the Okanagan has been one of experimentation, and along the way more unusual varietals such as ehrenfelser and auxerrois have been grown with success, make tasting local wines all the more interesting.

The best introduction to the valley's vino offerings is the **British Columbia Wine Information Centre** (553 Railway St., Penticton, 250/490-2006; summer daily 9 A.M.-8 P.M., the rest of the year daily 10 A.M.-5 P.M.). As much a wine shop as anything else, it offers plenty of information along with wine tour maps and knowledgeable staff to set you off in the right direction.

Okanagan Valley vineyard

limited, although the public beach at Manitou Park is good for swimming.

Continue through Naramata and up into the mountains, where the road fizzles out near the south border of undeveloped Okanagan Mountain Provincial Park. The only way to get into this piece of untouched wilderness is to walk or boat over. Hike in for the day for a picnic, some fishing, or to explore the 24 kilometers (15 miles) of trails.

Skiing and Snowboarding

Sunniest of the Okanagan resorts is **Apex Mountain Resort** (250/292-8222 or 877/777-2739, www.apexresort.com), 31 kilometers (19 miles) west of Penticton, which provides 605 vertical meters (1,990 feet) and 56 runs over 450 hectares (1,100 acres). The slopes are served by a T-bar and two chairlifts, one of which—the Quickdraw Express—zips skiers and boarders to the summit of Beaconsfield Mountain and opens up most of the expert terrain. Boarders are catered to with a terrain park and half-pipe, or you can slide downhill on an inflatable tube in the tube park. Lift tickets are adult $55, senior $45, child $34, kids under seven free.

Events

Penticton seems to have festivals, parades, events, or competitions going on throughout the year. The biggest event is the annual **Penticton Peach Festival** (www.peachfest .com), held on the first full weekend of August;

it's a tradition going back more than 50 years. Events include peach tasting, the crowning of Miss Penticton, Kiddies Day (the Sunday), a sandcastle competition, fireworks, and nightly entertainment in Gyro Park.

Other annual happenings include **Mid-Winter Break-Out** (250/490-3078) in mid-February, which includes everything from ice carving to a Polar Bear Dip; the **Spring Wine Festival** (250/861-6654, www.owfs.com), hosted by many local wineries in late April; the **Penticton Highland Games** (www.penticton highlandgames.com), the first Sunday of July in Kings Park; the **Ironman Canada** (250/493-5922) triathlon the last Sunday in August; and the **Pentastic Jazz Festival** (www.pentastic jazz.com) the second weekend of September. Two major wine festivals are a valley highlight; for details see the *Kelowna* section or check the website www.owfs.com.

ACCOMMODATIONS AND CAMPING

In July and August, you'll need to make reservations far in advance to snag a room at any of Penticton's beachfront motels. A good summer alternative is Apex Mountain Resort, 31 kilometers (19 miles) west of Penticton, where on-hill lodgings provide steeply discounted rooms for visitors looking to escape the busy valley floor. Check the resort's website (www.apexresort.com) for packages.

Under $50

As you'd expect in a resort town, the only accommodation under $50 is in a dormitory. **HI-Penticton** (464 Ellis St., 250/492-3992, www.hihostels.ca) occupies a 1950s stucco residence close to the heart of downtown. Facilities include a kitchen, a laundry, bike rentals, and an outdoor barbecue area; $20 per night for members of Hostelling International, $25 for nonmembers, and private rooms for $50 s or d. Check-in is 8 A.M.–noon and 5–10 P.M.

$50-100

The **Village Motel** (244 Robinson Dr., Naramata, 250/496-5535, www.villagemotel.com)

will bring back memories of a bygone era. Located in the village of Naramata, 14 kilometers (8.7 miles) north of Penticton, the nine older guest rooms are nicely decorated and open to landscaped gardens and a communal barbecue area. Regular rooms are $85 s or d, or pay $137 for a kitchen unit. The motel is within walking distance of the lake.

$100-150

The least expensive of several lodgings on Lakeshore Drive, close to both the lake and downtown, is the 36-room **Rochester Resort** (970 Lakeshore Dr., 250/493-1128 or 800/567-4904; from $139 s or d, $169 for a one-bedroom unit). All units have a kitchen, and there's a communal barbecue area for guest use.

Over $150

A few blocks back from the beach, **Ramada Inn & Suites** (1050 Eckhardt Ave. W., 250/492-8926 or 800/665-4966, www.penticton ramada.com) is a family-friendly, self-contained resort adjacent to an 18-hole golf course. Amenities include an outdoor pool, a sprawling courtyard, a playground, a fitness center, a restaurant, and a poolside bar. The rooms are decorated in smart color schemes and are air-conditioned. Rates start at $159 s or d, but in the off-season you'll pay around the same for a Jacuzzi suite.

For the atmosphere of an old-fashioned resort, it's difficult to surpass the **❰ Naramata Heritage Inn & Spa** (3625 1st St., Naramata, 250/496-6808 or 866/617-1188, www.naramata inn.com; from $207 s or d), north of Penticton along the east side of the lake. Dating to 1908, the hotel has been completely renovated, yet none of its historic appeal has been lost. The guest rooms have mission-style beds covered with plush duvets, bathrooms with heated floors and claw-foot tubs, and either a balcony or patio. Other amenities include spa services, a wine bar with live jazz on Friday evenings, and a fine-dining restaurant.

Camping

South of downtown, **Wright's Beach Camp**

RV Park (4200 Skaha Lake Rd., 250/492-7120, www.wrightsbeachcamp.com; May–Sept.; $37–50) is right on the lake and has a huge playground and an outdoor pool.

If being by the lake isn't important, choose to stay at **Twin Lakes Golf & RV Resort** (Hwy. 3A, 250/497-8379, www.twinlakesgolfresort .com; Apr.–mid-Oct.), 19 kilometers (12 miles) southwest of Penticton. The campground is in the middle of a full-length golf course (greens fee $50, but discounted for campers), which is surrounded by barren cliffs. Amenities include modern washrooms, free firewood, a restaurant, and a lounge. Tent sites are $20, full hookups $28. A five-minute drive west of the campground, you can fish from the banks of Yellow Lake for brook trout and perch. To get to Twin Lakes, head south from Penticton and turn west off Highway 97 at Kaleden. If you're traveling east from Princeton, turn off Highway 3 at Keremeos.

OTHER PRACTICALITIES
Food
Penticton has a wide variety of restaurants spread along the beach and through downtown. My favorite is the **C Dream Café** (74 Front St., 250/490-9012; Mon.–Fri. 11 A.M.–8 P.M., Sat.–Sun. 10 A.M.–8 P.M.), away from the water but with a dreamy ambience (think eclectic furniture, colorful kites hanging from the ceiling, and soothing background music), friendly staff, and innovative cuisine. The menu takes inspiration from throughout Asia and steers clear of red meat: poached lime chicken panini, salmon spinach pie, rice noodle wraps, and tandoori chicken.

Across the road from the beach along the busy downtown tourist strip is **Salty's Beach House** (1000 Lakeshore Dr., 250/493-5001; daily from 11 A.M.), with tables inside and out. The menu blends conventional pub fare with Thai and Caribbean cuisine, such as pad thai ($11) and a mango chicken sandwich ($8). The fruity drink menu befits the location.

On Main Street between Okanagan and Skaha Lakes are several decent eateries. At **Theo's Restaurant** (687 Main St., 250/492-4019) you can tuck into European favorites such as lamb moussaka ($14) and herbed tiger prawns ($23) in a large open-plan eatery with lots of greenery.

Information and Services
Wine Country Visitor Centre (555 Railway Ave., 250/493-4055 or 800/663-5052, www .penticton.org; summer daily 8 A.M.–8 P.M., the rest of the year Mon.–Fri. 9 A.M.–6 P.M., Sat.–Sun. 10 A.M.–5 P.M.) is well worth searching out. Inside the adobe-style structure is free Internet access, a wine information center, and lots of local literature.

Okanagan Books (233 Main St., 250/493-1941) stocks a wide range of local reading and all the current best sellers. Across the road, **Books 'n Things** is the city's premier used bookstore. Both are closed Sunday.

Penticton Regional Hospital is on Carmi Avenue (250/492-4000). The **post office** is on the corner of Winnipeg Street and Nanaimo Avenue.

Getting There
Visitors flying into the Okanagan use Kelowna Airport, to the north, where they pick up rental cars. The **Greyhound Bus Depot** (307 Ellis St., 250/493-4101) is busy with services heading south to Osoyoos and north through the Okanagan Valley to Salmon Arm on the Trans-Canada Highway.

NORTH OF PENTICTON
Highway 97 links Penticton and Kelowna, running along the west side of Okanagan Lake for the entire 60 kilometers (37 miles). The first worthwhile stop is tiny **Sun-Oka Beach Provincial Park,** a sun-drenched, south-facing park with a sandy beach, paddle boat rentals, and a concession.

C Summerland
As you enter picturesque Summerland, nestled between Giants Head Mountain and the lake 16 kilometers (10 miles) north of Penticton, turn west (away from the lake) at either of the stoplights and follow the signs to Prairie Valley

Station, the departure point for **Kettle Valley Steam Railway** (250/494-8422 or 877/494-8424, www.kettlevalleyrail.org). This steam train, dating from the early 1900s, runs along a historic 10-kilometer (6.2-mile) stretch of track, through orchards and vineyards, and over a 75-meter-high (246-foot-high) trestle bridge. Departures are late May to mid-October Saturday–Monday at 10:30 A.M. and 1:30 P.M., with additional trips in July and August on Thursday and Friday. The fare for the 90-minute round-trip is adult $19, senior $18, child $11.

Another interesting stop is the **Summerland Sweets** factory (Canyon View Rd., 250/494-0377) to see syrups, jams, and candy being made from fresh and frozen fruit. From Highway 97 take the Dunn Street or Arkell Road exit west, turn right on Gartrell Road, left on Happy Valley Road, right on Hillborn Street, then left on Canyon View Road.

Sumac Ridge Estate (one kilometer/.6 mile north of Summerland on the lake side of the highway, 250/494-0451) was British Columbia's first estate winery. Today, this well-recognized name appears on a wide variety of red and white wines, including an award-winning

cabernet franc and one of the Okanagan's few sparkling wines. Tours and tastings are offered May–October daily 10 A.M.–4 P.M. on the hour, and a bistro is open daily for lunch.

Continuing Toward Kelowna

On the way to Kelowna you pass two entrances to **Okanagan Lake Provincial Park,** a grassy, beach-fringed park popular for boating and swimming. Ponderosa pines line the shore while exotic trees such as maple and oak shade dozens of picnic tables. Camping is $22 a night.

Farther along is the community of **Peachland.** Crammed between a rocky bluff and Okanagan Lake, Peachland was founded in 1808 by Manitoba entrepreneur and newspaperman John Robinson, who came to the Okanagan in search of mining prospects but turned his talents to developing the delicious locally grown dessert peaches. The drive through downtown is a pleasant diversion from Highway 97. On one side are the lake and a long pebbly beach dotted with grassed areas of parkland and supervised swimming areas. On the other is a collection of shops and cafés.

Kelowna

British Columbia's largest city outside the Lower Mainland and Victoria, Kelowna (pop. 130,000) lies on the shores of 170-kilometer-long (106-mile-long) Okanagan Lake, approximately halfway between Penticton in the south and Vernon in the north. The city combines a scenic location among semiarid mountains with an unbeatable climate of long, sunny summers and short, mild winters. The low rolling hills around the city hold lush terraced orchards, and the numerous local vineyards produce some excellent wines. Visitors flock here in summer to enjoy the area's sparkling lakes, sandy beaches, numerous provincial parks, and golfing; in winter they come for great skiing and boarding at nearby Big White Ski Resort.

History

For thousands of years before the arrival of the first Europeans, the nomadic Salish people inhabited the Okanagan Valley, hunting (*kelowna* is a Salish word for grizzly bear), gathering, and fishing. The first European to settle in the valley was an oblate missionary, Father Pandosy, who established a mission in 1859. Since the first apple trees were planted at the mission, Kelowna has thrived as the center of the Okanagan fruit, vegetable, and vineyard industry (the valley is Canada's largest fruit-growing region).

SIGHTS
Along the Waterfront

Right downtown, beautiful **City Park** is the

© ANDREW HEMPSTEAD

Kelowna waterfront

largest of Kelowna's many parks. Its 14 hectares (35 acres) hold lots of flowers and large shady trees, expansive lawns, and a long sandy beach. You can rent a boat, houseboat, and fishing equipment at one of several marinas. Water-skiing and parasailing are also popular activities. Near the entrance to the park is the large, sparkling-white, attention-grabbing Dow Reid sculpture *Sails,* as well as a replica of the famed lake-dwelling serpent, Ogopogo (see sidebar).

At the south end of the park is one end of the **Okanagan Lake Bridge.** Built in 1958, this 1,400-meter-long (4600-foot-long) floating bridge, anchored to the lakebed in 24 spots, is the only such structure in Canada.

A promenade leads north from the Ogopogo statue past a large marina and a prime waterfront site undergoing redevelopment. Beyond the construction is the **Grand Okanagan,** the Okanagan's most luxurious accommodation. Even if you can't afford a lakefront suite, the resort holds a bar and restaurant with water views, and full spa services. Beyond the resort,

the promenade crosses a small lock, which allows boaters to travel between the higher water level of an artificial lagoon and the lake itself.

Other Downtown Sights

Okanagan Heritage Museum (470 Queensway Ave., 250/763-2417; Mon.–Fri. 10 A.M.–5 P.M., Sat. 10 A.M.–4 P.M.; donation) is opposite the post office; look for the brightly painted totem pole marking the entrance. The museum holds a mishmash of fascinating displays, including horse-drawn carriages; fossils found in the Princeton area; indigenous arts, crafts, clothing, jewelry, beads, and furs; children's books and games; radio equipment; pioneer artifacts; re-creations of an 1861 Kelowna trading post and a Chinese store; and a display of the interior of a Salish winter dwelling. Behind the museum is **Kasugai Gardens.** Built with the cooperation of Kelowna's Japanese sister city, Kasugai, the gardens are a quiet retreat from the downtown business district; admission is free and the gates are locked at dusk.

In an old downtown packing house, complete

OKANAGAN VALLEY

with exposed red-brick walls and hand-hewn wooden beams, the **British Columbia Orchard Industry Museum** (1304 Ellis St., 250/763-0433; Mon.–Sat. 10 A.M.–5 P.M.; donation) tells the story of the local orchard industry through rare photographs, displays, and a hands-on discovery corner. In the same building, the **Wine Museum** (250/868-0441; Mon.–Sat. 10 A.M.–5 P.M., Sun. 11 A.M.–5 P.M.) has information on local wineries and tours, and sells the finished product.

Historic Sights

Benvoulin Heritage Park (east of downtown at 2279 Benvoulin Rd.) surrounds the Gothic-revival Benvoulin Church, which dates to 1892. The church and a historic residence also within the grounds are closed to the public, but the garden holds the most interest. It is a xeriscape garden, designed to take advantage of the local climate and environment. In this case, plants grown here require little moisture, reflective of problems encountered by professional and amateur gardeners along the entire valley.

Farther south along Benvoulin Road is **Pandosy Mission Provincial Heritage Site,** the site of the mission established by Father Pandosy in 1859. Father Pandosy, an oblate priest, operated a church, school, and farm here, ministering to native people and settlers until his death in 1891. His mission claimed a lot of firsts: first White settlement in the Okanagan Valley, first school in the valley, first fruit and vine crops in the valley, and first Roman Catholic mission in the BC interior. Not much has changed within the broken-down wooden fences that hold the mission—four of the eight buildings on-site date to Pandosy's era, including a chapel and barn. The mission is open daily from 8 A.M. to dark, and the $2 donation includes an informative tour of the buildings, grounds, and antique farming equipment.

Wineries

Viticulture has been a mainstay of the Okanagan's economy for almost a century, but it has really taken off in the last decade, with local wines exported and winning awards worldwide.

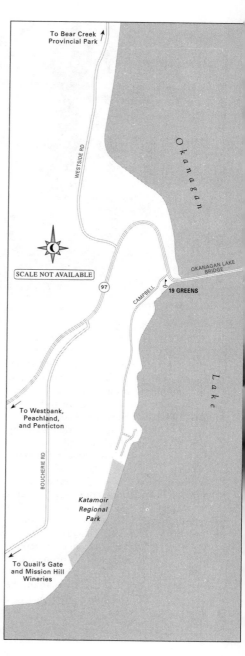

OKANAGAN VALLEY

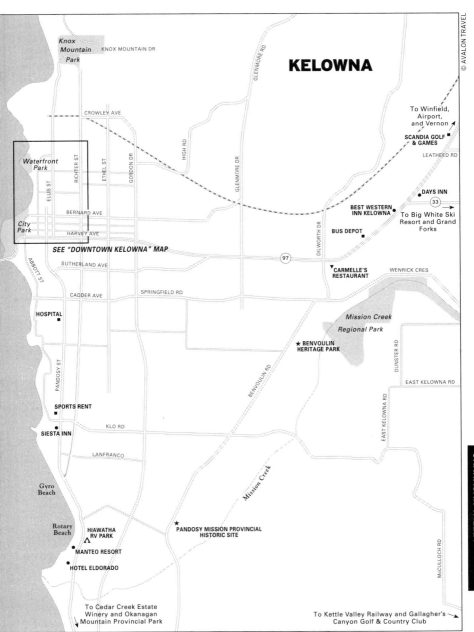

© AVALON TRAVEL

Knox Mountain Park

KNOX MOUNTAIN DR

KELOWNA

GLENMORE RD

CROWLEY AVE

Waterfront Park

RICHTER ST

ETHEL ST

GORDON DR

HIGH RD

ELLIS ST

GLENMORE DR

To Winfield, Airport, and Vernon

SCANDIA GOLF & GAMES

LEATHEED RD

BERNARD AVE

DAYS INN

33

BEST WESTERN INN KELOWNA

To Big White Ski Resort and Grand Forks

City Park

HARVEY AVE

BUS DEPOT

DILWORTH DR

SEE "DOWNTOWN KELOWNA" MAP

SUTHERLAND AVE

97

CARMELLE'S RESTAURANT

WENRICK CRES

ABBOTT ST

CADDER AVE

SPRINGFIELD RD

HOSPITAL

Mission Creek Regional Park

PANDOSY ST

★ BENVOULIN HERITAGE PARK

DUNSTER RD

BENVOULIN RD

EAST KELOWNA RD

SPORTS RENT

EAST KELOWNA RD

SIESTA INN

KLO RD

LANFRANCO

Mission Creek

Gyro Beach

Rotary Beach

HIAWATHA RV PARK

★ PANDOSY MISSION PROVINCIAL HISTORIC SITE

McCULLOCH RD

MANTEO RESORT

HOTEL ELDORADO

To Cedar Creek Estate Winery and Okanagan Mountain Provincial Park

To Kettle Valley Railway and Gallagher's Canyon Golf & Country Club

OKANAGAN VALLEY

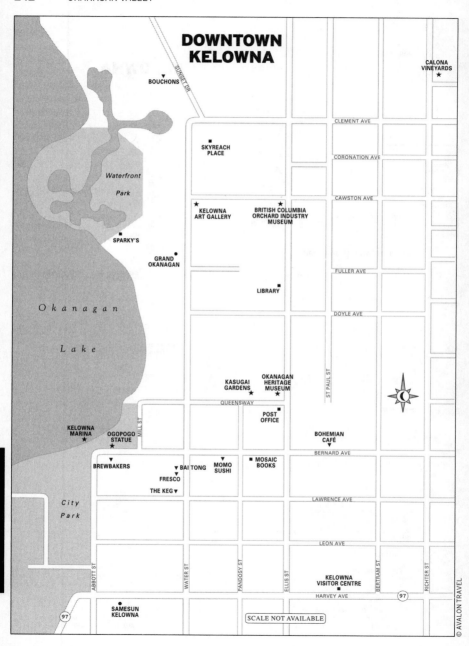

DOWNTOWN KELOWNA

BOUCHONS ▼

CALONA VINEYARDS ★

SKYREACH PLACE

Waterfront Park

CLEMENT AVE

CORONATION AVE

CAWSTON AVE

★ KELOWNA ART GALLERY

★ BRITISH COLUMBIA ORCHARD INDUSTRY MUSEUM

SPARKY'S ■

GRAND OKANAGAN ●

Okanagan

FULLER AVE

■ LIBRARY

DOYLE AVE

Lake

KASUGAI GARDENS ★

OKANAGAN HERITAGE MUSEUM ★

ST PAUL ST

QUEENSWAY

KELOWNA MARINA ★

POST OFFICE ■

OGOPOGO STATUE ★

MILL ST

BOHEMIAN CAFÉ ■

BERNARD AVE

BREWBAKERS ▼

▼ BAI TONG

MOMO SUSHI ▼

■ MOSAIC BOOKS

FRESCO ▼

THE KEG ▼

LAWRENCE AVE

City Park

LEON AVE

ABBOTT ST

WATER ST

PANDOSY ST

ELLIS ST

KELOWNA VISITOR CENTRE ■

BERTRAM ST

RICHTER ST

97

SAMESUN KELOWNA ●

HARVEY AVE

97

SCALE NOT AVAILABLE

OGOPOGO

Ogopogo is the friendly Loch Ness–style sea serpent that allegedly lives on the bottom of "bottomless" Okanagan Lake. Local native people told the first White settlers who came to live in the Okanagan Valley that a fast-swimming monster called N'ha-a-tik, meaning "devil of the lake," lived in a deep part of the lake near present-day Kelowna. Whenever they had to canoe near that particular point, they unceremoniously threw an animal overboard as a sacrifice.

Since 1942, when the mysterious monster became known as Ogopogo, thousands of sightings have allegedly been made, and the creature has been the subject of feature stories on the television shows *Unsolved Mysteries* and *Inside Edition*. Consensus is that Ogopogo is a snakelike creature with small humps, green skin, and a nice big smile – the latter feature confirmed by enterprising locals who print his image on T-shirts, posters, and postcards.

© ANDREW HEMPSTEAD

Although many times a prize has been put up for anyone providing definitive proof of Ogopogo's existence – the most recent is $2 million – no one has yet claimed the reward. Anyway, keep your eyes open and your camera at hand; you just never know, you may be one of the few (sober) ones to spot him.

Most of the local wineries welcome visitors with tours and free tastings year-round (but call ahead outside of summer to check hours). Because of the popularity of visiting the wineries, most now charge a small fee for tasting. **Okanagan Wine Country Tours** (250/868-9463 or 866/689-9463, www.okwinetours.com) has a variety of tours, including a full day of touring and tasting for $130 per person.

One of the province's oldest wineries, in operation since 1932, is **Calona Vineyards** (downtown at 1125 Richter St., 250/762-9144; daily 9 A.M.–6 P.M.). There's no actual vineyard, just a large winery that uses grapes grown throughout the valley. Calona offers tours throughout the year at 2 P.M. (more frequently in summer), with tastings and sales in a room set up as a cellar.

Across Okanagan Lake from Kelowna is **Mission Hill Family Estate** (1730 Mission Hill Rd., Westbank, 250/768-7611), high atop a ridge and surrounded by vineyards with stunning lake views. Mission Hill, British

Columbia's most successful winery, completed massive expansions in 2001, including a 45-meter-high (148-foot-high) bell tower, open for the public to climb. Tours depart three times daily, each ending with an informal tasting session at the Wine and Food Interpretation Centre (summer daily 9:30 A.M.–7 P.M., the rest of the year daily 10 A.M.–6 P.M.). At nearby **Quail's Gate Estate Winery** (3303 Boucherie Rd., 250/769-4451), the reserve pinot noir is a signature wine—enjoy a glass or two alfresco at the winery bistro (May–Oct. 11 A.M.–4 P.M. and 5 P.M.–dusk). Winery tours are conducted May–October up to six times daily.

Back on the main highway and farther south is **Hainle Vineyards Estate Winery** (5355 Trepanier Bench Rd., Peachland, 250/767-2525; Tues.–Sun. 10 A.M.–5 P.M.). Walter Hainle was a pioneer in the development of ice wines, and while this is the style that the vineyard is best known for, limited quantities of red and white wines are also produced. Lunch and dinner are served daily.

OKANAGAN VALLEY

Across the lake from these wineries is the much-heralded **Cedar Creek Estate Winery** (5445 Lakeshore Dr., 250/764-8866), where the vineyards and extensive gardens overlook Lake Okanagan. Tours are offered in summer daily 11 A.M.–4 P.M.

Gray Monk Estate Winery (22 kilometers/13.7 miles north of Kelowna on Camp Rd., Winfield, 250/766-3168) is a family affair most recognized for its German-style wines, including gewürztraminer and a pinot gris. Tours are offered April–October on the hour 11 A.M.–4 P.M., the rest of the year on Sunday at 2 P.M.

RECREATION
On the Lake

During the warm and sunny months of summer, Okanagan Lake comes alive with a colorful array of watercraft, anglers, and swimmers out on the water, and sunbathers dot the surrounding sandy beaches. The busiest spot is the stretch of sand fronting City Park, right downtown. Beyond the beach's northern end, you can rent watercraft from **Sparky's** (250/862-2469), in front of the Grand Okanagan; rent small powerboats at **Kelowna Marina** (250/861-8001); or go parachuting behind a boat with **Kelowna Parasail Adventures** (250/868-4838) for $50 per person.

Gyro Beach and adjacent **Rotary Beach** are beautiful stretches of sand south of downtown along Lakeshore Drive. Less crowded are the beaches in **Okanagan Mountain Provincial Park,** farther south.

Sports Rent (3000 Pandosy St., 250/861-5699) rents kayaks from $35 per day, canoes for $45 per day, and wetsuits.

Hiking and Biking

The **Kettle Valley Railway** bed, which winds around the back of Kelowna, may be protected as a national historic site, but unfortunately nothing could protect its 18 trestle bridges from 2003 wildfires. Plans are in place to have them rebuilt, but until then, opportunities for extended trips along the rail bed are somewhat limited. It's still an interesting spot, well worth the effort to reach. To get there take K.L.O. Road to McCulloch Road, turn south (right) and then south (right) again, following Myra Forest Service Road for 8.5 kilometers (5.3 miles). From the parking lot at this point, it's under one kilometer (0.6 mile) to the first of the burnt trestles.

The cacti-covered top of **Knox Mountain** offers great lake and city views. A hiking trail and a paved road popular with bicyclists both lead to the summit. To get there head north out of town along the lakeshore, passing pretty, lakeside Sutherland Park (with good views of Crown Forest Mill and log rafts), then take Knox Mountain Drive up to Knox Mountain Park, stopping at Crown Viewpoint on the way to the top. Trails lead off the summit in all directions, and in May the mountain swarms with activity as cars and motorcycles race up the mountain during the **Knox Mountain Hill Climb.**

Skiing and Snowboarding

Big White Ski Resort (250/765-3101 or 800/663-2772, www.bigwhite.com), 57 kilometers (35 miles) east of Kelowna on Highway 33, is one of the Okanagan's three major winter resorts and British Columbia's second largest. Its network of modern lifts, including a gondola and four high-speed quads, opens up over 850 hectares (2,100 acres) of terrain. Lifts operate December through mid-April daily 8:30 A.M.–3:30 P.M., and for night skiing and boarding Tuesday–Saturday 5–9 P.M. Lift tickets are adult $64, senior $55, child $32, 70 and over and under five free. Adjacent to the main lift-served area is Happy Valley Adventure Centre, a tube park with its own lift. Big White is also home to a terrain park, a half-pipe, cross-country trails, and an ice-skating rink. On-mountain facilities in the 9,000-bed base village include rental shops, a ski and snowboard school, accommodations, restaurants and cafés, and a large mall.

Fun Parks

North of downtown, **Scandia Golf & Games** (2898 Hwy. 97 N., 250/765-2355) is a sprawling complex of indoor and outdoor mini-golf courses, with one of the indoor layouts lit only by fluorescent lights and glowing golf balls. Head south from downtown and immediately after crossing the lake, turn left to access **19 Greens** (2050 Campbell Rd., 250/769-0213; Apr.–Oct. 11 A.M.–midnight), a mini-putt golf course that uses real grass to create fun for all ages.

ENTERTAINMENT AND EVENTS
Nightlife

Enjoy a drink overlooking Okanagan Lake in the stylish lounge at the **Hotel Eldorado** (500 Cook Rd., 250/763-7500; daily from 11 A.M.). Right downtown, **Sgt. O'Flaherty's,** in the Royal Anne Hotel (348 Bernard Ave., 250/860-6409), is a friendly pub with bands churning out a variety of music styles nightly from 9 P.M.

At **Lake City Casino** (Grand Okanagan, 1310 Water St., 250/860-9467), don't expect the ritz and glitz of Las Vegas—this is gambling Canadian style, with the action restricted to slot machines, blackjack, roulette, Caribbean stud poker, and mini baccarat, and everyone's ushered out the front door at 2 A.M.

Sunshine Theatre (250/763-4025) puts on 3–4 plays throughout the summer; pick up a schedule at the information center. The **Uptown Cinema Centre** (1521 Water St., 250/762-0099) screens films.

Festivals and Events

The **Okanagan Spring Wine Fest** (250/861-6654, www.owfs.com) is somewhat less pretentious than the fall equivalent, with many wineries not normally open to the public offering tours and tasting sessions through late April. The **Knox Mountain Hill Climb,** North America's longest paved motor-vehicle hill climb, has been contested annually since 1957; it's on in late May. The valley's biggest event is the **Okanagan Fall Wine Fest** (250/861-6654, www.owfs.com), held annually over 10 days from the last full weekend of September to celebrate the end of the grape harvest. Thousands of visitors participate in food and wine tastings, releases of new wines, cooking classes, and art displays with all sections of the industry participating. The **apple harvest** is celebrated during the same period at the Orchard Museum (1304 Ellis St., 250/763-0433), with apple tastings and displays.

ACCOMMODATIONS AND CAMPING
Under $50

Samesun Kelowna (245 Harvey St., 250/763-5013 or 888/562-2783, www.samesun.com) is a centrally located, purpose-built backpacker lodge. Inside the distinctive three-story building are 120 beds, many in private rooms (with shared bathrooms), with communal kitchens, bathrooms, a large lounge area, and public Internet access. Out back are a pleasant grassed barbecue area and a beach volleyball court. Rates are $28 for a dorm bed, $68 s or d in a private room.

$50-100

High in the highlands northeast of Kelowna, **(Beaver Lake Mountain Resort** (250/762-2225, www.beaverlakeresort.com; May–Oct.) is very different from the beachy resort complexes

Beaver Lake Mountain Resort

OKANAGAN VALLEY

down on the valley floor. Set in a forest on the edge of a lake famed for rainbow trout fishing, the resort comprises a restaurant, a horseback-riding operation (with afternoon pony rides for kids), and a fishing shop. Boat rentals are well priced at $55 per 24 hours, including gas. Canoes, kayaks, and belly boats are $30 per day. Cabins range from tiny "camping cabins" that share bathrooms ($45 s or d) to peeled log chalets with full kitchens ($140). Cabin 9 is typical: It's rustic but enjoys an absolute lakefront setting, with a private floating dock, a big deck, a full kitchen, a log fireplace, one bedroom, and a loft, all for under $120 per night. Make cabin reservations well in advance—locals know a bargain when they see one and book their favorite cabin up to a year in advance. Camping is $20 (no hookups). To get there, head north to Winfield, then 16 kilometers (10 miles) east on Beaver Lake Road.

$100-150

South of downtown, the **Siesta Inn** (3152 Lakeshore Rd., 250/763-5013 or 800/663-4347, www.siestamotorinn.com) offers a beachside atmosphere one block from the water. Rooms open onto a wide balcony overlooking a courtyard and pool. They range $129–279 s or d; many have kitchenettes.

Highway 97 (also known as Harvey Avenue) north of downtown holds many motels tucked between shopping malls, gas stations, and fast-food restaurants. Along this strip is **Days Inn Kelowna** (2469 Hwy. 97 N., 250/868-3297 or 800/337-7177, www.daysinn.com), with large, modern rooms decorated in Santa Fe style, as well as an outdoor pool and hot tub; the smallest rooms cost $139 s or d, but it's worth an extra $30 for a much larger suite. As at all Days Inns, rates include a light breakfast.

$150-200

North of downtown, **Best Western Inn Kelowna** (2402 Hwy. 97 N., 250/860-1212 or 888/860-1212, www.bestwesterninnkelowna .com) is a good choice for those who want the amenities of a full resort but don't want to pay for a waterfront location. Rooms are set around a grassed courtyard, complete with putting greens and an outdoor hot tub. Other facilities include an indoor pool, spa services, a fitness room, and a restaurant and pub. The rooms are spacious and modern and come filled with niceties such as air-conditioning, bathrobes, hairdryers, Internet access, and free local calls. Rates start at $184 s or d, which includes continental breakfast, but as always, check the hotel website for deals and packages.

Built in 1926 and moved to its present location in 1989, the **◖ Hotel Eldorado** (500 Cook Rd., south of downtown along Pandosy St., 250/763-7500 or 866/608-7500, www .eldoradokelowna.com) is a delightful lakeside accommodation offering 19 rooms furnished with antiques, and many offering a lake view and private balcony. Rooms in the Eldorado Arms wing are larger and have a distinct contemporary feel. Hotel facilities include a lakefront café, a restaurant, a lounge, and a marina with boat rentals. Summer rates range $189–389 s or d, with only the more expensive rooms having water views. Off-season rates start at $99.

Over $200

Overlooking the same stretch of lake as the Hotel Eldorado is the colorful and modern **Manteo Resort** (3766 Lakeshore Rd., 250/860-1031 or 888/462-6836, www .manteo.com). This self-contained complex includes a 78-room hotel and guest and resident facilities such as a private beach, a marina with boat rentals, a pool complex with a water slide, tennis courts, a small movie theater, a lounge with billiard table, and a barbecue area. Rates start at $255 s or d for a contemporary-styled hotel room ($275 with a water view), but villas that sleep six can be rented for $535 per night. Outside of summer, bed and breakfast is around $150 per couple.

The grandest of Kelowna's accommodations is **The Grand Okanagan** (1310 Water St., 250/763-4500 or 800/465-4651, www.grand okanagan.com), a sprawling lakeside development right downtown and integrated with local walking paths. Along the lake side of the resort is a lagoon with its own private lock and watercraft rentals, while farther along are eateries and a bar with outdoor seating. Inside, once past the cavernous lobby, you'll find a fitness center, spa services, restaurants, a lounge bar, and 205 luxuriously appointed rooms. In summer, standard rooms are $289 s or d, with suites from $425.

Camping
The closest campground to downtown is **Hiawatha RV Park** (3787 Lakeshore Rd., 250/861-4837 or 888/784-7275, www .hiawatharvpark.com; tent sites $39, hookups $42–47). It has a tenting area, showers, a laundry, a game room, and a playground.

Two provincial parks in the vicinity of Kelowna offer camping. The closest is **Bear Creek Provincial Park,** across the bridge from downtown and then nine kilometers (5.6 miles) north on Westside Road. The campground holds 122 sites nestled under cottonwood trees. Campers also enjoy a short beach and trails that cross back over Westside Road and into desertlike terrain above the lake. **Fintry Provincial Park** lies a further 23 kilometers (14.3 miles) north along Westside Road in the same beachside setting as Bear Creek, although the campground is less developed; $22 per night. A trail leads from the campground to a deep canyon along Shorts Creek.

FOOD
Downtown Kelowna has a great number of dining choices, for everything from a quick coffee to a full meal, but many of the city's finer restaurants are away from the business core, along quiet country roads or at the many golf clubs.

Cafés
Bohemian Café (524 Bernard Ave., 250/862-3517; Mon.–Fri. 7:30 A.M.–4:30 P.M., Sat. 9 A.M.–3 P.M.) has a loyal local following for gourmet coffee, bagels baked in-house, and inexpensive cooked breakfasts. One block farther west is **Brewbakers** (227 Bernard Ave., 250/979-0222; daily from 8 A.M.), also notable for inexpensive breakfasts. Lunch is also worthwhile, highlighted by healthy sandwiches

made to order with chicken roasted in-house, homemade quiche, and the like.

If you're browsing for a book at Mosaic Books, follow the aroma of freshly brewed coffee through to the adjacent **Mosaic Coffee Shop** (411 Bernard Ave., 250/763-4418; Mon.–Fri. 7:30 A.M.–4 P.M., Sat. 9 A.M.–4:30 P.M., Sun. 11 A.M.–4:30 P.M.).

Asian
Bai Tong (upstairs at 1530 Water St., 250/763-8638; Mon.–Fri. 11:30 A.M.–2:30 P.M. and 5–10 P.M.) is a step above your average small-town Asian restaurant. Feast on chicken cooked in a black bean sauce then wrapped in lettuce leaves, or stir-fry combos of vegetables and noodles with your choice of meat.

You'll find Kelowna's best Japanese food at **Momo Sushi** (377 Bernard Ave., 250/763-1030; Tues.–Sat. for lunch and dinner, Sun. dinner only).

Pacific Northwest
Fresco (1560 Water St., 250/868-8805; daily from 5:30 P.M.) is the latest addition to Kelowna's dining scene. In the surrounds of a heritage commercial building are elegant table settings, a martini bar, and comfortable sofas. The menu is typically West Coast, but more adventurous than you'd expect this far from Vancouver. Mains range $22–32, including signature dishes such as oat-crusted arctic char.

French
(Bouchons (1180 Sunset Dr., 250/763-6595; daily from 5:30 P.M.) is a little slice of France in the heart of downtown Kelowna. The setting is elegant yet welcoming, with an extensive collection of wines stored in a stone cellar in the middle of the main dining room. You could start with a classic baked French onion soup ($8) then move onto duck confit ($26) or a roasted rack of lamb with green-tea-infused jus ($34).

INFORMATION AND SERVICES
Kelowna Visitor Centre (544 Harvey Ave., 250/861-1515 or 800/663-4345, www.tourism

OKANAGAN VALLEY

kelowna.com; summer daily 9 A.M.–7 P.M., the rest of the year daily 9 A.M.–5 P.M.) is beside Highway 97 as it passes through the center of the city—watch for the signs. Coming into town from the south on Highway 97, turn left on Richter Street at the traffic lights and go back one block. A good map for immediate orientation is posted outside the center; it also incorporates a legend of motels and attractions.

Mosaic Books (411 Bernard Ave., 250/763-4418 or 800/663-1225; Mon.–Wed. 8 A.M.–6 P.M., Thurs.–Fri. 8 A.M.–9 P.M., Sat. 9 A.M.–6 P.M., Sun. 11 A.M.–5 P.M.) is an independent bookseller that has been serving the valley for over 30 years. Besides an excellent collection of western Canadian titles, it has a wide selection of magazines and an in-house coffee bar. The eye-catching, semicircular building on Ellis Street is **Kelowna Library** (1380 Ellis St., 250/762-2800; Mon. 10 A.M.–5:30 P.M., Tues.–Thurs. 10 A.M.–9 P.M., Fri.–Sat. 10 A.M.–5:30 P.M.).

The **post office** is right downtown on Queensway Avenue. **Kelowna General Hospital** is on the corner of Strathcona Avenue and Pandosy Street (250/862-4000).

GETTING THERE AND AROUND

Modern **Kelowna Airport,** the province's third busiest, is 15 kilometers (9.3 miles) north of downtown along Highway 97. It's served by **Air Canada** (250/542-3302) and **WestJet** (800/538-5696), both of which offer daily flights to and from Vancouver, Calgary, and Edmonton. At the airport are car-rental outlets, a lounge bar, and a casual café.

Greyhound (2366 Leckie Rd., 250/860-3835 or 800/661-8747) provides bus service throughout the Okanagan and beyond. Local buses are run by **Kelowna Regional Transit System.** Get schedule and route information from the downtown terminal (Bernard Ave. at Ellis St., 250/860-8121).

For a taxi, call **Kelowna Cabs** (250/762-2222) or **Checkmate Cabs** (250/861-1111). Another taxi service is offered by **Okanagan Shuttle** (250/766-4280, www.okanagan shuttle.com), which schedules personalized drop-offs at local wineries, golf courses, and the airport.

Rental car agencies include **Avis** (250/491-9500), **Budget** (250/491-7368), **Hertz** (250/765-3822), **National** (250/762-0622), **Rent-a-wreck** (250/763-6632), and **Thrifty** (250/868-2151). All these companies have vehicles out at the airport, but call in advance to ensure availability, especially in midsummer and during the ski season.

Sports Rent (3000 Pandosy St., 250/861-5699) rents mountain bikes for $7–10 per hour and $21–30 per day.

Vernon and Vicinity

The city of Vernon (pop. 36,000) lies between Okanagan, Kalamalka, and Swan Lakes, at the north end of the Okanagan Valley 50 kilometers (31 miles) from Kelowna. The city itself holds little of interest; the surrounding area boasts the main attractions. Among the area highlights: many sandy public beaches; local provincial parks; Silver Star Mountain Resort, a year-round recreation paradise east of the city; and fishing in more than 100 lakes within an hour's drive of the city.

SIGHTS AND RECREATION
In Town

Greater Vernon Museum and Archives (3009 32nd Ave., 250/542-3142; Tues.–Sat. 11 A.M.–5 P.M.) holds photos from the early 1900s and a large collection of pioneer and native artifacts. Displays cover natural history, recreation, period clothing, and steamships. In the same vicinity is **Vernon Public Art Gallery** (3228 31st Ave., 250/545-3173; Mon.–Fri. 10 A.M.–5 P.M., Sat. 11 A.M.–4 P.M.), featuring works by local artists as well as touring exhibitions.

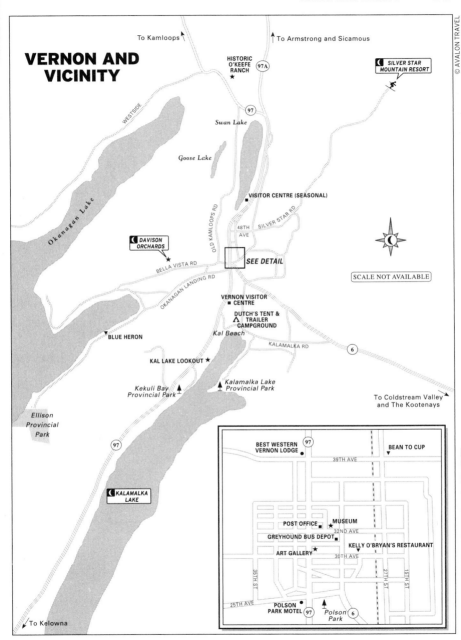

VERNON AND VICINITY

To Kamloops

To Armstrong and Sicamous

HISTORIC O'KEEFE RANCH ☆

97A

SILVER STAR MOUNTAIN RESORT

97

Swan Lake

Goose Lake

WESTSIDE

Okanagan Lake

OLD KAMLOOPS RD

VISITOR CENTRE (SEASONAL)

48TH AVE

SILVER STAR RD

DAVISON ORCHARDS ☆

BELLA VISTA RD

SEE DETAIL

SCALE NOT AVAILABLE

OKANAGAN LANDING RD

VERNON VISITOR CENTRE

DUTCH'S TENT & TRAILER CAMPGROUND

Kal Beach

BLUE HERON

KALAMALKA RD

6

KAL LAKE LOOKOUT ☆

Kekuli Bay Provincial Park

Kalamalka Lake Provincial Park

Ellison Provincial Park

To Coldstream Valley and The Kootenays

97

KALAMALKA LAKE

To Kelowna

BEST WESTERN VERNON LODGE

97

BEAN TO CUP

39TH AVE

POST OFFICE

MUSEUM ☆

32ND AVE

GREYHOUND BUS DEPOT ☆

KELLY O'BRYAN'S RESTAURANT

ART GALLERY ☆

30TH AVE

36TH ST

27TH ST

15TH ST

25TH AVE

POLSON PARK MOTEL

97

Polson Park

6

OKANAGAN VALLEY

Polson Park (off Hwy. 97 at 25th Ave.) has a Chinese teahouse, a small Japanese garden, and paths along a willow-lined creek, but most people go to stare at the spectacular floral clock: nine meters (30 feet) wide, made up of more than 3,500 plants, and the only one of its kind in western Canada.

Historic O'Keefe Ranch

Established in 1867, the O'Keefe Ranch (250/542-7868; May–Sept. daily 9 A.M.–5 P.M., until 6 P.M. in July and Aug.; adult $12, senior $11, child $10), 13 kilometers (eight miles) north of Vernon toward Kamloops on Highway 97, was one of the Okanagan's first cattle ranches. Today you can tour the opulent, fully furnished O'Keefe Mansion and other noteworthy outbuildings, including a furnished old log house that was the O'Keefes' original home; a working blacksmith's shop; the still-in-use St. Ann's Church, where services have been held since 1889; a fully stocked general store where you can buy postcards and old-fashioned candy; and the Chinese cook's bunkhouse. If you worked up an appetite in your explorations, visit the **Homestead Restaurant** (daily for lunch and weekends for dinner).

C Davison Orchards

Dozens of farms surround Vernon, but one in particular, Davison Orchards (west of downtown off Bella Vista Rd., 250/549-3266; mid-May–early Nov. daily 8 A.M.–8 P.M.), is worth a visit. Set on a sloping hill with views extending across Kalamalka Lake and up the Coldstream Valley, this family-operated business is a hive of tourist activity throughout the warmer months. A self-guided walk leads through a garden where everything from cucumbers to cantaloupe is grown, a wagon tour traverses the entire 20-hectare (50-acre) property, and there's a Critter Corral, a café with outside dining, an ice cream stand, and, of course, a fruit and vegetable market.

Ellison Provincial Park

Follow Okanagan Landing Road (from 25th Ave. off Hwy. 97) west to access the northern reaches of Okanagan Lake and this 200-hectare (494-acre) lakefront park, 16 kilometers (10 miles) from downtown. Most of the park is on a bench, with trails leading to and along the rocky shore. Ellison is best known by divers as British Columbia's first freshwater marine park. Enjoy shallow-water snorkeling and diving, weed beds full of life, underwater rock formations, a plastic bubble "Dive Dome," a deep-water wreck, and beach showers. Camping is $17.

C Kalamalka Lake

If you've driven up to Vernon from Kelowna, this was the beautiful lake that Highway 97 paralleled for much of the way. It's known as a "marl" lake, because as summer warms the water, the limestone bedrock forms crystals that reflect the sunlight, creating a distinctive aquamarine color that is all the more stunning with surrounding parched hills as a backdrop. The continuously changing emerald and turquoise water and surrounding mountain panorama is best appreciated from **Kal Lake Lookout,** five kilometers (3.1 miles) back toward Kelowna along Highway 97. Just south of the information center, a steep road winds down to the lakeshore and fine **Kal Beach,** fringed by trees. Parking is across the railway line from the beach (access is under the rail bridge). Also on the beach is a concession and, at the east end, a pub with a huge deck.

Continue beyond the beach for eight kilometers (five miles) to **Kalamalka Lake Provincial Park.** Within this 978-hectare (2,420-acre) park, a 1.5-kilometer (0.9-mile) trail winds down through bunchgrass and ponderosa pines to Turtle Head Point, while other trails lead to a low-lying wetland and lofty viewpoint.

PRACTICALITIES
Accommodations

Downtown and around the outskirts of Vernon is the usual collection of hotels and motels of greatly varying standards. These are handy for a simple overnight stay, but to make the most of your time in the area, book a room at Silver Star Mountain Resort (see following section).

Polson Park Motel (3201 24th Ave.,

© ANDREW HEMPSTEAD

Kal Beach is a wonderful spot to cool off on a summer day.

250/549-2231 or 800/480-2231, www .polsonparkmotel.com; $65 s, $75 d) is the least expensive of Vernon's 20-odd motels. Across from Polson Park, the three-story motel has an outdoor pool and basic rooms.

Moving up in price and quality is **Best Western Vernon Lodge** (3914 32nd St., 250/545-3385 or 800/663-4422, www.rpb hotels.com; $119 s, $129 d), where stylishly decorated rooms overlook an enclosed three-story tropical atrium.

Camping

Dutch's Tent and Trailer Campground, three kilometers (1.9 miles) south of downtown (Kalamalka Rd., 250/545-1023), is a five-minute walk from Kal Beach and Kalamalka Lake. The park has hot showers, a laundry, and a snack bar. Tent sites are $19, hookups $21–26.

Two provincial parks within a 15-minute drive of downtown provide campsites. Sixteen kilometers (10 miles) southwest of town on Okanagan Landing Road is **Ellison Provincial Park,** on the east shore of Okanagan Lake ($17 per night),

while south along Highway 97 toward Kelowna, **Kekuli Bay Provincial Park** slopes down to a boat launch and pebbly beach on Kalamalka Lake, but it's open to the elements ($22).

Food

The dining choices in Vernon have improved vastly in recent years, as has the coffee scene. The best coffee joint is **Bean to Cup** (3903 27th St., 250/503-2222; daily 6 A.M.–midnight), in a converted residential house. It offers a wide range of hot drinks and light meals, best enjoyed on the heated patio.

At **Kelly O'Bryan's Restaurant** (2933 30th Ave., 250/549-2112; open daily 11 A.M.–midnight), tuck in to burgers, steak, seafood, salads, and pasta in the setting of an Irish pub. **Intermezzo** (3206 34th Ave., 250/542-3853) has a casual yet somewhat romantic setting and is a locals' favorite for its wide choice of pastas. Daily specials are the best value—usually around $18 for two courses. For more of a dinnertime splurge try the **Garden Grill** at the Best Western Vernon Lodge (3914 32nd

OKANAGAN VALLEY

© ANDREW HEMPSTEAD

Silver Star Mountain Resort, a short drive from Vernon

St., 250/545-3385; daily for lunch from 11 A.M. and dinner from 5 P.M.). The dining room is set in a lush tropical garden with a stream flowing through the middle, and the menu features continental cuisine with nightly specials.

The **Blue Heron** (7673 Okanagan Landing Rd., 250/542-5550; daily from 11 A.M.) is a few kilometers west of downtown but well worth the drive. It sits right on Okanagan Lake, and a large deck right on the water is the most popular of the pub's three dining areas. The menu is fairly standard, with lots of dishes to share, but as it's off the tourist path, prices are reasonable.

Information and Services

Vernon Visitor Centre (250/542-3256 or 800/665-0795, www.vernontourism.com; daily 8:30 A.M.–6 P.M., till 6:30 P.M. in summer) is in a spruced-up heritage house on Highway 97 at the south end of town. If you're driving in from the north, make a stop at the seasonal info center (6326 Hwy. 97 N.). The **post office** is on the corner of 31st Street and 32nd Avenue. The **Greyhound** bus depot is on the cor-

ner of 30th Street and 31st Avenue (250/545-0527). For local bus information and schedules, contact **Vernon Regional Transit System** (250/545-7221).

◖ SILVER STAR MOUNTAIN RESORT

For summer or winter recreation, head up to Silver Star Mountain Resort (250/542-0224 or 800/663-4431, www.skisilverstar.com), a colorful gold-rush- style, fully self-contained resort town 22 kilometers (13.6 miles) northeast of Vernon (take 48th Ave. off Hwy. 97). The views of Vernon as you climb the mountain are worth the fairly long, steep drive, and the resort at the top offers great skiing and snowboarding, plus summer recreation to suit all ages.

Summer Activities

Silver Star offers the biggest range of summer recreation of any alpine resort in the interior. Starting at the end of June, a chairlift runs from the village to the top of Silver Star Mountain (1,915 meters/6,280 feet) for terrific views of Vernon and surrounding lakes. Much of the alpine area around the summit is protected by 8,714-hectare (21,500-acre) **Silver Star Provincial Park;** pick up a hiking guide in the village. The summer lift operates June–September daily 10 A.M.–4 P.M.; $15 for one ride, or buy an all-day pass for $30 (the day pass includes access to hiking and biking trails). To learn more about the mountain's natural history, take the naturalist-led three-hour wildflower tour Thursday–Sunday at 1 P.M.; $30 per person, which includes a chairlift ride. Mountain-bike rentals are $18 for one hour, $30 for two hours, and $45 for a full day.

Skiing and Snowboarding

November–April, skiers and boarders mob Silver Star, coming for great terrain and the facilities of an outstanding on-hill village. The two main faces—Vance Creek, good for beginners, and Putnam Creek, for intermediates and experts—are served by six chairlifts and a couple of T-bars. The resort's 80 runs cover 1,240 hectares (3,065 acres) with a vertical rise of 760 meters (2,500 feet). Lift tickets are adult $58, senior $42, child $32; those over 70 and under six ski free. For snow reports call 250/542-1745.

Silver Star Cross-Country Centre features 35 kilometers (22 miles) of groomed and set tracks, while beyond these are 50 kilometers (31 miles) of backcountry trails. A day pass is $18 per person; rentals are available for an additional $20.

Accommodations

The base village contains numerous types of accommodations; book year-round through central reservations (800/663-4431, www .skisilverstar.com) or contact each accommodation directly. The rates quoted here are for summer, which is low season. Through winter, expect to pay double (except at the Samesun property).

Least expensive is **Samesun Silver Star** (250/545-8933 or 877/972-6378, www.samesun .com; dorms $25, private rooms $60 s or d), one of Canada's only ski-in, ski-out backpacker lodges. Facilities include a modern communal kitchen, plenty of table space for dining, and 140 beds in dorms and private rooms.

The **Kickwillie Inn** (250/542-4548 or 800/551-7466, www.pinnacles.com) is part of the adjacent and much larger Pinnacles Suite Hotel but has the better value rooms; from $129 s or d with a kitchen. The **Lord Aberdeen Hotel** (250/542-1992 or 800/553-5885, www.lordaberdeen.com) also offers self-contained suites and is similarly priced. The most luxurious on-mountain lodging is **Silver Star Club Resort** (250/549-5191 or 800/610-0805, www.silverstarclubresort .com), which offers standard hotel rooms and self-contained suites spread through three buildings. Guests enjoy use of all facilities at the nearby National Altitude Training Centre. Summer rates start at $105 s or d, rising to $145 for a suite.

THE KOOTENAYS

The wild and rugged Kootenays region of British Columbia lies east of the Okanagan Valley and south of the TransCanada Highway. It is bordered by the United States to the south and Alberta to the east. Three north-to-south-trending mountain ranges—the Monashees, Selkirks, and Purcells—run parallel to each other across the region, separated by lush green valleys and narrow lakes up to 150 kilometers (93 miles) long. The snowcapped mountains and forested valleys abound with wildlife, including large populations of deer, elk, moose, black bears, and grizzly bears.

Europeans first entered the Kootenays in the late 1800s, searching for precious metals such as gold, silver, lead, and zinc, all of which were found in large quantities. While many of the boomtowns from this era have slipped into oblivion, others live on: Sandon is a ghost town, Fort Steele survives as a heritage theme park, and the grand old city of Nelson is today a heritage masterpiece, its streets lined with restored buildings.

Recreational opportunities abound throughout the Kootenays in all seasons. In summer, anglers flock to the lakes and rivers for trout, kokanee, and bass. Other visitors enjoy canoeing, swimming, or sunbathing on the beaches, or take to the mountains for hiking and wildlife viewing. Much of the region's higher elevations are protected in rugged and remote parks, including the spectacular Valhalla, Kokanee Glacier, Top of the World, and Purcell Wilderness Conservancy Provincial Parks. While these natural preserves offer plenty of opportunities for day-trippers, it takes extended backcountry trips to fully experience their beauty.

HIGHLIGHTS

Red Mountain Resort: Rossland is a beautiful town to visit at any time of year, but in wintertime, the steep slopes of nearby Red Mountain draw experienced skiers and boarders from across the land (page 259).

Sandon: In the late 1800s, Sandon was home to over 5,000 miners. Today, you could fit the entire population in the back of a pickup truck – not that they'd want to leave western Canada's most authentic ghost town (page 264).

Kokanee Glacier Provincial Park: This remote park takes some effort to reach, but the rewards are many, including alpine lakes, ancient glaciers, and abundant wildlife (page 270).

Crawford Bay: Even if the crafty shops don't appeal to you, the price of visiting will: The village is accessed by the world's longest free ferry ride (page 272).

Creston Valley Wildlife Management Area: Protecting vital resting grounds along the Pacific Flyway, this site provides a haven for more than 250 species of birds, including osprey, the rare Forester's tern, and a nesting colony of western grebe (page 273).

Fort Steele Heritage Town: The gold-rush era comes to life through costumed interpreters and musical theater. You can even try your hand at panning for gold (page 280).

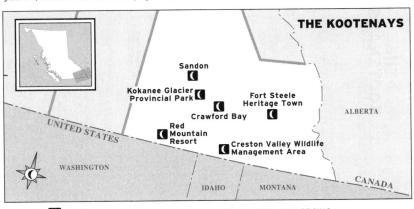

THE KOOTENAYS

LOOK FOR **(** TO FIND RECOMMENDED SIGHTS, ACTIVITIES, DINING, AND LODGING.

PLANNING YOUR TIME

The most important thing to remember when planning a driving tour through the Kootenays is that the region is very mountainous. Roads are generally narrow and winding, with mountain passes and ferry crossings slowing down travel time considerably. The main east–west thoroughfare is Highway 3, which runs through the southern extent of the region, traversing no less than five mountain passes between Osoyoos in the west and Cranbrook in the east. Even without detours north, allow a

couple of days to travel this route from one end to the other. Besides official attractions like **Creston Valley Wildlife Management Area,** you might be tempted to linger at the many roadside parks and mountain lookouts. Two main roads lead north from Highway 3, both eventually making their way north to the Trans-Canada Highway (Central British Columbia). Highway 6 is the westernmost of the two, passing the historic town of Nelson and the ghost town of **Sandon.** In the East Kootenays, Highway 3 continues its eastward course to

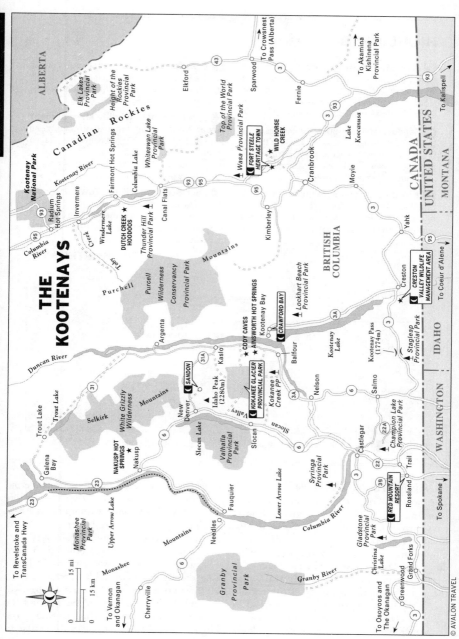

southern Alberta while Highway 93/95 jogs north through the Columbia Valley, where historic parks such as Fort Steele Heritage Town and natural highlights like Fairmont Hot Springs are the main attractions.

In colder months the mountains of the Kootenays catch a phenomenal amount of snow, turning the whole region into a winter wonderland. You won't find any major resorts here; however, three small but legendary ski areas— **Red Mountain,** Whitewater, and Fernie— attract adventurous powderhounds with some of North America's highest snowfalls and steepest lift-served slopes.

West Kootenays

Clustered on the edge of the Monashee Range in the western Kootenays are several communities that seem a world away from the hustle and the bustle of the nearby Okanagan Valley. Grand Forks, Rossland, Trail, and Castlegar all boomed at the turn of the 20th century, when thousands of gold-hungry prospectors descended on the slopes of Red Mountain. Today Red Mountain draws more powderhounds than prospectors, and lakes, rivers, parks, and peaks are the area's main attractions.

In addition to mining history, the West Kootenays are also known as the home of the Doukhobors, a religious sect of Russian immigrants who arrived in the early 1900s to till the land and practice their faith in peace. Aspects of their unique culture and lifestyle can be seen today in Grand Forks and elsewhere in the region.

GRAND FORKS

Perched at the confluence of the Granby and Kettle Rivers, Grand Forks (pop. 4,200) is a quiet town with tree-lined streets, historic homes, and an interesting history. It was once a rough-and-ready mining town, when the Doukhobors, a religious sect practicing pacifism and vegetarianism, arrived in the early 1900s after fleeing persecution in their Russian homeland. Although they no longer live in communal villages, local Doukhobor descendants still follow their beliefs and speak Russian, which is taught in local schools. To find out more about the intriguing Doukhobor lifestyle, visit **Boundary Museum** (7370 5th St., 250/442-3737; June–Oct. daily

10:30 A.M.–4:30 P.M.). While most of the original settlements have disappeared, **Hardy Mountain Doukhobor Village,** one kilometer (0.6 miles) west of town on Hardy Mountain Rd., is an exception. Comprising a smattering of redbrick buildings in various states of disrepair, the site is undergoing restoration. Although no buildings are currently open to the public, it's an interesting place to visit.

Practicalities

In a pleasant setting on the west edge of town, **Pinegrove Motel** (2091 Central Ave., 250/442-8203) offers rooms from $80 s, $90 d (with a huge discount for travelers aged 50 or older). Campers gravitate to the riverside **municipal campground** (mid-May–mid-Oct.; $12–18) at the end of 5th Street. Showers and hookups are offered.

At first glance, **Omega II Restaurant** (7400 Hwy. 3, 250/442-3124; daily 8 A.M.–9 P.M.), on the east side of town, looks no different from any other small-town restaurant, but on closer inspection you'll see the roots of Grand Forks show themselves with Russian dishes such as borscht and *galooptsi* (meat-filled cabbage rolls). Try a little of everything by ordering a platter of Russian specialties for $20 per person.

Adjacent to the museum on 5th Street is **Grand Forks Visitor Centre** (7362 5th St., 250/442-2833, www.grandforkschamber.com; Mon.–Fri. 9:30 A.M.–4:30 P.M.).

CHRISTINA LAKE

This 19-kilometer-long (12-mile-long) lake, 25 kilometers (16 miles) east of Grand Forks along Highway 3, is a summer favorite for folks from throughout the West Kootenays, who come for the lake's warm waters and fishing for rainbow trout, bass, and kokanee. On the western edge of town is **Christina Lake Golf Club,** a pleasant 18-hole layout; greens fees are $55, or play after 4 P.M. for $37.

The town of Christina Lake is spread around the southern end of the lake, where the best beach is protected from development by a small day-use area. The best-value motel is the **New Horizon Motel** (250/447-9312 or 888/859-0159, www.newhorizonmotel.com; $95–195 s or d), along the highway at the eastern edge of town. Rooms are spacious and comfortable, and a light breakfast is included in the rates. **Texas Creek Campground,** which is within **Gladstone Provincial Park,** has campsites for $14 per night.

Along Highway 3 is a grocery store, gas, a seasonal information center, and a bunch of eateries. At **Moon Beans** (Johnson Rd., 250/447-9591; daily 8 A.M.–4:30 P.M.), you can sip coffee while checking your email on the public computers—or forget about the outside world and blend in with vacationers by ordering lunch to stay.

ROSSLAND

Clinging to the slopes of an extinct volcanic crater deep in the tree-covered Monashee Mountains, Rossland (pop. 4,000) was once a gold-rush boomtown known as "The Golden City." The precious yellow metal was discovered on 1,580-meter (5,180-foot) Red Mountain by Joe Moris in 1890. Moris, like thousands of other prospectors unaware of the nearby wealth, had been traveling eastward on the Dewdney Trail to goldfields farther away. He nevertheless staked five claims on Red Mountain, the richest of which, Le Roi, later sold for $3 million. When word got out, thousands of diggers rushed in, and the township of Rossland was born. The town's population peaked at 7,000 in 1897. At that time, the city boasted four newspapers, 40 saloons, and daily rail service south to Spokane. By 1929, the mountain had yielded six million tons of ore worth $165 million. Today, tourism supplies

The streets of downtown Rossland are lined with restored buildings from the gold rush era.

© ANDREW HEMPSTEAD

the bulk of Rossland's gold; the town serves as a hidden haven for mountain-bike enthusiasts and adventurous skiers and boarders.

Sights

Downtown Rossland is a picturesque place full of historic buildings and old-fashioned street lamps. On the west side of downtown is the **Rossland Museum** (Hwy. 3B and Columbia Ave., 250/362-7722; summer daily 9 A.M.–5 P.M., adult $5, senior $4, child $3). At the entrance of the Le Roi mine, the museum catalogs the area's lustrous geological and human history. The museum also holds the Western Canada Ski Hall of Fame, which honors such luminaries as Olaus Jeldness—instigator of the local ski craze—and champion skier Nancy Greene, a local heroine who won a gold medal in the 1968 Olympics. To experience the day-to-day life of the early hard-rock miners, tour **Le Roi Gold Mine,** next to the museum complex. The 45-minute tour includes detailed explanations of how ore is mined, trammed, drilled, and blasted, and tells you how to differentiate igneous, metamorphic, and sedimentary rocks. Museum admission is included in the tour cost of adult $10, senior $8, child $5.

Mountain Biking

Each spring, Rossland comes alive with pedal power as mountain-bike enthusiasts take advantage of the maze of old logging and mining trails surrounding the city. Now known as the "Mountain Bike Capital of Canada," Rossland has hosted both the Canadian and North American championships. Rent bikes from **The Powderhound** (2040 Columbia Ave., 250/362-5311).

◖ Red Mountain Resort

The site of what was once one of the world's richest gold mines is now part of an alpine resort offering some of North America's most challenging lift-served runs. Facilities on the mountain have certainly improved since the days of Olaus Jeldness, but Red Mountain (250/362-7384 or 800/663-0105, www.redresort.com) is no megaresort. Nevertheless, the skiing and

---

OLAUS JELDNESS

In the late 1890s, after the first frantic summer of gold mining on Red Mountain, a group of prospectors put on a winter carnival, including a ski race down the slopes of Red Mountain. The organizer was Olaus Jeldness, a legendary Norwegian who had prospected all over the western United States before moving north of the border. Jeldness admitted that the mountain was "far too steep and the snow conditions too extreme" for a proper race. But it went ahead nevertheless. First the competitors hiked all the way to the summit. Then Jeldness gave the signal to go before strapping on his own skis and schussing off after the rest of the field. Despite their head start, Jeldness easily passed the other racers to become Canada's first national champion. His wooden skis and trophies are housed in the Western Canada Ski Hall of Fame in the Rossland Museum.

Jeldness was the first of many heroes to have skied the legendary slopes of "Red" – the mountain has been a breeding ground for more members of the Canadian National Ski Team than any other resort. Not bad, considering the adjacent town has just 4,000 residents.

---

boarding are still world-class. While two mountains provide opportunities for all ability levels, the resort holds most appeal for experts—and as any local will tell you, the advertised 640 hectares (1,580 acres) of terrain doesn't do justice to the opportunities for skiing in the backcountry. The heart-stopping face of Red Mountain is the star of the show. But adjacent Granite Mountain offers a vertical rise of 880 meters (2,890 feet) and almost unlimited intermediate, expert, and extreme skiing and boarding, mostly on unmarked trails through powder-filled glades. Beginners are catered to with a magic carpet while shredders will gravitate to the terrain park. Lift tickets are adult $58, senior $38, child under 12 $29, and those 6 and under ski for free.

Accommodations

The **Ram's Head Inn** (250/362-9577 or 877/267-4323, www.ramshead.bc.ca), one of Canada's premier small lodges, lies in the woods at the base of Red Mountain. Primarily designed for wintertime, the inn offers 14 ultra-comfy guest rooms that ooze mountain magnetism. Factor in a congenial dining room (breakfast only in summer), a game room, a sauna, an outdoor hot tub, and a spacious communal lounge with luxurious chairs and a large fireplace, and you have the perfect place to spend a couple of nights. Summer rates are very reasonable at $95 s or d, including a cooked breakfast. Winter packages average around $120–150 per person per night, including lift tickets.

Food

Each morning, locals converge on the **Sunshine Café** (2116 Columbia Ave., 250/362-5099; Mon.–Sat. 7 A.M.–7 P.M., until 3 P.M. outside of the winter ski season) for hearty cooked breakfasts from $6. The rest of the day, the café offers a diverse menu including Mexican and Indian dishes. **Goldrush Books and Espresso** (2063 Washington St., 250/362-5333; Mon.–Sat. 7 A.M.–3:30 P.M., Sun. 7 A.M.–1 P.M.) sets a few tables around bookshelves full of local and Canadian literature.

On the road up to Red Mountain, **Rock Cut Neighbourhood Pub** (250/362-5814; daily from 11 A.M.) is busiest in winter but opens year-round. It offers typical pub fare, smartly presented and well priced. Enjoy the mountain surroundings by eating on the heated deck.

Information

Rossland Visitor Centre (250/362-7722 or 888/448-7444, www.rossland.com; summer daily 9 A.M.–5 P.M.) is in the museum complex south of downtown, at the corner of Highway 3B and Columbia Avenue.

TRAIL AND VICINITY

Sprawling along both sides of the mighty Columbia River, Trail (pop. 8,000) lies 10 kilometers (6.2 miles) and 600 vertical meters (2,000 feet) below Rossland. It's probable that neither your first nor your subsequent impression of Trail will be positive. The world's largest lead and zinc smelter dominates the downtown area, its 120-meter-high (394-foot-high) smokestacks belching thick plumes of smoke into the atmosphere 24 hours a day. The smelter is the foundation of Consolidated Mining and Smelting Co. (Cominco), one of the world's largest mining companies, and poor Trail is often described as "Cominco with a town built around it." Head to the **Cominco Interpretive Centre** (1199 Bay Ave.) to learn about the smelting process. Free tours of the **Cominco complex** show you the area where ores are melted and separated and tell you about the byproducts, such as fertilizers, converted from the waste. The tours depart from the interpretive center, but to book a tour contact the visitor center (1199 Bay Ave., 250/368-3144 or 877/636-9569; summer daily 9 A.M.–5 P.M.).

Champion Lakes Provincial Park

Escape the smokestacks in this 1,426-hectare (3,520-acre) park, 23 kilometers (14.3 miles) east along Highway 3B toward Nelson, then a few kilometers farther along the access road. The park encompasses a chain of three small lakes nestled in the Bonnington Range. Hiking trails connect the lakes; First Lake, accessed from a trail at road's end, is the least busy. Camping is $17.

Salmo Toward Creston

East of Trail on Highway 3, the small village of Salmo (pop. 1,100) features old-fashioned wooden buildings, a small museum (open in summer daily 1–5 P.M.), and streets decorated in summer with huge hanging flower baskets bursting with brilliant color. The promise of quick fortune brought prospectors to gold diggings in the Salmo River watershed through the 1860s, but as in so many other boomtowns in the Kootenays, the riches were short-lived.

About 35 kilometers (21.7 miles) east of Salmo, at 1,133-hectare (2,800-acre) **Stagleap Provincial Park,** travelers can pause to picnic by Bridal Lake or go for a short hike. Continuing east, you'll crest 1,774-meter (5,820-foot)

Kootenay Pass, where a beautiful alpine lake makes a pleasant stop. The parking lots at either end of the lake are linked by a short trail showcasing stunted trees of this high alpine environment. From the pass, Highway 3 descends to Creston (see *Kootenay Lake and Creston*).

CASTLEGAR

Though endowed with the rich history of the Doukhobors, Castlegar (pop. 7,400) is not a particularly attractive place. Spread out along the barren Columbia River Valley, it's a real crossroads town. Here the Kootenay River drains into the much larger Columbia River, Highway 3 passes through east to west, Highway 3A leads north to Nelson, and Highway 22 leads south to Rossland and Trail. The town is also the major air gateway for the Kootenays.

The area's first nonnative residents, the Doukhobors, arrived in 1908. These pacifist Russian immigrants planted orchards, built sawmills, and even operated a jam factory while living in segregated villages along the valley floor. Many of their descendants still live in the area.

Doukhobor Sights

Castlegar's major attraction is the **Doukhobor Discovery Centre** (east side of the river along Hwy. 3A, 250/365-5327; May–Sept. daily 10 A.M.–5 P.M.; adult $8, student $5). The village allows a glimpse of the traditional lifestyle of these intriguing Russian immigrants. Admission includes a guided tour, led by Doukhobor descendants, through the main building and the simply furnished brick dwellings and outbuildings. Along the way you'll see some of the sect's artifacts, including handwoven clothing, crocheted bedspreads and shawls, a barn full of antique farming implements, and carved wooden spoons and ladles. At the Village Bistro you can dine on simple yet hearty Doukhobor fare.

Zuckerberg Island, at the confluence of the Kootenay and Columbia Rivers, was the home of Russian immigrant Alexander Zuckerberg, who came to Castlegar to teach Doukhobor children in 1931. Connected to the mainland by a 150-meter (492-foot) suspension bridge, the tree-covered two-hectare (five-acre)

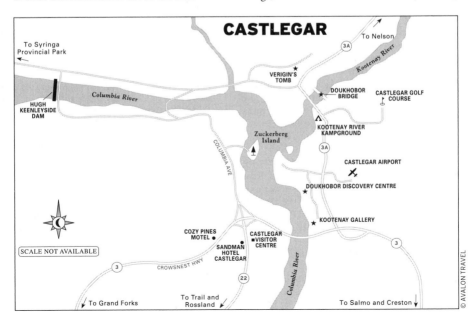

CASTLEGAR

To Syringa Provincial Park
To Nelson
Columbia River
HUGH KEENLEYSIDE DAM
VERIGIN'S TOMB
DOUKHOBOR BRIDGE
CASTLEGAR GOLF COURSE
Kootenay River
KOOTENAY RIVER KAMPGROUND
Zuckerberg Island
COLUMBIA AVE
CASTLEGAR AIRPORT
DOUKHOBOR DISCOVERY CENTRE
KOOTENAY GALLERY
SCALE NOT AVAILABLE
COZY PINES MOTEL
SANDMAN HOTEL CASTLEGAR
CASTLEGAR VISITOR CENTRE
CROWSNEST HWY
Columbia River
To Grand Forks
To Trail and Rossland
To Salmo and Creston

© AVALON TRAVEL

island is interesting to explore. A one-kilometer (0.6-mile) trail passes a full-scale model of a *ckukuli* (native winter pit house), as well as a Russian Orthodox chapel house, a cemetery, a log house, and many other Zuckerberg creations. To get there, turn off Highway 22 at 9th Street, turn left on 7th Avenue, then immediately turn right.

While you're in a Russian frame of mind, visit the old **Doukhobor Bridge,** which crosses the Kootenay River along Highway 3A. It was built by the Doukhobors in the 1910s as a link from their community to Nelson; none of them had any bridge-building experience, but the 100-meter-long (328-foot-long), hand-poured concrete suspension bridge was used until 1968, and the remains can still be seen today. On the north side of the river just west of the bridge lies **Verigin's Tomb,** the final resting place of Peter Verigin, the spiritual leader who led the Doukhobors to the Kootenays. To get there from the north side of the Kootenay River, head west toward Robson and take Terrace Road to the right. The tomb sits on a high bluff, surrounded by manicured gardens.

Practicalities

The comfortable and reasonably priced **Cozy Pines Motel** (2100 Crestview Cres., 250/365-5613, www.cozypines.com; $65 s, $70 d) offers spotless rooms with kitchenettes and high-speed Internet. Immediately south of the Highway 3 and Highway 22 intersection is the **Sandman Hotel Castlegar** (1944 Columbia Ave., 250/365-8444 or 800/726-3626, www.sandman.ca; $115 s, $125 d), with an indoor pool and a 24-hour restaurant. Campers looking for hookups should head to **Kootenay River Kampground** (651 Rosedale Rd., 250/365-5604, www.kootenayriverrv.com; $15–25), beside the river north of the airport. The setting at **Syringa Provincial Park** ($17), on the banks of Lower Arrow Lake north out of town toward Nelson, then west off Highway 3A, is much nicer, but facilities are limited.

Castlegar Visitor Centre (off Columbia Ave. at 1995 6th Ave., 250/365-6313) is open in summer daily 8 A.M.–7 P.M., the rest of the year Monday–Friday 9 A.M.–5 P.M.

THE SLOCAN VALLEY

The historically rich Slocan Valley, or "Silvery Slocan," nestles snugly between the Slocan and Valhalla Ranges of the Selkirk Mountains. In the 1890s the valley sprang into the limelight when silver was discovered at Sandon. It's much quieter today, offering many picturesque towns and an abundance of outdoor-recreation opportunities.

New Denver

Western gateway to "Silver Country," this picturesque town of 600 is on Slocan Lake, opposite Valhalla Provincial Park. Originally called Eldorado and renamed after Denver, Colorado, the town reached its mining peak in the 1890s.

Today the short main street is lined with funky false-front stores and pioneer-style buildings left over from the prosperous silver days.

VALHALLA WILDERNESS SOCIETY

Originally founded in the 1970s to lobby for the establishment of Valhalla Provincial Park, the Valhalla Wilderness Society was instrumental in convincing the BC government to designate the Khutzeymateen Valley, north of Prince Rupert, as Canada's first grizzly bear sanctuary. Closer to home, the organization also successfully campaigned for the creation of the White Grizzly Wilderness. Its latest crusade is for protection for the habitat of the Kermode bear in the north of the province and more generalized wilderness protection, such as saving the world's boreal forests.

The society is still headquartered in New Denver. The office (307 6th St., under the Valhalla Trading Post sign) holds a small retail outlet selling books, posters, calendars, and shirts. For more information, contact the Valhalla Wilderness Society directly (250/358-2333, www.vws.org).

© ANDREW HEMPSTEAD

Heritage buildings line the streets of New Denver.

Visit the **Silvery Slocan Museum** (6th Ave. and Bellevue Dr., 250/358-2201; July–Aug. daily 10 A.M.–4 P.M., weekends only spring and fall; adult $2) to find out all about New Denver's heyday.

Down on the lake within easy walking distance of the main street, **Sweet Dreams Guesthouse** (702 Eldorado St., 250/358-2415, www.newdenverbc.com) offers five large guest rooms and a cooked breakfast for $60 s, $80–95 d. Out of New Denver to the south, **Silverton Resort** (250/358-7157, www.silvertonresort.com; $190–310 s or d) takes advantage of its watery location with self-contained cottages that are as close to the water as any I've seen in British Columbia. Campers can head to a **municipal campground** (May–Sept.; $18–20), on the south side of the town and with full hookups, or to **Rosebery Provincial Park,** on Wilson Creek six kilometers (3.7 miles) north of town ($14).

New Denver Visitor Centre (202 6th Ave., 250/358-2719, www.slocanlake.com; July–early Sept. daily 9 A.M.–5 P.M.) is a friendly little place with lots of ideas that will tempt you to linger longer in the area.

Valhalla Provincial Park

This 49,893-hectare (123,290-acre) park preserves the high peaks, deep valleys, and magnificent alpine lakes between the Valhalla Range of the Selkirk Mountains on the west and the west shores of Slocan Lake on the east. The most imposing peaks are in the south of the park, where spectacular spires rise above alpine meadows to a height of 2,800 meters (9,190 feet). With no roads, the most popular access is by boat from New Denver or Slocan, across the lake. An eight-kilometer (five-mile) lakeshore trail also connects Slocan with the west shore. There, hiking trails lead into the heart of the park. The most rewarding and popular is the **Beatrice Lake Trail,** 12.5 kilometers (7.8 miles) each way. As with all trails starting from the lake, elevation gain is steady; you'll climb just under 1,000 vertical meters (3,280 feet) as you pass Little Cahill and Cahill Lakes and enter the massive cirque in which Beatrice Lake lies. The best source of trail and transportation information is **Valhalla Wilderness Society** (307 6th Ave., New Denver, 250/358-2333), a group of local environmentalists who were instrumental in the establishment of the park. At the society's office you can pick up a copy of the detailed *Trail Guide to Valhalla Provincial Park.*

Sandon

The original Slocan Valley boomtown, Sandon was once a thriving town of 5,000 people. After the discovery of silver on the slopes of Idaho Peak, Sandon grew quickly and at one time boasted 24 hotels, 23 saloons, banks, general stores, mining brokers' offices, and a newspaper. Its main link to the outside world was the Kaslo & Slocan Railway, built in 1895 to connect Sandon with sternwheeler transportation on Kootenay Lake. Sandon was destroyed by fire in 1902 but quickly rebuilt and incorporated as a city in 1908. The Great Depression of 1929 put an end to the heyday, but the town remained the "soul of the Silvery Slocan" until the spring of 1955. That year the creek running through town flooded, sweeping away most of the city and leaving a ghost town. Today you can count the population on two hands.

The best place to start a visit to Sandon is the 1900 city hall, where the *Sandon Walking Tour Guide* is sold ($2). The brochure details all the original structures—only a fraction of which remain—with a map that makes exploring on foot more enjoyable. Up the creek from city hall is **Sandon Museum** (250/358-7920), where exhibits bring the old town back to life. Also on this side of the creek is the road to 2,280-meter (7,480-foot) **Idaho Peak**. The road is very rough, passable only in July and August. From the end of the 12-kilometer (7.5-mile) road, a steep one-kilometer (0.6-mile) trail leads to the summit and spectacular 360-degree views of the Kootenays.

NAKUSP

Forty-eight kilometers (30 miles) northwest of New Denver, Nakusp (pop. 1,800) was

an interesting building in Sandon

© ANDREW HEMPSTEAD

established during the mining-boom years. Today the small town is best known for its hot springs and its stunning location on Upper Arrow Lake at the foot of the Selkirk Mountains.

Nakusp Hot Springs

To get to these hot springs (250/265-4528; summer daily 9:30 A.M.–10 P.M., the rest of the year daily 10 A.M.–9:30 P.M.; adult $11, senior and child $10), take Highway 23 north out of town for one kilometer (0.6 mile), then follow the signposted road along Kuskanax Creek for 12 kilometers (7.5 miles).

To see the source of the springs, take the sandy 500-meter (0.3-mile) trail that starts behind the pools. You'll cross the river and clamber through damp rainforest crammed with ferns and mosses, then come to an impressive waterfall where you can smell the sulfur from the springs.

Practicalities

A nearby resort, with its own private hot springs, is **Halcyon Hot Springs Village**

& Spa (32 kilometers/20 miles north of Nakusp, 250/265-3554 or 888/689-4699, www.halcyon-hotsprings.com). Accommodations are in cabins, cottages (my favorite), chalets, or a luxury family-oriented Lodge Suite, with rates ranging $139–399 s or d. Tent camping with full hookups is $33.50, and tepees $68 (bring your own bedding). **Nakusp Village Campground** (8th St., 250/265-4019; May–Oct.; unserviced sites $18, powered sites $21), within walking distance of the beach and

the main street, has large shaded sites, coin-operated showers, and firewood.

The place to be seen in Nakusp is the **Broadway Deli Bistro** (408 Broadway St. W., 250/265-3767; daily from 7 A.M.), where you'll find great coffee and a constant stream of muffins coming out of the oven.

The **Nakusp Visitor Centre** (92 6th Ave., 250/265-4234 or 800/909-8819) is open summer daily 8 A.M.–4 P.M. and the rest of the year on weekdays only.

Nelson

The elegant city of Nelson (pop. 9,400) lies in a picturesque setting on the West Arm of Kootenay Lake, 660 kilometers (410 miles) east of Vancouver. Its relaxed pace, hilly tree-lined streets, and late-19th-century architectural treasures have helped attract a mix of jaded big-city types, artists, and counterculture seekers. For visitors there is much to see and do around town, many good places to eat, and an eclectic atmosphere unlike anywhere else in the province. But while the city itself is uniquely charming, the surrounding wilderness of the Selkirk Mountains is Nelson's biggest draw. The area's many lakes provide excellent fishing, sailing, and canoeing, as well as some of British Columbia's best inland beaches. Trails suitable for hikers of all fitness levels lace Kokanee Glacier Provincial Park's alpine reaches. Old logging and mining trails attract happy hordes of mountain bikers. And nearby hot springs provide a welcome relief at the end of a hard day's play. In addition, when the snow starts flying, powderhounds flock to Whitewater Winter Resort for some of North America's best lift-served powder skiing and boarding.

SIGHTS

Nelson has 350 designated heritage buildings, more per capita than any other city in British Columbia, save Victoria. Most can be viewed by walking around the downtown core between Baker and Vernon Streets. Pick up the

detailed *Heritage Walking Tour* or *Heritage Motoring Tour* brochures from the information center. The walking-tour brochure details 26 downtown buildings, including the 1909 courthouse on Ward Street and the impressive stone-and-brick 1902 city hall on the corner of Ward and Vernon Streets.

Touchstones Nelson

Named for an instrument used to test for the purity of precious minerals, Touchstones Nelson: Museum of Art & History (502 Vernon St., 250/352-9813; summer Mon. and Wed.–Sat. 10 A.M.–6 P.M., Sun. 10 A.M.–4 P.M., the rest of the year Wed.–Sat. 10 A.M.–6 P.M., Sun. noon–4 P.M.; adult $10, senior $6, child $4) is in the historic stone post office building. The focus is on local history, with bright, modern displays covering native peoples, explorers, miners, traders, early transportation, Nelson's contribution to World War I, and the Doukhobors.

Nelson Artwalk

Organized by the local arts council (250/352-2402, www.nda.ca), Nelson's annual Artwalk highlights the work of up to 100 local artists. Throughout summer, works are displayed citywide at various venues such as restaurants, hotels, the theater building, art galleries, and even the local pool hall. On one Friday of every month, receptions are held at each of the venues. The receptions feature live entertainment, refreshments, and the artists themselves, on hand to discuss their work. A brochure available at the information center and motels and galleries around town contains biographies of each featured artist, tells where his or her work is displayed, and provides a map showing you the easiest way to get from one venue to the next.

RECREATION

In summer, the focus is on **Lakeside Park,** by the Orange Bridge (known locally as "BOB," an acronym for Big Orange Bridge). It has a sandy beach, tennis courts, and a picnic area. Another pleasant spot to escape suburbia is **Cottonwood Falls,** which tumble from below a highway overpass off Baker Street. The surrounding area has been nicely landscaped and is well worth a visit, especially when spring run-off creates a massive flow of water.

Outdoor Recreation

The best nearby hiking is in **Kokanee Glacier Provincial Park** (see *Kootenay Lake and Creston*),

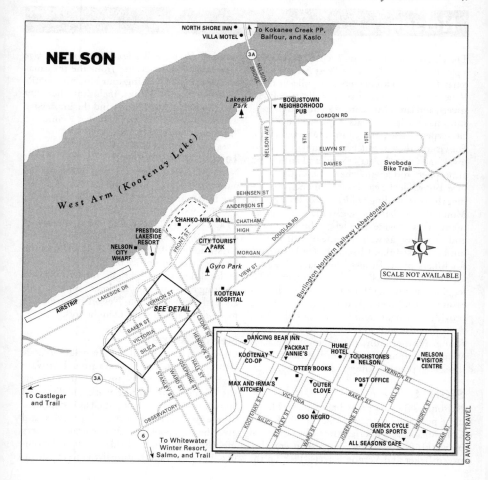

Nelson's historic buildings today hold many cafés and restaurants.

but the bed of the Burlington Northern Railway, built in 1893, provides an interesting nine-kilometer (5.5-mile) trek right on Nelson's back doorstep. Access the railway from the top end of South Cherry Street. The many old logging and mining roads surrounding the city are great for mountain biking; one favorite is the **Svoboda Bike Trail,** accessed along Elwyn Street beyond the college. For bike rentals and a trail map, head to **Gerick Cycle and Sports** (702 Baker St., 250/354-4622).

Legendary powder and an off-the-beaten-path location make **Whitewater Winter Resort** (250/354-4944 or 800/666-9420, www.skiwhitewater.com) a hidden gem. The small resort 20 kilometers (12 miles) south of Nelson sits beneath a string of 2,400-meter (7,900-foot) peaks that catch an amazing amount of snow. Three double chairlifts access 18 marked trails (the Summit Chair opens up the best powder-packed slopes). The area's abundant snowfall makes for a long season, but conditions are best in February and March. Whitewater has no on-mountain

accommodations—just the lifts and a day lodge with a cafeteria, rental shop, and ski/snowboard school. Lift tickets are adult $52, senior and youth $38.

ENTERTAINMENT

The **Hume Hotel** (422 Vernon St., 250/352-5331) is the center of Nelson's after-dark scene. This old hotel contains **Mike's Place,** a bar that comes alive on weekends; **Spiritbar,** a live music venue; and the elegant **Library Lounge,** with tapestried chairs by a fireplace, books to read, and an elaborate draped ceiling—the perfect place to head to for a quiet drink. Down on the water, the bar in the **Prestige Lakeside Resort** (701 Lakeside Dr., 250/352-7222) has an expansive deck that catches the afternoon sun. Another popular drinking hole is **Bogustown Neighbourhood Pub,** toward the Nelson Bridge (712 Nelson Ave., 250/354-1313), with a fireplace and outdoor patio. (The pub's intriguing name was coined by miners who were attracted to the city for its supposed wealth but were never paid).

ACCOMMODATIONS
Under $50

Right downtown, ◖ **Dancing Bear Inn** (171 Baker St., 250/352-7573 or 877/352-7573, www .dancingbearinn.com) offers clean and comfortable accommodations at a very reasonable price. It features a cozy lounge area with a TV, reading material, information on local attractions and restaurants, and a cupboard full of board games. Other facilities include wireless Internet, a kitchen, a laundry, and lockers. The dorm-style rooms are spacious, with a maximum of six beds in each. A few doubles and a single room are also available. Members of Hostelling International pay $19 per night, nonmembers $23; private rooms are $48–52 d.

$50-100

Villa Motel (250/352-5515 or 888/352-5515, www.thevillamotel.com) and **North Shore Inn** (250/352-6606 or 800/593-6636, www .nshoreinn.com) are directly across the Orange Bridge from downtown. Both offer regular motel rooms of a respectable standard for $75 s, $85 d, while the former has a small indoor pool.

$100-150

The 1898 **Hume Hotel** (422 Vernon St., 250/352-5331 or 877/568-0888, www.hume hotel.com) is a city landmark. It provides attractive, recently refurbished rooms, some with lake views, for $99–139 s, $109–149 d, including breakfast in the downstairs restaurant. The more expensive rooms are larger and generally have better views.

The pick of Nelson's many guesthouses is the ◖ **Kiwi Vine Guest House** (215 Houston St., 250/352-2297, www.kiwivine.com), named for fruit-filled vines running along the back fence. Accommodation is in two suites, one with two bedrooms ($135) and the other with three ($155). Each is decorated with inspiring color schemes and comes with a full kitchen, lounge with TV/DVD combo, and outdoor space that comes together at a great little playground that young children won't want to leave. Highly recommended.

The construction of the **Prestige Lakeside Resort** (701 Lakeside Dr., 250/352-7222, www

.prestigeinn.com; $159–229 s or d) is the first stage in the redevelopment of Nelson's waterfront. This resort features a spa facility, fitness center, swimming pool, private marina, and restaurants.

FOOD

Nelson's reputation as a center of good eating has come ahead in leaps and bounds during recent years, but a few old Chinese places hang on along Baker Street and remain open later than all the other restaurants listed.

The best place for breakfast is the **General Store Restaurant** (Hume Hotel, 422 Vernon St., 250/352-5331; daily 7:30 A.M.–8:30 P.M.). Cooked breakfasts are huge, especially the omelets (from $8.50), which come piled high with delicious hash browns.

Cafés

The counterculture of Nelson is evident at the **Kootenay Co-op** (295 Baker St., 250/354-4077), where you can pick up goat's milk ice cream, organic apple juice, hemp toaster waffles, west coast salmon caught by Nisga'a natives, eco-sweet chocolate, and preservative-free bread. If you're looking for lunch on the run, pick up healthy snacks, such as sweet curry rolls and vegan carrot cake, from the deli counter.

Over the last few years, the ◖ **Vienna Café** (411 Kootenay St., 250/354-4646; Mon.–Fri. 9 A.M.–5:30 P.M., Sat. 9 A.M.–5 P.M.), in Packrat Annie's bookstore, has lost its counterculture vibe, but the food has gotten better. You can't go wrong with a chicken burger—free range of course—loaded with feta cheese and green pepper ($9). A generous serving of vegetarian five-bean chili will set you back $5.50, or order a bowl of butternut squash soup livened up by a dash of maple syrup for $6.50. Excellent!

Up from the main street, duck in to **Oso Negro** (604 Ward St., 250/352-7661; Mon.–Sat. 7 A.M.–6 P.M., Sun. 8 A.M.–4 P.M.) for rich coffee roasted in-house. The bagels and other baked goods are also recommended.

Casual Dining

Outer Clove (536 Stanley St., 250/354-1667; Mon.–Sat. 11:30 A.M.–9 P.M.) is typical of Nelson's better restaurants, appealing to modern tastes but in a relaxed, low-key environment. The emphasis is on garlic (it's even an ingredient in a couple of the desserts), with tapas from $5 (you'd need three for a filling meal) and dinners $12–20. All lunch items are under $12.

The best pizza in town comes straight from the wood-fired oven at **Max & Irma's Kitchen** (515 Kootenay St., 250/352-2332; daily 11 A.M.–9 P.M.). Order your favorite off the standard menu ($12–14) or pay $7 for a base and build your own from a large assortment of mouthwatering toppings.

Tucked into a back alley behind the main street is ◖ **All Seasons Café** (620 Herridge Lane, 250/352-0101), a small yet stylish place with a delightful tree-shaded patio. Dishes such as rack of lamb baked with a fig-and-stilton-cheese crust will have you raving, while desserts like bourbon pecan pie will have you wishing you had more room. As a bonus, All Seasons has a small but well-thought-out selection of wines by the glass from $6.

INFORMATION AND SERVICES

All the information you'll need on Nelson and the Kootenays is available at **Nelson**

Visitor Centre (225 Hall St., 250/352-3433 or 877/663-5706, www.discovernelson .com; summer daily 8:30 A.M.–6 P.M., the rest of the year Mon.–Fri. 8:30 A.M.–4:30 P.M.).

Otter Books (398 Baker St., 250/352-3434) has an excellent selection of books about the Kootenays ranging from ghost town guides to the history of the Kettle River Railway. **Packrat Annie's** (411 Kootenay St., 250/354-4722) sells used books, tapes, and CDs, and offers good people-watching opportunities.

Kootenay Hospital is east of downtown (3 View St., 250/352-3111). The **post office** is at 514 Vernon Street.

GETTING THERE AND AROUND

Long-distance bus transportation is provided by **Greyhound.** The depot is at the Chahko-Mika Mall (1112 Lakeside Dr., 250/352-3939). From Vancouver, buses come into Nelson via Castlegar, then continue east to Cranbrook via Salmo.

Local car-rental agencies include **Rent-a-wreck** (250/352-5122) and **Thrifty** (250/352-2811). For details of local bus transportation, call the **Nelson Transit System** (250/352-8201).

Kootenay Lake and Creston

Heading first north, then east from Nelson, Highway 3A follows a narrow arm of Kootenay Lake before coming to the main, 100-kilometer-long (62-mile-long) body of water at Balfour. From there, you have a choice of routes. You can cross Kootenay Lake by ferry and follow the east shore of the lake down to Creston, or you can continue north up the west shore of the lake, passing through Ainsworth Hot Springs and Kaslo before arcing back west to Slocan Valley and Arrow Lake.

NELSON TO KASLO

It's 70 kilometers (44 miles) north from Nelson to Kaslo. A number of parks and small com-

munities dot the route, and Kootenay Lake is nearly always in view.

Kokanee Creek Provincial Park

This 257-hectare (630-acre) lakefront park 20 kilometers (12.4 miles) northeast of Nelson features a great sandy beach and one of the Kootenays' most popular campgrounds. Short walking trails crisscross the park, and kokanee (freshwater salmon) can be viewed in Kokanee Creek at the end of summer (access is from the visitor center). Instead of migrating in from the ocean like their anadromous cousins, kokanee spend their lives in the larger lakes of British Columbia's interior, spawning each summer in

feeding ducks along Kootenay Lake

© ANDREW HEMPSTEAD

the rivers and streams draining into the lakes. The super-popular day-use area runs the length of a one-kilometer (0.6-mile) sandy beach. The large campground's sites have showers, but no hookups, and they fill fast through summer; $22 per night. A visitor center (250/825-4421, mid-June–mid-Sept. daily 9 A.M.–9 P.M.) holds displays on local ecosystems, a room filled with children's games and books, and trail reports for Kokanee Glacier Provincial Park.

◖ Kokanee Glacier Provincial Park

Straddling the highest peaks of the Selkirk Mountains, this 32,035-hectare (79,160-acre) mountain wilderness park can be seen from downtown Nelson. This is one of British Columbia's premier provincial parks, filled with magnificent scenery and abundant wildlife and providing some unrivaled opportunities for backcountry travel. The park is named for a massive glacier that, along with two other glaciers and 30 lakes, feeds dozens of creeks and rivers flowing west to Slocan Lake and

east to Kootenay Lake. Almost entirely above 1,800 meters (5,900 feet), the park's environment is very different from the valley floor—dominated by barren peaks and, for a few short weeks in the middle of summer, meadows of lush subalpine wildflowers.

The heart of the park is too steep and rugged to be penetrated by roads, so all the best features must be reached on foot. The main access is via an unsealed road that spurs off Highway 3A 20 kilometers (12.4 miles) from Nelson and follows Kokanee Creek 16 kilometers (10 miles) to **Gibson Lake.** A 2.5-kilometer (1.6-mile) trail circles the lake, but the best hiking is farther afield. From Gibson Lake, it's four kilometers (2.5 miles) uphill to beautiful **Kokanee Lake.** There the trail flattens out, continuing three kilometers (1.9 miles) to Kaslo Lake and a further two kilometers (1.2 miles) to **Slocan Chief Cabin,** a century-old structure that sleeps 12 ($15 per person).

The park can also be accessed from a rough, 24-kilometer (15-mile) unsealed road that begins six kilometers (3.7 miles) west of Kaslo and ends at the **Joker Millsite** trailhead. From here a steep five-kilometer (3.1-mile) trail leads to Slocan Chief Cabin and a trail of similar length (with an elevation gain of 450 meters/1,480 feet) goes to a backcountry campground at **Joker Lakes,** two beautiful bodies of water in a glacial cirque surrounded by towering peaks.

Because of the park's remote location, it's vital to pick up information on road and hiking-trail conditions at the **visitor center** in Kokanee Creek Provincial Park (250/825-4421; summer 9 A.M.–9 P.M.). In years of high snowfall, some hiking trails are impassable until late July.

World's Longest Free Ferry Ride
Back in the 1890s, sternwheelers plied Kootenay Lake, dropping off prospectors and supplies at isolated mining camps and settlements along its shores. But completion of the railway in the early 1900s quickly put most of the sternwheelers out of action. Today one public ferry remains, and it's the "world's longest free ferry ride." The 45-minute trip across Kootenay Lake from Balfour to Kootenay Bay offers majestic lake and mountain scenery and makes a good route to Creston and points east (see *Across Kootenay Lake to Creston*).

Ainsworth Hot Springs
Overlooking Kootenay Lake from a hillside 17 kilometers north of Balfour, these springs were discovered in the early 1800s by local native people who found that the hot, odorless water helped heal their wounds and ease their aches and pains. Today the springs have been commercialized and include a main outdoor pool, a hot tub, a steam bath, and a cold plunge pool. Rates are $7 for a single entry or $11 per day (discounts for seniors and children). The pools are open year-round, with summer hours 10 A.M.–9:30 P.M. (from 8:30 A.M. for resort guests).

If you want a bit more pampering, stay at **Ainsworth Hot Springs Resort** (250/229-4212 or 800/668-1171, www.hotnaturally.com), which features exercise and massage

rooms, a lounge, and a restaurant overlooking the main pool and beautiful Kootenay Lake. Room rates are $118 s or d, but you'll pay $128–158 for a lake view.

Cody Caves Provincial Park
On the mountain slope high above Ainsworth Hot Springs, this cave system was discovered by prospector Henry Cody in the 1890s. Made up of several large chambers totaling 800 meters (2,600 feet) in length, the caves also hold an underground creek that drops over Cody Falls. To get to the caves, turn off Highway 31 3.5 kilometers (2.2 miles) north of Ainsworth Hot Springs, follow a narrow 15-kilometer (9.3-mile) gravel road to a trailhead, then hike 15 minutes along a forested trail. Experienced spelunkers can explore the caves unguided, but others will want to join a tour with **Hiad Venture Corp.** (250/353-7364, www.codycaves.ca). The one-hour option ($15 per person) departs from the parking lot between 10 A.M. and 4 P.M. The three-hour tour ($60) is more adventurous and passes formations you won't see on the shorter trip; departures at 9 A.M.

KASLO
Tree-lined streets graced by elegant late-19th-century architecture, lake and mountain views from almost every street, and the world's oldest passenger sternwheeler tied up at the wharf make Kaslo (pop. 1,100), 70 kilometers (44 miles) north of Nelson, a worthwhile stop.

Another of the Kootenays' great boomtowns, Kaslo began as a sawmill community in 1889. But nearby silver strikes in 1893 quickly turned the town into a bustling city of 3,000 and an important commercial hub; a railway brought silver down from Sandon to Kaslo, where it was loaded onto steamers and shipped out to Creston and the outside world. The town's 1898 city hall is one of only two wooden buildings in the country that are still the seats of local government.

SS *Moyie*
Dry-docked by the lakefront stands the 50-meter-long (164-foot-long) SS *Moyie* (324 Front St., 250/353-2525; mid-May–mid-Oct.

© ANDREW HEMPSTEAD

The SS *Moyie* was the last sternwheeler on Kootenay Lake.

daily 10 A.M.–5 P.M.; adult $5, senior $4, child $2), the last Canadian Pacific Railway sternwheeler to splash up Kootenay Lake. Built in 1897 and launched the following year at Nelson, the grand old red-and-white vessel was used for transportation of passengers, freight, and mail right up until its retirement in 1957. Today the ship serves as a museum containing a fine collection of photos, antiques, and artifacts of the region.

Practicalities

Right downtown, the **Kaslo Motel** (330 D Ave., 250/353-2431 or 877/353-2431, www .kaslomotel.ca; $57–68 s or d) has clean and convenient but basic rooms, some with small kitchens. North of town, the **Lakewood Inn** (Kohle Rd., 250/353-2395, www.lakewoodinn .com) has been taking in guests since the 1920s. Lakefront cabins are $90–120, while campers pay from $19.50.

Front Street is lined with small town businesses, many with historic facades. If you're hungry, the ones to look for are **Landmark**

Bakery (416 Front St., 250/353-2250; closed Sun.), with good coffee, a wide range of sweet treats, and public Internet access; **Sunnyside Naturals** (404 Front St., 250/353-9667), for freshly squeezed juices and organic foods; and, at the top end, **Rosewood Café** (213 5th St., 250/353-7693; summer daily for lunch and dinner) for more substantial meals.

In a restored railway station that also serves as the entrance to the SS *Moyie* is **Kaslo Visitor Centre** (324 Front St., 250/353-2525; mid-May–mid-Oct. daily 10 A.M.–5 P.M.).

ACROSS KOOTENAY LAKE TO CRESTON

From Balfour, the world's longest free ferry ride takes you across Kootenay Lake to **Kootenay Bay**. The *Osprey* offers lots of outside spots at which to sit and soak up the surrounding mountain panorama.

◖ Crawford Bay

From the ferry dock, Highway 3A traverses a low ridge before dropping into Crawford Bay, a small community sandwiched between the Purcell Mountains and the water. Artisan outlets have put this village of 200 on the map. On the left as you descend the hill is **North Woven Broom** (250/227-9245; Apr.–mid-Oct. daily 9 A.M.–5 P.M.), western Canada's only traditional broom manufacturer. The raw materials (from California and Mexico) are handcrafted into brooms using 19th-century methods. Stop in anytime and you're likely to find craftspeople hard at work and eager to share their knowledge of this lost art. The workshop is crammed with brooms of all shapes and sizes, ranging in price $35–80. A little farther along is **Kootenay Forge** (877/461-9466; May–mid-Oct. daily 9 A.M.–5 P.M.), a traditional blacksmith shop where you can watch artisans practicing this ancient trade.

Also at Crawford Bay is **Kokanee Springs Golf Resort** (250/227-9226 or 800/979-7999; mid-Apr.–early Oct.), one of the province's most picturesque courses. Featuring water views, forested fairways, huge greens, large elevation drops, and colorful flower beds around the tee boxes, it's not only a beautiful place to golf, it's also very challenging. Greens fees are a reasonable $69 (twilight rates $39). Right on the golf course is **Lodges of Kokanee Springs** (same contacts). The 64 rooms and suites are decorated in a stylish deep-blue color, offset by the natural colors of wooden trim and furniture. High-season rates start at $139–164 s or d, but most guests stay as part of a golfing package (from $140 pp per night).

The pick of local accommodations is **C Wedgwood Manor** (250/227-9233 or 800/862-0022, www.wedgewoodcountryinn .com; Apr.–Oct.; $105–145 s or d). Set on 20 beautiful hectares (50 acres) adjacent to the golf course and within walking distance of a beach, this 1910 home offers six heritage-style rooms, each with a private bathroom and modern elements such as wireless Internet.

South Along Kootenay Lake

From Crawford Bay, it's 80 kilometers (50 miles) of lake-hugging road to Creston. Along the way you'll pass small clusters of houses

and a number of resorts. **Mountain Shores Marina & Resort** (13 kilometers/eight miles from Crawford Bay, 250/223-8258, www .mtnshores.com; camping $19–25, motel rooms $72–107 s or d) is a lakefront resort with a beach, outdoor pool, and marina. Continuing south, **Lockhart Beach Provincial Park** has a small campground with sites for $14 per night.

CRESTON

In a wide, fertile valley at the extreme southern end of Kootenay Lake lies Creston, a thriving agricultural center of 4,800. Although the town is south of the Kootenays' most spectacular mountains, the scenery is still impressive; the Selkirk Mountains flank the valley to the west, while the Purcell Mountains do the same to the east. Fruit stands lining Highway 3 on the east side of Creston from the west are a sign of the district's most obvious industry. Stop for locally grown asparagus (May–early June), strawberries (July), cherries (mid-July–mid-Aug.), peaches (late July–Sept.), and apples (Aug.–Oct.).

C Creston Valley Wildlife Management Area

This 7,000-hectare (17,300-acre) wildlife reserve lies 10 kilometers (6.2 miles) west of Creston (250/428-3259; May–June Tues.–Sun. 9 A.M.–4 P.M., July–Sept. daily 9 A.M.–4 P.M.; donation). It extends from Kootenay Lake to the Canada–U.S. border. Protecting vital resting grounds along the Pacific Flyway, the site provides a haven for more than 250 species of birds, including a large population of osprey, a flock of the rare Forester's tern, and a nesting colony of western grebe. Start a visit at the park's wildlife center, where displays focus on the abundant birdlife, as well as on mammals and reptiles present in the reserve. From the center, hiking trails lead along dikes separating wetlands and ponds. Walking and canoe tours are adult $7, child $5, and leave four times daily. Even along the boardwalk leading into the center you may spy some local residents: turtles that sun themselves on half-submerged logs. Special events through the year coincide with various natural cycles, such as the spring **Osprey Festival.**

Other Sights

Creston Museum (219 Devon St., 403/428-9262; summer daily 10 A.M.–3:30 P.M.; adult $3, child $2), on the west side of town and south across the railway tracks, is home to a Kutenai canoe, unlike any other in North America but similar to the style used by the Gilyaki people in Russia, leading ethnologists to speculate about the possible links. West of the museum is **Kootenay Candles** (1511 Northwest Blvd., 250/428-9785), where candles are handcrafted and sold at a factory retail outlet.

Creston is home to the **Columbia Brewery** (1220 Erickson St., 250/428-9344), producer of British Columbia's popular Kokanee beer. Tours are offered in summer Monday–Friday at 9:30 A.M., 11:30 A.M., 1 P.M., and 2:30 P.M. At the brewery entrance is the Kokanee Beer Gear retail outlet (Mon.–Fri. 9 A.M.–4 P.M.).

Accommodations and Food

The best lodging options are north of town (see *South Along Kootenay Lake*), but you could stay right downtown at the aptly named **Downtowner Motor Inn** (1218 Canyon St., 250/428-2238 or 800/665-9904; from $60 s, $70 d), which sports an easily recognized blue-and-white exterior. Rooms are air-conditioned and come with wireless Internet. **Scottie's RV Park** (1409 Erickson Rd., 250/428-4256 or 800/982-4256, www.scottiesrv.com; $20–26.50) enjoys a pleasant treed setting across the road from the Columbia Brewery.

The busiest place in town each morning is **Creston Valley Bakery** (113 10th Ave., 250/428-2661), where you'll find plenty of tables and a large selection of freshly baked cakes and pastries.

Information

Creston Visitor Centre is in a small log building at the top end of the main street (1711 Canyon St., 250/428-4342; summer daily 9 A.M.–6 P.M., the rest of the year weekdays 9 A.M.–5 P.M.).

East Kootenays

In the southeastern corner of the province, the East Kootenays encompass the Purcell Mountains and the upper reaches of the Columbia River, with the Rocky Mountains rising abruptly from the Columbia Valley to the Continental Divide and the British Columbia–Alberta border to the west. The crossroads of the region is the service center of **Cranbrook,** from where Highway 3 heads west to **Fernie** and the neighboring province of Alberta, and Highway 93/95 parallels the Columbia River northward through a region dotted with golf courses, hot springs, and many provincial parks.

EAST FROM CRESTON

From Creston, the Crowsnest Highway (Highway 3) crosses the **Purcell Mountains** and descends to Cranbrook, the region's largest town. The distance between the two towns is a little over 100 kilometers (62 miles).

Yahk

Yahk grew into a thriving lumber town in the 1920s but was abandoned by the 1930s. Today empty houses and a still-operating hotel are all that remains along the main street, but the pioneer **museum** keeps history alive with its displays of household artifacts and costumes from the past. Tiny **Yahk Provincial Park** lies beside the rushing Moyie River east of town. Fishing in the river is good for rainbow trout and Dolly Varden; camping is $14 per night (this campground has only 26 sites, so arrive in early afternoon to be assured of a spot).

South of Yahk is the **Kingsgate port of entry,** open daily 24 hours.

Moyie

North from Yahk, Highway 3/95 parallels the Moyie River to its source at **Moyie Lake,** a deep-blue body of water backed by cliffs. Halfway

© ANDREW HEMPSTEAD

Canadian Museum of Rail Travel

along the lake, Moyie, once boasting a population of 1,500, today holds nothing more than a few historic buildings, a pub, and a gas station; the 1904 church on Tavistock Street and the 1907 fire hall beside the highway are among the original survivors. Miners working the nearby St. Eugene Mine for lead and silver were the first settlers. The old mine is visible back up the hill by wandering down to the lakeshore.

Around 13 kilometers (eight miles) north of town is 91-hectare (220-acre) **Moyie Lake Provincial Park,** which has a sandy swimming beach, short interpretive trails, and the chance to view kokanee spawning on gravel river beds. The large campground has semiprivate sites, hot showers, and a weekend interpretive program; $22 per site.

CRANBROOK

Crossroads of the eastern Kootenays, Cranbrook (pop. 19,000) nestles at the base of the Purcell Mountains 106 kilometers east of Creston and provides spectacular views eastward to the Canadian Rockies. The main touristy

reason to stop is the rail museum, but with the surrounding wilderness, nearby Fort Steele Heritage Town, and the development of a 36-hole Gary Player golf course well under way, it's a good base for further exploration.

Canadian Museum of Rail Travel

Cranbrook's main attraction, this museum is on a siding of the main Canadian Pacific Railway line directly opposite downtown (57 Van Horne St., 250/489-3918; mid-Apr.–mid-Oct. daily 10 A.M.–6 P.M., mid-Oct.–Mar. Tues.–Sat. 10 A.M.–5 P.M.). Most of the displays are outdoors, spread along three sets of track, including the only surviving set of railcars from the Trans-Canada Limited, a luxury train (also called "The Millionaires' Train") built for the Canadian Pacific Railway in 1929. The dining, sleeping, and solarium lounge cars sport inlaid mahogany and walnut paneling, plush upholstery, and brass fixtures. Restoration displays, a viewing corridor, a model railway display, a slide show, guided tours of the car interiors, and tea and scones in the Argyle Dining Car are included in the price of the

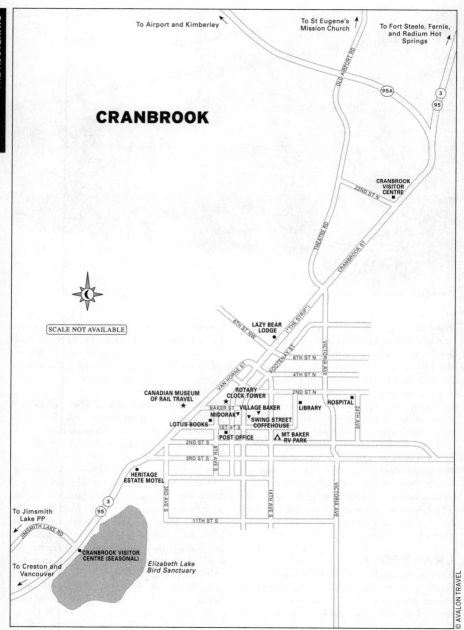

THE KOOTENAYS

CRANBROOK

To Airport and Kimberley

To St Eugene's Mission Church

To Fort Steele, Fernie, and Radium Hot Springs

OLD AIRPORT RD

95A

3

95

CRANBROOK VISITOR CENTRE

22ND ST. N

THEATRE RD

CRANBROOK ST

SCALE NOT AVAILABLE

LAZY BEAR LODGE

6TH ST NW

KOOTENAY ST ("THE STRIP")

VICTORIA AVE

6TH ST N

VAN HORNE ST

4TH ST N

2ND ST N

CANADIAN MUSEUM OF RAIL TRAVEL

ROTARY CLOCK TOWER

BAKER ST

MIDORAK

VILLAGE BAKER

LIBRARY

HOSPITAL

24TH AVE

LOTUS BOOKS

1ST S S

SWING STREET COFFEEHOUSE

POST OFFICE

MT BAKER RV PARK

2ND ST S

9TH AVE S

3RD ST S

HERITAGE ESTATE MOTEL

3RD AVE S

14TH AVE S

VICTORIA AVE

3

95

11TH ST S

To Jimsmith Lake PP

JIMSMITH LAKE RD

CRANBROOK VISITOR CENTRE (SEASONAL)

Elizabeth Lake Bird Sanctuary

To Creston and Vancouver

© AVALON TRAVEL

two-hour Deluxe Tour (adult $14, senior $12, child $7.50). You can choose abbreviated tours (from adult $6, senior $5, child $2.50), but you'll miss the best of the museum. Even if you don't take the full tour, you can wander through the railway garden to enjoy a light snack in the dining car (11:30 A.M.–2 P.M.) and to see, but not use, the railway's silver, china, and glassware collection.

Heritage Walking and Driving Tour

The locals are proud of their downtown heritage buildings, which you can view on a self-guided walking tour by picking up the handy *Cranbrook Heritage Tour* brochure from either of the information centers or the railway museum (stop number one on the tour). You can still see the home of Colonel Baker—the original Cranbrook developer for whom downtown's main street is named—in Baker Park off 1st Street South. Many other heritage homes are found between 10th and 13th Avenues and 1st and 4th Streets South.

If you're still in a heritage mood and heading for Kimberley, take Old Airport Road (a continuation of Theatre Road) north to **St. Eugene's Mission Church,** between Cranbrook and Kimberley. Built in 1897, this is the finest Gothic-style mission church in the province; it features beautiful, hand-painted Italian stained-glass windows.

Elizabeth Lake Bird Sanctuary

Beside the highway at the southern city limits (park at the information center), this large area of wetlands is a haven for many species of waterfowl, including Canada geese, teal, and ringneck, scaup, redhead, bufflehead, goldeneye, and ruddy ducks. You can also see coots, grebes, black terns, and songbirds. Mammals present include muskrats, white-tailed deer, and occasionally moose.

Accommodations and Camping

Most motels are along Highway 3 through town. The highway is known as Van Horne Street south of 4th Street North and Cranbrook Street to the north. On average, motel prices here are among the lowest in the province, making it a good spot to rest overnight.

The flower-basket-adorned **Heritage Estate Motel** (362 Van Horne St., 250/426-3862; $60 s, $65 d) is definitely the best value-for-money choice. The rooms are spacious, and each contains complimentary tea and coffee. I'm not the only one who regards this place as a bargain, so book ahead in summer. Continuing north, in the heart of the commercial strip, **Lazy Bear Lodge** (621 Cranbrook St., 250/426-6086 or 888/808-6086, www.lazybear-lodge.ca; $70 s, $75 d) is an old roadside motel snazzed up with

SAM STEELE

In uniform by age 16, Sam Steele was part of the famous march west by the North West Mounted Police in 1874. In 1887, Steele led 75 Mounties across the mountains to the Kootenays, establishing a post where miners had been crossing the Kootenay River on their way to the Wild Horse Creek goldfields. Steele and his men settled land-ownership disputes between local native people and new ranchers, easing friction and maintaining order. As more mineral discoveries were made through the region, Fort Steele, as the post had become known, grew into a bustling town. But when the railway bypassed the town in 1898, Fort Steele's population plummeted. Steele meanwhile had moved on, bringing law and order to the Klondike goldfields and leading a regiment that fought the Boers in South Africa. After a lifetime of serving his country, Steele passed away in 1919, aged 70.

Today, the memory of the man lives on at **Fort Steele Heritage Town** and during Cranbrook's **Sam Steele Days** (250/426-4161, www.samsteeledays.com), which take place over the third weekend in June. Expect a huge parade, the Sweetheart Pageant, loggers' sports, bicycle and wheelchair races, a truck rodeo, sporting events, live theater, and whatever else the Sam Steele Society comes up with each year.

log trim, beds of bright flowers, and a colorful coat of paint. The rooms remain basic, but each has a coffeemaker, and some have a fridge and microwave. Out front is a small swimming pool for guest use.

One of the area's most attractive campgrounds is in **Jimsmith Lake Provincial Park,** four kilometers (2.5 miles) off the main highway at the southern outskirts of the city. The park has a sandy beach on a small lake (swimming, fishing); wooded campsites are $14 per night. Downtown, **Mt. Baker RV Park** (14th Ave. and 1st St. S., 250/489-0056, www.mtbakerrvpark.com) provides grassy tent sites for $21 and hookups for $23–27.

Food
The earliest opener of Cranbrook's many cafés is the **Village Baker** (12 12th Ave. S., 250/489-2863; Mon.–Fri. 5 A.M.–5:30 P.M., Sat. 5 A.M.–4 P.M.), where you can relax with a massive muffin and a coffee for just $4. Another local café is **Swing Street Coffeehouse** (16 11th Ave. S., 250/426-5358; Mon.–Fri. 8 A.M.–5 P.M., Sat. 9 A.M.–5 P.M.).

Casual **Midorak** (1015 Baker St., 250/489-4808; Mon.–Sat. 11 A.M.–2:30 P.M., daily 5–9 P.M.) has a menu that suits all tastes—think Thai chicken curry ($17), feta herb-crusted rack of lamb ($26), and a creamy shellfish pasta ($18).

Information and Services
Cranbrook has two information centers, one at each end of the city. The main **Cranbrook Visitor Centre** (2279 Cranbrook St. N., 250/426-5914 or 800/222-6174, www.cranbrookchamber.com) is open in summer daily 8:30 A.M.–7 P.M., the rest of the year Monday–Friday 8:30 A.M.–4:30 P.M. At the southern entrance to the city is a seasonal center (July–Aug. daily 9 A.M.–5 P.M.). **Lotus Books** (33 10th Ave. S., 250/426-3415) is loaded with local reading material, including some interesting books on the gold-rush era.

Cranbrook Regional Hospital is off 2nd Street on 24th Avenue North (250/426-5281). The **post office** is downtown (corner of 10th Ave. and 1st St. S.).

FERNIE AND VICINITY
Fernie (pop. 5,200) nestles in the Elk Valley 100 kilometers (62 miles) east of Cranbrook on Highway 3. Town center is a couple of blocks south of the highway, holding the usual array of historic buildings and small-town shops. Look for an impressive redbrick courthouse on 4th Avenue and a good bakery on 2nd Avenue. The main attraction is winter, when one of British Columbia's great little alpine resorts comes alive nearby.

About 12 kilometers (7.5 miles) south of town is 259-hectare (850-acre) **Mount Fernie Provincial Park,** where hiking trails lead along a picturesque creek and to a waterfall.

Fernie Alpine Resort
Fernie Alpine Resort (14 kilometers/8.7 miles south of Fernie, 250/423-4655, www.skifernie.com) is another of British Columbia's legendary winter resorts, boasting massive annual snowfalls, challenging skiing and riding, and uncrowded slopes. The 1,000-hectare (2,500-acre) lift-serviced area lies under a massive ridge that catches an incredible nine meters (30 feet) of snow each year, filling a wide open bowl with enough of the white fluffy stuff to please all powderhounds. A few runs are groomed, but the steeper stuff—down open bowls and through trees—is the main attraction. The resort's total vertical rise is 857 meters (2,810 feet), with many of the challenging slopes at higher elevations and in Cedar and Timber Bowls. Lift tickets cost adult $72, senior $58, child $24; under six ski free.

In July and August, one chairlift operates, opening up hiking and mountain-biking terrain. Hikers pay $15 per ride or $30 for a day pass. Use the lift to take the hard work out of mountain biking for $30 for a full day. Bikes can be rented at the base village for $35–50 per day. Other summer activities include horseback riding, guided hikes, tennis, and photography courses. Accommodations are available on the hill, and visitors with RVs are offered hookups and shower facilities.

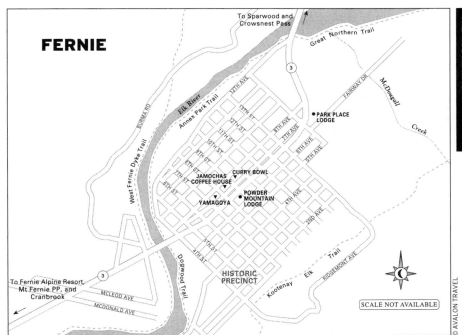

FERNIE

To Sparwood and
Crowsnest Pass

Great Northern Trail

Elk River

BURMA RD

West Fernie Dyke Trail

Annex Park Trail

12TH AVE

13TH ST

12TH ST

8TH AVE

7TH AVE

11TH ST

10TH ST

9TH ST

8TH AVE

7TH ST

JAMOCHAS
COFFEE HOUSE

CURRY BOWL

6TH AVE

5TH AVE

YAMAGOYA

POWDER
MOUNTAIN
LODGE

4TH AVE

3RD AVE

2ND AVE

• PARK PLACE
LODGE

FAIRWAY DR

McDougall

Creek

5TH ST

4TH ST

Dogwood Trail

HISTORIC
PRECINCT

Kootenay

Elk

Trail

RIDGEMONT AVE

To Fernie Alpine Resort,
Mt Fernie PP, and
Cranbrook

MCLEOD AVE

MCDONALD AVE

SCALE NOT AVAILABLE

© AVALON TRAVEL

Accommodations and Camping

Best of the bunch for budget-conscious travelers is **Powder Mountain Lodge** (892 Hwy. 3, 250/423-4492, www.powdermountainlodge .com). This converted motel has a game room, a communal kitchen, loads of parking, a laundry, Internet access, and even an outdoor pool. Accommodations are in dorms ($24 per bed) and private rooms ($69–139 s or d). In between the high summer and winter seasons, regular motel rooms go for as low as $50—a great deal. **Park Place Lodge** (742 Hwy. 3, 250/423-6871 or 888/381-7275, www.parkplacelodge.com; $99 s, $109 d) is a modern three-story hotel along the main road. Amenities include spacious and elegant rooms opening to an atrium-enclosed pool, the Max Restaurant, and a pub.

Up at the alpine resort, **Griz Inn** (250/423-9221 or 800/661-0118, www.grizinn.com) offers a mix of hotel rooms and kitchen-equipped suites, an indoor pool, a hot tub, and a restaurant. Through summer, room rates start at a reasonable $85 s or d, while a one-bedroom suite is $132 for up to four people.

The best bet for campers is **Mount Fernie Provincial Park** (mid-May–Sept.; $14), 12 kilometers (7.5 miles) south of town and four kilometers (2.5 miles) north of the Akamina–Kishinena Provincial Park access road. Facilities are basic, but it's a pleasant setting, and a short trail leads along Lizard Creek to a waterfall.

Other Practicalities

You will find a good selection of restaurants scattered through the downtown core, but my best picks are along the highway. **Jamochas Coffee House** (851 7th Ave., 250/423-6977) is the pick of many local caffeine joints (and it serves up some delicious homemade soups). Opposite Powder Mountain Lodge, the **Curry Bowl** (931 7th Ave., 250/423-2695; Tues.–Sun. 5–10 P.M.) won't win any design awards, but with delicious dishes like mango shrimp curry ($14) and a Vietnamese chicken stir-fry ($11), it really doesn't matter. (**Yamagoya** (741 7th Ave., 250/430-0090) is a stylish dining room that offers top-notch Japanese cuisine at equally reasonable prices.

Beside the highway, through town to the north, is **Fernie Visitor Centre** (250/423-6868, www.ferniechamber.com), a good source of information for those interested in exploring the surrounding wilderness.

Akamina-Kishinena Provincial Park

Bordering Glacier National Park (Montana, U.S.) and Waterton Lakes National Park (Alberta), this remote tract of 10,921 hectares (27,000 acres) protects the extreme southeastern corner of British Columbia. The park is named for its two main waterways, which flow southward into Montana. The landscape has changed little in thousands of years, since the Kootenay rested in the open meadows beside Kishinena Creek before crossing the Continental Divide to hunt bison on the prairies.

The only access is on foot from one of two trailheads. The longer option is from the end of an unsealed road that leaves Highway 3 at 16 kilometers (10 miles) south of Fernie. The road leads 110 kilometers (68 miles) into the Flathead River Valley, where trails climb along Kishinena then Akamina Creek into the park. The most popular and easiest access is by hiking trail from the Akamina Parkway in Waterton Lakes National Park (Alberta).

Sparwood

Thirty kilometers (18.6 miles) northeast of Fernie, Sparwood (pop. 3,800) is a small coal-mining community (the coal seams and part of the mining operations can be seen on the ridge high above town), but a more eye-catching element of the local industry is the world's largest truck, which sits beside Highway 3 in the center of town. Beside the truck is **Sparwood Visitor Centre** (250/425-2423 or 877/485-8185, www.sparwood.bc.ca), where you can arrange a tour of the mines. Those looking for a roof over their

head should plan on staying down the road in Fernie, while campers will enjoy **Mountain Shadows Campground** (Hwy. 3, 250/425-7815, www.sparwood.bc.ca/camping; May–Oct.; unserviced sites $15, hookups $20–25), set among trees immediately south of town.

Elkford and Vicinity

Surrounded by towering peaks, this coal-mining community of 2,500 lies 35 kilometers (22 miles) north of Sparwood on Highway 43. Abundant recreation opportunities in the area include fishing in the Elk River, wildlife viewing, and hiking and mountain biking along logging and mining roads. The community has few services, but there's a small **municipal campground** ($18) within walking distance of downtown. On Front Street is the **Elkford Visitor Centre** (250/865-4614 or 877/355-9453, www.tourismelkford.ca).

Elk Lakes Provincial Park encompasses more than 17,000 hectares (42,000 acres) of rugged wilderness 67 kilometers (42 miles) north of Elkford. From the end of the road, it's an easy one-kilometer (0.6-mile) walk to **Lower Elk Lake** and then another kilometer beyond the end of the lake to **Upper Elk Lake.** At the lower lake, a narrow trail climbs to a lookout. Aside from the long drive in, the ratio of effort to reward in reaching these lakes is unmatched in the Kootenays.

NORTH FROM CRANBROOK

From Cranbrook, the highway north divides, with the western option passing through Kimberley and a more direct route following the Kootenay River through an area that was flooded with miners after gold was discovered on Wild Horse Creek in 1865.

(Fort Steele Heritage Town

At Fort Steele Heritage Town (250/417-6000; mid-May–early Oct. daily 9:30 A.M.–6 P.M.; adult $13, senior $9, child $2), 16 kilometers (10 miles) north of Cranbrook, you'll see over 60 restored, reconstructed, fully furnished buildings, including log barracks, hotels, a courthouse, jail, museum, dentist's office, ferry office, printing office, and general store crammed to the rafters with intriguing historical artifacts. In summer, the park staff brings Fort Steele back to life with appropriately costumed working blacksmiths, carpenters, quilters, weavers, bakers, ice-cream makers, and many others. Hop on a stagecoach or a steam train, heckle a street politician, witness a crime and testify at a trial, pan for gold, watch a silent movie, and view operatic performances in the Opera House. Some of the theatrical performances inside cost extra. One of the highlights is Fort Steele Follies, a professional 1880s-style live-theater company performing a musical comedy at the Wild Horse Theatre. Showtimes are at 2 P.M. daily during the summer only (adult $7.50, senior $6, child $3).

A few commercial facilities surround the main entrance to Fort Steele. The largest is **Fort Steele Resort and RV Park** (250/489-4268, www .fortsteele.com; unserviced sites $22, hookups $28–34), which offers a heated pool, showers, a laundry, and a barbecue and cooking facility.

Wild Horse Creek

To get to the original Wild Horse Creek diggings, continue north from Fort Steele and take the logging road to Bull River and Kootenay Trout Hatchery (turn at the campground), then the first road on the left (before the creek crossing). Fisherville—the first township in the East Kootenays and once home to over 5,000 miners—was established at the diggings in 1864 but was relocated upstream when it was discovered that the richest seam of gold was right below the main street.

About five kilometers (three miles) from the highway is Wild Horse Graveyard. From this point you can hike a section of Wild Horse Creek to see a number of historic sites, including the Chinese burial ground, the site of the Wild Horse post office, the remains of Fisherville, and the diggings. It takes about two hours to do the trail, allowing for stops at all the plaques along the way. Hikers can also saunter down the last 2.5 kilometers (1.6 miles) of the Dewdney Trail, imagining all the men and packhorses, loaded to the hilt, that once

struggled from the Fraser Valley to the East Kootenays in search of fortune.

KIMBERLEY

Kimberley (pop. 7,000), 31 kilometers (19 miles) north of Cranbrook on Highway 95A, is a charming little town with no commercial strip or fast-food outlets, just streets of old stucco mining cottages and a downtown that's been "Bavarianized." In fact, Kimberley is also known as the "Bavarian City." Most downtown shops and businesses, and some of Kimberley's homes, have been decorated Bavarian-style with dark wood finish and flowery trim, steep triangular roofs, fancy balconies, brightly painted window shutters, and flower-filled window boxes.

Although named for a famous South African diamond mine, Kimberley boomed as a result of the silver and lead deposits unearthed on nearby North Star Mountain. The deposits were discovered in 1892, and by 1899 over 200 claims had been staked. As was so often the case, only operations run by larger companies

Bavarian Platzl in Kimberley

THE KOOTENAYS

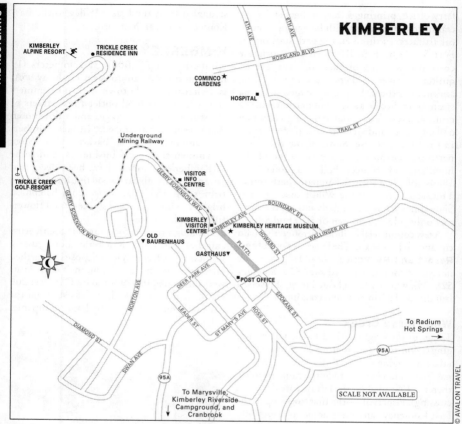

KIMBERLEY

proved profitable. The last of these, and one of the world's largest lead and zinc mines, Cominco's **Sullivan Mine,** closed in late 2001 as reserves became exhausted.

Sights

Strolling the **Bavarian Platzl,** you'll feel as though you've just driven into a village high in the Swiss Alps, with only bell-wearing cows and brightly dressed milkmaids missing. This is the focus of downtown: a cheerful, redbrick, pedestrian plaza complete with babbling brook, ornamental bridges, and the "World's Largest Cuckoo Clock" ("Happy Hans" pops out and

yodels on the hour). Shops, many German restaurants, and delis line the plaza, selling European specialties. At the far end of the Platzl, **Kimberley Heritage Museum** (250/427-7510; summer Mon.–Sat. 9 A.M.–4:30 P.M., the rest of the year Mon.–Fri. 1–4 P.M.; donation) houses mining-history exhibits, a stuffed grizzly bear, a hodgepodge of artifacts, and displays relating to all the locally popular outdoor sports.

Cominco Gardens enjoys a hilltop location (4th Ave., 250/427-2293; $3). Originally planted in 1927 to promote a fertilizer developed by Cominco, the one-hectare (2.5-acre) gardens now hold close to 50,000 flowers.

Departing up to six times daily through summer (weekends only in spring and fall), the **Underground Mining Railway** (250/427-0022; adult $15, senior $12, child $7) was constructed from materials salvaged from mining towns around the province. From just west of the Platzl, the seven-kilometer (4.3-mile) track climbs a steep-sided valley, crosses a trestle bridge, passes through a tunnel, and stops at particularly impressive mountain viewpoints and the original town site before arriving at Kimberley Alpine Resort.

Recreation

The Columbia Valley is one of British Columbia's premier golfing destinations, and while most of the best courses are farther north, Kimberley is home to **Trickle Creek Golf Resort** (250/427-5171 or 877/282-1200), along the lower slopes of North Star Mountain. The layout features huge elevation changes (such as the par-3 11th hole, which drops over 20 meters/66 feet from tee to green) and stunning mountain scenery. Greens fees are $109, or play after 2:30 P.M. for $83.

From early December to early April, **Kimberley Alpine Resort** (250/427-4881 or 800/258-7669, www.skikimberley.com) provides great skiing and snowboarding on a wide variety of slopes four kilometers (2.5 miles) west of downtown. Beginners and intermediates will be content on the well-groomed main slopes, while more experienced skiers and boarders will want to head to the expert terrain served by the Eastern Chair. Additional facilities at the resort include two snowboard parks, a cross-country ski area, an ice-skating rink, accommodations, and restaurants. Lift tickets are adult $55, senior $44, child $18.

Summer activities include chairlift rides, hiking, mountain biking, and luge rides; head to the Adventure Desk in the Marriott Hotel (250/427-6743) for details.

Accommodations and Camping

If you plan on a golfing or winter vacation in Kimberley, contact **Kimberley Vacations** (250/427-4877 or 800/667-0871, www.kimberley vacations.bc.ca) for the best package deals. Otherwise contact one of the following choices.

If you don't mind being a couple of kilometers out of town, **Travellaire Motel** (toward Marysville at 2660 Warren Ave., 250/427-2252 or 800/477-4499) provides excellent value. It's only a small place, but it is regularly revamped and decked out with new beds and furniture. There's also a barbecue area for guest use. Rates are $55 s, $65 d, or pay an extra $8 for a room with a small kitchenette. **Trickle Creek Residence Inn** is a Marriott affiliate at the base of Kimberley Alpine Resort (250/427-5175 or 877/282-1200, www.skikimberley.com). This stunning log and stone structure holds 80 spacious rooms, each with a kitchen, balcony, and fireplace. Guest facilities include a fitness center and a year-round outdoor heated pool. Summer rates are $149 s or d for a studio room and $169 for a one-bedroom suite. Check the website for golf and ski packages.

Kimberley Riverside Campground (250/427-2929 or 877/999-2929, www

Kimberley's best accommodation, the Trickle Creek Residence Inn, is up at the alpine resort.

.kimberleycampground.com; May–mid-Oct.) is seven kilometers (4.3 miles) south of downtown on Highway 95A and then three kilometers (1.9 miles) west along St. Mary's River Road. Tent sites are $18, hookups $22–26.

Other Practicalities

The **Gasthaus** in the Platzl (250/427-4851; daily except Tues. 11:30 A.M.–10 P.M.) features German lunches, such as goulash ($8), and German dinner specialties, such as bratwurst, *rheinischer sauerbraten,* Wiener schnitzel, and *kassler rippchen* ($12–18.50). Away from the Platzl, **Old Baurenhaus** (280 Norton Ave., 250/427-5133; dinner only, closed Tues.) features Bavarian specialties and plenty of atmosphere. It's in a post-and-beam building originally constructed about 350 years ago in southern Bavaria. The building was taken apart, shipped to Canada, and painstakingly rebuilt.

For information on Kimberley and the surrounding area, drop by **Kimberley Visitor Centre** (270 Kimberley Ave., 250/427-3666, www.kimberleychamber.com, summer daily 9 A.M.–7 P.M., the rest of the year Mon.–Fri. 9 A.M.–5 P.M.).

CONTINUING NORTH TOWARD INVERMERE

This stretch of highway passes through a deep valley chock-full of commercial facilities like world-class golf courses, resorts, and hot springs. The low elevation makes for relatively mild winters and an early start to the summer season. And with the Purcell Mountains on one side and the Rockies on the other, the valley certainly doesn't lack for scenery.

Wasa Provincial Park

Unlike the several backcountry parks in the area, 144-hectare (360-acre) Wasa Provincial Park, 30 kilometers (19 miles) north of Kimberley, is easily accessible off the main highway. The lake is warm, making for good summer swimming. Facilities include picnic tables, a nature trail, and swimming and water-sports areas. The park is open year-round, but the $17 camp fee is collected only May–September.

© ANDREW HEMPSTEAD

Whiteswan Lake

Whiteswan Lake Provincial Park

Continuing north, the Rockies close in and the scenery becomes unbelievably beautiful. Twenty-eight kilometers (17 miles) north of Skookumchuck and five kilometers (3.1 miles) south of Canal Flats, an unsealed logging road takes off east into the mountains, leading to 1,994-hectare (4,930-acre) Whiteswan Lake Provincial Park. The road climbs steadily from the highway, entering Lussier Gorge after 11 kilometers (6.8 miles). Within the gorge, a steep walking trail descends to **Lussier Hot Springs.** Two small pools have been constructed to contain the odorless hot (43°C/110°F) water as it bubbles out of the ground and flows into the Lussier River. Within the park itself, the road closely follows the southern shorelines of first **Alces Lake** and then the larger **Whiteswan Lake.** The two lakes attract abundant birdlife; loons, grebes, and herons are all common. They also attract anglers, who come for great rainbow trout fishing. Both lakes are stocked and have a daily quota of two fish per person.

The park road passes four popular campgrounds. The sites are $14 per night and fill on a first-come, first-served basis. There are no hook-ups or showers and reservations aren't taken.

Top of the World Provincial Park

If you thought the scenery around Whiteswan Lake was wild and remote, wait till you see this 8,790-hectare (21,720-acre) wilderness a rough 52 kilometers (32 miles) from Highway 95 (turn off the Whiteswan Lake access road at Alces Lake). You can't drive into the park, but it's a fairly easy six-kilometer (3.7-mile) hike from the end of the road to picturesque **Fish Lake,** the park's largest body of water. The trail climbs alongside the pretty Lussier River to the lake, which is encircled with Engelmann spruce and surrounded by peaks up to 2,500 meters (8,200 feet) high.

Canal Flats and Vicinity

The small lumber-mill town of Canal Flats lies between the Kootenay River and **Columbia Lake.** In 1889 the two waterways were connected by a canal with a single lock, but the passage was so narrow and dangerous that only two steamboats ever got through.

North of Canal Flats, the highway passes tiny **Thunder Hill Provincial Park,** which overlooks turquoise-and-blue Columbia Lake. The highway then approaches and passes the weirdly shaped **Dutch Creek Hoodoos,** a set of photogenic rock formations carved over time by ice, water, and wind.

Fairmont Hot Springs

Kootenay native people used these springs as a healing source for eons prior to the arrival of Europeans, but they wouldn't recognize the place today. Surrounding the site is **Fairmont Hot Springs Resort** (250/345-6311 or 800/663-4979, www.fairmontresort.com), comprising a four-star resort, three golf courses, a small ski resort, and an airstrip long enough to land a Boeing 737. Despite all the commercialism, the **hot springs** (daily 8 A.M.–10 P.M.; adult $9, child $6.50) are still the main attraction. Their appeal is simple: Unlike most other springs, the hot water bubbling up from underground here contains calcium, not sulfur with its attendant smell. The pools are a magical experience, especially in the evening. Lazily swim or float around in the large warm pool,

© ANDREW HEMPSTEAD

It's impossible to miss the Dutch Creek Hoodoos driving north from Canal Flats.

dive into the cool pool, or sit 'n' sizzle in the hot pool and watch the setting sun color the steep faces of the Canadian Rockies immediately behind the resort.

A lodge and a campground provide accommodations for all budgets. Lodge rooms are $179–265 s or d, with the more expensive having a loft and kitchen. Discounted ski, golf, and spa packages are usually available; check the website. Campers have a choice of over 300 sites spread around tree-shaded grounds, all just a one-minute stroll from the hot pools and open year-round. Unserviced sites are $23 while hookups range $32–42. Just south of the resort is **Spruce Grove Resort** (Hwy. 3, 250/345-6561 or 888/629-4004, www .sprucegroveresort.com; Apr.–early Oct.; $24–32), where campsites are spread through a tree-shaded area and along a quiet eddy in the Columbia River. Amenities for children include an outdoor pool and playground, while everyone gets a discount at the local golf course.

INVERMERE AND VICINITY

The next area to lure travelers off Highway 93/95 is large and busy **Windermere Lake.** Overlooking the lake's north end, **Invermere** (pop. 4,100) is the commercial center of the Columbia Valley. The lake and surrounding wilderness is a recreational playground, especially popular among landlocked Albertans. The area was the site of an 1807 trading post set up by David Thompson to trade with Kootenay native people (a small plaque along the road to Wilmer marks the exact spot), the first such post along the Columbia River. The original lakefront town site is now a popular recreation spot, where a pleasant grassy area dotted with picnic tables runs right down to a sandy beach and the warm, shallow waters of the lake. It's on the left as you travel along the Invermere access road. As you approach the town itself, consider a stop at **Windermere Valley Museum** (622 3rd St., 250/342-9769), where the entire history of the valley is contained in seven separate buildings. The main street itself (7th Ave.) is lined with restored heritage buildings and streetlights bedecked with hanging baskets overflowing with colorful flowers.

Practicalities
On a Saturday morning in downtown Invermere, you'll find all sorts of goodies at the outdoor market, which happens right on the main street. Farther down the hill, the **Quality Bakery** (888/681-9977) lives up to its name with a huge range of ultra-healthy sandwiches and not-so-healthy cakes and pastries.

Along the highway, just south of the Invermere turnoff, is the **Invermere Visitor Centre** (corner of 5th St. and 7th Ave., 250/342-2844, www.adventurevalley.com; July–Aug. daily 9 A.M.–5 P.M.).

Panorama Mountain Village
In the Purcell Mountains immediately west of Invermere, Panorama (250/342-6941 or 800/663-2929, www.panoramaresort.com) is an ambitious year-round resort and residential development highlighted by a ski resort and challenging **Greywolf Golf Course** (250/341-4100; greens fees $129), where the signature sixth hole, "the Cliffhanger," requires an accurate tee shot across a narrow canyon to a green backed by towering cliffs. During the warmer months, there are also chairlift rides, whitewater rafting and inflatable kayak trips down Toby Creek, and horseback riding, and in the village itself you'll find tennis, a climbing wall, and a network of connected hot pools.

Skiing first put Panorama on the map, mainly because the resort boasts one of North America's highest vertical rises (1,200 meters/3,940 feet). Lift tickets are adult $67, senior $56, child $27. The village is also home to **R.K. Heli-Ski** (250/342-3889 or 800/661-6060, www.rkheli ski.com), operating out of a "heli-plex," complete with a lounge and restaurant. The company is one of the few heli-ski operations that specialize in day trips; from $699 for three runs.

Accommodations in Panorama Mountain Village are all relatively new and well priced; book through the resort. Outside of the resort's marketing department, summer is still thought of as the off-season, and there are some great summer deals to be had, such as two nights' accommodation and unlimited use of the chairlift for $109 per person.

CANADIAN ROCKIES

The highest peaks of the Canadian Rockies form British Columbia's eastern boundary, separating the province from neighboring Alberta. On the British Columbia side of the Canadian Rockies (often called the BC Rockies) are Kootenay and Yoho National Parks and their gateway towns of Radium Hot Springs and Golden. The two national parks may lack the bustling resort towns of their famous Albertan neighbors, Banff and Jasper, but they boast the same magnificent mountain vistas, glacially fed streams and rivers, unlimited hiking opportunities, and abundant wildlife.

Many factors combine to make the Canadian Rockies so beautiful. The peaks themselves exhibit drastically altered sedimentary layers visible from miles away, especially when accentuated by a particular angle of sunlight or a dusting of snow. Between the peaks lie numerous cirques: basins gouged into the mountains by glaciers. These cirques fill with glacial meltwater each spring, creating lakes that shimmer a trademark translucent green. And thanks to a climate that keeps the tree line low and the vegetation relatively sparse, fantastic views of the wide sweeping valleys are assured.

Encompassing close to 20,000 square kilometers (7,700 square miles) of Mother Nature's finest offerings, Kootenay and Yoho, along with neighboring Banff and Jasper National Parks (both of which lie across the Continental Divide in Alberta), have been declared a World Heritage Site by UNESCO. For detailed coverage of the entire mountain

HIGHLIGHTS

◖ **Radium Hot Springs:** After a long day hiking, the best recipe for soothing aching muscles is a soak in hot springs (page 298).

◖ **Paint Pots:** The Paint Pots are a unique natural wonder that make for a colorful stop along Highway 93 (page 300).

◖ **Stanley Glacier Trail:** Although it takes around 90 minutes to reach the end of the trail, the stunning views make it worth every step (page 301).

◖ **Emerald Lake:** At Emerald Lake, you can hike, canoe, fish, or simply soak up the mountain scenery (page 307).

◖ **Lake O'Hara:** Quite simply, this is a magical lake. Access is limited by a quota system, so take heed of the reservation information and be prepared for a day of hiking you will always remember (page 307).

◖ **Kicking Horse Mountain Resort:** I've ridden each of the four gondolas in the Canadian Rockies, and my favorite for unbeatable top-of-the-world views is at Kicking Horse Mountain Resort, near Golden (page 315).

LOOK FOR ◖ TO FIND RECOMMENDED SIGHTS, ACTIVITIES, DINING, AND LODGING.

range north of the 49th parallel, see *Moon Canadian Rockies.*

PLANNING YOUR TIME

Lay out a map of British Columbia, and you'll see that visiting both Kootenay and Yoho National Parks as part of a loop through the Canadian Rockies is an obvious extension to a trip to the Kootenay region. What the map won't tell you is that nowhere in British Columbia is the scenery-to-distance-traveled ratio as good as it is in this part of the province. For the traveler, this means you should schedule a little longer than you may think to see everything.

Just one road passes through Kootenay National Park, and you can travel from one end

to the other in under two hours. But plan to spend at least a full day in the park, making stops at the hot springs and the **Paint Pots,** and allowing time to hike the **Stanley Glacier Trail.** The town of **Radium Hot Springs** is an excellent base for exploring the BC Rockies. Not only are lodgings relatively inexpensive, but the town's commercial campgrounds have more facilities than those in the parks (especially notable if you're traveling with children), there's good golfing, and bird-watchers will delight in exploring the Columbia River Wetlands.

Yoho National Park is a gem of a destination, well worth visiting even for just a day. If you make the loop through Kootenay via Lake Louise (Banff National Park),

© ANDREW HEMPSTEAD

Lake O'Hara

plan on overnighting in Yoho before continuing west along the TransCanada Highway to Golden. Scheduling a full day in the park allows enough time to drive to Takakkaw Falls, hike the loop trail around **Emerald Lake,** and enjoy lunch in between at one of the restaurants I recommend. The highlight of a visit to Yoho is **Lake O'Hara,** one of the most special places in the Canadian Rockies. Unlike at the region's other famous lakes, you can't simply drive up to O'Hara. Instead, you must make advance reservations for a shuttle bus that trundles up a restricted-access road to the lake.

The summer tourist season in the BC Rockies

is shorter than it is in the rest of the province. Emerald Lake doesn't become ice-free until early June, and the road to Takakkaw Falls remains closed until mid-June. While July and August are the prime months to visit, September is also pleasant, both weather- and crowdwise. Lake O'Hara doesn't become snow-free until early July, but the best time to visit is the last week of September, when the forests of larch have turned a brilliant gold color.

If you follow the loop this chapter takes, you'll end up in Golden, where a gondola ride at **Kicking Horse Mountain Resort** is the highlight.

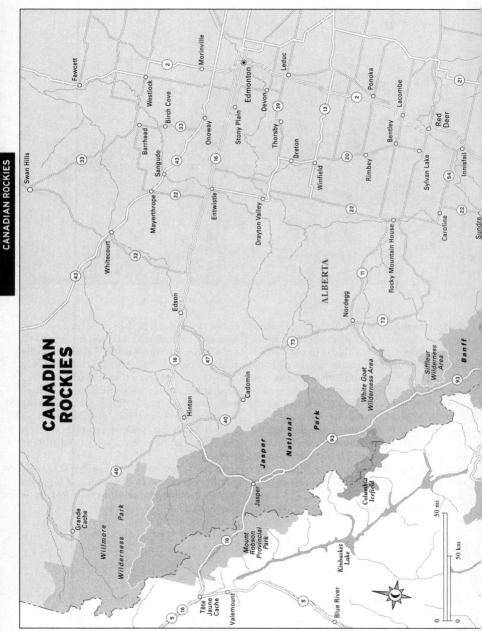

CANADIAN ROCKIES

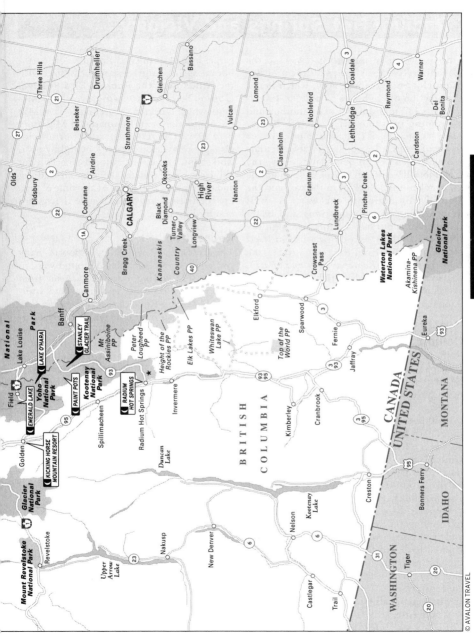

© AVALON TRAVEL

Radium Hot Springs and Vicinity

One of two main western gateways to the Canadian Rockies is the small town of Radium Hot Springs (pop. 900), which lies at the junction of Highways 93 and 95, 140 kilometers (87 miles) north of Cranbrook and a stunning two-hour drive through Kootenay National Park from the famous resort town of Banff. Its setting is spectacular; most of town lies on benchlands above the Columbia River, from where the panoramic views take in the Rockies to the east and the Purcell Mountains to the west. As well as providing accommodations and other services for mountain visitors and highway travelers, Radium is a destination in itself for many. Aside from the town's namesake (see the section *Kootenay National Park*), the area boasts a wildlife-rich wetland, two excellent golf courses, and many other recreational opportunities.

SIGHTS AND RECREATION
Columbia River Wetland
Radium sits in the Rocky Mountain Trench, which has been carved over millions of years by the Columbia River. From its headwaters south of Radium, the Columbia flows northward through a 180-kilometer-long (110-mile-long) wetland to Golden, continuingnorth for a similar distance before reversing course and flowing south into the United States. The wetland nearby Radium holds international significance, not only for its size (26,000 hectares/64,250 acres), but also for the sheer concentration of wildlife it supports. More than 100 species of birds live among the sedges, grasses, dogwoods, and black cottonwoods surrounding the convoluted banks of the Columbia. Of special interest are blue herons in large numbers and ospreys in one of the world's highest concentrations.

The wetland also lies along the Pacific Flyway, so particularly large numbers of ducks, Canada geese, and other migratory birds gather here in spring and autumn. The northbound spring migration is celebrated with the **Wings over the Rockies Bird Festival** (250/342-3210, www.wingsovertherockies .org), which is held in the second week of May in conjunction with International Migratory Bird Day. The festival features ornithologist speakers, field trips on foot and by boat, workshops, and events tailored especially for children, all of which take place in Radium and throughout the valley. At any time of year, use the festival website to source the valley's best birding spots.

Recreation
The Columbia River Valley supports many golf courses and is marketed around western Canada as a golfing destination. Aside from the excellent resort-style courses and stunning Canadian Rockies scenery, golfers here enjoy the area's mild climate. Warm temperatures allow golfing as early as March and as late as October—a longer season than is typical at other mountain courses. The 36-hole **Springs at Radium Golf Resort** is a highlight of golfing the Canadian Rockies, comprising two very different courses. One of them, the 6,767-yard, par-72 **Springs Course** (250/347-6200 or 800/667-6444), is generally regarded as one of British Columbia's top 10 resort courses. It lies between the town and steep cliffs that descend to the Columbia River far below. Immaculately groomed fairways following the land's natural contours, near-perfect greens, and more than 70 bunkers filled with imported sand do little to take away from the surrounding mountainscape. Greens fees are $115 for 18 holes (discounted to $83 after 4 P.M.). The resort's second course, the **Resort Course** (250/347-6266 or 800/667-6444) is much shorter (5,306 yards from the tips), but tighter and still challenging. Greens fees are $65, discounted to $44 after 4 P.M.

Kootenay River Runners (250/347-9210

or 800/599-4399) offer white-water rafting trips for adult $64, child $49 for a half-day trip, adult $90, child $64 full-day. This company also offers a more relaxing evening float through the Columbia River Wetland in large and stable voyageur canoes. The floats depart daily at 5:30 P.M., and the cost is adult $49, child $35.

ACCOMMODATIONS

Radium, with a population of just 900, has more than 20 motels, an indication of its importance as a highway stop for overnight travelers. Motels along the access road to Kootenay National Park come alive with color through summer as each tries to outdo the others with floral landscaping. When booking any of these accommodations, ask about free passes to the hot pools.

Under $50

At the top end of the motel strip, closest to the national park, **((Misty River Lodge** (5036 Hwy. 93, 250/347-9912, www.radium

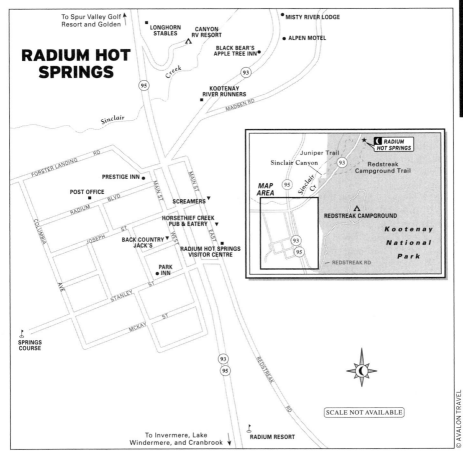

hostel.bc.ca) provides an excellent base for travelers on a budget. This converted motel has 11 beds in dormitories ($23 pp) and rooms that include a $55 room with shared bathroom and an $80 room that combines valley views with a full kitchen. Amenities include a communal kitchen, a lounge, and a big deck with even bigger views to the distant Purcell Mountains. You can also rent bikes and canoes.

$50-100

Kootenay Motel is along Highway 93, up the hill from the junction of Highway 95 (250/347-9490 or 877/908-2020). The rooms are nothing special (but air-conditioned) and rent from $70 s, $80 d, $10 extra for a kitchenette. Also on-site is a barbecue area and pleasant gazebo.

Up the hill a little and across the road is **Black Bear's Apple Tree Inn** (250/347-9565 or 800/350-1511, www.blackbearsinn.com; Apr.–Oct.), with a pleasant outdoor barbecue area; basic sleeping rooms are $80 s or d, or pay $90 for a room with a private balcony overlooking the valley.

Several older motels lie in the quiet residential streets west of highways 93/95. The best of these is the **Park Inn** (4873 Stanley St., 250/347-9582 or 800/858-1155, www.parkinn.bc.ca), which has similar rates to the rest of the bunch, features an indoor pool, and has a covered barbecue area. Standard rooms are $85 d, while those with kitchenettes start at $95 d.

Over $100

Along Highway 93 toward the park, the **Alpen Motel** (250/347-9823 or 888/788-3891, www.alpenmotel.com; $139–149) has the best and brightest flowers along the motel strip. It also has the nicest rooms, each of which are air-conditioned. Rates include passes to the hot springs.

Three kilometers (1.9 miles) south of town, **Radium Resort** (250/347-9311 or 800/667-6444, www.radiumresort.com) is surrounded by an 18-hole golf course and holds a wide

variety of facilities, including a health club, an indoor pool, a restaurant, and a lounge. Guest rooms overlook the golf course and are linked to the main lodge building by a covered walkway. Regular motel rooms range $160–190 s or d, while kitchen-equipped condos sleeping up to six people start at $240 per night. Check the website or call for specials (rooms are often sold for around $100, even in the middle of summer). Additionally, golf, ski, and spa packages lower rates considerably, especially before and after summer's peak season.

The modern **Prestige Inn** (7493 Main St. W., 250/347-2300 or 877/737-8443, www.prestigeinn.com; from $180 s or d) sits at the town's main intersection. Facilities include a fitness room, an indoor pool, a gift shop, spa services, an Italian restaurant, and a lounge bar.

Campgrounds

Within Kootenay National Park, but accessed from in town off Highway 93/95, is **Redstreak Campground** (see *Kootenay National Park*).

The closest commercial camping is at **Canyon RV Resort,** nestled in its own private valley immediately north of the Highway 93/95 junction (250/347-9564, www.canyonrv.com; Apr.–Oct.; $25–35 per site). Treed sites are spread along a pleasant creek, and all facilities are provided. **Spur Valley Golf Resort,** 18 kilometers (11 miles) north of Radium along Highway 95 (250/347-9822, www.spurvalley.com; $24–30) has 100 sites set around a large grassy area. Part of the resort is a full-length nine-hole golf course (across the road) and tennis courts.

Perfectly described by its name, **Dry Gulch Provincial Park** offers 26 sites four kilometers (2.5 miles) south of town. Typical of provincial park camping, each site has a picnic table and fire pit but no hookups, and reservations are not taken; $17 per night.

FOOD

The town of Radium Hot Springs holds several good choices for a food break. For breakfast, head to 🌙 **Springs Course** restaurant (Stanley St., 250/347-9311; Apr.–Oct. daily 7 A.M.–9 P.M.), at the golf course on the west side of the highway. The view from the deck, overlooking the Columbia River and Purcell Mountains, is nothing short of stunning. The food is good and remarkably inexpensive; in the morning, for example, an omelet with three fillings, hash browns, and toast is just $9. Lunch and dinner are also well priced, with a massive Caesar salad for $8 and main meals $12–21.50, including pastas for $14.

Back in town, **Back Country Jack's** (Main St. W., 250/347-0097; daily 11 A.M.–11 P.M.) is decorated with real antiques and real hard bench seats in private booths. There's a wide variety of platters to share, including Cowboy Caviar (nachos and baked beans) for $8.50 and a surprisingly good barbecued chicken soup ($5.50). For a main, the half chicken, half ribs, and all the extras for two ($26) is a good deal. Across the road, **Horsethief Creek Pub and Eatery** (Main St. E., 250/347-6400) serves up similar fare in more modern surroundings. Both places have a few outdoor tables.

Along the main drag is **Screamer's,** the place to hang out with an ice cream on a hot summer's afternoon. The ice cream here has been researched many times, most often when returning from camping trips in the Columbia Valley. Also along this strip is **Mountainside Market,** with an excellent choice of groceries and an in-house deli and butcher.

The restaurant at the **Radium Resort** (three km/1.9 miles south of town, 250/347-9311) caters mostly to golfers throughout the day and resort guests in the evening, but everybody is welcome. Enjoy lunch on the outdoor patio for around $10, or dine on sea bass smothered with a fruit-filled salsa for $24 in the evening. Buffets are offered on Wednesday and Friday nights from 6 P.M. ($22).

INFORMATION

On the east side of the highway, just south of the Highway 93/95 junction, is the **Radium**

Hot Springs Visitor Centre (250/347-9331 or 800/347-9704, www.radiumhotsprings.com). This building is also home to the national park information center. It's open weekdays year-round and daily in the busier summer months, 9 A.M.–7 P.M.

NORTH FROM RADIUM ALONG HIGHWAY 95

From Radium, most travelers head into Kootenay National Park, but another option is to continue north for 105 kilometers (65 miles) to Golden, from where the TransCanada Highway heads east, through Yoho National Park and across the Continental Divide to Banff National Park, which is in the neighboring province of Alberta. From this point it is possible to continue south and link up with Highway 93, making a 350-kilometer loop through the three parks.

Between Radium and Golden several small, historic towns are worthy of a stop. The first is **Edgewater,** where a farmers market is held each Saturday. Farther north is **Brisco.** Named for a member of the 1859 Palliser expedition, Brisco was founded on the mining industry and later grew as a regional center for surrounding farmland. Brisco General Store is a throwback to those earlier times, selling just about everything. Nearby **Spillimacheen,** meaning "white-water" to the area's native people, sits at the confluence of the Spillimacheen River and Bugaboo Creek.

Bugaboo Glacier Provincial Park

Inaccessible to all but the most experienced hikers and climbers, this vast tract of wilderness in the Purcell Mountains northwest of Radium Hot Springs is reached along a 45-kilometer (28-mile) gravel road west from Brisco. At road's end, a trail climbs steeply to a glaciated area that rivals the Canadian Rockies in beauty. Aside from the ice fields covering half the park, the most dominant features here are spectacular granite spires rising to elevations above 3,000 meters (9,840 feet). While the Purcell Mountains are an ancient range 1.5 billion years old, the spires formed as intrusions thrust skyward only about 70 million years ago. Since then, erosion has shaped them into today's granite needles towering over the surrounding ice fields.

The **Conrad Kain Hut,** a base for hikers and climbers wanting to explore the park, is a five-kilometer (3.1-mile) hike from the end of the road, up a valley carved by the retreating Bugaboo Glacier. The trail gains around 700 meters (2,300 feet) in elevation; allow at least two hours. Camping is also possible near the hut. No set trails lead from the hut to the spires or ice fields, and you'll need climbing and glacier-travel experience to continue deeper into the park.

The Bugaboos were the birthplace of heliskiing. It was here in the mid-1960s that Hans Gmoser used a helicopter to transport skiers into normally inaccessible areas. **Canadian Mountain Holidays** (403/762-7100 or 800/661-0252, www.cmhski.com), the company Gmoser founded, now has a lodge deep in the Bugaboos.

MOUNT ASSINIBOINE PROVINCIAL PARK

Named for one of the Canadian Rockies' most spectacular peaks, this 39,050-hectare (96,500-acre), roughly triangular park lies northeast of Radium Hot Springs, sandwiched between Kootenay National Park to the west and Banff National Park to the east. It's inaccessible by road; access is on foot or by helicopter. A haven for experienced hikers, the park offers alpine meadows, lakes, glaciers, and many peaks higher than 3,050 meters (10,000 feet) to explore. The park's highest peak, 3,618-meter (11,870-foot) Mount Assiniboine (seventh-highest in the Canadian Rockies), is known as the Matterhorn of the Rockies for its resemblance to that famous Swiss landmark. The striking peak can be seen from many points well outside the boundaries of the park, including Buller Pond in Kananaskis Country and Sunshine Village winter resort in Banff National Park.

Lake Magog is the destination of most park visitors. Here you'll find the park's only facilities and the trailheads for several interesting and varied day hikes. One of the most popular walks is along the Sunburst Valley/Nub Ridge Trail. From Lake Magog, small Sunburst Lake is reached in about 20 minutes, then the trail continues northwest a short distance to Cerulean Lake. From this lake's outlet, the trail descends slowly along the Mitchell River to a junction four kilometers (2.5 miles) from Lake Magog. Take the right fork, which climbs through a dense subalpine forest to Elizabeth Lake, nestled in the southern shadow of Nub Peak. From this point, instead of descending back to Cerulean Lake, take the Nub Ridge Trail, which climbs steadily for one kilometer (0.6 mile) to a magnificent viewpoint high above Lake Magog. From the viewpoint, it's just less than four kilometers (2.5 miles), downhill all the way, to the valley floor. The total length of this outing is 11 kilometers (6.8 miles), and as elevation gained is only just over 400 meters (1,310 feet), the trail can comfortably be completed in four hours.

Approaching the Park on Foot

Three trails provide access to **Lake Magog,** the park's largest body of water. The most popular comes in from the northeast, starting at Sunshine Village winter resort in Banff National Park and leading 29 kilometers (18 miles) via Citadel Pass to the lake. Not only is this trail spectacular, but the high elevation of the trailhead (2,100 meters/6,890 feet) makes for a relatively easy approach. Another approach is from the east, in Spray Valley Provincial Park (Kananaskis Country). The trailhead is at the southern end of Spray Lake; take the Mount Shark staging area turnoff 40 kilometers (25 miles) south of Canmore. By the time the trail has climbed the Bryant Creek drainage to 2,165-meter (7,100-foot) Assiniboine Pass, all elevation gain (450 meters/1,480 feet) has been made. At 27 kilometers (17 miles), this is the shortest approach, but its elevation gain is greater than the other two trails. The longest and least-used access is from Highway 93 at Simpson River in Kootenay National Park. This trail climbs the Simpson River and Surprise Creek drainages and crosses 2,270-meter (7,450-foot) Ferro Pass to the lake for a total length of 32 kilometers (20 miles).

The Easy Way In

If these long approaches put visiting the park out of your reach, there's one more option: you can fly in by helicopter from the Mount Shark Helipad, at the southern end of Spray Valley Provincial Park, 40 kilometers (25 miles) southwest of Canmore. Flights depart at 11:30 A.M. Wednesday, Friday, and Sunday and cost $145 per person each way, including an 18-kilogram (40-pound) per-person baggage limit. Although **Alpine Helicopters** operates the flights, all bookings must be made through the Mount Assiniboine Lodge (403/678-2883, www.assiniboinelodge.com; Mon.–Fri. 8 A.M.–2 P.M.).

If you're planning on hiking into the park, Alpine Helicopters will fly your gear in for $2 per pound (0.45 kilogram).

Mount Assiniboine Lodge

Getting to and staying at ◖ Mount Assiniboine Lodge isn't cheap, but the number of repeat guests is testament to an experience that you will never forget. The mountain scenery may take most of the kudos, but the lodge's congenial atmosphere, overseen by longtime hosts the Renners, makes the stay equally memorable. The main building holds six double rooms that share bathroom facilities, and a dining area where hearty meals (included in the rates) are served up communal-style. Scattered in the surrounding trees are six one-room cabins that sleep 2–5 people. Each has running water and uses propane to heat and light the space. Outhouses and showers are shared. The rate for lodge rooms and shared cabins is $235 per person; private cabin accommodations

range $295–395. Children 12 and under are $170. You can reach the lodge on foot (see *Approaching the Park on Foot*) or fly in with Alpine Helicopters from a helipad in Kananaskis Country (see *The Easy Way In*). The fare and departure days are the same as for campers; the only difference is that lodge guests depart at 1 P.M. If you decide to hike in (or out), the charge for luggage transfers is $2 per pound (0.45 kilogram).

The operating season is mid-June to the first weekend of October and then mid-February to mid-April for cross-country skiing. There is a minimum stay of two nights and a weight limit of 18 kilograms (40 pounds) on luggage for the flight. The lodge has no land-line phone; for reservations or information you will need to call 403/678-2883 (Mon.–Fri. 8 A.M.–2 P.M.) or check the website www .assiniboinelodge.com.

Campgrounds

Lake Magog is the park's main facility area, such as it is. A designated camping area on a low ridge above the lake's west shore provides a source of drinking water, pit toilets, and bear-proof food caches. Open fires are prohibited. Sites are $5 per person per night. No reservations are taken, but even those who visit frequently have told me they've never seen it full. Also at the lake are the **Naiset Huts,** where bunk beds cost $20 per person per night (book through Mount Assiniboine Lodge: 403/678-2883, www.assiniboine lodge.com; Mon.–Fri. 8 A.M.–2 P.M.). The cabins contain nothing more than bunk beds with mattresses, so you'll need a stove, food, a sleeping bag, and your own source of light.

Information

In addition to contacting the government agency responsible for the park (Ministry of Water, Land, and Air Protection, www .bcparks.ca), information and up-to-date trail conditions are available at park information centers located in Radium Hot Springs, Lake Louise, and Banff.

Kootenay National Park

Shaped like a lightning bolt, this narrow 140,600-hectare (347,400-acre) park lies northeast of Radium Hot Springs, bordered to the east by Banff National Park and Mount Assiniboine Provincial Park and to the north by Yoho National Park. Highway 93, extending for 94 kilometers (58 miles) through the park, provides spectacular mountain vistas. Along the route you'll find many short and easy interpretive hikes, scenic viewpoints, hot springs, picnic areas, and roadside interpretive exhibits. The park isn't particularly noted for its day-hiking opportunities, but backpacker destinations such as Kaufmann Lake and the Rockwall rival almost any other area in the Canadian Rockies.

Even if you never leave the highway, the scarred hillsides from wildfires that swept through the park in 2001 and 2003 will be obvious. The fires jumped the highway in places, burnt bridges and information booths, and forced the closure of some trails because of the danger of falling trees; check at local information centers for the latest updates.

Day-use areas, a gas station and lodge, and three campgrounds are the only roadside services inside the park; Radium Hot Springs, at the junction of Highways 93 and 95 (see *Radium Hot Springs and Vicinity*), is the park's main service center. The park is open year-round, although you should check road conditions in winter, when avalanche-control work and snowstorms can close Highway 93 for short periods of time.

DRIVING HIGHWAY 93

Climbing eastward from the town of Radium Hot Springs, Highway 93 (still known locally as the Banff–Windermere Highway) enters the boundary of Kootenay National Park at narrow **Sinclair Canyon,** a natural gateway to the wonders beyond. After squeezing through the canyon, the highway emerges at the actual springs that give the town of Radium Hot Springs its name.

◖ Radium Hot Springs

This soothing attraction (250/347-9485; summer daily 9 A.M.–11 P.M., the rest of the year daily noon–9 P.M.) lies inside the park but just three kilometers (1.9 miles) northeast of the town of the same name, which is outside the park boundary. It was discovered many centuries ago by the Kootenay people, who, like today's visitors, came to enjoy the odorless mineral water that gushes out of the Redwall Fault at 44°C (111°F).

Steep cliffs tower directly above the hot pool, whose waters are colored a milky blue by dissolved salts, which include calcium bicarbonate and sulfates of calcium, magnesium, and sodium. The hot pool (39°C, 97°F) is particularly stimulating in winter, when it's edged by snow and covered in steam—your head is almost cold in the chill air, but your submerged body melts into oblivion. Admission is adult $6.40,

Make time to stop for a soak at Radium Hot Springs.

© ANDREW HEMPSTEAD

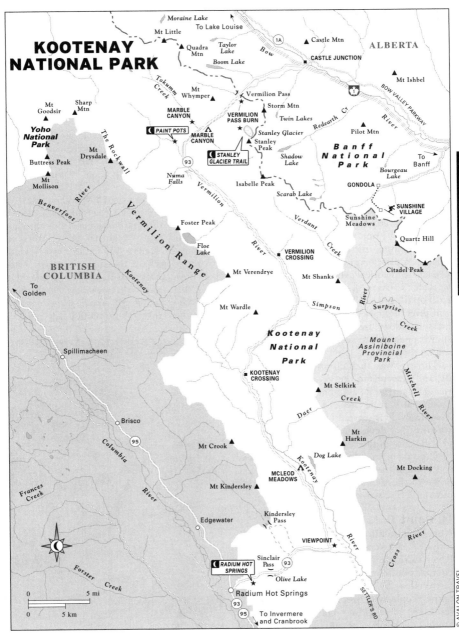

KOOTENAY NATIONAL PARK

senior and child $5.45. Towel and locker rentals are available, as are spa services. If you're camping at the park's Redstreak Campground, you can reach the complex on foot.

To Kootenay Valley

Leaving the hot springs, the road parallels Sinclair Creek, crests 1,486-meter (4,870-foot) Sinclair Pass, and passes small Olive Lake, which is ringed with bright yellow wildflowers in summer. At **Kootenay River Viewpoint** a splendid view overlooks the wild Kootenay River Valley below and the snowcapped mountains along the Continental Divide.

The highway then descends to the valley floor, passes two riverside picnic areas, and crosses the pretty Kootenay River at **Kootenay Crossing.** The official ribbon-cutting ceremony opening the Banff–Windermere Road took place here in 1923. Today you'll find a roadside historical exhibit, hiking trails, and a warden's station. As you cross the river and pass small, green Kootenay Pond, your eyes will revel in views of milky-green rivers, lush grassy meadows, tree-covered hills, and craggy, snowcapped peaks; keep your eyes peeled for mountain goats.

The highway then climbs over a low saddle and descends to the Vermilion River. On the descent, you'll pass a particularly nice picnic spot at Wardle Creek. Across the river, the mountainside is scarred black, the result of a wildfire that devastated over 4,000 hectares (9,900 acres) of forest in the summer of 2001. Left to take its natural course, the fire spread south along the Simpson River drainage and down to the Vermilion River, burning itself out as the first winter snow fell.

◖ Paint Pots

A scenic one-kilometer (0.6-mile) trail (20 minutes each way) leads over the Vermilion River to this unique natural wonder: three circular ponds stained red, orange, and mustard yellow by oxide-bearing springs. The native people, who believed that animal spirits resided in these springs, collected ocher from around the pools. They mixed it with animal fat or fish oil and then used it in ceremonial body and rock painting. The ocher had a spiritual association and was used in important rituals. Europeans, seeing an opportunity to "add to the growing economy of the nation," mined the ocher in the early 1900s and shipped it to paint manufacturers in Calgary.

Marble Canyon

Be sure to stop and take the enjoyable self-guided trail, one kilometer (0.6 mile) each way, that leads along this ice-carved, marble-streaked canyon. The walk takes only about 30 minutes or so, yet as one of several interpretive plaques says, it takes you back more than 500 million years.

From the parking lot, the trail follows a fault in the limestone and marble bedrock through Marble Canyon, which has been eroded to depths of 37 meters (130 feet) by fast-flowing Tokumm Creek. As the canyon narrows, water roars down through it in a series of falls. The trail ends at a splendid viewpoint where a natural rock arch spans a gorge. Marble Canyon is also the trailhead for the Kaufmann Lake Trail.

© ANDREW HEMPSTEAD

Marble Canyon

East to the Continental Divide

Well before the Paint Pots, you'll see entire hillsides burnt by a devastating fire in 2003. As the highway climbs, the burnt areas become more apparent. Started by lightning, the blaze began as a number of fires, which came together to cross the highway, burn entire watersheds, and extend high up surrounding mountains to the extent of the tree line.

Continuing eastward from Marble Canyon, Highway 93 climbs steadily to the **Vermilion Pass Burn.** Lightning started the fire that roared through this area in 1968, destroying thousands of hectares of trees. Lodgepole pine, which requires the heat of a fire to release its seeds, and fireweed were the first plant species to sprout up through the charred ground. From the highway everything seems pretty dead, but along the 0.8-kilometer (half-mile) **Fireweed Trail** you'll see the growth of a new forest on the floor of the old.

The burn area is immediately west of the Continental Divide, which the highway crosses at an elevation of 1,640 meters (5,380 feet). The divide marks the border between Kootenay National Park to the west and Banff National Park in Alberta to the east. From the divide, it's 11 kilometers (6.8 miles) to Highway 1, from which point the Town of Banff lies 29 kilometers (18 miles) southeast and Lake Louise lies 27 kilometers (16.8 miles) northwest.

HIKING

Some 200 kilometers (124 miles) of trails lace Kootenay National Park. Hiking opportunities range from short interpretive walks to challenging treks through remote backcountry. All trails start from Highway 93 on the valley floor, so you'll be facing a strenuous climb to reach the park's high alpine areas, especially those in the south. For this reason, many hikes require an overnight stay in the backcountry. The following hikes are listed from west to east. The best source of detailed hiking information is the *Canadian Rockies Trail Guide,* available for sale at both park information centers.

NATIONAL PARK PASSES

Permits are required for entry into all national parks of the Canadian Rockies. A **National Parks Day Pass** is adult $8.90, senior $7.65, child $4.45, to a maximum of $17.80 per vehicle. It is interchangeable between parks and is valid until 4 P.M. the day following its purchase.

An annual **National Parks of Canada Pass,** good for entry into national parks across Canada, is adult $62.40, senior $53.50, to a maximum of $123.80 per vehicle. Both types of pass are available at the entrances to Kootenay and Yoho National Parks, at all park information centers, and at campground fee stations. For more information, check online at the Parks Canada website (www.pc.gc.ca).

CANADIAN ROCKIES

Short Walks

The most popular short walks are to Paint Pots and through Marble Canyon. Just west of the Radium Hot Springs park gate is the **Juniper Trail,** an easy 3.2-kilometer (two-mile) loop. Named for the abundance of juniper along one section, this trail traverses a variety of terrain in a relatively short distance. You'll pass Sinclair Creek, an avalanche slope, and a lookout offering views of Windermere Valley and the Purcell Mountains. Beginning on the north side of the road just inside the park boundary, this trail rejoins the highway 1.5 kilometers (0.9 mile) farther into the park. There you can retrace your steps back to the start or return along the highway via Sinclair Canyon. Allow one hour.

◖ Stanley Glacier Trail

The Stanley Glacier Trail starts along Highway 93 seven kilometers (4.4 miles) west of the Continental Divide. Although this glacier is no more spectacular than those alongside the Icefields Parkway, the sense of achievement from traveling on foot makes this trail well worth the effort. From Highway 93, the trail crosses the

The view from the end of the Stanley Glacier Trail is inspiring.

© ANDREW HEMPSTEAD

CANADIAN ROCKIES

upper reaches of the Vermilion River, then begins a steady climb through an area burned by devastating fires in 1968. After two kilometers (1.3 miles), the trail levels off and begins winding through a massive U-shaped glacial valley, crossing Stanley Creek at the 2.4-kilometer (1.5-mile) mark. In open areas, fireweed, harebells, and yellow columbine carpet the ground. To the west, the sheer face of Mount Stanley rises 500 meters (1,640 feet) above the forest. The trail officially ends atop the crest of a moraine after 4.2 kilometers (2.6 miles), with distant views to Stanley Glacier. Allow 90 minutes to reach this point. It's possible (and worthwhile) to continue 1.3 kilometers (0.8 mile) to the tree-topped plateau visible higher up the valley. Surprisingly, once on the plateau, you'll find a gurgling stream, a healthy population of marmots, and incredible views west to Stanley Glacier and north back down the valley. Be especially careful on the return trip—it's extremely easy to lose your footing on the loose rock.

Other Long Hikes

For fit hikers only, sweeping mountain views from **Kindersley Summit** make up for the pain endured along the way. Starting from Highway 93 two kilometers (1.2 miles) west of Sinclair Pass, the trail gains 1,050 meters (3,445 feet) in 10 kilometers (6.2 miles); allow four hours one-way.

Overnight backcountry trips are somewhat limited, but the **Rockwall** is a classic. The 54-kilometer (33.6-mile), three-day trek focuses on a 30-kilometer-long (19-mile-long) escarpment that rises more than 1,000 meters (3,280 feet) from an alpine environment. Four different routes provide access to the spectacular feature; each begins along Highway 93 and traverses a steep valley to the Rockwall's base. Hikers will need to make arrangements for shuttle transportation between the beginning and end of this route—about 13 kilometers (eight miles) apart—or allow extra time to hike back. As with elsewhere in the park, all hikers spending the night in the backcountry must register and pick up a permit ($8 pp per night) at either of the park information centers.

ACCOMMODATIONS AND CAMPING

Accommodations within the park are limited, but the recommendations below are good ones. If you feel the need to be in town, see *Radium Hot Springs and Vicinity*, which has a dozen or so inexpensive motels.

$100-150

The only lodging in the heart of the park is **Kootenay Park Lodge** (403/762-9196, www.kootenayparklodge.com; mid-May–late Sept.), a cabin complex at Vermilion Crossing, 65 kilometers (40 miles) from Radium Hot Springs. Although no railway passes through the park, the 1923 lodge was one of many built by the Canadian Pacific Railway throughout the Canadian Rockies. It consists of a main lodge with a restaurant, 10 cabins, and a gas station/grocery store. The most basic cabins ($100 s or d) have a bathroom, small fridge, and coffeemaker, with rates rising to $120–145 for a cabin with cooking facilities and a fireplace. Utensil and cooking kits are $10 per day.

Over $150

The well-kept [Cross River Cabins (250/271-3296 or 877/659-7665; May–Sept.) have a real sense of privacy and of being away from the well-worn tourist path of Highway 93. And they are—tucked in a riverside setting 15 kilometers (9.3 miles) down Settler's Road, which branches off the highway 32 kilometers (20 miles) from Radium Hot Springs. The eight cabins are equipped with wood-burning fireplaces, log beds draped in down duvets, a toilet, and a sink. Showers are in the main building, along with the main lounge, cooking facilities (no meals supplied in the off-season), a dining area, and a deck. As you can imagine, the atmosphere is convivial, with the cabins attracting outdoorsy types who want to enjoy the Canadian Rockies in their natural state—without room service and fine dining. The cost is $225 s, $145 per person d, inclusive of meals. Children under $12 are $35 extra.

Nipika Mountain Resort (250/342-6516 or 877/647-4525, www.nipika.com) offers the same wilderness experience as the Cross River Cabins, and it's in the same vicinity—along Settler's Road, which branches off Highway 93 114 kilometers (71 miles) from Banff and 32 kilometers (20 miles) from Radium Hot Springs. Sleeping up to eight people, the cabins are larger than those at Cross River and have full en suite bathrooms and kitchens with wood-burning stoves ($170 s, $240 d). The cabins are modern but were constructed in a very traditional manner: The logs were milled on-site and construction is dovetail notching. Guests bring their own food and spend their days hiking, fishing, and wildlife watching. In winter, an extensive system of trails is groomed for cross-country skiing.

Campgrounds

The park's largest camping area is **Redstreak Campground** (mid-May–mid-Oct.), on a narrow plateau in the extreme southwest—vehicle access is from Highway 93/95 on the south side of Radium Hot Springs township. It holds 242 sites as well as showers and kitchen shelters. In summer, free slide shows and talks are presented by park naturalists five nights a week and typically feature topics such as wolves, bears, the park's human history, or the effects of fire. Trails lead from the campground to the hot springs, town, and a couple of lookouts. Unserviced sites are $26, hookups $32–36. Fire permits cost $6 per site per night. A percentage of sites can be reserved through the Parks Canada Campground Reservation Service (877/737-3783, www.pccamping.ca).

The park's two other campgrounds lie to the north of Radium Hot Springs along Highway 93. Both offer fewer facilities (no hookups or showers). The larger of the two is **McLeod Meadows Campground,** beside the Kootenay River 27 kilometers (16.8 miles) from Radium Hot Springs. Facilities include flush toilets, kitchen shelters, and a fire pit and picnic table at each of the 98 sites. **Marble Canyon,** across the highway from the natural attraction of the same name, offers 61 sites and similar facilities. Both are open mid-May to early September, and all sites cost $21. No reservations are taken in national park campgrounds, but for information, contact the park headquarters at 250/347-9615.

INFORMATION

Kootenay Park Information Centre (250/347-9615; summer daily 9 A.M.–7 P.M., the rest of the year weekdays only 9 A.M.–5 P.M.) is outside the park in the town of Radium Hot Springs, at the base of the access road to Redstreak Campground. Here you can collect a free map with hiking trail descriptions, find out about trail closures and campsite availability, get the weather forecast, browse through a gift shop, buy park passes and fishing licenses, and register for overnight backcountry trips.

The other source of park information is at **Kootenay Park Lodge,** at Vermilion Crossing (Apr.–May Fri.–Sun. 11 A.M.–6 P.M., June–Sept. daily 10 A.M.–7 P.M., and the early part of Oct. Fri.–Sun. 11 A.M.–6 P.M.).

CANADIAN ROCKIES

Yoho National Park

Yoho, a Cree word of amazement, is a fitting name for this 131,300-hectare (324,450-acre) national park on the western slopes of the Canadian Rockies. East of Golden, the Trans-Canada Highway bisects the park. Kootenay National Park lies immediately to the south, while Banff National Park (Alberta) borders Yoho to the east. The park's only watershed is that of the **Kicking Horse River,** which is fed by the Wapta and Waputik Icefields. The Kicking Horse, wide and braided for much of its course through the park, flows westward, joining the mighty Columbia River at Golden.

Yoho is the smallest of the four contiguous Canadian Rockies national parks, but its wild and rugged landscape holds spectacular waterfalls, extensive ice fields, a lake to rival those in Banff, and one of the world's most intriguing fossil beds. In addition, you'll find some of the finest hiking in all of Canada on the park's 300-kilometer (186-mile) trail system.

Within the park are four lodges, four campgrounds, and the small railway town of **Field,** offering basic services. The park is open year-round, although road conditions in winter can be treacherous, and occasional closures occur on Kicking Horse Pass. The road out to Takakkaw Falls is closed through winter, and it often doesn't reopen until mid-June.

ROAD-ACCESSIBLE SIGHTS

As with all other parks of the Canadian Rockies, you don't need to travel deep into the backcountry to view the most spectacular features—many

BURGESS SHALE

High on the rocky slopes above Mount Field is a layer of sedimentary rock known as the Burgess Shale, which contains what are considered to be the world's finest fossils from the Cambrian Period. The site is famous worldwide because it has unraveled the mysteries of a major stage of evolution.

In 1909, Smithsonian Institute paleontologist Charles Walcott was leading a pack train along the west slope of Mount Field, on the opposite side of the valley from the newly completed Spiral Tunnel, when he stumbled across these fossil beds. Encased in the shale, the fossils here are of marine invertebrates about 510 million years old. Generally, fossils are the remains of vertebrates, but at this site some freak event – probably a mudslide – suddenly buried thousands of soft-bodied animals (invertebrates), preserving them by keeping out the oxygen that would have decayed their delicate bodies. Walcott excavated an estimated 65,000 specimens from the site. Today paleontologists continue to uncover perfectly preserved fossils here – albeit in far fewer numbers than in Walcott's day. They've

also uncovered additional fossil beds, similar in makeup and age, across the valley, on the north face of Mount Stephen.

Protected by UNESCO as a World Heritage Site, the two research areas are open only to those accompanied by a licensed guide. The **Burgess Shale Geoscience Foundation** (call 250/343-6006 or 800/343-3006 Mon.-Fri. 10 A.M.-3:30 P.M., www.burgess-shale.bc.ca) guides trips to both sites between July and mid-September. The access to **Burgess Shale (Walcott's Quarry)** is along a strenuous 10-kilometer (6.2-mile) each way trail that gains 760 meters (2,500 feet) in elevation. Trips leave Friday-Monday at 8 A.M. from the trading post at the Field intersection, returning around 6:30 P.M.; adult $69, child under 12 $16. Trips to the **Mount Stephen Fossil Beds** depart Saturday and Sunday at 8:30 A.M., returning at around 4:30 P.M.; adult $48, child $16. The trail to the Mount Stephen beds gains 780 meters (2,560 feet) of elevation in three kilometers (1.9 miles). The trails to both sites are unrelenting in their elevation gain – you must be fit to hike them. Reservations are a must.

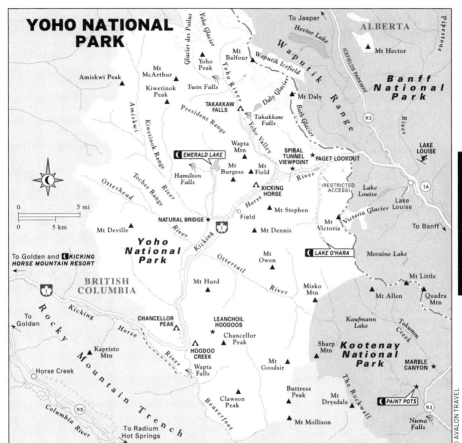

YOHO NATIONAL PARK

To Jasper

ALBERTA

Banff National Park

Yoho National Park

BRITISH COLUMBIA

To Golden and **KICKING HORSE MOUNTAIN RESORT**

Kootenay National Park

are visible from the roadside. The following sights are listed from east to west, starting at the park boundary (the Continental Divide).

Spiral Tunnel Viewpoint

The joy that Canadian Pacific Railway president William Van Horne felt upon completion of his transcontinental rail line in 1886 was tempered by massive problems along a stretch of line west of Kicking Horse Pass. Big Hill was less than five kilometers (3.1 miles) long, but its gradient was so steep that runaway trains, crashes, and other disasters

were common. A trail from Kicking Horse Campground takes you past the remains of one of those doomed trains. Nearly 25 years after the line opened, railway engineers and builders finally solved the problem. By building two spiral tunnels down through two kilometers (1.2 miles) of solid rock to the valley floor, they lessened the grade dramatically and the terrors came to an end. Today the TransCanada Highway follows the original railbed. Along the way is a viewpoint with interpretive displays telling the fascinating story of Big Hill.

TAKAKKAW FALLS

The torrent, issuing from an icy cavern, rushes tempestuously down a deep, winding chasm till it gains the verge of the unbroken cliff, leaps forth in sudden wildness for a hundred and fifty feet, and then in a stupendous column of pure white sparkling water, broken by giant jets descending rocket-like and wreathed in volumed spray, dashes upon the rocks almost a thousand feet below, and, breaking into a milky series of cascading rushes for five hundred feet more, swirls into the swift current of the Yoho River.

– Sir James Outram, *In the Heart of the Canadian Rockies*

Much discussion is made of which is Canada's highest waterfall. Della Falls, on Vancouver Island, also in British Columbia, is 440 meters (1,440 feet), but this drop is broken by a ledge. Takakkaw Falls is considerably lower, at 254 meters (830 feet), but the drop is unbroken, which, officially, makes it Canada's highest. There is one thing of which there is no doubt: Takakkaw Falls will leave you breathless, much as it did famous alpinist Sir James Outram and everyone who has viewed the spectacle since.

© ANDREW HEMPSTEAD

Yoho Valley

Fed by the Wapta Icefield in the far north of the park, the **Yoho River** flows through this spectacularly narrow valley, dropping more than 200 meters (660 feet) in the last kilometer before its confluence with the Kicking Horse River. The road leading up the valley passes the park's main campground, climbs a *very* tight series of switchbacks (watch for buses reversing through the middle section), and emerges at **Upper Spiral Tunnel Viewpoint,** which offers a different perspective on the aforementioned tunnel. A further 400 meters (0.25 mile) along the road is a pullout for viewing the confluence of the Yoho and Kicking Horse Rivers—a particularly impressive sight, as the former is glacier-fed and therefore silty, while the latter is lake-fed and clear.

Yoho Valley Road ends 14 kilometers (8.7 miles) from the main highway at **Takakkaw Falls,** the most impressive waterfall in the Canadian Rockies. The falls are fed by the Daly and Des Poilus Glaciers of the Waputik Icefield, which straddles the Continental Divide. Its name meaning "wonderful" in the language of the Cree, Takakkaw tumbles 254 meters (830 feet) over a sheer rock wall at the lip of the Yoho Valley, creating a spray bedecked by rainbows. It can be seen from the parking lot, but it's well worth the easy 10-minute stroll over the Yoho River to appreciate the sight in all its glory.

Natural Bridge

Three kilometers (1.9 miles) west of Field is the turnoff to famous Emerald Lake. On your way out to the lake, you pass another intriguing sight. At Natural Bridge, two kilometers (1.2 miles) down the road, the Kicking Horse River has worn a narrow hole through a limestone wall, creating a bridge. Over time, the bridge will collapse and, well, it won't be such an intriguing sight anymore. A trail leads to several viewpoints—try to avoid the urge to join the foolish folks clambering over the top of the bridge.

Emerald Lake

◖ Emerald Lake

Outfitter Tom Wilson stumbled on stunning Emerald Lake while guiding Major A. B. Rogers through the Kicking Horse River Valley in 1881. He was led to the lake by his horse, which had been purchased from natives. He later surmised that the horse had been accustomed to traveling up to the lake, meaning that the horse's former owners must have known about the lake before the Europeans arrived.

One of the jewels of the Canadian Rockies, the beautiful lake is surrounded by a forest of Engelmann spruce, as well as many peaks more than 3,000 meters (9,840 feet) high. It is covered in ice most of the year but comes alive with activity for a few short months in summer. In addition to hiking (see *Other Hiking in Yoho*), you can paddle across the lake by renting a canoe from **Emerald Lake Canoe Rentals** (250/343-6000; June–Sept. 9 A.M.– 8 P.M.; $25 per hour, $40 for two hours, or $70 all day). **Emerald Lake Stables,** along the lake access road (250/344-8982), rents

horses through the mid-June to early September season. A one-hour trip along the west shore of Emerald Lake costs $40 per person. Two-hour rides are $75, three-hour rides $110, four-hour rides $140, and all-day rides with lunch go for $185. **Emerald Lake Lodge** is the grandest of Yoho's accommodations, offering a restaurant, café, lounge, and recreation facilities for both guests and nonguests (see *Accommodations and Camping*).

◖ LAKE O'HARA

Nestled in a high bowl of lush alpine meadows, Lake O'Hara, 11 kilometers (6.8 miles) from the nearest public road, is surrounded by dozens of smaller alpine lakes and framed by spectacular peaks permanently mantled in snow. As if that weren't enough, the entire area is webbed by a network of hiking trails established over the last 90 years by luminaries such as Lawrence Grassi. Trails radiate from the lake in all directions; the longest is just 7.5 kilometers (4.7 miles), making Lake O'Hara an especially fine hub for day hiking. What makes this

golden larch near Lake O'Hara

© ANDREW HEMPSTEAD

destination all the more special is that a quota system limits the number of visitors.

Book the Bus

It's possible to walk to Lake O'Hara, but most visitors take the shuttle bus along a road closed to the public. The departure point is a signed parking lot 15 kilometers (9.3 miles) east of Field and three kilometers (1.9 miles) west of the Continental Divide. Buses for day visitors depart between mid-June and early October at 8:30 A.M. and 10:30 A.M., returning at 4:30 P.M. and 6:30 P.M. To book a seat, call the dedicated reservations line (250/343-6433). Reservations are taken up to three months in advance, but as numbers are limited, you will need to call *exactly* three months prior to get a seat; even then, call as early in the day as possible. The reservation fee is $12 per booking and the bus fare is $15 per person round-trip. The procedure is simple enough, but to be assured of a seat, it's important you get it right: for example, to visit on September 30 (when the larch are at their colorful peak), start dialing at 8 A.M. on June 30

(with a credit card ready). Six seats per day are set aside for those who haven't made advance reservations. They are allotted via the reservation phone number on a first-come, first-served basis the day prior. No-shows are filled on a standby basis by folks waiting around at the parking lot on the day of departure (generally, arrive around 7 A.M., head to the covered shelter, and you'll be the first in line). You have the best chance of snagging a seat on the 8:30 A.M. bus, especially if the weather is bad.

All times—bus departures and reservation center hours—are mountain standard time.

Other Considerations

After the 20-minute bus trip to the lake, day hikers are dropped off at **Le Relais,** a homely log shelter where books and maps are sold, including the recommended Gem Trek *Lake Louise and Yoho* map. Hot drinks and light snacks are served—something to look forward to at the end of the day, as this is also the afternoon meeting place for the return trip (no reservations necessary).

Several overnight options are available at the lake—including a lodge, a campground, and a rustic hut—but each should be booked well in advance (see *Accommodations and Camping*).

Hiking

A basic trail map is available at Le Relais, or invest in the *Canadian Rockies Trail Guide,* the premier hiking guide to the region (pick up a copy from the park information center in Field).

The most obvious trail is the **Lake O'Hara Shoreline,** a 2.8-kilometer (1.7-mile) loop that can be completed in 40 minutes. Starting from the warden's cabin across from Le Relais, most visitors use sections of this circuit to access the other trails detailed here, but it is an enjoyable walk in its own right, especially in the evening.

Three kilometers (1.9 miles) each way, the trail to **Lake Oesa** gains 240 meters (790 feet) of elevation before reaching a small aqua-colored lake surrounded by talus slopes—one of the area's gems. The Continental Divide peaks of Mount Victoria (3,464 meters/11,365 feet) and Mount Lefroy (3,423 meters/11,230 feet) rise dramatically behind the lake.

One of my favorite hikes in all of the Canadian Rockies is the 5.9-kilometer (3.7-mile) **Opabin Plateau Circuit,** especially in late September, when larches have turned a golden shade of yellow. Separated from Lake Oesa by 2,848-meter (9,344-foot) Mount Yukness, this plateau high above the tree line is dotted with small lakes. Two trails lead up to the plateau, which itself is laced with trails. The most direct route is the Opabin Plateau West Circuit, which branches right from the Shoreline Trail 300 meters (0.2 mile) beyond Lake O'Hara Lodge. It then passes Mary Lake, climbs steeply, and reaches the plateau in a little less than two kilometers (1.2 miles). Opabin Prospect is an excellent lookout along the edge of the plateau. From this point, take the right fork to continue to the head of the Cirque and Opabin Lake. This section of trail passes through a lightly forested area of larch that comes alive with color in late September.

Lake McArthur is the largest and (in my opinion) most stunning body of water in the Lake O'Hara area. Beginning from behind Le Relais, the 3.5-kilometer (2.2-mile) access trail passes Schäffer Lake after 1.6 kilometers (one mile). At a junction beyond that lake, take the left fork, which climbs steeply for 800 meters (0.5 mile) then levels out and traverses a narrow ledge before entering the Lake McArthur Cirque. (Stay high, even if trails descending into the McArthur Valley look like they offer an easier approach.) After leveling off, the trail enters the alpine and quickly reaches its maximum elevation and the first views of Lake McArthur. Backed by Mount Biddle and the Biddle Glacier, the deep-blue lake and colorful alpine meadows are an unforgettable panorama.

OTHER HIKING IN YOHO
Emerald Lake

One of the easiest yet most enjoyable walks in Yoho is the **Emerald Lake Loop,** which, as the name suggests, encircles Emerald Lake. The best views are from the western shoreline, where a massive avalanche has cleared away the forest of Engelmann spruce. Across the lake from this point, Mount Burgess can be seen rising an impressive 2,599 meters (8,530 feet). Traveling in a clockwise direction beyond the avalanche slope, and at the 2.2-kilometer (1.4-mile) mark, a small bridge is crossed. Views from this point extend back across the Emerald Lake Lodge to the Ottertail Range. Beyond the lake's inlet, the vegetation changes dramatically. A lush forest of towering western red cedar creates a canopy, protecting moss-covered fallen trees, thimbleberry, and bunchberry extending to the water's edge. Just over one kilometer (0.6 mile) from the bridge, the trail divides: The left fork leads back to the parking lot via a small forest-encircled pond, while the path straight ahead passes through the grounds of Emerald Lake Lodge. Allow 90 minutes for the 5.2-kilometer (3.2-mile) circuit. From along the loop, a trail climbs steadily to **Emerald Basin,** which is reached in 4.5

Elk are a common sight in Yoho National Park.

© ANDREW HEMPSTEAD

kilometers (2.8 miles). The most impressive sight awaiting you there is the south wall of the President Range, towering 800 vertical meters (2,630 feet) above. Allow three to four hours for the round-trip.

From the parking lot at Emerald Lake, it's just 800 meters (0.5 miles) to **Hamilton Falls.** It's an easy walk through a forest of Engelmann spruce and subalpine fir to a viewpoint at the base of the falls. A little farther along, the trail begins switchbacking steeply and offers even better views of the cascade. The trail continues beyond the waterfall to **Hamilton Lake,** which lies in a small glacial cirque a steep 880 vertical meters (2,890 feet) above Emerald Lake. Total distance from Emerald Lake to Hamilton Lake is 5.5 kilometers (3.4 miles) one-way; allow two to three hours each way.

Yoho Valley

The valley for which the park is named lies north of the TransCanada Highway. As well as the sights discussed previously, it provides many fine opportunities for serious day

hikers to get off the beaten track. The following day hikes begin from different trailheads near the end of the road up Yoho Valley. In each case, leave your vehicle in the Takakkaw Falls parking lot.

One of the most spectacular day hikes in the Canadian Rockies is the **Iceline Trail.** Gaining 690 meters (2,260 feet) of elevation over 6.4 kilometers (four miles), it's a relatively strenuous hike, one that you should dedicate a full day to. The length given is from Whiskey Jack Hostel (across from the Takakkaw parking lot) to the highest point along the trail, 2,250 meters (7,380 feet). From the hostel, the trail begins a steep and steady one-kilometer (0.6-mile) climb to a point where three options present themselves: the Iceline Trail is to the right, Yoho Pass is straight ahead, and Hidden Lakes is a 300-meter (0.2-mile) detour to the left. The Iceline Trail option now enters its highlight: a four-kilometer (2.5-mile) traverse of a moraine below Emerald Glacier. Views across the valley improve as the trail climbs. Many day hikers return from this point, although officially the trail continues into Little Yoho River Valley. Another option is to continue beyond Celeste Lake and loop back to Takakkaw Falls and the original trailhead, a total distance of 18 kilometers (11.2 miles). The trail to **Yoho Pass** can be combined with the Iceline. It leads 3.7 kilometers (2.3 miles) to picturesque, spruce-encircled Yoho Lake, then continues another easy one kilometer (0.6 mile) to the pass. The pass is below the tree line, so views are limited, but from this point it's 5.5 kilometers (3.4 miles) and an elevation loss of 530 meters (1,740 feet) down to Emerald Lake, or 2.4 kilometers (1.5 miles) north, with little elevation gain or loss, to an intersection with the Iceline Trail.

ACCOMMODATIONS AND CAMPING
Under $50
In downtown Field, **Fireweed Hostel** (313 Stephen Ave., 250/343-6441 or 877/343-6999, www.fireweedhostel.com; $35 pp) opened in 2007. It offers modern dorm rooms, complete with solid pine beds and pillow-top mattresses, hardwood floors, and tiled bathrooms. The mountain-rustic theme continues through to a communal living room centered on a fireplace. The reception is staffed 9 A.M.–noon and 4–9 P.M.

Hostelling International operates **HI-Whiskey Jack Wilderness Hostel** (403/760-7580 or 866/762-4122, www.hihostels.ca; mid-June–Sept.) in a meadow opposite Takakkaw Falls. Basic dormitory accommodation is provided for up to 27 guests, who have use of a communal kitchen and showers. Members of Hostelling International pay $21 per night, nonmembers $25. Check-in is 5–11 P.M.

$100-150
The streets of Field are lined with private homes offering reasonably priced overnight accommodations in rooms of varying privacy and standards. One of the better choices is the **Alpine Guesthouse** (313 2nd Ave., 250/343-6878 or 866/634-5665, www.alpineguesthouse

.ca), with a two-bedroom suite—complete with a kitchen, cable TV, outdoor patio, and private entrance—for $180 per night ($85 in low season). Like everywhere else in Field, it's within walking distance of the general store.

Also in Field is simple yet elegant **Kicking Horse Lodge** (100 Centre St., 250/343-6303 or 800/659-4944, www.kickinghorselodge .net), which offers 14 well-furnished motel-like rooms, a large comfortable lounge, and a restaurant (open in summer only). In July and August, rates are $145–180 s or d, discounted as low as $70 the rest of the year.

Over $150
€ Emerald Lake Lodge (403/410-7417 or 800/663-6336, www.crmr.com) is a grand, luxury-class accommodation along the southern shore of one of Canada's most magnificent lakes. Guests lap up the luxury of richly decorated duplex-style units and freestanding cabins. Each spacious unit is outfitted in an earthy heritage theme and has a wood-burning fireplace, private balcony, luxurious bathroom, comfortable bed topped by a plush duvet, and in-room coffee. Other lodge amenities include a hot tub and sauna, swimming pool, restaurant, lounge, and café. Guests can also go horseback riding or go boating and fishing on Emerald Lake. Rack rates start at $480 s or d, but book online for as low as $330 in summer and as low as $150 in November.

Comprising beautiful log cabins set around a timber-frame main lodge alongside the Kicking Horse River, the **€ Cathedral Mountain Lodge** complex (250/343-6442, www.cathedral mountain.com; mid-May–Sept.; $305–625 s or d) lies one kilometer (0.6 mile) along Yoho Valley Road from the TransCanada Highway. Many cabins have log fireplaces, and all have magnificent log beds, super-comfortable mattresses, private balconies, and an interior stylishly outfitted with mountain-themed antiques. Rates include a light breakfast, and dinner, with the emphasis on perfectly presented regional cuisine, is served à la carte in the main lodge.

Spending a night at **Lake O'Hara Lodge**

(250/343-6418, www.lakeohara.com) is a special experience, and one that draws familiar faces year after year. On a practical level, it allows hikers not equipped for overnight camping the opportunity to explore one of the finest hiking destinations in all of the Canadian Rockies at their leisure. The 15 cabins, each with a private bathroom, are spread around the lakeshore, while within the main lodge are eight rooms, most of which are twins and share bathrooms. Rates of $380 s, $485 d for a room in the main lodge (shared bathrooms) and $675–710 d for a lakeside cabin include all meals, taxes, gratuities, and transportation mid-June to September. Guests are transported to the lodge, which is 13 kilometers (eight miles) from Highway 1, by shuttle bus from a parking lot three kilometers (1.9 miles) west of the Continental Divide and 15 kilometers (nine miles) east of Field. Between February and April, the eight rooms in the main lodge are available for cross-country skiers for $275 per person, inclusive of meals and ski tours.

Campgrounds

Unlike other national parks, no reservations are taken for camping in Yoho's vehicle-accessible campgrounds. All sites have a picnic table and fire ring, with a fire permit costing $6 (includes firewood). When all campgrounds are filled, campers will be directed to overflow areas.

The park's main camping area is **Kicking Horse Campground** (mid-May–mid-Oct.; $26 per site), five kilometers (3.1 miles) northeast of Field along the road to Takakkaw Falls. Facilities include coin showers ($1), flush toilets, and kitchen shelters. Back toward the TransCanada Highway, **Monarch Campground** ($16.80 per site) offers more-limited facilities and less-private sites; **Hoodoo Creek Campground,** along the TransCanada Highway 23 kilometers (14 miles) southwest of Field, provides 106 private sites among the trees for $20.80 per vehicle. Facilities include flush toilets, hot water, kitchen shelters, and an interpretive program.

At the end of the road up the Yoho Valley, **Takakkaw Falls Campground** (July–mid-Sept.; $16.80) is designed for tent campers only. Park at the end of the road and load up the carts with your gear for a pleasant 400-meter (0.2-mile) walk along the valley floor. No showers are provided, and the only facilities are pit toilets and picnic tables.

Just below **Lake O'Hara,** alongside the access road, is a delightful little campground surrounded by some of the region's finest hiking. Each of 30 sites has a tent pad, fire pit, and picnic table, while other facilities include pit toilets, two kitchen shelters with woodstoves, and bear-proof food caches. Reservations for sites are made in conjunction with the bus trip along the restricted-access road from Highway 1 to Lake O'Hara; for bus information see *Lake O'Hara.* Even though access is aboard a bus, you should treat the trip as one into the backcountry; passengers are limited to one large or two small bags, and no coolers or fold-up chairs are permitted on board the shuttle. Camping is $9.90 per person per night, the bus costs $15 per person round-trip, and the reservation fee is $12 per booking.

FOOD

In downtown Field, **Truffle Pigs Café** (318 Stephen St., 250/343-6462) is one of those unexpected finds that make traveling such a joy. It's at the back of a general store, beyond racks of food basics and rental movies, with seating in a section off to the side or outside on a small patio. The best of the breakfast and lunch dishes are described on a massive blackboard, with freshly baked cookies and locally brewed coffee complementing sandwiches made to order from the glass-fronted deli. In the evening this place really shines, with dishes as adventurous as the spinach maple-pecan salad ($13.50) and as simple as an Alberta-raised buffalo rib-eye steak served with a port-based au jus and a baked potato ($28). It's open in summer daily 7:30 A.M.–10 P.M.; the rest of the year it's also open daily, but dinner is served only Friday and Saturday.

Across the road, the **Kicking Horse Lodge** (250/343-6303; daily 8–11 A.M., noon–2:30 P.M., and 5–9 P.M.) has a small restaurant that has views over the valley floor. It offers a short but varied dinner menu featuring dishes of wide-ranging appeal (including a delicious herb-crusted pork tenderloin smothered in a mango apple chutney) as well as a daily special and a soup of the day, both of which actually are *special.*

Overlooking an arm of Emerald Lake, **Cilantro on the Lake** (250/343-6321; summer only) is a casual café featuring magnificent views from tables inside an open-fronted, log chalet-style building or out on the lakefront deck. The menu is varied—you can sit and sip a coffee or have a full lunch or dinner. Starters—such as thick and creamy corn and potato chowder—are all less than $12, while mains, such as an extravagantly rich beef tenderloin served with a lobster and mushroom cream sauce, range $25–37. The café is part of the **Emerald Lake Lodge** resort complex, which also includes a more formal but historically attractive dining room, where dinner dishes such as grilled caribou with huckleberry sauce ($35) are served daily from 6 P.M. This restaurant is open year-round for breakfast and lunch also, or choose the more casual lounge bar and sink into one of the comfy couches with an abbreviated but still appealing menu.

INFORMATION

The main source of information about the park is the **Field Visitor Centre** on the TransCanada Highway at Field (250/343-6783; summer daily 9 A.M.–7 P.M., the rest of the year daily 9 A.M.–4 P.M.). Inside you'll find helpful staff, information boards, and interpretive panels. This is also the place to pick up backcountry camping permits, buy topographical maps, and find out schedules for campground interpretive programs. For more information, contact Yoho National Park (P.O. Box 99, Field, BC V0A 1G0, www.pc.gc.ca). For park road conditions, call 403/762-1450; for avalanche reports, call 403/762-1460.

Golden

From the western boundary of Yoho National Park, the TransCanada Highway meanders down the beautiful Kicking Horse River Valley to the town of Golden (pop. 5,000), at the confluence of the Kicking Horse and Columbia Rivers. As well as being a destination in itself, Golden makes a good central base for exploring the region or as an overnight stop on a tour through the Canadian Rockies that takes in the national parks on the western side of the Continental Divide.

Although Golden is an industrial town through and through—with local mines and huge logging operations that include a lumber mill that opened in 1999—it's also gaining a reputation for local outdoor-recreation opportunities, most notably for its new four-season resort and white-water rafting trips down the Kicking Horse River.

SIGHTS AND RECREATION

Take Highway 95 off the TransCanada Highway, and you'll find yourself in the old section of town, a world away from the commercial strip along the main highway. There's not really much to see in town, although you may want to check out the small museum on 14th Street. The 8.8-kilometer (5.5-mile) **Rotary Loop** is a paved walking and biking trail that leads across the river from downtown via an impressive timber-frame pedestrian bridge, then upstream across Highway 95 (10th Ave. S.) to the campground.

The **Columbia River Wetland** (see *Radium Hot Springs and Vicinity*) extends as far north as Golden. One easily accessible point of the wetlands is **Reflection Lake,** on the southern outskirts of Golden. A small shelter provides a telescope for viewing the abundant birdlife.

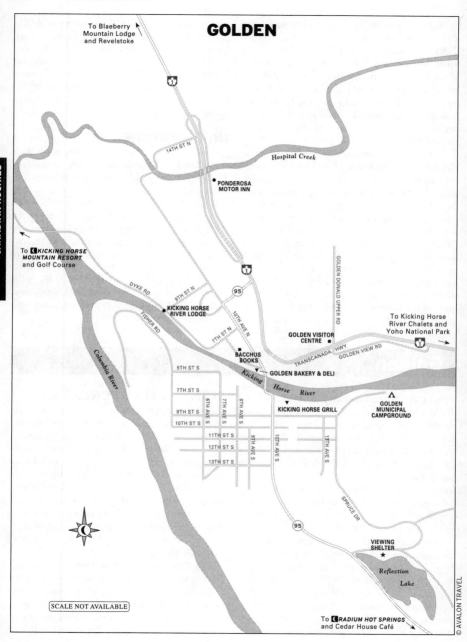

GOLDEN

To Blaeberry
Mountain Lodge
and Revelstoke

14TH ST N

Hospital Creek

● PONDEROSA
MOTOR INN

To **KICKING HORSE
MOUNTAIN RESORT**
and Golf Course

DYKE RD

9TH ST N

FISHER RD

95

■ KICKING HORSE
RIVER LODGE

7TH ST N

10TH AVE N

GOLDEN DONALD UPPER RD

To Kicking Horse
River Chalets and
Yoho National Park

■ GOLDEN VISITOR
CENTRE

TRANSCANADA HWY   GOLDEN VIEW RD

Columbia River

5TH ST S

7TH ST S

■ BACCHUS
BOOKS

▼ GOLDEN BAKERY & DELI

Kicking   Horse   River

9TH ST S

6TH AVE S

7TH AVE S

8TH AVE S

▼ KICKING HORSE GRILL

⌂ GOLDEN
MUNICIPAL
CAMPGROUND

10TH ST S

11TH ST S

9TH AVE S

10TH AVE S

13TH AVE S

12TH ST S

13TH ST S

SPRUCE DR

95

VIEWING
SHELTER
★

Reflection
Lake

To **RADIUM HOT SPRINGS**
and Cedar House Café

SCALE NOT AVAILABLE

© ANDREW HEMPSTEAD

Take a gondola to the top of Kicking Horse Mountain Resort to enjoy the sublime view.

Kicking Horse Mountain Resort

Summer or winter, as you descend into Golden from Yoho National Park, it's easy to make out the ski slopes of Kicking Horse Mountain Resort (250/439-5400 or 866/754-5425, www.kickinghorseresort.com) across the valley. The eight-person detachable Golden Eagle Express gondola transports visitors high into the alpine mid-June through September in just 18 minutes. The 360-degree panorama at the summit is equal to any other accessible point in the Canadian Rockies, with the Purcell Mountains immediately to the west and the Columbia Valley laid out below. Graded hiking trails lead from the upper terminal through a fragile, treeless environment, while mountain bikers revel in a challenging descent in excess of 1,000 meters (3,280 feet). A single gondola ride is adult $24, senior $21, child $12. A better deal is the SkyLunch combo ticket for adult $42, senior $36, child $18. A Sunset Dinner, also inclusive of the gondola ride, is adult $50, senior $45, child $20. Mountain bikers pay $32 for a single ride while a rent-and-ride package costs $100 for the full day, including a full-suspension bike. The gondola operates through the warmer months daily 10 A.M.–6:30 P.M.

With a vertical rise of 1,260 meters (4,130 feet), 45 percent of terrain designated for experts, lots of dry powder snow, and minimal crowds, Kicking Horse has developed a big reputation since opening for the 2000–2001 winter season. In addition to the 3.5-kilometer-long (2.2-mile-long) gondola ride, four other lifts transport skiers and boarders to hidden bowls and to a high point of 2,450 meters (8,040 feet), giving the resort North America's second-highest vertical rise (1,260 meters/4,135 feet). Lifts operate mid-December to early April, and tickets are adult $64, senior $54, child $32. Facilities in the base lodge include rentals, a cafeteria, and a ski school.

To get to Kicking Horse, follow the signs from Highway 1 into town and take 7th Street North west from 10th Avenue North; it's over the Columbia River and 13 kilometers (eight miles) uphill from this intersection.

White-Water Rafting

Anyone looking for white-water rafting action will want to run the Kicking Horse River. The rafting season runs mid-May to mid-September, with river levels at their highest in late June. The Lower Canyon, immediately upstream of Golden, offers the biggest thrills, including a three-kilometer (1.9-mile) stretch of continuous rapids. Upstream of here, the river is tamer but still makes for an exciting trip, while even farther upstream, near the western boundary of Yoho National Park, it's more of a float—a good adventure for the more timid visitor. The river is run by several companies, most of which offer the option of half-day ($60–80) or full-day ($100–150) trips. The cost varies with inclusions such as transportation and lunch.

Alpine Rafting (250/344-6778 or 888/599-5299, www.alpinerafting.com) offers trips ranging from a family-friendly float to the excitement of descending the Lower Canyon. They operate from a signposted base 25 kilometers (15.5 miles) east of Golden, where there is also primitive camping. Other local companies include **Wet 'n' Wild Adventures** (250/344-6546 or 800/668-9119) and **Glacier Raft Company** (250/344-6521).

ACCOMMODATIONS AND CAMPING

You can stay in one of the regular motels lining the highway, but don't. Instead choose one of the unique mountain lodgings that surround the town.

Under $50

HI-Golden (801 9th St. N., 250/439-1112) epitomizes the new wave of hostelling. It is a modern, riverfront log building with amenities that include high-speed Internet, a living area with a large-screen TV, and a café with outdoor seating overlooking the Columbia River. Members pay $29 per night for a dorm bed or $81–145 s or d for a private room. Nonmembers pay a few dollars extra.

$50-100

Blaeberry Mountain Lodge (1680 Moberly School Rd., 250/344-5296, www.blaeberry mountainlodge.bc.ca) is on a 62-hectare (150-acre) property among total wilderness. Rooms are in the main lodge or self-contained cabins, with plenty of activities available to guests. Standard rooms with shared bathroom are $85–95 s or d, and the large cabins, which feature a separate bedroom and full kitchen, are $145. The three-bedroom cottage is $300 for up to four people. Breakfast and dinner are offered for $14 and $28, respectively. Blaeberry is nine kilometers (5.6 miles) north of Golden along Highway 1, then seven kilometers (4.3 miles) farther north along Moberly School Road.

If you must stay in a motel, and don't want to spend a fortune, choose the distinctive two-story, lime-green **Ponderosa Motor Inn,** on the highway by 12th Avenue. (1206 TransCanada Hwy., 250/344-2205 or 800/881-4233, www.ponderosamotorinn.bc.ca), which has 85 older rooms but offers impressive mountain

views, a hot tub, a picnic area and gazebo, and a playground, making it a good value at just $78 s, $88 d ($52 s, $60 d outside of summer).

$100-150

The folks who operate the **Cedar House Café** (735 Hefti Rd., 250/344-4679, www.cedar housecafe.com) have restored an adjacent cabin, infusing it with a modern feel without losing any of the property's original charm. Sleeping up to four people, the cabin is spacious and comes with a full kitchen, a wood-burning stove, a laundry, and TV/VCR. It costs just $175 per night.

Over $150

Of many new accommodations at the base of Kicking Horse Mountain Resort, **Copper Horse Lodge** (250/344-7644 or 877/544-7644, www.copperhorselodge.com; from $180 s or d including breakfast) comes highly recommended. Guest rooms are outfitted in earthy yet stylish color schemes, and luxuries such as bathrobes, Internet access, and TV/DVD combos. Other amenities include a restaurant, lounge, and outdoor hot tub.

Along Highway 1, a 20-minute drive from Golden back toward Yoho National Park, **Kicking Horse River Chalets** (2924 Kicking Horse Rd., 866/502-5171, www.kicking horseriverchalets.com) comprises luxurious peeled-log cabins, each with full kitchen and dishwasher, wood-burning fireplace, balcony, and loft. The rate is $265 per night for up to four people.

Campgrounds

Continue south through the old part of town over the Kicking Horse River and take 9th Street South east at the traffic lights to reach **Golden Municipal Campground** (250/344-5412; mid-May–mid-Oct.; $18–20). It's a quiet place, strung out along the river and two kilometers (1.2 miles) from downtown along a riverfront walkway. Facilities include picnic shelters, hot coin-operated showers, and 70 sites with fire pits. Adjacent is a recreation center with a swimming pool and fitness facility. Golfers can stay out at the golf course for $18 per night.

FOOD

Start your day with the locals at the **Golden Bakery & Deli** (419 9th Ave., 250/344-2928; Mon.–Sat. 6:30 A.M.–6 P.M.), where the coffee is always fresh and the faces friendly. Baked goodies include breads, pastries, cakes, and meat pies, with inexpensive daily specials displayed on a blackboard in a seated section off to the side of the main counter.

At an elevation of 2,347 meters (7,700 feet), the **Eagle's Eye Restaurant** is the crowning glory of Kicking Horse Mountain Resort (250/439-5400 or 866/754-5425) and is Canada's highest restaurant. Access is by gondola from the resort's base village, 13 kilometers (eight miles) west of downtown Golden. As you'd expect, the views are stunning and are set off by a stylish timber and stonework interior, including a floor-to-ceiling fireplace and a wide wraparound deck protected from the wind by glass paneling. It's open daily at 10 A.M. for a lunch costing adult $42, senior $36, child $18, which includes the gondola ride. Between 7 and 10 P.M., the setting becomes more romantic and the food more adventurous but still distinctly Canadian. Dinner mains range $25–40 and include such delights as salmon baked in a saffron-vanilla cream and served with strawberry salsa ($28). All evening diners enjoy a complimentary gondola ride, or pay $45 for the ride and a fixed-course dinner. Reservations required.

A five-minute drive south of Golden off Highway 95, the **Cedar House Café** (735 Hefti Rd., 250/344-4679; daily 5–10:30 P.M.) is a good choice for wonderfully flavored food that takes advantage of seasonal Canadian produce. The soup of the day is a good way to get things going, then choose between mains such as portobello mushroom strudel ($18) or green Thai prawn curry ($20). The dining room is in a log building, but on warmer evenings you'll want to be outside on the patio.

INFORMATION AND SERVICES

Golden Visitor Centre is ensconced in an architecturally striking building beside the highway before it descends into town from the east (120 Golden Upper Donald Rd., 250/344-7125 or 800/622-4653, www.tourismgolden.com; daily 9 A.M.–5 P.M.). Interpretive displays describe the valley's natural and human history, as well as the scope of road construction through the Kicking Horse Canyon.

While accommodations, fast-food restaurants, and gas stations line the TransCanada Highway, downtown Golden holds other basic services, including the **post office** (502 9th Ave.). Ninth Avenue also holds outdoor equipment shops and **Bacchus Books** (506 9th Ave., 250/344-5600; Mon.–Sat. 10 A.M.–6 P.M.), offering a wide selection of new and used books, with plenty of local reading and detailed maps of the Columbia Valley.

CENTRAL BRITISH COLUMBIA

Ranging from the western slopes of the Rocky Mountains to the Pacific Ocean, central British Columbia holds such varied natural features as the massive Fraser River, the lofty peaks of the Cariboo and Coast Mountains, and the deeply indented coastal fjords around Bella Coola.

The region's history is dominated by colorful sagas of Canada's biggest gold rush, when over 100,000 miners and fortune seekers passed through the area on their way to the goldfields. But the best-remembered man in these parts was not a miner but an explorer. In 1793, Alexander Mackenzie left the Fraser River for the final leg of his epic transcontinental journey. Fourteen days later he reached the Pacific Ocean, becoming the first person to cross the continent.

Today the most heavily traveled route through central BC is the TransCanada Highway, which for the purposes of this book also forms the region's southern boundary. In the east of the province, the highway bisects Glacier National Park, a small but spectacular park of glaciers and towering peaks. Heading west from the park, the highway passes the heli-skiing hub of Revelstoke and the watery playground of Shuswap Lake before coming to the large population center of Kamloops.

From Kamloops, two highways lead north. Highway 5 accesses Wells Gray and Mount Robson Provincial Parks, the former a vast forested wilderness and the latter named for one of the most spectacular mountain peaks in all of Canada. The other route, Highway 97, runs through Cariboo Country, best-known for the 1860s gold-rush town of Barkerville,

HIGHLIGHTS

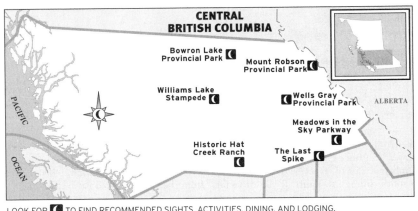

Meadows in the Sky Parkway: From the TransCanada Highway, this road climbs to a magnificent alpine meadow high above the tree line (page 326).

The Last Spike: Railway buffs in particular will enjoy seeing the spot where the final link was made in Canada's transcontinental railway (page 330).

Wells Gray Provincial Park: Waterfalls and wildlife combine to make this a worthwhile detour between Kamloops and Jasper (page 338).

Mount Robson Provincial Park: It's impossible not to be impressed on the drive into Mount Robson Provincial Park, unless of course clouds are covering the

highest peak in the Canadian Rockies (page 341).

Historic Hat Creek Ranch: Over 100 years since the Cariboo Wagon Road bustled with miners heading north in search of their fortune, it's still possible to experience the frontier feeling at this historic ranch (page 345).

Williams Lake Stampede: Rodeos take place across British Columbia, but none are bigger than the Williams Lake Stampede, on the first weekend of July (page 349).

Bowron Lake Provincial Park: The main attraction in this park is the wilderness canoe circuit, but it's also worth visiting for its scenic locale – and hopefully you'll find time to go for a quick paddle (page 355).

CENTRAL BRITISH COLUMBIA

Bowron Lake Provincial Park

Mount Robson Provincial Park

Williams Lake Stampede

Wells Gray Provincial Park

ALBERTA

Meadows in the Sky Parkway

Historic Hat Creek Ranch

The Last Spike

PACIFIC

OCEAN

CENTRAL B.C.

LOOK FOR ◖ TO FIND RECOMMENDED SIGHTS, ACTIVITIES, DINING, AND LODGING.

now completely restored and one of the highlights of a trip north.

PLANNING YOUR TIME

Planning how to spend your time in central British Columbia has as much to do with integrating the region with the rest of your itinerary as it does with trying to work out how to hit all the highlights. The main route through the region is the east–west TransCanada Highway,

which runs from Golden to Kamloops and on to Vancouver. This can easily be traveled in one day, but with two national parks and a string of interesting towns en route, the trip calls for at least one overnight stop (Revelstoke is a good choice). Even if you're in a hurry, detour along the **Meadows in the Sky Parkway** in Mount Revelstoke National Park. The region's biggest city is Kamloops, from where highways lead in four directions. Hands down, the most scenic is

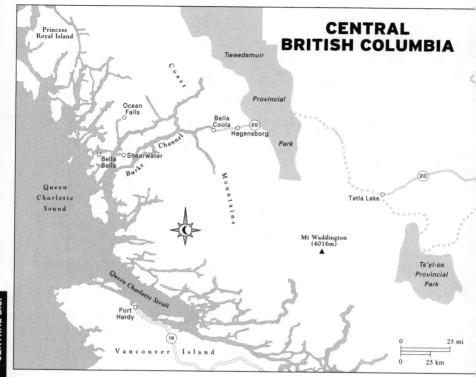

CENTRAL BRITISH COLUMBIA

Highway 5 north to **Mount Robson Provincial Park,** from where the choices are to head northwest to Prince George (Northern British Columbia) or east to Jasper National Park and then south through to Banff. If you drive far enough north along Highway 97 from Kamloops, you'll reach Prince George. A good way to kick off the long drive north is with a stop at **Historic Hat Creek Ranch,** where buildings from the Cariboo Gold Rush still stand.

Glacier National Park

Encompassing 135,000 hectares (333,600 acres) of the Selkirk Mountains, this park is a wonderland of jagged snowcapped peaks, extensive ice fields, thundering waterfalls, steep-sided valleys, and fast-flowing rivers. The TransCanada Highway bisects the park, cresting at 1,327-meter (4,350-foot) **Rogers Pass.** From this lofty summit, Golden is 80 kilometers (50 miles) east and Revelstoke is 72 kilometers (45 miles) west.

Those from south of the 49th parallel probably associate the park's name with the American national park in Montana. The two parks share the same name and glaciated environment, but the similarities end there. In the "other" park, buses shuttle tourists here and there and the backcountry is crowded with hikers. Here in the Canadian version, commercialism is almost totally

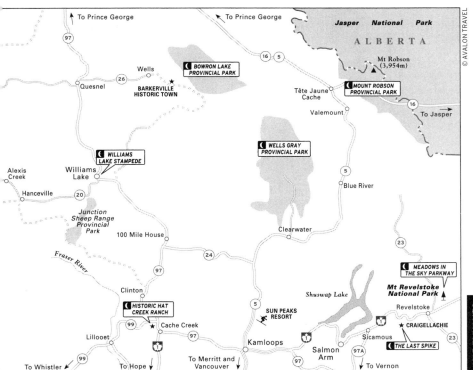

lacking and use of the backcountry is blissfully minimal.

The best place to start a visit to the park is **Rogers Pass Information Centre.** Looking south from the center, you can see the **Illecillewaet, Asulkan,** and **Swiss Glaciers.** As far as actual "sights" go, driving through the park you'll be surrounded by one of the most awe-inspiring panoramas visible from any Canadian highway. Each roadside viewpoint seems to outdo the last. You can also get out of the car and go hiking to get a better feeling for the park, but most of the trails entail strenuous climbs.

Through-traffic excepted, permits are required for entry into Glacier National Park; they're available from the information center. A one-day permit is $6.90 per person to a maximum of $17.30 per vehicle.

THE LAND

Regardless of whether you approach the park from the east or west, you'll be climbing from a valley only 600 meters (1,970 feet) above sea level to 1,327-meter (4,350-foot) Rogers Pass in under 15 kilometers (9.3 miles). The pass is not particularly high, but it's impressive. Surrounding peaks, many topping 3,050 meters (10,000 feet), rise dramatically from the pass and draw massive amounts of precipitation from eastward-moving clouds. The resulting heavy snows feed more than 400 glaciers and permanently cloak some 14 percent of the park's landscape in snow and ice. Most of the glaciers lie in the park's southern half. Notable among them are Deville Icefield, which surrounds 3,393-meter (11,130-foot) Mount Dawson, the park's highest peak, and Illecillewaet Icefield, whose glacial arms can be viewed

© ANDREW HEMPSTEAD

The snowcapped peaks of Glacier National Park can be seen from the highway.

up close from hiking trails starting at the Illecillewaet Campground.

Flora and Fauna

Three distinct vegetation zones can be seen within the park: montane (600–1,300 meters/1,970–4,260 feet), subalpine (1,300–1,900 meters/4,260–6,230 feet), and alpine (1,900 meters/6,230 feet to over 3,050 meters/10,000 feet). The montane forest supports a lush variety of tree species, including mountain hemlock, subalpine fir, Engelmann spruce, western red cedar, western hemlock, lodgepole pine, whitebark pine, western white pine, black cottonwood, Douglas fir, aspen, and white birch. Flower lovers will be impressed by the 600 species of flowering plants that have been identified within the park. The best time to see wildflowers in the high meadows and forests is early August.

The rugged terrain and long hard winters in Glacier National Park mean that resident mammals are a tough and hardy bunch. Healthy populations of both black and grizzly bears

inhabit the park. The black bears often feed along the roadside in late spring. Grizzlies are less common and tend to remain in the backcountry, but early in the season, lingering snow can keep them at lower elevations; look for them on avalanche slopes.

HISTORY

In a scenario familiar throughout western Canada, the proclamation of Glacier National Park was influenced by the Canadian Pacific Railway's desire to see tourists use its rail line. For CPR engineers, finding a passable train route through the Columbia Mountains proved a formidable challenge. The major obstacle was the threat of avalanche—high snowfall was coupled with narrow valleys and steep approaches from both east and west, all attributes spelling danger. Through three summers rail workers toiled with picks and shovels, finally completing a railbed on November 7, 1885. A national park was proclaimed, protecting the pass and surrounding wilderness and, much to the delight of the cash-strapped CPR, bringing visitors to the area—by rail of course. For the next three decades the CPR operated passenger and freight services over the pass, thrilling thousands of pioneer passengers. Unfortunately, despite railway engineering ingenuity, frequent and devastating avalanches took their toll, killing over 200 workers in the first 30 years of operation. Forced to stop the carnage, the CPR rerouted the line, tunneling under the pass in 1916. The rerouted line bypassed the park's most spectacular scenery, and the number of visitors to the park dropped dramatically.

In the early 1950s, a new team of engineers tackled the same problem—this time in an effort to build a highway across the pass. The tunnel approach that had worked for the railway was deemed impractical for a highway, so a new solution to the avalanche danger was required. In 1962 a route through the national park and over the pass was completed—this time with the addition of concrete snowsheds over sections of the highway.

HIKING

The park's 21 hiking trails cover 140 kilometers (87 miles) and range from short interpretive walks to long, steep, difficult climbs. Aside from the interpretive trails, most gain a lot of elevation, rewarding the energetic hiker with outstanding views. Along flat ground, reasonably fit hikers can usually cover four kilometers in an hour, but on Glacier National Park's steep trails, up to double that time should be allowed.

Interpretive Trails

The two most popular interpretive trails are the **Abandoned Rails Interpretive Trail** (one kilometer/0.6 mile; 20 minutes round-trip), which starts to the west of the information center, and the **Meeting of the Waters Trail** (one kilometer/0.6 mile; 25 minutes round-trip), which starts behind Illecillewaet Campground, four kilometers (2.5 miles) south of the information center.

Longer Hikes

Of the trails beginning from the Illecillewaet Campground, the 4.8-kilometer (three-mile)

Great Glacier Trail has the least elevation gain. But hard-core hikers will get the opportunity to scramble up rocky slopes to the toe of the Illecillewaet Glacier, 340 vertical meters (1,110 feet) higher. The **Avalanche Crest Trail** begins behind the Illecillewaet Campground, climbing 800 vertical meters (2,620 feet) in 4.2 kilometers (2.5 miles). As you face the campground's information board, the trail leads off to your left, climbing steeply through a subalpine forest for the first three kilometers (1.9 miles), then leveling out and providing stunning views below to Rogers Pass and south to Illecillewaet and Asulkan Glaciers. While elevation gain on the **Asulkan Valley Trail** is similar to that of others in the steep-sided Illecillewaet River Valley, it is gained over a longer distance (6.5 kilometers/4 miles), meaning a less-strenuous outing. Nevertheless, a full day should be allowed round-trip. The trail follows Asulkan Brook through a valley of dense subalpine forest. Whereas other trails lead to panoramic overlooks, the highlight of this trail's final destination is a view of the immense ice field rising high above you.

From the park information center, the five-kilometer (3.1-mile) **Balu Pass Trail** climbs a gut-wrenching 1,020 vertical meters (3,350 feet) between Mount Cheops to the south and a ridge of 2,700-meter (8,860-foot) peaks to the north. As elevation is gained, the valley closes in and the trail becomes steeper, finally ending at a pass 2,300 meters (7,450 feet) above sea level.

From the west side of the highway one kilometer (0.6 mile) north of the information center, the **Hermit Trail** climbs *very* steeply through a subalpine forest, breaking out above the tree line and ending at a view of glaciated peaks towering 1,000 meters (3,300 feet) above. Total elevation gain is 940 meters (3,080 feet) over 2.8 kilometers (1.7 miles). This trail is for fit hikers only.

PRACTICALITIES
Accommodations and Camping

Glacier Park Lodge (250/837-2126 or 800/528-1234, www.glacierparklodge.ca; $145 s,

TIME TRAVEL

Glacier National Park falls within two time zones. If you pass through the park westbound, turn your watch *back* one hour to **Pacific time.** If you're eastbound, turn it *forward* one hour to **Mountain time.**

$155 d) is a Best Western affiliate beside the main information center atop Rogers Pass. It offers 50 midsize rooms, a 24-hour café, a restaurant offering reasonably priced buffets through all three meals, and a lounge.

At **Illecillewaet Campground** (3.5 kilometers/ 2.2 miles south of Rogers Pass; late June–Sept.; $21), facilities include kitchen shelters, flush toilets, picnic tables, firewood, and an evening interpretive program. Sites are not particularly private, and the surrounding peaks and towering cedar trees mean little sunshine before noon, but the campground is the perfect base for exploring because it's the trailhead for the park's main concentration of hiking trails. When this campground fills, campers are directed to an overflow area in the nearby Sir Donald Picnic Area ($15). Smaller **Loop Brook Campground** (three kilometers/1.9 miles beyond the Illecillewaet Campground toward Revelstoke; July–Sept.; $21) holds just 20 sites.

If the above options are full or don't appeal to your budget and tastes, head 40 kilometers (25 miles) west to **Canyon Hot Springs Resort** (250/837-2420, www.canyon hotsprings.com; May–Sept.), a family-style complex of accommodations and activities with something for everyone. Two outdoor swimming pools (daily 9 A.M.–9 P.M.) filled with water pumped from nearby hot springs are the advertised highlight, while the short trail to historic Albert Canyon is a good way to escape the crowds. Aside from the solitude, you can explore the broken-down remains of log cabins dating to the days of highway construction. The resort offers showers, a laundry, and a restaurant. Unserviced sites are $28, serviced sites $36, and basic sleeping cabins with no bathrooms $68.

Information
Rogers Pass Information Centre (250/837-7500, www.pc.gc.ca; May–mid-June 8:30 A.M.–4:30 P.M., mid-June–Aug. 7:30 A.M.–8 P.M., Sept.–Nov. Thurs.–Mon. 9 A.M.–5 P.M., Dec.–Apr. daily 7 A.M.–5 P.M.) is beside the highway 1.2 kilometers (0.7 mile) north of the actual pass and resembles the old-fashioned snowsheds that once protected the railroad from avalanches. The center's fascinating displays focus on the park's natural and human history. Videos on various aspects of the park are shown on the TV (the viewing area by the fireplace is a great spot to while away time waiting for the clouds to lift), and the center's theater screens documentaries on mountain wildlife and avalanche protection. Staff members provide information on trail conditions and closures, operate a small bookstore, and conduct interpretive programs. The center is also the only place in the park to buy park passes, necessary for those planning any hiking or camping. If you already have a National Parks of Canada Pass, it must be presented for admission to the information center.

Revelstoke

Revelstoke lies 72 kilometers (45 miles) west of Rogers Pass at the confluence of the Illecillewaet River and the mighty Columbia, surrounded by mountains—the Monashees to the west and the Selkirks to the east. The setting couldn't be more spectacular.

An 1850s gold rush along the Columbia River brought the first Europeans to the area, but the town really began to grow with the coming of the railroad in the 1880s. In fact, the city is named for Lord Revelstoke, who provided funding for completion of the Canadian Pacific Railway's line through town. Finally, the TransCanada Highway came to town early in the 20th century, helping turn Revelstoke into today's midsize city of 8,500.

The town holds a couple of museums, but the main attractions are farther afield, including two massive dams, a national park on the back doorstep, and great skiing and snowboarding on Mount Mackenzie.

SIGHTS

The TransCanada Highway makes a lazy loop around the back of Revelstoke, missing downtown completely. It's well worth the detour to downtown, not just for the best dining, but to enjoy the laid-back atmosphere of a small city that has done an excellent job of preserving

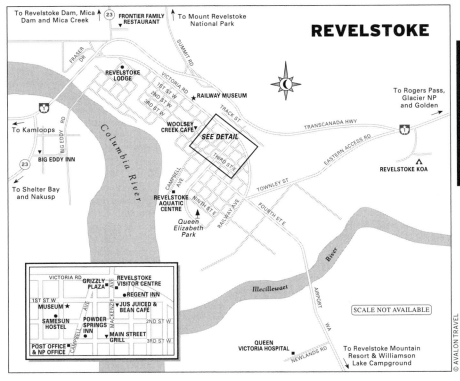

CENTRAL B.C.

its heritage. The rejuvenated downtown core centers around the appealing, all-brick Grizzly Plaza. Southwest from the plaza along Mackenzie Avenue are many frontier-style false fronted buildings and the art deco–style Roxy Theatre. Pick up the *Heritage Walking & Driving* brochure at the information center for routes that take in the historic highlights.

Museums

Railway buffs shouldn't miss **Revelstoke Railway Museum** (Victoria Rd., 250/837-6060; summer daily 9 A.M.–8 P.M., spring and fall daily 9 A.M.–5 P.M., winter Fri.–Tues. 11 A.M.–5 P.M.; adult $8, senior $6, child $4), a re-creation of an early Canadian Pacific Railway station. Reflecting the importance of this mode of transportation in Revelstoke's history, the museum centers on a massive 1948 steam locomotive and Business Car No. 4, the ultimate in early rail-travel luxury.

Revelstoke Museum (corner of Boyle Ave. and 1st St., 250/837-3067; summer Mon.–Sat. 10 A.M.–5 P.M., the rest of the year Mon.–Fri. 1–4 P.M.; adult $2.50, senior $2, child $1) fills two stories of a historic downtown post office building. It preserves plenty of pioneer memorabilia and a great collection of historical black-and-white photos, and offers displays on local industries, early Chinese miners, and winter recreation.

Dams

The 1,900-kilometer (1,180-mile) Columbia River, North America's third-longest, is controlled by many dams. Four of these are in British Columbia and two are in the vicinity of Revelstoke. The local dams provide the necessary water for two massive hydroelectric operations. These generating stations are each capable of producing 1,800 megawatts of electricity—or, combined, 30 percent of the province's needs.

Revelstoke Dam, eight kilometers (five miles) north of the city on Highway 23, was completed in 1985. It's 470 meters (1,540 feet) wide and 175 meters (590 feet) high. The massive reservoir behind the dam stretches over 130 kilometers (81 miles). Nestled in the valley downstream of the dam is the generating station. Exhibits at the two-story **Revelstoke Dam Visitor Centre** (250/814-6697; May–Sept. daily 9 A.M.–5 P.M.; free), above the generating station, explain the valley's history and the operation and impact of the dams. From the center, a high-speed elevator whisks visitors to the top of the dam for an excellent view.

Upstream of Revelstoke Dam is **Mica Dam,** 140 kilometers (87 miles) via Highway 23 to the north. This dam is much larger—in fact, it's North America's highest earth-filled dam (240 meters/790 feet), stretching 792 meters (2,600 feet) at the crest across the Columbia River Valley. It backs up 200-kilometer-long (124-mile-long) **Kinbasket Lake,** extending north to Valemount and south to a point just north of Golden.

MOUNT REVELSTOKE NATIONAL PARK

Visitors to this 26,000-hectare (64,250-acre) national park on the northern outskirts of Revelstoke can experience a high alpine environment from the enticingly named Meadows in the Sky Parkway, without any strenuous hiking.

The park protects the highest peaks of the **Clachnacudiann Range,** a northern arm of the Selkirk Mountains. The forested slopes of the range come to an icy apex around the Clachnacudiann Glacier and surrounding peaks, such as **Mount Coursier** and **Mount Inverness,** both 2,637 meters (8,650 feet) high. The park's diverse vegetation includes forests of ancient cedar along the Illecillewaet River, subalpine forests of Engelmann spruce and fir on higher slopes, and finally, above the tree line, meadows of low-growing shrubs that come alive with color for a few weeks in midsummer.

As with all Canadian national parks, a permit is required for entry; in this case it applies only for travel on the Meadows in the Sky Parkway. Permits are issued at the park gate, at the lower end of the parkway. A one-day permit is $6.90 per person to a maximum of $17.30 per vehicle.

◖ Meadows in the Sky Parkway

This 26-kilometer (16-mile) road one kilometer

(0.6 mile) west of the downtown Revelstoke turnoff climbs from the TransCanada Highway to a magnificent alpine meadow high above the tree line. The road is very steep, gaining well over 1,000 meters (3,280 feet) of elevation as it climbs seemingly endless hairpin bends through a sub-alpine forest of Engelmann spruce, hemlock, and the odd towering cedar. The summit area is snowed in until mid- to late July, depending on how much snow has fallen the previous winter. The public road ends one kilometer (0.6 mile) before the true summit. From this point, you have the option of taking a free shuttle bus (daily 10 A.M.–4:20 P.M., starting as soon as the snow melts off the road) or walking (20 minutes each way) to **Heather Lake.** From this point, the panoramic view takes in the Columbia River Valley and the distant Monashee Mountains, with hiking trails beckoning further exploration.

Heather Lake is the trailhead for the one-kilometer (round-trip) **Meadows in the Sky Trail,** which features signs explaining the flora of the fragile alpine environment. From the east side of Heather Lake, a nine-kilometer (5.6-mile) trail leads through alpine meadows to the **Jade Lakes.** Along the route, short side trails lead to **Miller** and **Eva Lakes.**

The park's main gate is closed 10 P.M.–7 A.M., prohibiting access.

More Hiking Opportunities

The park doesn't have an extensive network of hiking trails—just 10 marked trails totaling 65 kilometers (40 miles) in length. Most take under an hour and are posted with interpretive panels. Two of these start beside the TransCanada Highway east of Revelstoke, where the Illecillewaet River forms the park's southern boundary. The 500-meter (0.3-mile) **Giant Cedars Boardwalk** (allow 10 minutes) traverses a meadow before disappearing into an ancient cedar forest and then along a sparkling creek. Farther west along the highway is the trailhead for **Skunk Cabbage Interpretive Trail,** which leads 1.2 kilometers (0.7 mile) down to the Illecillewaet River; allow 40 minutes for the round-trip.

The park's most demanding trail is the 10-kilometer (6.2-mile) **Summit Trail,** which begins—or, more sensibly, ends—at the entrance to the Meadows in the Sky Parkway and runs to the Balsam Lake warden's cabin. The trail makes an elevation gain of 1,200 meters (3,940 feet), so allow at least 3.5 hours for this strenuous uphill slog. The eight-kilometer (five-mile) **Lindmark Trail** is equally strenuous, gaining 950 meters (3,120 feet) in elevation as it traverses up to Balsam Lake from the lookout eight kilometers (five miles) from the park gate.

Park Information

Services within the park are limited to picnic areas. Although backcountry camping is allowed in designated areas (permit required; $9.90 pp per night), no road-accessible campgrounds lie within the park.

Revelstoke is home to the park's **administration office** (300 3rd St., 250/837-7500; year-round Mon.–Fri. 8:30 A.M.–4:30 P.M.). Other sources of information are **Rogers Pass Information Centre,** in nearby Glacier National Park, and the Parks Canada website (www.pc.gc.ca).

RECREATION

In summer, recreation revolves around the national park, the local golf course (250/837-4276), and the Columbia River. In winter, an expanding alpine resort draws the visitors. One of the most attractive things about Revelstoke in winter is the prices, with local accommodations combining with the resort to offer some of the best-priced packages to be found anywhere in Canada.

Revelstoke Aquatic Centre (600 Campbell Ave., 250/837-9351; Mon.–Fri. 6:30 A.M.–9 P.M., Sat. 10 A.M.–8 P.M., Sun. noon–8 P.M.; adult $4.50, senior $3.25, child $2.75) is an excellent facility comprising multiple indoor saltwater pools, waterslides, a slow-moving "lazy river," and a climbing wall built over one pool. Many local accommodations, including the Samesun Hostel and Revelstoke Lodge, provide guests with pool passes.

Skiing and Snowboarding

The first phase of development at **Revelstoke**

Mountain Resort (250/837-4675, www .discoverrevelstoke.com) included the installation of an eight-person gondola and high-speed quad for the 2007–2008 winter season. The vertical rise of 1,400 meters (4,600 feet) is slated to increase to 1,800 meters (6,000 feet), North America's highest, and there are plans in place for a 5,000-unit base village complete with golf course and heli-skiing base. In the meantime, lift tickets are a reasonable adult $56, senior $42, child #2.

Nestled between the Selkirk and Monashee Mountains, Revelstoke is also the center of much heli-skiing. **Selkirk Tangiers Heli-skiing** (250/837-5378 or 800/663-7080, www .selkirk-tangiers.com) operates from town, offering all-inclusive packages—including seven days heli-skiing (over 30,000 meters/100,000 feet vertical), accommodations (at the Coast Hillcrest Resort Hotel), and meals. Prices range from $2,200 for three days in December to $7,050 for seven days in February.

ENTERTAINMENT

In July and August, free entertainment takes place nightly at the **Grizzly Plaza band shell,** at the bottom end of Mackenzie Avenue. Whether it be comedy or country, crowds of up to a couple hundred gather, sitting in plastic chairs, snagging a table at a surrounding restaurant, or just standing in the background. For music and dancing of a more formal nature, the young crowd heads for **Big Eddy Inn** (2108 Big Eddy Rd., 250/837-9072). Downtown in the Regent Inn (112 1st St., 250/837-2107), you'll find live music or a DJ Wednesday–Saturday at the **River City Pub,** and plenty of quiet corners at the more subdued **One Twelve Lounge.**

ACCOMMODATIONS AND CAMPING
Under $50

The best value of all accommodations in town is the **◖ Samesun Hostel** (400 2nd St. W., 250/837-4050 or 877/962-6378, www.samesun .com), within easy walking distance of downtown. Providing a true home away from home, this heritage house has been fully restored,

complete with hardwood floors and comfortable beds with linen. Amenities include kitchen facilities, a laundry, free wireless Internet access, bike rentals, and a game room. The 26 double and twin rooms share bathrooms, but beds are comfortable and linen is supplied. Rates are $22.40 per person for a dorm bed or $48 s or d in a private room.

$50-100

Downtown, the **Powder Springs Inn** (200 3rd St. W., 250/837-5151 or 800/991-4455, www .powdersprings.ca; $69 s, $79 d) is a centrally located renovated motel providing good value year-round. A restaurant, spa services, and a hot tub are also on the premises.

Other motels are spread through downtown and out on the highway. The best is the **Revelstoke Lodge** (601 1st St. W., 250/837-2181 or 888/559-1979, www.revelstokelodge .com; $89 s, $99 d), with air-conditioned guest rooms set around a heated outdoor pool.

$100-150

To experience Revelstoke's most appealing accommodation, head 20 kilometers (12 miles) south of town on Highway 23 to **Mulvehill Creek Wilderness Inn** (250/837-8649 or 877/837-8649, www.mulvehillcreek.com). This well-designed property centers on a main cedar lodge trading on outdoor opportunities (canoeing, swimming, and fishing) and modern conveniences (heated pool, hot tub, en suite guest rooms). Rates of $125–225 s or d include a big breakfast buffet of egg dishes courtesy of the inn's chickens and homemade goodies such as breads and jams.

Camping

Revelstoke KOA (250/837-2085 or 800/562-3905, www.revelstokekoa.com; May–mid-Oct.) is off the TransCanada Highway six kilometers (3.7 miles) east of downtown. The well-kept campground offers grassy sites, lots of trees, a swimming pool, propane-filling facilities, a well-stocked store, free hot showers, laundry facilities, and a main lodge that looks like a Swiss chalet. Tent sites are $27, RV sites range $32–42, tepees $46, camping cabins (no bathrooms) $59, and chalets $115–145. The fun stuff includes a heated outdoor pool, two playgrounds, rock-climbing lessons, evening campfires, and pancake breakfasts.

Quiet **Williamson Lake Campground** (seven kilometers/4.3 miles south of town on Airport Way, 250/837-5512 or 888/676-2267; mid-Apr.–Oct.; $16–28) lies on the edge of a warm lake perfect for swimming. Mini-golf, canoe rentals, a general store, free hot showers, and a quiet atmosphere help make this an appealing choice.

FOOD

Jus Juiced and Bean Café pours freshly squeezed juices and a range of coffee concoctions in canary-yellow surroundings (204 Mackenzie Ave., 250/837-5960; Mon.–Thurs. 7 A.M.–5:30 P.M., Fri. 7 A.M.–7 P.M., Sat. 7 A.M.–5 P.M.). Up the hill, in a restored heritage home, the ambience at the **Main Street Grill** (317 Mackenzie Ave., 250/837-6888; Tues.–Sat. 7 A.M.–5 P.M., Sun. 7 A.M.–3 P.M.) is a little more reserved. Cooked breakfasts are around $8 and lunches, including a tangy Thai salad, are all under $10.

A few blocks from the heart of downtown is my favorite restaurant in all of Central British Columbia, the ◖ **Woolsey Creek Café** (600 2nd St. W., 250/837-5500; daily 4–9:30 P.M.). It has a warm, friendly atmosphere but is always full and noisy with locals enjoying a wide range of healthy, well-prepared, and remarkably inexpensive dishes.

Despite the many good choices downtown, **Frontier Family Restaurant** (TransCanada Hwy., 250/837-5119; daily 5 A.M.–10 P.M.) may appeal to hurried highway travelers because of its location. It's a typical roadside diner with nothing fancy that doesn't need to be. The wood interior is decorated with red-and-white checkered curtains, cowboy boots, hats, antlers, and cattle horns; the waitresses wear jeans; and a sign outside says "Y'all come back, y'hear!"

INFORMATION AND SERVICES

Facing downtown's Grizzly Plaza, **Revelstoke Visitor Centre** (204 Campbell Ave., 250/837-5345 or 800/487-1493, www.revelstokecc.bc.ca; summer daily 8:30 A.M.–9 P.M., the rest of the year Mon.–Fri. 8:30 A.M.–4:30 P.M.) has public Internet access. **Mount Revelstoke National Park administration office** (313 3rd St., 250/837-7500) is in the post office building and is open year-round (Mon.–Fri. 8:30 A.M.–4:30 P.M.).

Queen Victoria Hospital is on Newlands Road (off Airport Way), on the southeast side of town (250/837-2131). The **post office** is a couple of blocks from downtown at 307 3rd Street.

Greyhound buses come through Revelstoke 4–7 times daily in both directions along the TransCanada Highway. The depot is by the Sandman Inn (1899 Fraser Dr., 250/837-5874).

West Toward Kamloops

Continuing west along the TransCanada Highway from Revelstoke, it's 62 kilometers (39 miles) to the next town, Sicamous, then 42 kilometers (26 miles) farther to the much larger center of Salmon Arm. The first stop along the way should be intriguingly black **Summit Lake,** lying in a heavily forested ravine and fed by a waterfall that plunges over a cliff face high above. A few kilometers farther west is similarly black **Victor Lake,** also fed by a waterfall. Shoreside **Victor** Lake Provincial Park makes a good spot for a picnic.

Three Valley

Several attractions on the next stretch of road compete for your tourist dollar. On the shore of Three Valley Lake is the difficult-to-miss **Three Valley Gap** "ghost" town (250/837-2109; Apr.–mid-Oct. daily 8 A.M.–dusk; adult $8, child $4), a rebuilt pioneer community with more than 20 historic buildings moved to the site from around the province. Part of the same complex is **Three Valley Lake Chateau** (250/837-2109 or 888/667-2109, www.3valley .com; Apr.–mid-Oct.), a large motel (200 rooms) overlooking extensive gardens and the lake. Amenities include a café, a restaurant, and an indoor pool. Standard rooms are $115–150 s or d, while the Cave Honeymoon Suite—complete with stone walls, roof, fireplace, and bathroom—is $175 s or d.

The next commercial attraction, eight kilometers (five miles) west, is **Enchanted Forest** (250/837-9477; Apr.–early Oct. daily 9 A.M.–sunset; adult $8, child $6), where a trail through towering trees meanders past more than 250 handcrafted figurines to fairyland buildings and western Canada's biggest tree house.

Farther west, **Beardale Miniatureland** (250/836-2268; May–Sept. daily 9 A.M.–6 P.M.; adult $8, child $6) takes miniature appreciators through several European towns and a Haida fishing village, into the world of nursery rhymes and fairy tales, and on into the world of trains. Most of the displays are indoors, making Beardale a good rainy-day diversion.

The Last Spike

At **Craigellachie,** signs point off the highway to the Last Spike. It was here on November 7, 1885, that a plain iron spike joined the last two sections of Canadian Pacific's transcontinental rail line, finally connecting Canada from sea to sea. A cairn with a plaque and a piece of railway line marks the spot. **Craigellachie Station** (May–Oct.) is home to a small information center/gift shop selling ice cream.

Sicamous

This town of 3,000, 62 kilometers (39 miles) west of Revelstoke, lies on the shore of **Shuswap Lake** and is known as the "Houseboat Capital of Canada." The lake itself is a convoluted body of water with four distinct arms, edged by secluded beaches, rocky coves, 25 marine

A freight train passes by Craigellachie, famous as the spot where the final section of Canada's transcontinental rail line was completed in 1885.

parks, and more than 1,000 kilometers (620 miles) of shoreline. Houseboating is the number-one activity in these parts, and Sicamous is headquarters to major agencies, including **Blue Water Houseboats** (250/836-2255 or 800/663-4024, www.bluewaterhouseboats.ca), **Three Buoys Houseboat Vacations** (250/836-2403 or 800/663-2333, www.threebuoys.com), and **Twin Anchors Houseboat Vacations** (250/836-2450 or 800/663-4026, www.twinanchors.com). Rates vary greatly through the May–early Oct. season. Expect to pay around $1,900 for four days' rental in July, with the same boat going for around $1,000 in September.

Sandwiched between the two natural features referenced in its name, **Hyde Mountain on Mara Lake Golf Course** (250/836-4653; Apr.–Oct.) is not particularly long, but golfers enjoy fantastic lake views from elevated greens. Rates, including cart rental, are $88. To get there, head three kilometers (1.9 miles) south of town on Old Spallumcheen Road, which branches off the TransCanada Highway immediately west of the bridge. The clubhouse restaurant (daily 6:30 A.M.–midnight) combines good food with views to make it the best place in town to eat, even for nongolfers.

Highway 97A, south from Sicamous, is the main northern artery leading into the Okanagan Valley. Even if you're not planning on heading that far, it's worth taking this route a short way along the shoreline of Mara Lake. Aside from being particularly picturesque, the warm water tempts swimming.

SALMON ARM

Known as the "Gem of the Shuswap," Salmon Arm (pop. 15,000) lies along the Salmon Arm of Shuswap Lake, surrounded by lush farmland and forested hills. Legend has it that the name was coined in the days when the rivers here were chockablock with salmon. Farmers used to spear the fish with pitchforks and use them for fertilizer.

Sights

From downtown, follow the Salmon Arm Wharf signs to lakeside **Marine Park**, where picnic

tables dot the lawns, and colorful flower boxes hang from the lampposts. The attractive **Salmon Arm Wharf**, the largest marina structure in British Columbia's interior, lures you out over the water, past a boat-launching area, a snack bar, and businesses renting motorboats and houseboats. A wide swath of lakefront on either side of the wharf is undeveloped, inviting exploration on foot. Immediately west of the wharf, you'll find a bird-watching hide tucked into the trees above a marshy area rich with birds.

Two kilometers (1.2 miles) east of Salmon Arm on Highway 97B, **R. J. Haney Heritage Village & Museum** (250/832-5243; June–early Sept. daily 10 A.M.–5 P.M.; adult $5, child $2.50) holds the town's main historic attractions, including Salmon Arm Museum, which relates the town's earliest days through a slide show, photo albums, and the adjacent **Haney House,** an early-20th-century farmhouse on beautiful, parklike grounds. The park also holds a blacksmith's shop, an old fire hall, and a church.

This church is one of the many historic buildings preserved at R. J. Haney Heritage Village & Museum.

CENTRAL B.C.

© ANDREW HEMPSTEAD

Practicalities

Salmon River Motel and RV Park (one kilometer/0.6 mile west of Salmon Arm, 250/832-3065; $69–89) offers 10 rooms of a reasonable standard. Out back are a few tree-shaded campsites with hookups ($25). The landscaped **KOA Salmon Arm** (381 Hwy. 97B, 250/832-6489 or 800/562-9389, www.salmonarmkoa.com; mid-May–mid-Oct.) has hot showers, a laundry, a pleasant outdoor pool area, a convenience store, miniature golf, a playground, and a petting zoo. Tent sites are $35, full hookups $45, and rustic cabins $70. Highway 97B branches south toward Vernon just east of town.

Head down through the center of town and over the rail line toward the main wharf to reach **Java Cabana** (680 Marine Park Dr., 250/832-2329; daily from 7:30 A.M.), a corner coffeehouse where patrons take full advantage of sunny outdoor table settings. With your coffee, try the Thai salad ($7), then check your email on the public terminals. Right on the lakefront here is the Prestige Inn, home to **Forster's** (251 Harbourfront Dr., 250/833-1154), specializing in prime rib ($20–25). The restaurant itself is as stylish as dining out gets in Salmon Arm, but if it's a warm evening, you'll want to be outside on the deck.

Salmon Arm Visitor Centre (200 Trans-Canada Hwy., 250/832-2230) is open in summer daily 9 A.M.–6 P.M., the rest of the year Monday–Friday 9 A.M.–5 P.M. For information on the region before leaving home, visit the **Tourism Shuswap** website (www.shuswap.bc.ca).

CONTINUING WEST
Squilax

Squilax lies at the turnoff to Roderick Haig-Brown Provincial Park, 48 kilometers (30 miles) west of Salmon Arm. The town's one remaining building was originally a general store and is now the Hostelling International–affiliated **HI-Shuswap Lake** (250/675-2977 or 888/675-2977, www.hihostels.ca). The hostel office and a store selling organic products are in the building, while the dorm beds and communal kitchen are in three railway cabooses (the living quarters for railway workers in days gone by). The carriages sit on a short stretch of rail line overlooking the west end of Shuswap Lake. Members pay $17 for a dorm or $38 s or d for a private room; nonmembers pay a $4 surcharge. Check-in is after noon (Mon.–Tues. after 5 P.M.).

Adams River Sockeye Run

Turn off at the Squilax Bridge to get to 988-hectare (2,440-acre) **Roderick Haig-Brown Provincial Park,** named for noted British Columbian conservationist and writer Roderick Haig-Brown, but best known for protecting in its entirety the Adams River sockeye salmon run, North America's biggest such run. The salmon runs occur annually, but every four years (2008, 2012, etc.) a dominant run brings up to two million fish congregating in the river. These salmon are near the end of their four-year life cycle, having hatched in the same section of the Adams River four years previously. Unlike other species, after hatching sockeye spend up to two years of their life in a "nursery" lake, which in the case of the Adams River run is Shuswap Lake. It is estimated that in conjunction with dominant runs, 15 million Adams River sockeye enter the Pacific, with about 10 million running back toward their birthplace, of which just one in five make it past fishing nets to their goal. After an arduous 500-kilometer (310-mile) swim from the Pacific Ocean, the salmon spawn on shallow gravel bars here during the first three weeks of October (numbers generally peak in the second week).

Forested with Douglas fir, cottonwood, birch, hemlock, and cedar, the park flanks the Adams River between Adams Lake and Shuswap Lake, protecting the spawning grounds in their entirety. When the salmon aren't filling the river, the park is still interesting and interpretive boards describe the salmon run you've missed.

Kamloops

Kamloops (pop. 84,000), 110 kilometers (68 miles) west of Salmon Arm and 355 kilometers (220 miles) northeast of Vancouver, is the province's sixth-largest city and a main service center along the TransCanada Highway. The city holds a few interesting sights but is certainly no scenic gem—the surrounding landscape is dominated by barren, parched rolling hills. The downtown area, however, lies along the south bank of the Thompson River and is set off by well-irrigated parkland.

Entering the city from the west, the Trans-Canada Highway descends the Aberdeen Hills, passing shopping malls, motels, and Kamloops Visitor Centre. The highway bypasses downtown; take Columbia Street West to get to the city center. From the east, the TransCanada Highway parallels the Thompson River through almost 20 kilometers (12.4 miles) of industrial and commercial sprawl.

History

The Secwepemc, whose descendents are now known as Shuswap, were the first people to live in this region, basing their lifestyle on hunting and salmon fishing. They knew the area as T'kumlups, meaning "meeting of the rivers." The first nonnative settlement occurred in 1812, when the North West Company established a fur-trading post at the confluence of the north and south branches of the Thompson River. Prospectors began arriving in 1858, followed by entrepreneurs who began setting up permanent businesses. Kamloops grew as a transportation center, and today the economy revolves around the forest-products industry, copper mining, cattle and sheep ranching, and tourism.

SIGHTS
Kamloops Museum and Art Gallery

Excellent displays at the three-story, gold-colored **Kamloops Museum** (207 Seymour St., 250/828-3576; summer Mon.–Fri. 9 A.M.–8 P.M., Sat. 10 A.M.–5 P.M., and Sun. 1–5 P.M., the rest of the year Tues.–Sat. 9:30 A.M.–4:30 P.M.; adult $3, child $1) cover local native culture, the fur trade (peek in the reconstructed fur trader's cabin), pioneer days, natural history (many stuffed and mounted critters), industry, and transportation. You'll see a furnished late-19th-century living area, a stable complete with tack and carriage, a blacksmith shop, paddle wheels, old wall clocks and cameras, and a 15-minute slide presentation on the city's history.

Kamloops Art Gallery (465 Victoria St., 250/377-2400; Mon.–Sat. 10 A.M.–5 P.M., Sun. noon–4 P.M.; adult $3, child $2) features an impressive collection of more than 1,000 works by contemporary artists in all sorts of media—quite a contrast to the museum. The gallery stays open until 9 P.M. on Thursday, when admission is by donation after 5 P.M.

© ANDREW HEMPSTEAD

Kamloops Museum

CENTRAL B.C.

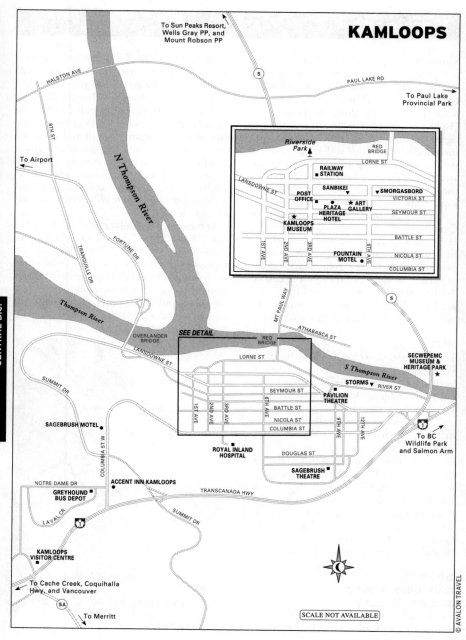

KAMLOOPS

To Sun Peaks Resort, Wells Gray PP, and Mount Robson PP

HALSTON AVE

PAUL LAKE RD

To Paul Lake Provincial Park

8TH ST

To Airport

N Thompson River

FORTUNE DR

TRANQUILLE DR

Thompson River

OVERLANDER BRIDGE

LANSDOWNE ST

MT PAUL WAY

ATHABASCA ST

SEE DETAIL

RED BRIDGE

LORNE ST

S Thompson River

SECWEPEMC MUSEUM & HERITAGE PARK

SUMMIT DR

STORMS ▼

RIVER ST

SEYMOUR ST

1ST AVE

2ND AVE

3RD AVE

6TH AVE

BATTLE ST

NICOLA ST

COLUMBIA ST

PAVILION THEATRE

9TH AVE

12TH AVE

SAGEBRUSH MOTEL ●

COLUMBIA ST W

ROYAL INLAND HOSPITAL

DOUGLAS ST

To BC Wildlife Park and Salmon Arm

NOTRE DAME DR

ACCENT INN KAMLOOPS ●

TRANSCANADA HWY

SAGEBRUSH THEATRE

GREYHOUND BUS DEPOT ■

SUMMIT DR

LAVAL CR

KAMLOOPS VISITOR CENTRE ■

To Cache Creek, Coquihalla Hwy, and Vancouver

5A

To Merritt

Detail (inset)

Riverside Park

RED BRIDGE

LORNE ST

LANSDOWNE ST

RAILWAY STATION ■

SANBIKEI ▼

▼ SMORGASBORD

VICTORIA ST

POST OFFICE

★ ART GALLERY

SEYMOUR ST

PLAZA HERITAGE HOTEL

BATTLE ST

KAMLOOPS MUSEUM ★

1ST AVE

2ND AVE

3RD AVE

FOUNTAIN MOTEL ■

6TH AVE

NICOLA ST

COLUMBIA ST

SCALE NOT AVAILABLE

Secwepemc Museum & Heritage Park

A living-history museum dedicated to the Shuswap tribe, this cultural attraction (250/828-9801; Mon.–Fri. 8:30 A.M.–4:30 P.M., until 8 P.M. in summer; adult $6, senior $4, child $4) offers numerous exhibits focusing on the Shuswaps' traditions and rich mythology. Highlights include an archaeological site dating back 2,000 years, a re-created Shuswap winter village, a salmon-fishing station, a garden filled with native plants for food and medicinal purposes, and a re-creation of a traditional summer shelter. To get to the park, follow Highway 5 north across the Thompson River and take the first right.

British Columbia Wildlife Park

This nonprofit park (TransCanada Hwy. 16 kilometers/10 miles east of Kamloops, 250/573-3242; June–Aug. 9 A.M.–7 P.M., Sept.–Oct. 9:30 A.M.–4 P.M.; adult $12, senior $11, child $9) is primarily a wildlife rehabilitation center, but among the more than 150 furry inhabitants are many species of mammals from western Canada, including a couple of grizzly bears, wolves, cougars, and lynx. Other attractions are a huge visitor center, the BC-themed Discovery Centre, an outdoor amphitheater, a glass-walled beehive, and, for the kids, a petting zoo.

RECREATION
Paul Lake Provincial Park

This small provincial park northeast of Kamloops is a relaxing, grassy, tree-shaded spot to take a picnic, go swimming in warm Paul Lake, or camp. And the drive out there, following Paul Creek past scrub-covered rolling hills and flower-filled meadows, is an enjoyable ramble through the countryside. At the park's day-use area you'll find the best beach, picnic tables, toilets, and changing rooms. Before settling down at the beach, take the 1.6-kilometer (one-mile) trail out to a bluff overlooking the valley. To get to the park, head north of Kamloops five kilometers (3.1 miles) on Highway 5, then 17 kilometers (10.5 miles) east on Paul Lake Road.

Sun Peaks Resort

In the 1990s, this mountain village north of the city along Highway 5 (250/578-5474, www.sunpeaksresort.com) has evolved from a medium-sized local ski hill to a year-round resort, with ongoing development both on the slopes and at the base village, where a golf course spreads out along the valley floor.

In summer, the Sunburst Express lift takes the hard work out of reaching the alpine for hikers and bikers. From the top of this lift, it's easy to descend back to the village on foot in less than an hour, but if the weather is good, consider exploring higher elevations, including the 2,152-meter (7,060-foot) summit of Mount Tod. Mountain-bike enthusiasts have many options, but the most popular destination is McGillivray Lake, accessed along a wide 6.2-kilometer (3.8-mile) trail from the village. Ride the lift all day for $15 ($33 with a mountain bike). Other activities include golfing a shortish resort-style 18-hole course, tennis, horseback riding, and fishing. High season for the resort is wintertime, when three high-speed lifts whisk skiers up the mountain. One of these—the Sunburst Express—links up with more lifts that access intermediate and expert terrain above the tree line and an easy eight-kilometer (five-mile) cruising run back to the village. The total vertical rise is 882 meters (2,900 feet) over almost 1,490 hectares (3,678 acres) of terrain. Facilities at the resort include eateries, a rental shop, and the Snow Sports School. Lift tickets are adult $67, senior $50, child $34. On-mountain accommodation packages are good value—from $100 per person per night, including a lift ticket.

ENTERTAINMENT

British Columbia's third-largest theater company, Kamloops-based **Western Canada Theatre,** presents live theatrical productions by top Canadian actors, producers, and designers. Performances take place in the **Pavilion Theatre** (1025 Lorne St., 250/372-3216) and at the **Sagebrush Theatre** (821 Munro St., 250/372-5000). The latter is also home to the **Kamloops Symphony Society.**

ACCOMMODATIONS AND CAMPING

You won't find quaint or memorable here. Instead, expect reliable motels serving the needs of highway travelers spread throughout the city. On the western approach to the city many newer motels offer clean and comfortable rooms but no particular bargains. The top end of Columbia Street West has some unspectacular older motels for travelers on a budget.

$50-100

It's nothing to write home about, but the **Fountain Motel** (506 Columbia St., 250/374-4451 or 888/253-1569, www.fountain.kamloops.com) offers a higher standard of rooms than the exterior may suggest; $65–80 s or d and kitchenettes an extra $10. The best of other similarly priced choices along a wide sweeping bend of Columbia Street West between the TransCanada Highway and downtown is the **Sagebrush Motel** (660 Columbia St. W., 250/372-3151, www.sagebrush.kamloops.com; $55 s, $68 d). This place has air-conditioned rooms, each with a coffeemaker and biggish TV, as well as an adjacent restaurant open daily from 7 A.M.

$100-150

Just off the highway near the westside access to downtown, **Accent Inn Kamloops** (1325 Columbia St. W., 250/374-8877 or 800/663-0298, www.accentinns.com) charges $129 s, $139 d for a modern and spacious room, with guests having use of an outdoor pool, a hot tub, and a fitness room. Other pluses include a national paper delivered to your door and free wireless Internet.

Right downtown is the **Plaza Heritage Hotel** (405 Victoria St., 250/377-8075 or 877/977-5292, www.plazaheritagehotel.com), first opened in 1928 as one the interior's finest accommodations. Its restoration and opening as a boutique hotel is only recent. The 68 rooms feature rich woods, a heritage color scheme, and comfortable beds covered in plush duvets. The Heritage Restaurant and a stylish lounge bar are at street level. The smallest rooms are $149 s or d, but the king rooms are only $10 more.

Camping

The city's most scenic campground is at **Paul Lake Provincial Park,** north of Kamloops five kilometers (3.1 miles) on Highway 5, then 17 kilometers (11 miles) east on Paul Lake Road. Facilities are basic (no hookups or showers), but the treed setting just a short walk to the beach makes up for it. All sites are $14.

FOOD

Kamloops has the usual family-style and fast-food restaurants along the highway, as well as some good dining choices in the downtown core.

A reliable lunch spot slightly off the main downtown thoroughfare is the old-fashioned **Smorgasbord** (225 7th Ave., 250/377-0055; Mon.–Sat. 7 A.M.–5 P.M.), which is not a smorgasbord as the British know it, but a small café offering a wide range of soups, salads, and sandwiches, with a daily special offering the best value.

Superb sushi is the draw at ◖ **Sanbiki** (476 Victoria St., 250/377-8857; daily 11:30 A.M.–2:30 P.M. and 5:30–9:30 P.M.), in a distinctive orange building with a sun-splashed patio out front. The chefs do a great job of sourcing the freshest of ingredients, including—most importantly—seafood. A popular lunch combo dish is teriyaki chicken, tempura, California rolls, salad, and miso soup for $11. Other choices include asparagus Shira-ae (salad), douced in a creamy sesame sauce; hearty rice bowls; and crumbed panko prawns.

Information and Services

Kamloops Visitor Centre (250/374-3377 or 800/662-1994, www.tourismkamloops.com; summer daily 9 A.M.–7 P.M., the rest of the year Mon.–Fri. 9 A.M.–5 P.M.) is beside the TransCanada Highway on the western outskirts of town (at Hillside Rd. opposite the Aberdeen Mall).

Royal Inland Hospital (311 Columbia St., 250/374-5111) is at the south end of 3rd Avenue. The **post office** is at 301 Seymour Street.

GETTING THERE AND AROUND

Kamloops Airport is on Airport Road, seven kilometers northwest of the city center; follow Tranquille Road through the North Shore until you come to Airport Road on the left. **Air Canada** (888/247-2262) has scheduled flights between Kamloops and Vancouver and **Central Mountain Air** (888/865-8585) flies north to Prince George. **VIA Rail** (800/561-8630) runs scheduled service three times weekly west to Vancouver and east to Jasper from the downtown railway station (north end of 3rd Ave.). **Greyhound** provides daily service to most parts of the province from its Kamloops bus depot (725 Notre Dame Dr., off Columbia St. W. at the west end of town, 250/374-1212).

Local bus transportation (including out to the airport) is provided by **Kamloops Transit System** (250/376-1216); adult fare is $2, while a day pass is just $4. Taxi companies include **Kami Cabs** (250/374-5151) and **Yellow Cabs** (250/374-3333). For a rental car, call **Budget** (250/376-5423), **Hertz** (250/376-3022), or **National** (250/374-5737).

North to Mount Robson

From Kamloops, Highway 5 follows the North Thompson River to Tete Jaune Cache on Highway 16. This stretch of highway is part of the most direct route between Vancouver and Jasper National Park, and is also worthwhile for two excellent provincial parks: **Wells Gray,** a vast wilderness of rivers and mountains, and **Mount Robson,** protecting a spectacular peak that is the highest point in the Canadian Rockies.

Barriere

In the summer of 2003, Barriere, 66 kilometers (41 miles) north of Kamloops, was evacuated as wildfires surrounded the small town during a hot spell of weather that kept the surrounding mountains alight for six weeks. A sawmill, the town's main employer, and 70 homes were lost in the blaze. Driving through today, you will see scarred hillsides and open areas along the valley floor where burnt trees and buildings have been cleared.

Along the highway through town, the **Monte Carlo Motel** (4380 Hwy. 5, 250/672-9676 or 888/660-5050; from $60 s, $70 d) is good value. The medium-sized rooms are air-conditioned, and if it's a hot day, take a dip in the outdoor pool or take advantage of the barbeque area.

CLEARWATER

The small town of Clearwater (pop. 1,600), 125 kilometers (78 miles) north of Kamloops, is the gateway to Wells Gray Provincial Park. A few motels, restaurants, gas stations, services, and an information center are on the highway; the rest of the community is off the highway to the south.

Practicalities

A couple of good overnight options lie along the park access road (see Wells Gray *Accommodations and Camping*), or stay beside a pleasant lake in Clearwater at **Dutch Lake Resort & RV Park** (361 Ridge Rd., 250/674-3351 or 888/884-4424, www.dutchlake.com; March–Nov.), where tent camping is $24 and hookups range $28–32. Cabins are $95–215, with the largest having two bedrooms and full kitchens. Resort activities revolve around families and the water; the on-site restaurant (daily 8:30 A.M.–3 P.M. and 5–9 P.M.) has a wide patio.

Housed in a massive log building a few hundred meters along the park access road, the **[C] Flower Meadow Bakery** (444 Clearwater Valley Rd., 250/674-3654; Mon.–Fri. 5 A.M.–6 P.M., Sat. 5 A.M.–5 P.M.) is impossible to miss—and you won't want to either. The breakfast burritos ($6) are healthy and huge; the lemon meringues are also supersized (but probably not as good for you), and the carrot cake will melt in your mouth. There's plenty of room for everyone, with the outdoor seating filling first. On your way out, buy an extra

CENTRAL B.C.

TERRY FOX

Terry Fox is a name that is sure to come up at some point on your Canadian travels. In 1977, as a college-bound teenager, Fox lost his right leg to cancer. On April 12, 1980, after three years of training, with next to no sponsorship and little media coverage, he set off from Newfoundland on his **Marathon of Hope**, with the aim of raising money for cancer research. After he ran over 5,000 kilometers (3,100 miles) in 144 days, a recurrence of the cancer forced him to stop just outside Ontario's Thunder Bay. Cancer had begun spreading to his lungs, and on June 28, 1981, aged just 22, he died. As his run had progressed, the attention had grown, and, more important, the donations poured in. In total, his Marathon of Hope raised $24 million, far surpassing all goals.

The legacy of Terry Fox lives on in many ways, including 2,650-meter (8,700-foot) **Mount Terry Fox**, along the Yellowhead Highway; the **Terry Fox Run**, an annual fall event in many Canadian towns; Vancouver's **Terry Fox Plaza** and a tribute in the adjacent BC Sports Hall of Fame and Museum; and an annual $5 million scholarship fund.

loaf of bread or a stacked sandwich to go for a picnic in the park.

At the turnoff to Wells Gray Provincial Park is **Clearwater Visitor Centre** (250/674-2646; summer daily 8 A.M.–6 P.M., the rest of the year weekdays 9 A.M.–5 P.M.). Look for the moose sculpture out front. It's a popular spot for tour buses (a handy restroom stop between Jasper and Kamloops, I was told by a coach driver), so if the center is crowded, bide your time with an ice cream from the adjacent log cabin.

◀ WELLS GRAY PROVINCIAL PARK

Snow-clad peaks, extinct volcanoes, and ancient lava flows. Amazing waterfalls—so many the park is often referred to as the "Waterfall Park." Icy mineral springs, subalpine forest, and flower-filled meadows. Prolific wildlife (I counted six bears, five deer, and two moose on my last visit). An abundance of lakes and rivers where anglers can fish to their heart's content for rainbow trout and Dolly Varden.

The main access road into the 540,000-hectare (1,334,000-acre) park leads north from Clearwater for 37 kilometers (23 miles) to the park boundary. From there it continues 11 kilometers (6.8 miles) to one of the park's highlights, Helmcken Falls, where it turns to gravel and continues another 18 kilometers (11 miles) to its end at Clearwater Lake. Although this access road barely penetrates the park, driving its length is enough to get a taste of the rugged northern reaches. If it's not, you can take a canoe trip or boat tour from the end of the road.

Sights and Hikes

Make your first stop 10 kilometers (6.2 miles) from Clearwater, where a short trail leads through an old-growth forest of cedar and hemlock to a colorful lava canyon where 61-meter-high (200-foot-high) **Spahats Creek Falls** plummets over multicolored bedrock into the Clearwater River.

Continuing through the park, take a signposted gravel road to the west to **Green Viewing Tower** atop Green Mountain. The viewpoint provides panoramic views of a volcanic cone and many spectacular, rugged peaks, including snow-covered Garnet Peak, highest in the park.

Wells Gray is best known for its waterfalls, the two most spectacular of which are accessible by road. Southernmost is **Dawson Falls**, four kilometers (2.5 miles) into the park, where the **Murtle River** cascades over a 90-meter-wide (295-foot-wide) ledge. A little farther along the main road is the **Mush Bowl** (or Devil's Punchbowl), where the river has carved huge holes in the riverbed. But save some film for incredible **Helmcken Falls**, British Columbia's fourth-highest falls, where the Murtle River cascades off the edge of Murtle Plateau in a sparkling, 137-meter-high (449-foot-high) torrent to join the Clearwater River. In winter, the frozen falls create an enormous ice cone as tall as a 20-story building.

For an enjoyable short walk from the road (20 minutes each way), hike the one-kilometer (0.6-mile) trail out to **Ray Farm,** former home of one of the area's first settlers. The picturesque abandoned farm buildings sit among rolling meadows full of wildflowers.

Farther north up the road, a 500-meter (0.3-mile) trail (10 minutes each way) winds through a stand of towering cedar trees to **Bailey's Chute,** a narrow rapids-filled passage. In fall, large numbers of chinook salmon battle the torrent, trying in vain to leap up the chute. After a number of valiant attempts, they're washed back downstream to the gravel beds where they spawn and die.

Clearwater Lake

The road ends at a boat ramp/canoe dock beside the southern end of Clearwater Lake, 66 kilometers (41 miles) from the town of Clearwater. To make the most of the lake, you really need to take to the water. Based just before the end of the road (take the Clearwater Campground turnoff), **Clearwater Lake Tours** (250/674-2121, www.clearwaterlaketours .com) offers a couple of options. A three-hour motorboat cruise to Azure Lake, including a short walk, departs daily at 11 A.M. and 2:30 P.M.; adult $70, senior $65, child $40. The company rents canoes ($40 per day) and kayaks ($40–55 per day) for those who would rather propel themselves.

Accommodations and Camping

Around halfway between Clearwater and Helmcken Falls, **(** **Wells Gray Guest Ranch** (250/674-2792 or 866/467-4346, www .wellsgrayranch.com; mid-May–Sept.) is surrounded by grassy meadows full of wildflowers and grazing horses. Activities organized for guests include horseback riding ($40 for a 1.5-hour ride), wildlife viewing ($20–55), canoeing, white-water rafting, fishing, and

western-style barbecues. Overnight options are: well-furnished, kitchen-equipped cabins ($120 s, $130 d); ranch house rooms with shared bathrooms ($90 s or d); tepees ($15 per person); a bunkhouse ($15 per person); and a limited number of campsites ($15). The ranch also has a restaurant and saloon (daily 4 P.M.–midnight).

Continuing north, **Helmcken Falls Lodge** (250/674-3657, www.helmckenfalls.com) overlooks a golf course and seemingly endless forested hills. The main lodge was constructed as a fishing camp in the 1940s but has been revamped since, with motel-like rooms costing $134–165 s or d and the on-site restaurant cooking up simple, well-priced meals. Camping with hookups is $22–30.

Each of the four park campgrounds along the access road has drinking water, toilets, and picnic tables; none have hookups or showers. Sites cost $14 per night. Heading up the road from Clearwater, you'll pass, in order, **Spahats Creek Campground,** within walking distance of the falls; **Pyramid Campground,** just beyond Dawson Falls; **Falls Creek Campground,** with large riverside sites; and finally **Clearwater Lake Campground,** which is almost at the end of the road, right on the lake, and is the first to fill each night. Although no reservations are taken, you can find out about campsite availability at the Clearwater Visitor Centre. If you need a serviced site, stay at tranquil **Wells Gray Golf Resort & RV Park** (35 kilometers/ 22 miles north of Clearwater, 250/674-0072; May–Oct.), which has 50 campsites set in the middle of a full-length nine-hole golf course (greens fee $18). Rates of $20–27 include hookups, free firewood, and use of modern shower facilities.

Information

Park information is available at **Clearwater Visitor Centre** (250/674-2646; summer daily 8 A.M.–6 P.M., the rest of the year weekdays 9 A.M.–5 P.M.). The center sells two invaluable guidebooks to the park: *Exploring Wells Gray Park* and *Nature Wells Gray.*

CENTRAL B.C.

BLUE RIVER

Although right on busy Highway 5, 215 kilometers (134 miles) north of Kamloops, this one-time railway division point has remained small, holding just a few hundred residents along with services for passing travelers. Lake Eleanor, in the middle of town, offers a good beach and swimming, but most visitors head into the surrounding wilderness—the Cariboo Mountains to the north, Wells Gray Provincial Park to the west, and the northern reaches of the North Thompson River just to the east. Access to the eastern reaches of Wells Gray Provincial Park is by a 24-kilometer (15-mile) gravel road heading west from the middle of Blue River. From the trailhead at the end of the road, it's a 2.5-kilometer (1.5-mile) walk to **Murtle Lake,** the park's largest freshwater lake.

Accommodations and Camping

◖ **Mike Wiegele Resort** (250/673-8381 or 800/661-9170, www.wiegele.com) is designed for the wintertime heli-skiing crowd, but it's open year-round. Mike Wiegele was instrumental in the development of "fat boy" skis that helped revolutionize powder skiing by making it easier for everyone. His resort has grown from humble beginnings to a world-class facility, featured in many ski movies and the host of the annual Powder 8 Championship. Wintertime visitors enjoy some of the world's most famous powder skiing in the Cariboo and Monashee Mountains, then kick back each evening at the upscale resort in Blue River. Accommodation is in large two- to six-room log chalets in a private setting beside Lake Eleanor. In the off-season (Apr.–Nov.), if the resort hasn't been booked by a tour group, the rooms are one of British Columbia's best bargains: $128–290 s or d for a luxurious suite with a full kitchen, log fireplace, and comfortable lounge.

Glacier Mountain Lodge (250/673-2393 or 877/452-2686, www.glaciermountainlodge.com) is another stylish Blue River accommodation, this one offering 33 well-appointed guest rooms. Summer rates of $92–189 s or d,

including a continental breakfast buffet and use of a hot tub, make this place good value.

The least expensive place to stay in town is **Blue River Campground** (250/673-8203, www.bluerivercampground.ca; May–mid-Oct.), where sites range $20–32 per night, or you can stay in a tepee for $40 s or d. The campground is within walking distance of Lake Eleanor.

VALEMOUNT AND BEYOND

North of Blue River, Highway 5 follows the North Thompson River through the Cariboo Mountains to Valemount, 20 kilometers (12 miles) south of the Yellowhead Highway. This small town boasts two scenic golf courses, overnight horseback trips with **Headwaters Outfitting** (250/566-4718, www.davehenry.com), lots of fishing holes (ask for a brochure at the information center), and mountain scenery all around. If you're passing through between mid-August and late September, be sure to visit **Swift Creek,** below the information center, where chinook salmon spawn after a 1,200-kilometer (745-mile) journey from the Pacific Ocean. At the south end of town is the spring-fed Cranberry Marsh, where you can expect to see Canada geese, teal, ducks, and red-winged blackbirds. Park at the Holiday Inn and follow the marked trail 500 meters (0.3 mile) to a bird tower for the best viewing opportunities.

Practicalities

◖ **Mica Mountain Lodge** (15658 Old Tete Jaune Rd., 250/566-9816 or 888/440-6422, www.micamountainlodge.bc.ca) is in a wilderness setting on the northwest side of town. During summer, guests ride horses, canoe, fish, and mountain bike. Come winter, it's cross-country skiing, dog sledding, and snowmobiling that are the major draws. The cabins are charming and practical, with full kitchens, three-piece en suite bathrooms, decks, TVs, and pine log beds. Summer rates are quoted at $135 s or d, but many visitors stay as part of an activity package. **Irvin's Park and Campground** (one kilometer/

0.6 mile north of town, 250/566-4781, www.irvins.ca; $24–30) has a few tent sites along one side, but it's best suited for RVs and trailers.

Cariboo Grill (1002 5th Ave., 250/566-8244; daily from 4:30 P.M.) is in an oversized log building beyond the downtown core along 5th Avenue. It's a good place for enjoying simple, hearty food, such as pastas under $16, steaks from $22 to $30, and a few Canadian specialties, such as caribou stew for $28.

Tourism Valemount (785 Cranberry Lake Rd., 250/566-4846, www.valemount.org) operates a **visitor center** along Highway 5, across from the turnoff to downtown. It's open mid-May to mid-September.

Valemount to Mount Robson

From the Yellowhead Highway junction 20 kilometers (12 miles) north of Valemount, Prince George is 270 kilometers (168 miles) to the west, and the BC–Alberta border is 76 kilometers (47 miles) east. Although most of the distance to the border is through Mount Robson Provincial Park, two worthwhile stops lie between the highway junction and the park. The first of these is **Rearguard Falls,** a one-kilometer (0.6-mile) hike (20 minutes each way) from the highway. Eight kilometers (five miles) downstream from the falls—some 1,200 kilometers (745 miles) up the Fraser River from the Pacific Ocean—is a spawning ground for Pacific salmon; many of the hardy fish make it all the way to the falls. Farther east along the highway is a viewpoint for **Mount Terry Fox** (see sidebar, *Terry Fox*).

◀ MOUNT ROBSON PROVINCIAL PARK

Spectacular Mount Robson Provincial Park was created in 1913 to protect 224,866 hectares (555,650 acres) of steep canyons and wide forested valleys; icy lakes, rivers, and streams; and rugged mountain peaks permanently blanketed in snow and ice. Towering over the park's western entrance is magnificent 3,954-meter (12,970-foot) Mount Robson,

© ANDREW HEMPSTEAD

The approach to Mount Robson Provincial Park is stunning.

highest peak in the Canadian Rockies. The park lies along the Continental Divide, adjacent to Jasper National Park. The main watershed is the Fraser River, one of British Columbia's most important waterways. Highway 16, from where many roadside sights present themselves, splits the park in two, but for experienced backpackers it is the super-scenic Berg Lake Trail that attracts.

Roadside Sights

If you're approaching the park from the west along Highway 16, you'll see **Mount Robson** long before you reach the park boundary (provided the weather is cooperating). It's impossible to confuse this distinctive peak with those that surround it—no wonder it's known as the "Monarch of the Canadian Rockies." Once inside the park boundary, the highway climbs gradually to the main facility area, where you'll find a visitor center, campgrounds, a gas station, and a restaurant. From this point, the sheer west face of Mount Robson

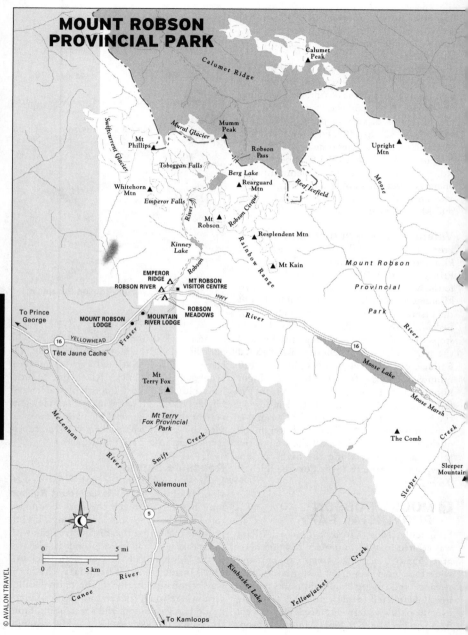

MOUNT ROBSON PROVINCIAL PARK

Calumet Peak

Calumet Ridge

Mumm Peak

Upright Mtn

Robson Pass

Moose

Mural Glacier

Mt Phillips

Toboggan Falls

Berg Lake

Reargard Mtn

Reef Icefield

Whitehorn Mtn

Emperor Falls

Robson Cirque

Mt Robson

Resplendent Mtn

Kinney Lake

Mount Robson

Mt Kain

Rainbow Range

Provincial

Park

River

EMPEROR RIDGE

ROBSON RIVER

MT ROBSON VISITOR CENTRE

Robson

HWY

ROBSON MEADOWS

River

To Prince George

MOUNT ROBSON LODGE

MOUNTAIN RIVER LODGE

YELLOWHEAD

Moose Lake

Fraser

Tête Jaune Cache

Moose Marsh

Mt Terry Fox

Mt Terry Fox Provincial Park

Swift Creek

The Comb

Sleeper Mountain

McLennan River

Valemount

River

Sleeper Creek

N

0 5 mi

0 5 km

Kinbasket Lake

Yellowjacket Creek

Canoe River

To Kamloops

slices skyward just seven kilometers away across a flower-filled meadow. This is as close as you can get to the peak in your vehicle.

From the visitor center, the highway climbs steeply then parallels photogenic **Moose Lake.** Waterfalls on the far side of the lake create a scenic backdrop. The Moose River drains into the Fraser River at **Moose Marsh,** a good spot for wildlife watching at the southeast end of the lake. Moose often feed here at dawn and dusk, and waterfowl are present throughout the day. Continuing westward, the highway crosses the upper reaches of the Fraser River before passing long and narrow Yellowhead Lake at the foot of 2,458-meter (8,060-foot) **Yellowhead Mountain.**

Finally, Highway 16 exits the park at the 1,066-meter (3,500-foot) **Yellowhead Pass,** on the BC–Alberta border 60 kilometers (37.2 miles) east of the visitor center. It's the lowest highway pass over the Continental Divide. Right before the pass is picturesque **Portal Lake,** with a small lakeside picnic area.

Berg Lake Trail

The 19.5-kilometer (12-mile) Berg Lake Trail is the most popular overnight hike in the Canadian Rockies, but don't let the crowds put you off—the hike is well worth it. Beautiful aqua-colored Berg Lake lies below the north face of Mount Robson, which rises 2,400 meters (7,880 feet) directly behind the lake. Glaciers on the mountain's shoulder regularly calve off into the lake, resulting in the icebergs that give the lake its name.

Starting from two kilometers (1.2 miles) north of the visitor center along a narrow access road, the trail follows the Robson River 4.5 kilometers (2.8 miles) through dense subalpine forest to glacially fed **Kinney Lake.** There the trail narrows, crossing the fastflowing river at the eight-kilometer (five-mile) mark and climbing alongside it. The next four kilometers (2.5 miles), through the steep-sided Valley of a Thousand Falls, are the most demanding, but views of four spectacular waterfalls ease the pain of the

CENTRAL B.C.

500-vertical-meter (1,640-foot) climb. The first glimpses of Mount Robson come soon after reaching the head of the valley, from where it's another kilometer to the outlet of Berg Lake, 17.5 kilometers (10.9 miles) from the trailhead. While the panorama from the lake is stunning, most hikers who have come this far want to spend some time exploring the area. From the north end of the lake, trails lead to Toboggan Falls and more mountain views, to the head of Robson Glacier, and to Robson Pass, which opens up the remote northern reaches of Jasper National Park.

It's possible to traverse the trail's first section and return the same day, but to get all the way to Berg Lake and back you need to stay in the backcountry overnight. Along the route are seven primitive campgrounds, including three along the lakeshore. Overnight hikers must register at the visitor center and pay a camping fee of $6 per person per night. Bookings are taken at the visitor center or through BC Parks (604/689-9025 or 800/689-9025). Book early as the quota fills quickly.

If the walk in seems too ambitious, **Robson Helimagic** (250/566-4700 or 877/454-4700, www.robsonhelimagic.com) makes drop-offs at Robson Pass from Valemount every Monday and Friday, from where day hikers can return to the visitor center in one long day. The cost is $199 per person (minimum four).

Accommodations and Camping

(**Mountain River Lodge** (four kilometers/2.5 miles west of the visitor center, 250/566-9899, www.mtrobson.com) is in a delightful setting right alongside the Fraser River. The main lodge holds four guest rooms, each with a different character, a balcony, and private bathroom. The smallest of the rooms (with twin beds and a private bathroom down the hall) is $89 s or d, while the other three are $119; rates include a cooked breakfast. Self-contained cabins cost $149 per night, with breakfast available at an extra charge. One kilometer (0.6 mile) west of Mountain River Lodge is **Mount Robson**

Lodge (250/566-4821 or 888/566-4821, www.mountrobsonlodge.com; May–Oct.), with 18 freestanding cabins ($70–130 s or d); the more expensive ones have kitchens, or eat at the small coffee shop.

Within the park are four auto-accessible campgrounds, with another just outside the park boundary. Three of these are park operated. Closest to the visitor center (and my favorite) is **Robson River Campground,** where numerous trails lead down to the river for the classic upstream view of Mount Robson. It's also only a short walk to the visitor center and a café. Across the highway is the larger **Robson Meadows Campground,** with 125 sites set on a spiral road system that centers on an outdoor theater that hosts evening interpretive programs through summer. A number of sites at Robson Meadows can be reserved through www .discovercamping.ca. Both campgrounds have flush toilets and showers but no hookups; $17 per site. Beside the east end of Yellowhead Lake (swimming for the brave), 50 kilometers (31 miles) from the visitor center, is the more rustic **Lucerne Campground,** where sites are $14. All facilities are open May to mid-September. **Emperor Ridge Campground** (250/566-8438; mid-May–late Sept.) is a small commercial facility right behind the visitor center; $16.50 per site including hot showers but no hookups. **Robson Shadows Campground** is part of Mount Robson Lodge (250/566-4821 or 888/566-4821, www.mountrobsonlodge .com; May–Oct.; $15), outside of the park and five kilometers (3.1 miles) west of the visitor center. It also has showers but no hookups.

Information

At the park's western entrance, **Mount Robson Visitor Centre** (250/566-9174, www.bcparks .ca; mid-June–mid-Sept. daily 8 A.M.–8 P.M., mid-May–mid-June and mid-Sept.–mid-Oct. daily 8 A.M.–5 P.M.) features informative slide shows, an evening interpretive program, and trail reports updated daily.

Cariboo Country

The wild, sparsely populated Cariboo region extends from Kamloops north to Prince George and west to the Pacific Ocean. Its most dramatic natural features are the mountain ranges rising like bookends on either side. In the west, the **Coast Mountains** run parallel to the coast and rise to a height of 4,016 meters (13,200 feet) at **Mount Waddington.** In the east, the **Cariboo Mountains** harbor numerous alpine lakes, high peaks, and several provincial parks. Between the two ranges flows the **Fraser River,** which is flanked to the west by expansive plateaus home to British Columbia's biggest ranches.

This is cowboy country, where horseback holidays and the Williams Lake Stampede are the main visitor drawcards. This was once gold-rush country—most of the region's towns began as stopping places along the Gold Rush Trail. Those such as **100 Mile House** owe their names to the trail but have remained small, while others, such as **Williams Lake** and **Quesnel,** have continued to grow and are service centers for the ranching and forestry industries. The only coastal access in Cariboo Country is via Highway 20, which runs through **Tweedsmuir Provincial Park** to **Bella Coola,** at the head of a long fjord.

CACHE CREEK

A town born with the fur trade at a spot where traders cached furs and food supplies, Cache Creek was once the largest town between Vancouver, 337 kilometers (200 miles) to the south, and Kamloops, 80 kilometers (50 miles) to the east. But since the Coquihalla Highway opened in the 1980s, the town is but a shadow of its former self. The surrounding desertlike climate is intriguing: Sagebrush and cacti grow on the relatively barren volcanic landscape, and tumbleweeds blow through town. Due to the town's former highway prominence, the main drag is lined with motels, roadside diners, and gas stations.

◖ Historic Hat Creek Ranch

Between 1885 and 1905, the Cariboo Wagon Road bustled with stagecoaches and freight wagons. One of the few sections of the original road still open to the public is at Hat Creek Ranch, 11 kilometers north of Cache Creek on Highway 97 (250/457-9722 or 800/782-0922, www.hatcreekranch.com; mid-May–mid-Oct. daily 10 A.M.–6 P.M.). Many of the original buildings—some dating as far back as 1861—still stand, and visitors can watch the blacksmith at his forge, appreciate a collection of antique farm machinery, enjoy a picnic lunch in the orchard, or take a guided tour of the ranch house. Admission to the ranch is free, but a donation is requested after touring the house.

For those looking for accommodations, a lack of creature comforts is a trade-off for experiencing the western atmosphere of this historic property. Cabins with shared bathrooms and no linen are least expensive ($65 s or d), but the en suite cabins with both queen and bunk beds, linen, and a coffeemaker ($85) are a better deal. Other overnight options include tepees ($35), Miners' Tents ($35), unserviced campsites ($10), powered sites ($15), and a native pit house ($100). Other amenities include modern bathrooms, native sweat lodges (similar to a sauna), and a restaurant.

Accommodations and Camping

The **Sage Hills Motel** (1390 Hwy. 97, 250/457-6451, www.sagehillsmotel.com; $55, $65 with a kitchen) is one of many local motels that would have filled every night before the highway was rerouted. Today, it's seen better days, but the owners try their best, keeping the place clean and planting a colorful bed of flowers out front each spring.

Summer temperatures around Cache Creek can get very high, so the outdoor pool at **Brookside Campsite** (TransCanada Hwy., east of town, 250/457-6633; Apr.–Oct., www.brooksidecampsite.com; $18–25) is a good enough reason to choose this commercial

CENTRAL B.C.

ECHO VALLEY RANCH & SPA

You can choose between several guest ranches in Cariboo Country, but none comes close to the luxury offered at Echo Valley Ranch & Spa (northwest of Clinton, 250/459-2386 or 800/253-8831, www.evranch.com; mid-Mar.-Oct.). Deep in the heart of ranching country, the resort provides the opportunity to immerse yourself in Western culture while indulging in the amenities of an upmarket lodge. The emphasis is on horseback riding, with lessons and guided rides scheduled each day, but there are plenty of other things to do, such as taking a four-wheel-drive excursion into the nearby Fraser River Canyon, watching a falcon trainer at work, and learning about native culture. The centerpiece of the sprawling property is an impressive main lodge built entirely of glistening spruce logs. Inside is a comfortable lounge area, the communal dining room overlooking an open kitchen, and a downstairs billiards and TV room. Adjacent is an impressive Baan Thai structure, with full spa services, and the Pavilion, for quiet contemplation.

Rooms in the main lodge are beautifully furnished, and each has a private balcony, while the Honeymoon Cabin sits high above a deep ravine and has a wraparound deck complete with hot tub. Dining is ranch style, at a couple of long tables with plenty of interaction between guests. But the food – from a one-time chef to European royalty – is anything but chili and beans.

As you'd expect, staying at Echo Valley isn't cheap (from $300 pp per night in high season), but it's a very special place that my wife and I hold dear memories of from our own honeymoon.

campground with all facilities, including wireless Internet.

LILLOOET

This historic town of 2,400 was founded as Mile Zero of the 1858 Cariboo Wagon Road—also known as the Gold Rush Trail—which led north to the Barkerville and Wells goldfields. Several towns along the Gold Rush Trail—70 Mile House, 100 Mile House, and 150 Mile House, among them—were named for their distance up the wagon road from Lillooet. With thousands of prospectors passing through in the mid-1800s, Lillooet was the scene of its own gold rush. By this time the city held some 16,000 residents, making it the second-largest population center north of San Francisco and west of Chicago. But as with most other boomtowns, the population explosion was short-lived.

Sights and Recreation

A row of rusty farming relics out front marks **Lillooet Museum** (790 Main St., 250/256-4308; May–Oct. Tues.–Sat. 10 A.M.–4 P.M., extended to daily 9 A.M.–7 P.M. in July and Aug.). Inside are ore samples and details about the one-time boomtown's mining history and growth. Within the museum is the local visitor info center. After visiting here, saunter along wide Main Street and pretend you're back in the gold-rush era—which won't be hard if you happen to be here in June during **Only in Lillooet Days.** During this weeklong celebration, the town re-creates the Old West with all sorts of entertaining events.

Lillooet is also home to the unique **Sheep Pasture Golf Course** (five kilometers/3.1 miles southwest of town, 250/256-4484; Apr.–Oct.; $13), a nine-hole layout on a working sheep farm.

Accommodations and Camping

One block up the hill from the museum, **4 Pines Motel** (108 8th Ave., 250/256-4247 or 800/753-2576, www.4pinesmotel.com) has older rooms ($65 s or d) and a newer wing ($85 s or d). **Cayoosh Creek Campground** (no reservations

taken; $18–22) is a treed spot near the south end of town, where Cayoosh Creek drains into the much larger Fraser River. Facilities include hot showers and power hookups.

CLINTON TO 100 MILE HOUSE
Clinton

The old-fashioned town of Clinton lies 40 kilometers (25 miles) north of Cache Creek on Highway 97. **South Cariboo Historical Museum** (Hwy. 97, 250/459-2442; summer Mon.–Fri. 10 A.M.–6 P.M.) occupies an old schoolhouse made of handmade bricks fired locally in the 1890s. The museum contains pioneer belongings, guns, historical photos, native and Chinese artifacts, freight wagons, and all sorts of items from the gold-rush days. A nearby natural attraction worth seeing is Painted Chasm, in **Chasm Provincial Park,** 16 kilometers (10 miles) north of town, then four kilometers (2.5 miles) east. During the last ice age, glacial meltwater carved a 300-meter-deep (984-foot-deep) box canyon out of mineral-laden volcanic bedrock. It's quite a spectacle when the sunlight brings out the sparkling reds, yellows, and purples of the minerals. Every May, the town hosts the **Clinton Ball** (250/459-2146, www.clintonannualball .com), a fancy-dress wingding that has been held every year since 1868, making it Canada's oldest annual celebration.

The huge log structure on the main street is **Cariboo Lodge Resort** (250/459-7992 or 877/459-7992, www.cariboolodgebc.com). Although the rooms are motel-like, rates are reasonable ($64 s, $69 d) and a downstairs restaurant and western-style pub mean you don't have to leave the building after checking in.

North to 100 Mile House

Back on the main highway, between 70 Mile House and 100 Mile House, are several turn-offs leading to hundreds of lakes, big and small. All information centers in Cariboo Country stock the invaluable *Cariboo-Chilcotin Fishing Guide.* Updated annually, the booklet features essential fishing information (where, when, and with what) for many of the lakes, plus maps, camping spots, and even recipes for the ones that didn't get away.

The most accessible provincial park between Clinton and 100 Mile House is at **Green Lake,** 14 kilometers (8.7 miles) east of Highway 97 (turn off Highway 97 16 kilometers/10 miles northeast of 70 Mile House). This large, emerald-colored lake lies along an old Hudson's Bay Company fur-brigade trail; you can see traces of the trail along the lake's shoreline. The park has a shaded lakeside picnic area, a playground, horseshoe pits, relatively warm water for swimming, and a campground (mid-May–Sept.; $14).

Passing through 100 Mile House, it's difficult to miss the **South Cariboo Visitor Centre**—just look for the world's largest cross-country skis out front (250/395-5353 or 877/511-5353, www.southcaribootourism.com; Mon.–Fri. 8:30 A.M.–4:30 P.M., longer hours in summer). An area of wetland lies directly behind the information center, with signage depicting the many species that are often present.

Toward Williams Lake

Three kilometers (1.9 miles) north of 100 Mile House, a road heads east off the highway, leading 30 kilometers (18.6 miles) to **Ruth Lake,** which is stocked with rainbow trout; 44 kilometers (27 miles) to **Canim Beach Provincial Park,** with campsites for $14; and 70 kilometers (43.4 miles) to **Canim River Falls,** between Canim and Mahood Lakes.

Back out on the highway and continuing north, you'll come to 19-kilometer-long (12-mile-long) **Lac La Hache,** one of the most picturesque bodies of water in Cariboo Country (and known by boat anglers for its hungry kokanee and lake trout). At the lake's south end is the small community of Lac La Hache, with a small museum and information center on the east side of the highway. At the lake's north end, a provincial park offers campsites for $14.

The next main turnoff, at **150 Mile House,** takes you on a 65-kilometer (40-mile) scenic drive (the last 10 kilometers/6.2 miles are unpaved) northeast to **Horsefly Lake Provincial Park,** protecting a forest of old-growth western

red cedar and Douglas fir. You can swim, rent a canoe, or just relax on the pebbly beach. The small campground has sites for $14.

WILLIAMS LAKE

Originally bypassed by the builders of the Cariboo Wagon Road because of protests from a stubborn landowner, Williams Lake (pop. 11,000), 95 kilometers (59 miles) north of 100 Mile House, has ironically become the Cariboo region's largest city. Today the ranching and forestry center is best known for the Williams Lake Stampede, one of Canada's biggest rodeos.

Sights and Recreation

The highlight of the large **Museum of the Cariboo Chilcotin** (113 4th Ave. N., 250/392-7404, summer Mon.–Sat. 10 A.M.–4 P.M., the rest of the year Tues.–Sat. 11 A.M.–4 P.M.; adult $2) is the BC Cowboy Hall of Fame and associated rodeo, ranching, and Stampede displays. Other exhibits include historical photos, remains of the Chinese settlement at Quesnel Forks, and all kinds of picks, pans, and axes from the gold-mining days. **Station House Gallery,** in the original railway station (1 Mackenzie Ave. N., 250/392-6113) displays an excellent collection of western-themed art.

On the eastern outskirts of the city, **Scout Island Nature Centre** (250/398-8532, May–mid-Sept. Mon.–Fri. 9 A.M.–4 P.M., Sun. 1–4 P.M.; free) is surrounded by wetlands that serve as a staging area for migratory waterfowl. Colorful displays inside the center catalog the surrounding ecosystem, but the idea is to get out into the wetlands. Wander along one of the short hiking trails or climb the observation tower for a bird's-eye view of the wild landscape.

The region's diverse waterways provide plenty of opportunities for boating. Numerous gently flowing streams and serene lakes make perfect spots for canoe and kayak discovery trips, while the Fraser River provides opportunities for exciting rafting trips down steep-walled canyons, through semi-arid hill country, and past abandoned boom towns. **Chilko River Rafting Co.** (250/267-5258, www.chilkoriver.com) offers a full-day trip in

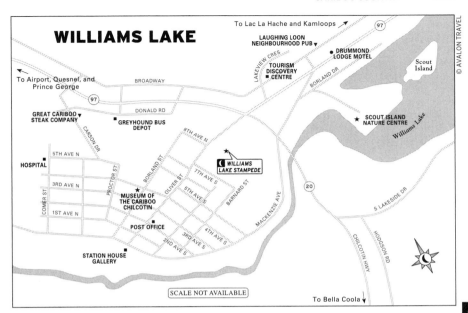

rafts and inflatable kayaks for $125 per person. At **Springhouse Trails Ranch** (Dog Creek Rd., 250/392-4780; May–Sept.), horse rental is $20 an hour or $80 per day, and you can stay out on the ranch overnight (see *Accommodations and Camping*). The ranch is 20 kilometers (12 miles) southwest of town off Highway 20.

Williams Lake Stampede
On the first weekend of July, the town comes alive as North America's best cowboys and cowgirls compete for over $100,000 in the Williams Lake Stampede (250/392-6585 or 800/717-6336, www.williamslakestampede .com). The whole town dresses up for the occasion; the locals put on Western garb, and the shop fronts are decorated accordingly. The highlight of each day's action is the rodeo, and events that include bareback riding, saddle-bronc riding, calf-roping, steer-wrestling, barrel racing, chuckwagon racing, and the crowd favorite: bull riding. Scheduled around these traditional rodeo events are cow-milking contests, tractor pulls, cattle penning, chariot races, raft races, a parade, barn dances, all-you-can-eat breakfasts and steak-outs, and a host of other decidedly Western-flavored activities.

Accommodations and Camping
If you're after somewhere to simply rest your head, stay on the east side of town at the **Drummond Lodge Motel,** set on extensive grounds overlooking the lake (1405 Hwy. 97 one kilometr/0.6 mile east of downtown, 250/392-5334 or 800/667-4555, www .drummondlodge.com; $85–95 s or d including a light breakfast).

For a more memorable overnight experience—longer if you can afford it—plan on spending time at **Tyee Lake Resort** (Tyee Lake Rd., 250/989-9850 or 866/989-9850, www.tyeelak-eresort.com; May–Oct.). Set on a perfect little lake, the main lodge holds 18 guest rooms, each decked out with handcrafted wooden furniture and a small balcony. The rates top out at a very reasonable $144 in July and August, including breakfast. Fishing is the most popular outdoor activity—troll for rainbow trout for best results—with canoes, motor-boats, and fishing tackle for rent. The resort restaurant is also worth mentioning. Open daily for lunch and dinner, it offers meals like New York steak pan-fried with a sweet mustard glaze ($27). Tyee Lake requires some effort to reach, so you should plan on spending at least two nights at the resort. The turnoff is 47 kilometers (29 miles) north of Williams Lake toward Quesnel; turn east at McLeese Lake, following Beaver Lake Road for 10 kilometers (6.2 miles), then following the resort signs for 12 kilometers (7.4 miles) south.

If a ranching vacation is more your style, consider **Springhouse Trails Ranch,** 20 kilometers (12 miles) southwest of town (on Dog Lake Rd., 250/392-4780, www.springhouse trails.com), where basic but comfortable rooms are $71 s, $79 d, and all-inclusive package deals are available from $145 per person per day, including accommodations, meals taken in a communal dining room, and riding. You can also camp here for $26 a night, with full hookups. Children especially will love this place.

Food

Williams Lake lacks outstanding eateries but has no shortage of typical family-style restaurants. One of these is the **Great Cariboo Steak Company,** in the Fraser Inn Hotel (285 Donald Rd., 250/398-7055; daily for lunch, breakfast, and dinner). Breakfast ranges $7–11; all-you-can-eat lunch buffets are $12; dinners range from $9.50 for the all-you-can-eat salad bar to $16–25 for steak, prime rib, chicken, seafood, and pasta dishes. On the northern edge of town, the **Laughing Loon Neighbourhood Pub** (1730 S. Broadway, 250/398-5666) offers a wide-ranging menu of beef, chicken, and pork dishes in a welcoming heritage-style atmosphere.

Information

Beside the highway on the east side of town is impressive log and timber-frame **Tourism Discovery Centre** (1660 Broadway, 250/392-5025, www.williamslake.ca; summer daily 8 A.M.–8 P.M., the rest of the year Mon.–Fri. 9 A.M.–5 P.M.). Inside is the local visitor center,

a café, a gift shop, and displays on local natural and human history.

HIGHWAY 20

Highway 20 west of Williams Lake leads 485 kilometers (301 miles) to Bella Coola, the only road-accessible town along the 500 kilometers (310 miles) of coastline between Powell River and Prince Rupert. The highway is paved less than half its length; the rest of the way it's mostly all-weather gravel and can be slow going in spots. But experiencing the vast and varied wilderness of the **Chilcotin Coast** is worthy of as much time as you can afford. And with a ferry at the end of the road providing a link to Port Hardy (Vancouver Island), you'll only need to make the trip one-way.

Services along Highway 20 are spaced at regular intervals, but don't take the trip too lightly; make sure your vehicle is in good condition, and carry tools and spare tires to alleviate the necessity of an expensive tow-truck ride.

West from Williams Lake

The road west from Williams Lake meanders through the Fraser River Valley before beginning a steady climb to the **Chilcotin Plateau,** the heart of British Columbia's ranching country.

The first worthwhile detour is **Junction Sheep Range Provincial Park,** at the end of a 20-kilometer (12-mile) unpaved road that branches south off Highway 20 at Riske Creek, 47 kilometers (29 miles) west of Williams Lake. The triangular park protects 4,573 hectares (11,300 acres) of mostly semi-arid grasslands between the Fraser and Chilcotin Rivers, home to around 600 bighorn sheep. The confluence of these two major rivers forms the southern tip of the park and can be reached on foot in well under one hour from the end of the access road.

Back on Highway 20, the first community with services is **Alexis Creek,** 114 kilometers (71 miles) west of Williams Lake. Beside the Chilcotin River, 10 kilometers (6.2 miles) west of Alexis Creek, is **Bull Canyon Provincial Park,** at a bend in the Chilcotin River. Camping is $14.

Continuing west, the highway follows the Chilcotin River for 60 kilometers (37 miles) to Chilanko Forks; here a spur road leads 10 kilometers (6.2 miles) north to **Puntzi Lake.** This picturesque body of water is home to a number of low-key fishing resorts, including **Poplar Grove Resort** (250/481-1186 or 800/578-6804, www.poplargroveresort.com). Small lakeside cabins come with basic cooking facilities and shared washrooms ($48–85 s or d), or choose the en suite lodge units ($65–90 s or d). Camping with hookups is $16–20. If you plan on rising early to fish for kokanee, make arrangements to rent a motorboat the night before.

Chilko Lake

Continuing toward the coast, Highway 20 narrows and turns to gravel at the small community of Tatla Lake, which is also the turnoff to remote **Ts'il-os Provincial Park.** Pronounced "SIGH-loss," Ts'il-os is the native Chilcotin name for the park's highest peak, 3,066-meter (10,060-foot) Mount Tatlow, but its most magnificent feature is 84-kilometer-long (52-mile-long), glacially fed Chilko Lake, which is ringed by the highest peaks of the Coast Mountains. The park is home to a wide variety of wildlife, including grizzly and black bears, bighorn sheep, and, at higher elevations, mountain goats. Fishing in the lake is legendary for rainbow trout (to 2.7 kilograms/six pounds). The park access road parallels the lake's northeast shore and holds a number of accommodations. For outdoor enthusiast, the best of these, 60 kilometers (37 miles) south of Highway 20, is ◖ **The Lodge at Chilko Lake** (250/481-3333 or 888/639-1114, www.chilkolake.com), which charges $795 per person for a two-night package.

Toward the Coast

From Tatla Lake, Highway 20 continues westward, climbing steadily to **Nimpo Lake,** where more self-contained resorts put the emphasis on fishing. From this point, it's 10 kilometers (6.2 miles) west to **Anahim Lake,** where anglers will be tempted to linger at **Anahim**

Lake Resort (250/742-3242 or 800/667-7212, www.anahimlakeresort.com; May–Oct.), where rainbow trout fishing is consistently good throughout summer. All but one cabin share a communal bathroom facility, but they all have a woodstove, fridge, running water, and screened-in veranda. A restaurant is open for all meals, and you can rent boats from the resort marina. Cabins are $75–125 s or d, and camping is $22–26.

From Anahim Lake, it's a steady climb of another 30 kilometers (19 miles) to 1,524-meter (5,000-foot) **Heckman Pass** over the Coast Mountains. West across the pass, you face **"The Hill."** This infamous descent from Heckman Pass to the Bella Coola Valley drops nearly the full 1,524 meters (5,000 feet) in less than 10 kilometers (6.2 miles). Be prepared for numerous switchbacks and a gradient as steep as 18 percent.

Tweedsmuir Provincial Park

At nearly a million hectares (2.5 million acres), this is British Columbia's largest provincial park. Roughly triangular, the park is bounded by Ootsa Lake on the north, the high peaks of the Coast Mountains on the west, and the Rainbow Range—so named for its colorful volcanic formations—on the east. Within these boundaries lies an untouched landscape, wild and remote, holding numerous river systems, forested valleys, alpine meadows, waterfalls, and glaciers. Most of those park highlights are accessible only on foot. Although the park's resident populations of large mammals are high, viewing opportunities are limited. Black and grizzly bears, mountain goats, caribou, wolves, and moose are all present, but they tend to remain well away from the highway. In early fall, grizzlies can occasionally be seen feeding on spawned-out salmon along the Atnarko River. Highway 20 meanders through the southern section of the park, but aside from two campgrounds and a handful of picnic areas along this route, the park is devoid of facilities.

One of the few short hiking trails is to a series of kettle ponds formed by a receding glacier that stalled many thousands of years ago. This

CENTRAL B.C.

trail is four kilometers (2.5 miles) each way, beginning from a picnic area 16 kilometers (10 miles) west of Atnarko River Campground.

Campgrounds are on the north bank of the Atnarko River (at the base of The Hill) and 30 kilometers (18.6 miles) west at Fisheries Pool. Facilities at both include pit toilets, drinking water, and picnic tables; $14 a night.

BELLA COOLA

The urge to see what's at the end of the road brings many travelers over The Hill and down to Bella Coola (pop. 800), 485 kilometers (301 miles) west of Williams Lake. Here the Bella Coola River drains into North Bentinck Arm, a gateway to the Inside Passage and the Pacific Ocean. The town lies in a coastal valley that was originally the home of the Nuxalk tribe.

Sights and Recreation

Housed in a historic schoolhouse, the **Bella Coola Museum** (250/799-5767; June–early Sept. Mon.–Sat. 10 A.M.–5 P.M.; $2) features artifacts of early Norwegian settlers and the Hudson's Bay Company, which established a post here in 1869. Over in Hagensborg, 15 kilometers (nine miles) inland, the many hand-hewn timber buildings still standing are testament to the construction skills of Norwegian settlers, who first arrived in the valley in 1894.

There's plenty of outdoor recreation to keep visitors busy. Unfortunately, most of the action is out on the water and requires the services of a boat charter company (not cheap). Fishing is the most popular activity; expect to pay from $150 per hour for four persons. Those with a sense of history will want to visit **Mackenzie Rock,** in the Dean Channel and accessible only by boat, where Alexander Mackenzie in his own words, "mixed up some vermillion and melted grease and inscribed in large characters on the face of the rock on which we slept last night, this brief memorial: Alexander Mackenzie, from Canada, by Land, the Twenty Second of July, One Thousand Seven Hundred and Ninety Three." In doing so, he became the first person to cross continental North America. For boat charter

information, contact **Bella Coola Outfitting** (604/946-0060, www.bcoutfitting.com).

Accommodations and Camping

Right on the river is **Bella Coola Motel** (Clayton St., 250/799-5323, www.bellacoolavalley .com; $95 s, $100 d, camping $20), with clean and comfortable rooms each with a full kitchen. Between Bella Coola and Hagensborg, the friendly hosts at **Eagle Lodge** (250/799-5587 or 866/799-5587, www.eaglelodgebc .com; June–Oct.) will make you feel welcome the moment you step through the front door. Each of eight rooms is configured differently, with the smallest having a twin bed ($80 s) and the largest a two-bedroom suite complete with a kitchen and fireplace ($135 s or d). A breakfast buffet is $7.50 per person, and guests have use of an outdoor hot tub positioned to take full advantage of the rural setting. **Gnome's Home Campground and RV Park** (Hagensborg, 250/982-2504, www.gnomes home.ca; Apr.–Oct.; $15–18) has showers, a cook shelter, and a laundry, and is the starting point for a short trail leading through the temperate rainforest.

DISCOVERY COAST PASSAGE

BC Ferries (250/386-3431 or 888/223-3779, www.bcferries.com) sailings from Bella Coola open a remote section of the British Columbia coastline that would otherwise be inaccessible. The main route is between Bella Coola and Port Hardy (Vancouver Island). The direct sailing takes 13 hours, or 31 hours with all stops. Study the timetable (on the BC Ferries website) to see which sailing suits your needs. When the ferry does make a stop, it's only for around two hours each time, so if you want to get off, plan on overnighting until the next ferry comes by. Peak one-way fares for the entire trip are adult $145, child 5–11 $80, vehicle $290.

Shearwater

The most accessible and interesting stop along the Discovery Coast Passage is Shearwater, on Denny Island. Shearwater is an old cannery village that has also been a logging camp, a base for flying boats patrolling the coast during World War II, and a stop for major shipping lines. The community was sold off to a private enterprise and today operates as **Shearwater Resort & Marina** (250/957-2666, www.shearwater .ca), complete with two lodges ($75–125 s or d) and an RV park ($25). The accommodations are fairly basic, and aimed toward anglers chasing salmon and halibut, but the resort does have a marina with boat rentals and fishing charters, kayak rentals, a general store, and the waterfront Fisherman's Bar & Grill. Rates are $65 s, $75–90 d, with the least expensive rooms sharing bathrooms. Some guests arrive on the scheduled BC Ferries service, others on an inexpensive boat shuttle operated by the resort.

QUESNEL

Back inland, Highway 97 north from Williams Lake takes you to Quesnel. The town (pop. 8,000) began during the Barkerville gold rush of the 1860s. Today the town's economy continues to thrive, with an asphalt plant, ranching, mining, and, especially, forestry industries (Two Mile Flat, east of downtown, is North America's most concentrated wood-products manufacturing area).

Sights

At **Heritage Corner** (Carson Ave. and Front St.), you can see the Old Fraser Bridge, the remains of the steamer *Enterprise,* a Cornish waterwheel used by gold miners, and the original Hudson's Bay Store. To learn all about Alexander Mackenzie or the gold-rush days, head to **Quesnel and District Museum** (Hwy. 97 at Carson Ave., 250/992-9580; summer daily 9 A.M.–6 P.M., Sept.–Apr. Tues.–Sat. 8:30 A.M.–4:30 P.M.; adult $3, child $1.50), which holds almost 30,000 artifacts. The scenic four-kilometer (2.5-mile) **Riverfront Walking Trail** loops around the downtown core, with plaques honoring early residents; start at any point along the river (allow 75 minutes).

CENTRAL B.C.

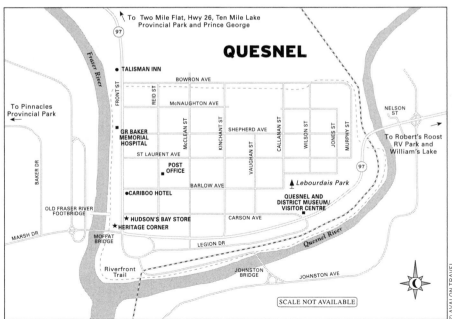

© AVALON TRAVEL

Eight kilometers (five miles) west of Quesnel on Baker Drive are the geologically intriguing, glacially eroded hoodoos at **Pinnacles Provincial Park.** The viewpoint is one kilometer (0.6 mile) from the day-use area; allow 40 minutes for the round-trip. Another local provincial park is **Ten Mile Lake,** 11 kilometers (6.8 miles) north of town. Fishing is regarded as good for rainbow trout, and there's a large beaver dam near the day-use area.

Billy Barker Days

The main event in Quesnel is Billy Barker Days (250/992-1234, www.quesnelbc.com/billy barkerdays), named for the prospector who made the first gold strike in the Cariboo. Over the third weekend of July, downtown streets are closed to traffic in favor of an outdoor crafts fair, parade, and dancing. Residents casually stroll around town in period costumes from the gold-mining days—men in cowboy hats, women in slinky long dresses with brightly feathered hats. The Quesnel Rodeo is one of some 150 events staged during the festival.

Accommodations and Camping

Right downtown, the restored 1896 **Cariboo Hotel** (254 Front St., 250/992-2333 or 800/665-3200, www.cariboohotel.com) has nine guest rooms with TVs and phones; rates of $70 s, $75 d include a continental breakfast. Farther north and across Highway 97 is the **Talisman Inn** (753 Front St., 250/992-7247 or 800/663-8090, www.talismaninn.bc.ca). Most of the 85 rooms are slightly dated ($70 s, $80 d), although the larger rooms, with more modern furnishings and particularly spacious bathrooms, along with microwaves and toasters, are best value ($90 s, $100 d).

For campers who don't need services, the best bet is to head north 11 kilometers (6.8 miles) to **Ten Mile Lake Provincial Park.** Of the park's two campgrounds, Lakeside is best (sites 4–9 are closest to the water) and has hot showers and flush toilets ($17 per night). During the week, snagging a spot isn't usually a problem, but on weekends the campground fills with Quesnel locals who come for the

swimming, fishing, and canoeing. Closer to town is **Robert's Roost RV Park** (3121 Gook Rd., 250/747-2015 or 888/227-8877, www .robertsroostcampsite.ca; Apr.–Oct.; $19–28) on the west side of Dragon Lake. To get there, take Highway 97 south, turn east on Gook Road, and go to the end. Amenities include coin showers, a laundry, boat rentals, and a beach with swimming.

Information

Quesnel Visitor Centre is beside Lebourdais Park (703 Carson Ave., 250/992-8716 or 800/992-4922, www.northcariboo.com; summer daily 8 A.M.–8 P.M., the rest of the year Mon.–Fri. 8:30 A.M.–4:30 P.M.).

EAST FROM QUESNEL
Cottonwood House

About 28 kilometers (17.4 miles) east of Quesnel on Highway 26, Cottonwood House (250/992-2071; mid-May–early Sept. daily 10 A.M.–5 P.M.; adult $4.50, senior $3.50, child $2) is a roadhouse built in 1864 to serve Barkerville-bound gold seekers. In addition to the old guesthouse, structures at the site include a barn, stable, and other outbuildings. You'll also find an interpretive center, displays of old farming equipment, a country-style café, and a shop selling handmade woodcrafts. Camping beside the Cottonwood River is $12.50–15, and cabins with shared bathrooms are $35 s or d, which includes site admission.

Wells

A few kilometers before reaching Barkerville, Highway 26 passes the village of Wells. Most local businesses hand out historic walking tour brochures of the town, which includes points of interest such as a one-time illegal gambling hall below a barbershop. In the center of the village is the 1933 **C Wells Hotel** (2341 Pooley St., 250/994-3427 or 800/860-2299, www.wellshotel.com), which has been wonderfully restored without losing its historic charm. Lounging in front of the log fireplace, surrounded by historic photos and with polished hardwood floors underfoot, is the perfect way to end a day of sightseeing. Or relax over dinner at a sidewalk table and watch the world of Wells go by. Rooms are in the original hotel or in a new wing, but all are well-furnished and good value at $90 s or d, including a continental breakfast.

Barkerville Historic Town

In 1862 Billy Barker struck gold on Williams Creek, 88 kilometers (55 miles) east of Quesnel. One of Canada's major gold rushes followed, as thousands of prospectors streamed in to what soon became known as Barkerville. The area turned out to be the richest of the Cariboo mining districts, yielding over $40 million in gold. By the mid-1860s Barkerville's population had peaked at over 10,000. But fortunes began to fade after the turn of the 20th century. In 1916 Barkerville was destroyed by fire. Although the town was quickly rebuilt, the gold played out soon thereafter, and many of the miners lost interest and moved on. Today the town is mostly restored, and is claimed to be North America's largest heritage site (250/994-3332 or 888/994-3332, www.barkerville.ca), comprising over 120 restored buildings. The grounds are open year-round 8 A.M.–8 P.M., although many of the attractions and rides operate June–September and for shorter hours. A day pass is adult $13, senior $11.75, child $7.50; entry for a second day is just $2 per person. Historic reenactments take place throughout summer, when the town's shops, stores, and restaurants all operate in a century-old time warp. Highlights include the town bakery, which sells some of the most mouthwatering baked goods in the province; stagecoach rides ($10); the chance to try your hand at gold-panning ($6); and the musical comedy performances at the Theatre Royal, presented 2–3 times daily ($12).

You can spend the night in one of two historic buildings within the town. Inside and out, **Kelly House** (250/994-3328, www.kellyhouse.ca; $89 s or d shared bath, $109 en suite) fits the heritage theme of Barkerville. Rates include a cooked breakfast that may include delightful apple pancakes topped with real cream. More

upscale, the 1898 **St. George Hotel** (250/994-0008 or 888/246-7690, www.stgeorgehotel.bc.ca; $120–140 s or d including breakfast) has been fully restored and offers seven guest rooms, some of which share bathrooms; all are tastefully furnished with comfortable beds and authentic antiques. The pick of three BC Parks-operated campgrounds (mid-June–Sept.) is **Lowhee Campground** ($19), with showers and a playground. **Forest Rose** ($17) also has shower facilities. **Government Hill Campground** ($16) is closest to the historic site, but as all three campgrounds are within walking distance, this is of little consequence. It's also the most rustic, with pit toilets and no showers.

Bowron Lake Provincial Park

Best known for the **Bowron Lake Canoe Circuit,** Bowron Lake Provincial Park encompasses 149,207 hectares (386,700 acres) of magnificent forests, lakes, and rivers in the Cariboo Mountains. To get there, take Highway 26 east of Quesnel toward Barkerville, but just past Wells take a signposted gravel road to the north.

The park boundary follows a chain of six major lakes—Indianpoint, Isaac, Lanezi, Sandy, Spectacle, and Bowron—and some smaller lakes and waterways that, roughly, form a diamond-shaped circuit. Campsites, cabins, and cooking shelters are strategically spaced along the way. To circumnavigate the entire 116-kilometer (72-mile) route takes 6–10 days of paddling and requires seven portages, the most difficult being a 2.5-kilometer (1.5-mile) uphill hike at the very start. As well as being proficient in the use of canoes, those attempting the route should be well prepared for backcountry travel and wet weather. July and August are the most popular months; try to avoid departing on a weekend if you like solitude. September is one of the most colorful months, with lakeside trees in their fall colors.

Before setting out on the circuit, paddlers must obtain a permit from the BC Parks Registration Centre (May 15–Sept. 30 daily 7 A.M.–8 P.M.) at the end of the park access road.

Permits cost $60 per person to a maximum of $120 per canoe. Because a limited number of persons are permitted on the circuit at any given time, you should reserve a spot as far in advance as possible (lines open January 2 for the following season) by calling 250/387-1642 or 800/435-5622. The reservation fee is $19.26 per canoe. A few spots are set aside each day for drop-ins, but the sensible course of action is to reserve as far ahead as possible. More information is online at www.bcparks.ca.

Two privately owned lodges near the end of the park access road provide meals and accommodations, and are as popular with those attempting the canoe circuit as with travelers who drive out simply to take in the wilderness setting. Both are right on Bowron Lake and offer canoe rentals and full outfitting services for those doing the lake circuit. Taking in guests since the 1930s, **Bowron Lake Lodge** (250/992-2733 or 800/519-3399, www.bowronlakelodge

.com) has both lake and river frontage, including its own private sandy beach. Motel-style rooms, some with kitchens and separate bedrooms, are $70–150 s or d. Campers pay $25 per site and have access to a cook shelter and coin showers. **Beckers Lodge** (250/992-8864 or 800/808-4761, www.beckerslodge.ca; May–early Oct.) has a choice of cabins ranging $80–220 s or d. The Trapper Cabins with shared bathrooms are the most basic, and the best is the family-friendly Betty Wendle Cabin ($220), with an upstairs loft that has water views, a full kitchen, a practical bathroom, separate bedrooms, and solid wooden furnishings throughout. Camping is $20–25. The restaurant, in the original lodge building, sits on a high bluff and oozes historic charm. It's open June through mid-September for breakfast and dinner. At the very end of the access road is a provincial park campground with 25 sites but no hookups (mid-May–Sept.; $14).

NORTHERN BRITISH COLUMBIA

Wild, remote northern British Columbia extends from the Yellowhead Highway (Highway 16) north to the 60th parallel. Its mostly forested landscape is broken by two major mountain ranges—the Rockies and the Coast Mountains—and literally thousands of lakes, rivers, and streams. Wildlife is abundant here; the land is home to moose, deer, black and grizzly bears, elk, Dall's sheep, and mountain goats.

The region's largest city is Prince George, a forestry and service center 780 kilometers (484 miles) north of Vancouver in the heart of a recreational paradise. From Prince George, the Yellowhead Highway runs west to the towns of Vanderhoof, Burns Lake, Smithers, and Terrace, all jumping-off points for fishing and boating adventures on surrounding lakes and rivers.

The western terminus of the Yellowhead Highway is Prince Rupert, a busy coastal city at the north end of the BC Ferries network and a stop on the Alaska Marine Highway. It's northern British Columbia's sole coastal city; north of here the coastline is part of Alaska.

Off the coast from "Rupert" are the Queen Charlotte Islands, part of British Columbia yet entirely unique. The islands beckon adventure, with legendary fishing, great beachcombing, ancient Haida villages, and a typical laid-back island atmosphere.

Two routes head north off the Yellowhead Highway. The Stewart-Cassiar Highway begins west of Prince George and parallels the Coast Mountains, passing the turnoff to the twin towns of Stewart and Hyder and some remote provincial parks. It ends at its junction

© ANDREW HEMPSTEAD

HIGHLIGHTS

🌙 Fort St. James National Historic Site: It's a little out of the way, but the detour to Canada's largest collection of buildings from the fur-trade era is well worthwhile (page 366).

🌙 'Ksan Historical Village: Learn about native culture at this village, where totem poles, longhouses, and Gitxsan arts and crafts are on display (page 373).

🌙 North Pacific Historic Fishing Village: Step back in time to experience the sights and sounds of the West Coast's oldest cannery village (page 381).

🌙 Gwaii Haanas National Park Reserve: Traveling to the Queen Charlotte Islands is

an adventure in itself, but to *really* get off the beaten track, schedule a trip to the Gwaii Haanas National Park Reserve (page 396).

🌙 Hyder: Defining the tiny hamlet of Hyder is difficult. It's scenic, it's eccentric, and it's unforgettable – especially in late summer when bears are as common as visitors along the main street (page 400).

🌙 Liard River Hot Springs: This is more of a must-soak than a must-see (page 411).

🌙 Atlin: British Columbia's most remote town, Atlin is also one of the most scenic. Take a trip out on to Atlin Lake to fully appreciate the surrounding wilderness (page 412).

LOOK FOR 🌙 TO FIND RECOMMENDED SIGHTS, ACTIVITIES, DINING, AND LODGING.

with the other route north—the famous Alaska Highway. Mile Zero of the Alaska Highway is at Dawson Creek, northeast of Prince George. From there the highway winds through kilometer after kilometer of boreal forest, past lakes and mountains to the great northland of Alaska.

PLANNING YOUR TIME

The most important thing to remember when planning your time in northern British Columbia is that this part of the province is vast.

It is as big as all the other regions combined, so plan accordingly. Though you can loop up through Williams Lake to Prince George and then head south again, you'll be missing all the highlights. If you want to see the best of the region, schedule at least three days to drive the length of Highway 16 west to Prince Rupert. To drive the Alaska/Cassiar Highway loop will take at least another four days, including a stop at **Liard River Hot Springs** and detours to **Hyder** and **Atlin.** Add another three days in the Queen Charlotte Islands for good

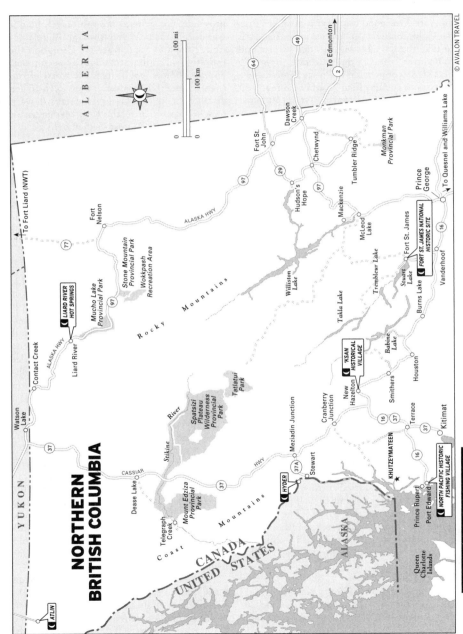

© AVALON TRAVEL

NORTHERN BRITISH COLUMBIA

NORTHERN B.C.

measure. One good way to visit northern British Columbia without retracing your steps is to take the ferry between Prince Rupert and Vancouver Island in one direction. If you do make ferry connections in Prince Rupert, allow at least one full day in town and be sure to visit the **North Pacific Historic Fishing Village.**

The summer season in northern British Columbia is shorter than elsewhere in the province. For general interest travel, plan a trip during the peak July through August period. June and September are also good for traveling—it's still warm enough to camp out, and as a bonus, you'll miss the worst of the high-summerbug season. Those keen to see grizzly bears in their natural habitat will want to schedule a visit to the Khutzeymateen in June or to Hyder August–September.

Prince George

British Columbia's seventh-largest city, Prince George (pop. 77,000) lies roughly at the geographical center of the province, at the confluence of the historically important Fraser and Nechako Rivers. Early trappers and explorers used the rivers as transportation routes into the northern reaches of the province. When they discovered the region's wealth of wolf, fox, lynx, mink, wolverine, otter, and muskrat, they quickly established forts and trading posts by rivers and lakes so that furs could be sent out and supplies could be brought in. In 1807, Simon Fraser of the North West Company began construction of Fort George. The railroad reached the area in 1908, and in 1915 the Grand Trunk Pacific Railway platted the town site of Prince George a few kilometers south of the original Fort George. The new town went on to become a major logging, sawmill, and pulp-mill town, the center of the white spruce industry in British Columbia's central interior. Hundreds of sawmills started cutting local timber, and Prince George became the self-proclaimed "Spruce Capital of the World." The city has continued from strength to strength and has grown to become northern British Columbia's economic, social, and cultural center.

SIGHTS

The best place to start a Prince George sightseeing trip is the top of **Connaught Hill,** which affords a panoramic view of the city. To get there from downtown, take Queensway Street south,

turn right on Connaught Drive, then right again on Caine Drive. At the summit are grassy tree-shaded lawns, picnic spots, and several well-kept gardens bursting with color in summer.

Exploration Place and Vicinity

This museum (333 Becott Pl., 250/562-1612; July–Aug. daily 10 A.M.–5 P.M., the rest of the year Wed.–Sun. 10 A.M.–5 P.M.; adult $10.95, senior $9.95, child $8.95) is an excellent place to discover the fascinating natural and human history of Prince George and the lifestyle and culture of the indigenous Carrier tribe. The facility is filled with modern exhibits that go beyond the meaning of a museum in the usual sense. You'll find a technological dinosaur display, a small IMAX-style theater, high-speed Internet terminals, and many hands-on exhibits. Among the items on display in the History Hall are many stuffed and mounted specimens of wild animals and birds native to British Columbia—including two towering grizzly bears in the foyer—fine crafts of the local Carrier people, an impressive sternwheeler anchor, snowshoes, guns, horrific animal traps and other relics of the fur trade, artifacts from early sawmilling days, an old buggy, mock-ups of early business establishments, and a hands-on Science Centre.

Exploration Place is within **Fort George Park,** a 36-hectare (90-acre) riverside site where Simon Fraser established Fort George in 1807. Walking trails lead through the park along the Fraser River and to the Indian Burial Grounds.

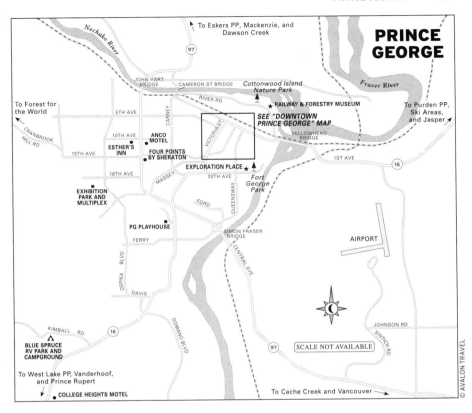

Art Galleries

The architecturally stunning **Two Rivers Gallery** (Civic Plaza, corner of 10th Ave. and Dominion St., 250/614-7800; Tues.–Sat. 10 A.M.–5 P.M., Sun. noon–5 P.M.; adult $5, senior $4, child $2) is Prince George's major cultural attraction. The large permanent collection is the main drawcard, but temporary shows that change every four to five weeks are included in the admission fee. It's also a good place to buy high-quality local artwork at a reasonable price. Look for paintings, sculpture, pottery, beadwork, woven and painted silk items, and jewelry. On Thursday, admission is free after 3 P.M. and the gallery stays open until 9 P.M.

To see and buy all sorts of native arts and crafts, head for the **Native Art Gallery** in the Prince George Native Friendship Centre (1600 3rd Ave., 250/564-3568; Tues.–Sat. 10 A.M.–4:30 P.M.). Throughout summer you can watch experienced carvers and painters teaching their students. Moccasins, jewelry, carvings, hand-printed cards, and sweatshirts with native designs are all for sale.

North of Downtown

Prince George Railway and Forestry Museum (250/563-7351; summer daily 10 A.M.–5 P.M., the rest of the year Tues.–Sat. 11 A.M.–4 P.M.; adult $6, senior $5, child $3) catalogs the region's industrial history. Take a self-guided tour through some of the antiquated railway cars and buildings, clamber on retired railway equipment, and chug back in time via

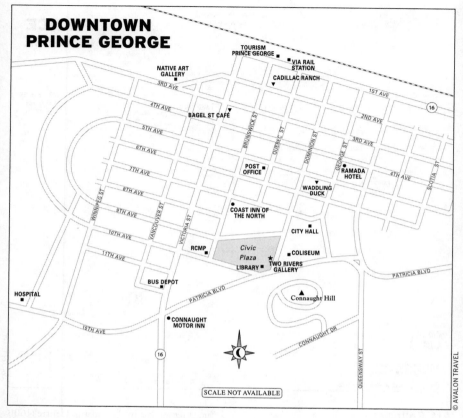

the black-and-white photo displays and assorted memorabilia. To get there from downtown, take Highway 16 east to the River Road exit (just before the Yellowhead Bridge over the Fraser River) and continue north down River Road one kilometer (0.6 miles) to the museum.

Just down River Road from the railroad museum is the entrance to beautiful 33-hectare (81-acre) **Cottonwood Island Nature Park**—one of Prince George's 16 city parks and a beautiful spot for a quiet stroll or picnic. The park lies beside the Nechako River, which overflows each spring; over time, sediment from the overflow has built up an island. The park's dominant feature is an extensive forest of northern black cottonwood trees. In spring sticky buds

cover the cottonwoods, and in summer the air is thick and the ground white with seed-bearing tufts of fluff. You'll see all sorts of birds, and might spy the occasional beaver, fox, or moose. The park's trail system is extensive; the short walk between the main parking lot and the river is popular.

RECREATION
Hiking
Hikers can follow the **Heritage River Trail** through the city, past interpretive signs detailing local natural history. The clearly marked gravel trail, open to hikers, joggers, cyclists, and cross-country skiers, runs between Cameron Street Bridge and Carrie Jane Gray Park.

You can make an 11-kilometer (6.8-mile) loop of it if you complete the circuit by following Carney Street. Ask for the *Heritage River Trails* pamphlet at the information center.

Forest for the World, a 106-hectare (262-acre) recreation area set aside for forest demonstrations, hiking, and cross-country skiing, was established in 1986 to commemorate Prince George's 75th anniversary. To get there, take 15th Avenue to the west end of the city, continue onto Foothills Boulevard, and turn left on Cranbrook Hill Road, which steeply climbs Cranbrook Hill. At the signs for Forest for the World, turn left on Kueng Road and continue to the end. From the parking lot, hiking trails lead to Shane Lake (10 minutes one-way), where beavers and waterfowl are present, and to a hilltop viewpoint northwest of Shane Lake (15 minutes one-way).

Farther out is **Eskers Provincial Park,** 40 kilometers (25 miles) northwest of Prince George (access is off Highway 97 along Pine Marsh Rd.). Named for the park's main features, the eskers, or long gravel ridges, were deposited by a receding glacier at the end of the last ice age. Fifteen kilometers (9.3 miles) of hiking trails lead around Circle Lake to two viewing platforms and through forests of aspen, lodgepole pine, and Douglas fir.

ENTERTAINMENT
Nightlife

Of the city's many pubs and nightclubs, one of the most popular is **Steamers** (2595 Queensway St., 250/562-6654), with typical pub meals and bands playing most weekends. For country music, it's impossible to go past the **Cadillac Ranch** (1380 2nd Ave., 250/563-7720), with a mixture of bands and DJ music, but it's always hard-core country and always busy. For a quiet drink in typical hotel surroundings, head for **Coaches Corner** (Ramada Hotel, 444 George St., 250/563-0055).

Studio 2880 (2820 15th Ave., 250/562-4526; closed Sun.) is the local arts center, operated by the Community Arts Council. It hosts many cultural activities, acts as a ticket office for events, and organizes workshops, art classes, concerts, ballets, special events, and two major craft markets each year. In a similar vein, **Theatre North West** (556 North Nechako Rd., 250/563-6969) offers a five-play season running late September–May. The **Prince George Symphony Orchestra** (250/562-0800, www.pgso.com) combines professional and amateur musicians to produce a September–May performance season at Vanier Hall (2901 Griffiths St.).

Festivals and Events

Prince George is certainly not short on year-round celebrations and goofy seasonal events. In early February, **Festival d'Hiver** or **Fete d'hiver** is a winter carnival featuring logging sports, scuba diving, dogsledding, and car races on the ice at nearby Tabor Lake. Over the next two weeks, the city goes berserk with a 10-day **Snow Daze,** featuring a snow ball and snow golf in bright crazy costumes, *knurdling* (jousting using padded poles), bed races on ice, and other hog-wild events. It's all finished off with a fireworks display.

In early June, the warmer half of the annual events calendar kicks off with the biennial (even years) **Forest & Resources Expo** (www.forestexpo.bc.ca), held at Exhibition Park. The expo, North America's largest forestry exposition, is interesting even for those not involved in the industry, especially the displays of new technology. On the last weekend of July, the **Prince George Folkfest** (www.pgfolkfest.com) attracts a good range of performers from throughout Canada to Fort George Park.

ACCOMMODATIONS AND CAMPING
Under $50

With no hostels, Prince George holds just one accommodation that falls into this price range. It's the **College Heights Motel** (five kilometers/3.1 miles west of downtown along Highway 16, 250/964-4708). It has no toll-free number, no website, not even cable TV, but for $42 s, $50 d in high season, what do you expect? It's on the south side of the highway at the top of the rise.

NORTHERN B.C.

$50-100

Most Prince George accommodations fall into the $50–100 range, and they are spread throughout the city. A few blocks south from downtown, where the Yellowhead Highway crosses Patricia Boulevard, is **Connaught Motor Inn** (1550 Victoria St., 250/562-4441 or 800/663-6620; $75 s, $80 d). It's a large place, with close to 100 air-conditioned rooms and a pool, sauna, and restaurant.

The most concentrated area of accommodations is along the Highway 97 bypass west of downtown. Least expensive of these is the **Anco Motel** (1630 Central St., 250/563-3671 or 800/663-3290; $70 s, $75 d). The least expensive rooms at **Esther's Inn** (1151 Commercial Cres., 250/562-4131 or 800/663-6844, www.esthersinn.bc.ca; $68–96 s or d) are priced similarly to those at the Anco, but are dark and on the small side. Instead, request a renovated 3rd-floor room, with Internet access and a king bed. Esther's is a tropical-themed hotel, with rooms surrounding a lush tropical atrium packed with palms and philodendrons, waterfalls, Polynesian artifacts, swimming pools, a water slide, and a thatched-roof restaurant.

Over $100

The **C Four Points by Sheraton** (1790 Hwy. 93 S., 250/564-7100, www.starwoodhotels.com; $140–170 s or d) is a standout in Prince George. Not because it's a fantastic place to stay, but because the other choices are all a little tired. Opened in 2007, it features large rooms with modern conveniences like high-speed Internet and LCD TVs. Amenities include a restaurant, a fitness room, and an indoor pool.

Two major downtown hotels are more convenient for business travelers but come with older rooms and overpriced dining. They are **Ramada Hotel** (444 George St., 250/563-0055 or 800/830-8833, www.ramadaprincegeorge.com, $150 s or d) and **Coast Inn of the North** (770 Brunswick St., 250/563-0121 or 800/716-6199, www.coasthotels.com; from $165 s or d). Both have indoor pools.

Camping

Privately operated **Blue Spruce RV Park and Campground** (Kimball Rd., 250/964-7272 or 877/964-7272; Apr.–mid-Oct.; $22–28) is five kilometers (3.1 miles) west on Highway 16 from the junction of Highway 97. It's a popular spot, filling up each night during the busy summer months. Each site has a picnic table and a barbecue grate, and the facilities include spotlessly clean heated bathrooms, a coin-operated laundry, a swimming pool, mini-golf, and a playground.

The closest provincial park to Prince George is at **Purden Lake,** 55 kilometers (34 miles) east of the city on Highway 16. The picturesque lake has a small stretch of sandy beach and offers fishing for rainbow trout and burbot. Sites are $14 a night.

FOOD

A few blocks from downtown is **Bagel Street Café** (1493 3rd Ave. at Victoria St., 250/563-0071). It's small—just one long row of stools—and gets crowded when workers from the government offices across the road are on a break, but it's inexpensive; coffee $1.80, hearty lunches from $5.50.

A reliable place for lunch is **Papaya Grove Restaurant** (Esther's Inn, 1151 Commercial Cres., 250/562-4131). You can choose from three different seating areas: under a thatched roof, around the pool, or in the bar. All are enclosed within a massive tropical indoor atrium. A set menu is offered, but the buffet is the most popular choice. The daily lunch buffet (11 A.M.–2 P.M.) is around $12, with a different theme each day. Sunday brunch is particularly good; for $17.95 you get all the usual breakfast choices, along with salmon, prawns, roast beef, and a staggering number of desserts. The dinner buffet is $18.95 Sunday–Thursday, and $21.95 on Friday and Saturday when prime rib is served.

With its thoughtful menu and casually elegant setting, the **Waddling Duck** (1157 5th Ave., 250/561-5550; daily 11 A.M.–11 P.M.) stands out as the restaurant of choice for a nice night out in Prince George. The setting is a big, old stone-and-brick building, with lots of exposed beams and polished wood throughout. The weekday lunch buffet is $10, while the nightly specials provide good pub-style food value. But it is the main menu that is most notable, with dinner entrées such as wild coho salmon drizzled with basil pear emulsion ($19) making this restaurant a standout. I'm not usually a fan of chocolate fudge brownies, but the Waddling Duck's version ($4) was delectable.

OTHER PRACTICALITIES
Information

Tourism Prince George operates an excellent information center right downtown (1300 1st Ave., 250/562-3700 or 800/668-7646, www .initiativespg.com; Mon.–Fri. 8:30 A.M.– 5 P.M., with extended summer hours of daily 9 A.M.–8 P.M.).

Prince George Public Library (887 Dominion St., 250/563-9251; Mon.–Thurs. 10 A.M.–9 P.M., Fri.–Sat. 10 A.M.–5:30 P.M.) has newspapers and magazines from across North America, as well as a good display of native art and artifacts. **Books & Company** (1685 3rd Ave., 250/563-6637) features a great selection of local and northern BC literature, plus major Canadian newspapers.

Services

The main **post office** is on the corner of 5th Avenue and Quebec Street. **Prince George Regional Hospital** is at 2000 15th Avenue, 250/565-2000 (routine calls) or 250/565-2444 (emergencies). A private health clinic deals with walk-in problems; turn off 15th Avenue on Edmonton by the hospital. The Royal Canadian Mounted Police (RCMP) is on the corner of Brunswick and 10th Avenue, behind the library (250/562-3371).

Getting There and Around

Prince George Airport is 18 kilometers (11 miles) east of town. It is linked to Vancouver by **Air Canada** (888/247-2262) and **WestJet** (800/538-5696) and to many regional centers, including Kelowna, by **Central Mountain Air** (888/865-8585). The **Airporter Shuttle Service** bus (250/563-2220) provides shuttle service between the airport and downtown. **VIA Rail** operates transcontinental service from Prince George west to Prince Rupert and east through Jasper and Edmonton to Toronto and beyond. The VIA Rail station is on 1st Avenue between Brunswick and Quebec Streets (250/564-5233). **Greyhound** (1566 12th Ave., 250/564-5454 or 800/661-1145) runs regularly scheduled services from Prince George south to Kamloops and Vancouver (via Williams Lake and Quesnel); west along the Yellowhead Highway to Terrace and Prince Rupert; north to Dawson Creek via Chetwynd; and east along the Yellowhead Highway to Jasper and Edmonton.

The **Prince George Transit System** operates buses throughout the city daily except Sunday. Pick up a current *Prince George Rider's Guide* from the information center or call 250/563-0011 for an automated timetable. For a cab call **Prince George Taxi** (250/564-4444). Car-rental agencies with desks out at the airport are **Budget** (250/563-2662), **National** (250/564-4847), and **Thrifty** (250/564-3499).

West from Prince George

VANDERHOOF

The first town west of Prince George, at 65 kilometers (40 miles), is Vanderhoof (pop. 4,400), a service center for the Nechako Valley and British Columbia's geographical center (the exact spot is marked by a cairn five kilometers east of town). Vanderhoof grew as a stop on the Grand Trunk Pacific Railway. Today it's a prosperous farming and logging town.

Sights

The 1914 building at the corner of Highway 16 and Pine Avenue houses **Vanderhoof Heritage Museum** (250/567-2991; late May–Aug. daily 10 A.M.–5 P.M.; adult $2). The museum displays mounted specimens of birds and animals, pioneer equipment, blacksmithing tools, a rock collection, and plenty of local history from goldrush and pioneer days. Surrounding the main building are 11 restored heritage buildings, among them a jail, a 1922 schoolhouse, and a restored gambling room. Also here is the **OK Café** (mid-May–Sept. daily 8:30 A.M.–8 P.M., the rest of the year Tues.–Sat. 11 A.M.–8 P.M.), where you can tuck in to hearty homemade soup and rolls, salads, and tasty pie and ice cream. It's inside a heritage building that was Vanderhoof's first restaurant.

Vanderhoof's town symbol is the Canada goose. You can see these beautiful birds and other waterfowl in spring and fall at their transient home, **Nechako Bird Sanctuary,** along the banks of the Nechako River. Access it via the wooden bridge at the north end of Burrard Avenue, the town's main street.

Practicalities

Inexpensive accommodations are available at the **Hillview Motel** (Hwy. 16, 250/567-4468 or 888/387-9788; $55 s, $65 d), on the east side of town. Similarly priced, but right downtown and home to Vanderhoof's best restaurant, is **North Country Inn** (2575 Burrard Ave., 250/567-3047; $59 s, $68 d).

Riverside Park Campground (250/567-4710; May–Sept.) enjoys a pleasant setting beside the Nechako River. Turn north off Highway 16 onto Burrard Avenue and continue through town; the campground is to the west side of Burrard Avenue. Showers and firewood are supplied. Tenters pay $15, those looking for hookups $17–21.

For delicious food at reasonable prices, head to the comfortable **North Country Inn** (2575 Burrard Ave., 250/567-3047), where the restaurant is in a stunning alpine-style log building. Breakfasts are hearty and cost from $5; lunch is mostly burgers and sandwiches ranging $5–9. In the evening the soup and salad bar is $8, and steak, seafood, and pasta dinners run $10–29. Try the delicious chicken lasagna.

Vanderhoof Visitor Centre (2353 Burrard Ave., 250/567-2124 or 800/752-4094)

is open year-round Monday–Friday 9 A.M.–5 P.M., with extended summer hours: daily 8:30 A.M.–6 P.M.

FORT ST. JAMES

A sealed road leads 60 kilometers (37 miles) north from Vanderhoof to Fort St. James (pop. 2,000), the earliest nonnative settlement in northern British Columbia. While it's worth a detour to check out Fort St. James Historic Site, you can also see other historic buildings, including the lakefront Our Lady of Good Hope Catholic Church, built in 1873. The town fronts 90-kilometer-long (56-mile-long) **Stuart Lake,** the province's seventh largest body of water. North of Fort St. James, Germanson Landing North Road (well-maintained but unpaved) leads to the **Takla-Nation Lakes** region—a favorite with campers in search of untouched wilderness and with anglers wanting to pull grayling, char, rainbow trout, and Dolly Varden from the region's dozens of fish-filled lakes.

◖ Fort St. James National Historic Site

In the early 1800s, Fort St. James (250/996-7191; late May–Sept. daily 9 A.M.–5 P.M.; adult $7, senior $6, child $3.50) was the chief fur-trading post and capital of the large and prosperous district of New Caledonia—the name originally given to central British Columbia by Simon Fraser, who was instrumental in expanding the fur trade west of the Rockies. It continued to operate until the early 1900s, and today the restored fort forms the centerpiece of a historic site holding Canada's largest collection of original fur-trade buildings. Enter the fort through the Visitor Reception Centre, which holds displays on pioneer explorers, fur traders, and the indigenous Carrier people. An audio recording and a map trace the route of the early explorers, and a slide show fills you in on the restoration of the fort's original buildings. Free guided walking tours leave from the center May–September. In July and August, characters dressed in pioneer garb lurk in the log-constructed general store, the fish cache, the single men's bunkhouse, the main house, and the veggie garden. You're actively encouraged to get into the spirit of things and play along. Tell them you've just arrived by canoe, want to stay the night in the men's house, and need a good horse and some provisions…then see what happens!

Practicalities

The best place to stay in the area is **Stuart Lodge** (Stones Bay Rd., 250/996-7917, www .stuartlodge.ca; $72–90 s, $78–100 d), on the shore of Stuart Lake five kilometers (3.1 miles) west of Fort St. James. The complex's five cottages come with cooking facilities, decks, and TVs. **Paarens Beach Provincial Park** and **Sowchea Bay Provincial Park,** west of Fort St. James, both offer lakeside tent and vehicle camping, swimming, fishing, picnic areas, and washrooms; open May–September with a $14 nightly fee for campers.

To get the scoop on the entire area, stop at **Fort St. James Visitor Centre** (115 Douglas Ave., 250/996-7023; July–Aug. daily 8 A.M.– 6 P.M. and May, June, and Sept. Mon.–Fri. 8:30 A.M.–4:30 P.M.).

FORT FRASER TO FRASER LAKE

Heading west from Vanderhoof, the Yellowhead Highway passes through low rolling terrain before crossing the wide **Nechako River** and passing the turnoff to **Beaumont Provincial Park.** The park offers boating on Fraser Lake, a short interpretive trail, and a campground (May–Oct.; $17 per site). The park also marks the eastern edge of an area known as the **Lakes District,** comprising more than 300 fish-filled lakes. Traveling this stretch of the highway in summer, you'll notice all the vehicles hauling canoes, kayaks, or small fishing boats.

The town of Fraser Lake (pop. 1,300), 60 kilometers (37 miles) west of Vanderhoof, lies on a chunk of land sloping gently down to its namesake lake. In winter, trumpeter swans settle in at each end of the lake. In summer, a salmon run on the **Stellako River**—a short stretch of water between Fraser and Francois Lakes—draws scores of eager anglers. Over-looking Fraser Lake, **Piper's Glen Resort** (250/690-7565, www.pipersglenresort.com; May–Sept.) has a grassy lakeshore camping area with full hookups and showers; $15–18 per night for campers, $40 s or d in basic cabins. Guests can rent canoes and motorboats. **Fraser Lake Visitor Centre,** along the highway through town (250/699-8844; July–Aug. daily 8 A.M.–6 P.M.), offers tourism information and a small museum out back.

Just west of Fraser Lake, a turnoff leads south to **Francois Lake,** another popular fishing hole. **Glenannan Tourist Area,** at the lake's east end, boasts a handful of resorts providing everything an angler could possibly desire. Right on the lake, **Noralee Resort** (49400 Colleymount Rd., 250/695-6399, www.noraleeresort.com) is well suited for anglers (tackle shop, boat rentals), but everyone is welcome. Cabins rent for $70–80 s or d, camping is $15–20 per night, and the on-site restaurant offers inexpensive meals.

BURNS LAKE AND VICINITY

The first thing you see when you enter Burns Lake (pop. 1,900) is an enormous chainsaw-carved trout with the inscription "Three Thousand Miles of Fishing!" That pretty much sums up what attracts visitors to the town and surrounding Lakes District.

Sights and Recreation

Continue west along the highway through town for about one kilometer (0.6 mile) until you come to the green-and-white **Heritage Centre** (250/692-3773; daily 1–5 P.M.; $2), comprising a museum and the local information center. The museum is housed in a 1919 home whose furnished rooms contain an odd assortment of articles, including a collection of foreign currency, memorabilia from an old ship (viewed through a porthole), and typewriters that have seen better days. The museum provides a map showing other local heritage buildings, including the **Bucket of Blood,** a historic fur-trading depot and gambling den where a murder occurred during a poker game. For a wonderful view of the area, follow 5th Avenue up the hill out of town, then take the turnoff to **Boer Mountain Forestry Lookout.** Rockhounds will prefer to head 6.5 kilometers (four miles) south of town to **Eagle Creek Agate Opal Site,** one of the province's few opal deposits. From the parking lot, a two-kilometer (1.2-mile) trail (40 minutes each way) leads to the creekside deposit and an intriguing outcrop of hoodoos.

More than 300 lakes dot the region around Burns Lake, and all are renowned fishing spots. To even mention all the lakes and their fishing possibilities would take a whole other book. Ask at the information center for the free *Burns Lake 3,000 Miles of Fishing* map and information sheet. The center also stocks brochures on local fishing resorts and guides, boat rentals, and floatplane adventures.

Practicalities

On the east side of town before Highway 16 descends to the main street, the low-slung **Wanakena Motel** (250/692-3151 or 888/413-3151, www.blwana.com; $60 s, $65–75 d) is an older place, but rooms are cheery and clean. KOA-affiliated **Burns Lake Campground** (Freeport Rd., 250/692-3105 or 800/562-0905; May–Sept.; unserviced sites $22, hookups $24–31) is off Highway 16 about seven kilometers (4.3 miles) east of Burns Lake. Its picturesque tent sites lie up in a forested area, and each site has a picnic table. The large RV section below is out in the open and has full hookups. Amenities include free showers and a laundry, store, and gift shop. The nearest provincial park with a campground is along a gravel road north of Burns Lake.

Burns Lake Visitor Centre is along the highway west of downtown (250/692-3773; summer Mon.–Fri. 8 A.M.–7 P.M., Sat.–Sun. 9 A.M.–5 P.M.).

TWEEDSMUIR PROVINCIAL PARK (NORTH)

The town of Burns Lake is not only near British Columbia's smallest provincial park (Deadman's Island in Burns Lake), it also happens to be the northern gateway to the largest: 981,000-hectare

(2.42-million-acre) Tweedsmuir Provincial Park. The park extends over 200 kilometers (124 miles) from north to south. Its northern boundary, formed by **Ootsa** and **Whitesail Lakes,** is accessed along a network of gravel roads south from Burns Lake. The only road *within* the park is Highway 20 (see *Cariboo Country* in the *Central British Columbia* chapter). Most of the park's northern section is made up of the **Quanchus Mountain Range,** holding many peaks topping 1,900 meters (6,230 feet), and the **Nechako Plateau,** which is riddled with lakes and streams. Wildlife abounds. If you're in the right place at the right time, you can see caribou, mountain goats, moose, black and grizzly bears, mule deer, wolves, smaller mammals such as hoary marmots and wolverines, and many birds. The lakes are filled with fish, including rainbow trout, kokanee, mountain whitefish, and burbot. Aside from fishing, the most popular activity in the park's northern reaches is boating, canoeing, or kayaking the circular route through Ootsa, Whitesail, Eutsuk, Tetachuck, and Natalkuz Lakes. Some portaging is required. Ootsa Lake is the main access to the park, but the shoreline has been described as a forest of drowned trees and floating hazards—very dangerous, with few places to land when frequent strong winds funnel across the lakes.

Practicalities

Wilderness campsites sprinkle some of the lakes within the park. To get to Ootsa Lake, follow Highway 35 for 16 kilometers (10 miles) south from Burns Lake to Francois Lake, take the free vehicle ferry across Francois Lake, then continue south another 44 kilometers (27 miles) to the settlement of Ootsa Lake. To get *into* the park itself, you'll need a canoe, kayak, motorboat, or chartered floatplane. **Lakes District Air Services** (250/692-3229, www.lakesdistrictair.com) flies charters year-round from a base along Francois Lake Road—on floats in summer and skis in winter. Rates are $455 per hour for the three-passenger Cessna 185 and $585 per hour for the six-passenger Beaver. This company also services fly-in cabins on Tesla and Coles Lakes. See their website for package details.

TOPLEY TO TELKWA
Babine Lake

At Topley, 51 kilometers (32 miles) west of Burns Lake, a side road leads north to 177-kilometer-long (110-mile-long) Babine Lake, the province's largest natural lake and yet another spot known for producing trophy-size rainbow trout, Dolly Varden, kokanee, coho salmon, and whitefish.

Topley Landing, 30 kilometers (19 miles) from the Yellowhead Highway, is a former trapping and trading center dating back to the 1700s. Beyond the landing, over the Fulton River, is **Red Bluff Provincial Park,** named for iron-impregnated cliffs nearby. The park's small campground enjoys a picturesque riverside location, but facilities are limited; $14 per night.

The road terminates at **Granisle,** formerly a company town where life revolved around a copper mine. In 1992 the mine closed, many residents moved out, and a developer moved in, attempting to attract retirees and holiday-makers. The preexisting mining-employee accommodations were refurbished to be sold as condominiums, and the former Granisle Village Inn was revamped and renamed the **Granisle Resort** (250/697-6322 or 800/671-4475, www.granisleresort.com). The latter is excellent value, with basic but comfortable kitchenette units from $70 s or d. The sockeye salmon run in August and September, but other than that there's little reason to come out here. A free municipal campground is one kilometer (0.6 mile) south of town.

Houston

Like Burns Lake, Houston's welcoming sign also proudly bears a carved fish—this time a steelhead. Houston calls itself "Steelhead Country," for the only species of trout that migrates to the ocean. The forestry town of 4,000 lies at the confluence of the Bulkley and Morice Rivers in the stunning Bulkley Valley, which enjoys the snowcapped Telkwa and Babine Ranges for a backdrop. As in the rest of

© ANDREW HEMPSTEAD

NORTHERN B.C.

Fishing draws many visitors to Babine Lake.

this region, the local fishing is superb. At the information center, pick up a copy of the local forestry district recreation map, showing the area's rivers, lakes, logging roads, and campgrounds. The best steelhead fishing is in the Morice River—take the highway west toward Smithers, turn left at the Northwood Pulp Mill sign, and continue about 1.6 kilometers (one mile) to the end. At the dirt road, turn right (at the bridge). Both bait fishing and fly-fishing are popular here.

Houston Visitor Centre (Hwy. 16 at Benson Ave., 250/845-7640; summer daily 9 A.M.– 5 P.M., weekdays only the rest of the year) is easy to spot—out front is the world's largest fly-fishing rod.

Telkwa

As you continue west, the scenery just keeps getting better. You'll pass open fields and rolling, densely forested hills, all the while surrounded by snowcapped mountains peeking tantalizingly out of clouds. The neat little village of Telkwa lies at the confluence of the Bulkley and Telkwa Rivers, almost exactly halfway between Prince George and Prince Rupert. Several species of anadromous fish make spawning runs up the rivers here at various times of year—spring chinook salmon in late June, coho salmon in August, and steelhead between fall and freeze-up. The area also appeals to canoeists, offering stretches of water to suit novices through intermediates. Many of the buildings in the village were put up between 1908 and 1924.

On the highway through town, the 【 **Two Rivers Lodge** (250/846-6000, www.tworivers lodge.ca) is one of the best places to stay between Prince George and the coast. It offers a beautiful riverside setting and is surrounded by gardens. Motel rooms with wireless Internet are $75–105 s or d, while self-contained log cabins, complete with fireplaces, are $105–245 s or d. Nearby **Tyhee Lake Provincial Park** has a good swimming beach, picnic facilities, and a campground with hot showers ($20 per site May–Sept., free the rest of the year).

SMITHERS AND VICINITY

The Coast Mountains surround the town of Smithers (pop. 5,400), while the splendid 2,560-meter (8,400-foot) Hudson Bay Mountain towers directly above. It's a vibrant community with some excellent accommodations, fine restaurants, and interesting arts-and-crafts shops. Hiking trails close to town lead to a magnificent glacier, intriguing fossil beds, and a remote recreation area.

Town Sights

With a backdrop of magnificent mountains, it's no surprise that Main Street is done up in a Bavarian theme. Visitors shop here for native crafts and tourist paraphernalia. The grand old 1925 courthouse, at the junction of the Yellowhead Highway and Main Street, is home to **Bulkley Valley Museum** (250/847-5322) and **Smithers Art Gallery** (250/847-3898). The museum has a predictable collection of historic artifacts, highlighted by an interesting collection of black-and-white photos. Both the museum and gallery are open in summer Monday–Saturday 11 A.M.–5 P.M.

Natural Attractions

Many millions of years ago, the Bulkley Valley had a subtropical climate and the area north of present day Smithers was a low wetland of swamps and shallow lakes. Over eons, deposited sediments covered and preserved the remains of the plants and animals that died in the water. Around a million years ago, a lava flow covered the entire region. But then during the last ice age, melting ice carved out a canyon that sliced right through the ancient wetlands, exposing the fossil beds. The site is now protected as **Driftwood Canyon Provincial Park.** It is 17 kilometers (11 miles) northeast of town; take Highway 16 three kilometers (1.9 miles) east, head north on Old Babine Lake Road, turn left on Telkwa High Road, then right on Driftwood Road. A short walk from the road leads to a viewing platform over the east bank of Driftwood Creek, where interpretive panels describe the site's significance. Excavated specimens can be viewed in the Bulkley Valley Museum.

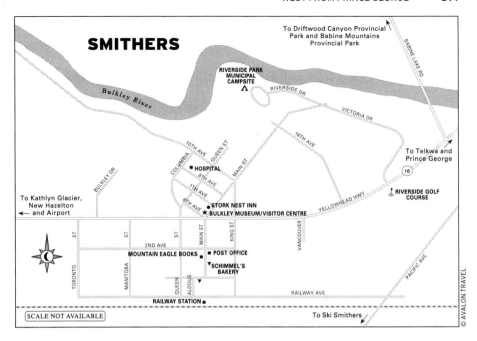

SMITHERS

To Driftwood Canyon Provincial
Park and Babine Mountains
Provincial Park

BABINE LAKE RD

RIVERSIDE PARK
MUNICIPAL
CAMPSITE

Bulkley River

RIVERSIDE DR

VICTORIA DR

10TH AVE

QUEEN ST

16TH AVE

COLUMBIA ST

■ HOSPITAL

8TH AVE

7TH AVE

6TH AVE

MAIN ST

BULKLEY DR

To Kathlyn Glacier,
New Hazelton
← and Airport

★ STORK NEST INN
★ BULKLEY MUSEUM/VISITOR CENTRE

To Telkwa and
Prince George

16

RIVERSIDE GOLF
COURSE

YELLOWHEAD HWY

ST

ST

ST

MAIN ST

KING ST

VANCOUVER

2ND AVE

MOUNTAIN EAGLE BOOKS ■

■ POST OFFICE

TORONTO

MANITOBA

QUEEN

ALDOUS

▼ SCHIMMEL'S
BAKERY

PACIFIC AVE

RAILWAY AVE

© AVALON TRAVEL

RAILWAY STATION ■

SCALE NOT AVAILABLE

To Ski Smithers

From Driftwood Canyon, Driftwood Road continues five kilometers (3.1 miles) to a parking lot—the trailhead for trails leading into remote **Babine Mountains Provincial Park,** protecting 32,400 hectares (80,000 acres) of the Skeena Mountains. From this trailhead, the **McCabe Trail** leads eight kilometers (five miles) one-way to the alpine meadows between Mounts Hyland and Harvey, while the **Silver King Basin Trail** climbs steadily through a subalpine forest for nine kilometers (5.6 miles) one-way to another alpine meadow. Allow three hours one-way for either option.

About eight kilometers (five miles) west of Smithers on the Yellowhead Highway, take the **Hudson Bay Mountain Lookout** turnout for magnificent views of the mountain and the quickly receding Kathlyn Glacier on its north face. In the same vicinity, turn south off the highway at Lake Kathlyn Road to the trailhead for **Glacier Gulch,** a strenuous 1,000 vertical meters (3,280 feet) above the parking lot. The trail is only six kilometers (3.7 miles) one-way, but allow at least three hours to reach the toe of Kathlyn Glacier. Just 500 meters (0.3 mile) along the trail is dramatic **Twin Falls,** a worthy destination in itself. Beyond the Glacier Gulch trailhead, Lake Kathlyn Road ends, appropriately enough, at **Lake Kathlyn,** a photogenic body of water at the base of Hudson Bay Mountain.

Ski Smithers

This smallish winter resort (250/847-2058, www.skismithers.com) on Hudson Bay Mountain is mostly geared to beginners and intermediates, but a few of the 19 designated runs challenge more experienced skiers and boarders. Four lifts serve a vertical rise of 553 meters (1,750 feet) and 120 hectares (300 acres) of mostly intermediate terrain. Facilities include two day lodges, a rental shop, and a ski and snowboard school. A day pass is adult $45, senior $35, child $25. Cross-country skiers can

NORTHERN B.C.

choose from a 2.5-kilometer (1.6-mile) groomed trail on the mountain or the 10-kilometer (6.2-mile) **Pine Creek Loop** on the road to the resort. To get to the mountain, take either Main Street or King Street south onto Railway Avenue and turn left; the base area is 23 kilometers (14 miles) from downtown Smithers.

Accommodations and Camping

Because skiers and snowboarders from throughout the north flock to the slopes of Hudson Bay Mountain when the snow falls, the local lodgings are apt to be as busy in winter as in summer. The 23-room **Stork Nest Inn** (1485 Main St., 250/847-3831, www.storknestinn.com; $75 s, $85 includes breakfast) is styled on a Bavarian lodge. It features 23 comfortable rooms with air-conditioning, Internet access, and small fridges. The premier accommodation in this region is the (**Logpile Lodge** (3105 McCabe Rd., 250/847-5152, www.logpilelodge .com; Mar.–late Dec.; $85–135 s or d), north of town (call for directions) and surrounded by a magnificent mountain panorama. Guest rooms on the upper floor have vaulted ceilings, while exposed log walls dominate those on the lower floor. All seven rooms have solid log beds and private balconies. A big breakfast, cooked to order, will set you up for an activity-filled day (horseback riding, canoeing, fishing, and more) with local operators.

Riverside Park Municipal Campsite (May–Oct.; $14–18) is beside the Bulkley River, north of town. It provides shaded sites, a few electrical hookups, showers, and a cooking shelter. **Riverside Golf Course** (Hwy. 16 east of town, 250/847-3229; mid-Apr.–mid-Oct.) has better facilities and is within the bounds of a golf course; unserviced sites $20, hookups $21–25.

Other Practicalities

Mountainside Café (3763 4th Ave., 250/847-3455; Mon.–Sat. 11 A.M.–8 P.M.) is a funky little space with a stylish yet uncomplicated decor. The varied menu includes everything from fish and chips to a Thai curry ($16).

Expect live music on Thursday evening. At **Schimmel's Bakery** (1172 Main St., 250/847-9044; Tues.–Sat. 5:30 A.M.–5 P.M.), enjoy a range of delicious cakes and pastries, or enjoy a bowl of homemade soup ($3–5) with a sandwich ($4–7) made to order.

Tourism Smithers (250/847-5072 or 800/542-6673, www.tourismsmithers.com) operates the **Smithers Visitor Centre,** upstairs in the museum building (corner of Main St. and the Yellowhead Hwy.; summer daily 9 A.M.–6 P.M., the rest of the year Mon.–Fri. 8:30 A.M.–4:30 P.M.). A good source of northern literature is **Mountain Eagle Books** (1237 Main St., 250/847-5245).

Continuing West from Smithers

The next place to stop and stretch your legs is the viewpoint at **Moricetown Canyon,** where the 500-meter-wide (1,640-foot-wide) Bulkley River funnels and roars its way down through a 15-meter-wide (49-foot-wide) canyon. Salmon desperately hurl themselves up these spectacular rapids in autumn. Below the canyon the river pours into a large pool, one of the best fishing spots in the area. The canyon is part of **Moricetown Indian Reserve,** which recognizes an area that has been a Carrier village site for more than 5,000 years. Villagers still fish the canyon using traditional spears and nets; look for the locals congregated around the canyon in summer.

Continuing west, the scenery changes dramatically; suddenly pine trees line the Bulkley River and cover the hills and mountains. About 50 kilometers (31 miles) from Smithers, a four-kilometer (2.5-mile) unpaved road to the north leads to 307-hectare (760-acre) **Ross Lake Provincial Park,** named for a lake with crystal-clear waters full of trout and Dolly Varden. The backdrop is one of forested hills and spectacular snowcapped peaks. In the early mornings you can hear loons; in the evenings beavers slide into the water, slapping their tails. Facilities include a boat-launching area (no powerboats allowed), barbecue pits, picnic tables, and pit toilets. The park is a day-use area only, with no campsites.

NEW HAZELTON AND VICINITY

It's easy to be confused by the three Hazeltons—Hazelton, New Hazelton, and South Hazelton—situated at the most northerly point on the Yellowhead Highway. As usual, the arrival of the Grand Trunk Pacific Railway caused the confusion. The original Hazelton (called Old Town) was established 50 years or so before the railway came. The other two Hazeltons were founded because each of their respective promoters thought he owned a better spot for a new railway town. Today the largest of the three small communities is New Hazelton (pop. 900), a service center watched over by spectacular Mount Rocher Deboule (French for "mountain of the rolling rock").

Hazelton

From New Hazelton, Highway 62 leads about eight kilometers (five miles) northwest to Hazelton. Along the way it crosses the one-lane **Hagwilget Suspension Bridge,** 79 meters (260 feet) above the turbulent Bulkley River. Stop and read the plaque about the original footbridge—made from poles and cedar rope—that once spanned the gorge here; you'll be glad you live in modern times.

At the junction of the Bulkley and Skeena Rivers, Hazelton has retained its unique 1890s-style architecture and pioneer settlement atmosphere. Along the waterfront sits a museum (open daily 10 A.M.–5 P.M.), a landing with river views, and a café.

◖ 'Ksan Historical Village

'Ksan, which means "between the banks," is an authentically reconstructed Gitxsan village on the outskirts of Hazelton (250/842-5544 or 877/842-5518; Apr.–Sept. daily 9 A.M.–5 P.M.; adult $10, senior and student $8.50). In the main building a museum features cedar boxes and cedar-bark mats, woven and button blankets, masks, coppers (the most valuable single object a chief possessed), rattles used by shamans, and an art gallery with changing exhibitions. In the adjacent gift shop are the works of on-site artists. Beyond the museum is the main village, which can be visited only as part of a fascinating guided tour (included in admission). Tours leave every hour on the hour, visiting the burial house, food cache, smokehouse, community houses, and 'Ksan artists' carving shop and studio. You'll see traditional Northwest Coast carved interiors, paintings and painted screens, totem poles, and fine examples of native artifacts, arts and crafts, tools and implements, and personal possessions. And you'll learn how the people lived and all about their beliefs and legends. On Friday nights from mid-July to mid-August, performances of traditional Gitxsan song and dance take place starting around 8 P.M.

Kispiox

The traditional Gitxsan village of Kispiox lies 16 kilometers (10 miles) north of Hazelton along Kispiox Valley Road (turn off on the Smithers side of Hazelton). Sights include a large group of red cedar **totem poles** near the confluence of the Skeena and Kispiox Rivers and the locally operated, log-constructed **Kispiox Salmon Hatchery** (daily 8 A.M.–5 P.M.). The hatchery can rear 500,000 salmon fry per year.

The Seven Sisters

These impressive peaks lie west of New Hazelton, immediately south of the junction of the Yellowhead Highway and Highway 37. From the highway you'll get only occasional glimpses of the range; for the best panorama take Highway 37 north across the Skeena River, turn west (left) toward Cedarvale, and stop after about 10 kilometers (6.2 miles) at the picnic area by Sedan Creek. Several walking trails also lead to good views of the peaks. The one-kilometer (0.6-mile) **Gull Creek Trail** climbs about 200 vertical meters (660 feet) from the trailhead at Gull Creek, which is signposted along Highway 16. Serious hikers can take any of a number of routes up into the heart of the range, but each is a strenuous slog. The easiest to follow is **Coyote Creek Trail,** an old mining road beginning from where Highway 16 crosses Coyote Creek. The nine-kilometer (5.6-mile) road ends at a few cabins often used by climbers. From there it's a six-kilometer (3.7-mile) climb along a rough trail that becomes increasingly difficult to follow. The trail ends on a high alpine ridge at the base of a large ice field.

Practicalities

Along the highway through New Hazelton is the **28 Inn** (250/842-6006 or 877/842-2828, www.28inn.com; $55 s, $60 d), with slightly nicer rooms than the rates may suggest. It also has a restaurant and pub.

Between the highway and "Old" Hazelton is the log (**Hummingbird Restaurant** (250/842-5628; Mon.–Sat. 11 A.M.–2 P.M. and 5–9 P.M.), the best spot for a meal in all the Hazeltons. The wood interior is decorated with etched glass and hanging lamps, and you'll be dazzled by the million-dollar picture-window view of Mount Rocher Deboule. Tiny hummingbirds flit back and forth between the feeders outside the windows. At lunch, expect to pay around $6–9 for sandwiches, hamburgers, or a huge taco salad. At dinner choose from steaks, chicken, and pasta dishes, all for around $16–20.

At the intersection of Highways 16 and 62, **Hazelton Visitor Centre** (250/842-6071; mid-May–Sept. daily 8 A.M.–7 P.M.) has all the usual literature and holds a display detailing local history.

TERRACE AND VICINITY

Terrace (pop. 12,500) lies on the Yellowhead Highway, 580 kilometers (360 miles) west of Prince George and 146 kilometers (91 miles) east of Prince Rupert. The city is built on a series of terraces along the beautiful Skeena River, the province's second-largest river system, and is completely surrounded by the spectacular Hazelton and Coast Mountains. The town offers basic tourist services and little else. But the surrounding area makes up for it with a mix of intriguing sights, beautiful parks, and outstanding recreation opportunities.

Heritage Park Museum

At this outdoor-indoor museum (4113 Sparks

© ANDREW HEMPSTEAD

Heritage Park Museum is a good place to learn about Terrace's history.

St., 250/635-4546; June–Aug. daily 10 A.M.–6 P.M., Sept.–May Mon.–Thurs. 10 A.M.–4 P.M.; adult $4, senior $2), a one-hour guided tour takes you through an old, beautifully furnished log hotel, a dance hall, a barn, and six authentic log cabins dating from between 1910 and 1955. Some of the cabins are furnished; others contain historical artifacts or collections of antique farming and mining equipment. The guide fills you in on the early history of Terrace—covering gold, copper, and lead mining; fur trading; construction of the telegraph line; logging; and the homesteaders of the late 1800s and early 1900s. To get there from downtown, head north up Skeenaview Street.

Nisga'a Memorial Lava Bed Provincial Park

Protecting Canada's youngest lava flow, the fascinating landscape of this 17,683-hectare (43,700-acre) park is unique within the province. The flow is about 18 kilometers (11 miles) long and three kilometers (1.9 miles) wide;

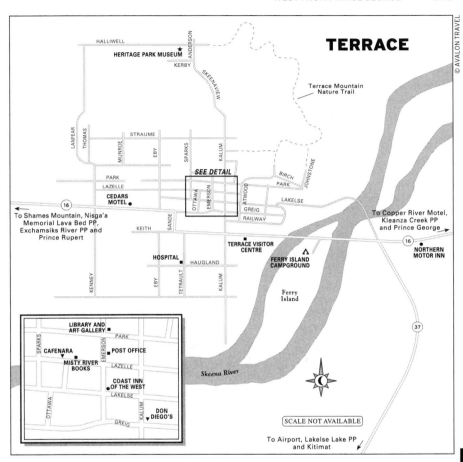

TERRACE

Map labels:
HALLIWELL
HERITAGE PARK MUSEUM
KERBY
ANDERSON
SKEENAVIEW
Terrace Mountain Nature Trail
STRAUME
LANFEAR
THOMAS
MUNROE
EBY
SPARKS
KALUM
BIRCH
JOHNSTONE
PARK
LAZELLE
CEDARS MOTEL
OTTAWA
EMERSON
ATWOOD
PARK
LAKELSE
GREIG
RAILWAY
16
To Shames Mountain, Nisga'a Memorial Lava Bed PP, Exchamsiks River PP and Prince Rupert
KEITH
SANDE
HOSPITAL
HAUGLAND
KENNEY
EBY
TETRAULT
KALUM
TERRACE VISITOR CENTRE
FERRY ISLAND CAMPGROUND
Ferry Island
To Copper River Motel, Kleanza Creek PP and Prince George
16
NORTHERN MOTOR INN
37
Skeena River
SCALE NOT AVAILABLE
To Airport, Lakelse Lake PP and Kitimat

Detail map:
LIBRARY AND ART GALLERY
SPARKS
CAFENARA
MISTY RIVER BOOKS
EMERSON
PARK
POST OFFICE
LAZELLE
COAST INN OF THE WEST
LAKELSE
OTTAWA
KALUM
DON DIEGO'S
GREIG
SEE DETAIL

experts think the molten rock spewed through the earth's crust between 1650 and 1750, killing an estimated 200 indigenous people. You can see all different types of lava, as well as crevasses, spiky pinnacles, sinkholes, craters, and bright blue pools where underground rivers have risen to the surface. Explore the lava with caution—in some parts the surface may be unstable, and it's very hard on footgear. The only facilities are a day-use area and a couple of short hiking trails.

To get to the park, take Highway 16 west out of town for three kilometers (1.9 miles), then head north around the back of the sawmill on Kalum Lake Drive. The park is 78 kilometers (48.5 miles) along this road; watch for logging trucks during the week. The information center in Terrace has an interesting brochure on the lava beds.

Summer Recreation

Many trails in the area tempt hikers. For an easy stroll, take the three-kilometer (1.9-mile) path (50 minutes or less) around **Ferry Island,** in the middle of the Skeena River east of downtown (reached via Highway 16). More demanding

Lakelse Lake Provincial Park has a pleasant sandy beach, hiking trails, and a campground.

is **Terrace Mountain Nature Trail,** a five-kilometer (3.1-mile) trail providing great views of the city and the surrounding area. It takes about two hours round-trip, because much of it is uphill. Start at the intersection of Halliwell Avenue and Anderson Street (by Heritage Park Museum), climbing the lower slopes of Terrace Mountain to a cleared area where views are best, then descending to the end of Johnstone Street. Complete the circle by walking down Johnstone Street, turning right on Park Avenue, right again on Kalum Avenue, then continuing straight onto Skeenaview Avenue back to the trailhead. Farther afield, consider scenic **Clearwater Lakes Trail,** which begins from Highway 37, 27 kilometers (16.8 miles) south of Terrace. The trail leads 1.8 kilometers (1.1 miles) to Little Clearwater Lake, then another 700 meters (0.4 mile) to Big Clearwater Lake. The two lakes are linked by a shallow creek, along the banks of which are many good picnic spots and berries to pick in season. From the same parking lot, a trail leads

1.8 kilometers (1.1 miles) to a lookout with outstanding views of Lakelse Lake. To get the rundown on all the best hikes in the area, ask for the handy *Terrace Hiking Trails* brochure at the visitor center.

When locals want to cool down on a hot summer's day, they head south along Highway 37 for 26 kilometers (16 miles) to 354-hectare (874-acre) **Lakelse Lake Provincial Park,** at the north end of beautiful Lakelse Lake. It offers good swimming beaches backed by shaded picnic areas, a hiking trail through an old-growth forest of towering spruce, and a large campground (see *Accommodations and Camping*).

The Skeena River is chock-full of salmon and other fish. Steelhead can be caught April–May and August–November. Chinooks make their upstream migration in late May and again July through early August. Coho salmon run from August to early fall. Be sure to get a license and read up on the latest rules and regulations before hitting the rivers and lakes.

Skiing and Snowboarding

Shames Mountain (250/635-3773, www.shamesmountain.com) offers a vertical rise of 488 meters (1,600 feet) and virtually guaranteed good snow coverage. In the opening season (1990–1991) an amazing 2,400 centimeters (944 inches) of snow fell at the resort—nearly twice as much as at any other resort in North America. Current facilities include a day lodge, ski and snowboard school, chairlift, T-bar, and rope tow. Lift tickets are adult $37, senior $29, child $19. Lifts operate between Christmas and early April Wednesday–Sunday only.

Accommodations and Camping

The less expensive motels are strung out along Highway 16 on the eastern and western outskirts of the city. To the west, your best bet is **Cedars Motel** (4830 Hwy. 16, 250/635-2258 or 866/635-2258, www.cedarsmotel.com; $56 s, $65 d), which is nothing special but comes with free wireless Internet and a light breakfast. On the other side of town is **Copper River Motel,** three kilometers (1.9 miles) east (4113 Hwy. 16,

250/635-6124 or 888/652-7222, www.copper rivermotel.com; $70 s, $75 d), set up for anglers, with fishing supplies and guides, 4WD rentals, and free ice. Rooms are clean and have coffee- and tea-making appliances. On the down side are the paper-thin walls. Right downtown is **Coast Inn of the West** (4620 Lakelse Ave., 250/638-8141 or 800/663-1144, www.coasthotels.com; $145 s, $155 d), where each of the 60 air-conditioned rooms is decorated in stylish pastel colors. Facilities include a family-style restaurant and lounge.

On Ferry Island in the Skeena River, just over three kilometers east of downtown, **Ferry Island Campground** (250/635-7391; mid-Apr.–mid-Oct.; unserviced sites $15, powered sites $18) offers sheltered sites among birch and cottonwood trees, berry bushes, and wildflowers. A few sites have excellent views of the river and mountains, and a hiking trail runs through the woods and around the island. Facilities include picnic tables and shelters, fire grates, firewood, and pit toilets, but no showers. A short drive from Terrace, three provincial parks have campgrounds. **Kleanza Creek Provincial Park,** site of a short-lived gold rush, is 20 kilometers (12 miles) east of Terrace on Highway 16; $14 a night. In the opposite direction, 50 kilometers (31 miles) west of the city on Highway 16 is **Exchamsiks River Provincial Park;** $14 a night. **Lakelse Lake Provincial Park,** 16 kilometers (10 miles) south of Terrace along Highway 37, is the most developed of the three parks, offering a sandy beach, safe swimming, an interpretive amphitheater, hot showers, and flush toilets. Sites are $20 a night.

Other Practicalities

One of the most popular places to go for breakfast is the **Northern Motor Inn,** near the Chevron gas station on Highway 16 just east of Terrace (250/635-6375). Large omelets, hash browns, toast, and coffee run around $7–8. Head to **Cafenara** (4716 Lazelle Ave., 250/638-1662; Mon.–Sat. 7 A.M.–9 P.M., Sun. 9 A.M.–4 P.M.) for your daily quota of caffeine in a big-city coffeehouse atmosphere. For delicious Mexican food, head downtown to **Don**

THE ELUSIVE KERMODE

The Tsimshian called the Kermode "Spirit Bear" and often rendered it in human form in their artwork. Little known outside British Columbia, the Kermode (pronounced kerr-MO-dee) is an elusive subspecies of black bear (Ursus americanus kermodei) inhabiting only the vast tract of wilderness north of Terrace as well as uninhabited Princess Royal Island south of Kitimat, where it is protected by the Spirit Bear Conservancy.

First studied by Francis Kermode, director of the provincial museum at the turn of the 20th century, the bear was originally thought to be a distinct species. It's slightly larger than other black bears, has a different jaw structure, and, although its color varies, some individuals are pure white. These white bears are not albinos, but instead contain a recessive gene that results in the light coloring.

Once close to extinction, the Kermode is now fully protected and is the mammal emblem of British Columbia.

Diego's (3212 Kalum St., 250/635-2307; Mon.–Sat. 11 A.M.–9 P.M., Sun. 10 A.M.–2 P.M. and 5–9 P.M.), where a few outdoor tables catch the evening sun. It's a small, bright restaurant with lots of plants and Mexican wall hangings. Lunch is $7–10 (the shrimp crepes are superb). Dinner entrées start at around $12. It's always busy, so you may have to wait for a table.

Terrace Visitor Centre is beside Highway 16 on the east side of town (4511 Keith Ave., 250/635-2063 or 800/499-1637, www.terrace tourism.bc.ca; summer Mon.–Fri. 8:30 A.M.–8 P.M. and Sat.–Sun. 9 A.M.–8 P.M., the rest of the year Mon.–Fri. 9 A.M.–5 P.M.). In addition to a solid collection of northern literature, **Terrace Public Library** (4610 Park Ave., 250/638-8177; Tues.–Sat. noon–3 P.M. and 7–9 P.M., Sun. 1–4 P.M.) holds a community art gallery offering exhibitions that change monthly. For local reading and a good selection of Canadiana, head to **Misty River Books** (4710 Lakelse Ave., 250/635-4428).

KITIMAT

The planned industrial community of Kitimat (pop. 10,000), at the northern end of Douglas Channel 62 kilometers (39 miles) south of Terrace, was founded by the aluminum giant **Alcan** (Aluminum Company of Canada) in the 1950s. Described at the time by *National Geographic* as "the most expensive project ever attempted by private industry," the project included one of the world's largest aluminum smelters, a company town to serve the workers, and a massive hydroelectric scheme 75 kilometers (47 miles) south of Kitimat.

Tours

The highlight of a visit to British Columbia's self-proclaimed "Aluminum City" is a guided industrial tour. The town's Alcan smelter, **Kitimat Works,** produces 270,000 tons of aluminum products worth $350 million annually. Tours, offered in summer Monday–Friday at 10:30 A.M. and 1:30 P.M., start with an audiovisual presentation, then it's into a bus for a drive around the works and down to the wharf. Tours are free, but book ahead (250/639-8259).

Methanex, Kitimat's newest industry and northern British Columbia's only **petrochemical plant,** offers tours June–August Monday and Wednesday at 3 P.M. Bearded men (or women) are not permitted on this tour. Book at 250/639-9292.

If all this industrial hooey gives you a headache, get back to nature at **Kitimat River Fish Hatchery** (250/639-9616), which releases 11 million trout and salmon annually. Tours are conducted three times daily through summer.

Other Sights

In **Radley Park,** along the Kitimat River, stands the province's largest living tree, a 50-meter-high (164-foot-high), 500-year-old Sitka spruce. It's behind the Riverlodge Recreation Centre. The **Centennial Museum** (293 City Centre, 250/632-7022; June–Aug. Mon.–Sat.

10 A.M.–5 P.M., the rest of the year Mon.–Fri. 10 A.M.–5 P.M. and Sat.–Sun. noon–5 P.M.) tells the story of the planned town and displays historic and native artifacts; a gallery features locally produced artwork.

Practicalities

Channel's Edge Inn (1487 Albatross Ave., 250/632-8478 or 888/632-8478, www.channels edgeinn.com; $125–150 s or d) is a modern home built for Alcan executives that has been converted to an upscale bed and breakfast. It features seven en suite rooms, a comfortable living area, and a dining room where a cooked breakfast is served. Kitimat's premier accommodation is **Minette Bay Lodge** (2255 Kitimat Village Rd., 250/632-2907, www .minettebaylodge.com; $175 s, $200 d, or $250 pp with meals), a grand estate that looks like it has been transported from the English countryside to the Kitimat waterfront. Guests enjoy activities such as heli-hiking, jet boat tours, and fishing charters through the day, and then kick back in the lap of luxury. The guest rooms are spacious and feature a pinky pastel color scheme; most have water views. **Radley Park Campground** (May–Sept.; $18–20) has a riverside setting, showers, a few electrical hookups, and a kitchen shelter.

Kitimat Visitor Centre is at the entrance to town (2109 Forest Ave., 250/632-6294 or 800/664-6554, www.visitkitimat.com).

WEST TOWARD PRINCE RUPERT

The 147-kilometer (91-mile) stretch of the Yellowhead Highway between Terrace and Prince Rupert rivals any stretch of road in the province for beauty. For almost the entire distance, the highway hugs the north bank of the beautiful Skeena River (Skeena is a Gitxsan word for "river of mist"). On a fine day, views from the road are stunning—forested mountains, ponds covered in yellow water lilies, and waterfalls like narrow ribbons of silver, snaking down vertical cliffs from the snow high above. In some sections the highway shrinks to two extremely narrow lanes neatly sandwiched between the railway tracks and the river—drive defensively.

Exchamsiks River Provincial Park, on the north side of the highway 50 kilometers (31 miles) west of Terrace, features a grassy picnic area where the deep green Exchamsiks River drains into the much larger Skeena River.

Camping is $14 a night. As the highway continues westward, the Skeena widens, eventually becoming a tidal estuary. Sandbars and marshes, exposed at low tide, are a mass of colorful mosses, and wading birds feed in shallow pools. Keep an eye out for bald eagles on the sandbars or perched in the trees above the highway.

Prince Rupert

Prince Rupert (pop. 16,000), on hilly Kaien Island 726 kilometers (451 miles) west of Prince George, is busy with travelers throughout the summer. The city itself holds an odd but intriguing mixture of cultural icons—totem poles, old English coats of arms and street names, highrise hotels and civic buildings—all crammed together on the edge of the Pacific Ocean. Wildlife is varied and prolific. Prince Rupert is gateway to the Khutzeymateen Grizzly Bear Sanctuary, but even from town, you're likely to spot bald eagles, seals, and even black bears.

The city has always been a hub for travelers but has never been seen as a destination in itself. That began changing in the early 1990s, with the redevelopment of Cow Bay, and in 1999 the first cruise ship arrived at the newly constructed Atlin Dock. The area south along the waterfront from Cow Bay is still a wasteland of rail yards and disused docks, but work has already begun on sprucing up this part of the city, and it will continue for many years to come. Plan to spend at least a day in the area, visiting the excellent museum, exploring an old cannery village, or maybe taking a harbor tour.

SIGHTS
Museum of Northern British Columbia

You can easily spend several hours at this fascinating museum, which occupies an imposing post-and-beam building overlooking the harbor (corner of 1st Ave. W. and McBride St., 250/624-3207; early June–Aug. Mon.–Sat. 9 A.M.–8 P.M. and Sun. 9 A.M.–5 P.M., the rest of the year Mon.–Sat. 9 A.M.–5 P.M.;

adult $5, child $2). Exhibits trace the history of Prince Rupert from 5,000-year-old Tsimshian settlements through fur-trading days to the founding of the city in 1914 as the western terminus of the Grand Trunk Pacific Railway. Many of the most fascinating displays spotlight the Coast Tsimshian natives—their history, culture, traditions, trade networks, and potlatches. Among the Tsimshian artifacts on display: totem poles, pots, masks, beautiful wooden boxes, blankets, baskets, shiny black argillite carvings, weapons, and petroglyphs. The Monumental Gallery—filled with contemporary art—is worth visiting for the sweeping harbor views alone.

Other Town Sights

Right by the Museum of Northern British Columbia is **Pacific Mariner's Memorial Park,** a grassed area with benches strategically placed for the best ocean views. A statue of a mariner staring out to sea is surrounded by plaques remembering those lost at sea. Also in the park is the *Kazu Maru,* a small fishing boat that drifted across the Pacific from Japan after its owner was lost. It washed up on the Queen Charlotte Islands in 1987, two years after it was reported missing. On the other side of the museum to the memorial park and beside the fire hall is the **Firehall Museum** (200 1st Ave. W., 250/627-4475), which features a 1925 REO Speedwagon along with various other firefighting memorabilia. It's open July and August daily 10 A.M.–4 P.M., but closes when there's a fire being fought in town. From this museum, continue south along 1st Avenue, then head to

NORTHERN B.C.

PRINCE RUPERT

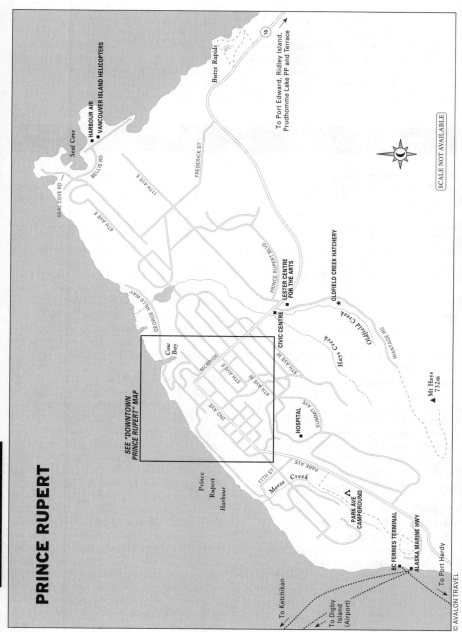

To Ketchikan

To Digby Island (Airport)

To Port Hardy

© AVALON TRAVEL

BC FERRIES TERMINAL

ALASKA MARINE HWY

PARK AVE CAMPGROUND

Prince Rupert Harbour

Morse Creek

PARK AVE

11TH ST

2ND AVE

MCBRIDE

Cow Bay

SEE "DOWNTOWN PRINCE RUPERT" MAP

5TH AVE E

6TH AVE E

5TH AVE W

6TH AVE W

8TH AVE W

HOSPITAL

SUMMIT AVE

CIVIC CENTRE

LESTER CENTRE FOR THE ARTS

PRINCE RUPERT BLVD

GEORGE HILLS WAY

6TH AVE E

5TH AVE E

11TH AVE

FREDERICK ST

BELL'S RD

SEAL COVE RD

Seal Cove

HARBOUR AIR

VANCOUVER ISLAND HELICOPTERS

Butze Rapids

To Port Edward, Ridley Island, Prudhomme Lake PP and Terrace

16

OLDFIELD CREEK HATCHERY

Oldfield Creek

Hays Creek

WANTAGE RD

Mt Hays 732m

SCALE NOT AVAILABLE

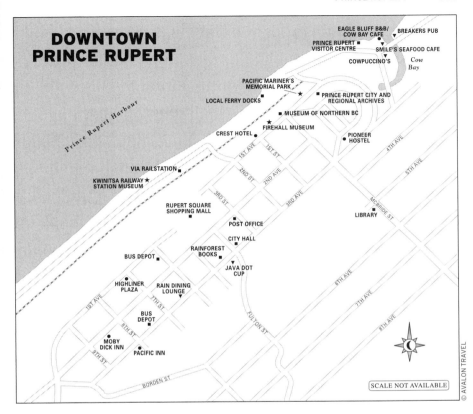

DOWNTOWN PRINCE RUPERT

EAGLE BLUFF B&B/ COW BAY CAFE
BREAKERS PUB
PRINCE RUPERT VISITOR CENTRE
SMILE'S SEAFOOD CAFE
COWPUCCINO'S
Cow Bay

PACIFIC MARINER'S MEMORIAL PARK
LOCAL FERRY DOCKS
PRINCE RUPERT CITY AND REGIONAL ARCHIVES
MUSEUM OF NORTHERN BC
CREST HOTEL
FIREHALL MUSEUM
PIONEER HOSTEL

Prince Rupert Harbour

VIA RAILSTATION
KWINITSA RAILWAY STATION MUSEUM
RUPERT SQUARE SHOPPING MALL
LIBRARY
POST OFFICE
CITY HALL
BUS DEPOT
RAINFOREST BOOKS
JAVA DOT CUP
HIGHLINER PLAZA
RAIN DINING LOUNGE
BUS DEPOT
MOBY DICK INN
PACIFIC INN
BORDEN ST

1ST AVE · 1ST ST · 2ND ST · 2ND AVE · 3RD ST · 3RD AVE · 4TH AVE · 5TH AVE · MCBRIDE ST · 6TH AVE · 7TH AVE · 8TH AVE · FULTON ST · 7TH ST · 8TH ST · 9TH ST

SCALE NOT AVAILABLE

© AVALON TRAVEL

NORTHERN B.C.

the foot of 2nd Street, which ends harborside. Here you'll find the **Kwinitsa Railway Station Museum** (250/624-3207; summer daily 9 A.M.– noon and 1–5 P.M.), housed in a small railway station—one of only four such remaining buildings that were once part of a chain of 400 identical stations along the Grand Trunk Railway. Displays tell the story of the railway and its implications for Prince Rupert.

🌊 North Pacific Historic Fishing Village

South of Prince Rupert in Port Edward, the North Pacific Historic Fishing Village (250/628-3538; mid-May–Sept. daily 9 A.M.– 6 P.M.; adult $12, senior $10, under six free) is the oldest remaining cannery village from

over 1,000 similar facilities that were once operating along the west coast of North America. Dating to 1889 and now classified as a national historic site, this living museum is one of the highlights of a visit to Prince Rupert. You can find out everything you've ever wanted to know about fish, the fishing industry, canning—even which fish tastes the best (locals say it's red snapper every time). You're free to stroll at your own pace along the boardwalk through the riverside settlement with its many original buildings, including a church, schoolroom, general store, and living quarters. Guided tours are included in the entry fee, as is a seat at the *Skeena River Story,* a live performance and slide show presented through summer daily at 11:30 A.M., 1 P.M., 2:30 P.M., and 4 P.M.

THE KHUTZEYMATEEN

Officially protected as a provincial park, the Khutzeymateen is a rugged and remote 44,300-hectare (109,500-acre) tract of wilderness 50 kilometers (31 miles) northeast of Prince Rupert that is Canada's only grizzly bear sanctuary. To the Tsimshian people, the area was known as the K'tzim-a-Deen, which translates to "the long inlet surrounded by a steep valley." To Canadian conservationists, the name Khutzeymateen is synonymous with one of their earliest victories: a 1984 decision to set aside an area where grizzly bears would be safe from hunters. In 1994, further protection was given with the proclamation of a provincial park where grizzly numbers were highest within the no-hunting zone. The park extends from the upper reaches of Khutzeymateen Inlet to the high peaks of the Kitimat Range, protecting the tidal zone at the head of the inlet where approximately 50 grizzly bears,

fresh out of hibernation in May and June, come down to the water's edge to feed on sedges and grasses. Through summer, the bears remain in the area, feeding in the salmon-rich Khutzeymateen and Kateen Rivers.

Given the inaccessibility of the region, most visitors arrive on a guided trip. For adult $155, child $135, **West Coast Launch** (250/624-3151 or 800/201-8377, www.westcoastlaunch.com; mid-May–July) runs visitors into the area by boat from Prince Rupert, but most of the six-hour trip is spent traveling. Overnight tours are run by **SunChaser Eco-Tours** (250/624-5472), which offers trips on a live-aboard motor cruiser. Departing from Prince Rupert and taking half a day to reach the sanctuary, the trips emphasize bear viewing, but time is also spent exploring other aspects of the area's natural and human history; from $1,800 for four days.

When you're done with the sightseeing, take lunch at the cannery café—ordering seafood of course. To get to the village, head out of Prince Rupert on the Yellowhead Highway and take the first road to the right after leaving Kaien Island.

Touring Local Waterways

Once you're done with Prince Rupert's land-based attractions, plan on taking at least one water-based tour. There are no tour boats as such; instead, choose from scenic ferry rides, fishing charters, kayaking (see *Recreation*), or a grizzly bear viewing excursion into the Khutzeymateen (see sidebar).

Jump aboard the small ferries that run around the harbor to communities with no road connections for an inexpensive harbor cruise. Head down to the small docks at the bottom of McBride Street for route and schedule information, or call 250/624-3337. The shortest trip is a 15-minute run to **Dodge Cove** on Digby Island. There's not much to do on the island, but it's a nice cruise there and back, and it costs just $8 round-trip. The *Centurion*

IV departs Prince Rupert Monday and Friday at 8:30 A.M. and makes a short stop before returning midafternoon; $15 one-way. For details call **BC Ferries** (250/624-5411).

Ask at the Museum of Northern British Columbia or call 250/624-5645 about tours to **Laxspa'aws** (Pike Island), where shell middens, petroglyphs, and depressions from prehistoric houses point to human habitation up to 2,000 years ago. The website www.pikeisland.ca has more information. **Seashore Charters** (Atlin Terminal, Cow Bay, 250/624-5645 or 800/667-4393, www.seashorecharters.com) is a longtime booking agent representing local charter operators. Some of the options available include yacht trips; day-long cruises looking for eagles, waterfowl, seals, otters, porpoises, and killer whales; and fishing trips for salmon, halibut, or cod, with gear and bait supplied. Expect to pay from $100 per person for a fishing trip.

RECREATION
Outdoor Activities

Walking trails lead from town to Cow Bay,

Hays Creek, Morse Creek, the ferry terminals, and the low summit of Mount Oldfield. Pick up a map and descriptions for all the local trails at the information center. On one of my first visits to Prince Rupert, I blindly led a group of three others to the summit of 732-meter (2,400-foot) Mount Hays via an old gondola cut line. Halfway up we got tangled in head-high undergrowth, and then knee-deep snow. Therefore, I heartily recommend you take the more conventional route, a gravel road that leads off where Wantage Road ends. Once at the top, the views of Prince Rupert, the sound, southeastern Alaska, and bald eagles soaring through updrafts are second to none.

The calm waters of Prince Rupert Harbour are perfect for kayaking. Even if you have had no experience in a kayak, **Blackfish Kayaking** (250/638-1887, www.blackfish.ca) will take you on an easy full-day paddle to a remote beach for $75 per person. An overnight excursion to Laxspa'aws (Pike Island) costs $200.

ENTERTAINMENT

In the same complex as the recreation facilities listed above is the **Lester Centre for the Arts** (1100 McBride St., 250/627-8888, www.lestercentre.ca), where just about anything could be happening. Symphony concerts, plays, lectures, and operas are among the events scheduled.

The most popular spot in town for a beer is **Breakers Pub** (117 George Hills Way, Cow Bay, 250/624-5990; daily noon–midnight). This waterfront drinking hole boasts plenty of atmosphere, an outdoor deck with harbor views, and a bistro-style restaurant. Downtown and also with great water views, **Charley's Lounge** (Crest Hotel, 222 1st Ave. W., 250/624-6771) is more subdued than Breakers. It also has an impressive-for-this-far-north wine list and a semicreative menu.

The major annual celebration is **Seafest,** on the second weekend of June. All sorts of wacky events involving the sea are scheduled—a canoe-dunking contest (the water's icy so no one wants to lose), bathtub races, and fish-filleting competitions. There's also a more serious side to the weekend: a memorial

KING PACIFIC LODGE

King Pacific Lodge (604/987-5452 or 888/592-5464, www.kingpacificlodge.com; mid-May–mid-Sept.) provides an unforgettable wilderness experience, far removed from what the casual highway traveler might encounter. The floating lodge is on remote Princess Royal Island, best known for its population of Kermode, the albino-like "Spirit Bear." Its three-story timber structure is built over the waters of a protected cove, the perfect base for searching out abundant marine mammals, kayaking, and fishing. It is this last that attracts most guests, with chinooks (kings) biting best May–July and peak season for other salmon August–September.

The minimum stay is three nights, with all packages including floatplane transportation from Prince Rupert, all meals and drinks, and all activities. The lodge itself holds 17 spacious guest rooms, each with ample amenities and luxurious furnishings. The Great Room is a sea-level lounge centered on a huge stone fireplace; a wraparound veranda faces the ocean out front. Gourmet meals are served in an elegant setting overlooking the water, with fresh seafood the order of the day.

barbecue for those lost at sea, followed by a ceremony to dedicate new bricks at the mariner's statue. Another event held in June (the 21st) is **National Aboriginal Day,** featuring a salmon feast and plenty of authentic native dancing and singing.

ACCOMMODATIONS AND CAMPING

Prince Rupert's 700 motel rooms fill fast every summer night (late June–early Sept.) with travelers waiting for ferries—so book well in advance (if you're traveling onward from Prince Rupert, you should have already made ferry reservations, so you know which nights you'll be in town). Accommodation choices are wide-ranging, and although no one property stands out as being good value, all are moderately priced. On the other hand, Prince Rupert has a great campground within easy walking distance of the ferry terminals.

Under $50

The distinctive blue and green **Pioneer Hostel** (167 3rd Ave. E., 250/624-2334 or 888/794-9998; dorms $22–28, 56 d) has had the reputation of being a bit rough around the edges, but new owners and a new name have turned things around. It's still mostly full of "steadies" in winter, but in summer daily and weekly accommodations are offered. Facilities include dorm rooms with shared bathrooms, a couple of private doubles, an outside yard with a barbecue, free use of bicycles, a living room with TV, and a small but well-equipped kitchen.

$50-100

My favorite Rupert accommodation is the **(Eagle Bluff Bed and Breakfast** (201 Cow Bay Rd., 250/627-4955 or 800/833-1550). The house is built out over the water, overlooking the marina and harbor, and lies within easy walking distance of cafés and restaurants. Rates are $45 s, $65 d for a shared bath; $85 s, $95 d for a private bath; and $100 for a large suite sleeping five. A cooked breakfast—complete with freshly baked muffins—is included.

One of many reasonably priced motels is the **Moby Dick Inn** (935 2nd Ave. W., 250/624-6961 or 800/663-0822, www.mobydickinn .com; $84 s, $94 d), which is home to the best-priced breakfast restaurant in town. Also in the area is the **Pacific Inn** (909 3rd Ave. W., 250/627-1711 or 888/663-1999, www.pacific inn.bc.ca; $95–140 s or d), with larger rooms, each with stylish decor.

$100-150

The massive building right downtown is the 15-story **Highliner Plaza** (815 1st Ave. W., 250/624-9060 or 888/561-7666, www.highliner plaza.com; from $130 s or d). Rooms are no nicer than at the aforementioned Pacific Inn,

Eagle Bluff Bed and Breakfast

but the location is central and many have balconies with water views.

In a prime harborside location, the full-service **Crest Hotel** (222 1st Ave. W., 250/624-6771 or 800/663-8150, www.cresthotel.bc.ca) holds a glass-enclosed waterfront café, a dining room, and a lounge with water views. Rates for the stylishly decorated rooms start at $157 s or d. Upgrade to Crest Class for $187 s or d and enjoy water views and in-room amenities that include Internet access, a cordless phone, and coffee-making facilities.

Camping

Like the rest of Rupert's accommodations, **Park Avenue Campground** (1750 Park Ave., 250/624-5861 or 800/667-1994) fills and empties on a daily basis with the arrival and departure of the ferries. If you know when you're arriving in the city, phone ahead to avoid any hassles. The campground is a one-kilometer (0.6-mile) hike from both the city center and ferry terminals. Facilities include hot showers, cooking shelters, a grassy tenting area, pay phones, a mail drop, and visitor information. Unserviced sites are $16, full hookups $26. The other alternative is **Prudhomme Lake Provincial Park,** along the Yellowhead Highway 16 kilometers (10 miles) east of downtown; $14 per night.

FOOD
Breakfast

Most of Rupert's larger motels have restaurants, but the place to head for substantial and inexpensive breakfasts is the **Moby Dick Inn** (935 2nd Ave. W., 250/624-6961, daily 6:30 A.M.–9:30 P.M.). You can order anything from a bowl of fruit and a muffin ($4) to eggs, bacon, and toast ($5) or steak and eggs ($8). It's always crowded, and service can be slow. Just around the corner, the **Raffles Inn** (1080 3rd Ave. W., 250/624-9161) offers similar fare and is open similar hours.

Java Dot Cup (516 3rd Ave. W., 250/622-2822, Mon.–Fri. 7:30 A.M.–6 P.M., Sat.–Sun. 10 A.M.–6 P.M.) combines a wide range of coffee drinks with public Internet access.

Cow Bay Cafés

East of downtown is Cow Bay, originally a fishy-smelling, rough-and-tumble part of town home to a large fishing fleet. The boats are still there, moored in a marina, and a few old buildings still stand. But for the most part, the bay is a changed place. Rowdy dives have been replaced by trendy art and crafts shops, restaurants, and two of the city's best cafés.

Cowpuccino's (25 Cow Bay Rd., 250/627-1395; daily 7:30 A.M.–10 P.M.) is a great little coffeehouse with freshly brewed coffee, magnificent muffins, delicious desserts, newspapers and magazines to read, and a laid-back atmosphere. Across the way and right on the harbor is **Cow Bay Cafe** (205 Cow Bay Rd., 250/627-1212; Tues.–Sun. 11 A.M.–8 P.M.), where you can sit at an outside table and take in the smells of the ocean, or stay inside and enjoy the greenery. Good home-cooked meals, including vegetarian dishes, and daily specials start at $7.

Seafood and Pacific Northwest

Ask a local where to go for good seafood and the answer is invariably **(Smile's Seafood Cafe** (113 Cow Bay Rd., 250/624-3072; July–Aug. daily 9 A.M.–10 P.M., the rest of the year daily 11 A.M.–8 P.M.). This diner-style café, decorated with black-and-white fishing photos and colored-glass floats, has been serving seafood since 1934. It's always busy, mobbed by local anglers, residents, and visitors no matter what time of day. The extensive menu includes seafood salads and sandwiches, burgers, fish and chips, shellfish, and seafood specialties. Prices range $6–25 per plate.

Combining seasonal seafood with cooking as creative as it gets in northern British Columbia is **Rain Dining Lounge** (737 3rd Ave. W., 250/250/627-8272; daily for lunch and dinner). Almost all entrées are under $20, including lobster ravioli with saffron-cream sauce, salmon cakes with green-curry coconut-lime sauce, and pan-seared halibut doused with fruity salsa.

Combining water views, good food, and pleasant surroundings, the **Waterfront Restaurant** (Crest Hotel, 222 1st Ave. W., 250/624-6771) is as upscale as it gets in Prince Rupert. You could start with alder-smoked steelhead and then move on to oven-roasted salmon in a lemony Dijon crust. Or give seafood a break and choose beef tenderloin with a rosemary jus. Either way, you'll pay $22–36 for a main.

INFORMATION AND SERVICES
Information
Prince Rupert Visitor Centre is in a converted fish plant along the Cow Bay waterfront (215 Cow Bay Rd., 250/624-5637 or 800/667-1994, www.tourismprincerupert.com; early June–early Sept. Mon.–Sat. 9 A.M.–8 P.M. and Sun. 9 A.M.–5 P.M., the rest of the year Mon.–Sat. 9 A.M.–5 P.M.). It's one of the best information centers around, with a knowledgeable staff and lots of printed material on Prince Rupert sights, walking tours, restaurants, services, and ferry schedules.

Books
The **library** is just off McBride Avenue (101 6th Ave., 250/627-1345); an adjacent room provides public Internet access for a minimal charge. If you're looking for books, especially on BC native art or history, spend some time at **Rainforest Books** (515 3rd Ave. W., 250/624-9053; Mon.–Sat. 8:30 A.M.–6 P.M.). This bookstore also stocks a good selection of Queen Charlotte Islands material.

Services
Prince Rupert Regional Hospital is south of downtown (1305 Summit Ave., 250/624-2171). The **post office** is on 2nd Avenue at 3rd Street. **Laundries** are at 226 7th Street and 745 2nd Avenue West.

GETTING THERE AND AROUND
Air
Prince Rupert Airport is served by **Air Canada** (888/247-2262) and **Hawk Air** (800/487-1216), both with scheduled flights from Vancouver, and the latter also from other provincial centers. The airport is west of town on Digby Island. It is linked to the city by

a ferry that takes buses and foot passengers only—no vehicles. Airlines provide free bus transportation between the airport and downtown, via the ferry, but passengers must pay the ferry fare of $12 per person each way. The downtown pickup point for passengers is the Highliner Plaza (815 1st Ave. W.).

Seal Cove Air Base lies at the east end of town and serves as the seaplane base for Prince Rupert. To get there, take 5th Avenue east from McBride Street and follow the signs to Seal Cove. The largest operator is **North Pacific Seaplanes** (250/627-1341 or 800/689-4234, www.northpacificseaplanes .com), which makes scheduled flights throughout the region and out to Sandspit ($238). The company also offers flightseeing excursions, including a 30-minute flight over the city for $145 per person and an hour-long trip to the Khutzeymateen Valley grizzly bear sanctuary for $295 per person.

Rail and Bus
Prince Rupert is the western terminus of Canada's transcontinental rail system, which runs east from here to Prince George and Edmonton, across the prairies to Toronto, and on to the Atlantic provinces. The route through British Columbia is the highlight of the trip, especially the couple of hundred kilometers just outside Prince Rupert, where the line follows the Skeena River. To get to the **VIA Rail** station (250/627-7589) take 2nd Street north over the rail line. Trains arrive in Prince Rupert on Monday, Thursday, and Saturday at 8 P.M. and depart on Wednesday, Friday, and Sunday at 8 A.M.

From the local **Greyhound** bus depot (112 6th St., 250/624-5090), buses travel east along the Yellowhead Highway to Terrace and Prince George, then either north to the Alaska Highway, east to Jasper National Park and Edmonton, or south through Cariboo Country to Kamloops and on to Vancouver. The run between Prince George and Prince Rupert leaves twice daily. Reservations are not taken—just turn up and buy your ticket on the day you want to go.

Ferry

Prince Rupert is the northern terminus of the BC Ferries network (250/386-3431 or 888/223-3779, www.bcferries.com), which offers regular services south to Port Hardy on Vancouver Island and west to the Queen Charlotte Islands. The terminal is two kilometers (1.2 miles) from downtown, right alongside the Alaska Marine Highway terminal. Ferries serving Prince Rupert have both day rooms and sleeping cabins, shower facilities, food service, and plenty of room to sit back and relax. During the busy summer months, it's imperative that you book well in advance, especially if you plan to transport a vehicle.

The 15-hour, 440-kilometer (273-mile) ferry trip between Prince Rupert and Port Hardy is a beautiful ride, with ferries departing through summer every second day, less frequently the rest of the year. The summer one-way fares are adult $125, child 5–11 $62.50, vehicle $300. Discounts are available outside of summer and for BC seniors. Cabins ($60–90) and recliner chairs ($20) are available by reservation.

The **Alaska Marine Highway** (907/465-3941 or 800/642-0066, www.alaska.gov/ferry) operates an extensive network of ferries through southeastern Alaska and down to Prince Rupert. The first stop north from Prince Rupert is Ketchikan, six hours away. Walk-on passengers need not make reservations, but if you require a cabin or have a vehicle, make reservations as far in advance as possible (up to one year), especially for sailings between May and September. Check-in time is three hours ahead of sailing time—it takes up to two hours to go through Customs and one hour to load up. Foot passengers must be there one hour ahead of sailing.

Getting Around

Local bus service along four routes is provided by **Prince Rupert Transit System** (2nd Ave. W., 250/624-3343). Adult fare starts at $2.50. All-day passes cost $4 and are available from the driver. Have exact fare ready—drivers don't carry change. The only car-rental agencies in town are **Budget** (250/627-7400) and **National** (250/624-5318). For a cab call **Skeena Taxis** (250/624-2185).

Queen Charlotte Islands

Wild. Quiet. Mysterious. Primordial. Inhabited by the proud and ferocious Haida people for over 10,000 years, the Queen Charlotte Islands spread like a large upside-down triangle approximately 100 kilometers (62 miles) off the northwest coast of mainland British Columbia, linked to the mainland by scheduled ferry and air services. Visitors have the opportunity to immerse themselves in native culture, view the abundant wildlife, explore the rugged coastline, and share a laid-back island camaraderie with the 4,000 permanent residents.

Of the chain's 150 mountainous and densely forested islands and islets, the main ones are **Graham Island** to the north and **Moresby Island** to the south, separated by narrow **Skidegate Channel.** The islands stretch 290 kilometers (180 miles) from north to south and up to 85 kilometers (53 miles) across. Running down the west side of the islands are the Queen Charlotte and San Christoval ranges, which effectively protect the east side from Pacific battering. Nevertheless, the east coast, where most of the population lives, still receives over 1,000 millimeters (39 inches) of rain annually.

Life on the islands is very different from elsewhere in the province. Visitors can expect a friendly reception and adequate services. Motel-style accommodations are available in each town, but bed-and-breakfasts provide a better glimpse of the island lifestyle. Other services are similar to any small town, though choices of fresh fruit and vegetables can be limited. Gasoline is only slightly more expensive

NORTHERN B.C.

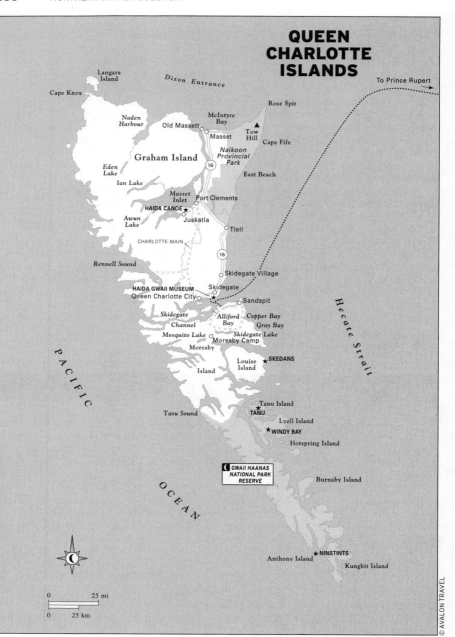

QUEEN CHARLOTTE ISLANDS

Langara Island

Dixon Entrance

To Prince Rupert

Cape Knox

Naden Harbour

Rose Spit

McIntyre Bay

Old Massett

Masset

Tow Hill

Cape Fife

Graham Island

Naikoon Provincial Park

16

Eden Lake

Ian Lake

East Beach

Masset Inlet

Port Clements

HAIDA CANOE ★

Awun Lake

Juskatla

CHARLOTTE MAIN

Tlell

16

Rennell Sound

Skidegate Village

HAIDA GWAII MUSEUM
Queen Charlotte City

Skidegate

Sandspit

Skidegate Channel

Alliford Bay

Copper Bay

Gray Bay

Mosquito Lake

Skidegate Lake

Moresby Camp

Moresby

Louise Island

★ SKEDANS

Island

PACIFIC

Tasu Sound

Tanu Island

★ TANU

Lyell Island

★ WINDY BAY

Hotspring Island

Hecate Strait

GWAII HAANAS
NATIONAL PARK
RESERVE

Burnaby Island

OCEAN

Anthony Island

★ NINSTINTS

Kunghit Island

0   25 mi

0   25 km

© ANDREW HEMPSTEAD

Many island homes and businesses are decorated with colorful buoys, driftwood, and just about anything that floats.

than on the mainland, and raging nightlife is nonexistent.

The Haida

The Haida people have lived on the Queen Charlottes since time immemorial. Fearless warriors, expert hunters and fishermen, and skilled woodcarvers, they owned slaves and threw lavish potlatches. They had no written language, but they carved records of their tribal history, legends, and important events on totem poles rising up to 104 meters (340 feet) high. Living in villages scattered throughout the islands, they hunted sea otters for their luxuriant furs, fished for halibut and Pacific salmon, and collected chitons, clams, and seaweed from tidepools.

The first contact the Haida had with Europeans occurred in 1774, when Spanish explorer Juan Perez discovered the Charlottes. At the turn of the 19th century, White settlers from the mainland began moving over to the Charlottes to live along the low-lying east coast and the protected shores of Masset Inlet. By the 1830s the traditional lifestyle of the Haida was coming to an end. The governments on the mainland prohibited the Haida from owning slaves and throwing potlatches—an important social and economic part of their culture—and forced all Haida children to attend missionary schools. The Haida abandoned their village sites and moved onto reserves at Skidegate and Masset on Graham Island.

For many years the Haida struggled alongside the Island Protection Society to preserve their heritage. Their longtime efforts paid off in two major events: in 1981 the best-known of the abandoned Haida villages, **Ninstints,** was declared a UNESCO World Heritage Site, and in 1988 the southern section of the archipelago was proclaimed **Gwaii Haanas National Park Reserve.**

GETTING THERE AND AROUND
Air

The main gateway is Sandspit, where the small air terminal holds car-rental agencies

NORTHERN B.C.

BEACHCOMBING ON THE CHARLOTTES

Beachcombing on the Queen Charlotte Islands is popular year-round, but it's especially good after heavy winter storms. You may find fishing floats from countries around the Pacific (glass balls from Japan are especially prized), bottles, rope, driftwood, shells, whale bones, semiprecious agate, or just about anything that floats. A few years back, a container of Nike runners broke apart somewhere in the Pacific; they were found scattered on beaches throughout the Charlottes and as far south as the Oregon coast. Before that, an abandoned fishing boat from Japan washed ashore and caused excitement; it's now on display in Prince Rupert.

(book ahead) and an information center, and across the road is the Sandspit Inn. **Air Canada** (888/247-2262) flies daily between Vancouver and Sandspit. **Hawk Air** (250/635-4295) offers daily service between Prince Rupert and Sandspit. The Airporter bus meets all Sandspit flights and transports passengers to Queen Charlotte City for $16.

From Prince Rupert's Seal Cove Air Base, **North Pacific Seaplanes** (250/627-1341 or 800/689-4234) has scheduled flights to Masset ($152) and Sandspit ($238).

Ferry

In summer, **BC Ferries** (250/386-3431 or 888/223-3779, www.bcferries.com) operates the *Queen of Prince Rupert* between Prince Rupert and Skidegate five or six times a week, less frequently the rest of the year. Departure times vary, but most often it's 11 A.M. from Prince Rupert (arriving Skidegate at 5:30 P.M.) and 11 P.M. from Skidegate (arriving Prince Rupert at 6 A.M. or 7:30 A.M.). Peak one-way fares: adult $29, child $14.50, vehicle $109. BC seniors get a discount, as do all travelers outside the peak summer season. Cabins are available

for $55. The ferry terminal is five kilometers (3.1 miles) east of Queen Charlotte City at Skidegate. Taxis usually wait at the terminal when the ferry arrives; expect to pay around $15 to get into town.

Getting Around

A ferry connects Graham and Moresby Islands, departing hourly in each direction 7 A.M.–10 P.M.; peak round-trip fare is adult $7, child $4, vehicle $15. Apart from that, the islands have no public transportation. Handiest for vehicle-less ferry travelers is **Rustic Car Rentals,** based in Queen Charlotte City (250/559-4641), with vehicles from $40 per day. Both **Budget** (250/637-5688) and **Thrifty** (250/637-2299) have offices in Sandspit.

QUEEN CHARLOTTE CITY

Known to the locals simply as "Charlotte," Queen Charlotte City is spread along the shores of Bearskin Bay, five kilometers (3.1 miles) west of the dock for the mainland ferry. It's not really a city at all—most places that include "city" in their name aren't—but instead a laid-back fishing village of 1,000 people. Heritage buildings dating back to the early 1900s (most along the main road) are interspersed with all the services of a small town, with a colorful array of private residences sprawling east and west, overlooking the water and backed by forested wilderness. The main street is 3rd Avenue, a continuation of the road from the ferry dock.

Accommodations and Camping

Queen Charlotte City is a good base for exploring the islands and has a wide variety of accommodations. Built in 1910, the old Premier Hotel has been totally renovated and now operates as **❰ Premier Creek Lodging** (3rd Ave., 250/559-8415 or 888/322-3388), offering beds to suit all budgets. In the main lodge, single "sleeping rooms" with shared facilities cost $35 per person, but definitely worth the extra money are the rooms with private bathrooms, balconies, and harbor views (some with kitchens) for $65 s, $75 d. Behind the main lodge is the simple **Premier Creek Hostel** (same telephone numbers as the lodge). It has two four-bed dorms and one double room, a kitchen, a living room, a laundry, a gas barbecue, and bike rentals ($30 per day); rates are $23 per person.

The least expensive rooms at **Dorothy and Mike's Guest House** (3127 2nd Ave., 250/559-8439) are $49 s, $69 d and share baths, but my favorite is the en suite Kumdis Room ($84 s or d), where a sliding door opens to a private deck with fantastic views. Common areas include a kitchen, a TV room, a large deck area, and a library overflowing with island literature. A hearty cooked breakfast will get you going each morning.

Moonglow Guest House (3611 Highway 33, 250/559-8831; $65 s, $75 d) has just one guest room, but it's a good one, with cooking facilities, a patio with views of Skidegate Inlet, and a private entrance. Behind the property, a trail leads along a creek to a waterfall.

Haydn Turner Park, through town to the west, has toilets, picnic tables, and fire rings for campers, but no showers or hookups; $8 per night.

Food and Drink

The place to go for breakfast is **Lam's** (3223 Wharf St., 250/559-4204; Mon.–Sat. 6:30 A.M.–3 P.M., Sun. 8 A.M.–3 P.M.). All the locals congregate here. In addition to water views, this place has plenty of atmosphere, and the food is good and plentiful for the price (cooked breakfasts from $7.50), but be prepared to wait for a table. For something more substantial, head to **Sea Raven Motel** (3301 3rd Ave., 250/559-4423). Specializing in local seafood, the motel's no-frills dining room is open daily 7 A.M.–2 P.M. and 5–9 P.M. The seafood chowder ($5) is delicious. **Howler's Pub and Bistro** (3rd Ave., 250/559-8602; 11 A.M.–10 P.M.) has a downstairs pub and upstairs dining room. Menus in both are pub-like, but with a surprising number of vegetarian choices and a good selection of desserts.

Information and Services

Down on the waterfront, **Queen Charlotte**

Visitor Centre (3220 Wharf St., 250/559-8316; mid-May–mid-Sept. daily 10 A.M.–7 P.M.) offers natural history displays, a wide variety of brochures and information on everything that's going on around the islands, and current weather forecasts. The *Guide to the Queen Charlotte Islands,* which includes maps, details on all the villages, and more, is available at the center. The best online source of information is www.haidagwaiitourism.ca. For island and North Coast literature, head to **Northwest Coast Books** (3205 3rd Ave., 250/559-4681, www.nwcbooks.com). The selection of new and used titles is incredible, with the bookstore wholesaling hard-to-find titles to galleries and museums across North America.

Emergency services in Queen Charlotte City include **Queen Charlotte Islands General Hospital** (3209 3rd Ave., 250/559-4300) and the **Royal Canadian Mounted Police** (250/559-4421). The **post office** and a **laundry** are in the City Centre Building off 2nd Avenue.

NORTH TO PORT CLEMENTS

From Queen Charlotte City, Graham Island's main road follows the eastern coastline past the ferry terminal and Haida Heritage Centre to the Haida community of Skidegate Village, from where it's a pleasant 65-kilometer (40-mile) coastal drive to Port Clements.

Haida Heritage Centre at Qay'llnagaay

While totem poles and other ancient Haida art can be seen in various places around the islands, this **museum** (250/559-4643; summer Mon.–Fri. 9 A.M.–6 P.M., Sat.–Sun. 9 A.M.–5 P.M.; adult $12, child $5), on the north side of the Skidegate Landing ferry terminal, gives visitors the opportunity to see a variety of such art under one roof. Inside the impressive log building are striking Haida wood and argillite carvings, pioneer artifacts, a beautiful woven blanket, jewelry, historic black-and-white photos, stunning prints by Haida artist Robert Davidson, ancient totems from Tanu and Skedans dating to 1878, the skull of a humpback whale, shells galore, and a collection of stuffed birds. Outside, be sure to visit the longhouse-style **cedar carving shed,** where the fantastic 15-meter-long (49-foot-long) canoe *Loo Taas* (which means "wave eater") is housed.

Between late April and early June, migrating **gray whales** rest and feed on shallow gravel bars of Skidegate Inlet in front of the museum on their annual 15,000-kilometer (9,300-mile) odyssey between Mexico and Alaska. Behind the museum, a wooden deck overlooking the water is a great vantage point for watching these magnificent creatures, or continue a few hundred yards farther around the bay and search them out from the roadside.

Skidegate Village and Vicinity

Continuing north from the museum you'll soon come to Skidegate Village, a Haida reserve of 700 residents. A weathered totem pole, over 100 years old, still stands here, as do six newer ones. Facing the beach is a traditional longhouse, home to the Skidegate Haida Band Council House, where local artisans fashion miniature totem poles, argillite ornaments, and jewelry in traditional designs. Cross the road from the local recreation center to the trailhead of a hiking trail to **Spirit Lake.** The trail passes through an old-growth forest of hemlock, Sitka spruce, and red cedar and passes two picturesque bodies of water, one with picnic tables. The round-trip is three kilometers (1.9 miles)—an easy hour's walk.

From Skidegate, the road follows the shoreline of Hecate Strait, past driftwood-strewn beaches, an attractive old graveyard, and **Balance Rock,** one kilometer (0.6 mile) north of Skidegate Village. A highway sign and turnout mark the start of a short trail down to the rock. Continuing north, the scenery becomes rural, as the road skirts land cleared by early settlers for cattle-grazing; watch for black-tailed deer in this area. Near **Lawn Hill** look for tree stumps that have been carved into the shapes of animals and birds.

Naikoon Provincial Park (Southern End)

Just north of Tlell, 48 kilometers (30 miles)

north of Queen Charlotte City, is the southern tip of Naikoon Provincial Park. While the park's main entrance is farther north out of Masset, visitors exploring the Tlell area will find interesting things to see and do here in the park's south end as well. The main attraction down here is the wreck of the *Pesuta,* a wooden log barge that ran aground in 1928. To get there, park at the picnic area on the north side of the Tlell River and follow the river to its mouth, then walk north along the beach. It's about six kilometers (3.7 miles) each way. Keen hikers may want to attempt the **East Beach Hike,** a 94-kilometer (58-mile) trail that leads all the way north from the Tlell River to Tow Hill via Rose Spit.

Misty Meadows Campground, immediately north of park headquarters, is uncrowded and costs only $14 per site for one of 30 scenic campsites. Facilities include a picnic area and pit toilets.

Port Clements

Weather-beaten houses decorated with driftwood, shells, fishing floats, and other sea-washed treasures line the streets of this logging and fishing village on the shore of Masset Inlet. **Port Clements Museum** (Bayview Dr., 250/557-4255; summer daily 1–5 P.M.; donation) houses an intriguing selection of pioneer artifacts from the area, as well as black-and-white photos of logging camps and early village life.

Charlotte Main

This rough logging road links Port Clements to Queen Charlotte City via an inland route, a good alternative to returning via Tlell. To get to it, take Bayview Drive southwest out of Port Clements. Twelve kilometers (7.5 miles) from town, a short trail leads through the forest to an unfinished **Haida canoe,** estimated to have been abandoned around 100 years ago. Continuing south, the road passes through **Juskatla,** a logging camp established in the 1940s to supply spruce for World War II airplanes. From this point on, you are driving on a road used by logging trucks, so travel is safest outside of operating hours (Mon.–Fri.

7 A.M.–6 P.M.). Check in at the office or call 250/559-4224 to check the status of the road before heading any farther.

From Juskatla, the logging road continues south to Queen Charlotte City. A turnoff to the west (signposted) leads to **Rennell Sound,** the only point on the remote west coast accessible by road. At the end of the road await great beachcombing opportunities and free primitive campsites. The final descent to the shore is a hair-raising 24 percent gradient, one of the steepest public roads in North America.

MASSET AND VICINITY

Known as Graham City when founded in 1909, Masset (pop. 800) lies just south of a Haida community named Massett. Over time, Massett became known as Old Massett or Haida, and Graham City was incorporated as Masset (with one "t"). The population has decreased since downsizing began on the local Canadian Armed Forces Station, where at one time half the local population lived. Today, Masset's economy revolves around the ocean, with most workers involved in the fishing industry—either as fisherfolk or as workers in the local fish canning and freezing plant.

Delkatla Wildlife Sanctuary

Bordering Masset to the east is Delkatla Wildlife Sanctuary, where you can observe Canada geese, sandhill cranes, trumpeter swans, great blue herons, many varieties of ducks, and other waterfowl resting during migration. Several short walking trails wind through the preserve near town; follow Hodges Avenue west onto Trumpeter Drive and continue alongside the inlet to the trailhead. For better views, drive along Tow Hill Road toward Naikoon Provincial Park, turning left at the sanctuary sign onto Masset Cemetery Road. Along this road, more signs mark trails or other points of interest. You first pass a turnout for the **Bird Walk Trail,** which winds along the edge of a marshy area. Then farther down the road, you come to **Simpson Viewing Tower,** where you may spy waterfowl, bald eagles, peregrine falcons,

and other birds of prey, as well as four-legged marsh animals such as muskrats.

Back on Tow Hill Road, continue east to a parking lot and a trail to the beach. Just across from the parking lot is beautiful **Masset Cemetery,** where the graves are marked by large aboveground mounds of moss planted with flowering bulbs and surrounded by bushes and trees. It's a peaceful place to ponder the beauty of the Charlottes.

Old Massett

If you're in search of Haida treasures, head for the village of Old Massett, also known as Haida. It's just a five-minute drive from Masset, west down the coastal road. Go as far as the road takes you and you'll end up at the old blue schoolhouse, now **Ed Jones Haida Museum** (summer Sat.–Sun. 9 A.M.–5 P.M.; donation). Exhibits include a large collection of fascinating old photographs showing how the villages used to look, Haida art and prints, and some of the original totem poles from around the Queen Charlottes. Outside you'll find a partly completed canoe and a field sprinkled with more totems, these from a more recent era. Across from the museum is a carving shed where artists can be seen working throughout summer. Continue up behind the museum to the impressive weathered building with the two totem poles out front; this is **Sarah's Haida Arts and Jewellery** (387 Eagle Rd., 250/626-5560; Mon.–Sat. 11 A.M.–5 P.M., Sun. noon–5 P.M.), where you can buy custom argillite carvings, silk-screen prints, handcrafted silver and abalone jewelry, books on native culture, and greeting cards.

Accommodations and Camping

Several B&Bs in Masset provide lodgings and local flavor. Next to the pier, rustic ❰ **Copper Beech House** (1590 Delkatla Rd., 250/626-5441, www.copperbeechhouse.com) is a New England–style saltbox, decorated with sea treasures and with a beautiful flower garden. Rates of $75 s, $100 d ($125 for an en suite) include a delicious breakfast prepared by David Phillips, whose enthusiasm for the islands is infectious.

Phillips does wonders with local produce—smoking his own seafood and making jams and preserves from locally harvested berries.

Alaska View Lodge (12 kilometers/7.5 miles east of Masset on Tow Hill Rd., 250/626-3333 or 800/661-0019, www.alaskaviewlodge.ca) is right on the beach and backed by dense temperate rainforest of Sitka spruce. Accommodations in the main building share bathrooms and range $60–70 s, $80–90 d, depending on the view. Closer to the beach, two rooms in the "Guesthouse" feature practical beach furniture and a joined deck; $80 s, $90 d. Continuing toward Tow Hill, **Rapid Ritchie's Rustic Rentals** (250/626-5472, www.beachcabins .com) is a similar setup, with cedar-shaked cabins spread through the forest. If you can do without modern conveniences, you'll love this place—and the rates ($40–75, cash only)—but be prepared for outhouses, no electricity, and no phones.

Village of Masset RV Site and Campground is on Tow Hill Road two kilometers (1.2 miles) north of Masset, opposite the Delkatla Wildlife Sanctuary. The campground features large, fairly private campsites with tables among the trees, and washrooms with coin-operated hot showers. Unserviced sites are $12, powered sites $18. Another option for campers is to continue 20 kilometers (12 miles) along the road into Naikoon Provincial Park.

Food

Even though Masset has a large fishing fleet, most of the catch ends up in mainland canneries. Your best choice for seafood is **Sandpiper Restaurant** (corner of Collison Ave. and Orr St., 250/626-3672; Mon.–Sat. 8:30 A.M.–9 P.M.), where the daily lunch specials are around $9 and dinner entrées range $14–24. **Pearl's** (corner of Main St. and Collison Ave., 250/626-3223; Mon.–Sat. for lunch and daily for dinner) features Chinese cuisine in an almost hospital-like atmosphere. For around $12 you can get an enormous helping of chicken and vegetables in black bean sauce, along with a large bowl of steamed rice, tea, and the mandatory fortune cookie.

NAIKOON PROVINCIAL PARK

This wild coastal park encompasses some 72,640 hectares (179,500 acres) along the northeast tip of Graham Island. Tlell marks the park's southern boundary, while access to the northern reaches is via the road out to Tow Hill, 26 kilometers (16 miles) east of Masset. The park's dominant features are its beaches, 97 kilometers (60 miles) of them, bordering Hecate Strait on the east and the turbulent Dixon Entrance on the north. Most of the rest of the park is lowlands, surrounded by stunted lodgepole pine, red and yellow cedar, western hemlock, and Sitka spruce. Wildlife is abundant; black-tailed deer, black bears, marten, river otters, raccoons, red squirrels, beavers, muskrats, small herds of wild cattle, and many species of birds inhabit the park. Dolphins, orcas, porpoises, and seals swim offshore year-round, and northern fur seals and California gray whales migrate north past the park in May and June.

Sights

The drive out to the park from Masset is superb, passing through seemingly endless moss-draped trees. Along the way you pass **Tow Hill Ecological Reserve,** a beautiful spruce forest where birds tweet from the treetops, and the ground and most of the trees are completely cushioned by spongy yellow moss.

The road passes the base of Tow Hill and ends at the southern end of long, sandy **North Beach.** This strip of sand is a beachcomber's delight, as it is strewn with shells, driftwood, and shiny, sea-worn pebbles of every color under the sun. The beach is best known for semiprecious agate, ranging from light yellow in color to almost-translucent, which is found among piles of pebbles that become exposed at low tide starting about three kilometers (1.9 miles) along the beach. At the end of North Beach is **Rose Spit.** Known to the Haida as Naikoon, meaning "long nose," this narrow point of land separates the waters of Hecate Strait and Dixon Entrance. From the end of Tow Hill Road, it's about 10 kilometers (6.2 miles) of easy beach walking

a victim of the sea, Naikoon Provincial Park

© ANDREW HEMPSTEAD

to the end of the spit; if you allow six hours for the round-trip, you'll have enough time to enjoy a picnic lunch among the driftwood along the way.

Head back toward Masset, along the beach from the end of the road, and **Tow Hill** is impossible to miss. A one-kilometer (0.6-mile) trail leads to the top of this 130-meter-high (430-foot-high) basalt monolith, or satisfy yourself with exploring the tidal pools at its base.

Cape Fife Trail

From near the end of the park access road, the Cape Fife Trail (three hours each way) heads in a southeasterly direction, passing boglands and stunted pine trees on its 10-kilometer (6.2-mile) route to **Fife Point,** overlooking Hecate Strait. The shore above the high-tide line is blanketed by a mass of driftwood logs, crushed together during the fierce storms that regularly lash this coast. A rough shelter at the end of the trail provides some protection from the elements. Backcountry camping is permitted;

hide among the trees on especially windy days. From this point you can hike north along the beach to Rose Spit (described earlier), then continue back along North Beach to the parking lot at Hiellen River—a total of 34 kilometers (21 miles) and an easy two-day trip. Well-equipped adventurers can continue south from Fife Point along **East Beach** to finish at Tlell, a total distance of 72 kilometers (45 miles). This has become a popular hike—take your time (allow 4–5 days) and bring adequate food and water.

Camping

Agate Beach Campground is near Tow Hill, about 26 kilometers (16 miles) from Masset. The campsites lie along the back of the beach and offer outstanding views. A shelter and pit toilets are provided, but no showers. In summer you need to nab a spot early in the day—by late afternoon they're all taken. The campground is open year-round. Sites cost $14 per night May–September; the rest of the year they're free.

SANDSPIT AND VICINITY

Across Skidegate Channel from Queen Charlotte City, Sandspit (pop. 560) is the only community on Moresby Island. Home to the islands' main airport and linked to Graham Island by a short ferry trip, the town occupies a low-lying, windswept spit overlooking Shingle Bay. The northern half of Moresby Island is largely given over to logging, while the southern half and over 100 outlying islands fall within Gwaii Haanas National Park Reserve, which protects a high concentration of abandoned Haida villages.

Those determined to tour the forests in their own vehicle can make an enjoyable loop trip south out of Sandspit. Logging roads lace the forest, leading to beaches strewn with driftwood, streams alive with salmon and steelhead, and beautiful Skidegate and Mosquito Lakes (good trout fishing). Free campgrounds are available at Gray Bay and Mosquito Lake.

Practicalities

Sandspit lacks the appeal of communities on Graham Island, but services are available. Friendly **Moresby Island Guest House** (385 Beach Rd., 250/637-5300, www.moresby island-bnb.com; $30–75 d) is a popular kayakers' hangout across the road from Shingle Bay. Some of the 10 rooms share bathrooms, but everyone has use of a kitchen, laundry, and wide deck with water views. Bike rentals are also available.

Sandspit Visitor Centre is a small desk inside the airport terminal (250/637-5362; mid-May–mid-Sept. daily 9 A.M.–6 P.M.).

◖ GWAII HAANAS NATIONAL PARK RESERVE

Renowned around the world for its ancient Haida villages dotted with totem poles, this park encompasses the southern half of Moresby Island as well as 137 smaller islands in the south of the archipelago—1,480 hectares (3,660 acres) of land and 1,600 kilometers (1,000 miles) of coastline. It's a remarkable place. Ancient, brooding totems and remnants of mighty Haida longhouses stand against a backdrop of lush wilderness: dense trees, thick spongy moss, and rock-strewn beaches with incredibly clear water. Colonies of nesting seabirds and an abundance of marinelife—killer and minke whales, sea lions, tufted puffins—all add to the atmosphere.

Jointly managed by Parks Canada and the Haida nation, the park was established in 1988 after a long, bitter struggle between the Haida and forestry companies. The area now protected was home to seafaring Haida for almost 10,000 years, but by the early 1900s, less than 100 years after their first contact with Whites, their communities were abandoned, the inhabitants having been wiped out by disease or having moved to Old Massett and Skidegate.

Nan Sdins (Ninstints) on tiny SGaang Gwaii (Anthony Island) near the south end of the park, was once home to around 300 Haida and had been occupied for thousands of years before the arrival of Europeans. Today, weathered totem poles stretch along the shoreline, with the nearby ruins of cedar longhouses slowly being consumed by the surrounding rainforest. Anthony Island was declared a UNESCO World Heritage Site in 1981, just 97 years after the last Haida families had abandoned their remote home. **Gandle K'in** (Hotspring Island), the site of another abandoned village, has the bonus of oceanfront hot pools that held special healing and spiritual qualities to the Haida. Other well-known villages include **Kuuna** (Skedans), closest to Sandspit; **T'aanuu** (Tanu); and **Hik'yah** (Windy Bay).

Park Practicalities

The only access to the park is by air or sea. If you aren't visiting the park as part of an organized tour, reserve a permit through Tourism BC (250/387-1642 or 800/435-5622; $15 per booking). Six spots are set aside on a standby basis; claim them from the Haida Heritage Centre at 8:30 A.M. on the day of departure. Either way, you must also purchase the permit itself (adult $20, senior $18, child $9 per day) and participate in an orientation session; these are held at the Haida Heritage Centre daily at 9:30 A.M. **Moresby Explorers** (250/637-2215 or 800/806-7633, www.moresbyexplorers .com) provides drop-offs and pickups for those heading into the park unguided. Sample cost is $700 for two for kayak rental, use of a VHF radio, and boat transportation to the company's base camp in Crescent Inlet. **South Moresby Air Charters** (250/559-4222, www.smair.com) is a floatplane operation based at the wharf in Queen Charlotte City. Charter rates for four people (book in advance for the best chance of making up the numbers) are $480 to Skedans, $765 to Hotspring Island, and $1,800 to Nan Sdins. Rates include an hour's ground time at the destination, with the Nan Sdins rate also including a short boat ride—the planes are unable to land right at Nan Sdins.

The above permit information is irrelevant if, like many visitors, you travel as part of a guided tour (although the operator will charge you the permit fee). **Archipelago Ventures** (604/940-6309 or 888/559-8317, www.tourhaidagwaii.com) combines the best of the park into a six-day tour that costs $2,000. The main mode of transportation is a stable 42-foot mother ship, with the focus on kayaking,

hiking, and soaking up culture in the abandoned Haida villages, including Nan Sdins. Along the way, freshly caught shrimp and halibut create enticing meals. The turnaround point for these tours is Rose Harbour; travel is by boat in one direction and floatplane in the other, which allows for a relaxed pace in one direction and a spectacular ride above the park in the other. **Ocean Light II Adventures** (604/328-5339, www.oceanlight2.bc.ca) has been conducting sailing trips through the south end of the archipelago since well before the proclamation of a park. Board the company's 71-foot *Ocean Light II* for eight days of sailing, visiting all the best-known abandoned Haida villages, exploring the waterways, and searching out land and sea mammals. All meals and accommodations aboard the boat are included in the rate of $3,800 per person.

For general park information, click through the links on the Parks Canada website (www.pc.gc.ca). To contact the local park office, call 250/559-8818.

Stewart-Cassiar Highway

An alternative to the Alaska Highway, this route—often referred to simply as "the Cassiar"—spurs north off the Yellowhead Highway 45 kilometers (28 miles) west of New Hazelton and leads north to the Yukon, joining the Alaska Highway just west of Watson Lake. The highway opens up a magnificent area of northern wilderness that in many ways rivals that along the more famous Alaska Highway. The highlight of the Stewart-Cassiar Highway is definitely the side trip west to the twin coastal villages of **Stewart** and **Hyder.**

From the Yellowhead Highway it's 155 kilometers (96 miles) north to Meziadin Junction, then 65 kilometers (40 miles) west to Stewart, official beginning of the Stewart-Cassiar Highway. Total length of the trip between the Yellowhead and Alaska Highways is 733 kilometers (455 miles), excluding the 130 kilometers (80 miles) round-trip for the jaunt out to Stewart.

Be Prepared
The highway is mainly paved, but improved gravel sections are found on the 80-kilometer (50-mile) stretch north of Meziadin Junction, the 40-kilometer (25-mile) stretch south of Kinaskan Lake, and for around 30 kilometers (19 miles) each side of Dease Lake. Be prepared for washboard conditions on these sections, especially after heavy rain. Dust and mud can also be problematic, and many narrow, one-lane bridges call for extra caution. Gas stations and services can be found along the highway, but it's not a bad idea to fill up with gas wherever and whenever you get the opportunity. And to be on the safe side, take two spare tires, a basic tool kit, a gas can (filled!), and drinking water. In summer, there's a regular flow of traffic, so if you do get stranded it shouldn't be too long before someone comes along.

NORTHERN B.C.

lakeside camping along the Stewart-Cassiar Highway

© ANDREW HEMPSTEAD

FROM YELLOWHEAD HIGHWAY TO MEZIADIN JUNCTION

Tree-covered hills, dense patches of snow-white daisies, banks of pink-and-white clover and purple lupine, craggy mountains and distant peaks, beautiful lakes covered in yellow water lilies, and lots of logging trucks flying along the road—these are images of the 155 kilometers (96 miles) between the Yellowhead Highway and Meziadin Junction, the turnoff to Stewart.

Kitwanga

This small village just north of the Yellowhead Highway is home to **Kitwanga Fort National Historic Site,** the first national historic site commemorating native culture in western Canada. The site protects 13-meter-high (43-foot-high) Battle Hill, where in the early 1800s a native warrior named Nekt fought off attacks from hostile neighbors. A trail leads from the parking lot down to the flat area around the bottom of the hill, where you can read display panels describing the hill's history. The site is on Kitwanga Valley Road, overlooking the Kitwanga River, and is open year-round.

Gitanyow Totem Poles

Continuing north, you're paralleling what was commonly called the Grease Trail, the route coastal native people took to the interior to trade their *oolichan* (tiny oily fish) with other tribes. At the native village of Gitanyow (also called Kitwancool), 23 kilometers (14 miles) from Kitwanga, is the world's greatest remaining concentration of totem poles still in their original location. The oldest, "Hole in the Ice," is approximately 140 years old; some say it's the oldest standing totem pole in the world. It tells the story of a man preventing his people from starving by chopping a hole in the ice and doing a spot of ice fishing.

STEWART (AND HYDER) SIDE TRIP

At Meziadin Junction is 335-hectare (830-acre) **Meziadin Lake Provincial Park** (mid-May–Oct., $14), one of the most picturesque camping spots along the Cassiar, including some sites right on the lakeshore.

From Meziadin Junction, Stewart is 65 kilometers (40 miles) west along a spectacular stretch of highway that crosses the glaciated Coast Mountains. The first 40 kilometers (25 miles) is all uphill, through thick subalpine forests and past lakes, waterfalls, and a string of glaciers sitting like thick icy slabs atop almost-vertical mountains. Suddenly, and quite unexpectedly, the highway rounds a corner and there in front of you is magnificent, intensely blue **Bear Glacier.** The glacier tumbles down into small Strohn Lake, where small icebergs float across the surface in the breeze. From Bear Glacier it's downhill all the way to Stewart. Keep an eye out for three mighty waterfalls on the north side of the highway, one after another.

Stewart

The twin towns of Stewart, British Columbia, and Hyder, Alaska, straddle the international boundary at the headwaters of the **Portland Canal,** the world's fourth-longest fjord. Stewart (pop. 900) enjoys a stunning setting, with snowcapped peaks rising abruptly from the surrounding fjord. After a 1910 gold strike, Stewart's population mushroomed to 10,000. But the boom was short-lived and what's left of the local economy revolves around the lumber industry. To get the lowdown on the town's interesting past, head to **Stewart Historical Museum,** in the original city hall (Columbia St. between 6th St. and 7th St., 250/636-2568; mid-June–Aug. daily 9:30 A.M.–4:30 P.M.; donation). Displays include a tool collection and exhibits on the town's boom-and-bust mining industry.

The premier accommodation is the **Ripley Creek Inn** (250/636-2344, www.ripley creekinn.homestead.com; $59–99 s, $59–120 d), a funky collection of 32 guest rooms in historic buildings centrally located to downtown. One is an old hotel, another was once home to a brothel, another is above the Bitter Creek Café. All rooms have modern bathrooms and most are in a contemporary style. Those in the main lodge overlook the estuary and have wireless Internet. Nestled below the towering peaks of the Coast Mountains at the

STEWART AND HYDER: SOME QUICK FACTS

The twin towns of Stewart (Canada) and Hyder (United States) are separated by an international border, but you'd hardly know it. Crossing into Hyder comes without any of the formalities or checkpoints you'd expect at a border, and upon reentering Canada, an ATCO trailer serves as the port of entry (until the mid-1990s there were no border checks at all), mostly in place to check for cheap U.S. booze purchased at the Hyder liquor store.

RESIDENTS OF BOTH TOWNS...

- Send their kids to school in Canada.

- Are supplied power by BC Hydro.

- Use the Canadian phone system (area code 250).

- Are policed by the Royal Canadian Mounted Police.

- Never have to wait for a drink – Hyder has one bar for every 30 residents.

NOTES FOR THE TRAVELER

- Buy your booze in Hyder – it's cheaper (but is only tax-free if you have been in town for more than 48 hours).

- Watch for bears – they often wander along the streets.

- Use Canadian currency in both towns.

- Post your mail on whichever side of the border saves the cost of international postage.

- Bring your passport – border checks are made when reentering Canada.

- Don't miss the drive to Salmon Glacier.

back of town is **Rainey Creek Campground** (8th Ave., 250/636-2537; $14–19).

NORTHERN B.C.

The small but ever-busy **Brothers Bakery** (5th Ave.) serves delicious cakes and breads at reasonable prices. Next-door in an old three-story building is **Bitter Creek Café** (250/636-2166), serving light meals at lunchtime.

Stewart Visitor Centre overlooks the estuary at the north end of 5th Avenue (250/636-9224 or 888/366-5999; mid-May–Sept. daily 8:30 A.M.–7 P.M.). The staff offers a wealth of local information, including directions out to Salmon Glacier, hiking-trail brochures, and history sheets.

◖ Hyder

Continue through Stewart along the Portland Canal, and next thing you know you've crossed an international border and you're in Hyder, Alaska—without all the formalities and checkpoints you'd expect at an international border. The "Friendliest Little Ghost Town in Alaska" is a classic end-of-the-road town, with a population of 90 people, unpaved roads, and a motley assortment of buildings. Local residents send their kids to school in Canada and use the Canadian phone system. Everyone sets their clocks to Pacific Standard Time (except the postmaster, who's on Alaska Time). Prices are quoted in Canadian dollars (except for that same postmaster, who only accepts U.S. currency). Finally, no one ever has to wait for a drink: Hyder has one bar for every 30 residents.

Soak up the historic charm of Hyder by wandering the main street and poking your nose in the few remaining businesses. Join the tradition and tack a bill to the wall of the **Glacier Inn** to ensure that you won't return broke, then toss back a shot of 190-proof, pure grain alcohol in one swallow to qualify for your "I've Been Hyderized" card. At the end of the main drag, head left out to the wharf, where the mountain panorama extends for 360 degrees. Head right and you're on the way to **Fish Creek,** the most accessible place in all of North America to watch bears feasting on salmon (late July–Sept.).

If you want to stay the night in Hyder, choose between basic rooms at the **Sealaska Inn** (250/636-2486, www.sealaskainn.com; $64–72 s or d), set up your tent at the adjacent campground ($15), or pull up your rig into the parking lot up the road ($18–22). If you want to stay forever, marry a local.

The Road to Salmon Glacier

Continuing beyond Hyder, the unpaved road

Salmon Glacier

continues up Fish Creek, passing an abandoned mining operation and then the ruins of a covered bridge that provided access to a remote mine up the Texas Creek watershed. From this point the road narrows considerably and becomes increasingly steep (travel is not recommended for RVs), crossing back into Canada and winding through former living quarters for the abandoned gold and mineral ore Premier Mine. The road makes a loop around tailing ponds and continues climbing steeply, with **Salmon Glacier** first coming into view 25 kilometers (15.5 miles) from Hyder. The road parallels the glacier and climbs to a high point after another 10 kilometers (6.2 miles), where the best lookout point is. This glacier, fifth largest in North America but also one of the most accessible, is one of British Columbia's most awesome sights, snaking for many kilometers through the highest peaks of the Coast Mountains.

NORTH OF MEZIADIN JUNCTION
Meziadin to Dease Lake

Around 100 kilometers (62 miles) from the junction, **Bell II Lodge** (604/639-8455 or 800/530-2167, www.bell2lodge.com; $120–160 s or d, tent sites $18, RVs and trailers $21–30) comes into view. It's the winter base for Last Frontier Heli-skiing but is a lot more than a spot to spend the night before heading north through the rest of the year. Fishing is the biggest attraction, especially through summer for chinook salmon and late September to early November for steelhead. Also here is a restaurant (daily 7 A.M.–9 P.M.) and a bar. The lodge sells all the fishing tackle you'll need and offers a variety of daily guiding services, including heli-fishing.

At the 200-kilometer (124-mile) mark is 1,800-hectare (4,450-acre) **Kinaskan Lake Provincial Park** (camping $14), known for its hungry rainbow trout. In the south of the park, a trail leads one kilometer (0.6 miles) to another reliable fishing hole, **Natadesleen Lake,** then a further kilometer (0.6 mile) along an overgrown trail to beautiful, tiered **Cascade Falls.**

The small Tahltan town of **Iskut** has a post office, gas station, and grocery store (daily 8 A.M.–9 P.M.). North of Iskut is **Bear Paw Ranch Resort** (250/234-3005), where you have the choice of staying in the main lodge building ($95 s or d) or Northern "themed" cabins ($75). The ranch offers horseback riding, fishing, and canoe trips, and amenities including a restaurant, lounge, hot tub, and sauna. Continuing north, the highway runs through the **Stikine River Provincial Park,** a long and narrow 217,000-hectare (536,200-acre) park straddling the Stikine River. The park also links **Spatsizi Plateau Provincial Park** and **Mount Edziza Provincial Park.** The former is British Columbia wilderness at its wildest—656,780 hectares (1.62 million acres) of broad plateaus, stunning glacier-capped peaks, roaring rivers, and fish-filled lakes. Wildlife abounds: Grizzly bears, moose, wolves, wolverines, mountain goats, woodland caribou, and more than 100 species of birds are all present, but access is by foot or float-plane only. Mount Edziza Provincial Park protects a moonlike volcanic landscape, above the tree line and dominated by 2,787-meter (9,140-foot) **Mount Edziza,** an extinct volcano whose glaciated crater is over two kilometers (1.2 miles) wide.

The small community of **Dease Lake,** on the shores of its namesake lake 65 kilometers (40 miles) north of Iskut, provides basic tourist services and a bit more. The best place to eat is the **Boulder Café** (250/771-3021; daily 8 A.M.–9 P.M.), where an always-busy waitperson will serve you breakfast ($6–9), lunch, or dinner (burgers $8, main dishes from $13.50) while you admire the old photographs lining the walls.

Telegraph Creek

From Dease Lake an unsealed road leads 119 kilometers (74 miles) west along the Tanzilla River to Telegraph Creek (pop. 300), which lies on a terraced hill overlooking the Stikine River. The town boasts friendly people, gorgeous scenery, and heritage buildings dating back to the 1860s. Jet boat tours are popular—by the hour or day, upstream through Stikine River

Provincial Park or down to Wrangell or Petersburg, Alaska (book through Stikine RiverSong Lodge, 250/235-3196). A 20-kilometer (12.5-mile) road leads west from town to **Glenora,** which had 10,000 residents in its gold-rush heyday. Nowadays, only one or two of the original buildings remain. Originally a Hudson's Bay Company store, the **Stikine RiverSong Lodge** (250/235-3196, www.stikineriversong.com; $65 s, $70 d) has eight guest rooms with shared baths. Use of a kitchen and Internet access incur a small extra charge. Also at the lodge are a café, general store, and gas station.

Continuing to the Alaska Highway

As you continue north from the turnoff to Telegraph Creek, the road parallels the east shore of Dease Lake. Good campsites are found by the lake, along with the occasional chunk of jade on the lakeshore—the area has been called the jade capital of the world. From Dease Lake to the Alaska Highway it's clear sailing for 235 kilometers (146 miles) along the northern slopes of the Cassiar Mountains.

The next worthwhile stop is 4,597-hectare (11,360-acre) **Boya Lake Provincial Park,** 150 kilometers (92 miles) north of Dease Lake. White, claylike beaches ring the incredibly clear lake. Walking along the shoreline is worthwhile, or take the short hiking trail that leads to an active beaver pond. The park also has a primitive campground (mid-May–Sept.; $14). From Boya Lake, the highway traverses the Liard Plain across the border and into the Yukon. From the border it's another four kilometers (2.5 miles) to the junction of the Alaska Highway, then 21 kilometers (13 miles) east to Watson Lake, which is covered below in the *Prince George to the Alaska Highway* section.

Prince George to the Alaska Highway

Most travelers use the route north from Prince George to access Mile Zero of the Alaska Highway at Dawson Creek. But this direct route, a distance of 405 kilometers (252 miles), bypasses the region's highlight at **Hudson's Hope,** halfway between Chetwynd and Fort St. John. Whichever route you take, there's plenty to see and do, with interesting provincial parks and towns offering northern hospitality.

TO HUDSON'S HOPE

The first worthwhile stop along Highway 97 is 970-hectare (2,300-acre) **Crooked River Provincial Park,** 80 kilometers (50 miles) north of Prince George. The park's centerpiece is Bear Lake, with a sandy beach, forested picnic area, and good canoeing. At the end of the park access road, a largish campground has well-spaced sites (mid-May–Sept.; $14), easy access to a beach, pit toilets, drinking water, and a playground.

Carp Lake Provincial Park lies 140 kilometers (87 miles) north of Prince George, then 32 kilometers (20 miles) west (turn off at McLeod Lake) along a sometimes rough unsealed road. The park's epicenter is Carp Lake, a picturesque body renowned for its rainbow trout fishing (although you really need a canoe or motorboat to get out to the best fishing grounds). Despite its name, you won't catch carp—the lake was named by explorer Simon Fraser, who noted that the Carrier Indians journeyed to the lake for fish "of the carp kind." The park holds two campgrounds with facilities limited to pit toilets, picnic tables, and fire rings. Both are open mid-May to mid-September and cost $14 per night. The larger of the two, right on Carp Lake, is a 15-minute walk to a sandy beach inaccessible by road.

To Powder King

The forestry town of **Mackenzie** (pop. 6,200) lies 180 kilometers (112 miles) north of Prince George on the southern arm of massive Williston Lake, North America's largest manmade reservoir. At the town's entrance is the world's largest tree crusher, used during that logging operation. Nearby **Morfee Lake** has swimming

DINOSAURS IN THE PEACE RIVER VALLEY

During construction of Peace Canyon Dam, fossilized remains of the plesiosaur, a marine reptile, were discovered. This wasn't the first time evidence of prehistoric life had been discovered in the Peace River Valley. As early as 1922, dinosaur footprints over 100 million years old were found in the area where Hudson's Hope now lies. The footprints belonged to several species of dinosaurs, most common among them the hadrosaur. This plant-eater was around 10 meters (33 feet) long and weighed about four tons. It was amphibious but preferred the land, walking around on its hind legs ever-alert for the ancestors of the dreaded tyrannosaurus.

Footprints are as important as skeletons in unraveling the mysteries of dinosaurs. They provide clues about the ratios of various dinosaurs in a particular area, and information on herds and how they traveled. Most of the 1,500 dinosaur footprints discovered in the valley have been excavated and transported to museums throughout Canada (a couple are on display in the Hudson's Hope Museum). Plant and shell fossils can still be found. The best time for searching them out is after heavy rain – try looking downstream from the dam (a few short trails lead from the highway into the canyon, but it's a bit of a scramble). The best opportunity to learn more about local dinosaurs is in the **Peace Canyon Dam Visitor Centre** (250/783-9943; May–Oct. daily 8 A.M.-4 P.M., weekdays only the rest of the year).

---

off a sandy beach. Take the logging road to the summit of Morfee Hill for lake views. Stay in a regular motel room at **Williston Lake Lodge** (Mackenzie Blvd., 250/997-3266 or 800/663-2964, www.willistonlakelodge.com; $58 s, $68 d) or park your rig at **Mackenzie Municipal RV Park** ($14–18) with showers and hookups.

Continuing east toward Chetwynd, the landscape becomes more dramatic as the highway climbs steadily up the western slopes of the Rocky Mountains. Near Pine Pass, **Powder King** (250/964-0645, www.powderking.com) is a remote skiing and boarding destination legendary for its incredible snowfall—over 12 meters (40 feet) annually. One triple chair and two surface lifts serve a vertical rise of 640 meters (2,100 feet) and 600 hectares (1,500 acres). The lifts run Thursday–Sunday only. Lift tickets are adult $40, senior $30, child $22.

Chetwynd

The touristy highlight of Chetwynd (pop. 2,800), at the junction of Highways 97 and 29, are the numerous log sculptures carved with chainsaws. **Pinecone Motor Inn** (5224 53rd Ave., 250/788-3311 or 800/663-8082; $68 s, $72 d) has largish rooms with comfortable

beds. On the east side of town, **Westwind RV Park** (Hwy. 97 N., 250/788-2190) has pull-through sites, a laundry, showers, and an RV wash; sites range $16–25 per night. **Chetwynd Visitor Centre** (250/788-1943, www.go chetwynd.com; summer daily 8:30 A.M.–6 P.M.) is in a railway caboose beside the highway through town to the south.

HUDSON'S HOPE

This small town of 1,000 is the only settlement between Chetwynd and Fort St. John. Founded as a fur-trading post in 1805, it is a picturesque spot with two nearby dams attracting the most attention.

Sights

Across from Hudson's Hope Visitor Centre is **Hudson's Hope Museum** (9510 Beattie Dr., 250/783-5735; mid-May–early Sept. daily 9:30 A.M.–5:30 P.M.; donation), comprising historic buildings, such as a trapper's cabin and the log-walled St. Peter's Church, that were moved to the site from throughout the Peace River Valley. The site itself is of some historical significance: Simon Fraser spent the winter of 1805–1806 here.

NORTHERN B.C.

The **W.A.C. Bennett Dam,** seven kilometers (4.3 miles) west of town, is one of the world's largest earth-filled structures. The 183-meter-high (600-foot-high) structure backs up **Williston Lake,** British Columbia's largest lake, which extends more than 300 kilometers (186 miles) along three flooded valleys. At the top of the dam's control building is **Bennett Dam Visitor Centre** (888/333-6667; May–Oct. daily 9 A.M.–6 P.M.; free), where displays catalog the construction tasks, a film celebrates the dam's opening, and the uses of electricity are detailed. Free guided bus tours of the dam are scheduled daily May–Oct. 9:30 A.M.–4:30 P.M. The much smaller Peace Canyon Dam is downstream from Bennett Dam, nine kilometers (5.6 miles) south of Hudson's Hope on Highway 29. The visitor center (250/783-9943; May–Oct. daily 8 A.M.–4 P.M., weekdays only the rest of the year) focuses on the fascinating natural history, exploration, and pioneers of the area, and the building of the Peace Canyon Project. You can also see the central control system, powerhouse, and switchgear station. Don't miss a trip up to the outside observation deck.

Accommodations and Camping

Neither of the town's accommodations is outstanding, but the **Sportsman Inn** (10501 Beattie Dr., 250/783-5523; $80 s or d) has the biggest rooms and an in-house pub and restaurant. The town's three municipal campgrounds each cost $12 per night. Closest to civilization is **King Gething Campground,** on the south end of town, which has flush toilets, coin-operated showers, and plenty of firewood. **Alwin Holland Park,** southeast of town, is more primitive (pit toilets) but is off the main highway and has some nice hiking trails. The third, **Dinosaur Lake Campground,** seven kilometers (4.3 miles) southeast, has pit toilets, firewood, and good fishing and swimming.

Alaska Highway

When the Japanese threatened invasion of Canada and the United States during World War II, the Alaska Highway was quickly built to link Alaska with the Lower 48. It was the longest military road ever constructed in North America—an unsurpassed road-construction feat stretching 2,288 kilometers (1,422 miles) between Dawson Creek, BC, and Delta Junction, Alaska.

Construction began March 9, 1942, and was completed, incredibly, on November 20 that same year. In less than nine months troops had bulldozed a rough trail snaking like a crooked finger through almost impenetrable muskeg and forest, making literally hundreds of detours around obstacles and constructing 133 bridges. At a cost of more than $140 million, the highway was the major contributing factor to the growth of northern British Columbia in the 1940s. At the height of construction, the region's population boomed. Dawson Creek's population alone rose from 600 to over 10,000,

and Whitehorse replaced Dawson City as a more convenient capital of the Yukon.

Driving the highway was notoriously difficult in its earliest days. Highway travelers returned with tales of endless mud holes and dust, washed-out bridges, flat tires, broken windshields and smashed headlights, wildlife in the road, mosquitoes the size of hummingbirds, and sparse facilities. But they also sported "I drove the Alaska Highway" bumper stickers as though they'd won a prize. Nowadays the route doesn't merit quite the bravado—it's paved most of the way, has roadside lodges fairly frequently, and can easily be driven in three days, or two at a pinch. What hasn't changed is the scenery. You'll still see kilometer after kilometer of unspoiled wilderness, including boreal forests of spruce and aspen, the majestic, snow-dusted peaks of the northern Canadian Rockies, and gorgeous rivers and streams (and you can still buy the stickers).

Although official signage along the Alaska

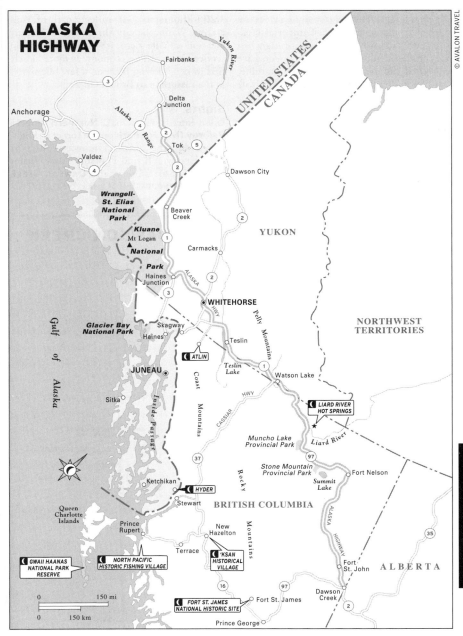

ALASKA HIGHWAY

© AVALON TRAVEL

Fairbanks

Yukon River

UNITED STATES
CANADA

Anchorage

Delta
Junction

Alaska

Range

Tok

Valdez

Dawson City

YUKON

Beaver
Creek

Wrangell-
St. Elias
National
Park

Kluane
Mt Logan

National

Carmacks

Park

Haines
Junction

ALASKA

WHITEHORSE

Pelly Mountains

NORTHWEST
TERRITORIES

Glacier Bay
National Park

Skagway

Haines

HWY

Teslin

ATLIN

Teslin
Lake

JUNEAU

Gulf

Coast

of

Sitka

Alaska

Mountains

Watson Lake

HWY

CASSIAR

LIARD RIVER
HOT SPRINGS

Liard River

Inside

Muncho Lake
Provincial Park

Passage

Rocky

Stone Mountain
Provincial Park

Summit
Lake

Fort Nelson

Ketchikan

HYDER

Stewart

BRITISH COLUMBIA

Queen
Charlotte
Islands

Prince
Rupert

New
Hazelton

Mountains

ALASKA

HIGHWAY

Fort
St. John

ALBERTA

Terrace

'KSAN
HISTORICAL
VILLAGE

GWAII HAANAS
NATIONAL PARK
RESERVE

NORTH PACIFIC
HISTORIC FISHING VILLAGE

FORT ST. JAMES
NATIONAL HISTORIC SITE

Fort St. James

Dawson
Creek

Prince George

0   150 mi

0   150 km

NORTHERN B.C.

Highway is in kilometers, many services are marked in miles, a legacy of imperial measurement. This only becomes confusing when you consider that highway improvements have shortened the original route. For example, Liard River Hot Springs is still marked as Mile 496, though it's now only 462 miles (754 kilometers) from Dawson Creek.

DAWSON CREEK

Although Dawson Creek (pop. 11,800) marks the southern end of the Alaska Highway, it's still a long way north—over 400 kilometers (250 miles) northeast of Prince George and 1,200 kilometers (746 miles) north of Vancouver. While the city thrives on its historic location at Mile Zero, it's also an important service center whose economy is more closely tied to neighboring Alberta, a few kilometers to the east, than to British Columbia.

Sights

Upon entering town, make **Northern Alberta Railway (N.A.R.) Park** on the corner of Highway 2 and the Alaska Highway your first stop. Here you'll find Dawson Creek Visitor Centre, an art gallery, and **Dawson Creek Station Museum** (900 Alaska Ave., 250/782-

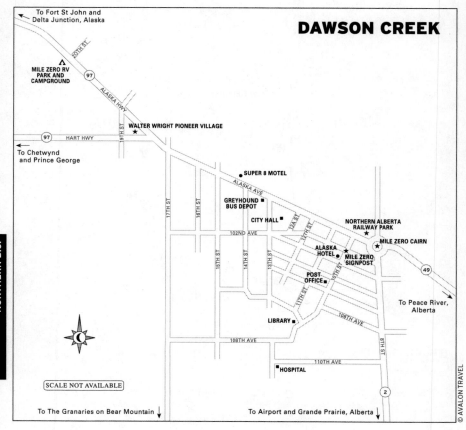

DAWSON CREEK

To Fort St John and Delta Junction, Alaska

MILE ZERO RV PARK AND CAMPGROUND

70TH ST

97

ALASKA HWY

19TH ST

WALTER WRIGHT PIONEER VILLAGE

97 HART HWY

To Chetwynd and Prince George

SUPER 8 MOTEL

ALASKA AVE

GREYHOUND BUS DEPOT

CITY HALL

102ND AVE

17TH ST

16TH ST

12A ST

13TH ST

17TH ST

NORTHERN ALBERTA RAILWAY PARK

MILE ZERO CAIRN

ALASKA HOTEL

MILE ZERO SIGNPOST

POST OFFICE

16TH ST

14TH ST

13TH ST

11TH ST

10TH ST

49

To Peace River, Alberta

LIBRARY

108TH AVE

108TH AVE

110TH AVE

HOSPITAL

8TH ST

SCALE NOT AVAILABLE

To The Granaries on Bear Mountain ↓

To Airport and Grande Prairie, Alberta ↓

2

© AVALON TRAVEL

9595; May–early Sept. daily 8 A.M.–7 P.M., the rest of the year Tues.–Sat. 10 A.M.–noon and 1–5 P.M.; $4). This marvelous and curious museum, housed in the original 1931 Northern Alberta Railway station, offers exhibits on a wide variety of topics, including construction of the Alaska Highway, the area's railroad history, pioneer life, and local flora and fauna. Among the unusual items on display: a rack of antlers estimated to be several thousand years old, a gas pump from the 1920s, a 1941 Massey-Harris cream separator, and the largest mammoth tusks found in western Canada. In the annex of the towering grain elevator adjacent to the museum is the **Dawson Creek Art Gallery** (250/782-2601; June–Aug. daily 9 A.M.–5 P.M., the rest of the year Tues.–Fri. 10 A.M.–5 P.M.). The elevator itself is fascinating. It was saved from demolition and redesigned with a spiral walkway around the interior walls to make the most of the building's height.

In front of N.A.R. Park is the **Mile Zero Cairn,** the Alaska Highway's official starting point. (The original marker was mowed down by a car in the 1940s). Despite the cairn's official status, the Mile Zero signpost in the center of 102nd Avenue at 10th Street is more often photographed. It reads "You are now entering the world famous Alaska Highway" and notes the following distances: Fort St. John, 49 miles; Fort Nelson, 300 miles; Whitehorse, 918 miles; and Fairbanks, 1,523 miles.

One kilometer (0.6 miles) west of N.A.R. Park at the Highway 97 split, **Walter Wright Pioneer Village** (250/782-7144; June–Sept. daily 10 A.M.–6 P.M.; donation) holds two pioneer churches, a furnished log house, a general store, the Napoleon Loiselle Blacksmith Shop (containing many of his inventions), a trapper's cabin with handmade furniture, and two old schoolhouses.

Accommodations and Camping

Dawson Creek's oldest and most colorful accommodation is the downtown **Alaska Hotel** (10209 10th St., 250/782-7998, www.alaska hotel.com; $40–65 s, $45–75 d). Known as the Dew Drop Inn when it first opened in 1928,

the hotel has been renovated in a colorful heritage style. Rooms remain very basic, with no televisions or phones and shared bathroom facilities. For something a little more modern, you can choose among a number of regular motels spread along the Alaska Highway, such as the **Super 8 Motel** (1440 Alaska Ave., 250/782-8899 or 800/800-8000, www.super8 .com; $109 s or d). Southwest of town, ◖ **The Granaries on Bear Mountain** (2106 Ski Hill Rd., 250/782-6304 or 888/782-6304, www .thegranaries.com; $160–190 s or d) is a wonderful surprise in a part of the province where roadside motels dominate. The guest rooms are ensconced in three circular granaries set around a manmade lake, with a profusion of colorful flowerbeds lining the shoreline. Each granary has been given a complete makeover—a snazzy new conical corrugated metal roof, sliding doors that open to a circular deck facing the lake, and a smart interior decor. Other features include cast-iron fireplaces, cooking facilities, jetted tubs, and a breakfast delivered to the door.

Mile Zero RV Park and Campground (250/782-2590; $20–28) isn't at Mile Zero of the famous highway—it's about one kilometer (0.6 miles) north from downtown—but it's the pick of Dawson Creek's numerous campgrounds. Sites sit around a large shaded grassy area, and each one has a picnic table. Facilities include hot showers and a laundry. Take Highway 97S west from town to reach **Northern Lights RV Park** (250/782-9433 or 888/414-9433, www.nlrv.com; May–Oct.; $18–28), which holds a mix of RV and tent sites, an RV wash, free showers, and a laundry.

Information

An almost obligatory stop for travelers heading north on the famous highway is **Dawson Creek Visitor Centre,** in the railway station at N.A.R. Park on Alaska Avenue (250/782-9595 or 866/645-3022, www.tourismdawson creek.com; May–Aug. daily 8 A.M.–7 P.M., Sept. Mon.–Sat. 9 A.M.–5 P.M., Oct.–Mar. Tues.–Sat. 10 A.M.–5 P.M., Apr. Mon.–Sat. 9 A.M.–6 P.M.).

DIGGING UP THE PAST

Overlooking Charlie Lake is **Charlie Lake Cave,** where buffalo bones and artifacts such as stone tools, a fluted basalt spear point, and a handmade stone bead have been discovered. Hunters may have hid there while chasing buffalo. Dated at 10,500 years old, this is the oldest such site discovered on the continent, leading archaeologists to postulate that this area was one of the earliest North American sites occupied by humans.

During the period of earliest occupation, Charlie Lake was a much larger body of water, an enormous ice-dammed lake where larger mammals were common. In the ensuing centuries, silt has built up on the floor of the cave, decreasing its original size.

The cave is on private property. Although access is not possible, a display in the Fort St. John-North Peace Museum tells the story of the cave dwellers and the archaeologists who excavated the site.

FORT ST. JOHN

As the second-largest community along the Alaska Highway (only Whitehorse, Yukon, is larger), Fort St. John (pop. 15,500), 72 kilometers (45 miles) northwest of Dawson Creek, is an important service center for local industries, including oil, gas, and coal extraction; forestry; and agriculture. It's one of the province's oldest nonnative settlements—the Beaver and Sekani tribes both occupied the area when European traders arrived in the 1790s—and served as a fur-trading post until 1823. But it wasn't until construction of the Alaska Highway began that Fort St. John really boomed.

Sights

Fort St. John-North Peace Museum (9323 100th St., 250/787-0430; summer daily 8 A.M.–8 P.M., the rest of the year Mon.–Sat. 9 A.M.–5 P.M., adult $2.50, senior and child

$1.50) is difficult to miss as you drive through town—look for the outside exhibits, including a 40-meter-high (130-foot-high) **oil derrick.** In the museum, local history springs to life with reconstructed historical interiors. A trapper's cabin recalls the original Rocky Mountain fort and fur-trading days, while the pioneer days are commemorated in fully furnished rooms, including a kitchen, bedroom, schoolroom, dentist's office, post office, outpost hospital, and blacksmith's shop. Don't miss the fur press, the birch-bark canoe, and the grizzly bear with claws big enough to send shivers up your spine.

Peace River Canyon Lookout provides splendid panoramic views taking in the wide, deep-green Peace River, its rocky canyon walls, and the lush fields along the canyon rim. From the museum, head south along 100th Street, crossing the Alaska Highway and continuing along the gravel road, which ends at the edge of the canyon.

Practicalities

One of the least expensive motels along the highway is **Blue Belle Motel** (9705 Alaska Hwy., 250/785-2613, $64 s, $70 d), where rooms have such amenities as microwaves and coffeemakers, while guests also have use of a barbeque and laundry facility. The six-story **Quality Inn Northern Grand** (9830 100th Ave., 250/787-0521 or 800/663-8313, www .qualityinnnortherngrand.com; $109 s, $119 d) is a modern, full-service hotel with regularly revamped rooms that come with luxuries such as heated bathroom floors. There's also an indoor pool, a fitness room, a lounge, and a family-style restaurant.

Two small provincial parks with campgrounds lie along the shoreline of Charlie Lake, just over six kilometers (3.7 miles) north of town. **Charlie Lake Provincial Park,** at the junction of the Alaska Highway and Highway 29, is mainly a campground ($14 per site), while 312-hectare (770-acre) **Beatton Provincial Park,** on the lake's east shoreline, features beautiful aspen-lined hiking trails, a beach, boating, fishing, swimming, and camping

($14 per site). For more facilities, check in to the **Rotary RV Park,** also beside Charlie Lake (Mile 52, Alaska Hwy., 250/785-1700; unserviced sites $16, hookups $18–26). Amenities include hot showers and a laundry, and it's within walking distance of a general store and Jackfish Dundee's restaurant.

My favorite place to eat in Fort St. John isn't in town, but 6.5 kilometers (four miles) north at Mile 52 of the Alaska Highway. **C Jackfish Dundee's** (250/785-3233; daily 11 A.M.–10 P.M.) is in a big wooden building that has an inviting atmosphere and lake views. The food is delicious and well priced. Start with calamari with a tangy Thai sauce ($9) and choose from mains such as crab-stuffed sole ($16) and a juicy slab of Alberta beef ($20). Back in town, grab an inexpensive breakfast at **Fogg 'n' Suds** (Ramada Hotel, 10103 98th Ave., 250/787-0779; daily from 6 A.M.) or city-style coffee at **Cosmic Grounds** (10430 100th St., 250/261-6648; daily 7 A.M.–10 P.M.).

Fort St. John Visitor Centre (9523 100th St., 250/785-3033, www.cityfsj.com) is open May through mid-June daily 8 A.M.–6 P.M., mid-June through mid-September daily 8 A.M.–8 P.M., the rest of the year Monday–Friday 8 A.M.–5 P.M.

TO FORT NELSON

The 374-kilometer (232-mile) stretch of the Alaska Highway between Fort St. John and Fort Nelson passes through boreal forest and a landscape that becomes more and more mountainous. It also provides one of your best chances of spotting wildlife, especially if you travel in the cool of the early morning. Species you may spy are moose, bears, deer, elk, and bison.

From Wonowon, the highway climbs steadily to **Pink Mountain,** at Mile 147. Numerous services perch on the low summit, where snow can fall year-round. On the west side of the highway, **Pink Mountain Campsite** (250/772-5133) provides tent and RV sites for $18 (power hookups). Showers are an extra $2.50. In typical northern fashion, it also has liquor, a laundry, and gas. A few kilometers beyond the summit

is **C Mae's Kitchen** (250/772-3215; Mon.–Sat. 7 A.M.–10 P.M.), where breakfasts are huge and the pancakes ($7) and blueberry muffins ($3) are especially good. For lunch, try the house special Buffalo Burger, complete with fries and salad for $10.50.

Sikanni Chief to Prophet River

The next services are 30 kilometers (18.6 miles) north of Pink Mountain at **Sikanni River RV Park** (250/772-5400; tents $15, hookups $20, cabins $55 s, $65 d). Twenty kilometers (12.5 miles) north from Sikanni Chief you'll pass the small **Buckinghorse River Wayside Provincial Park.** The river is alive with arctic grayling, providing the perfect meal for campers ($14 per site). From here north, a newer, scenic stretch of the highway runs through **Minaker River Valley** then parallels the **Prophet River,** passing a rustic campground (May–Sept.; $10) where a hiking trail leads down to the river.

FORT NELSON

At Mile 300 of the Alaska Highway, 454 kilometers (281 miles) north of Dawson Creek, Fort Nelson (pop. 4,300) is the largest town between Fort St. John and the Yukon. The earliest of many trading posts was built here in 1800. Over 200 years later, the town continues to be a supply center—now for the surrounding forestry, oil, and gas industries.

Sights

On the west side of the highway at the north end of town, **Fort Nelson Heritage Museum** (250/774-3536; summer daily 8:30 A.M.–7:30 P.M.; adult $5, senior or child $3) contains a great collection of Alaska Highway construction items and native and pioneer artifacts. An interesting 30-minute movie, shown throughout the day, uses footage taken during the construction of the highway to effectively convey what a mammoth task the project was. The building is surrounded by machinery and vehicles used during the early days. Around back is a trapper's cabin crammed with antiques. At the end of Mountain View Drive is the **Native**

NORTHERN B.C.

Trail, a four-kilometer (2.5-mile) self-guided interpretive trail that passes two native-style shelters and holds signs describing native foods, local wildlife, and trapping methods. Allow at least one hour round-trip.

Practicalities

Fort Nelson has many hotels and motels spread out along the Alaska Highway. The nicest is **Blue Bell Inn** (4103 50th Ave., 250/774-6961 or 800/663-5267, www.bluebellinn .ca; $79–99), next to the Petro-Canada gas station. The modern two-story lodging has air-conditioned rooms, a laundry, and an adjacent 24-hour restaurant. Beside the museum is **Westend Campground** (250/774-2340; Apr.–Oct.; $17–24), where you can choose from tent sites in an open area or hookups surrounded by trees. Facilities include coin-operated showers, a laundry, a grocery store, RV service bays, and free firewood.

As you enter town from the south, modern **Dan's Neighbourhood Pub** (4204 50th Ave. N., 250/774-3929; daily 11 A.M.–midnight) wouldn't look out of place in a big city—and it's always busy.

At Mile 300.5 of the Alaska Highway is **Fort Nelson Visitor Centre** (5319 50th Ave., 250/774-6868; mid-May–Sept. daily 8 A.M.–8 P.M., the rest of the year Mon.–Fri. 9:30 A.M.–4:30 P.M.). Here you can get information on road conditions and find out the current topics for the Welcome Visitor Program—a series of entertaining talks on local subjects, offered Monday through Thursday at 6:45 P.M.

CONTINUING TO WATSON LAKE

Awaiting the traveler on this 525-kilometer (326-mile) portion of the Alaska Highway are mountain peaks, glacial lakes, mountain streams, provincial parks with some great scenery, and the mighty Liard River.

Soon after leaving Fort Nelson, you'll come to a junction with the gravel **Liard Highway,** which runs north 175 kilometers (109 miles) to Fort Liard in the Northwest Territories. From this junction, the Alaska Highway climbs the lower slopes of **Steamboat Mountain,** which, with a certain amount of imagination, resembles an upturned boat.

Summit Lake

This intensely blue lake 140 kilometers (87 miles) west of Fort Nelson is a popular stopping point for travelers. It lies at the north end of 25,691-hectare (63,480-acre) **Stone Mountain Provincial Park,** a vast wilderness at the northern reaches of the Rocky Mountains. Named for the predominantly stony nature of mountains that have been folded and faulted by massive forces deep below the Earth's surface, the park is predominantly above the tree line. For super-fit hikers, the best way to appreciate the landscape is by hiking the 2.6-kilometer (1.6-mile) **Summit Peak Trail,** which ends in a treeless alpine area a strenuous 1,000 vertical meters (3,300 feet) above the trailhead; allow at least two hours each way. The trailhead is on the north side of the highway, across from the campground. Much easier is the 2.5-kilometer (1.5-mile) trail to **Flower Springs Lake,** nestled in alpine peaks south of the highway. Allow one hour each way. The trailhead is three kilometers (1.9 miles) along Microwave Tower Road, which spurs south at the café.

At Summit Lake's eastern end is an exposed campground ($14) with pit toilets and picnic tables.

Muncho Lake Provincial Park

Lying among mountains and forested valleys at the north end of the Rocky Mountains, this 86,079-hectare (212,700-acre) park surrounds stunning **Muncho Lake,** one of the scenic highlights of the Alaska Highway. The magnificent, 12-kilometer-long (7.7-mile-long) body of water is encircled by a dense spruce forest, which gives way to barren rocky slopes at higher elevations. Around three kilometers (1.9 miles) beyond the north end of the lake, natural mineral licks attract Stone sheep and woodland caribou to a roadside quarry. In the vicinity, a hiking trail leads to an escarpment above the Trout River; allow 20 minutes to walk the 1.5-kilometer (0.9-mile) loop.

At around Mile 462 of the Alaska Highway, the small community of Muncho Lake spreads out along the eastern banks of the lake, providing services for park visitors. If you plan to overnight here, try to book ahead; motel rooms and campgrounds all fill up well in advance for July and August. **J & H Wilderness Motel & RV Resort** (250/776-3453), offers simple motel rooms for $74 s or d as well as campsites with clean and modern facilities, including free hot showers, for $20–28. The resort's restaurant (daily 7 A.M.–10 P.M.) dishes up portions with the trucker's appetite in mind. Spread along the lakeshore, **(Northern Rockies Lodge** (250/776-3481 or 800/663-5269, www.northernrockieslodge.com; $115 s, $125 d) has a variety of accommodations, but a huge common room with a stone fireplace and towering cathedral ceiling brings it all together. Choose from rustic cabins or more comfortable rooms in the main lodge, or park your rig at a lakeside campsite ($35–47). Many guests visit as part of a fishing package, staying in luxurious lakeside log chalets (around $2,200 per week inclusive of flights from Vancouver, meals, and some activities). Campers who don't need serviced sites have the option of staying at two campgrounds in the provincial park itself, north of the town. Sites at these two campgrounds are all $14 a night, but with only 15 sites in each one, they fill up fast.

(Liard River Hot Springs

One of the most wonderful places to stop on the whole highway is this 1,082-hectare (2,670-acre) park, 40 kilometers (25 miles) north of Muncho Lake. Most travelers understandably rush to soak their tired, dusty limbs in the hot pools. But the rest of the park is also worth exploring. Hot gases deep underground force heated groundwater upward through a fault in the sedimentary rock. The water fills rock pools constructed by Alaska Highway workers in the 1940s, then overflows into a wide area of marshland. Even in the middle

of winter, the water doesn't freeze, creating a microclimate of aquatic plants not normally associated with the northern latitude. Also inhabiting the swamp are many species of small fish, plus mammals such as moose, woodland caribou, and black bear, as well as 100 species of birds.

A 500-meter (0.3-mile) boardwalk leads from the main parking lot over warm-water swamps to **Alpha Pool,** where water bubbles up into a long, shallow concrete pool. The pool area, surrounded by decking, has pit toilets and changing rooms. A rough trail leads farther to undeveloped **Beta Pool,** which is cooler, much deeper, and not as busy.

At the entrance to the hot springs is a campground (May–mid-Oct., $17) providing toilets and showers. In summer, a percentage of sites can be booked through www.discovercamping .ca. The rest (only 20 sites) are first-come, first-served and are usually filled by noon each day. Gates to the hot springs and campground are locked between 11 P.M. and 6 A.M.

To Watson Lake and Beyond

Anglers will find good fishing for grayling in the Liard River below **Smith River Falls,** 30 kilometers (19 miles) or so northwest of the hot springs. Canyon and river views dot the highway heading north and west, and visitor services are available at **Coal River** and **Fireside.** The highway crosses the 60th parallel and enters the Yukon just before Contact Creek Lodge (all services). It then meanders back and forth across the border six times before reaching the final crossing, 58 kilometers (36 miles) farther west.

Watson Lake (pop. 1,600), a major service center along the highway, lies just north of the BC–Yukon border. The town is best known for the famous **Signpost Forest** started by Carl K. Lindley, a GI who was working on the Alaska Highway. Instructed to repair a directional sign, he added a mileage sign to his hometown of Danville, Illinois. Over the years others followed his lead, and today over 20,000 signs have been added. Behind the "forest" is the excellent

signpost forest at Watson Lake

© ANDREW HEMPSTEAD

Watson Lake Visitor Information Centre (corner of Alaska Hwy. and Robert Campbell Hwy., 867/536-7469; early May–early Sept. daily 8 A.M.–8 P.M.). This facility provides visitors with historic information on the highway through extensive displays and an audiovisual presentation.

Twenty-one kilometers (13 miles) west of Watson Lake, the Alaska Highway meets the Stewart-Cassiar Highway, which leads south to the Yellowhead Highway between Prince George and Prince Rupert. The distance between Prince George and Watson Lake is almost identical via either the Alaska Highway or the Stewart-Cassiar Highway. The loop trip up one and back down the other is around 2,450 kilometers (1,522 miles).

Continuing north on the Alaska Highway, it's 444 kilometers (276 miles) to Whitehorse, capital of the Yukon; 524 kilometers (326 miles) to Skagway, northernmost point of the Alaska Marine Highway; and 1,990 kilometers (1,237 miles) to Delta Junction, Alaska, the official end of the Alaska

Highway. An excellent source of information for those continuing north is Don Pitcher's *Moon Alaska.*

◖ ATLIN

The small community of Atlin lies 100 kilometers (62 miles) south of Jake's Corner, back over the border in British Columbia. It is British Columbia's northernmost and westernmost settlement. Although isolated from the rest of British Columbia, it is one of that province's most picturesque communities. The glaciated peaks of the Coast Mountains form a stunning backdrop for the town, which is on a gently sloping hill overlooking beautiful 140-kilometer-long (85-mile-long) **Atlin Lake.**

Atlin was a boomtown with more than 8,000 people during the 1898 Klondike gold rush, when gold was discovered in nearby Pine Creek. Today they're still finding some color hereabouts, but the town's population has dwindled to about 400.

The highlight of Atlin is the surrounding

scenery. Wandering along the lakeshore, you'll have outrageous views of sparkling peaks, glaciers, waterfalls, and mountain streams. Tied up on the lake in front of town is the **SS Tarahne,** a 1916 steamer that has been restored. If you want to get out on the lake yourself, contact **Norseman Adventures** (250/651-7535, www.atlin.net/norseman), which rents small motorboats ($20 per hour) and modern houseboats ($625–1,000 for four days), and offers guided fishing and wildlife-watching trips ($60 per hour).

Sights

Atlin Historical Museum (3rd St. and Trainor St., 250/651-7522; June–early Sept. daily 9 A.M.–5 P.M.; $3), housed in a 1902 schoolhouse, lets you relive the excitement of the gold rush. Scattered through town are many historic buildings and artifacts pretty much untouched from the gold-rush era.

South of Atlin along Warm Springs Road are various lakes, camping areas, and, at the end of the road, **warm springs.** The springs bubble out of the ground at a pleasant 29°C (84°F) into shallow pools surrounded by flower-filled meadows.

Practicalities

Holding a prime downtown, lakefront location is the **Atlin Inn** (1st St., 250/651-7546 or 800/682-8546) which comprises 18 motel rooms ($115 s or d) and a string of similarly priced kitchen-equipped cottages. It also has a restaurant open daily at 7 A.M. and a lounge with a great patio.

RVers can park their rigs on the lakeshore at the **Norseman Adventures** marina (250/651-7535) for $18 per night, including power and water hookups. For more primitive camping, the first of four spots through Atlin to the south is **Pine Creek Campground** ($5), with pit toilets and firewood (no drinking water).

BACKGROUND

The Land

British Columbia is Canada's third-largest province in area, behind Ontario and Quebec. Covering 948,596 square kilometers (366,252 square miles), it's four times larger than Great Britain, two and a half times as large as Japan, larger than all U.S. states except Alaska, and larger than California, Oregon, and Washington combined. The province is long north to south, relatively narrow east to west, and lies between the 49th and 60th parallels. Its largest city, Vancouver, is on the same latitude as Paris and the same longitude as San Francisco. To the south are the U.S. states of Washington, Idaho, and Montana; to the west the Pacific Ocean and the narrow panhandle of southeastern Alaska. To the north are Canada's Yukon Territory and Northwest Territories; to the east, across the Continental Divide, lies the Canadian province of Alberta. The land within those borders is dominated by mountain ranges, which trend northwest–southeast and are highest in the south.

Mountains

Mountains dominate British Columbia; half of the land area lies more than 1,000 meters (3,300 feet) above sea level. The province occupies part of the mountainous terrain that runs down the entire western margin of the Americas. It lies mainly in the Cordilleran Region,

which is composed of Precambrian to Cenozoic rock formed into mountain ranges, deep intermountain troughs, and wide plateaus.

The landscape is defined by parallel north–south mountain ranges and a series of parallel valleys. The steep **Coast Mountains,** an unbroken chain extending for 1,500 kilometers (932 miles), rise abruptly from the Pacific Ocean. Their high point, and the highest peak completely in British Columbia, is 4,016-meter-high (13,180-foot-high) **Mount Waddington.** The province's highest point is shared with Alaska; 4,663-meter (15,300-foot) **Mount Fairweather** (sixth highest in Canada) is part of the **St. Elias Range,** a northern extension of the Coast Mountains that straddles the BC–Alaska border in the extreme northwest corner of the province. The province's eastern border is defined by the **Continental Divide** of the **Rocky Mountains,** which reach a high point north of the 49th parallel at 3,954-meter (13,000-foot) **Mount Robson.** In the south of the province between the Coast Mountains and the Rockies lie the **Columbia Mountains,** the collective name for the **Cariboo, Monashee, Selkirk,** and **Purcell Ranges.** These ranges rise to peak elevations of just over 3,000 meters (9,900 feet) and are separated by deep valleys and long, narrow lake systems. Only the highest of the Columbia Mountains—including some glaciated peaks in the Selkirks and Purcells—are snow-covered year-round. In the northern half of the province, the ranges are lower, wider, and less well-defined, rising to vast plateaus that extend hundreds of kilometers in all directions. The least obvious of the province's mountain ranges lies mostly underwater, off the west coast. The range rises above sea level at thousands of points, forming a string of islands, including Vancouver Island, whose high point is 2,200-meter (7,200-foot) **Mount Golden Hinde.**

Waterways

The province enjoys more than its share of waterways. Some 24,000 lakes, rivers, and streams contribute to British Columbia's two million hectares of freshwater surface area

(approximately 2 percent of the province's landmass). The largest watershed is drained by the **Fraser River.** With its headwaters around Mt. Robson, this mighty river drains 233,000 square kilometers (90,000 square miles), almost 25 percent of the province, on its 1,368-kilometer (850-mile) journey to the Pacific Ocean at Vancouver. The Fraser is not the province's longest river, though. That title belongs to the 2,000-kilometer-long (1,240-mile-long) **Columbia River,** which follows a convoluted course through southeastern British Columbia before crossing the U.S. border and draining into the Pacific Ocean in Oregon.

The northern half of British Columbia comprises three major drainage basins: The 580-kilometer-long (360-mile-long) **Skeena River** flows westward through the heart of the province to the Pacific Ocean at Prince Rupert; the 1,900-kilometer-long (1,180-mile-long) **Peace River,** the only river system to cut across the Rocky Mountains, flows in a northeasterly direction into the Mackenzie River System, whose waters eventually flow into the Arctic Ocean; and in the far north, the **Liard River** drains a vast area of remote wilderness to also join the Mackenzie River.

Islands

British Columbia's deeply indented coastline comprises 6,500 islands. While most of these are uninhabited and many unexplored, the largest, 31,284-square-kilometer (12,100-square-mile) **Vancouver Island,** is home to over 500,000 people and holds the provincial capital. (This island confusingly shares its name with the province's largest city, which lies on the mainland 50 kilometers/31 miles to the east.) Between the mainland and Vancouver Island, 200 islands dot the Strait of Georgia, some of which are populated and all of which are protected from the wind- and wave-battering action of the Pacific Ocean by Vancouver Island. The other major island group is the **Queen Charlottes,** a remote archipelago linked geologically to Vancouver Island but with its own unique natural and human history.

CLIMATE

British Columbia's varied topography makes for radically varying **temperatures,** which rise or fall with changes in elevation, latitude, slope aspect, and distance from the ocean. The coastal region boasts the mildest climate in all of Canada, but this comes with one drawback: It rains a lot. The two main cities, Vancouver and Victoria, lie within this zone. Most of the interior is influenced by both continental and maritime air, resulting in colder, relatively dry winters and hot, dry summers. And the northern latitudes are influenced by polar continental and arctic air masses, making for extremely cold, snowy winters and short, cool, wet summers.

Precipitation in British Columbia is strongly influenced by the lay of the land and the waft of the wind, resulting in an astonishing variation in rainfall from place to place. For example, Lillooet, in the sheltered Fraser River Valley, is Canada's driest community, whereas Port Renfrew on Vancouver Island's west coast averages 4,000 millimeters (157 inches) of precipitation annually. The amount of precipitation any given area receives is greatly determined by its location on the windward or lee side of the major mountain ranges—the windward side usually cops most of the downpour. Hence, the western side of the Coast Range is wet, the Interior Plateau on the east side of the Coast Range is relatively dry, and the western, windward side of the Rockies along the Alberta border is once again wet.

ENVIRONMENTAL ISSUES

Humans have been exploiting British Columbia's abundant natural resources for 10,000 years. Indigenous people hunting and fishing obviously had little effect on ecological integrity, but over time, the clearing of land for agriculture and development did. Today, the province is minimizing the effects of logging operations, global warming, fish farming, and offshore oil and gas exploration that are hot-button environmental issues in the region.

As rising population numbers have put ever-increasing demands on the region's plentiful natural resources, conservation measures have become necessary. The province has imposed fishing and hunting seasons and limits, a freeze on rezoning agricultural land, and mandatory reforestation regulations, and has restrained hydroelectric development to protect salmon runs. By preserving its superb physical environment, the province will continue to attract outdoor enthusiasts and visitors from around the world, ensuring a steady stream of tourism revenues. But the ongoing battle between concerned conservationists and profit-motivated developers continues.

Forestry

The issue of forestry management in British Columbia, and most notably on Vancouver Island, is very complex, and beyond the scope of a guidebook. In British Columbia, where a couple of mega-companies control an industry worth $17 billion annually to the local economy, many forestry decisions have as much to do with politics as they do with good management of the natural resource. The most talked about issue is **clear-cutting,** where entire forests are stripped down to bare earth, with the practice in old-growth forests especially contentious. The effect of this type of logging goes beyond just the removal of ancient trees—often salmon-bearing streams are affected. Clayoquot Sound, on the west coast of Vancouver Island, is synonymous with environmentalists' fight against the logging industry. The sound is home to the world's largest remaining coastal temperate forest. Environmentally friendly options are practiced, with companies such as the Eco-Lumber Co-op selling wood that is certified as being from responsibly managed forests.

You can see the extent of logging through British Columbia when you arrive, but visit Google Maps (http://maps.google.com) and click on the Satellite link. Then zoom into British Columbia—northern Vancouver Island is a good example—to see just how extensive the clear-cut logging is.

Contacts

For more information on any of these issues, contact the following local environmental organizations: **Canadian Parks and Wilderness Society** (www.cpaws.org), **Greenpeace** (www.greenpeace.ca), **Society Promoting Environmental Conservation** (www.spec.bc.ca), and **Valhalla Wilderness Society** (www.vws.org).

Flora and Fauna

FLORA

Two colors invariably jump to mind when you say "British Columbia": green and blue. Just about everywhere you travel in British Columbia you see trees, trees, and more trees—around two-thirds of the province is forested. But the types of trees differ in each geographic and climatic region. Coastal regions are dominated by temperate rainforest, which requires at least 1,000 millimeters (40 inches) of rain annually and is predominantly evergreens. This biome is extremely rare: at the end of the last ice age it is estimated that 0.2 percent of the world's land area was temperate rainforest. Only 10 percent of these forests remain, 25 percent in British Columbia. This forest is mostly hemlock, western red cedar, and Sitka spruce. **Arbutus** (known as Pacific madrone in the United States) is an evergreen hardwood distinctive for its red bark and glossy oval-shaped leaves. It grows near saltwater at the southern end of Vancouver Island and on the Southern Gulf Islands. Forests of Douglas fir thrive in drier areas of the coast. Engelmann spruce is common throughout the interior at subalpine elevations. The interior also supports a mixture of Douglas fir and ponderosa pine in the south; interior western hemlock in the southeast; aspen and lodgepole pine in the central reaches; subboreal spruce, birch, and willow in the north; Sitka spruce in the west; and white spruce and black spruce in the northeast. The Queen Charlottes' rainforest is thickly covered in spongy pale green moss, which grows alongside coastal Douglas fir. In the region's subalpine areas you'll find mountain hemlock.

The official provincial floral emblem is the **Pacific dogwood,** a small tree sporting huge clusters of cream-colored flowers in spring and bright foliage and red berries in autumn. The tree is a protected plant in British Columbia; it's a punishable offense to pick from it or destroy it.

In summer, British Columbia turns on a really magnificent floral display. Wildflowers every color of the rainbow pop up on the roadsides: white and yellow daisies, purple lupines, pale pink and dark pink wild roses, bloodred Indian paintbrush, orange and black lilies, red and white clover, yellow buttercups, to name but a handful. And if you venture off the beaten track and up into the alpine meadows, the floral beauty is hard to believe. You can pick up a wildflower guide at most any local bookshop, and most of the national park visitor centers stock brochures on wildflower identification.

MAMMALS

British Columbia is one of the best provinces in Canada for wildlife watching. Thanks to a diverse topography that provides a wide variety of habitat, more species of mammals are found here than in any other province or territory in the country.

Bears

Two species of bears—black bears and grizzlies—are present in British Columbia. Both species are widespread and abundant across the province. The two can be differentiated by size and shape. Grizzlies are larger than black bears and have a flatter, dish-shaped face and a distinctive hump of muscle behind the neck. Color is not a reliable way to tell them apart. Black bears are not always black. They can be brown or cinnamon, causing them to be confused with the brown grizzly.

If you spot a bear feeding beside the road,

WILDLIFE AND YOU

British Columbia's abundance of wildlife is one of its biggest drawcards. To help preserve this unique resource, obey fishing and hunting regulations and use common sense.

- Do not feed the animals. Many animals may seem tame, but feeding them endangers yourself, the animal, and other visitors. Animals become aggressive when looking for handouts.

- Store food safely. When camping, keep food in your vehicle or out of reach of animals. Just leaving it in a cooler isn't good enough.

- Keep your distance. Although it's tempting to get close to animals for a better look or a photograph, it disturbs the animal and, in many cases, can be dangerous.

- Drive carefully. The most common cause of premature death for larger mammals is being hit by cars.

BEARS

Bears are dangerous, and while bear-human encounters happen regularly, their infamous reputation far exceeds the actual number of attacks that occur (in the last 20 years, black bears have accounted for 12 fatalities and grizzly bears for 5 within British Columbia). That said, common sense is your best weapon against an attack. First and foremost, **keep a safe distance,** particularly if cubs are present – the protective mother will not be far away. **Never harass or attempt to feed a bear,** and resist the temptation to move in for an award-winning close-up photo; they are wild animals and are totally unpredictable.

Before heading out on a hike, **ask local park or forest-service staff about the likelihood of encountering bears in the area,** and heed their advice. **Travel in groups,** never by yourself. Out on the trail, **watch for signs of recent bear activity,** such as fresh footprints or scat. **Make noise** when traveling through dense woods (take a noisemaker – a few rocks in a soft-drink can or a bell – or let out a loud yell every now and again to let wildlife know you're coming). **Bear spray** has become popu-

lar in recent years, but don't trust your life to it by taking unnecessary risks.

Bears will usually avoid you; however, you may come across the odd bruin. Bear talk is a favorite topic in the north, and everyone who has ever spent time in the wilderness has his or her own theory about the best course of action in the event of an encounter or an unlikely attack. On a few things, everyone agrees: **Stay in a group and back away slowly,** talking firmly the whole time; **do not run** – a bear can easily outrun a human. Black bears can climb trees but grizzlies can't. If an attack seems imminent and it's a black bear, the general consensus is to try to fight the animal off; if it's a grizzly, drop to the ground in a hunched-up position, covering your neck, and play dead.

Park staff can supply you with bear-aware literature, and many books have been written on the subject. One of the best is *Bear Attacks: Their Causes and Avoidance* (Lyons Press, 2002), by Canadian bear expert Stephen Herrero.

© ANDREW HEMPSTEAD

Grizzly bears are recognized by the distinctive hump behind the neck.

chances are it's a **black bear.** These are the most common of all large mammals in British Columbia, estimated to number around 120,000, with the highest concentrations on Vancouver Island and the Queen Charlotte Islands. Their weight varies considerably (the larger ones are found in coastal areas), but males average 150 kilograms (330 pounds), females 100 kilograms (220 pounds). Their diet is omnivorous, consisting primarily of grasses and berries but supplemented by small mammals. They are not true hibernators, but in winter they can sleep for up to a month at a time before changing position. Young are born in late winter, while the mother is still asleep.

British Columbia's estimated 10,000 **grizzlies** are widespread in all mainland areas of the province but are only occasionally seen by casual observers. Most sightings occur along coastal areas (where they are generally called **brown bears**) during salmon runs (the Khutzeymateen, near Prince Rupert, is world-renowned as a grizzly viewing spot) and in spring and fall in alpine and subalpine zones. The bears' color ranges from light brown to almost black, with dark tan being the most common. On average, males weigh 250–350 kilograms (550–770 pounds). The bears eat small- and medium-sized mammals, and salmon and berries in fall. Like black bears, they sleep through most of the winter. When they emerge in early spring, the bears scavenge carcasses of animals that succumbed to the winter until the new spring vegetation becomes sufficiently plentiful.

The Deer Family

Mule deer and **white-tailed deer** are similar in size and appearance. Their color varies with the season but is generally light brown in summer, turning dirty gray in winter. While both species are considerably smaller than elk, the mule deer is a little stockier than the white-tailed deer. The mule deer has a white rump, a white tail with a dark tip, and large mule-like ears. It inhabits open forests along valley floors. The white-tailed deer's tail is dark on top, but when the animal runs, it holds its tail erect, revealing an all-white underside. White-tailed are common along valleys throughout British Columbia but especially prevalent on Vancouver Island. **Sitka** deer, a subspecies, inhabit the Queen Charlotte Islands.

The giant of the deer family, the **moose,** is an awkward-looking mammal that appears to have been designed by a cartoonist. It has the largest antlers of any animal in the world, stands up to 1.8 meters (5.9 feet) at the shoulder, and weighs up to 500 kilograms (1,100 pounds). Its body is dark brown, and it has a prominent nose, long spindly legs, small eyes, big ears, and an odd flap of skin called a bell dangling beneath its chin. Apart from all that, it's good-looking. Each spring the bull begins to grow palm-shaped antlers that by August will be fully grown. Moose are solitary animals, preferring marshy areas and weedy lakes, but they are known to wander to higher elevations searching out open spaces in summer. They forage in and around ponds on willows, aspen, birch, grasses, and all aquatic vegetation. They are most common in northern British Columbia.

The **elk** (also known as wapiti) has a tan body with a dark-brown neck, dark-brown legs, and a white rump. This second-largest member of the deer family weighs 250–450 kilograms (550–990 pounds) and stands 1.5 meters (4.9 feet) at the shoulder. Pockets of elk inhabit valleys in the east of the province, but the animals are not particularly common.

Small populations of **woodland caribou** are restricted to the far north of the province. You may see them feeding in open areas at higher elevations along the Alaska Highway. Native people named the animal *caribou* (hoof scraper) for the way in which they feed in winter, scraping away snow with their hooves. Caribou are smaller than elk and have a dark-brown coat with creamy patches on the neck and rump.

Wild Dogs and Cats

After being hunted to near extinction, **wolf** numbers have rebounded across the continent, including in British Columbia, where the vast wilderness is home to a widespread and stable population that numbers around 8,000 and is distributed across the province everywhere except the lower mainland and coastal islands. Wolves weigh up to 65 kilograms (145 pounds), stand a meter (3.3 feet) high at the shoulder, and resemble large huskies or German shepherds. Their color ranges from snow white to brown or black; those in British Columbia are most often shades of gray or brown. Unlike other predators, they are not solitary but are intriguing animals that adhere to a complex social order, living in packs of 5–10 animals and roaming over hundreds of kilometers in search of prey.

The **coyote** is often confused for a wolf, when in fact it is much smaller, weighing up to only 15 kilograms (33 pounds). It has a

WHALES OF BRITISH COLUMBIA

Whale-watching has gained great popularity off the BC coast in recent years. Most towns along the Vancouver Island coast offer trips out in various watercraft, many staying in sheltered waters where the whales are resting on migratory routes between Mexico and Alaska.

Once nearly extinct, today an estimated 20,000 **gray whales** swim the length of the BC coast twice annually between Baja Mexico and the Bering Sea. The spring migration (March-April) is close to the shore, with whales stopping to rest and feed in places such as Clayoquot Sound and the Queen Charlotte Islands.

Orcas, best known as killer whales, are the largest member of the dolphin family. Adult males can reach 10 meters (32.8 feet) in length and up to 10 tons in weight, but their most distinctive feature is a dorsal fin that protrudes more than 1.5 meters (five feet) from the back. Orcas are widespread in oceans around the world, but especially common along the BC coast, including Robson Bight, the world's only sanctuary established especially for the protection of the species. Three distinct populations live in BC waters: *resident* orcas feed primarily on salmon and travel in pods of up to 50; *transients* travel by themselves or in very small groups, feeding on marine mammals such as seals and whales; and *offshore* orcas live in the open ocean, traveling in pods and feeding only on fish. In total, they number around 500, with around 300 residents living in 15 pods.

Local waters are home to an abundance of other marine mammals. Porpoises, dolphins, and humpback whales frolic in coastal waters, and colonies of seals and sea lions can be viewed by boat or kayak.

© JIM BORROWMAN

pointed nose and long bushy tail. Its coloring is a mottled mix of brown and gray, with lighter-colored legs and belly. The coyote is a skillful and crafty hunter preying mainly on rodents. They are common and widespread at lower elevations throughout British Columbia (often patrolling the edges of highways and crossing open meadows in low-lying valleys).

Cougars (also called mountain lions, Mexican lions, pumas, and catamounts) are relatively plentiful in British Columbia, especially on Vancouver Island, where it is estimated the population numbers around 500. Adult males can grow to over two meters (6.5 feet) in length and weigh up to 90 kilograms (200 pounds). The fur generally ranges in color from light brown to a reddish-tinged gray, but occasionally black cougars are reported. Their athletic prowess puts Olympians to shame. They can spring forward more than eight meters (26 feet) from a standstill, leap four meters (13 feet) into the air, and safely jump from a height of 20 meters (66 feet). These solitary animals are versatile hunters whose acute vision takes in a peripheral span in excess of 200 degrees.

The elusive **lynx** is identifiable by its pointy black ear tufts and an oversized tabby cat appearance. The animal has broad, padded paws that distribute its weight, allowing it to "float" on the surface of snow. It weighs up to 10 kilograms (22 pounds) but appears much larger because of its coat of long, thick fur. The lynx, uncommon but widespread throughout the interior, is a solitary creature that prefers the cover of subalpine forests, feeding mostly at night on snowshoe hares and other small mammals.

Sheep and Goats

Dall's sheep (also known as Rocky Mountain or bighorn sheep) are one of the most distinctive mammals of Canada. Easily recognized by their impressive horns, they are often seen grazing on grassy mountain slopes or at salt licks beside the road. The color of their coat varies with the season; in summer it's a brownish gray with a cream-colored belly and rump, turning lighter in winter. Bighorn sheep are particularly tolerant of humans and often

approach parked vehicles; although they are not especially dangerous, you should not approach or feed them (as with all mammals).

The remarkable rock-climbing ability of nimble **mountain goats** allows them to live high in the mountains, retreating to rocky ledges or near-vertical slopes when threatened by predators.

Small Mammals

One of the animal kingdom's most industrious mammals is the **beaver.** Growing to a length of 50 centimeters (20 inches) and tipping the scales at around 20 kilograms (44 pounds), it has a flat, rudderlike tail and webbed back feet that enable it to swim at speeds up to 10 kph (6.2 mph). The exploration of western Canada can be directly attributed to the beaver, whose pelt was in high demand in fashion-conscious Europe in the early 1800s. The beaver was never entirely wiped out from the mountains, and today the animals inhabit almost any forested valley with flowing water. Beavers build their dam walls and lodges of twigs, branches, sticks of felled trees, and mud. They eat the bark and smaller twigs of deciduous plants and store branches underwater, near the lodge, as a winter food supply.

Several species of **squirrel** are common in British Columbia, including the golden-mantled ground, Columbian, and red squirrels. **Marmots** are common and widespread, with various species living in different habitats. They are stocky creatures, weighing 4–9 kilograms (9–20 pounds). The **porcupine,** a small, squat animal, is easily recognized by its thick coat of quills. It eats roots and leaves but is also known for being destructive around wooden buildings and vehicle tires.

REPTILES

Reptiles don't like cold climates, and therefore they don't like Canada. British Columbia is home to just 17 of the world's 10,000-odd reptile species. All 17 inhabit dry, hot valleys of grassland, such as the Okanagan Valley. The breakdown includes nine species of snakes, five turtles, two lizards, and one species of skink. The province's only poisonous snake is the extremely rare **western rattlesnake,** which lives in the southern interior. Like other rattlers, it waits for prey rather than actively hunting and won't bite unless provoked.

BIRDS

Of the 454 bird species recorded in British Columbia, 300 breed within the province (the most of any province or territory), and of these, 35 species nest nowhere else in Canada. The lower mainland is a migration stop for the million-odd birds that travel the Pacific Flyway each year. Huge populations of waterfowl winter at Boundary Bay near Vancouver, and large concentrations can also be seen around Fort St. James, Cranbrook, Prince George, and Lac La Hache. The province is home to half of the world's populations of both trumpeter swans and blue grouse, as well as a quarter of the world's bald eagles. You'll see beautiful Canada and snow geese, trumpeter and whistling swans, and all kinds of ducks.

British Columbia's official bird is the often-cheeky, vibrant blue-and-black **Steller's jay,** found throughout the province.

FISH

Of the 72 species of fish in British Columbia, 22 are considered sport fish. The two varieties most sought after by anglers are salmon, found in tidal waters along the coast, and trout, inhabiting the freshwater lakes and rivers of interior British Columbia. (For more information on fishing, please see *Recreation* in the *Essentials* chapter.)

Salmon

Five species of salmon are native to the tidal waters of British Columbia. All are *anadromous;* that is, they spend their time in both freshwater and saltwater. The life cycle of these creatures is truly amazing. Hatching from small red eggs often hundreds of miles upriver from the ocean, the fry find their way to the ocean, undergoing massive internal changes along the way that allow them to survive in saltwater. Depending on the species, they then spend 2–6 years in the open water, traveling as far as the Bering Sea. After reaching maturity, they begin the epic journey back to their birthplace, to the exact patch of gravel on the same

Wander along the shoreline at low tide and you'll come across a wealth of marine life.

© ANDREW HEMPSTEAD

river from where they emerged. Their navigation system has evolved over a million years, relying on, it is believed, a sensory system that uses measurements of sunlight, the earth's magnetic field, and atmospheric pressure to find their home river. Once the salmon are in range of their home river, scent takes over, returning them to the exact spot where they were born. Once the salmon reach freshwater they stop eating. Unlike other species of fish (including Atlantic salmon), Pacific salmon die immediately after spawning; hence the importance of returning to their birthplace, a spot the salmon instinctively know gives them the best opportunity for their one chance to reproduce successfully.

Largest of the five salmon species is the **chinook,** which grows to 30 kilograms (66 pounds) in BC waters. Known as king salmon in the United States, chinooks are a prized sport fish most recognizable by their size but also by black gums and silver-spotted tails.

Averaging 2–3 kilograms (4.4–6.6 pounds), **sockeye** (red salmon) are the most streamlined of the Pacific salmon. They are distinguished from other species by a silvery-blue skin and prominent eyes. While other species swim into the ocean after hatching, the sockeye remain inland, in freshwater lakes and rivers, for at least a year before migrating into the Pacific. When it's ready to spawn, the body of the sockeye turns bright red and the head a dark green.

Chum (dog) salmon are very similar in appearance to sockeye, and the bodies also change dramatically when spawning; a white tip on the anal fin is the best form of identification. Bright, silver-colored **coho** (silver) average 1.5–3 kilograms (3.3–6.6 pounds). This species can be recognized by white gums and spots on the upper portion of the tail.

Smallest of the Pacific salmon are the **pinks,** which rarely weigh over four kilograms (nine pounds) and usually average around two. Their most dominant feature is a tail covered in large oval spots. They are most abundant in northern waters in even-numbered years and in southern waters in odd-numbered years.

Freshwater Fish

Trout are part of the same fish family as salmon, but, with one or two exceptions, they live in freshwater their entire lives. Interestingly, the trout of British Columbia are more closely related to Atlantic salmon than to any of the species of Pacific salmon detailed here. The predominant species is the **rainbow trout,** common in lakes and rivers throughout the province. It has an olive-green back and a red strip running along the center of its body. Many subspecies exist, such as the large Gerrard rainbow trout of the southern interior; the steelhead, an ocean-going rainbow, inhabits rivers flowing into the Pacific Ocean.

Other trout species present include the **bull trout,** which struggles to survive through high levels of fishing and a low reproductive rate. **Cutthroat trout,** found in high-elevation lakes, are named for a bright red dash of color that runs from below the mouth almost to the gills. Colorful **brook trout** can be identified by their dark-green backs with pale splotches and purple-sheened sides. **Brown trout** are the only trout with both black and red spots.

The **lake trout,** which grows to 20 kilograms (44 pounds), is native to large, deep lakes throughout the province, but it is technically a member of the char family. The **kokanee** is a freshwater salmon native to major lakes and rivers of the southern interior. They are directly related to sockeye salmon and look similar in all aspects but size (kokanee rarely grow to over 30 centimeters/12 inches in length), spawning in the same freshwater range as sockeye.

The **whitefish,** a light gray fish, is native to lower elevation lakes and rivers across the province. **Arctic grayling** and **Dolly Varden trout** (named for a colorful character in a Charles Dickens story) inhabit northern waters. **Walleye** (also called pickerel) grow to 4.5 kilograms (10 pounds) and are common in sandy-bottomed areas of lakes in northeastern British Columbia. The monster freshwater fish of British Columbia is the **sturgeon,** growing to over 100 kilograms (220 pounds) in size and living for upwards of 100 years.

History

THE EARLIEST INHABITANTS

Human habitation of what is now British Columbia began around 15,000 years ago, when *Homo sapiens* migrated from northeast Asia across a land bridge spanning the Bering Strait. During this time, the northern latitudes of North America were covered by an ice cap, forcing these people to travel south down the west coast before fanning out across the ice-free southern latitudes. As the ice cap receded northward, the people drifted north also, perhaps only a few kilometers in an entire generation, and began crossing the 49th parallel about 12,000 years ago. By the time the ice cap had receded from all but the far north and the highest mountain peaks, two distinct cultures had formed: one along the coast and one in the interior. Within these two broad groups, many tribes formed, developing distinct cultures and languages.

The Northwest Coast

Around 12,000 years ago, Canada's west coast had become ice-free, and humans had begun settling along its entire length. Over time they had broken into distinct linguistic groups, including the **Coast Salish, Kwagiulth, Tsimshian, Gitxsan, Nisga'a, Haida,** and **Tlingit,** but all had two things in common: their reliance on cedar and on salmon. They lived a very different lifestyle from the stereotypical "Indian"—they had no bison to depend on, they didn't ride horses, nor did they live in tepees, but instead developed a unique and intriguing culture that remains in place in small pockets along the west coast. These coastal bands lived comfortably off the land and the sea, hunting deer, beaver, bear, and sea otters; fishing for salmon, cod, and halibut; and harvesting edible kelp. They built huge 90-meter-long (295-foot-long) cedar houses and 20-meter-long (65-foot-long) dugout cedar canoes, and developed a distinctive and highly decorative arts style featuring animals, mythical creatures, and oddly shaped human forms believed to be supernatural ancestors.

West coast native society emphasized the material wealth of each chief and his tribe, displayed to others during special events called potlatches. The potlatch ceremonies marked important moments in tribal society, such as marriages, puberty celebrations, deaths, or totem-pole raisings. The wealth of a tribe became obvious when the chief gave away enormous quantities of gifts to his guests—the nobler the guest, the better the gift. The potlatch exchange was accompanied by much feasting, speech-making, dancing, and entertainment, all of which could last many days. Stories performed by hosts garbed in elaborate costumes and masks educated, entertained, and affirmed each clan's historical continuity.

The Interior Salish

Moving north with the receding ice cap around 10,000 years ago, the Salish fanned out across most of southwestern and interior British Columbia. After spending summers in the mountains hunting and gathering, they would move to lower elevations to harvest their most precious natural resource: salmon. At narrow canyons along the Fraser River and its tributaries, the Salish put their fishing skills to the test, netting, trapping, and spearing salmon as the fish traveled upstream to spawn. Much of the catch was preserved by drying or roasting, then pounded into a powder known as "pemmican" for later use or to be traded. The Salish wintered in earth-covered log structures known as pit houses. Depressions left by these ancient structures can still be seen in places such as Keatley Creek, alongside the Fraser River. Within the Salish Nation, four distinct tribes have been identified: the Lillooet, the Thompson (Nlaka'pamux), the Okanagan, and the Shuswap. The Shuswap occupied the largest area, with a territory that extended from the Fraser River to the Rocky Mountains; they were the only Salish who crossed the Rockies to hunt buffalo on the plains.

The Kootenay

The Kootenay (other common spellings include

TOTEM POLES

Traveling through British Columbia, you can't help but notice all the totem poles decorating the landscape. Totem poles are made of red (or occasionally yellow) cedar painted black, red, blue, yellow, and white, with colored pigment derived from minerals, plants, and salmon roe. They are erected as validation or a public record or documentation of an important event. Six types of poles are believed to have evolved in the following order: house post (an integral part of the house structure), mortuary (erected as a chief's or shaman's grave post, often with the bones or ashes in a box at the top of the pole), memorial (commemorating special events), frontal (a memorial or heraldic pole), welcome, and shame poles. None is an object of worship; each tells a story or history of a person's clan or family. The figures on the pole represent family lineage, animals, or a mythical character.

Since 1951, when a government ban on potlatch ceremonies (of which the raising of totem poles is an integral part) was lifted, the art form has been revived. Over the years, many totem poles have been moved from their original locations. Both historic and more modern poles can be viewed in British Columbia. The Haida, of the Queen Charlotte Islands, were renowned for their totem poles; many totem villages, long since abandoned, remain on the remote southern tip of the archipelago. Of these, **Ninstints** is regarded as the world's best example of an ancient Haida

You'll see totem poles in coastal communities throughout British Columbia.

totem village. More modern totems can be found at **Stanley Park,** Vancouver; **Thunderbird Park,** Victoria; **Alert Bay,** Cormorant Island; and **Kitwancool,** at the south end of the Stewart-Cassiar Highway. The **Museum of Anthropology** in Vancouver also has an excellent collection.

Kootenai, Kootenae, and Kutenai) were once hunters of buffalo on the great American plains, but they were pushed westward by fierce enemies. Like the Salish did farther west, they then moved north with the receding ice cap. They crossed the 49th parallel around 10,000 years ago, settling in the Columbia River Valley, along the western edge of the Canadian Rockies. Like the Salish, they were hunters and gatherers and came to rely on salmon. The Kootenay were generally friendly, mixing freely with the Salish and treating the

earliest explorers, such as David Thompson, with respect. They regularly traveled east over the Rockies to hunt—to the wildlife-rich Kootenay Plains or farther south to the Great Plains in search of bison.

The Athabascans

Athabascan (often spelled Athapaskan) is the most widely spread of all North American linguistic groups, extending from the Rio Grande to Alaska. In 1793, when Alexander Mackenzie made his historic journey across the continent, he spent the last summer before reaching the west coast in Athabascan territory, which at that time included most of what is now northern British Columbia. The largest division of the Athabascans within this area was the **Carrier** group, so named for their custom requiring a widowed woman to carry the ashes of her husband with her for at least a year. Aside from the fact that they cremated their dead, the Carrier had similar traits to those found throughout the Athabascan peoples—they lived simply and were generally friendly toward each other and neighboring tribes. They lived throughout the northern reaches of the Fraser River basin and along the Skeena River watershed. The Carrier, along with Athabascan tribes that lived farther north (including the Chilcotin, Tahltan, and Inland Tlingit), adopted many traits of their coastal neighbors, such as potlatch ceremonies and raising totem poles. Another Athabascan group inhabiting British Columbia was the **Beaver,** who were forced westward, up the Peace River watershed, by the warlike Cree (the name Peace River originated after the two groups eventually made peace). With no access to salmon-rich waters west of the Rocky Mountains, the Beaver hunted bison, moose, and caribou and were strongly influenced by the fur trade. Over the subcontinental divide to the north is the upper watershed of the mighty Mackenzie River; extending into the northeast corner of the province, this area was the traditional home of the **Slavey,** one of seven groups of the Dene (DEN-ay) people. Like the Beaver, they were nomadic hunters and gatherers but also relied heavily on fishing.

EUROPEAN EXPLORATION AND COLONIZATION

It was only a little more than 200 years ago that the first European explorers began to chart the northwest corner of North America. The area's geography presented formidable natural barriers to the east (the lofty Rocky Mountains) and the west (long stretches of ocean away from other landmasses).

By Sea

In the second half of the 18th century, curiosity about a western approach to the fabled Northwest Passage and a common desire to discover rich natural resources lured Russian, Spanish, British, and American explorers and fur traders along the coastline that is now British Columbia. In 1774, the ship of Mexican **Juan Perez** was the first vessel to explore the coastline and trade with the natives. He was quickly followed by Spaniard **Don Juan Francisco de la Bodega y Quadra,** who took possession of the coast of Alaska for Spain. England's **Captain James Cook** arrived in 1778 to spend some time at Nootka, becoming the first nonnative to actually come ashore, trading with the natives while he overhauled his ship. Cook received a number of luxuriantly soft sea otter furs, which he later sold at a huge profit in China. This news spawned a fur-trading rush that began in 1785 and continued for 25 years. Ship after loaded ship called in along the coast, trading iron, brass, copper, muskets, cloth, jewelry, and rum to the natives in exchange for furs. The indigenous people were eager to obtain the foreign goods, but they were also known for driving a hard bargain. The traders took the furs directly to China to trade for silk, tea, spices, ginger, and other luxuries. In 1789, Bodega y Quadra established a settlement at Nootka, but after ongoing problems with the British (who also claimed the area), he gave it up. In 1792, **Captain George Vancouver,** who had been the navigator on Cook's 1778 expedition, returned to the area and sailed into Burrard Inlet, claiming the land for Great Britain.

By Land

In the meantime, adventurous North West Company fur traders were crossing the Rockies in search of waterways to the coast. The first European to reach the coast was **Alexander Mackenzie,** who traveled via the Peace, Fraser, and West Road Rivers—you can still see the rock in the Dean Channel (off Bella Coola) where he inscribed "Alexander Mackenzie from Canada by land 22nd July 1793." Not far behind came other explorers, including **Simon Fraser,** who followed the Fraser River to the sea in 1808, and **David Thompson,** who followed the Columbia River to its mouth in 1811. Today the names of these men grace everything from rivers to motels. In the early 19th century, the North West Company established trading posts in **New Caledonia** (the name Simon Fraser gave to the northern interior). These posts were taken over by Hudson's Bay Company after amalgamation of the two companies in 1821.

The Native Response

The fur trade brought prosperity to the indigenous society, which was organized around wealth, possessions, and potlatches. The Hudson's Bay Company had no interest in interfering with the natives and, in general, treated them fairly. This early contact with Europeans resulted in expanded trade patterns and increased commerce between coastal and interior tribes. It also spurred the production of indigenous arts and crafts to new heights, as chiefs required more carved headgear, masks, costumes, feast dishes, and the like for the increasingly frequent ceremonial occasions that came with increased wealth.

However, commerce between the Europeans and locals also caused the indigenous tribes to abandon their traditional home sites and instead to cluster around the forts for trading and protection. In addition, the Europeans introduced muskets, alcohol, and disease (most significantly smallpox), all of which took their toll on the native population, which stood at around 60,000 in 1850. Christian missionaries soon arrived and tried to ban the natives' traditional potlatches. But not until land-hungry White colonists showed up did major conflicts arise between native peoples and Whites. Those land-ownership conflicts proved tenacious, continuing to this day.

Vancouver Island

The British government decided in 1849 that Vancouver Island should be colonized to confirm British sovereignty in the area and forestall any American expansion. Though mostly content to leave the island in the hands of the Hudson's Bay Company, the Brits nevertheless sent **Richard Blanshard** out from England to become the island colony's first governor. Blanshard soon resigned and was replaced in 1851 by **James Douglas,** chief factor of the Hudson's Bay Company. Douglas had long been in control of the island, and his main concerns were to maintain law and order and to purchase land from the natives. He made treaties with the tribes in which the land became the "entire property of the white people forever." In return, tribes retained use of their village sites and enclosed fields, and could hunt and fish on unoccupied lands. Each indigenous family was paid a pitiful compensation.

In 1852, coal was discovered near Nanaimo, and English miners were imported to develop the deposits. Around the same time, loggers began felling the enormous timber stands along the Alberni Canal, and the Puget Sound Agricultural Association (a subsidiary of Hudson's Bay Company) developed several large farms in the Victoria region. By the 1850s, the town of Victoria, with its moderate climate and fertile soil, had developed into an agreeable settlement.

LAW, ORDER, AND GOLD
Firsts

In 1856 the first parliament west of the Great Lakes was elected, and Dr. J. S. Helmcken became speaker. (Today you can still see his house in Victoria.) Only two years later this still relatively unexplored and quiet part of the world was turned upside down with the first whispers of "gold" on the mainland, along the banks of the Fraser River. As the news spread, miners—mostly Americans—arrived by the shipload at Victoria, increasing the town's population from several hundred to more than 5,000. Fur trading faded as gold mining jumped to the forefront. Realizing that enormous wealth could be buried on the mainland, the British government quickly responded by creating a mainland colony that at first was named New Caledonia. Because France possessed a colony of the same name in the South Pacific, Queen Victoria was asked to change the name, which she did, using "Columbia," which appeared on local maps, and adding "British," making the name distinct from the Columbia River district across the border.

In 1858, Governor James Douglas of Vancouver Island also became governor of British Columbia, giving up his Hudson's Bay Company position to serve both colonies. In 1866 the two colonies were combined into one.

Cariboo Gold

The lucrative Cariboo gold rush resulted in construction of the Cariboo Wagon Road (also called the Gold Rush Trail), an amazing engineering feat that opened up British Columbia's interior. Completed in 1865, the road connected Yale with Barkerville, one of the richest and wildest gold towns in North America. Mule trains and stagecoaches plied the route, and roadhouses and boomtowns dotted its entire length. Among the colorful characters of this era was Judge Matthew Baillie Begbie, an effective chief of law and order during a time when law and order might as easily have been nonexistent.

In addition to the gold miners, groups of settlers soon began arriving in the Cariboo. One such group, a horde known as the **Overlanders,** left Ontario and Quebec with carts, horses, and oxen in summer 1862, intent on crossing the vast plains and the Rockies to British Columbia. One detachment rafted down the Fraser River, the other down the North Thompson. Both arrived in Kamloops in autumn that same year. Some continued north up the Cariboo Gold Rush Trail, but others headed for the coast, having had more than their fill of adventure on the trip across.

Rapid Development

In addition to the Cariboo Wagon Road, other trails opened up more of the province in the early 1860s. The Hope-Princeton and Dewdney Trails into the Kootenays led to settlement in British Columbia's eastern regions. Salmon canning was also developed in the 1860s, and several canneries on both the lower Fraser and Skeena Rivers had the world market in their pockets. (You can still see one of the old canneries near Prince Rupert today.)

It wasn't until 1862 that Burrard Inlet—site of today's city of Vancouver—sprang onto the map with the building of a small lumber mill on the north shore. The region's tall, straight trees became much in demand. More lumber mills started up, and a healthy export market developed in only a few years. Farmers began to move into the area, and by the end of the 1860s a small town had been established. "Gassy Jack" Deighton started a very popular saloon on the south shore of Burrard Inlet near a lumber camp, and for some time the settlement was locally called Gastown. After the town site was surveyed in 1870, the name was changed to Granville. Then in 1886, the town was officially renamed Vancouver, in honor of Captain George Vancouver. At this time, New Westminster was the official capital of the colony of British Columbia, much to the concern and disbelief of Vancouver Islanders, who strongly believed Victoria should have retained the position. Two years later, with the mainland gold rushes over, the capital reverted to Victoria, where it has remained ever since.

Confederation and Beyond

The next big issue to concern British Columbia was confederation. The eastern colonies had become one large dominion, and BC residents were invited to join. London and Ottawa both wanted British Columbia to join, to assist in counterbalancing the mighty U.S. power to the south. After much public debate, the southwesternmost colony entered the Confederation as the Province of British Columbia in July 1871—on the condition that the west coast be connected to the east by railway. Many roads were built during the 1870s, but it was the completion of the transcontinental railway in 1885 that really opened up British Columbia to the rest of the country. Other railways followed, steamships plied the lakes and rivers, more roads were built, and industries—including logging, mining, farming, fishing, and tourism—started to develop.

During the 20th century, British Columbia moved from roads to major multilane highways, from horses to ferries, and from gold mining to sportfishing. Yet it still attracts explorers—backcountry hikers and mountain climbers in search of untrammeled wilderness, plenty of which remains.

Government and Economy

GOVERNMENT

Canada is a constitutional monarchy. Its system of government is based on England's, and the British monarch is also king or queen of Canada. However, because Canada is an independent nation, the British monarchy and government have no control over the political affairs of Canada. An appointed **governor general** based in Ottawa represents the Crown, as does a **lieutenant governor** in each province. Both roles are mainly ceremonial, but their "royal assent" is required to make any bill passed by Cabinet into law.

Elected representatives debate and enact laws affecting their constituents. The head of the federal government is the **prime minister,** and the head of each provincial government is its **premier.** The **speaker** is elected at the first session of each parliament to make sure parliamentary rules are followed. A bill goes through three grueling sessions in the legislature—a reading, a debate, and a second reading. When all the fine print has been given the royal nod, the bill then becomes a law.

Provincial Politics

In the BC legislature, the lieutenant governor is at the top of the ladder. Under him are the members of the **Legislative Assembly** (MLAs). Assembly members are elected for a period of up to five years, though an election for a new assembly can be called at any time by the lieutenant governor or on the advice of the premier. In the Legislative Assembly are the premier, the cabinet ministers and backbenchers, the leader of the official opposition, other parties, and independent members. All Canadian citizens and BC residents 19 years old and over can vote, providing they've lived in the province for at least six months.

Provincial politics in British Columbia have traditionally been a two-party struggle. The province was the first in Canada to hold elections on a fixed date, with the next election scheduled for 2009. In the 2005 election, the Liberals defeated the New Democrats (NDP), who came to be reviled by the business community for tax burdens that stalled the local economy. The NDP first came to prominence in the late 1960s as the official opposition to the **Social Credit Party** (Socreds), advocating free enterprise and government restraint, who had ruled the province for two decades. After a 1972 NDP election win, the support of these two parties seesawed back and forth until 1991, when the Social Credit Party was almost totally destroyed by a string of scandals that went as high as the premier, Bill Vander Zalm.

The laws of British Columbia are administered by the cabinet, premier, and lieutenant governor; they are interpreted by a **judiciary** made up of the Supreme Court of BC, the Court of Appeal, and county or provincial courts.

For information on the provincial government, its ministries, and current issues, surf the web to www.gov.bc.ca.

parliament buildings in Victoria

© ANDREW HEMPSTEAD

ECONOMY

British Columbia's economy has always relied on resource-based activities. The first indigenous people hunted the region's abundant wildlife and fished in its trout- and salmon-filled rivers. Then Europeans arrived on the scene, reaping a bounty by cutting down forests for timber and slaughtering the wildlife for its fur. Luckily, the province is blessed with a wealth of natural resources. In addition to timber and wildlife, British Columbia holds rich reserves of minerals, petroleum, natural gas, and coal, and water for hydroelectric power is plentiful.

Forestry

Almost two-thirds of British Columbia—some 60 million hectares (148 million acres)—is forested, primarily in coniferous softwood (fir, hemlock, spruce, and pine). These forests provide about half the country's marketable wood and about 25 percent of the North American inventory. On Vancouver Island, the hemlock species is dominant. Douglas fir, balsam, and western red cedar are other valuable commercial trees in the region. The provincial government owns 94 percent of the forestland, private companies own 5 percent, and the national government owns the remaining 1 percent. Private companies log much of the provincially owned forest under license from the government. Around 75 million cubic meters of lumber are harvested annually, directly employing 85,000 workers. The forestry industry generates $10 billion annually in exports, more than all other industries combined.

Tourism

Tourism has rapidly ascended in economic importance; it's now the second-largest industry and the province's largest employer (more than 200,000 are directly employed in the industry). Vancouver and Victoria are the province's two major destinations, with Whistler one of North America's most visited ski resorts.

The tourism segment continues to grow, as more and more people become aware of outstanding scenery; numerous national, provincial, historic, and regional parks; and the bountiful outdoor recreation activities available year-round. **Tourism BC** promotes British Columbia to the world; latest figures record 26 million annual "visitor nights" (the number of visitors multiplied by the number of nights they stayed within British Columbia). Official visitor numbers are broken down to show that four million visitors were Canadians from outside British Columbia, four million were from the United States, while one million visitors originated from outside North America (Japan, Great Britain, and Germany provided most of these).

Mining

British Columbia is a mineral-rich province, and historically mining has been an important part of the economy. Since the first Cariboo gold rush in the late 1850s, the face of the industry has changed dramatically. Until the mid-1900s, most mining was underground, but today open-pit mining is the preferred method of mineral extraction. The province is home to 26 major mines and three mineral processing plants that produce $3.6 billion worth of exports. Coal is the most valuable sector of the mining industry, accounting for $800 million of exports (most to Japan and other Asian markets). Other mining is for metals (such as copper, gold, zinc, silver, molybdenum, and lead), industrial minerals (sulfur, asbestos, limestone, gypsum, and others), and structural materials (sand, gravel, dimension stone, and cement). In northeastern British Columbia, drilling for petroleum and natural gas also helps fuel the economy.

Agriculture

Cultivated land is sparse in mountainous British Columbia—only 4 percent of the province is arable, with just 25 percent of this land regarded as prime for agriculture. Nevertheless, agriculture is an important part of the provincial economy; 19,000 farms growing 200 different crops contribute $1.4 billion annually. The most valuable sector of the industry is dairy farming, which is worth $260 million (that works out to an output of 510 million liters/134.5 million gallons of milk a year). The best land for dairy cattle is found in the

© ANDREW HEMPSTEAD

commercial halibut fishermen at work

lower Fraser Valley and on southern Vancouver Island. Poultry farms, vegetables, bulbs, and ornamental shrubs are also found mostly in the Fraser River Valley and the southern end of Vancouver Island.

Fishing

Commercial fishing, one of British Columbia's principal industries, is worth $1 billion annually and comes almost entirely from species that inhabit tidal waters around Vancouver Island. The province has 6,000 registered fishing boats and 600 fish farms. The industry concentrates on salmon (60 percent of total fishing revenues come from six species of salmon), with boats harvesting the five species indigenous to the Pacific Ocean and the aquaculture industry revolving around Atlantic salmon, which is more suited to farming. Other species harvested include herring, halibut, cod, sole, and shellfish, such as crabs. Canned and fresh fish are exported to markets all over the world—the province is considered the most productive fishing region in Canada.

Japan is the largest export market, followed by Europe and the United States.

Film Industry

The film industry is the fastest-growing sector of the provincial economic pie; its value has quadrupled since 1997 to be worth $1.4 billion annually and to directly employ 35,000 locals. The province is ideal both as a location for shooting and as a production center (Vancouver ranks third behind only Los Angeles and New York as a production center, with 70 post-production facilities). Since the late 1970s, more and more Hollywood production companies have discovered the beauty of Vancouver, its studio facilities, on-site production crews, and support services, as well as more recently a favorable exchange rate. The industry is overseen by the **BC Film Commission** (604/660-2732, www.bcfilmcommission.com).

Shipping and Maritime Commerce

The province boasts year-round ports, deep-sea international shipping lanes, log-towing vessels, specialized freight and passenger steamers, and all the requisite marine facilities. The United States and Japan are British Columbia's main export and import trading partners.

PEOPLE AND CULTURE

When British Columbia joined the confederation to become a Canadian province in 1871, its population was only 36,000, and 27,000 of the residents were natives. With the completion of the Canadian Pacific Railway in 1885, immigration during the early 20th century, and the rapid industrial development after World War II, the provincial population burgeoned. Between 1951 and 1971 it doubled. Today 4.1 million people live in British Columbia (8 percent of Canada's total). The population is concentrated in the southwest, namely in Vancouver, on the south end of Vancouver Island, and in the Okanagan Valley. These three areas make up less than 1 percent of the province but account for 80 percent of the population. The overall population density is just 3.7 people per square kilometer.

British Columbia is third only to Alberta and Ontario as Canada's fastest growing province. Annual population growth has been averaging 5 percent over the last decade. Around 70 percent of this population growth can be attributed to westward migration across the country. Retirees make up a large percentage of these new arrivals, as to a lesser extent do young professionals.

Around 40 percent of British Columbians are of British origin, followed by 30 percent of other European lineage, mostly French and German. To really get the British feeling, just spend some time in Victoria—a city that has retained its original English customs and traditions from days gone by. First Nations make up 3.7 percent of the population. While the native peoples of British Columbia have adopted the technology and the ways of the European, they still remain a distinct group, contributing to and enriching the culture of the province. Asians have made up a significant percentage of the population since the mid-1800s, when they came in search of gold. More recently, the province saw an influx of settlers from Hong Kong prior to the 1997 transfer of control of that city from Britain to China.

LANGUAGE

The main language spoken throughout the province is English, though almost 6 percent of the population also speaks French, Canada's second official language. All government information is written in both English and French throughout Canada.

The indigenous people of British Columbia fall into 10 major ethnic groups by language: Nootka (west Vancouver Island), Coast Salish (southwest BC), Interior Salish (southern interior), Kootenay (in the Kootenay region), Athabascan (in the central and northeastern regions), Bella Coola and Northern Kwakiutl (along the central west coast), Tsimshian (in the northwest), Haida (on the Queen Charlotte Islands), and Inland Tlingit (in the far northwest corner of the province). However, most native people still speak English more than their mother tongue.

NATIVE ARTS AND CRAFTS

Indigenous artistry tends to fall into one of two categories: "arts," such as woodcarving and painting, argillite carving, jade- and silverwork, and totem restoration (all generally attended to by the men), and "handicrafts," such as basketry, weaving, beadwork, skinwork, sewing, and knitting (generally created by the women). Today, all of these arts and crafts contribute significant income to First Nations communities.

Painting and woodcarving are probably the most recognized art forms of the northern west coast tribes. Throughout British Columbia—in museums and people's homes, outdoors, and of course in all the shops—you can see brightly colored carved totems, canoes, paddles, fantastic masks, and ceremonial rattles, feast dishes, bowls, and spoons. Fabulous designs, many featuring animals or mythical legends, are also painstakingly painted in bright primary colors on paper. You can buy limited-edition, high-quality prints of these paintings at many Indian craft outlets. They are more reasonable in cost than carvings, yet just as stunning when effectively framed.

Basketry comes in a variety of styles and materials. Watch for decorative cedar-root (fairly rare) and cedar-bark baskets, still made on the west coast of Vancouver Island; spruce-root baskets from the Queen Charlotte Islands; and beautiful, functional, birch-bark baskets from the Hazelton area, between Prince George and Prince Rupert.

Beaded and fringed moccasins, jackets, vests, and gloves are available at most craft outlets. And all outdoor types should consider forking out for a heavy, water-resistant, raw-sheep-wool sweater; they're generally white or gray with a black design, much in demand because they're warm, good in the rain, rugged, and last longer than one lifetime. One of the best places to get your hands on one is the Cowichan Valley on Vancouver Island, although you can also find them in the Fraser Valley from Vancouver to Lytton and in native craft outlets. Expect to pay around $90–160 for the real thing, more in tourist shops.

Carved argillite (black slate) miniature totem poles, brooches, ashtrays, and other small items, highly decorated with geometric and animal designs, are created exclusively by the Haida on the Queen Charlotte Islands; the argillite comes from a quarry near Skidegate and can only be used by the Skidegate band. You can find argillite carvings in Skidegate and in craft shops in Prince Rupert, Victoria, and Vancouver. Silverwork is also popular, and some of the best is created by the Haida. Particularly notable is the work of Bill Reid, a Haida artist living in Vancouver. Jade jewelry can be seen in the Lillooet and Lytton areas.

Shops throughout British Columbia are generally open Monday–Friday 9 A.M.–5 P.M. and Saturday 9 A.M.–1 P.M. Major malls stay open all weekend.

ESSENTIALS

Getting There

AIR

Vancouver International Airport (YVR) is British Columbia's main gateway and Canada's second-busiest airport. Regularly scheduled service to and from Vancouver is offered by major airlines throughout the world. Victoria may be the capital, but it comes in a distant second when it comes to international flights; the only destinations served from its international airport are major Canadian cities and Seattle.

Air Canada

Air Canada (604/688-5515 or 888/247-2262, www.aircanada.ca or aircanada.com in the U.S.) is one of the world's largest airlines, serving five continents. It offers direct flights to Vancouver from the following North American cities: Calgary, Chicago, Edmonton, Halifax, Honolulu, Las Vegas, Los Angeles, Miami, Montreal, Ottawa, Phoenix, San Francisco, Seattle, Toronto, Whitehorse, and Winnipeg. Air Canada also flies into Victoria directly from most western Canadian cities as well as Seattle.

From Europe, Air Canada flies directly from London to Vancouver and from other major cities via Toronto. From the South Pacific, Air Canada operates flights from Sydney and, in alliance with Air New Zealand, from Auckland

and other South Pacific islands. Asian cities served by direct Air Canada flights from Vancouver include Beijing, Hong Kong, Nagoya, Osaka, Seoul, Shanghai, Taipei, and Tokyo. Air Canada's flights originating in the South American cities of Buenos Aires and São Paulo are routed through Toronto.

WestJet

Canada's second largest airline, **WestJet** (604/606-5525 or 800/538-5696, www.west jet.com), is a budget-priced airline with specials advertised year-round. The least expensive flights land at Abbotsford, 72 kilometers (45 miles) east of downtown Vancouver. Flights also terminate at Vancouver's main airport and in Victoria. As well as receiving flights from regional centers throughout British Columbia, these three airports take flights originating in Calgary, Edmonton, Hamilton, Ottawa, Regina, Saskatoon, Thunder Bay, and as far east as St. John's, Newfoundland.

U.S. Airlines

Air Canada offers the most flights into Vancouver from the United States, but the city is also served by the following U.S. carriers: **Alaska Airlines** (800/252-7522, www.alaksaair.com) from Anchorage and Los Angeles; **American Airlines** (800/433-7300, www.aa.com) from Chicago and Dallas; **Continental Airlines** (800/231-0856, www.continental.com) from its Houston hub and New York (Newark); **Delta** (800/221-1212, www.delta.com) with summer-only flights from Atlanta and Salt Lake City; **Frontier Airlines** (800/432-1359, www.frontierairlines.com) from Denver; **Harmony Airways** (866/868-6789, www .harmonyairways.com) from Honolulu, Kahului, and Los Angeles; **Horizon Air** (800/547-9308, www.horizonair.com) from nearby Seattle; **Northwest Airlines** (800/225-2525, www.nwa.com) from Detroit, Memphis, and Minneapolis; **Skywest** (800/221-1212, www .skywest.com) from Salt Lake City; and finally **United Airlines** (800/241-6522, www.united .com) from Chicago, Denver, San Francisco, and Seattle.

AIR TAXES

The advertised airfare that looks so tempting is just a base fare, devoid of a raft of fees and taxes collected by numerous government agencies. On domestic flights within Canada, expect to pay around $80-100 extra. This includes an **Air Travellers Security Tax** ($6 each sector for domestic flights, $17 for international flights), an insurance surcharge of $3 each way, and a fee of $9-20 each way that goes to **NAV Canada** for the operation of the federal navigation system. Advertised domestic fares are inclusive of **fuel surcharges,** but on international flights expect to pay up to $230 extra. All major Canadian airports charge an **Airport Improvement Fee** to all departing passengers, with Vancouver charging $15 per passenger. You'll also need to pay this fee from your original departure point, and if you're connecting through Toronto, another $8 is collected. And, of course, the above taxes are taxable with the Canadian government collecting the 6 percent goods and services tax. The bright side to paying these extras? It's often made easy for consumers, with airlines lumping all the charges together and into the final ticket price.

International Airlines

In addition to Air Canada's daily London–Vancouver flight, **British Airways** (800/247-9297, www.british-airways.com) also flies this route daily. Air Canada flights between Vancouver and Continental Europe are routed through Toronto, but **KLM** (800/447-4747, www.klm.nl) has a daily nonstop flight to Vancouver from Amsterdam, and **Lufthansa** (800/563-5954, www.lufthansa.de) flies from Frankfurt and Munich. **Air New Zealand** (800/663-5494, www.airnz.com) operates in alliance with Air Canada, with direct flights between Vancouver and Auckland. This airline also has flights with stops throughout the South Pacific, including Nadi. **Air Pacific**

(800/227-4446, www.airpacific.com) flies from points throughout the Pacific to Honolulu and then on to Vancouver.

Vancouver is the closest West Coast gateway from Asia, being more than 1,200 kilometers (750 miles) closer to Tokyo than Los Angeles. This and the city's large Asian population mean that it is well served by carriers from across the Pacific. In addition to Air Canada's Asian destinations, Vancouver is served by **Air China** (800/685-0921, www.airchina.com) from Beijing; **All Nippon Airways** (888/422-7533, www.ana.co.jp) from Osaka and Tokyo, in affiliation with Air Canada; **Cathay Pacific** (604/606-8888, www.cathaypacific.com) twice daily from Hong Kong; **Eva Air** (800/695-1188, www.evaair.com.tw) from Taipei; **Japan Airlines** (800/525-3663, www.jal.co.jp) from Tokyo; **Korean Air** (800/438-5000, www.koreanair.com) from Seoul; **Philippine Airlines** (800/435-9725, www.philippineair.com) from Manila; and **Singapore Airlines** (604/689-1223, www.singaporeair.com) from Singapore via Seoul.

CUTTING FLIGHT COSTS

Ticket structuring for air travel has traditionally been so complex that finding the best deal required some time and patience (or a good travel agent), but the process has gotten a lot easier in recent years. Air Canada leads the way, with streamlined ticketing options that are easy to understand.

The first step when planning your trip to British Columbia is to contact the airlines that fly to the West Coast and search out the best price they have for the time of year you wish to travel. The Internet has changed the way many people shop for tickets, but even if you use this invaluable tool for preliminary research, having a travel agent that you are comfortable dealing with – who takes the time to call around, does some research to get you the best fare, and helps you take advantage of any available special offers or promotional deals – is an invaluable asset in starting your travels off on the right foot. In addition to your local agent, **Travel Cuts** (866/246-9762, www.travelcuts.com) and **Flight Centre** (877/967-5302, www.flightcentre.ca), both with offices in all major cities, consistently offer the lowest airfares available, with the latter guaranteeing the lowest. Flight Centre offers a similar guarantee from its U.S. offices (866/967-5351, www.flightcentre.us), as well as those in Great Britain (tel. 0870/499-0040, www.flightcentre.co.uk), Australia (tel. 13-31-33, www.flightcentre.com.au), New Zealand (tel. 0800/24-35-44, www.flightcentre.co.nz), and South Africa (0860/400-727, www.flightcentre.co.za). All Flight Centre toll-free numbers will put you through to the closest office from where you are calling. In London, **Trailfinders** (215 Kensington High St., Kensington, tel. 020/7938-3939, www.trailfinders.com) always has good deals to Canada and other North American destinations. Or use the services of an Internet-only company such as **Travelocity** (www.travelocity.com) or **Expedia** (www.expedia.com). The Dream Maps function (http://dps1.travelocity.com/dreammap.ctl) on the Travelocity site is a fun and functional way to search for the best fares from your own home city. Also look in the travel sections of major newspapers – particularly in weekend editions – where budget fares and package deals are frequently advertised.

Many cheaper tickets have strict restrictions regarding changes of flight dates, lengths of stay, and cancellations. A general rule: The cheaper the ticket, the more restrictions. Most travelers today fly on APEX (advance-purchase excursion) fares. These are usually the best value, though some (and, occasionally, many) restrictions apply. These might include minimum and maximum stays, and nonchangeable itineraries (or hefty penalties for changes); tickets may also be nonrefundable once purchased.

Edward Hasbrouck's *Practical Nomad Guide to the Online Travel Marketplace* (Avalon Travel) is an excellent resource for working through the web of online travel-planning possibilities.

RAIL
VIA Rail

Government-run VIA Rail (416/366-8411 or 888/842-7245, www.viarail.ca) provides passenger-train service across Canada. The **Canadian** is a thrice-weekly service between Toronto and Vancouver via Edmonton, Jasper, Kamloops, Saskatoon, and Winnipeg. Service is provided in two classes of travel: **Economy** features lots of legroom, reading lights, pillows and blankets, and a Skyline Car complete with bar service, while **Silver and Blue** is more luxurious, featuring sleeping rooms, daytime seating, all meals, a lounge and dining car, and shower kits for all passengers.

Passes and Practicalities: If you're traveling to Vancouver from any eastern province, the least expensive way to travel is on a **Canrailpass,** which allows unlimited travel anywhere on the VIA Rail system for 12 days within any given 30-day period. During high season (June 1–Oct. 15) the pass is adult $837, senior (over 60) and child $753, with extra days (up to three are allowed) $71 and $64, respectively. The rest of the year, adult tickets are $523 and senior and student $471, with extra days $45 and $41, respectively. VIA Rail has cooperated with Amtrak (800/872-7245) to offer a North America Rail Pass, with all the same seasonal dates and discounts as the Canrailpass. The cost for unlimited travel over 30 days is adult $1,149, senior and child $1034; $815 and $734, respectively, through the low season.

On regular fares, discounts of 25–40 percent apply to travel in all classes Oct.–June. Those over 60 and under 25 receive a 10 percent discount that can be combined with other seasonal fares. Check for advance-purchase restrictions on all discount tickets.

The VIA Rail website (www.viarail.ca) provides route, schedule, and fare information, takes reservations, and offers links to towns and sights en route. Or pick up a train schedule at any VIA Rail station.

Rocky Mountaineer

Rocky Mountaineer Vacations (604/606-7245 or 877/460-3200, www.rockymountaineer .com) runs luxurious rail trips to Vancouver from Banff or Jasper and from Jasper to Whistler via Prince George. Travel is during daylight hours only so you don't miss anything. Trains depart in either direction in the morning (every second or third day), overnighting at Kamloops or Quesnel. One-way travel in RedLeaf Service, which includes light meals, nonalcoholic drinks, and accommodations, costs $769 per person d, $849 s from either Banff or Jasper and $869 and $949, respectively, from Calgary. GoldLeaf Service is the ultimate in luxury. Passengers ride in a two-story glass-domed car, eat in a separate dining area, and stay in luxurious accommodations. GoldLeaf costs $1,569 per person d, $1,649 s from Banff or Jasper to Vancouver. Outside of high season (mid-Apr.–May and the first two weeks of Oct.), fares are reduced around $150 per person in RedLeaf and $200 per person in GoldLeaf Services. The Rocky Mountaineer terminates behind Pacific Central Station at 1755 Cottrell Street (off Terminal Avenue).

BUS
Greyhound

Bus travel throughout Canada is easy with Greyhound (604/482-8747 or 800/661-8747, www .greyhound.ca). The company offers TransCanada Highway service from Toronto, Winnipeg, Regina, and Calgary through Kamloops to Vancouver, as well as a more southerly route from Calgary through Cranbrook and the Kootenays to Vancouver. Among the northern routes: Edmonton and Jasper southwest to Vancouver or west to Prince Rupert; and Grande Prairie northwest through Dawson Creek to Whitehorse. Reservations are not necessary—just turn up when you want to go, buy your ticket, and kick back. As long as you use your ticket within 30 days, you can stop over wherever the bus stops and stay as long as you want.

When calling for information, ask about any special deals—including the Go Anywhere Fare, on which you can travel between any two points in North America for one low fare. Other discounts apply to regular-fare tickets bought 7 and 14 days in advance, travelers 65 and over, and two people traveling together.

Greyhound's **Discovery Pass** comes in many forms, including passes valid only in Canada, in the western states and provinces, and in all of North America. The pass is sold in periods of 7 days ($329), 15 days ($483), 30 days ($607), and 60 days ($750) and allows unlimited travel west of Montreal. Passes can be bought 14 or more days in advance online, 7 or more days in advance from any Canadian bus depot, or up to the day of departure from U.S. depots.

FERRY

One of the most pleasurable ways to get your first view of British Columbia is from sea level. Many scheduled ferry services cross from Washington state to Victoria, on Vancouver Island, but no ferries run to Vancouver from south of the border.

From Washington State

From downtown Seattle (Pier 69), **Clipper Navigation** (800/888-2535, www.clippervacations.com) runs passenger-only ferries to Victoria's Inner Harbour. Full fare is adult US$86 one-way, US$140 round-trip. In summer, sailings are made five times daily, with the service running the rest of the year on a reduced schedule. Travel is discounted off-season, and year-round for seniors and children.

North of Seattle, Anacortes is the departure point for **Washington State Ferries** (206/464-6400, 250/381-1551, or 888/808-7977, www.wsdot.wa.gov/ferries) to Sidney (on Vancouver Island, 32 kilometers/20 miles north of Victoria), with a stop made en route in the San Juan Islands. Sample fares are adult US$16, senior US$8, child US$12.80, vehicle and driver US$53.70. Make reservations at least 24 hours in advance.

The final option is to travel from Port Angeles to Victoria. Two companies offer service on this route. The **MV Coho** (250/386-2202 or 360/457-4491, www.cohoferry.com) runs year-round, with up to four crossings daily in summer; adult US$11.50, child US$5.75, vehicle and driver US$44. The passenger-only **Victoria Express** (250/361-9144 or 360/452-8088, www.victoriaexpress.com) makes the crossing 2–4 sailings daily June–Sept.; US$12.50 per person each way.

Getting Around

The best way to get around British Columbia is via your own vehicle—be it a car, RV, motorbike, or bicycle. It's easy to get around by bus, but you can't get off the beaten track and, let's face it, that's exactly where most of British Columbia is. It's also easy to get around by air—all the larger airports are served by scheduled intraprovincial flights, and charter services fly out of many of the smaller ones.

AIR

For travel connections throughout British Columbia, **Air Canada Jazz** (www.flyjazz.ca), a connector airline for Air Canada (604/688-5515 or 888/247-2262, www.aircanada.ca), serves most major BC cities from both Vancouver and Victoria international airports.

Harbour Air (604/274-1277 or 800/665-0212, www.harbour-air.com) and **West Coast Air** (604/606-6888 or 800/347-2222, www.westcoastair.com) have scheduled floatplane flights between downtown Vancouver (the terminal is beside Canada Place) and Victoria's Inner Harbour. Expect to pay around $120 per person each way for any of these flights.

Pacific Coastal (604/273-8666 or 800/663-2872, www.pacific-coastal.com) has flights from Vancouver's South Terminal (connected to the main terminals by shuttle) and Victoria International Airport to Campbell River, Comox, Cranbrook, Port Hardy, Powell River, Williams Lake, and many remote coastal towns further north. **KD Air** (604/688-9957 or 800/665-4244, www.kdair.com) flies daily to Qualicum (Vancouver Island), with a connecting ground shuttle to Port Alberni. **Orca Airways**

(604/270-6722 or 888/359-6722, www.fly orcaair.com) flies from the South Terminal to Tofino/Ucluelet. **Hawk Air** (250/635-4295 or 800/487-1216, www.hawkair.ca) offers scheduled flights throughout northern British Columbia and from as far south as Vancouver.

BUS

British Columbia by bus is a snap. Just about all the cities have local bus companies providing transportation in town and, in many cases, throughout their local region—check the transportation sections of each individual chapter for more details. **Greyhound** operates daily bus service to just about anywhere in the province. You don't need to make reservations—just buy your ticket and go. All scheduled services are nonsmoking. The bus depot in Vancouver is Pacific Central Station (1150 Station St., 604/482-8747 or 800/661-8747).

FERRY
BC Ferries

Chances are, at some stage of your British Columbia adventure, you'll use the services of **BC Ferries** (250/386-3431 or 888/223-3779, www.bcferries.com), which serves 46 ports with a fleet of 40 vessels. All fares listed for "vehicles" in this book cover cars and trucks up to 6.1 meters (20 feet) long and under 2.1 meters (seven feet) high (or under two meters/six feet eight inches high on a few routes). Larger vehicles such as RVs pay more. Also note that prices listed for all types of vehicles are in addition to the passenger price; the vehicle's driver/rider/porter is not included in the vehicle fare.

Vancouver has two major ferry terminals. From **Tsawwassen,** south of downtown, ferries run regularly across the Strait of Georgia to the Vancouver Island centers of Swartz Bay (32 kilometers/20 miles north of Victoria) and Nanaimo. From **Horseshoe Bay,** west of downtown Vancouver, ferries ply the strait to Nanaimo. Also from Horseshoe Bay, ferries run across Howe Sound to **Langdale,** gateway to the Sunshine Coast. From **Powell River,** at the north end of the Sunshine Coast, ferries depart for **Comox** (Vancouver Island), making

© ANDREW HEMPSTEAD

soaking up the sun on the ferry crossing to Vancouver Island

it possible to visit both the island and the Sunshine Coast without returning to Vancouver.

BC Ferries also provides regular services from Vancouver Island and the mainland to the **Southern Gulf Islands.** Other islands in the Strait of Georgia linked to Vancouver Island by ferry include: Thetis and Kuper (from Chemainus), Gabriola (from Nanaimo), Lasqueti (from Parksville), Denman and Hornby (from Buckley Bay), Quadra and Cortes (from Campbell River), Malcolm and Cormorant (from Port McNeil), and Texada (from Powell River).

From **Port Hardy** at the northern tip of Vancouver Island, a ferry runs north up the coast to **Prince Rupert.** From the end of May through September the ferry goes every other day, from October through April once a week, and during May twice a week. The trip takes 15 hours and links up with the **Alaska Marine Highway.** Also from Prince Rupert, ferries run out to the **Queen Charlotte Islands;** these longer sailings require reservations, which should be made as far in advance as possible.

Inland Ferries

Many interior lakes and rivers are crossed by ferries owned and operated by the government. Of course, no service is available between freeze-up and breakup, but the rest of the year, expect daily service from 6 A.M. until at least 10 P.M. Some of the ferries are small, capable of carrying just 2 vehicles, while others can transport up to 50. Passage is free on all these ferries, including the 45-minute sailing across Kootenay Lake between Balfour and Kootenay Bay—the world's longest free ferry trip.

DRIVING IN CANADA

U.S. and International Driver's Licenses are valid in Canada. All highway signs give distances in kilometers and speeds in kilometers per hour. Unless otherwise posted, the maximum speed limit on the highways is 100 kph (62 mph).

Use of safety belts is mandatory, and motorcyclists must wear helmets. Infants and toddlers weighing up to nine kilograms (20 pounds) must be strapped into an appropriate child's car seat. Use of a child car seat for larger children weighing 9–18 kilograms (20–40 pounds) is required of British Columbia residents and recommended to nonresidents. Before venturing north of the 49th parallel, U.S. residents should ask their vehicle insurance company for a Canadian Non-resident Inter-provincial Motor Vehicle Liability Insurance Card. You may also be asked to prove vehicle ownership, so carry your vehicle registration form. If you're involved in an accident with a BC vehicle, contact the nearest Insurance Corporation of British Columbia (ICBC) office, 800/663-3051.

If you're a member in good standing of an automobile association, take your membership card—the Canadian Automobile Association provides members of related associations full services, including free maps, itineraries, excellent tour books, road and weather condition information, accommodations reservations, travel agency services, and emergency road services. For more information, contact the **British Columbia Automobile Association** (604/268-5600 or 877/325-8888, www.bcaa .com).

Note: Drinking and driving (with a blood-alcohol level of 0.08 percent or higher) in British Columbia can get you imprisoned for up to five years on a first offense and will cost you your license for at least 12 months.

Car Rental

All major car-rental companies have outlets at Vancouver International Airport, in downtown Vancouver, and in Victoria. Many companies also have cars available in towns and cities throughout the province. Try to book in advance, especially in summer. Expect to pay from $50 a day and $250 a week for a small economy car with unlimited kilometers.

Vehicles can be booked for Canadian pickup through parent companies in the United States or elsewhere using the Web or toll-free numbers. **Discount** (403/299-1202 or 800/263-2355, www.discountcar.com) is a Canadian company with 200 rental outlets across the country. Their vehicles are kept in service a little longer than the other majors, but they provide excellent rates—even through summer—especially if booked in advance. Other companies include **Alamo** (800/462-5266, www.alamo.com), **Avis** (800/974-0808, www.avis.ca), **Budget** (800/268-8900, www.budget.com), **Dollar** (800/800-4000, www.dollar.com), **Enterprise** (800/325-8007, www.enterprise.com), **Hertz** (800/263-0600, www.hertz.ca), **National** (800/227-7368, www.nationalcar.com), **Rent-a-wreck** (800/327-0116, www.rentawreck.ca), and **Thrifty** (800/847-4389, www.thrifty.com).

RV and Camper Rental

You might consider renting a camper-van or other recreational vehicle for your British Columbia vacation. With one of these apartments-on-wheels, you won't need to worry about finding accommodations each night. Even the smallest units aren't cheap, but they can be a good deal for longer-term travel or for families or two couples traveling together. The smallest vans, capable of sleeping two people, start at $150 per day with 100 free kilometers (62 miles) per day. Standard extra charges include insurance, a preparation fee (usually around $50 per rental), a linen/cutlery charge (around $60 pp per trip), and taxes. Major agencies with rental outlets in Vancouver include **Cruise Canada** (480/464-7300 or 800/327-7799, www.cruisecanada.com) and **Go West** (604/987-5288 or 800/661-8813, www.go-west.com). Remember to figure in higher ferry charges for crossing to Vancouver Island with an RV.

Visas and Officialdom

ENTERING CANADA
U.S. Citizens

Traditionally, U.S. citizens and permanent residents have needed only to present some form of identification that proves citizenship and/or residency, such as a birth certificate, voter-registration card, driver's license with photo, or alien card (essential for nonresident aliens to reenter the United States) to enter Canada. But as of January 1, 2008, the United States began requiring its citizens to present a passport for reentry to the United States in accordance with the Western Hemisphere Travel Initiative. Therefore, it is imperative to carry a passport, even though one is not technically required for entry to Canada. At the time of going to press, there was some talk of developing an alternative secure document less costly than a passport. For the latest, check out the travel section of the U.S. Department of State website (http://travel.state.gov).

Other Foreign Visitors

All other foreign visitors entering Canada must have a valid passport and may need a visitor permit or Temporary Resident Visa depending on their country of residence and the vagaries of international politics. At present, visas are not required for citizens of the United States, British Commonwealth, or Western Europe. The standard entry permit is for six months, and you may be asked to show onward tickets or proof of sufficient funds to last you through your intended stay. Extensions are available from the Citizenship and Immigration Canada office in Calgary. This department's website (www.cic.gc.ca) is the best source of information on the latest entry requirements.

CUSTOMS

You can take the following into Canada duty-free: reasonable quantities of clothes and personal effects, 50 cigars and 200 cigarettes, 200 grams of tobacco, 1.14 liters of spirits or wine, food for personal use, and gas (normal tank capacity). Pets from the United States can generally be brought into Canada, with certain caveats. Dogs and cats must be more than three months old and have a rabies certificate showing date of vaccination. Birds can be brought in only if they have not been mixing with other birds, and parrots need an export permit because they're on the endangered species list.

Handguns, automatic and semiautomatic weapons, and sawn-off rifles and shotguns are not allowed into Canada. Visitors with firearms must declare them at the border; restricted weapons will be held by Customs and can be picked up on exit from the country. Those not declared will be seized and charges may be laid. It is illegal to possess any firearm in a national park unless it is dismantled or carried in an enclosed case. Up to 5,000 rounds

of ammunition may be imported but should be declared on entry.

On reentering the United States, if you've been in Canada more than 48 hours, you can bring back up to US$400 worth of household and personal items, excluding alcohol and tobacco, duty-free. If you've been in Canada fewer than 48 hours, you may bring in only up to US$200 worth of such items duty-free.

For further information on all customs regulations contact **Canada Border Services Agency** (204/983-3500 or 800/461-9999, www.cbsa-asfc.gc.ca).

Recreation

The great outdoors: British Columbia certainly has plenty of it. The province encompasses some 948,600 square kilometers (366,250 square miles) of land area and a convoluted coastline totaling 25,000 kilometers (15,500 miles). With spectacular scenery around every bend, millions of hectares of parkland, and an abundance of wildlife, the province is an outdoorsperson's fantasy come true. Hiking, mountain climbing, fishing, hunting, boating, canoeing, white-water rafting, scuba diving, downhill and cross-country skiing—it's all here. For specific recreation information, contact **Tourism BC** (250/387-1642 or 800/435-5622, www.hellobc.com).

HIKING

Just about everywhere you go in British Columbia you'll find good hiking opportunities, from short, easy walks in city and regional parks to long, strenuous hikes in wilderness parks.

The mountains are great places to hike. Short trails lead to waterfalls, lakes, rock formations, and viewpoints, and longer trails wander high into alpine meadows tangled with wildflowers, past turquoise lakes, and up to snow-dusted peaks providing breathtaking views. Rustic huts are provided at regular intervals along wilderness trails. Perhaps the best known of British Columbia's hikes lies not

in the Rockies but along the wild and remote west shore of Vancouver Island; backpackers return time and again to the **West Coast Trail,** an unforgettable 77-kilometer (48-mile) trek through Pacific Rim National Park.

To get the most out of a hiking trip, peruse the hiking section of any major bookstore—many books have been written on BC hiking trails. The Don't Waste Your Time series (www.hikingcamping.com) covers interior regions while the *Canadian Rockies Trail Guide* (www.summerthought.com) is the book of choice for Kootenay and Yoho National Parks. Before setting off on a longer hike, study the trail guides and a topographical map of the area. Leave details of your intended route and itinerary with a relative or friend. And try to travel in groups of at least two in the backcountry.

CYCLING AND MOUNTAIN BIKING

Cycling is a great way to explore British Columbia. The casual pace allows riders time to stop and appreciate the scenery, wildlife, and flowers that can easily be overlooked at high speeds. Some of the most popular areas for cycling trips are the **Southern Gulf Islands** between Vancouver Island and the mainland (quiet, laid-back, loads of sunshine, rural scenery, and lots of artists), the **east coast of Vancouver Island** (following

PARKS AND PROTECTED AREAS

Visitors and locals alike enjoy over 800 protected areas totaling 11.7 million hectares (29 million acres) throughout British Columbia. From old-growth coastal rainforests to glaciated peaks, and ranging in size from less than one hectare to over a million hectares (2.5 million acres), these parks provide almost unlimited recreation opportunities.

NATIONAL PARKS

British Columbia holds 7 of Canada's 37 national parks. The most accessible is also the newest, **Southern Gulf Islands National Park,** which was created in 2003 by piecing together existing provincial and marine parks scattered throughout the archipelago. **Pacific Rim National Park** protects a stretch of Vancouver Island's rugged west coast, offering long beaches, remote islands, and the famous West Coast Trail to explore. In the east of the province, **Kootenay** and **Yoho National Parks** form a part of the UNESCO Rocky Mountains World Heritage Site; the two spectacular mountain parks lie just across the Continental Divide from the more famous Banff and Jasper National Parks in neighboring Alberta. Also protecting a mountainous landscape are **Glacier** and **Mount Revelstoke National Parks** along the TransCanada Highway. The most remote of British Columbia's national parks is **Gwaii Haanas** on the Queen Charlotte Islands. No roads access this park, which encompasses the southern half of an archipelago renowned the world over for ancient Haida villages. For general national park information, contact **Parks Canada** (www.pc.gc.ca).

PROVINCIAL PARKS

BC Parks manages more than 800 protected areas, including almost 500 provincial parks. Many are day-use areas, others have campgrounds, but all have one thing in common: They protect a particularly scenic area, a unique natural feature, a wildlife habitat, or maybe a fish-filled lake.

Among these are: **Cypress Provincial Park,** on Vancouver's city limits and offering great views; **Carmanah Walbran Provincial Park,** protecting a magnificent old-growth forest on Vancouver Island; **Manning Provincial Park,** a high alpine area of snowcapped peaks and colorful flower-filled meadows; **Kokanee Glacier Provincial Park,** named for its spectacular ice field; **Mount Assiniboine Provincial Park,** a rugged Rocky Mountain wilderness perfect for extended hiking trips; **Mount Robson Provincial Park,** protecting the Canadian Rockies' highest peak; **Bowron Lake Provincial Park,** famous for its wilderness canoe route; and **Naikoon Provincial Park,** on the Queen Charlotte Islands.

Major new parks added in the last decade include **Valhalla Provincial Park,** a remote wilderness area in the heart of the Kootenays; **Khutzeymateen Provincial Park,** an important coastal grizzly bear habitat; the 6.5-million-hectare (16-million-acre) **Muskwa-Kechika Wilderness Area** of the northern Canadian Rockies; and, in the province's extreme northwest corner, **Tatshenshini-Alsek Provincial Park,** part of the world's largest UNESCO World Heritage Site.

For information on provincial parks, contact **BC Parks** (www.bcparks.ca).

FOREST SERVICE LANDS

Over half of British Columbia (59 million hectares/146 million acres) is forested and under the control of the Ministry of Forests, which manages the land for timber harvesting, recreational activities, and just plain wilderness. Many recreation areas have been provided on forest land, but facilities are often limited. Get more information on recreation areas, forest roads, safety, and possible fire closures from the **Ministry of Forests** (www.gov.bc.ca/for), regional offices, or information centers throughout the province.

© ANDREW HEMPSTEAD

Yoho National Park

NATIONAL PARK PASSES

Permits are required for entry into all Canadian national parks. A **National Parks Day Pass** costs up to adult $7, senior $6, child $3.50, up to a maximum of $17.30 per vehicle. It is interchangeable among parks and is valid until 4 P.M. the day following its purchase. An annual **National Parks of Canada Pass,** good for entry into all of Canada's national parks for one year from the date of purchase, is adult $62.40, senior $53.50, child $31.70, up to a maximum of $123.80. The **Discovery Package** (adult $77.25, senior $66.35, child $38.60, to a maximum of $155.50 per vehicle) is a good choice for history buffs. It allows unlimited entry into both national parks and national historic sites (six of which are in British Columbia) for a full year from purchase.

Annual and day passes are available at park gates, at all park information centers, and at campground fee stations. Day passes are also available from automated ticket machines at popular stopping points in Pacific Rim National Park. For more information, check the Parks Canada website (www.pc.gc.ca).

© ANDREW HEMPSTEAD

Pacific Rim National Park

the Strait of Georgia past lazy beaches and bustling towns), the **Kootenays** (forest-clad mountains, deep lakes, curious old gold- and silver-mining communities, and ghost towns—good mountain-bike country), and the **Rockies** (outstanding mountain scenery second to none, abundant wildlife often right beside the highways, hot springs, and hiking trails). Rocky Mountain routes suit the intermediate to advanced cyclist.

For information on touring, tour operators, bicycle routes, and local clubs, contact **Cycling BC** (1367 W. Broadway, 604/737-3034, www.cyclingbc.net) or, in the same building, the **Outdoor Recreation Council of BC** (604/737-3058, www.orcbc.ca), which also publishes a series of maps covering much of British Columbia. These maps can by purchased directly from the council or at many sporting-goods stores and bookstores. A good source of online information is the **British Columbia Mountain Bike Guide** (www.bcmbg.com).

ON THE WATER
Canoeing and Kayaking

Canoes are a traditional form of transportation along British Columbia's numerous lakes and rivers. You can rent one at many of the more popular lakes, but if you bring your own you can slip into any body of water whenever you please, taking in the scenery and viewing wildlife from water level. One of the most popular canoe routes is in **Bowron Lake Provincial Park,** where a 117-kilometer (73-mile) circuit leads through a chain of lakes in the Cariboo Mountains. Shorter but no less challenging is the **Powell Forest Canoe Route,** on the Sunshine Coast. Other, less-traveled destinations include **Slocan Lake,** and **Wells Gray Provincial Park.** For information on canoe routes, courses, and clubs, contact the **Outdoor Recreation Council of BC** (604/737-3058, www.orcbc.ca).

Anywhere suitable for canoeing is also prime kayaking territory, although most keen kayakers look for white-water excitement. The best wilderness kayaking experiences are in the north, where access can be difficult but crowds are minimal. The **Stikine River** is challenging, with one stretch—the Grand Canyon of the Stikine—successfully run only a handful of times.

The province's long coastline is great for sea kayaking, and rentals are available in most coastal communities. The **Southern Gulf Islands** are ideal for kayakers of all experience levels, while destinations such as **Desolation Sound,** the **Broken Group Islands,** and the **Queen Charlotte Islands** are the domain of experienced paddlers. Most outfits offering kayak rentals also provide lessons and often tours. One such Vancouver operation is the **Ecomarine Ocean Kayak Centre** (604/689-7575, www.ecomarine.com) based on Granville Island. Tofino, on Vancouver Island's west coast, is a mecca for sea kayakers. **Tofino Sea Kayaking Company** (250/725-4222 or 800/863-4664, www.tofino-kayaking.com) rents kayaks and leads tours through local waterways. **Northern Lights Expeditions** (360/734-6334 or 800/754-7402, www.seakayaking.com) specializes in overnight expeditions along the BC coast. Each Northern Lights trip features three knowledgeable guides, all necessary equipment, and an emphasis on gourmet meals, such as shoreline salmon bakes, complete with wine and freshly baked breads. The six-day trip through the Strait of Georgia is $1,595.

White-Water Rafting

The best and easiest way to experience a white-water rafting trip is on a half- or full-day trip with a qualified guide. Close to Vancouver, the **Green, Fraser, Nahatlatch,** and **Thompson Rivers** are run commercially. In the Rockies, the **Kicking Horse River** provides the thrills. Expect to pay $90–120 for a full day's excitement, transfers, and lunch.

Boating

British Columbia's 25,000 kilometers (15,500 miles) of coastline, in particular the sheltered, island-dotted Strait of Georgia between Vancouver Island and the mainland, is a boater's paradise. Along it are sheltered coves, sandy beaches, beautiful marine parks, and facilities specifically designed for boaters—many accessible only by water. One of the most beautiful marine parks is **Desolation Sound,** north of Powell River; locals claim it's one of the world's best cruising grounds. Many of the enormous freshwater lakes inland are also excellent places for boating.

Yachties and yachties-to-be should head for **Cooper Boating** (1620 Duranleau St., Granville Island, 604/687-4110 or 888/999-6419, www.cooperboating.com), which boasts Canada's largest sailing school and also holds the country's biggest fleet for charters. For those with experience, Cooper's rents yachts (from $390 per day for a Catalina 32) for a day's local sailing, or take to the waters of the Strait of Georgia on a bareboat charter (from $1,750 per week for a Catalina 27).

Scuba Diving

Some of the world's most varied and spectacular cold-water diving lies off the coast of British Columbia. Diving is best in winter, when you can expect up to 40 meters of visibility. The diverse marinelife includes sponges, anemones, soft corals, rockfish (china, vermilion, and canary), rock scallops, and cukes. Plenty of shipwrecks also dot the underwater terrain. The most popular dive sites are off the Southern Gulf Islands, Ogden Point in Victoria, Nanaimo (for wreck diving), Telegraph Cove, Port Hardy, and Powell River (the scuba diving capital of Canada). Many of the coastal communities along Vancouver Island and the Sunshine Coast have dive shops with gear rentals and air tanks, and many can put you in touch with charter dive boats and guides.

A quick flip through the Vancouver Yellow Pages lets you know that scuba diving is alive and well north of the 49th parallel. The city's many scuba shops have everything you need, and they're excellent sources of information on all the best local spots. Coming highly recommended is **Rowand's Reef Scuba Shop** (1512 Duranleau St., Granville Island, 604/669-3483, www.rowandsreef.com; daily 10 A.M.–6 P.M.), a full-service dive shop offering rentals, sales, organized diving trips, and PADI dive-certification courses throughout the year. The local *Diver* magazine (www.divermag.com) is another good source of information; its scuba directory lists retail stores, resorts, charter boats, and other services.

FISHING
Freshwater

The province's freshwater anglers fish primarily for trout—mostly rainbow trout, but also Dolly Varden, lake, brook, brown, and cutthroat trout. One particular type of rainbow trout, the large anadromous **steelhead,** is renowned as a fighting fish and considered by locals to be the ultimate fishing challenge. Salmon are also abundant in the province; several seagoing species come up British Columbia's rivers to spawn. **Kokanee** rarely grow over one kilogram (2.2 pounds), but this freshwater salmon is an excellent sport fish inhabiting lakes of the southern interior. Feeding near the surface and caught on wet or dry artificial flies, they taste great, especially when smoked.

Fishing guides, tours, lodges (from rustic to luxurious), and packages are available throughout the province; one is sure to suit you. Expect to pay $200–400 a day for a guide, and up to several thousand dollars for several days at a luxury lodge with all meals and guided fishing included.

Fishing licenses are required, and prices vary according to your age and place of residence. British Columbia residents pay $36 for a freshwater adult license, good for one year. All other Canadians pay $20 for a one-day license, $36 for an eight-day license, or $55 for a one-year. International visitors pay $20, $50, and $80, respectively. For more information, contact **Ministry of Environment** (www.env .gov.bc.ca) and download the *British Columbia Freshwater Fishing Regulations Synopsis.*

Tidal

The tidal waters of the Pacific Northwest offer some of the world's best fishing, with remote lodges scattered along the coast catering to all budgets. And although most keen anglers will want to head farther afield for the best fishing opportunities, many top fishing spots can be accessed on a day trip from Vancouver. The five species of Pacific salmon are most highly prized by anglers. The chinook (king) salmon in particular is the trophy fish of choice. They commonly weigh over 10 kilograms (22 pounds) and are occasionally caught at over 20 kilograms (44 pounds); those weighing over 12 kilograms (26.5 pounds) are often known as "tyee." Other salmon present are coho (silver), pink (humpback), sockeye (red), and chum (dog). Other species sought by local recreational anglers include halibut, lingcod, rockfish, cod, perch, and snapper.

A tidal-water sportfishing license for residents of British Columbia, good for one year from March 31, costs $22.26 ($11.66 for those 65 and over); for nonresidents, the same annual license costs $107.06, or $7.42 for a single-day license, $20.14 for three days, and $32.86 for five days. A **salmon conservation stamp** is an additional $6.36. Licenses are available from sporting goods stores, gas stations, marinas, and charter operators. When fish-tagging programs are on, you may be required to make a note of the date, location, and method of capture, or to record on the back of your license statistical information on the fish you catch. Read the current rules and regulations. For further information, contact **Fisheries and Oceans Canada** (604/664-9250, www.pac .dfo-mpo.gc.ca).

The **Sport Fishing Institute of British Columbia** (604/270-3439, www.sportfishing .bc.ca) produces an annual free magazine, *Sport Fishing,* that lists charter operators and fishing lodges and details license requirements.

GOLFING

Relative to the rest of Canada, British Columbia's climate is ideal for golfing, especially on Vancouver Island, where the sport can be enjoyed year-round. Many of the province's 280 courses are in spectacular mountain, ocean, or lake settings. Municipal courses offer the lowest greens fees, generally $15–40, but the semiprivate, private, and resort courses usually boast the most spectacular locations. At these courses, greens fees can be as high as $200. At all but the

snowboarding at Whistler

smallest municipal courses, club rentals, power carts, and lessons are available, and at all but the most exclusive city courses, nonmembers are welcomed with open arms. The mild climate and abundance of water create ideal conditions for the upkeep of golf courses in the south of the province—you'll be surprised at how immaculately manicured most are. (In the north, many courses have oil-soaked or artificial-grass greens to make upkeep easier.)

SKIING AND SNOWBOARDING
Most of the developed winter recreation areas are in the southern third of the province. Whether you're a total beginner or an advanced daredevil, BC resorts have a slope to suit you. The price of lift tickets is generally reasonable, and at the smaller, lesser-known resorts, you don't have to spend half your day lining up for the lifts.

The best known of all Canadian winter resorts is **Whistler/Blackcomb,** north of Vancouver, but others scattered through the southern interior provide world-class skiing and boarding on just-as-challenging slopes. The best of these include: **Big White Ski Resort** and **Silver Star Mountain Resort** in the Okanagan Valley; **Red Mountain** and **Whitewater** near Nelson; **Fernie Alpine Resort** near Fernie; **Panorama Mountain Resort** near Invermere; and **Sun Peaks Resort** north of Kamloops. In the north, **Powder King,** north of Prince George, lives up to its name with an average annual snowfall around 12 meters (39 feet)—among the highest of any North American resort. You can even go skiing and boarding out on Vancouver Island at **Mt. Washington Alpine Resort.**

Heli- and Sno-Cat Skiing and Boarding
Alternatives to resorts are also available. If you're an intermediate or advanced skier or snowboarder, you can go heli-skiing and heli-boarding in the mind-boggling scenery and deep, untracked powder of the Coast and Chilcotin Ranges, the central Cariboo Mountains, the Bugaboos, and the BC Rockies. The

world's largest heli-ski operation is **CMH Heli-skiing** (403/762-7100 or 800/661-0252, www.cmhski.com), founded by Austrian mountain guide Hans Gmoser in the Bugaboos in 1965. Today the operation has grown to include almost limitless terrain over five mountain ranges accessed from 11 lodges. **Mike Wiegele Helicopter Skiing** (250/673-8381 or 800/661-9170, www.wiegele.com) offers heli-skiing and heli-boarding in the Monashee and Cariboo Mountains from a luxurious lodge at Blue River.

Another, less-expensive alternative is to hook up with one of the many Sno-Cat operations in the province. Sno-Cats are tracked, all-terrain vehicles that can transport skiers and boarders up through the snow to virgin slopes in high-country wilderness (similar to snow groomers but capable of carrying passengers). British Columbia has been a world leader in this type of skiing, and many operators are scattered through the province. Through its location amid some of the continent's most consistent powder snow and because of its luxurious lodgings, **Island Lake Lodge** near Fernie (250/423-3700 or 888/422-8754, www.islandlakelodge.com) has gained a reputation for both its Sno-Cat skiing and its accommodations.

Accommodations

The best lodging guide is the free *Accommodations* book put out annually by Tourism BC. It's available at all information centers, from the website www.hellobc.com, or by calling 250/387-1642 or 800/435-5622. The book lists hotels, motels, lodges, resorts, bed-and-breakfasts, and campgrounds. It contains no ratings, simply listings with facilities and rates.

Rates quoted in this book are for a standard double room through the high season, which generally extends from June to early September (except in alpine resort towns such as Whistler). Almost all accommodations are less expensive outside of these busy months, some cutting their rates by as much as 50 percent. You'll enjoy the biggest seasonal discounts at properties that rely on summer tourists, such as those in Vancouver, on Vancouver Island, and in the Okanagan Valley. The same applies in Vancouver and to a lesser extent Victoria on weekends—many of the big downtown hotels rely on business and convention travelers to fill the bulk of their rooms; when the end of the week rolls down, the hotels are left with rooms to fill at discounted rates Friday, Saturday, and Sunday nights.

HOTELS AND MOTELS
Prices for a basic motel room in a small town start at $50 s, $55 d. In Vancouver and Victoria

expect to pay at least double this amount for the least expensive rooms. The most luxurious lodgings in the province—Vancouver's Pan Pacific Hotel, Victoria's grand old Fairmont Empress, or any one of Whistler's resort hotels, for example—charge over $300 per night for a basic room. Room rates outside the two major cities fluctuate greatly. For example, few lodgings on Vancouver Island charge less than $70, but along the TransCanada Highway, in places like Kamloops and Revelstoke, you can pay as little as $55 for a room. Try to plan ahead for summer travel and book as far in advance as possible, especially for accommodations in Vancouver and Prince Rupert, on Vancouver Island, and on the Queen Charlotte Islands.

Making Reservations
While you have no influence over the seasonal and weekday/weekend pricing differences, *how* you reserve a room *can* make a difference in how much you pay. First and foremost, when it comes to searching out actual rates, the Internet is an invaluable tool. Most accommodation websites listed in *Moon British Columbia* show rates, and many have online reservation forms. Use these websites to search out specials, many of which are available only on the Internet.

Don't be afraid to negotiate during slower

times. Even if the desk clerk has no control over rates, there's no harm in asking for a bigger room or one with a better view. Just look for a Vacancy sign hanging out front.

Most hotels offer auto association members an automatic 10 percent discount, and whereas senior discounts apply only to those over 60 or 65 on public transportation and at attractions, most hotels offer discounts to those over 50, with chains such as Best Western also allowing senior travelers a late checkout. "Corporate Rates" are a lot more flexible than in years gone past; some hotels require nothing more than the flash of a business card for a 10–20 percent discount.

When it comes to frequent flyer programs, you really do need to be a frequent flyer to achieve free flights, but the various loyalty programs offered by hotels often provide benefits simply for signing up.

BED-AND-BREAKFASTS

Bed-and-breakfast accommodations are found throughout British Columbia. Styles run the gamut from restored heritage homes to modern townhouses. They are usually private residences, with up to four guest rooms, and as the name suggests, breakfast is included. Rates fluctuate enormously. In Vancouver and Victoria, for example, they range $60–180 s, $70–210 d. Amenities also vary greatly—the "bed-and-breakfast" may be a single spare room in an otherwise regular family home or a full-time business in a purpose-built home. Regardless, guests can expect hearty home cooking, a peaceful atmosphere, personal service, knowledgeable hosts, and conversation with like-minded travelers.

Reservation Agencies

The **Western Canadian Bed & Breakfast Innkeepers Association** (604/255-9199, www.wcbbia.com) represents more than 140 bed-and-breakfasts across Western Canada. The association produces an informative brochure with simple descriptions and a color photo of each property, and manages an easily navigable website. This association doesn't take bookings—they must be made directly. **Bed and Breakfast Online** (www.bbcanada

For something a little different, plan to spend a night or two in a tepee – such as this one pictured at Princeton Castle Resort, east of Vancouver.

© ANDREW HEMPSTEAD

.com) doesn't take bookings either, but links are provided and an ingenious search engine helps you find the accommodation that best fits your needs. If none of the recommendations in the destination chapters of this book catches your eye, contact a local agency such as **Vancouver B&B Ltd.** (604/298-8815 or 800/488-1941, www.vancouverbandb.bc.ca). Tell them what you're looking for and the price you're prepared to pay, and they'll find the right place for you.

BACKPACKER ACCOMMODATIONS

Budget travelers are enjoying more and more options in British Columbia, ranging from a converted downtown Vancouver hotel to a tree house on Salt Spring Island, all for around $20 per person per night. Hostelling International (formerly the Youth Hostel Association) has undergone a radical change in direction and now appeals to all ages, and privately run "hostels" within the province fill the gaps. Either way, staying in what have universally become known as "backpackers' hostels" is an enjoyable and inexpensive way to travel through the province. Generally, you need to provide your own sleeping bag or linen, but most hostels supply extra bedding (if needed) at no charge. Accommodations are in dormitories (2–10 beds) or double rooms. Each also offers a communal kitchen, a lounge area, and laundry facilities, while some have Internet access, bike rentals, and organized tours.

Hostelling International

You don't *have* to be a member to stay in an affiliated hostel of Hostelling International (HI), but membership pays for itself after only a few nights of discounted lodging. Aside from lower rates, benefits of membership vary from country to country but often include discounted air, rail, and bus travel; discounts on car rental; and discounts on some attractions and commercial activities.

For Canadians, the membership charge is $35 annually or $175 for a lifetime membership. For more information, contact **HI-Canada** (613/237-7884 or 800/663-5777, www.hihostels.ca).

Joining the HI affiliate of your home country entitles you to reciprocal rights in Canada, as well as around the world. In the United States, the contact address is **Hostelling International USA** (301/495-1240, www.hiusa.org); annual membership is adult US$28 and senior US$18, or become a lifetime member for US$250.

Other contact addresses include **YHA England and Wales** (0870/770-8868, www.yha.org.uk), **YHA Australia,** based in all capital cities, including at 422 Kent Street, Sydney (02/9261-1111, www.yha.com.au), and **YHA New Zealand** (03/379-9970, www.yha.org.nz). Otherwise, click through the links on the HI website (www.hihostels.com) to your country of choice.

CAMPING

Almost every town in British Columbia has at least one campground, often with showers

British Columbia is blessed with over 1,000 campgrounds, many enjoying prime lakefront locations.

© ANDREW HEMPSTEAD

and water, electricity, and sewer hookups. Prices range $10–25 in smaller towns, up to $50 in the cities and more popular tourist destinations. If you're planning a summer trip to Vancouver, Vancouver Island, the Sunshine Coast, Whistler, or the Okanagan Valley, try to book in advance. At other times and places, advance reservations aren't usually necessary.

National parks provide some of the nicest campgrounds in British Columbia. All have picnic tables, fire grates, toilets, and fresh drinking water, although only some provide showers. Prices range $14–28 depending on facilities and services. They are all open through summer, with each park having one area designated for winter camping. A percentage of sites can be reserved through the **Parks Canada Campground Reservation Service** (877/737-3783, www.pccamping.ca). Backcountry camping in a national park costs $8 per person per night.

Nearly 14,000 campsites lie scattered through 344 campgrounds in 275 provincial parks. Rates range $14–22 a night depending on facilities, most of which are basic. The fee is collected in different ways at different parks, but it's always *cash only*. Reserve a spot at the 60 most popular provincial parks by calling BC Parks' **Discover Camping** (604/689-9025 or 800/689-9025, www .discovercamping.ca). Reservations are taken between March 15 and September 15 for dates up to three months in advance. The reservation fee is $6.42 per night, to a maximum of $19.26, and is in addition to applicable camping fees.

Camping in the province's over 1,400 **Forest Service Campgrounds** costs $8–10 per site per night, which is collected on-site. For a list of site locations, pick up a Forest District recreation map from local information centers or surf the Internet to www.gov.bc.ca/for.

Commercial and provincial park campgrounds are listed in Tourism BC's invaluable *Accommodations* guide, available at all information centers, online at www.hellobc.com, or by calling 250/387-1642 or 800/435-5622.

Conduct and Customs

Liquor Laws

Liquor laws in Canada are enacted on a provincial level. The minimum age for alcohol consumption in British Columbia is 19.

Like the rest of North America, driving in Vancouver and Victoria under the influence of alcohol or drugs is a criminal offence. Those convicted of driving with a blood alcohol concentration above 0.08 face big fines and an automatic one-year license suspension. Second convictions (even if the first was out of province) lead to a three-year suspension. Note that in British Columbia drivers below the limit can be charged with impaired driving. It is also illegal to have open alcohol in a vehicle or in public places.

Smoking

Smoking is banned in virtually all public places across Canada. Most provinces have enacted province-wide bans on smoking in public places (including British Columbia, where a blanket law went into effect in 2001), which includes all restaurants and bars.

Tipping

Gratuities are not usually added to the bill. In restaurants and bars, around 15 percent of the total amount is expected. But you should tip according to how good (or bad) the service was, as low as 10 percent or up to and over 20 percent for exceptional service. The exception to this rule is groups of eight or more, when it is standard for restaurants to add 15 to 20 percent as a gratuity. Tips are sometimes added to tour packages, so check this in advance, but you can also tip guides on stand-alone tours. Tips are also given to bar tenders, taxi drivers, bellmen, and hairdressers.

Tips for Travelers

EMPLOYMENT AND STUDY

Whistler and the resort towns of Vancouver Island are especially popular with young workers from across Canada and beyond. Aside from Help Wanted ads in local papers, a good place to start looking for work is the Whistler Employment Resource Centre (www.whistler chamberofcommerce.com).

International visitors wishing to work or study in Canada must obtain authorization *before* entering the country. Authorization to work will only be granted if no qualified Canadians are available for the work in question. Applications for work and study are available from all Canadian embassies and must be submitted with a nonrefundable processing fee. The Canadian government has a reciprocal agreement with Australia for a limited number of **holiday work visas** to be issued each year. Australian citizens aged 30 and under are eligible; contact your nearest Canadian embassy or consulate. For general information on immigrating to Canada contact **Citizenship and Immigration Canada** (www.cic.gc.ca).

VISITORS WITH DISABILITIES

A lack of mobility should not deter you from traveling to Vancouver and Victoria, but you should definitely do some research before leaving home.

If you haven't traveled extensively, start by doing some research at the website of the **Access-Able Travel Source** (www.access-able .com), where you will find databases of specialist travel agencies and lodgings in Canada that cater to travelers with disabilities. **Flying Wheels Travel** (507/451-5005, www.flying wheelstravel.com) caters solely to the needs of travelers with disabilities. The **Society for Accessible Travel and Hospitality** (212/447-7284, www.sath.org) supplies information on tour operators, vehicle rentals, specific destinations, and companion services. For frequent travelers, the annual membership fee (adult US$45, senior US$30) is well worthwhile.

Emerging Horizons (www.emerginghorizons .com) is a U.S. quarterly magazine dedicated to travelers with special needs.

Access to Travel (800/465-7735, www .accesstotravel.gc.ca) is an initiative of the Canadian government that includes information on travel within and between Canadian cities, including Vancouver and Victoria. The website also has a lot of general travel information for those with disabilities. The **Canadian National Institute for the Blind** (800/563-2642, www .cnib.ca) offers a wide range of services from its Vancouver office (604/431-2121). Finally, the **Canadian Paraplegic Association** (613/723-1033 or 877/324-3611, www.canparaplegic .org), with a chapter office in Vancouver, is another good source of information.

TRAVELING WITH CHILDREN

Regardless of whether you're traveling with toddlers or teens, you will come upon decisions affecting everything from where you stay to your choice of activities. Luckily for you, Vancouver and Victoria are very family-friendly, with a variety of indoor and outdoor attractions aimed specifically at the younger generation.

Admission and tour prices for children are included throughout the destination chapters of this book. As a general rule, these reduced prices are for children aged 6–16 years. For two adults and two or more children, always ask about family tickets. Children under 6 nearly always get in free. Most hotels and motels will happily accommodate children, but always try to reserve your room in advance and let the reservations desk know the ages of your kids. Often, children stay free in major hotels, and in the case of some major chains—such as Holiday Inn—eat free also. Generally, bed-and-breakfasts aren't suitable for children and in some cases don't accept kids at all. Ask ahead.

As a general rule when it comes to traveling with children, let them help you plan the trip, looking at websites and reading up on the province together. To make your vacation more enjoyable if you'll be spending a lot of time on the road, rent a minivan (all major rental agencies have a supply). Don't forget to bring along favorite toys and games from home—whatever you think will keep your kids entertained when the joys of sightseeing wear off.

The websites of **Tourism BC** (www.hellobc .com) and **Tourism Vancouver** (www.tourism vancouver.com) have sections devoted to children's activities. Another handy source of information is **Kid Friendly!** (604/541-6192, www.kidfriendly.org), a Vancouver-based nonprofit organization that has compiled an online database of, you guessed it, kid-friendly attractions, lodgings, and restaurants throughout British Columbia. The website even has room for your children to write about their vacation. Another useful online tool is **Traveling Internationally with Your Kids** (www.travel withyourkids.com).

Health and Safety

Compared to other parts of the world, Canada is a relatively safe place to visit. Vaccinations are required only if coming from an endemic area. That said, wherever you are traveling, carry a medical kit that includes bandages, insect repellent, sunscreen, antiseptic, antibiotics, and water-purification tablets. Good first-aid kits are available at most camping shops. Health care in Canada is mostly dealt with at a provincial level.

Taking out a travel-insurance policy is a sensible precaution because hospital and medical charges start at around $1,000 per day. Copies of prescriptions should be brought to Canada for any medicines already prescribed.

Staying Safe in the City

Although Vancouver and Victoria are generally safer than U.S. cities of the same size, the same safety tips apply there as elsewhere in the world. Tourists, unused to their surroundings and generally carrying valuables such as cameras and credit cards, tend to be easy targets for thieves. You can reduce the risk of being robbed by using common sense. First and foremost in Vancouver, avoid East Hastings Street, especially at night. It is known as one of the seediest areas in all of Canada, so you should catch a bus or cab between downtown and Chinatown to avoid this area. Wherever you are, avoid traveling or using ATMs at night, try to blend in with the crowd by walking with a purpose (be discreet if reading a map out in public), and don't wear expensive jewelry.

Giardia

Giardiasis, also known as beaver fever, is a real concern for those heading into the backcountry. It's caused by an intestinal parasite, *Giardia lamblia,* that lives in lakes, rivers, and streams. Once the parasite is ingested, its effects, although not instantaneous, can be dramatic: Severe diarrhea, cramps, and nausea are the most common symptoms. Preventive measures should always be taken, including boiling all water for at least 10 minutes, treating all water with iodine, or filtering all water using a filter with a pore size small enough to block the giardia cysts.

Winter Travel

Travel to Vancouver and Victoria in winter is relatively easy, with snowfall only rarely falling in these cities. Traveling beyond the coast during winter months should not be undertaken lightly. Before setting out in a vehicle, check antifreeze levels, and always carry a spare tire and blankets or sleeping bags. **Frostbite** is a potential hazard, especially when cold temperatures are combined with high winds (a combination known as **windchill**). Most often, frostbite leaves a numbing, bruised sensation, and the skin turns white. Exposed areas of skin, especially the nose and ears, are most susceptible.

Hypothermia occurs when the body fails to produce heat as fast as it loses it. It can strike at any time of the year but is more common during cooler months. Cold weather, combined with hunger, fatigue, and dampness, creates a recipe for disaster. Symptoms are not always apparent to the victim. The early signs are numbness, shivering, slurring of words, dizzy spells, and, in extreme cases, violent behavior, unconsciousness, and even death. The best way to dress for the cold is in layers, including a waterproof outer layer. Most important, wear headgear. The best treatment is to get the victim out of the cold, replace wet clothing with dry, slowly give hot liquids and sugary foods, and place the victim in a sleeping bag. Warming too quickly can lead to heart attacks.

Information and Services

MONEY

As in the United States, Canadian currency is based on dollars and cents. Coins come in denominations of 1, 5, 10, and 25 cents, and one and two dollars. The one-dollar coin is the gold-colored "loonie," named for the bird featured on it. The unique two-dollar coin, introduced in 1996, is silver with a gold-colored insert. Notes come in $5, $10, $20, $50, and $100 denominations.

All prices quoted in this book are in Canadian dollars unless noted. American dollars are accepted at many tourist areas, but the exchange rate is more favorable at banks. Currency other than U.S. dollars can be exchanged at most banks, airport money-changing facilities, and foreign exchange brokers in Vancouver, Victoria, and Whistler. Travelers checks are the safest way to carry money, but a fee is often charged to cash them if they're in a currency other than Canadian dollars. All major credit and charge cards are honored at Canadian banks, gas stations, and most commercial establishments. Automatic teller machines (ATMs) can be found in almost every town.

Costs

The cost of living in Vancouver and Victoria is similar to that of all other Canadian major cities, but higher than in the United States. If you will be staying in hotels or motels, accommodations will be your biggest expense. Gasoline is sold in liters (3.78 liters equals one U.S. gallon) and is generally $1–1.30 a liter for regular unleaded.

Tipping charges are not usually added to your bill. You are expected to add a tip of 15–20 percent to the total amount for waiters and waitresses, barbers and hairdressers, taxi drivers, and other such service providers. Bellhops, doormen, and porters generally receive $1 per item of baggage.

Taxes

Canada imposes a 6 percent **goods and services tax (GST)** on most consumer purchases. The BC government imposes its own 7.5 percent tax (PST) onto everything except

---

CURRENCY EXCHANGE

At press time, exchange rates (into CDN$) for major currencies are:

US$1 = $1.05
AUS$1 = $0.87
EUR€1 = $1.43
HK$10 = $1.38
NZ$1 = $0.78
UK£1 = $2.15
¥100 = $0.90

On the Internet, check current exchange rates at www.xe.com/ucc.

All major currency can be exchanged in Vancouver, Victoria, and Whistler at banks, airport money-changing facilities, and foreign exchange brokers. Many Canadian businesses will accept U.S. currency, but you will get a better exchange rate from the banks.

groceries and books. So when you are looking at the price of anything, remember that the final cost you pay will include an additional 13.5 percent in taxes.

MAPS AND INFORMATION
Maps
Driving maps are available at bookstores, gas stations, and gift shops throughout the province. In Vancouver, pick up maps at these specialty bookstores: **International Travel Maps and Books** (530 W. Broadway, 604/879-3621, www.itmb.com), **The Travel Bug** (3065 W. Broadway, 604/737-1122, www.travelbug books.ca), or **Wanderlust** (1929 W. 4th Ave., Kitsilano, 604/739-2182). In Victoria, check out **Crown Publications** (521 Fort St., 250/386-4636). These stores stock many topographical maps and can order specific maps and marine charts for you.

If you're heading to the BC Rockies, look for **Gem Trek** maps (www.gemtrek.com), which use computer-generated "3D Imagery" to clearly define changes in elevation and GPS to plot hiking trails. The backs of the maps are filled with trail information and tidbits of history. Waterproofing is an added bonus.

Tourism Information
Begin planning your trip by contacting the government tourist office: **Tourism BC** (250/387-1642 or 800/435-5622, www.hello bc.com). The literature and maps can be downloaded from the website or ordered by phone. As well as being a great source of tourist information, the agency produces the invaluable *Accommodations* guide and a road map. Other handy web addresses are www .canadatourism.com, the official site of the Canadian Tourism Commission, and www .tbc.gov.bc.ca, the site of the Ministry of Small Business, Tourism, and Culture.

Each town of any size in British Columbia has a **visitor center;** hours vary, but most are open June–August. (The Vancouver Visitor Centre is at 200 Burrard St., 604/683-2000.) When these are closed, head to the local chamber of commerce for information. Most chamber offices are open Monday–Friday year-round.

COMMUNICATIONS
Postal Services
Canada Post (www.canadapost.ca) issues postage stamps that must be used on all mail posted in Canada. First-class letters and postcards sent within Canada are $0.52, to the United States $0.93, to foreign destinations $1.55. Prices increase along with the weight of the mailing. You can buy stamps at post offices, automatic vending machines, most hotel lobbies, airports, Pacific Central Station (Vancouver), many retail outlets, and some newsstands.

Telephone
The **area code** for Vancouver and the lower mainland, including the Sunshine Coast, as far north as Whistler, and east to Hope, is **604.** The are code for the rest of the province, including Victoria and all of Vancouver Island, is **250.** The area code **778** applies to new numbers, but its implementation means that you must add the relevant area code to all numbers dialed within Vancouver. All prefixes must be dialed for all long-distance calls, including those made within the province.

The country code for Canada is 1, the same as the United States. Toll-free numbers have the 800, 888, or 877 prefix, and may be good within British Columbia, in Canada, throughout North America, or, in the case of major hotel chains and car-rental companies, worldwide.

To make an international call from Canada, dial the prefix 011 before the country code or dial 0 for operator assistance.

Public phones accept 5-, 10-, and 25-cent coins; local calls are $0.35, and most long-distance calls cost at least $2.50 for the first minute. The least expensive way to make long-distance calls from a public phone is with a **phone card.** These are available from convenience stores, newsstands, and gas stations.

Public Internet Access

If your Internet provider doesn't allow you to access your email away from your home computer, open an email account with **Hotmail** (www.hotmail.com) or **Yahoo** (www.yahoo.com). Although there are restrictions to the size and number of emails you can store, and junk mail can be a problem, these services are handy and, best of all, free.

Public Internet access is available throughout British Columbia. All larger hotels have wireless or high-speed access. Those that don't—usually mid- and lower-priced properties—often have an Internet booth in the lobby. Except for wilderness hostels, backpacker lodges provide inexpensive Internet access. You'll also find wireless connections or Internet booths in many cafés and in public areas, such as Canada Place in Vancouver, where a credit card will get you as long as you need on the Net. Aside from a lack of privacy, the downside to these public access points is the lack of a mouse at most terminals—instead you must move around the screen using a touch pad.

WEIGHTS AND MEASURES

Canada officially adopted the **metric system** back in 1975, though you still hear grocers talking in ounces and pounds, golfers talking in yards, and seamen talking in nautical miles. Metric is the primary unit used in this book, but we've added imperial conversions for readers from the United States, Liberia, and Myanmar, the only three countries that have not adopted the metric system. You can also refer to the metric conversion chart in the back of this book.

Electricity

Electrical voltage is 120 volts, the same as in the United States.

Time Zones

Most of British Columbia, including Vancouver and Victoria, is in the **Pacific time zone,** the same as Los Angeles and three hours before eastern time. The **mountain time zone** extends west into southern British Columbia, which includes Yoho and Kootenay National Parks as well as the towns of Golden and Radium Hot Springs.

RESOURCES

Suggested Reading

NATURAL HISTORY

Campbell, Wayne. *Birds of British Columbia.* Edmonton: Lone Pine Publishing, 2008. A field guide to birds across the province's wide-ranging landscapes.

Cannings, Richard and Sydney. *British Columbia: A Natural History.* Vancouver: Douglas & McIntyre, 2004. The natural history of the province divided into 10 chapters, including Forests of Rain, Mountaintops, and The World of Fresh Water. A beautiful book with lots of color maps.

Fischer, George (photographer). *Haida Gwaii Queen Charlotte Islands: Land of Mountains, Mystery, and Myth.* Halifax: Nimbus Publishing, 2006. A magnificent coffee table book that depicts the unique and intriguing natural and human history of these remote islands.

Folkens, Peter. *Marine Mammals of British Columbia and the Pacific Northwest.* Vancouver: Harbour Publishing, 2001. In a waterproof, fold-away format, this booklet provides vital identification tips and habitat maps for 50 marine mammals, including all species of whales present in local waters.

Gadd, Ben. *Handbook of the Canadian Rockies.* Jasper: Corax Press, 1999. Although bulky for backpackers, this classic field guide is a must-read for anyone interested in the natural history of the Canadian Rockies.

Gill, Ian. *Haida Gwaii: Journeys through the Queen Charlotte Islands.* Vancouver: Raincoast Books, 1997. A personal and touching view of the Queen Charlottes complemented by the stunning color photography of David Nunuk.

Haig Brown, Roderick. *Return to the River.* Vancouver: Douglas & McIntyre, 1997. Although fictional, this story of the life of one salmon and its struggle through life is based on fact, and is a classic read for both anglers and naturalists. It was originally published in 1946 but has recently been reprinted and is available at most bookstores.

Herrero, Stephen. *Bear Attacks: Their Causes and Avoidances.* New York: Nick Lyons Books, 1995. Through a series of gruesome stories, this book catalogs the stormy relationship between people and bruins, provides hints on avoiding attacks, and tells what to do in case you're attacked.

Pojar, Jim. *Plants of Coastal British Columbia.* Edmonton: Lone Pine Publishing, 2005. This popular field guide makes the province's coastal flora easy to identify through detailed descriptions and illustrations.

Pyne, Stephen J. *Awful Splendor.* Vancouver: University of British Columbia Press, 2007. This big, beautiful book tells the story of wildfires in Canada, both through specific fires and the effects on the environment and humans.

HUMAN HISTORY

Barman, Jean. *The West Beyond the West: A History of British Columbia*. Toronto: University of Toronto Press, 2007. Authored by a local university professor, this book makes interesting reading for its exploration of the province's lesser-known history.

Coull, Cheryl. *A Traveller's Guide to Aboriginal B.C.* Vancouver: Whitecap Books, 1996. Although this book covers native sites throughout British Columbia, the Lower Mainland (Vancouver) chapter is very comprehensive. Also included are details of annual festivals and events and hiking opportunities with a cultural slant.

Coupland, Douglas. *City of Glass: Douglas Coupland's Vancouver*. Vancouver: Douglas & McIntyre, 2000. Best known for coining the term *Generation X* in his 1991 novel of the same name, local author Coupland delves deep into the cultural heart of Vancouver.

Duff, Wilson. *The Indian History of British Columbia: The Impact of the White Man*. Victoria: University of British Columbia Press, 1997. In this book, Duff deals with the issues faced by native peoples in the last 150 years, but also gives a good overview of their general history.

Johnson, Pauline. *Legends of Vancouver*. Vancouver: Douglas & McIntyre, 1998. First published in 1911, this small book contains the writings of Pauline Johnson, a well-known writer and poet in the early part of the 1900s. She spent much of her time with native peoples, and this is her version of myths related to her by Joe Capilano, chief of the Squamish. This most recent edition is the latest of many reprints over the years; search out others at Vancouver's many secondhand bookstores.

Lavallee, Omer. *Van Horne's Road*. Montreal: Railfare Enterprises, 1974. William Van Horne was instrumental in the construction of Canada's first transcontinental railway. This is the story of his dream, and the boom-towns that sprung up along the route. Lavallee devotes an entire chapter to telling the story of the railway's push through British Columbia to Vancouver.

Luxton, Donald. *Building the West: The Early Architects of British Columbia*. Vancouver: Talonbooks, 2007. Printed in two-tone, this beautiful reference book delves into the lives and work of prominent early architects, many of whom are represented by buildings that still stand today.

Murray, Tom. *Canadian Pacific Railway*. Osceola, Wisconsin: Zenith Press, 2006. Railway buffs are spoilt for choice when it comes to reading about the history of Canada's transcontinental railway, but this large format book stands apart for its presentation of historic images and coverage of the railway industry today.

Nicol, Eric. *Vancouver*. Toronto: Doubleday Canada, 1970. An often-humorous look at Vancouver and its colorful past through the eyes of Eric Nicol, one of Vancouver's favorite columnists of the 1960s. The book has been reprinted a few times, and although it has been out of print for many years, Vancouver's secondhand bookstores usually have multiple copies in stock.

Scott, Chic. *Pushing the Limits*. Calgary: Rocky Mountain Books, 2000. A chronological history of mountaineering in Canada, with special emphasis on many largely unknown climbers and their feats, as well as the story of Swiss guides in Canada and a short section on ice climbing.

Spaner, David. *Dreaming in the Rain: How Vancouver Became Hollywood North by Northwest*. Vancouver: Arsenal Pulp Press, 2003. Tells the story of Vancouver's short but dramatic rise as one of the world's premier filmmaking centers.

Valliant, John. *The Golden Spruce*. Toronto: Vintage Canada, 2006. The gripping true story of a man who chopped down one of the world's only golden spruce trees, then disappeared to leave many questions unanswered.

Verchère, Ian. *V0N 1B0: General Delivery, Whistler, B.C.* Vancouver: Douglas & McIntyre, 2006. An irreverent look at life in Whistler, including its short but dynamic history. Verchère is a local ski racer.

Wilson, Diana. *Heart of the Cariboo-Chilcotin: Stories Worth Keeping.* Vancouver: Heritage House, 2007. A series of short stories describing the native peoples, the gold rush, ranching, and the modern-day conservation movement.

Wynn, Graeme. *Vancouver and its Region.* Vancouver: University of British Columbia Press, 1992. An in-depth look at the city, its geography, and the history of its urbanization, through aerial photography, maps, graphs, and descriptive passages.

RECREATION

Aitchison, Catherine J. *Birder Guide to Vancouver and the Lower Mainland.* Vancouver: Whitecap Books, 2001. This spiral-bound field guide details 350 species recorded in the region and provides detailed directions to the best viewing spots.

Copeland, Craig and Cathy. *Done in a Day: Whistler: The 10 Premier Hikes.* Canmore: hikingcamping.com, 2007. A detailed look at 10 of the most popular day hikes in and around Whistler.

Kimantas, John. *BC Coastal Recreation and Small Boat Guide.* Vancouver: Whitecap Books, 2007. A two-volume, splash-proof atlas set that is an essential tool for kayakers.

Patton, Brian, and Bart Robinson. *Canadian Rockies Trail Guide.* Banff: Summerthought Publishing, 2007. This regularly updated guide, first published in 1971, covers 230 hiking trails and 3,400 kilometers (2,100 miles) in the Canadian Rockies.

Pratt-Johnson, Betty. *151 Dives in the Protected Waters of British Columbia and Washington State.* Vancouver: Adventure Publishing, 2007. This book is the best source of detailed information on diving in British Columbia.

Schreiner, John. *John Schreiner's Okanagan Wine Tour Guide.* Vancouver: Whitecap Books, 2007. A useful tool for travelers focusing their attention on local wineries. Includes information on wine styles, the climate, and the industry in general.

Woodsworth, Glenn. *Hot Springs of Western Canada.* West Vancouver: Gordon Soules Book Publishers, 1997. Details every known hot springs in western Canada, including both commercial and undeveloped sites. A short history, directions, and practicalities are given for each one.

OTHER GUIDEBOOKS AND MAPS

Backroad Mapbooks. Vancouver: Mussio Ventures. This atlas series is perfect for outdoor enthusiasts, with detailed maps, and highlights such as campgrounds, fishing spots, and swimming holes. www.backroadmapbooks.com.

Crockford, Ross. *Victoria: The Unknown City.* Vancouver: Arsenal Pulp Press, 2006. Filled with little-known facts and interesting tales, this book describes how to get the best seats on BC Ferries, where to shop for the funkiest used clothing, the history of local churches, and more.

Mackie, John. *Vancouver: The Unknown City.* Vancouver: Arsenal Pulp Press, 2003. Compiled from the author's many years uncovering city secrets revealed in his magazine writing, this book delves into the darkest corners of the city.

MapArt. Driving maps for all of Canada, including provinces and cities. Maps are published as old-fashioned fold-out versions, as well as laminated and in atlas form. www.mapart.com.

Moyer, Marybeth. *The Canadian Bed and Breakfast Guide.* Toronto: Fitzhenry &

Whiteside, 2008. Lists all bed-and-breakfasts that pay a fee, so the reviews aren't very objective. Also lists prices.

Neering, Rosemary. *Eating Up Vancouver Island.* Vancouver: Whitecap Books, 2003. A guide to everything culinary on Vancouver Island, from the brewpubs of Victoria to the farms of the Cowichan Valley.

MAGAZINES

Beautiful British Columbia. Victoria. This quarterly magazine depicts the beauty of the province through stunning color photography and informative prose. It's available by subscription (250/384-5456 or 800/663-7611, www.bcmag.ca).

Canadian Geographic. Ottawa: Royal Canadian Geographical Society. Bimonthly publication pertaining to Canada's natural and human histories and resources. www.canadiangeographic.ca.

Explore. Calgary. Bimonthly publication of adventure travel throughout Canada. www.explore-mag.com.

Nature Canada. Ottawa, Ontario. Quarterly magazine of the Canadian Nature Federation. www.cnf.ca.

Western Living. Vancouver. Lifestyle magazine for western Canada. Includes travel, history, homes, and cooking. www.westernliving.ca.

Internet Resources

TRAVEL PLANNING

Canadian Tourism Commission
www.canadatourism.com
Official tourism website for all of Canada.

Tourism British Columbia
www.hellobc.com
Learn more about the province, plan your travels, and order tourism literature.

Tourism Vancouver
www.tourismvancouver.com
An excellent resource for planning your time in Vancouver.

Tourism Victoria
www.tourismvictoria.com
The official site for British Columbia's capital.

Travel to Canada
www.westerncanadatravel.com
Website of the author, Andrew Hempstead. Includes general and up-to-date tips on travel to Canada.

PARKS

BC Parks
www.bcparks.ca
A division of the government's Ministry of Environment, this office is responsible for British Columbia's provincial parks. Website includes details of each park, as well as recreation and camping information.

Parks Canada
www.pc.gc.ca
Official website of the agency that manages Canada's national parks and national historic sites. Website has information on each of western Canada's national parks (fees, camping, and wildlife) and national historic sites.

Parks Canada Campground Reservation Service
www.pccamping.ca
Online reservation service for national park campgrounds.

GOVERNMENT

Canadian Parks and Wilderness Society
www.cpaws.org

Nonprofit organization that is instrumental in highlighting conservation issues throughout Canada. The link to the Vancouver chapter provides local information and a schedule of guided walks.

Citizenship and Immigration Canada
www.cic.gc.ca

Check this government website for anything related to entry into Canada.

Environment Canada
www.weatheroffice.ec.gc.ca

Five-day forecasts from across Canada, includingalmost 300 locations through western Canada. Includes weather archi ves such as seasonal trends and snowfall history.

Government of British Columbia
www.gov.bc.ca

The official website of the BC government.

Government of Canada
www.gc.ca

The official website of the Canadian government.

TRANSPORTATION AND TOURS

Air Canada
www.aircanada.ca

Canada's national airline.

BC Ferries
www.bcferries.com

Providing a link between Vancouver and Vancouver Island.

Rocky Mountaineer Vacations
www.rockymountaineer.com

Luxurious rail service to and from Vancouver to Banff and Jasper, including via Whistler.

VIA Rail
www.viarail.ca

Passenger rail service across Canada.

PUBLISHERS

Arsenal Pulp Press
www.arsenalpulp.com

Gastown is the perfect place for this fiercely independent publisher with a title list stacked with urban literature.

Heritage House
www.heritagehouse.ca

With over 700 nonfiction books in print, this large Vancouver publisher is known for its historical and recreation titles covering all of western Canada.

Raincoast Publishing
www.raincoast.com

A large Vancouver publishing house with titles covering all genres.

Whitecap
www.whitecap.ca

Best known for its Canadian coffee table books, this Vancouver publisher also produces respected cooking titles.

Index

www.moon.com

For helpful advice on planning a trip, visit www.moon.com for the **TRAVEL PLANNER** and get access to useful travel strategies and valuable information about great places to visit. When you travel with Moon, expect an experience that is uncommon and truly unique.

HANDBOOKS | METRO | OUTDOORS | LIVING ABROA